INTRODUCTION TO COMPUTER PROGRAMMING

STRUCTURED COBOL

ANAHEIM PUBLISHING COMPANY
Specialist In Data Processing Textbooks

INTRODUCTION TO DATA PROCESSING

The Computers In Our Society, Logsdon & Logsdon
The Computers In Our Society Workbook, Logsdon & Logsdon

BASIC

Programming In BASIC, Logsdon
Programming In BASIC With Applications, Logsdon

ASSEMBLER LANGUAGE

IBM System/360 Assembler Language, Cashman & Shelly
IBM System/360 Assembler Language Workbook, Cashman & Shelly
IBM System/360 Assembler Language Disk/Tape Advanced Concepts, Shelly & Cashman
DOS Job Control For Assembler Language Programmers, Shelly & Cashman

COBOL

Introduction To Computer Programming Structured COBOL, Shelly & Cashman
Introduction To Computer Programming ANSI COBOL, Shelly & Cashman
ANSI COBOL Workbook, Testing & Debugging Techniques & Exercises, Shelly & Cashman
Advanced ANSI COBOL Disk/Tape Programming Efficiencies, Shelly & Cashman
Introduction To Computer Programming System/360 COBOL, Cashman
IBM System/360 COBOL Problem Text, Cashman
IBM System/360 COBOL Disk/Tape Advanced Concepts, Shelly & Cashman
DOS Job Control For COBOL Programmers, Shelly & Cashman

RPG

Introduction To Computer Programming RPG, Shelly & Cashman
Computer Programming RPG II, Shelly & Cashman
IBM System/360 RPG Programming, Volume 1-Introduction, Fletcher & Cashman
IBM System/360 RPG Programming, Volume 2-Advanced Concepts, Fletcher & Cashman

FORTRAN

Introduction To Computer Programming Basic FORTRAN IV-A Practical Approach, Keys

PL/I

Introduction To Computer Programming System/360 PL/I, Shelly & Cashman

SYSTEMS ANALYSIS AND DESIGN

Business Systems Analysis And Design, Shelly & Cashman

FLOWCHARTING

Introduction To Flowcharting and Computer Programming Logic, Shelly & Cashman
Basic Logic For Program Flowcharting and Table Search, Jones & Oliver

JOB CONTROL-OPERATION SYSTEMS

Dos Utilities Sort/Merge Multiprogramming, Shelly & Cashman
OS Job Control Language, Shelly & Cashman

INTRODUCTION TO COMPUTER PROGRAMMING

STRUCTURED COBOL

By:

Gary B. Shelly
Educational Consultant
Fullerton, California

&

Thomas J. Cashman, CDP, B.A., M.A.
Long Beach City College
Long Beach, California

ANAHEIM PUBLISHING COMPANY
1120 E. Ash, Fullerton, CA, 92631
(714) 879-7922

First Printing
July 1977

Second Printing
September 1977

Third Printing
December 1977

Fourth Printing
March 1978

Library of Congress Catalog Card Number 77-089824

ISBN 0-88236-111-2

Printed in the United States of America

PREFACE

In the early 1970's numerous articles were written relative to the merits of a "new" approach to programming a computer called STRUCTURED PROGRAMMING. Discussion in these articles centered around the value of structured programming and the suitability of COBOL as a programming language for implementing structured programming methodologies. The controversy relative to the value of structured programming and the usefulness of COBOL as a structured programming language was quickly resolved as numerous companies successfully implemented structured programming using COBOL.

It soon became apparent, however, that a "structured program" could be just as poorly written as an "unstructured program"; that is, a structured program could be written that was difficult to understand, difficult to modify, and difficult to maintain. As industry's understanding of structured programming theory evolved, it was found that the production of "good" programs **must** be based upon the principles of STRUCTURED DESIGN in combination with the theories of STRUCTURED PROGRAMMING.

Thus, the most important question faced by industry, educators, and students as well, is not how to code a structured program, but how to DESIGN a program prior to the actual coding so that the program will be error free, reliable, and easy to modify and maintain. Unfortunately, an individual untrained in structured design may often be unable to recognize a "good" structured program from one that is poorly written until it becomes necessary to modify and maintain the program at some future time.

In today's data processing environment, data processing educators must do more than teach programming techniques that illustrate structured coding; they must provide students with a firm foundation in modern programming methodologies including not only Structured COBOL coding but Structured Program Design as well.

The objective of this textbook is to "teach students, from the very beginning, the proper methods of STRUCTURED DESIGN and STRUCTURED COBOL PROGRAMMING." In this text, the first program illustrated for analysis by the student has been carefully designed and could well serve as a model for industry. In the chapters that follow, the programs become more complex and introduce additional techniques of structured design. In every case, the COBOL coding is also carefully explained. Thus, beginning with the very first chapters, the student studies Structured Program Design as well as COBOL coding. Perhaps even more important, when students write their first programs they will be producing properly designed and coded COBOL programs.

The structured design methodologies used in this textbook are based upon Top-Down Design, Functional Decomposition, and Pseudocode, which are techniques widely advocated and used in structured design.

This textbook is designed to be used in a one quarter or one semester course to teach the beginning student of computer programming how to DESIGN and WRITE structured programs using COBOL: No prior knowledge of computer programming is required. A "problem-oriented" approach is used throughout the book, that is, the student is introduced to structured design and programming through a series of programs illustrating typical business applications. Only those statements and segments of the language necessary in the solution of the problem are explained. The student, therefore, learns programming in relation to the total problem, and is not burdened with the task of remembering a series of isolated facts concerning the individual segments of the language. Each of the chapters in the text introduces additional structured design and structured programming concepts. Upon completion of the text the student will have gained experience in designing and writing a variety of business-oriented programs using COBOL.

The programs explained in each of the chapters include the following operations or programming techniques: Basic Input/Output, Addition, Subtraction, Editing, Multiplication, Division, the Compute Verb, Comparing, Nested IF Statement, Single and Multiple Level Control Breaks, and Table Lookup and Table Search.

At the conclusion of each chapter there are three types of activities which should be performed by the student. The first activity is a set of Review Questions which require the student to apply the knowledge learned within the chapter to a set of questions. The second activity involves debugging COBOL programs, requiring the correcting of diagnostics within the program and/or the correcting of errors which occur in the execution of the program. Source listings, diagnostics, and output listings are given for the student to correct.

The third activity involves actually writing COBOL programs. Four programming assignments are included in each chapter. The first assignment is relatively close to the program illustrated in the text, and requires a basic understanding of the problem and the concepts presented in the text. The second programming assignment presents a slight variation of the sample program developed in the text and requires more creative thinking to arrive at the solution of the problem. The third and fourth assignments are increasingly complex and are designed to challenge the student with more difficult programming assignments. At the conclusion of the text, two case studies are presented. These case studies are designed to encompass many of the concepts discussed in previous chapters and to provide the student with the opportunity to write a program that closely approximates the type of problems that one would encounter in industry.

The Appendices also provide valuable information. The first appendix contains the two sets of test data which can be used for the programming assignments in the text. All of the programming assignments which are presented within the text will use one of the two sets of test data in the appendix. There is, therefore, no need to prepare extensive test data for each of the programming assignments. Appendix D contains the Environment Division, Data Division, and Procedure Division entries required for reading and writing sequential disk files. Therefore, if the test data for the programming assignments is to be placed on a sequential disk file for use by all students, a review of Appendix D should be conducted so the student will have the knowledge required to read sequential disk files. The Appendices also contain COBOL format notations, directions on reading source listings and diagnostics, and a reserved word list.

After the study of the material contained in the text has been completed, the student should have a firm foundation in the concepts and techniques of STRUCTURED PROGRAM DESIGN and STRUCTURED COBOL PROGRAMMING, and should be capable of solving a wide variety of business-type problems using COBOL. With the widespread use of STRUCTURED COBOL in industry and the implementation of the language by a variety of manufacturers, the student will have taken a significant step in gaining the knowledge required to enter the data processing profession.

The authors would like to thank Mike Broussard for the text illustrations, page design, cover photograph and design, and preparing the finished copy. They would also like to thank Marion Kenyon and Marilyn Martin for typesetting and proofreading the finished manuscript, and Steve Juarez for preparing the coding forms used in the text.

Gary B. Shelly

Thomas J. Cashman

ACKNOWLEDGEMENT

The following information is reprinted from **COBOL** Edition 1965, published by the Conference on Data Systems Languages (CODASYL).

TABLE OF CONTENTS

CHAPTER

INTRODUCTION TO STRUCTURED PROGRAMMING

1

1

> *Computer Programming as a practical human activity is some 25 years old, a short time for intellectual development. Yet computer programming has already posed the greatest intellectual challenge that mankind has faced in pure logic and complexity.* [1]

INTRODUCTION

The data processing industry has undergone dramatic changes since it first began in the late 1940's. Much of the drama has centered around the changes and improvements in computer hardware and the related peripheral equipment such as magnetic tape units and disk storage devices. Whereas in 1955 it required a large room with extensive cooling to operate a medium sized computer, today that same computing capacity can be stored on a single board about 3'' X 5'' in size. In fact, many of the microcomputers which are being produced today have many times the computing power which was found 10-20 years ago in large computers.

Figure 1-1 Computer Programmers at Work

---

1 Mills, Harlan D., "The New Math of Computer Programming", COMMUNICATIONS OF THE ACM, Vol. 18, No. 1, January, 1975

As computer hardware has gone through an evolutionary change, so too has the art or science of computer programming. This includes both the jobs done by programmers and the methods used by programmers for solving problems.

The basic task of a computer programmer is to write a program, or set of instructions, that will direct the computer to process data in a way which will solve a given problem. These programs are termed the **software** of the computer. The usefulness of computers stems from their ability to perform logical and arithmetic operations accurately and at very high speeds. But even with these capabilities, computers must always be controlled by some type of program which consists of a series of instructions which direct the operations of the computer. The job of the programmer is to produce these sets of instructions.

Computer programming may be broken down into two broad categories: **Systems Programming** and **Applications Programming**. The systems programmer is concerned with writing programs that make it easier to operate and program computers. Systems programmers produce control programs that operate input/output devices, test programs that detect errors and malfunctions within the computer, utility programs, such as sorts, which provide for easy manipulation of data, and programming languages and compilers which are available for the applications programmer to use when solving problems.

The applications programmer is concerned with writing programs that are needed to solve problems related to business, science, and government. There are two general areas in applications programming: Scientific Programming and Business Programming. The scientific applications programmer is normally involved in writing programs requiring a great deal of complex mathematical calculations. In many cases, scientific applications programmers are also mathematicians or engineers who are using the computer to solve problems with which they are directly concerned.

The business applications programmer writes programs to solve problems relating to the business transactions of a company. Applications such as payroll, billing, and inventory control are areas of concern to a business applications programmer. Business programming is not normally performed by a person such as an accountant or a production manager. Rather, in most businesses, the job of programming is assigned to an individual working in the data processing department. Thus, the business programmer is required to write a variety of programs for various applications within a company, and should not only be skilled in computer programming but should have a broad background in busines as well.

EVOLUTION OF COMPUTER HARDWARE AND SOFTWARE

Great changes have taken place in the development of both hardware and software in the past two decades. The first business computers were punched card-oriented computers on which single applications such as payroll, accounts receivable, or inventory control were processed. These so-called batch systems usually required the writing of a single, relatively simple program to process the required data.

The era of the 1960's, however, saw great growth in the use of larger, faster, and more powerful computers with an increasingly greater variety of input/output capabilities. Computers changed from batch oriented card systems to more powerful machines using magnetic tape and magnetic disks for storing data. In addition, computer terminals and data communications facilities which allow for remote access to the computer became more widely used.

With these great changes in computer hardware also came great changes in the design of applications which were run on the computer. Applications changed from single program, batch oriented, card systems to extremely complex systems such as on-line retrieval and updating systems used for air line reservations, and large data-base oriented communications systems. These types of systems are frequently composed of many interrelated programs each of which consist of many thousands or even tens of thousands of computer instructions.

In software the primary advances which have taken place in the past two decades include the development and widespread use of high level programming languages such as COBOL, RPG II, and PL/I, and the use of operating systems to control the overall operation of the computer.

It is interesting to note that the relative cost of hardware and software has changed dramatically during the past 20 years. Prior to 1960, hardware comprised the largest percentage of the budget for a typical installation as compared to the cost of software or programming the computer system. The chart below illustrates this relationship.

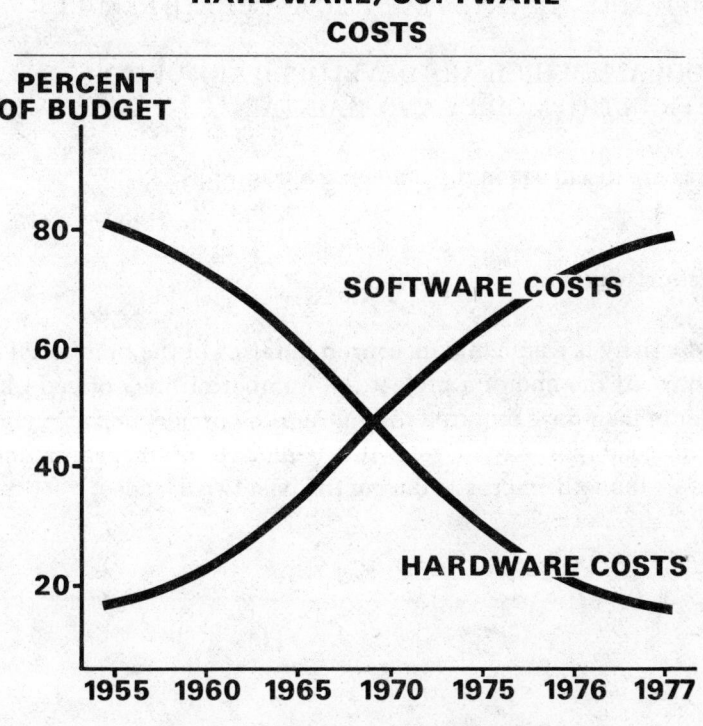

Figure 1-2 Hardware/Software Costs

It can be seen from the chart in Figure 1-2 that the development of software is now more expensive than the cost of computer hardware. This fact is due to the great decrease in the cost of the electronic components which make up modern computers and the increase in the cost of personnel needed to program computers. It is also apparent from the chart that significant improvements have not been made in increasing the efficiency of developing programs which would lead to a decrease in software development costs.

In addition, the great advances which have taken place in computer hardware have exceeded the ability of data processing personnel and management to utilize these new capabilities. Studies conducted by consulting firms have often indicated that computers are not being utilized effectively, costs are much greater than anticipated for programming the computer to perform desired tasks, programming projects are frequently late, and in many cases after years of effort in developing applications for use on the computer, projects have been abandoned altogether.

PROBLEMS IN SOFTWARE DEVELOPMENT

Although high level programming languages such as COBOL were designed to increase the productivity of computer programmers, numerous problems have arisen during the past several decades in software development. The major problems include:

1. LOW PROGRAMMER PRODUCTIVITY

2. PROGRAMS DEVELOPED ARE OFTEN UNRELIABLE
   AND DO NOT ALWAYS PRODUCE ACCURATE RESULTS

3. PROGRAMS WHICH ARE DEVELOPED ARE OFTEN
   DIFFICULT TO MODIFY AND MAINTAIN

Each of these areas are discussed in the following paragraphs.

Low Programmer Productivity

Programmer productivity is commonly measured in terms of the number of debugged lines of code written per day. At the end of a project the number of lines of code in the project is divided by the number of man-days required to program the project and this yields the number of debugged lines of code per day. Using this standard of measurement, programmer productivity has not substantially improved during the past two decades.

Studies of programmer productivity have indicated that the average applications programmer can produce between 10-15 debugged program statements per day, that is, less than two debugged statements per hour. For systems programmers working on large operating systems the number of debugged statements drops to as little as two or three debugged statements per day. Thus, in terms of salary, it can be estimated that every statement written by a programmer costs approximately $5.00, depending upon the salary paid. This is a staggering figure when realistically estimating the cost of programming a system for use on a computer.

It is also interesting to note that studies have been undertaken which point out that there are great variations in programmers' abilities within an installation. One study indicated that there is as much as a 25 to 1 ratio between good and bad programmers, that is, some programmers can design, code, and test a program some 25 times faster than others. Similarly, it was found that some programmers can produce code that is 10 times more efficient than code produced by others, that is, occupying ten times less memory and executing ten times faster on the computer. In addition, there does not appear to be any correlation between experience and the ability to program, nor are scores on an aptitude test relevant in determining "good" programmers from "bad" programmers.

Another fact discovered in studies of programmer productivity is that the number of computer instructions written by a programmer appears to be language independent, that is, the productivity of a programmer in terms of the number of debugged lines of code written does not vary significantly from language to language. This is attributed to the fact that much of a programmer's time is spent in activities other than writing source coding and any variation in the speed at which a programmer can write source code is not significant when measuring the overall productivity of the programmer. It should be noted, however, that high level programming languages tend to result in more production than machine languages because a single statement in a high level language can perform functions which may require a number of machine language instructions.

Thus, as can be seen, even with the development of sophisticated computer hardware and high level languages, the productivity of programmers has not been significantly increased; and with the rising cost of personnel, software costs have substantially increased over the past two decades.

Unreliable Software

As noted, the productivity of programmers has not increased over the past two decades. In addition, the coding produced by programmers has often been unreliable. Unreliability of software takes two forms—first, the program fails to execute; and second, the program produces incorrect output.

Examples of the first type of unreliable programs are consistently found in data processing installations. It is a rare programmer who has not been called in at 3 a.m. to fix a program which has "blown up", that is, ceased execution in the middle of processing data. Even more serious consequences can be found in the failure of operating systems software, such as when a major manufacturer's operating system contained over 1,000 errors. Because of these errors, installations were unable to operate their computers properly, costing them thousands of dollars.

The second type of unreliability where a program produces incorrect output has produced some spectacular results. Newspaper articles commonly contain such headlines as "Computerized voting system fails," "Welfare check issued for $480,000.00," or "Homeowner complains of $75,000.00 water bill."

An analysis of failures such as documented above frequently reveals a deficiency in the computer program written to process the data. Although the issuance of a check in an excessive amount is an important area of concern, with today's complex systems controlling space ships to the moon, on-line reservation systems, and electronic funds transfer systems, there is little margin for error, and the reliability of software is essential. Therefore, software reliability is an area to which much attention must be directed if computers are to be used efficiently and with confidence.

Programs Are Difficult to Modify and Maintain

Although it would appear to the casual observer that once a program is written and placed into operation that future changes or modifications would be unnecessary, the fact is that even those programs which are reliable must often be changed or modified at a later time. For example, with yearly changes in income tax laws, social security deductions, etc., payroll programs must be constantly modified and updated.

As the number of programs within an organization increases, a greater portion of the programming staff's time must be devoted to program maintenance, that is, modifying programs to ensure that they process data according to the latest system requirements.

Unfortunately, programs which have been poorly written and poorly documented are often difficult and time-consuming to modify. Today it is estimated that maintenance programming occupies 50-80% of the time of a typical organization's staff. Many authorities estimate that properly written programs could substantially reduce the time and effort spent in program maintenance.

In addition to modifying programs it is consistently found that programs must be corrected in order to work properly, that is, changes must be made so that the program will work in the manner in which it was designed. Frequent errors include not being able to process all the types of data which are input to the program, incorrect calculations being made on input data, and abnormal terminations of a program because of incorrect instructions or invalid data which is not handled properly by the program. When these types of errors occur, it is usually mandatory that the correction be made very quickly, since the programs which fail are in production and users are awaiting the output. Again, when programs are written poorly, these corrections are difficult to make and may result in long delays for the users.

CAUSES OF SOFTWARE DEVELOPMENT PROBLEMS

A number of areas have been identified which give insight into the reasons for the software problems which have existed in the data processing industry for the past several decades and which, in many instances, exist today. The causes of these problems are discussed in the following paragraphs.

1. PROGRAMMERS HAVE BEEN ASSIGNED A WIDE VARIETY OF JOB DUTIES - Although programming a computer requires a very specialized skill and knowledge, research studies have indicated that the average programmer spends very little of his time performing activities directly associated with programming, such as designing a program, coding a program, or testing and debugging a program. One study of a programmer's job duties indicated that only 27% of a programmer's time is devoted to programming and related tasks. The other 73% of the time is devoted to related clerical tasks. It would appear from these statistics that an environment should be created for the programmer which would provide for a greater percentage of his time to be spent in programming in order for maximum productivity to be achieved.

2. LACK OF STANDARDIZED APPROACH TO PROGRAM DESIGN - For many years, a programmer would learn the instruction set for a given computer or programming language and then set about to devise a solution to the problem to be solved. Using flowcharts as the primary design tool, the programmer would ''figure out'' the steps necessary to solve the problem using his own set of rules in the construction of the logic of the program. Little emphasis was placed upon how to design a ''good'' program, that is, a program that was both efficient and easy to maintain. As a result, programs were built on a trial and error basis, coping with each new combination of conditions as they were encountered. Thus, when similar problems were encountered by the programmer at some future time, it was highly unlikely that the logic or structure of the program would be developed in a similar manner. This approach has led to the development of programs that are often unreliable.

This approach has also led to programs which are virtually impossible to follow from start to finish, that is, someone following the logic of the program would not be able to determine what was taking place within the program. Obviously, if a person attempting to modify a program cannot figure out what is taking place within the program, then there is no possibility that proper corrections will be made to the program. Thus, the lack of program design has also caused programs to be very difficult to modify and maintain.

The reason that there has historically been little emphasis on program design is that most of the emphasis has been on program testing and debugging to obtain reliability. The program development cycle is commonly considered to consist of four phases: 1) Analyzing the programming specifications; 2) Designing the program; 3) Coding the program; 4) Testing and debugging the program. Estimates of the time spent in each phase of the program development cycle are given in the chart below.

10%	20%	20%	50%
ANALYZE SPECS.	DESIGN	CODE	TEST & DEBUG

As can be seen from the chart above, a very small portion of the programmer's time is typically spent in program design and an unusually large percentage of time is spent in testing and debugging the program, presumably to ensure a reliable program. The opposite result has been obtained, however. Because of the lack of design, even 50% of the time has often not been adequate to find all of the "bugs" and errors within a program and, as a result, programs frequently are unreliable even after extensive testing.

It has been suggested that if a much greater time were spent in designing a program, the time spent in testing and debugging could be substantially reduced and a better program would result.

3. LACK OF CONSIDERATION OF THE NEED FOR PROGRAM MAINTENANCE - In both the first and second generation of computers, internal storage was relatively limited and internal processing speeds were relatively slow. Therefore, programmers often found it necessary to resort to "clever" techniques to reduce the size of programs and to make their programs execute more efficiently. Little emphasis was placed upon the need to write programs that were easy to modify and maintain at some future date by someone other than the programmer who originally wrote the program.

Today, the shortage of internal storage is, in most instances, no longer a problem and the internal operating speeds of computers are much faster than in previous generations of computers. Unfortunately, the "old" habits of programming are too often retained at the expense of writing programs that are easy to modify and maintain. The result is that under the guise of writing efficient programs, programmers are producing programs which are quite difficult to understand by other programmers and are, therefore, quite difficult to modify and maintain.

It is interesting to note that studies have shown that although programmers say they are programming for efficiency, at the time of coding a program most programmers are unaware of which segments of the program will require the largest portion of execution time. Further, it has been shown that 75-85% of the execution time in a program takes place in only 5-10% of the coding within the program. Thus, even if there is concern with the efficiency in terms of execution time, the programmer need be concerned with only 5-10% of the entire program. This 5-10% which must be "optimized" normally cannot be identified at the time the program is written.

Because of these facts, it is generally accepted by most authorities today that programs should be initially written which are easy to modify and maintain. Only if it is shown that the program is not executing at acceptable speeds should the programmer optimize the program; and the only portions which should be optimized are that 5-10% which execute 75-85% of the time. If programs are written with this philosophy, most experts agree that the difficulty in maintenance programming and the related costs would be reduced dramatically.

NEEDS IN SOFTWARE DEVELOPMENT

In reviewing the history and development of software and projecting the needs of the future, it becomes apparent that within the data processing industry there is a great need to:

1. Improve programmer productivity
2. Develop programs that are reliable
3. Develop programs that are easy to modify and maintain

It is with these facts in mind that considerable research has been conducted during the past decade aimed at changing the profession of computer programming from an "art" to a "science"; that is, from the non-disciplined, individualized expression of one's ideas and approaches to a disciplined approach to solving a programming problem.

HISTORICAL DEVELOPMENT OF STRUCTURED PROGRAMMING

Research by computer scientists has indicated that a method of computer programming known as **STRUCTURED PROGRAMMING** can solve many of the problems that have existed since the inception of the stored program concept, and can result in improved programmer productivity, improved reliability, and the development of programs that are easy to modify and maintain.

Structured programming is a method of programming that involves the design and coding of programs using a limited number of control structures in the program to form highly structured units of code that are easily read and, therefore, more easily maintained.

The history of structured programming can be divided into four distinct areas which are outlined below and on the following pages. These areas are:

1. The Theoretical Foundation

2. The Advocation of GO TO-less Programming

3. The Application of Structured Programming Theory

4. The Widespread Use of Structured Programming in Industry.

THE THEORETICAL FOUNDATION [1964 - 1968]

The earliest beginning of structured programming theory can be traced to a paper presented by two mathematicians, Corrado Böhm and Guiseppe Jacopini, at the 1964 International Colloquium on Algebraic Linguistics and Automata Theory in Israel. This paper set out to prove that a few basic control structures could be used to express any programming logic, no matter how complex. Because of the highly theoretical nature of the paper, it did not attract significant attention at the time it was presented; however, the paper was published two years later in the **Communications of ACM**, a publication of the Association of Computing Machinery which is widely read by computer scientists. It is reportedly at this time that the article attracted the attention of other leading computer scientists throughout the world.

From the efforts of Böhm and Jacopini has developed a structured theorem which states that a "proper program," that is, a program with one entry and one exit and no infinite loops or unreachable code, can be written using as few as three types of control structures. These control structures are defined as 1) SEQUENCE; 2) IF-THEN-ELSE; 3) DO WHILE.

Sequence

The sequence control structure means that one sequence of events occurs after another. This is illustrated below.

SEQUENCE

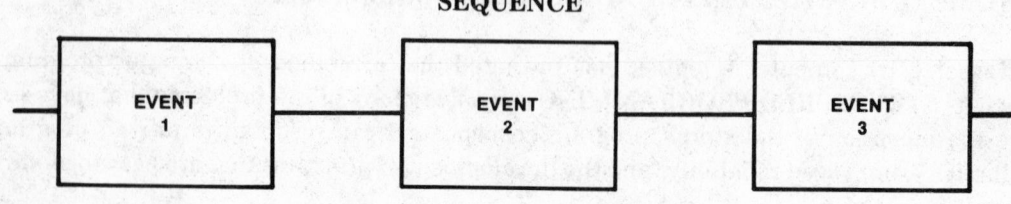

Figure 1-3 Example of SEQUENCE

Note in the example that the rectangular boxes are used to specify a particular event that is to take place; for example, a computer instruction that is to be executed. Each event is to take place in an exact sequence, one event followed by another. The simple sequence is the first of three basic control structures needed in order to solve any programming problem.

If-Then-Else

The second control structure is termed the IF-THEN-ELSE.

IF-THEN-ELSE

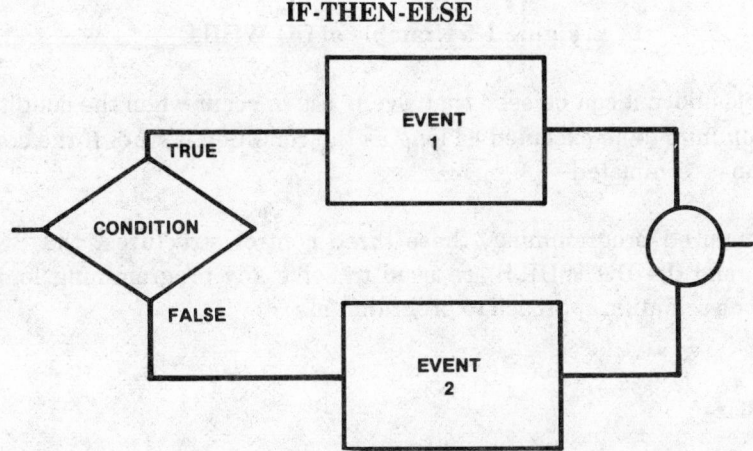

Figure 1-4 Example of IF-THEN-ELSE

The IF-THEN-ELSE structure is a conditional statement and specifies that certain events are to take place only upon given conditions. Note in the example that a condition is specified in the diamond shaped figure. If the condition is true, Event 1 will occur; if the condition is false, Event 2 will take place.

Do While

The third logical control structure is the DO WHILE. The DO WHILE structure allows a looping effect, that is, one or more events will take place while a given condition is true. This is illustrated in the following diagram.

DO WHILE

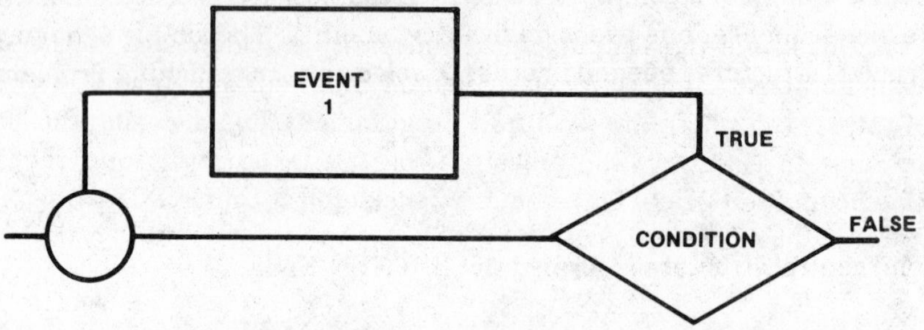

Figure 1-5 Example of DO WHILE

In the example above it can be seen that Event 1 is to occur when the condition is true, and this event will continue to be executed as long as the condition is true. If the condition is false, the looping action is terminated.

Thus, in structured programming, these three control structures, the SEQUENCE, the IF-THEN-ELSE, and the DO WHILE are used to solve any programming logic problem and form the basis for a scientific approach to programming.

Top-Down Corollary

Further research in structured programming has led to the development of what is known as the "Top-Down Corollary," which states that any program using these three structures can be written and read "top-down," that is, beginning with the first instruction in the program and continuing down to the last instruction in the program, at which time the execution of the program is complete. This means that each segment of a program can be determined to be correct without respect to the correctness of other segments within the program and provides a means of program design and testing which ensures a more reliable program.

Thus, the foundation for a new approach to computer programming called "structured programming" began to evolve.

GO TO-less PROGRAMMING [1968]

Edsger W. Dijkstra of the Technological University at Eindhoven, Netherlands, has made important contributions to the theory of structured programming. It is Dijkstra who led to the evolution of the second phase of structured programming by advancing the theory of GO TO less programming. In March of 1968, Dijkstra wrote a letter to the editor of the **Communications of ACM** which he entitled "GO TO Statement Considered Harmful." The opening paragraph of the letter to the editor is given below:

> **EDITOR:**
> For a number of years I have been familiar with the observation that the quality of programmers is a decreasing function of the density of go to statements in the programs they produce. More recently I discovered why the use of the go to statement has such disastrous effects, and I became convinced that the go to statement should be abolished from all "higher level" programming languages [i.e. everything except, perhaps, plain machine code]. At that time I did not attach too much importance to this discovery; I now submit my considerations for publication because in very recent discussions in which the subject turned up, I have been urged to do so. [2]

It should be noted at this time, however, that structured programming should not be characterized strictly by the absence of GO TO's. It occurs that when the basic control structures are properly utilized, the GO TO Statement is not necessary.

This letter attracted the attention of many individuals within the data processing community and was considered by many practicing business application programmers as a revolutionary concept. "We've always used Go To's in programming," "How can you write a COBOL program without the use of the Go To?" seemed to be the topic of conversation.

More importantly, however, this letter attracted the attention of Dr. Harlan Mills, a member of the IBM Corporate Technical Committee and F. Terry Baker, the manager of the Newspaper System Development Group at IBM.

Dr. Mills wrote several significant articles relative to structured programming, including the **Mathematical Foundations of Structured Programming**. These articles further influenced the advancement of the structured approach to programming. Mills and Baker became major advocates of structured programming at IBM and developed and defined structured programming techniques for use throughout the IBM Federal Systems Division. These two men are responsible for what may be considered the third phase in the development of structured programming—applying the theoretical foundation of structured programming to the development of a complex business-oriented programming project.

---

2 Dijkstra, E., "GO TO Statement Considered Harmful," COMMUNICATIONS OF THE ACM, Vol. 11, No. 3, March 1968

APPLICATION OF STRUCTURED PROGRAMMING THEORY [1969 - 1971]

The "New York Times project" is commonly considered and reported upon as being the first use of structured programming concepts in the solution of a large business-oriented programming project. The New York Times project was an on-line information system designed by IBM to provide access to the "morgue," that is, the past articles which had appeared in the newspaper. The system was designed so that users could make inquiries into a data base by selecting the date of publication, the section of the paper where an article appeared, etc. and view abstracts of those articles. It was designed to handle up to 500 terminals.

Under the guidance of Mills and Baker, the system, which was comprised of over 83,000 lines of code, was produced in an unusually short period of time with very few errors. The programs in the File Maintenance subsystem contained 12,029 lines of code and no errors were detected in this code during the testing phase of the system. A Conversational subsystem was written containing 38,990 lines of code and 20 errors were detected during testing. The Data Entry subsystem containing 13,421 lines of code had one error. Additional subsystems, consisting of 18,884 lines of code, contained no errors. Thus, for the entire project, 83,324 lines of code were written with only 21 errors. Indeed a remarkable record—approximately 4 errors for each 10,000 lines of code produced. Much of the success of the project has been attributed to the use of structured programming.

IMPROVED PROGRAMMING TECHNOLOGIES

In addition to utilizing the techniques of structured programming, several additional concepts have been implemented which have now become an important part of the overall approach to problem solving and programming. These concepts include:

1. CHIEF PROGRAMMER TEAM

2. STRUCTURED WALKTHROUGHS

3. PROGRAM SUPPORT LIBRARIES

These techniques are commonly called "Improved Programming Technologies" and have been widely adopted by industry.

Chief Programmer Teams

The chief programmer team is an organizational technique that complements the methodology of structured programming and the concept of top-down design. A chief programmer team is a group of personnel assigned to a programming project under the technical leadership of a senior level programmer. The chief programmer team consists of:

1. A Chief Programmer
2. A Backup Programmer
3. A Program Librarian
4. Programmers as needed

The chief programmer is responsible for the design of all the programs within the project and is vested with complete technical responsibility for the project. The chief programmer writes the main processing routines and defines other segments of the programs which are to be coded by other members of the team. In addition, the chief programmer will review all code produced by the programming team prior to its being tested. By the nature of the job, the chief programmer should be a "super programmer."

The backup programmer is a senior level programmer who works closely with the chief programmer and is available to assume the chief programmer's duties if necessary. In addition, the backup programmer is an active participant in the technical design of the programs being written by the team and is normally responsible for conducting the "structured walkthroughs" which will be performed by members of the programming team on the programs which are written. The backup programmer may also be responsible for the testing phase of the project.

The librarian is an important team member who must possess administrative skills in order to relieve the programmers of the clerical duties too often detracting from the programmers' prime responsibility of programming. The librarian is responsible for maintenance of project management statistics, arranges for the entry, compilation, and testing of programs as requested by team members, and manages the Program Support Library for the project. These responsibilities are critical to the proper functioning of the chief programmer team, and in large projects, the librarian will be a full-time job.

The additional programmers who are members of the team will be added as required by the project. They are responsibile for writing much of the detail code that is required in a large business application and also serve as reviewers in structured walkthroughs.

Structured Walkthroughs

In the past computer programming has been considered an individual effort. Although programmers have worked as a team on a major project, each programmer's approach to the problem, coding, testing, and debugging, etc. were considered "personal possessions." This approach has too frequently led to programs that were error prone and difficult to maintain.

To remedy this difficulty, the concepts of "egoless" programming and structured walkthroughs have evolved. Egoless programming refers to the idea that all programs written within an installation are essentially "public property," that is, the programs are available to anyone who wishes to review them. Thus, programmers are encouraged to write programs which are understandable by anyone who would review the code. This approach results in programs which are simpler and easier to modify and maintain. In addition, it emphasizes the fact that programs are written in order to solve a problem for a user of the system and not as a personal challenge to a programmer. Clever code and abstract solutions to problems have no place in egoless programming.

A structured walkthrough is a formal review of a programmer's or designer's work by other programmers on the team. It is designed to detect and remove errors as early as possible in the programming cycle when the cost of correction is lowest and the impact of errors smallest. It is estimated that it costs 50 times more to correct an error detected after a program has been written and implemented than it does to detect and correct an error during the structured walkthrough. Structured walkthroughs are normally conducted after the design effort has been completed and before coding is started; and also after the program has been coded but before testing has begun.

The structured walkthrough is normally conducted in the following manner. First, the programmer whose work is to be reviewed will select from 3 to 7 members of his team or other programmers within the department to act as reviewers. It should be noted that management personnel do not act as reviewers since the object of the walkthrough is to detect errors, not to assess the competence of the programmer whose work is being reviewed.

The programmer will then make copies of the work to be reviewed, whether it be program design material or the coding of a program on coding forms. These copies will be distributed to the reviewers several days before the review is to take place so that those who are reviewing the work will have an opportunity to look at the copies and formulate their questions concerning the program design or the program coding. In addition, prior to the meeting the reviewers will normally document any syntax errors, such as misspelled words or missing punctuation, which they find in the coding so that time is not spent on relatively minor errors such as these.

At the review meeting, that is, the actual structured walkthrough, the programmer whose work is being reviewed will ''walk through'' either the design or the coding, explaining why and how things were done. After this review, the reviewers will ask questions which they have formulated as a result of their prior examination of the work. These questions will normally focus on the completeness, accuracy, and general quality of the work produced. In particular, questionable areas in program logic and the organization of the program will be discussed. It should be noted that the reviewers will not tell the programmer how to make the corrections to cause the program to function correctly, that is, a walkthrough is not a session where the reviewers superimpose their solutions on the programmer's work. Rather, they are to point out syntax errors which they have discovered and they raise issues which they feel may cause the program to function incorrectly or inefficiently or which may cause the program to be unintelligible to others who may have to maintain or modify the program at a later time. During the walkthrough, it is many times the function of the backup programmer on the team to record all the remarks and give them to the programmer.

After the meeting, the programmer will go over the questions and suggestions made by the reviewers with a view of correcting his program. If the issues raised were relatively minor issues, such as syntax errors or minor logic problems, the programmer will normally make the necessary corrections and then continue on to the next phase of the program. If, however, significant questions were raised which require extensive changes, then it is likely that another structured walkthrough will be held after the changes are made. In either event, the programmer whose work was reviewed will document those corrections which he made and distribute this documentation to the programmers who did the review. In this manner, it is assured that the corrections will be made and will in all likelihood be made correctly.

It should be noted that although a structured walkthrough can be used independently of structured programming techniques and other techniques such as chief programmer teams, the concept of walkthroughs fits quite naturally with the philosophy that programs should be written that are easy to read, easy to understand, and easy to modify and maintain.

Program Support Libraries

A Program Support Library (variously called Development Support Library or Programming Production Library) is developed for the programming project in order to separate the clerical tasks involved in programming from the actual designing and coding which a programmer is trained to do. The library consists primarily of two entities: an "internal" library which is maintained in a disk file and contains the programs and job control statements which have been generated by the programming team; and an "external" library which consists of the program source listings, test results, etc.

It is the function of the team librarian to keep these libraries current and to perform those tasks which are necessary to ensure that whenever programmers need access to information developed for the project, the information is available. This is a critical function since the success of the entire project can center around the ability of the programming team to have access to and use of the information generated from the other programs and procedures within the project.

The use of program support libraries has alleviated much of the clerical work with which programmers had to be concerned and has allowed a greater percentage of their time to be dedicated to designing and writing programs, thus increasing the amount of programming which can be accomplished.

USE OF STRUCTURED PROGRAMMING BY INDUSTRY [1972 -   ]

After the completion of the New York Times project, Mills and Baker began publishing material and presenting papers concerning the project and the success which they had enjoyed with the use of structured programming and the related improved programming technologies. In addition, numerous other articles began appearing in popular data processing journals advocating the use of structured programming and relating "success stories" through its use. Thus, with increasing frequency, industry has been turning to the use of structured programming concepts and the improved programming technologies to ensure that their programs are written more quickly, with more reliability, and are easier to modify and maintain.

The remainder of this text will deal with the methods to be used in designing structured programs together with the elements of the COBOL language needed to implement structured programming and to solve those types of problems which are commonly found in business application programming.

CHAPTER 1

REVIEW QUESTIONS

1. What is the relative cost of hardware and software, today, compared to twenty years ago?

2. List three major problems in software development.

3. Historically, how many debugged lines of code has the ''typical'' applications programmer been able to write per day?

4. What is meant by the term ''unreliable'' software?

5. List three causes of software development problems.

6. List three important "needs" relative to the improvement of the software development process.

7. Draw and identify the three basic control structures used in structured programming.

8. Define the term "structured programming".

9. Briefly explain the organizational structure of the chief programmer team. What are the duties of each of the members of the team?

10. What is meant by ''egoless'' programming.

11. Briefly explain the purpose and technique of conducting a structured walkthrough

12. What is contained in a program support library?

INTRODUCTION TO STRUCTURED DESIGN

2

2

> *Most computer programs are never designed; they are created on the coding pad. This practice leads to programs that are poorly constructed, resulting in higher production costs, higher maintenance and modification costs, and unreliability. 1*

INTRODUCTION

As discussed in the previous chapter, historically the approach used in programming an application has consisted of briefly reviewing the programming specifications and, after sketching out the logic of the program, immediately setting about coding the program in the programming language used in the installation. This practice has resulted in the development of programs that are unreliable and programs that are difficult to modify and maintain.

Interestingly, this approach to problem solving is seldom used in other professions. For example, when building a house, an architect first prepares a detailed set of plans which are carefully followed in the actual construction of the house itself. Similarly, in constructing a program, the first step the programmer should take is to develop a detailed set of plans which will serve as a guideline for the actual writing of the instructions which will comprise the program; for it has become apparent through extensive research that program design offers the greatest source of improvement in the manner in which programs are efficiently developed and implemented.

---

1 *RELIABLE SOFTWARE THROUGH COMPOSITE DESIGN, Glenford J. Myers, Petrocelli/ Charter, 1976*

SAMPLE APPLICATION

Prior to discussing the development of a program, it is essential to have an overall understanding of how processing occurs within the computer for a "typical" application. To illustrate this basic concept a sample application is developed in this chapter in which a list of customers who have purchased magazine subscriptions is to be prepared. This Subscription List Report is to contain the Subscription Expiration Date, the Customer's Name, the Customer's Address, and the City and State of the customer. An example of the printed report that is to be prepared is illustrated below.

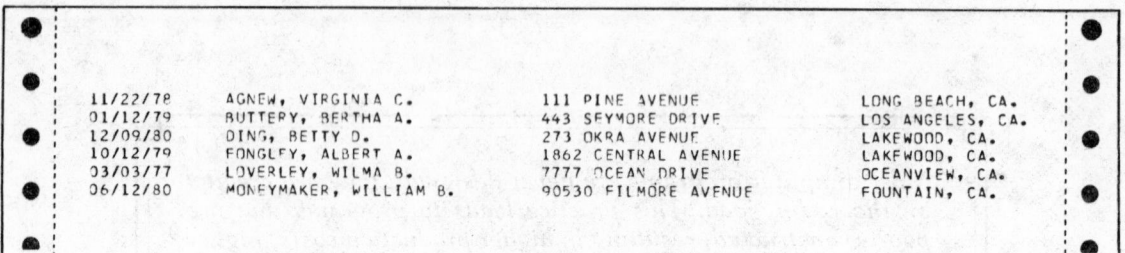

```
11/22/78     AGNEW, VIRGINIA C.         111 PINE AVENUE           LONG BEACH, CA.
01/12/79     BUTTERY, BERTHA A.         443 SEYMORE DRIVE         LOS ANGELES, CA.
12/09/80     DING, BETTY D.             273 OKRA AVENUE           LAKEWOOD, CA.
10/12/79     FONGLEY, ALBERT A.         1862 CENTRAL AVENUE       LAKEWOOD, CA.
03/03/77     LOVERLEY, WILMA B.         7777 OCEAN DRIVE          OCEANVIEW, CA.
06/12/80     MONEYMAKER, WILLIAM B.     90530 FILMORE AVENUE      FOUNTAIN, CA.
```

Figure 2-1 Output Report

The input to prepare the printed report is a Subscription List Card File. Each card within the file is to contain a Customer Name, a Customer Address, the Customer's City and State, and the Expiration Date of the subscription. An example of the input card is illustrated in Figure 2-2.

| NAME | ADDRESS | CITY/STATE | EXP DATE | |

Figure 2-2 Input Card

Thus, in the sample application, the Subscription List Cards are to be used to produce a Subscription List Report.

The processing required to prepare the Subscription List Report consists of reading an input card into an input area, moving each of the fields in the input area to the output area, and writing a line. This processing is repeated as long as there are cards to be processed. These steps are illustrated in the diagrams in Figure 2-3.

STEP 1: A Card containing a Name, Address, City/State and Expiration Date is read into an Input Area.

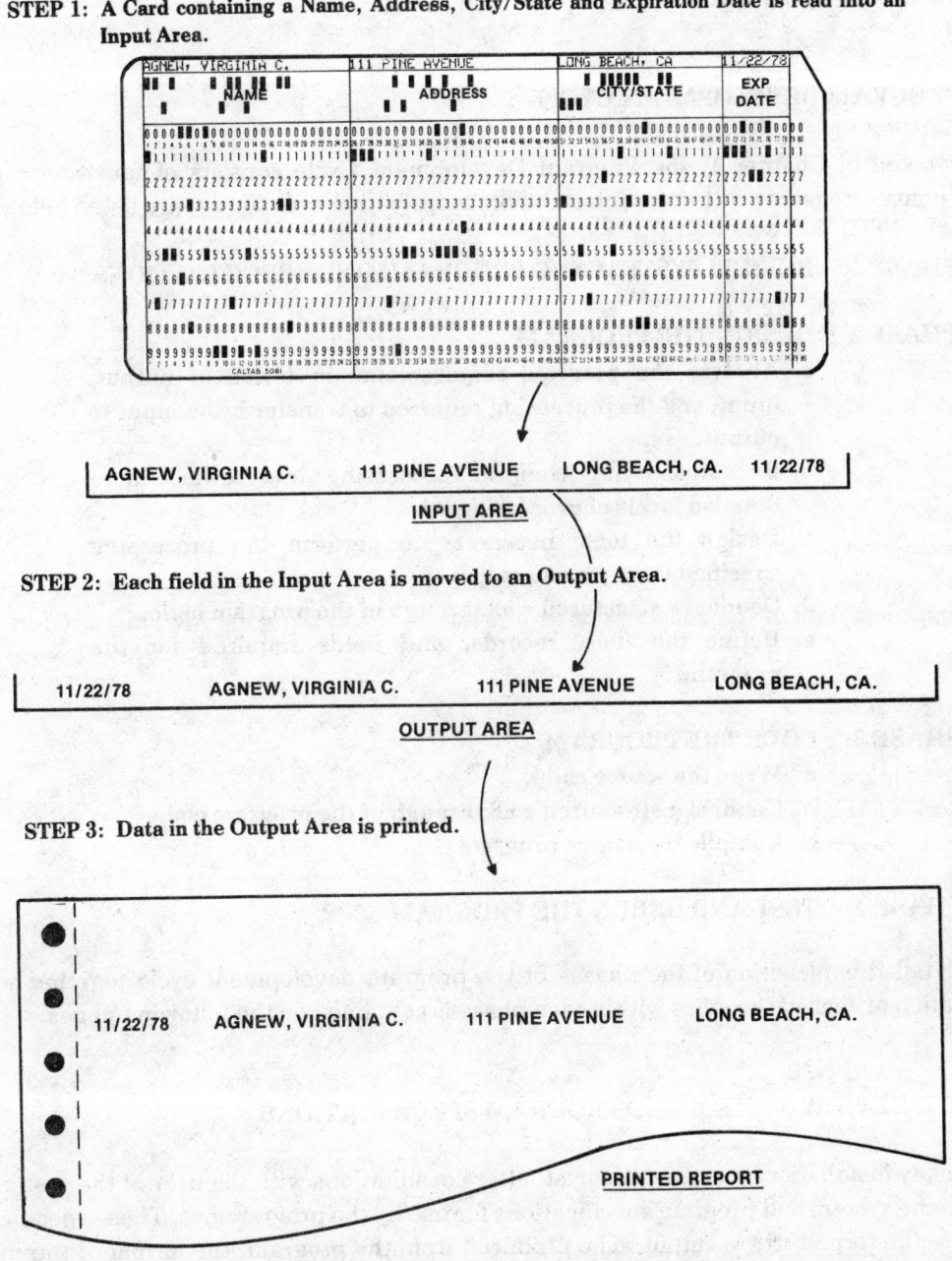

STEP 2: Each field in the Input Area is moved to an Output Area.

STEP 3: Data in the Output Area is printed.

Figure 2-3 Steps in Preparing Report

It can be seen in Figure 2-3 that the data in the card is read into an input area in computer storage. Each field in the input area is then moved to an output area, that is, an area reserved for the data which is to be printed on the report. The report is then written. This sequence of events will continue so long as there are cards to be processed.

Note in Figure 2-3 that the fields on the printed report are not in the same sequence as the fields on the input card, that is, the Expiration Date is the last field on the input card but is the first field to appear on the printed report. The arrangement of the fields on the report is under the control of the programmer when the program is written. It is important for the programmer to understand the basic processing that is to occur within the computer in order to be able to properly design a program.

THE PROGRAM DEVELOPMENT CYCLE

As noted in Chapter 1, the Program Development Cycle consists of four major phases. These phases, together with some intermediate steps within each phase, are listed below.

PHASE 1.   REVIEW SYSTEM AND PROGRAMMING SPECIFICATIONS

PHASE 2.   DESIGN THE PROGRAM
   a. Analyze the program requirements in terms of output, input, and the processing required to transform the input to output.
   b. Decompose any complex processing into lower, more detailed levels of processing.
   c. Design the logic necessary to perform the processing specified in step a and step b.
   d. Conduct a structured walkthrough of the program logic.
   e. Define the files, records, and fields required for the program.

PHASE 3:   CODE THE PROGRAM
   a. Write the source code.
   b. Conduct a structured walkthrough of the program code.
   c. Compile the source program.

PHASE 4.   TEST AND DEBUG THE PROGRAM

A detailed explanation of the phases of the program development cycle together with an explanation of each of the steps within each phase is contained on the following pages.

PHASE 1: REVIEW SYSTEM AND PROGRAM SPECIFICATIONS

In many installations a systems analyst, after consultations with the user of the system, will develop the system and program specifications for use by the programmer. These specifications illustrate the format of the output to be produced from the program, the format of the input to be used in the program, and the processing that is to occur within the program. These system and program specifications commonly consist of:

1. A Printer Spacing Chart defining the format of any printed report that is to be prepared.

2. A record layout form defining the fields that appear in the input record.

3. A narrative explaining the processing which is to occur.

As noted, to define the format of a report, that is, where the fields are to be printed on the report and to indicate whether the report is to be single or double spaced, a printer spacing chart is used. Figure 2-4 contains the printer spacing chart for the Subscription List Report.

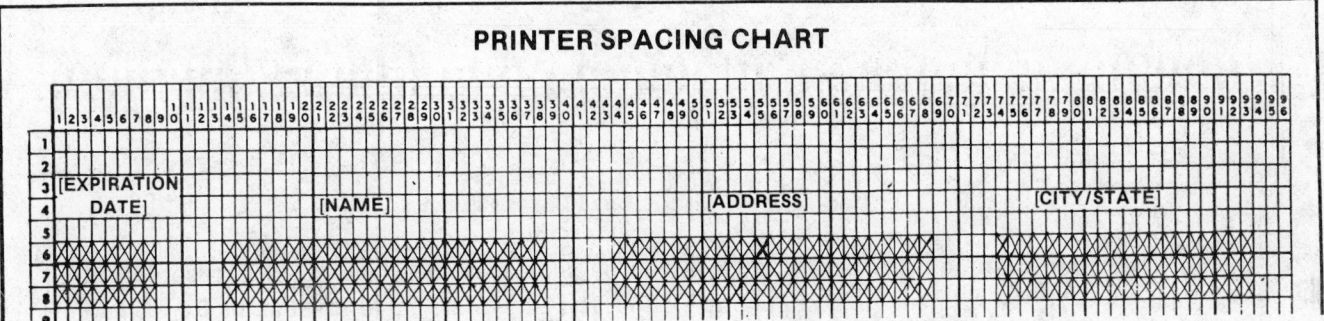

Figure 2-4 Printer Spacing Chart of Subscription Listing

The small numbers at the top of the printer spacing chart represent the actual printing positions on the computer's printer. To layout a report on a printer spacing chart, the programmer or analyst selects the print positions which are to be used to print the fields from the input record and makes an "X" notation in each print position. Thus, as can be seen from Figure 2-4, the Expiration Date will be printed in positions 1-8 on the report, the Name will be printed in positions 14-38, the Address will appear in positions 44-68, and the City/State is printed in positions 74-93.

At least two lines of X's should be recorded in order to indicate if the report is to be single, double, or triple spaced. For example, if the report is to be double spaced, a blank line would appear between each row of X's. Note in the example that the Subscription List Report is to be single spaced.

When input is to be in form of punched cards, the format of the cards is normally defined on a Multiple Card Layout Form. Figure 2-5 illustrates the layout of the Subscription List Cards.

MULTIPLE-CARD LAYOUT FORM

Application __Subscription List Cards__   by   __Shelly_____   Date _____   Job No. _____   Sheet No. _____

NAME	ADDRESS	CITY/STATE	EXP DATE	
9 9 9 9 9 9 9 9 9 9 9 9 9 9 9 9 9 9 9 9 9 9 9 9 9	9 9 9 9 9 9 9 9 9 9 9 9 9 9 9 9 9 9 9 9 9 9 9 9 9	9 9 9 9 9 9 9 9 9 9 9 9 9 9 9 9 9 9 9 9	9 9 9 9 9 9 9 9	9 9
1 2 3 4 5 6 7 8 9 10 11 12 13 14 15 16 17 18 19 20 21 22 23 24 25	26 27 28 29 30 31 32 33 34 35 36 37 38 39 40 41 42 43 44 45 46 47 48 49 50	51 52 53 54 55 56 57 58 59 60 61 62 63 64 65 66 67 68 69 70	71 72 73 74 75 76 77 78	79 80

| 9 9 9 9 9 9 9 9 9 9 9 9 9 9 9 9 9 9 9 9 9 9 9 9 9 9 9 9 9 9 9 9 9 9 9 9 9 9 9 9 9 9 9 9 9 9 9 9 9 9 9 9 9 9 9 9 9 9 9 9 9 9 9 9 9 9 9 9 9 9 9 9 9 9 9 9 9 9 9 9 |
| 1 2 3 4 5 6 7 8 9 10 11 12 13 14 15 16 17 18 19 20 21 22 23 24 25 26 27 28 29 30 31 32 33 34 35 36 37 38 39 40 41 42 43 44 45 46 47 48 49 50 51 52 53 54 55 56 57 58 59 60 61 62 63 64 65 66 67 68 69 70 71 72 73 74 75 76 77 78 79 80 |

Figure 2-5 Multiple Card Layout Form

From the Multiple Card Layout Form it can be seen that the Name field is recorded in columns 1-25, the Address field in columns 26-50, the City/State Field in columns 51-70, and the Expiration Date in columns 71-78. Card columns 79 and 80 are not used in this program and will contain blanks.

Processing

The processing which is to take place is normally recorded on a Programming Specifications form. The form used for the Subscription List Report is illustrated in Figure 2-6.

PROGRAMMING SPECIFICATIONS		
SUBJECT Subscription List Report	**DATE** December 8	**PAGE** 1 **OF** 1
TO Programmer	**FROM** Systems Analyst	

A program is to be written to prepare a Subscription List Report. The format of the input card and the printer spacing chart are included as a part of this narrative. The program should be written to include the following processing:

1. The program should read the input cards and create the Subscription List Report as per the format illustrated on the printer spacing chart. The report shall contain the Name, Address, City/State, and Expiration Date.

2. One line is to be printed on the report for each card which is read.

3. The report is to be single spaced.

4. The program should be written in COBOL.

Figure 2-6 Programming Specifications

Note that the programming specifications contain a narrative description of the processing which is to occur in the program. Thus, the printer spacing chart, record layout form, and programming specifications are commonly used by the analyst to provide the programmer with the information required to design the program and produce the required output.

When the programming specifications have been received from the systems analyst, the programmer must very carefully review the specifications so that every aspect of the program which is to be written is fully understood. Too much emphasis cannot be placed on the requirement that the programmer fully understand the processing which is to take place within a program. It is quite obvious that if the programmer does not understand what is required in a program, the program cannot possibly contain the proper coding to process the data. Beyond that basic truism, however, is the fact that a programmer can many times find errors or omissions within the programming specifications which must be corrected prior to the programming effort. An extremely detailed perusal of the programming specifications must always be undertaken before beginning the task of program design.

PHASE 2: DESIGN THE PROGRAM

Design means to plan out the form or method of solution of a given problem. To design a program, a series of well-defined steps must be followed. These steps are outlined below.

1. Analyze the programming specifications in terms of output, input and functions to be performed by the program, and determine the major processing tasks necessary to convert the input to output. Record this information on an IPO Chart (Input/Processing/Output Chart).

2. Further analyze the major processing tasks of the program. Decompose any complex processing into lower, more detailed levels of processing.

3. Design the logic necessary to perform the processing specified in step 1 and step 2 by recording the detailed steps using English-like statements. (Note: The English-like statements are commonly referred to as Pseudocode).

4. Conduct a structured walkthrough of the pseudocode.

5. Analyze the pseudocode and record all files, records, and fields required by the program.

It must be noted that program design is an iterative process in which the design is continuously reviewed at each step and revised if necessary so that the optimal solution to the program will result. In particular, steps 1 and 2 will be continually repeated since each time the processing is decomposed into more detailed levels of processing, a new IPO Chart will be prepared for the new level of processing.

In addition, it is not at all uncommon to have reached Step 3 or Step 4 only to find that the design of the program is not correct. In this case, it would be required to begin a redesign of the program with Step 1 and Step 2. Although it is preferable that this type of redesigning be kept to a minimum, in actual practice it occurs quite frequently, especially with more complex programming. Thus, the programmer should not feel that a poor job of design has been done if steps within the design process must be repeated. It must be kept in mind that the end result of the design phase is to have a program which will work the first time it is placed on the computer and will never fail subsequently. Therefore, any corrections which are necessary in the design phase of the program serve only to enhance the probabilities of a correct program and the programmer should be encouraged to continue the repetitive process of design until it is ensured that the program is correct.

A detailed explanation of each of the design steps is contained on the following pages.

Step 1: **Analyze the programming specifications in terms of Output, Input, and Processing to be performed.**

As the first step in program design, the programmer must specify: 1) the output to be produced from the program; 2) the input to be used to produce the output; 3) the major processing tasks which must occur to transform the input to the desired output. This information is recorded on an IPO Chart (Input/Processing/Output Chart).

The output from the sample program is the Subscription List Report. An entry reflecting this should be made on the IPO Chart as follows:

IPO CHART				
PROGRAM: Subscription List Report		**PROGRAMMER:** Shelly/Cashman		**DATE:** Dec.8
MODULE NAME: Create Subscription List Report	**REF:** AØØØ	**MODULE FUNCTION:** Create Subscription List Report		
INPUT		**PROCESSING**	**REF:**	**OUTPUT**
				1. Subscription List Report

Figure 2-7 Example of IPO Chart with Output Entry

Note from Figure 2-7 that the output to be produced from the program consists of the Subscription List Report, and that this entry is recorded in the OUTPUT portion of the IPO Chart. Note also that headings are included on the IPO Chart to identify the module which is being defined on the IPO Chart by both name and function. A module is a part of the program which is to accomplish a specific function within the program. In the sample program, the processing is not complex, so one module is all that is required to create the Subscription List Report. More complex programs are made up of more than one module, and each module has a particular function to perform. The Reference Number (REF) is a number given to each module for identification purposes. When the program consists of only one module, the reference number of A000.

The REF entry in the heading line with the Input, Processing, and Output is used to specify those processing tasks which will be separate modules within the program. As noted, in the sample program in this chapter there is only one module, so an entry in this field will not be required.

The input to the program is the Subscription List Card File and this information should be entered on the IPO Chart as illustrated in Figure 2-8.

IPO CHART

PROGRAM: Subscription List Report		PROGRAMMER: Shelly/Cashman		DATE: Dec.8
MODULE NAME: Create Subscription List Report	REF: A000	MODULE FUNCTION: Create Subscription List Report		
INPUT	PROCESSING		REF:	OUTPUT
1. Subscription List Card File				1. Subscription List Report

Figure 2-8 Example of IPO Chart with Input Entry

As can be seen from Figure 2-8, the input to the program and the output from the program are specified in their proper positions on the IPO Chart.

The programmer must then determine the **major processing tasks** which are necessary to accomplish the function of the module defined on the IPO Chart. In the example, the function of the module is to create the Subscription List Report. The major processing tasks to accomplish this are specified in the Processing portion of the form, as illustrated in Figure 2-9.

IPO CHART

PROGRAM: Subscription List Report		PROGRAMMER: Shelly/Cashman		DATE: Sept. 18
MODULE NAME: Create Subscription List Report	REF: A000	MODULE FUNCTION: Create Subscription List Report		
INPUT	PROCESSING		REF:	OUTPUT
1. Subscription List Input File	1. Initialization			1. Subscription List Report
	2. Obtain the input data			
	3. Format the print line			
	4. Write the report			
	5. Termination			

Figure 2-9 Example of IPO Chart with Processing Entry

The first entry on the IPO Chart under PROCESSING is "Initialization." Most computer programs require some type of initialization processing which will prepare files and fields for processing. In the sample program, one of the tasks which must be specified is Initialization.

Another major processing task which must normally be performed within a business program is obtaining the input data. In most business programs, the reason for the program is to process some input data and create some type of output. Thus, in order for this to occur, the input data must be obtained for processing within the program. Since the program in this chapter is to process the Subscription List Card File, this input data must be obtained for processing; and, therefore, "Obtain the input data" is one of the processing tasks which must be accomplished within the program.

Another task which must be accomplished within the program is to format the print line, that is, prepare the line to be printed as specified on the printer spacing chart. It should be noted that any detailed steps which may be involved in formatting the print line, such as moving individual fields from the input area to the output area, are not specified on the IPO Chart. At this step in the design process, only the major processing tasks are specified. At a later time the information on the IPO Chart will be further analyzed to define specific steps which must be taken.

In order to produce output from the program, the report must be printed. Therefore, another task to be done within the program is to Write the Report. In addition, most business programs will require some type of termination processing. Thus, Termination is one of the processing tasks which must be specified on the IPO Chart.

It should be noted that the entries in the Processing section of the IPO Chart do not specify the manner in which any of the processing is to be accomplished nor are they necessarily listed in the sequence in which the processing is to take place within the program. Instead, the IPO Chart is used to merely specify the major processing tasks which must occur within the program. Thus, the IPO Chart is used to specify WHAT is to take place within the program, not WHEN and HOW.

Step 2: Analyze the processing specified on the IPO Chart and decompose the module into more detailed modules if required.

As noted, the program module defined on the IPO Chart performs a given function and it is composed of major processing tasks which must be performed in order to accomplish the function of the module. After the tasks have been defined on the IPO Chart, the programmer should analyze the processing to determine if the module requires further "decomposition." A general rule used in structured programming is that no module within a program should require more than 50 lines of source statements in a given programming language. Modules requiring in excess of 50 statements are often difficult to comprehend.

Therefore, if it appears that the processing for the module, as specified on the IPO Chart, will require more than 50 statements, then those tasks which perform a unique function within the module should themselves be made modules of the program. Each of these new modules will accomplish a given function within the program. Whenever this occurs, an IPO Chart for these new modules will be made by the programmer. This process will continue until all modules have been broken down into less than 50 statements and perform a specific function. It should be noted that the primary idea is to decompose each module into more detailed modules, each of which perform a specific function. The general rule which limits modules to 50 statements is only a guideline to assist in the decomposition of modules and to lead to an effective program design.

In the sample program in this chapter, an analysis of the processing to be accomplished in the module whose function is to create the Subscription List Report reveals that none of the major processing tasks are of such a size so as to cause the entire module to be greater than 50 statements in length. Therefore, further decomposition of the module specified on the IPO Chart in Figure 2-9 is not required.

After the IPO Charts have been completed, the programmer would normally consult with the systems analyst who designed the system in which the program is to be used in order to ensure that the programmer has properly understood the problem to be solved and has provided a viable solution to the problem. Such elements as being sure the proper input and output have been identified and that the processing which is to take place will constitute all of the processing which should occur within the program will be discussed.

In large programming projects, the processing to be performed may be extremely complex, with many different functions to be performed. Therefore, at this time it may be desirable to conduct a structured walkthrough with other programmers to review the overall design of the program. If the basic design appears satisfactory, the programmer then begins the next step in the structured design process by defining the logic necessary in the solution of the problem.

Step 3: Design the logic necessary to perform the processing specified in Step 1 and Step 2.

After the input, processing, and output have been specified for a module, it is necessary to define on a more detailed level the steps and sequences of operations that are necessary in the solution of the problem, that is, the logic required to solve the problem must be designed. A design tool called PSEUDOCODE has been developed to facilitate this process.

The primary purpose of pseudocode is to enable the programmer to express thoughts in a form that uses regular English language prose but allows for the expression of the control flow of a program in a straight-forward, easy to understand manner. Pseudocode has few syntactical rules and merely uses English language phrases to express thoughts, with each phrase representing a programming statement or process which must be performed. Pseudocode is written at a level of completeness and detail which allows the coding of the program directly from it.

It should be noted that the pseudocode is developed from the processing which is specified in the Processing portion of the IPO Chart. Thus, the object of pseudocode is to specify the logic and methods of implementing the major processing tasks which are required to accomplish the function of the module. It will be recalled that the processing specified on the IPO Chart should indicate WHAT is to occur; the processing specified in pseudocode indicates WHEN and HOW this processing will be performed. The pseudocode for the production of the Subscription List Report is illustrated in Figure 2-10.

PSEUDOCODE SPECIFICATIONS

PROGRAM: Subscription List Report	PROGRAMMER: Shelly/Cashman	DATE: Dec 8

MODULE NAME: Create Subscription List Report	REF: A000	MODULE FUNCTION: Create Subscription List Report

PSEUDOCODE	REF:	FILES, RECORDS, FIELDS REQUIRED

Open the files
Read an input record
PERFORM UNTIL no more input records
    Clear the output area
    Move the expiration date, name, address,
        city/state to the output area
    Write the line on the report
    Read an input record
ENDPERFORM
Close the files
Stop run		

Figure 2-10 Pseudocode for Sample Program

Note from Figure 2-10 that the pseudocode is recorded on a form entitled "Pseudocode Specifications." This form is used to specify the logic which is to be employed in the program as well as the Files, Records, and Fields which are required in the program. The heading on the Pseudocode Specifications is the same as that on the IPO Chart. The REF (Reference) column in the center of the form is used to specify the Reference Number of other modules which are referenced within the pseudocode. In the sample program in this chapter, there is only one module so an entry in this portion of the form is not required.

As can be seen from Figure 2-10, pseudocode is a series of statements which indicate the sequence in which operations are to be executed within the program and also under what conditions they will be done. The first operation to occur is to "Open the files." This is the initialization processing which was noted previously and readies the files to be processed. Whenever a file is to be used for either input or output in a COBOL program, it must be opened.

The next statement is "Read an input record." Thus, the first record in the Subscription List Card File will be read into computer storage. It should be noted that the statements in the pseudocode are NOT COBOL statements; rather, they are English statements of what is to take place and the sequence in which they are to take place.

After the first input record is read, a PERFORM UNTIL statement is specified. This statement says "Perform the following statements until there are no more input records." All of the statements between the PERFORM UNTIL and the ENDPERFORM will be executed in a "loop," that is, they will be continually executed until there is no more data to be processed.

The first job of the PERFORM UNTIL statement is to determine if there are any more input records. Assuming there is at least one input record, and since it was read by the previous Read statement, the statements within the "Perform Loop" would be executed.

The first statement within the loop specifies "Clear the output area." This consists of placing blanks in the output area so that improper data will not appear in the print line. After the output area has been cleared, that is, the entire output area contains blanks, the data in the input area is moved to the output area. Thus, the Expiration Date, Name, Address, and City/State will be moved from the input area, where it was stored when read, to the output area, from which it will be printed.

After the data is moved from the input area to the output area, the data is ready for printing. Therefore, the next step is to "Write the line on the report." This will cause the data in the output area to be printed on the report.

After the line has been printed on the report, it has been completely processed. Thus, the next step is to read another input record, as is specified in the pseudocode in Figure 2-10. After the next input record is read, control passes back to the Perform Until statement which will determine if there is another input record to process. If there is, then the statements within the "Perform Loop" will again be executed. If there is no more data, then the statement following the ENDPERFORM statement will be executed. As can be seen, it is the Perform statement which determines when the looping process should be terminated.

After all of the records have been read and printed on the report, the loop will be terminated. At that time, the "Close the files" statement will be executed. The closing of the files is the termination processing which is required whenever files are processed using COBOL, that is, the files must be closed after being opened. After the files are closed, the program is stopped.

To further illustrate the processing which will occur as a result of the pseudocode statements in Figure 2-10, assume that there are three input cards in the input file. The following steps would take place within the program:

1. The files are opened.
2. The first input record is read.
3. Since there is a record to be processed, the following occurs:
    a. The output area is cleared.
    b. The data from the first card is moved from the input
       area to the output area.
    c. The data in the output area is printed.
    d. The second card is read from the input file.

4. Since there is another record to be processed, the following occurs:
   a. The output area is cleared.
   b. The data from the second card is moved from the input area to the output area.
   c. The data in the output area is printed.
   d. The third card is read from the input file.
5. Since there is another record to be processed, the following occurs:
   a. The output area is cleared.
   b. The data from the third card is moved from the input area to the output area.
   c. The data in the output area is printed.
   d. An attempt is made to read the next card; however, there are no more records to be processed.
6. Since there are no more records to be processed, the loop is terminated and the files are closed.
7. The program is stopped.

This concept of performing statements within a loop so long as there are more records to process is very important since virtually all COBOL programs employ this identical logic to process input records. Therefore, it is imperative that the programmer understand this concept and be able to use it in programs!

Note that as a result of the processing which is specified in the pseudocode, the tasks to be performed as specified on the IPO Chart in Figure 2-9 are accomplished. This relationship is illustrated below.

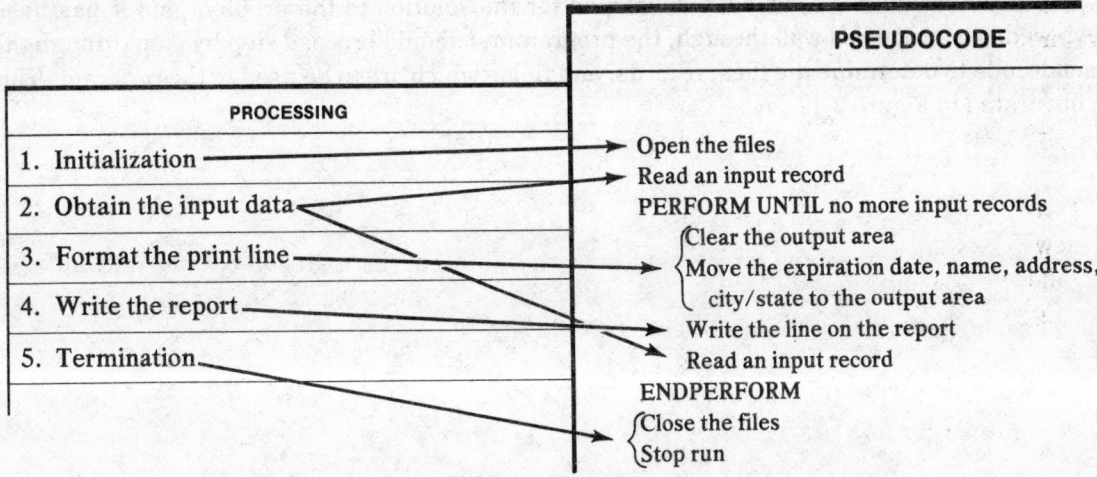

Figure 2-11 Relationship of IPO Chart and Pseudocode

As can be seen from Figure 2-11, all of the major processing tasks which had to be accomplished as specified in the Processing portion of the IPO Chart were accomplished by what is to take place in the program as a result of the sequence designed through the use of pseudocode. It must be noted again that the processing specified on the IPO Chart consists of the major processing tasks which must be performed; it does not specify the sequence in which events are to take place nor how they are to be accomplished. It is only when these tasks are translated into pseudocode that the methods to be used in the program are specified.

It will also be noted in the pseudocode illustrated in Figure 2-11 that the PERFORM UNTIL and ENDPERFORM words are in capital letters. This is because these words have special meaning within pseudocode—they indicate the beginning and end of the loop process as has been described. In addition, the statements which are to be executed within the looping process are indented so that they are more easily seen. This convention of capitalizing the PERFORM UNTIL and ENDPERFORM words and indenting the statements to be executed within the loop should always be followed.

Step 4: Conduct a structured walkthrough of the pseudocode.

After the pseudocode is completed and reviewed by the programmer to ensure its accuracy, it will normally be reviewed by 3-7 members of the programming team or other programmers within the programming staff to allow them to attempt to find any logic errors which have occurred within the pseudocode; that is, they will review the pseudocode to determine if the programmer has made any logical mistakes which would prevent the proper output from being produced from the input to the program. If they find any questionable logic and techniques used, then the original programmer should again review the pseudocode and justify what is taking place within the program to the reviewing programmers. After all reviewing programmers and the original programmer are satisfied that the program is correct as specified in the pseudocode, then the programmer should determine the Files, Records, and Fields required for the program.

Step 5: Record all files, records, and fields required by the program.

After the pseudocode has been developed for the solution to the problem and it has been reviewed in a structured walkthrough, the programmer should proceed step by step through the pseudocode to determine the files, records, and fields which are to be used in the program. This is illustrated in Figure 2-12.

PSEUDOCODE SPECIFICATIONS

PROGRAM: Subscription List Report	PROGRAMMER: Shelly/Cashman	DATE: Dec 8

MODULE NAME: Create Subscription List Report	REF: AØØØ	MODULE FUNCTION: Create Subscription List Report

PSEUDOCODE	REF:	FILES, RECORDS, FIELDS REQUIRED
Open the files		Subscription list card file ⟩ *input* file
		Subscription list report file ⟩ file
Read an input record		Input area for input record — *Record*
		Name ⟩
		Address ⟩ *Fields*
		City/State ⟩
		Expiration date
PERFORM UNTIL no more input records		Indicator for no more records —
Clear the output area		Printer output area — *Record*
		Expiration date ⟩
		Name ⟩ *Field*
		Address ⟩
		City/State ⟩
Move the expiration date, name, address, city/state to the output area		
Write the line on the report		
Read an input record		
ENDPERFORM		
Close the files		
Stop run		

Figure 2-12 Determination of Files, Records and Fields Required

Note from the example above that each statement within the pseudocode is examined to determine what files, records, or fields must be available for that particular statement. In order to "Open the files", the Subscription List Card File and the Subscription List Report File must be defined. When an input record is read, there must be an input area in which to store the input record. Therefore, the input area for the input record must be defined. Within that input area will be areas for the Name, Address, City/State, and Expiration Date because these fields must be referenced within the program (see Figure 2-2 for the input record format).

As has been noted, the loop to format the report, write the report, and read the next record will be performed until there are no more input records. Therefore, it is mandatory that some means be used to indicate there are no more input records so that the loop will be terminated. The method used is an "indicator" which can be tested to determine if there are no more data records. The definition of the indicator and the method in which it can be set to indicate no more data records will be discussed in detail in Chapter 3.

In order to clear the output area, the printer output area must be defined within the program. Therefore, the printer output area is specified together with the fields which are found within the printer output area (see Figure 2-1 for the output area format). The remainder of the statements in the pseudocode reference files, records, or fields which have already been specified, so there is no need for further entries on the form.

Once the pseudocode has been defined and approved in a walkthrough, and the files, records, and fields have been specified, the design phase of the program development cycle is complete. Therefore, the programmer must move on to the third phase—that of coding the program.

PHASE 3: CODE THE PROGRAM

The third phase of the program development cycle consists of coding the program in the programming language which is to be used for the program. This phase is made up of three steps:

1. Write the source code

2. Conduct a structured walkthrough of the source code

3. Compile the source program

A detailed explanation of each of these steps is contained in the following paragraphs.

Step 1: Write the source code.

As noted in Chapter 1, one of the major advances in data processing has been the development of high-level programming languages. These lanuages are designed in such a way that the programmer can write the source code, that is, the instructions and statements in the program, clearly and with ease, leading to a program which is easily understood by others. In addition, a high-level language is independent of the internal characteristics of a particular machine, which allows programs written in high-level languages to be used on many different machines.

COBOL, which is an acronym for COmmon Business Oriented Language, was released in 1960 after development by a committee composed of representatives from manufacturers, government agencies, and the Bureau of Standards. Since its initial release, there have been several changes in the language in order to ensure the compatibility of the language between different computer manufacturers. In 1968 and again in 1974 versions of COBOL were released from the American National Standards Institute. Although some manufacturers have added extensions to the language, the basic ANSI COBOL is found on almost all machines available for business data processing.

In order to write a program using the COBOL language, the programmer writes the program statements on predesigned coding forms. A portion of the COBOL program to solve the sample problem in this chapter is illustrated below.

```
COBOL Coding Form

SYSTEM
PROGRAM    SUBSCRIPTION LIST REPORT      GRAPHIC  O  Ø  2  Z  1  1
PROGRAMMER SHELLY/CASHMAN   DATE DEC. 13  PUNCH   11-6 ZERO TWO O-9 12-9 ONE

004010  PROCEDURE DIVISION.                                        SUBLIST
004020                                                             SUBLIST
004030 *************************************************************** SUBLIST
004040 *                                                           * SUBLIST
004050 *    THIS PROGRAM READS THE SUBSCRIPTION INPUT RECORDS AND  * SUBLIST
004060 *    CREATES THE SUBSCRIPTION LISTING. IT IS ENTERED FROM THE * SUBLIST
004070 *    OPERATING SYSTEM AND EXITS TO THE OPERATING SYSTEM.    * SUBLIST
004080 *                                                           * SUBLIST
004090 *************************************************************** SUBLIST
004100                                                             SUBLIST
004110  A000-CREATE-SUBSCRIPTION-LIST.                             SUBLIST
004120                                                             SUBLIST
004130      OPEN INPUT SUBSCRIPTION-INPUT-FILE                     SUBLIST
004140           OUTPUT SUBSCRIPTION-REPORT-FILE.                  SUBLIST
004150      READ SUBSCRIPTION-INPUT-FILE                           SUBLIST
004160          AT END                                             SUBLIST
004170              MOVE 'NO ' TO ARE-THERE-MORE-RECORDS.          SUBLIST
004180      PERFORM A001-FORMAT-PRINT-REPORT                       SUBLIST
004190          UNTIL ARE-THERE-MORE-RECORDS = 'NO '.              SUBLIST
```

```
COBOL Coding Form

SYSTEM
PROGRAM    SUBSCRIPTION LIST REPORT      GRAPHIC  O  Ø  2  Z  1  1
PROGRAMMER SHELLY/CASHMAN   DATE DEC. 13  PUNCH   11-6 ZERO TWO Ø-9 12-9 ONE

005010      CLOSE SUBSCRIPTION-INPUT-FILE                          SUBLIST
005020            SUBSCRIPTION-REPORT-FILE.                        SUBLIST
005030      STOP RUN.                                              SUBLIST
005040                                                             SUBLIST
005050                                                             SUBLIST
005060                                                             SUBLIST
005070  A001-FORMAT-PRINT-REPORT.                                  SUBLIST
005080                                                             SUBLIST
005090      MOVE SPACES TO SUBSCRIPTION-REPORT-LINE.               SUBLIST
005100      MOVE EXPIRATION-DATE-INPUT TO EXPIRATION-DATE-REPORT.  SUBLIST
005110      MOVE NAME-INPUT TO NAME-REPORT.                        SUBLIST
005120      MOVE ADDRESS-INPUT TO ADDRESS-REPORT.                  SUBLIST
005130      MOVE CITY-STATE-INPUT TO CITY-STATE-REPORT.            SUBLIST
005140      WRITE SUBSCRIPTION-REPORT-LINE                         SUBLIST
005150          AFTER ADVANCING 1 LINES.                           SUBLIST
005160      READ SUBSCRIPTION-INPUT-FILE                           SUBLIST
005170          AT END                                             SUBLIST
005180              MOVE 'NO ' TO ARE-THERE-MORE-RECORDS.          SUBLIST
```

Figure 2-13 Example of COBOL Program

Note from the example of the coding illustrated in Figure 2-13 that the COBOL statements are somewhat readable without having a proficiency in the structure of the language and they resemble the pseudocode which was developed for the solution of the problem (see Figure 2-10). As was noted, the program should be coded directly from the pseudocode so that the program will operate in the manner designed through the use of the pseudocode. A detailed explanation of the use of the COBOL language to solve the sample problem is contained in Chapter 3.

Step 2: Conduct a structured walkthrough of the program code

After the coding has been written on the coding forms, a structured walkthrough should be conducted to review the coding and detect any errors which have been incorporated into the program code. In particular, the reviewers should check the code to be sure that no syntax errors have occurred and that the coding corresponds to the pseudocode which was developed for the program. Syntax errors are errors which occur when the rules of the programming language are violated. For example, if required punctuation is omitted or punctuation is included where it cannot be, a syntax error has occurred and it is the function of this walkthrough to detect these errors so that they will not occur when the program is compiled.

When the structured walkthrough is completed, the programmer and the reviewers should be completely confident that the coding is correct, that no errors will occur as a result of misuse of the programming language, and also that the logic as implemented in the programming language is correct. The program should not be placed on the computer until all possible care has been taken to ensure that it is correct.

Step 3: Compile the source code

For processing on the computer, the COBOL program is punched onto cards or recorded on disk or tape for reading by an input device. The diagram in Figure 2-14 illustrates a segment of the COBOL program as it appears on punched cards. Note that for each line of coding on the form (see Figure 2-13), a single punched card is required.

EXAMPLE

```
005180              MOVE 'NO ' TO ARE-THERE-MORE-RECORDS.          SUBLIST
005170                AT END                                       SUBLIST
005160              READ SUBSCRIPTION-INPUT-FILE                   SUBLIST
005150                AFTER ADVANCING 1 LINES.                     SUBLIST
005140              WRITE SUBSCRIPTION-REPORT-LINE                 SUBLIST
005130              MOVE CITY-STATE-INPUT TO CITY-STATE-REPORT.    SUBLIST
005120              MOVE ADDRESS-INPUT TO ADDRESS-REPORT.          SUBLIST
005110              MOVE NAME-INPUT TO NAME-REPORT.                SUBLIST
005100              MOVE EXPIRATION-DATE-INPUT TO EXPIRATION-DATE-REPORT. SUBLIST
005090              MOVE SPACES TO SUBSCRIPTION-REPORT-LINE.       SUBLIST
005080                                                             SUBLIST
005070  A001-FORMAT-PRINT-REPORT.                                  SUBLIST
005060                                                             SUBLIST
005050                                                             SUBLIST
005040                                                             SUBLIST
005030          STOP RUN.                                          SUBLIST
005020              SUBSCRIPTION-REPORT-FILE.                      SUBLIST
005010          CLOSE SUBSCRIPTION-INPUT-FILE                      SUBLIST
004190              UNTIL ARE-THERE-MORE-RECORDS = 'NO '.          SUBLIST
004180          PERFORM A001-FORMAT-PRINT-REPORT                   SUBLIST
004170              MOVE 'NO ' TO ARE-THERE-MORE-RECORDS.          SUBLIST
004160                AT END                                       SUBLIST
004150          READ SUBSCRIPTION-INPUT-FILE                       SUBLIST
004140              OUTPUT SUBSCRIPTION-REPORT-FILE.               SUBLIST
004130          OPEN INPUT  SUBSCRIPTION-INPUT-FILE                SUBLIST
004120                                                             SUBLIST
004110  A000-CREATE-SUBSCRIPTION-LIST.                             SUBLIST
004100                                                             SUBLIST
004090 ***************************************************         SUBLIST
004080 *                                                  *        SUBLIST
004070 * OPERATING SYSTEM AND EXITS TO THE OPERATING SYSTEM. *     SUBLIST
004060 * CREATES THE SUBSCRIPTION LISTING. IT IS ENTERED FROM THE * SUBLIST
004050 * THIS PROGRAM READS THE SUBSCRIPTION INPUT RECORDS AND   * SUBLIST
004040 *                                                  *        SUBLIST
004030 ***************************************************         SUBLIST
004020                                                             SUBLIST
004010  PROCEDURE DIVISION.                                        SUBLIST
```

Figure 2-14 Segment of COBOL Program Punched on Cards

It should be noted that the computer can only understand instructions on a machine language level; therefore, COBOL statements written by the programmer must be translated into machine language instructions which can be understood by the computer. For example, the COBOL word "MOVE" must be converted to a code which can be understood by the computer in order for the move operation to be executed.

Because computers only understand instructions in machine language form, symbolic "translators" were developed. The "translator" program that converts the COBOL Source Statements, that is, the statements written by the programmer, into machine language instructions which can be understood by the computer is called a Compiler. The following diagram illustrates the basic steps to compile a COBOL language program, that is, convert the program from source statements written by the programmer into machine language.

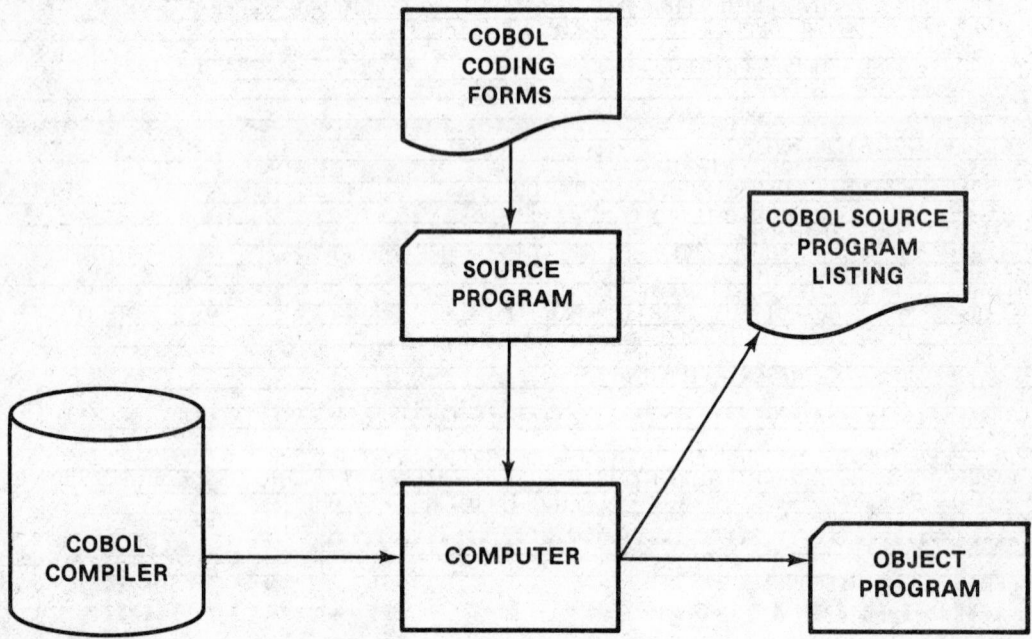

Figure 2-15 Steps in Compiling a Program

To "convert" a program from a symbolic form to machine language, the Compiler is read into the storage unit of the computer followed by the source program. The Compiler then "translates" the symbolic statements of the source COBOL program into a machine language form and produces an OBJECT PROGRAM. The Object Program is the machine language instructions generated by the Compiler from the COBOL Program and is typically stored on either cards or disk.

The Compiler also provides auxilary functions that assist the programmer in checking and documenting programs. Some of these functions are:

Program Listings: A listing of the source program statements may be produced by the COBOL Compiler for each source program compiled.

Error Indications: As a source program is compiled, it is analyzed for actual or potential errors in the use of the COBOL language. Detected errors are indicated in the program listing.

The following is a segment of a listing of a COBOL program generated by the Compiler and "diagnostics" or errors detected by the Compiler. These errors must be corrected before the computer can execute the object program and process the data.

EXAMPLE

```
3

00067  004090 PROCEDURE DIVISION.                                         SUBLIST
00068  004100                                                            SUBLIST
00069  004110**********************************************************  SUBLIST
00070  004120*                                                        *  SUBLIST
00071  004130*  THIS PROGRAM READS THE SUBSCRIPTION INPUT RECORDS AND  *  SUBLIST
00072  004140*  CREATES THE SUBSCRIPTION LISTING.  IT IS ENTERED FROM THE *  SUBLIST
00073  004150*  OPERATING SYSTEM AND EXITS TO THE OPERATING SYSTEM.    *  SUBLIST
00074  004160*                                                        *  SUBLIST
00075  004170**********************************************************  SUBLIST
00076  004180                                                            SUBLIST
00077  004190 A000-CREATE-SUBSCRIPTION-LIST.                              SUBLIST
00078  004200                                                            SUBLIST
00079  005010     OPEN INPUT SUBSCRIPTION-INPUT-FILE                      SUBLIST
00080  005020          OUTPUT SUBSCRIPTION-REPORT-FILE.                   SUBLIST
00081  005030     READ SUBSCRIPTION-INPUT-FILE                            SUBLIST
00082  005040        AT END                                              SUBLIST
00083  005050          MOVE 'NO ' TO ARE-THERE-MORE-RECORDS.             SUBLIST
00084  005060     PERFORM A001-FORMAT-PRINT-REPORT                       SUBLIST
00085  005070        UNTIL ARE-THERE-MORE-RECORDS = 'NO '.               SUBLIST
00086  005080     CLOSE SUBSCRIPTION-INPUT-FILE                          SUBLIST
00087  005090           SUBSCRIPTION-REPORT-FILE.                        SUBLIST
00088  005100 STOP RUN.                                                  SUBLIST
00089  005110                                                            SUBLIST
00090  005120                                                            SUBLIST
00091  005130                                                            SUBLIST
00092  005140 A001-FORMAT-PRINT-REPORT.                                  SUBLIST
00093  005150                                                            SUBLIST
00094  005170     MOVE EXPIRATION-DATE-INPUT TO EXPIRATION-DATE-REPORT.  SUBLIST
00095  005180     MOVE NAME-INPUT TO NAME-REPORT.                        SUBLIST
00096  005190     MOVE ADDRESS-INPUT TO ADDRESS-REPORT                   SUBLIST
00097  005200     MOVE CITY-STATE-INPUT TO CITY-STATE-REPORT.            SUBLIST
00098  006010     WRITE SUBSCRIPTION-REPORT-LINE                         SUBLIST
00099  006020        AFTER ADVANCING 1 LINES.                            SUBLIST
00100  006030     READ SUBSCRIPTION-INPUT-FILE                           SUBLIST
00101  006040        AT END                                             SUBLIST
00102  006050          MOVE 'NO ' TO ARE-THERE-MORE-RECORDS.            SUBLIST
```

```
5

CARD   ERROR MESSAGE

 41    ILA1043I-W   END OF SENTENCE SHOULD PRECEDE 01 . ASSUMED PRESENT.
 84    ILA3001I-E   A001-FORMAT-PRINT-REPORT NOT DEFINED. STATEMENT DISCARDED.
 88    ILA1087I-W   ' STOP ' SHOULD NOT BEGIN IN AREA A.
 95    ILA3001I-E   NAME NOT DEFINED. DISCARDED.
 96    ILA3001I-E   ADDRES-REPORT NOT DEFINED. DISCARDED.
102    ILA4001I-C   OUTCOME OF A PRECEDING CONDITION LEADS TO NON-EXISTENT 'NEXT SENTENCE'. 'GOBACK'
                    INSERTED.

ILA0004I- LINK OPTION RESET -- D OR E LEVEL ERROR FOUND
```

Figure 2-16 Example of COBOL Program and Diagnostics

It should be noted that with careful coding and a thorough structured walkthrough, there should never be any compilation errors to correct. Only if there are keypunch errors which go undetected should compilation errors be found. Once a "clean compilation" has been obtained, that is, once the compilation has been made without any diagnostics, then the programmer is ready for the fourth phase of the program development cycle, that of Program Testing and Debugging.

PHASE 4: TEST AND DEBUG THE PROGRAM

As has been noted, in the past there was a great emphasis on the testing and debugging phase of the program development cycle because it was felt that this was the proper place to be sure that a program did not contain any errors. Although this thinking has been largely discounted with the increased emphasis on program design, it still remains that the program must be tested prior to implementing it in a production environment.

In order to test a program, data must be produced which will allow the routines within a program to be executed in order to determine if the program is operating correctly. Although many times the programmer will be required to make up his own test data, it has been found that when a programmer makes test data to test his own program, the data is many times biased to test what the programmer knows his program should do, as opposed to testing what the program was designed to do. Therefore, in recent years, with the advent of chief programmer teams, the trend is to have the test data prepared by someone other than the programmer who wrote the program to be tested. In this manner, unbiased test data is produced and it is more likely that the program will be adequately tested.

The errors which are found in programs can be in many forms. Typical errors include logic errors which will produce results other than those intended for the program, errors or omissions which will cause the program to be unable to process all the types of input data which can be read by the program, and inadvertent omission of program statements which will cause invalid output from a program. An example of the latter type of error is the listing below, which was produced by an error in the sample program.

```
1/22/78 ZEROAGNEW, VIRGINIA C.      $$B111 PINE AVENUE          LONG BEACH, CA.     ABB  OX   B OX-  &G  G
1/12/79  3 HRUTTERY, BERTHA A.      D 2 443 SEYMORE DRIVE   J &BGLOS ANGELES, CA.   <J &3G&OFQ-OUGOO Q-&*G=NAO-- GOO GOOFQ-
2/09/80 ZERODING, BETTY D.          $$B273 OKRA AVENUE           LAKEWOOD, CA.      ABB  OX   B OX-  &G  G
0/12/79  3 HEONGLEY, ALBERT A.      D 2 1862 CENTRAL AVENUE  J &BGLAKEWOOD, CA.     <J &3G&OFQ-OUGOO Q-&*G=NAO-- GOO GOOFQ-
3/03/77 ZEROLOVERLEY, WILMA B.      $$H7777 OCEAN DRIVE          OCEANVIEW, CA.     ABB  OX   B OX-  &G  G
6/12/80  3 HMONEYMAKER, WILLIAM R.  D 2 90530 FILMORE AVENUE J &BGFOUNTAIN, CA.     <J &3G&OFQ-OUGOO Q-&*G=NAO-- GOO GOOFQ-
```

Figure 2-17 Example of Program Error

In the sample report illustrated in Figure 2-17 it can be seen that each print line contains "garbage," that is, meaningless data which should not appear on the report. When an error such as this occurs, the programmer must closely examine the source program to determine why the error occurred and then carefully make corrections to the program. In making a correction, the programmer must be sure that the correction which is made does not cause an error elsewhere in the program. This is not an infrequent occurrence and, therefore, must be considered by the programmer. If a program is properly designed, with each function in a separate module, the probability of this type of error when making a correction is reduced considerably, but it is something which the programmer must be aware of.

After any test run, the programmer must carefully examine the output to find all errors which occurred in the test. For example, in the output in Figure 2-17 it is obvious that the print line contains invalid data. It is less obvious, however, that the first digit of the Expiration Date is not included on the report. Thus, the test run which produced the output in Figure 2-17 revealed two distinct errors in the program. It is the responsibility of the programmer to find ALL of the errors which are produced from the test run and make the proper corrections. After corrections are made, the report will be printed correctly, as illustrated in Figure 2-18.

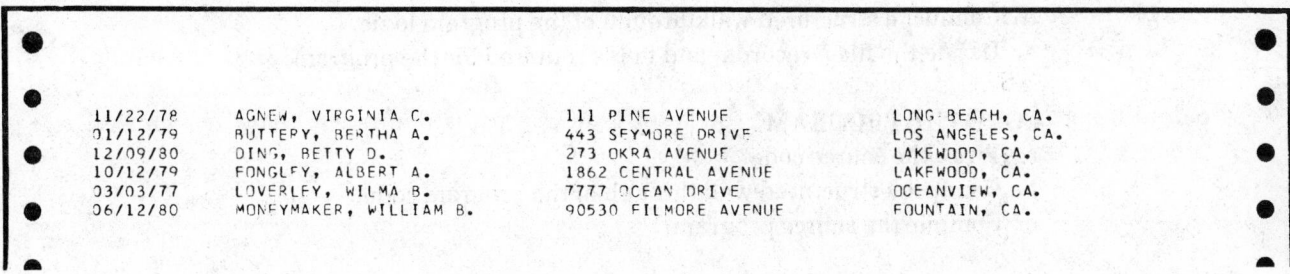

```
11/22/78    AGNEW, VIRGINIA C.           111 PINE AVENUE          LONG BEACH, CA.
01/12/79    BUTTERY, BERTHA A.           443 SEYMORE DRIVE        LOS ANGELES, CA.
12/09/80    DING, BETTY D.               273 OKRA AVENUE          LAKEWOOD, CA.
10/12/79    FONGLEY, ALBERT A.           1862 CENTRAL AVENUE      LAKEWOOD, CA.
03/03/77    LOVERLEY, WILMA B.           7777 OCEAN DRIVE         OCEANVIEW, CA.
06/12/80    MONEYMAKER, WILLIAM B.       90530 FILMORE AVENUE     FOUNTAIN, CA.
```

Figure 2-18 Example of Correct Report

Note from the report illustrated in Figure 2-18 that both of the previous errors have been corrected and the output is now correct. Again, although program testing and debugging is an important phase in the program development cycle, it must be emphasized that proper program design will keep the number of errors to a minimum; in fact, there should be NO errors when a program is compiled and tested. The programmer must constantly work toward this goal when designing and writing the program.

SUMMARY

Contrary to previous beliefs, computer programming is not naturally an error prone activity. Errors occur because of carelessness or poor design. It has been shown beyond doubt that programs can be written correctly the first time. This will not occur, however, unless the programmer follows a disciplined approach to writing a program and closely adheres to the steps in the program development cycle with care and diligence. These steps are again summarized below.

1. REVIEW SYSTEM AND PROGRAMMING SPECIFICATIONS

2. DESIGN THE PROGRAM
   a. Analyze the program requirements in terms of output, input and the processing required to transform the input to output.
   b. Decompose any complex processing into lower, more detailed levels of processing.
   c. Design the logic necessary to perform the processing specified in step a and step b.
   d. Conduct a structured walkthrough of the program logic.
   e. Define the files, records, and fields required for the program.

3. CODE THE PROGRAM
   a. Write the source code.
   b. Conduct a structured walkthrough of the program code.
   c. Compile the source program.

4. TEST AND DEBUG THE PROGRAM

With an emphasis in the design phase of the program development cycle, each program which is written should be correct the first time it is executed on the computer and should not fail when it is subsequently placed into production.

CHAPTER 2

REVIEW QUESTIONS

1. What is meant by the quotation ''Most computer programs are never designed; they are created on the coding pad''?

2. List the four phases in the program development cycle.

3. What are the steps in Phase 2?

4. What are the steps in Phase 3?

5. What types of information should be recorded on an IPO Chart?

6. In the sample program design developed in this chapter it is necessary to move the Customer's Name, Address, City/State and Expiration Date from the input area to the output area. Why is this information not recorded under PROCESSING on the IPO Chart?

7. What is the purpose of pseudocode?

8. What are the advantages of pseudocode?

9. What is a COMPILER?

10. What is an OBJECT PROGRAM?

CHAPTER 2

PROGRAM DESIGN ASSIGNMENT 1

INSTRUCTIONS

A Payroll Register is to be prepared. Design the program to create the Payroll Register by preparing the IPO Chart and writing the required pseudocode. Retain the IPO Chart and pseudocode for use in Chapter 3.

INPUT

Input is to consist of Payroll Cards that contain the Employee Number, the Employee Name, the Department Number and the Hours Worked. The format of the Payroll Cards is illustrated below.

OUTPUT

Output is to consist of a Payroll Register, listing the Employee Number, the Department Number, the Employee Name, and the Hours Worked. The printer spacing chart for the report is illustrated below.

CHAPTER 2

PROGRAM DESIGN ASSIGNMENT 2

INSTRUCTIONS

An Inventory Report is to be prepared. Design the program to create the Inventory Report by preparing the IPO Chart and writing the required pseudocode. Retain the IPO Chart and pseudocode for use in Chapter 3.

INPUT

Input consists of Inventory Cards that contain the Item Number, the Item Description, the Quantity On Hand, the Quantity Sold, and the Store Number. The format of the Inventory Cards is illustrated below.

OUTPUT

The output is to consist of a listing of the fields contained on the Inventory Cards and is to contain the Store Number, the Item Number, the Item Description, the Quantity On Hand and the Quantity Sold. The printer spacing chart is illustrated below. Note that the report is to be double spaced.

CHAPTER 2

PROGRAM DESIGN ASSIGNMENT 3

INSTRUCTIONS

Two listings of a company's customers are to be prepared. Since two listings are required, it has been decided to print each of the fields in the card twice on the same line of the report. Design the program to create the listing by preparing the IPO Chart and writing the required pseudocode. Retain the IPO Chart and pseudocode for use in Chapter 3.

INPUT

The input is to consist of Customer Name Cards that contain the Customer Number and the Customer Name. The format of the cards is illustrated below.

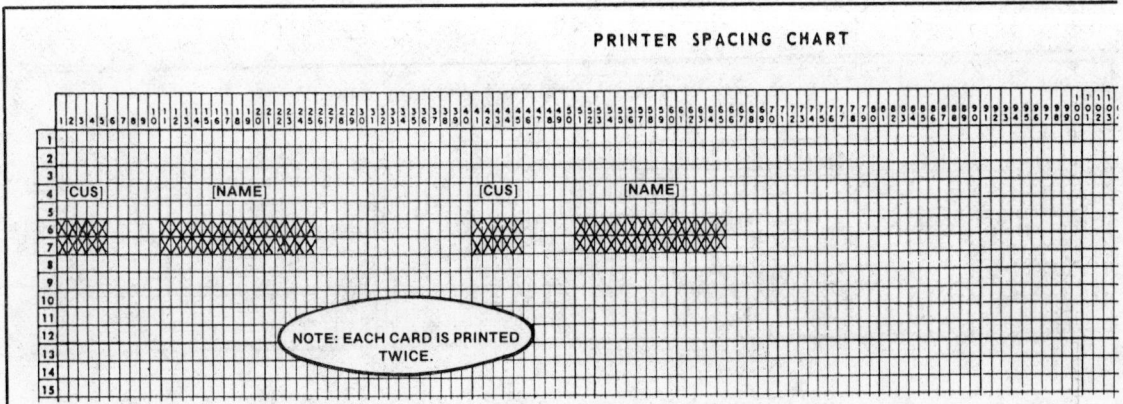

OUTPUT

The output is to consist of two listings of the card. The printer spacing chart is illustrated below.

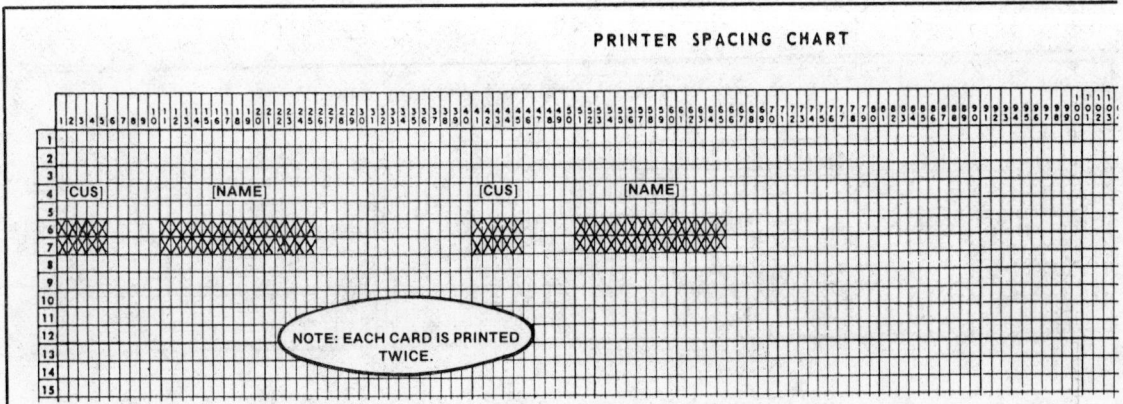

CHAPTER 2

PROGRAM DESIGN ASSIGNMENT 4

INSTRUCTIONS

An Employee Roster is to be prepared listing new employees. Design the program to create the Employee Roster by preparing the IPO Chart and writing the required pseudocode. Retain the IPO Chart and pseudocode for use in Chapter 3.

INPUT

The input to the program is the New Employee Card File. The records in the file contain the Department Number, the Employee Name, and the Social Security Number. The format of the records is illustrated below.

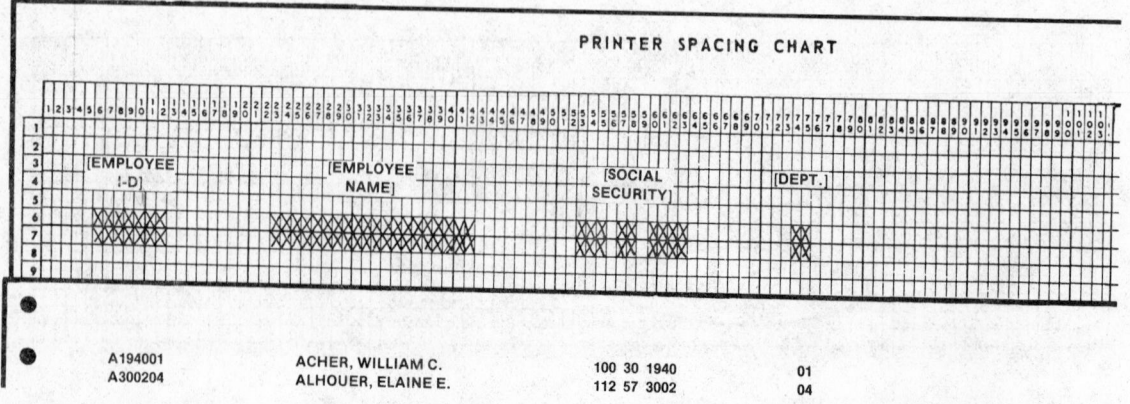

OUTPUT

The output from the program is the Employee Roster and it contains the Employee Identification, the Employee Name, the Social Security Number, and the Department. The Employee Identification is generated as follows: The first character is the first letter of the last name of the employee. This is followed by the last four digits of the social security number, followed by the department number. Thus, the Identification for employee Acher whose social security number is 100-30-1940 and who works in department 01 would be A194001. The printer spacing chart for the report is illustrated below.

INTRODUCTION TO COMPUTER PROGRAMMING INPUT/OUTPUT OPERATIONS

> *Now the new reality is that ordinary programmers, with ordinary care, can learn to consistently write programs which are error free from their inception.* [1]

INTRODUCTION

As explained in Chapter 2, the program development cycle consists of analyzing the problem to be solved, designing the program to solve the problem, coding the program, and testing and debugging the program. One of the steps in coding the program is to write the source code. This chapter is devoted to explaining the entries required to write the COBOL source code to produce the Subscription List Report from the Subscription List Cards.

OUTPUT

In review, the output from the program is a Subscription List Report containing a listing of magazine subscribers. The printer spacing chart for the report is illustrated in Figure 3-1.

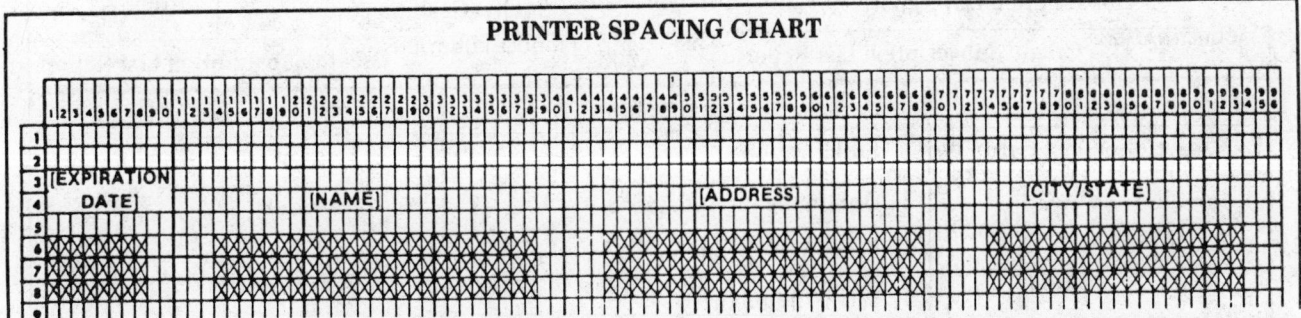

Figure 3-1 Printer Spacing Chart of Subscription Listing

Note in the printer spacing chart illustrated above that the Expiration Date, the subscriber's Name, Address, and City/State are to be printed on the report.

---

1 H. D. Mills, *HOW TO WRITE CORRECT PROGRAMS AND KNOW IT*, IBM Federal Systems Division, IBM, February 1973.

INPUT

The input to the program is the Subscription List Card File, with each card containing the Name, Address, City/State, and Expiration Date. The format of the input card is illustrated below.

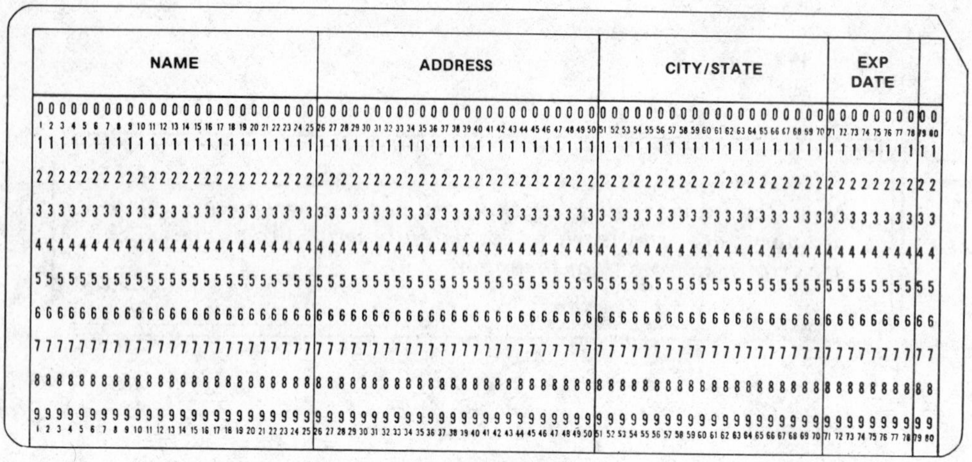

Figure 3-2 Input

Note from Figure 3-2 that the input card contains the Name, Address, City/State, and Expiration Date for each subscriber.

IPO CHART

The IPO Chart is again illustrated below. The IPO Chart contains the input, output, and major processing tasks that are to be performed to transform the input to output.

IPO CHART

PROGRAM: Subscription List Report		PROGRAMMER: Shelly/Cashman		DATE: Dec.8
MODULE NAME: Create Subscription List Report	REF: A000	MODULE FUNCTION: Create Subscription List Report		

INPUT	PROCESSING	REF:	OUTPUT
1. Subscription List Card File	1. Initialization		1. Subscription List Report
	2. Obtain the input data		
	3. Format the print line		
	4. Write the report		
	5. Termination		

Figure 3-3 IPO Chart

PSEUDOCODE-REQUIRED FILES, RECORDS AND FIELDS

The pseudocode, which specifies the detailed steps required in the solution of the problem, and a listing of the required files, records, and fields to be referenced in the program are illustrated below on the Pseudocode Specifications.

PSEUDOCODE SPECIFICATIONS

PROGRAM: Subscription List Report		PROGRAMMER: Shelly/Cashman		DATE: Dec 8
MODULE NAME: Create Subscription List Report	REF: A000	MODULE FUNCTION: Create Subscription List Report		

PSEUDOCODE	REF:	FILES, RECORDS, FIELDS REQUIRED
Open the files		Subscription list card file
Read an input record		Subscription list report file
PERFORM UNTIL no more input records		Input area for input record
Clear the output area		Name
Move the expiration date, name, address,		Address
city/state to the output area		City/State
Write the line on the report		Expiration date
Read an input record		Indicator for no more records
ENDPERFORM		Printer output area
Close the files		Expiration date
Stop run		Name
		Address
		City/State

Figure 3-4 Pseudocode Specifications

After the pseudocode has been written and the required files, records, and fields have been specified, the programmer is ready to write the COBOL program. The COBOL program written to process the Subscription List Card File and create the Subscription List Report is illustrated in Figure 3-5 and Figure 3-6.

EXAMPLE

```
                              COBOL Coding Form

SYSTEM                                        PUNCHING INSTRUCTIONS          PAGE 1 OF 6
PROGRAM    SUBSCRIPTION LIST REPORT      GRAPHIC  O  Ø  2  Z  1  1 .
PROGRAMMER SHELLY/CASHMAN    DATE DEC 9  PUNCH  11-6 ZERO TWO Ø-9 12-9 ONE

SEQUENCE  C   A   B            COBOL STATEMENT                          IDENTIFICATION
PAGE SERIAL O
001010  IDENTIFICATION DIVISION.                                        SUBLIST
001020                                                                  SUBLIST
001030  PROGRAM-ID.  SUBLIST.                                           SUBLIST
001040  AUTHOR.      SHELLY AND CASHMAN.                                SUBLIST
001050  INSTALLATION.  ANAHEIM.                                         SUBLIST
001060  DATE-WRITTEN.  12/09/76.                                        SUBLIST
001070  DATE-COMPILED.  Ø5/26/77.                                       SUBLIST
001080  SECURITY.      UNCLASSIFIED.                                    SUBLIST
001090                                                                  SUBLIST
001100  *************************************************************   SUBLIST
001110  *                                                          *    SUBLIST
001120  *   THIS PROGRAM PRODUCES A LISTING OF PERSONS ON A MAGAZINE *  SUBLIST
001130  *   SUBSCRIPTION LIST.                                      *   SUBLIST
001140  *                                                          *    SUBLIST
001150  *************************************************************   SUBLIST
001160                                                                  SUBLIST
001170                                                                  SUBLIST
001180  ENVIRONMENT DIVISION.                                           SUBLIST
001200                                                                  SUBLIST
```

```
SEQUENCE  C  A   B            COBOL STATEMENT                           IDENTIFICATION
PAGE SERIAL O
002010  CONFIGURATION SECTION.                                          SUBLIST
002020                                                                  SUBLIST
002030  SOURCE-COMPUTER.  IBM-37Ø.                                      SUBLIST
002040  OBJECT-COMPUTER.  IBM-37Ø.                                      SUBLIST
002050                                                                  SUBLIST
002060  INPUT-OUTPUT SECTION.                                           SUBLIST
002070                                                                  SUBLIST
002080  FILE-CONTROL.                                                   SUBLIST
002090      SELECT SUBSCRIPTION-INPUT-FILE                              SUBLIST
002100          ASSIGN TO SYSØØ7-UR-254ØR-S.                            SUBLIST
002110      SELECT SUBSCRIPTION-REPORT-FILE                             SUBLIST
002120          ASSIGN TO SYSØ13-UR-14Ø3-S.                             SUBLIST
002130      EJECT                                                       SUBLIST
002140  DATA DIVISION.                                                  SUBLIST
002150                                                                  SUBLIST
002160  FILE SECTION.                                                   SUBLIST
002170                                                                  SUBLIST
002180  FD  SUBSCRIPTION-INPUT-FILE                                     SUBLIST
002190      RECORD CONTAINS 80 CHARACTERS                               SUBLIST
002200      LABEL RECORDS ARE OMITTED                                   SUBLIST
```

```
SEQUENCE  C  A   B            COBOL STATEMENT                           IDENTIFICATION
PAGE SERIAL O
003010      DATA RECORD IS SUBSCRIPTION-INPUT-RECORD.                   SUBLIST
003020  01  SUBSCRIPTION-INPUT-RECORD.                                  SUBLIST
003030      05  NAME-INPUT              PICTURE X(25).                   SUBLIST
003040      05  ADDRESS-INPUT           PICTURE X(25).                   SUBLIST
003050      05  CITY-STATE-INPUT        PICTURE X(2Ø).                   SUBLIST
003060      05  EXPIRATION-DATE-INPUT   PICTURE X(8).                    SUBLIST
003070      05  FILLER                  PICTURE XX.                      SUBLIST
003080                                                                  SUBLIST
003090  FD  SUBSCRIPTION-REPORT-FILE                                    SUBLIST
003100      RECORD CONTAINS 133 CHARACTERS                              SUBLIST
003110      LABEL RECORDS ARE OMITTED                                   SUBLIST
003120      DATA RECORD IS SUBSCRIPTION-REPORT-LINE.                    SUBLIST
003130  01  SUBSCRIPTION-REPORT-LINE.                                   SUBLIST
003140      05  CARRIAGE-CONTROL        PICTURE X.                       SUBLIST
003150      05  EXPIRATION-DATE-REPORT  PICTURE X(8).                    SUBLIST
003160      05  FILLER                  PICTURE X(5).                    SUBLIST
003170      05  NAME-REPORT             PICTURE X(25).                   SUBLIST
003180      05  FILLER                  PICTURE X(5).                    SUBLIST
003190      05  ADDRESS-REPORT          PICTURE X(25).                   SUBLIST
003200      05  FILLER                  PICTURE X(5).                    SUBLIST
```

Figure 3-5 COBOL Source Coding - Part 1 of 2

EXAMPLE

COBOL Coding Form

SYSTEM				
PROGRAM	SUBSCRIPTION LIST REPORT	GRAPHIC	0 0 2 Z 1 1	PAGE 4 OF 6
PROGRAMMER SHELLY/CASHMAN DATE DEC 9		PUNCH	11-6 ZERO TWO O-9 12-9 ONE	

COBOL STATEMENT / IDENTIFICATION

```
004010        05  CITY-STATE-REPORT          PICTURE X(20).          SUBLIST
004020        05  FILLER                     PICTURE X(39).          SUBLIST
004030                                                               SUBLIST
004040  WORKING-STORAGE SECTION.                                     SUBLIST
004050                                                               SUBLIST
004060  01  PROGRAM-INDICATORS.                                      SUBLIST
004070      05  ARE-THERE-MORE-RECORDS  PICTURE X(3) VALUE 'YES'.    SUBLIST
004080      EJECT                                                    SUBLIST
004090  PROCEDURE DIVISION.                                          SUBLIST
004100                                                               SUBLIST
004110  ***************************************************************  SUBLIST
004120  *                                                          *  SUBLIST
004130  *   THIS PROGRAM READS THE SUBSCRIPTION INPUT RECORDS AND  *  SUBLIST
004140  *   CREATES THE SUBSCRIPTION LISTING.  IT IS ENTERED FROM THE *  SUBLIST
004150  *   OPERATING SYSTEM AND EXITS TO THE OPERATING SYSTEM.    *  SUBLIST
004160  *                                                          *  SUBLIST
004170  ***************************************************************  SUBLIST
004180                                                               SUBLIST
004190  A000-CREATE-SUBSCRIPTION-LIST.                               SUBLIST
004200                                                               SUBLIST
```

```
005010  OPEN INPUT  SUBSCRIPTION-INPUT-FILE                          SUBLIST
005020       OUTPUT SUBSCRIPTION-REPORT-FILE.                        SUBLIST
005030  READ SUBSCRIPTION-INPUT-FILE                                 SUBLIST
005040      AT END                                                   SUBLIST
005050          MOVE 'NO ' TO ARE-THERE-MORE-RECORDS.                SUBLIST
005060  PERFORM A001-FORMAT-PRINT-REPORT                             SUBLIST
005070      UNTIL ARE-THERE-MORE-RECORDS = 'NO '.                    SUBLIST
005080  CLOSE SUBSCRIPTION-INPUT-FILE                                SUBLIST
005090        SUBSCRIPTION-REPORT-FILE.                              SUBLIST
005100  STOP RUN.                                                    SUBLIST
005110                                                               SUBLIST
005120                                                               SUBLIST
005130                                                               SUBLIST
005140  A001-FORMAT-PRINT-REPORT.                                    SUBLIST
005150                                                               SUBLIST
005160  MOVE SPACES TO SUBSCRIPTION-REPORT-LINE.                     SUBLIST
005170  MOVE EXPIRATION-DATE-INPUT TO EXPIRATION-DATE-REPORT.        SUBLIST
005180  MOVE NAME-INPUT TO NAME-REPORT.                              SUBLIST
005190  MOVE ADDRESS-INPUT TO ADDRESS-REPORT.                        SUBLIST
005200  MOVE CITY-STATE-INPUT TO CITY-STATE-REPORT.                  SUBLIST
```

```
006010  WRITE SUBSCRIPTION-REPORT-LINE                               SUBLIST
006020        AFTER ADVANCING 1 LINES.                               SUBLIST
006030  READ SUBSCRIPTION-INPUT-FILE                                 SUBLIST
006040      AT END                                                   SUBLIST
006050          MOVE 'NO ' TO ARE-THERE-MORE-RECORDS.                SUBLIST
```

Figure 3-6 COBOL Source Coding - Part 2 of 2

An explanation of the entries on each line of the COBOL coding form is contained on the following pages.

COBOL Coding Form

The COBOL program is normally written on a special COBOL coding form. A segment of the coding form is illustrated below.

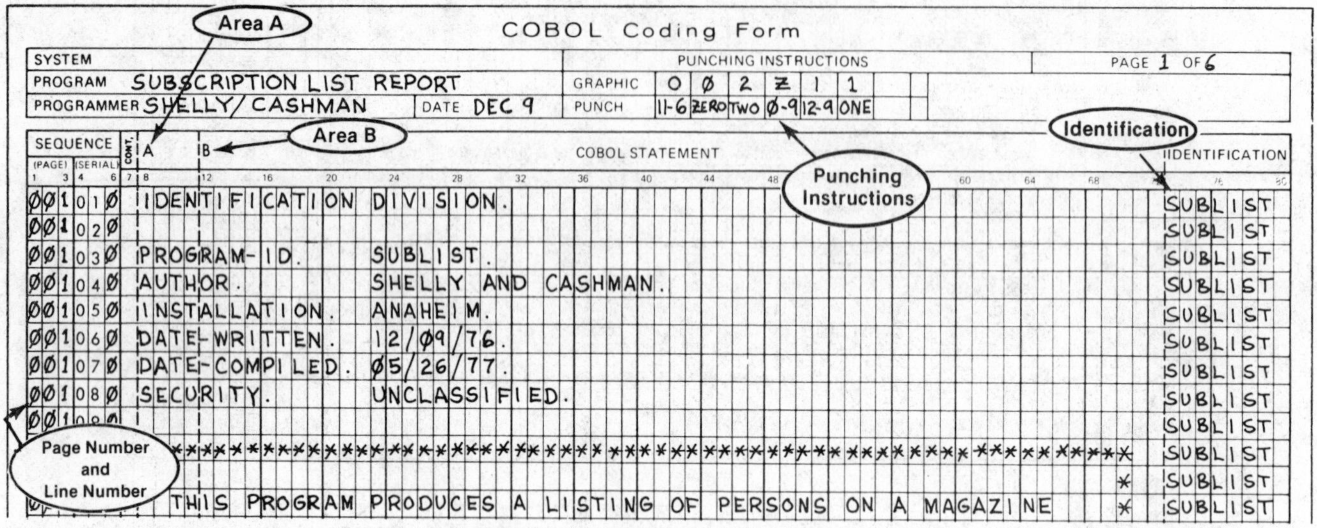

Figure 3-7 COBOL Coding Form

At the top of the form, space is provided for general information about the program, such as the name of the system, program, programmer, date, etc. Instructions to the keypunch operator can be given in the section labeled "Punching Instructions." A character that might create confusion when keypunching can be assigned a special symbol or "graphic" to identify the card code to be punched by the keypunch operator. For example in the coding sheet illustrated, it can be seen that the graphic "O" is to be punched as an 11-6. Thus, "O" is a letter of the alphabet. The graphic "Ø" is to be punched as a zero and is thus a numeric zero when encountered on the coding form. On the right side of the form, space is provided to record the Page Number and the total number of pages of coding.

In columns 73-80, space is reserved for the "Identification." This area on the form is used to give an identification to each of the source program cards. Any numbers, letters of the alphabet, or special characters, including blanks, may be used. The "Identification" has no effect on the object program or the compiler even though this information is punched into card columns 73-80 of the cards comprising the COBOL source program. It is used merely for identification purposes.

Columns 1-6, labelled "Sequence," are used to number the lines of coding on the form. Columns 1, 2, and 3 are used for page number identification, and columns 4, 5, and 6 are used to identify each line number (serial number). Each succeeding line is given a higher number. Columns 4 and 5 are usually prenumbered on the coding form. Use of the card columns 1-6 for sequence numbering program cards is optional and is not required for most COBOL compilers. Most compilers will accept the program cards in the order in which they appear. If these card columns have been used, however, the compiler will check the sequence of each input card. Every low or equal sequence number will produce a warning message on the program listing. This warning will not disturb the compilation or execution of the program.

If columns 1-6 are used, Page Number (1-3) and Serial Number (4-6) must contain only numeric digits. Letters of the alphabet or special characters are not allowed. Notice that the method of numbering in Figure 3-7 allows additional instructions to be inserted at a later date, if required, without disturbing the ascending sequence of instructions. For example, if an additional line of coding is to be inserted between line 010 and line 020, the line could be identified as line 015 and be inserted into the main program without disturbing the sequence of cards comprising the COBOL program.

The continuation indicator area (column 7) must be blank on all cards except when a special type of COBOL word called a non-numeric literal must be continued on a second line, or when comments are to be placed in the source program. This use of the continuation column is explained in detail later in the text.

Columns 8-72 are used for program entries. The columns are grouped into two areas, AREA A (columns 8-11) and AREA B (columns 12-72). Certain portions of the COBOL program must begin in Area A and certain portions must begin in Area B. The specific rules for recording the various entries are discussed in detail throughout this chapter.

IDENTIFICATION DIVISION

The Identification Division of a COBOL program is written first. This Division specifies information which serves to identify and document the program. The following is an illustration of the Identification Division of the COBOL program used to prepare the Subscription List Report.

EXAMPLE

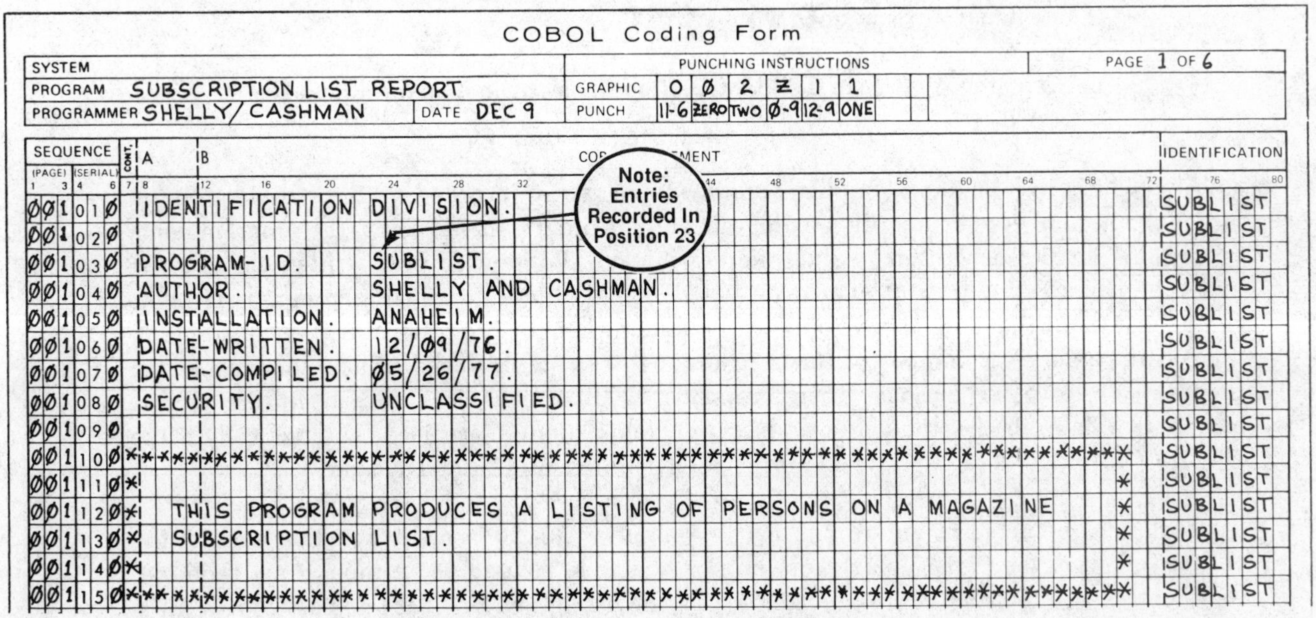


```
001010 IDENTIFICATION DIVISION.                                          SUBLIST
001020                                                                   SUBLIST
001030 PROGRAM-ID.    SUBLIST.                                           SUBLIST
001040 AUTHOR.        SHELLY AND CASHMAN.                                SUBLIST
001050 INSTALLATION.  ANAHEIM.                                           SUBLIST
001060 DATE-WRITTEN.  12/09/76.                                          SUBLIST
001070 DATE-COMPILED. 05/26/77.                                          SUBLIST
001080 SECURITY.      UNCLASSIFIED.                                      SUBLIST
001090                                                                   SUBLIST
001100******************************************************************SUBLIST
001110*                                                                *SUBLIST
001120*   THIS PROGRAM PRODUCES A LISTING OF PERSONS ON A MAGAZINE     *SUBLIST
001130*   SUBSCRIPTION LIST.                                           *SUBLIST
001140*                                                                *SUBLIST
001150******************************************************************SUBLIST
```

Figure 3-8 Example of Identification Division

When writing a COBOL program, the method of recording the Division Names and related entries, the spacing, and the presence or absence of the period is extremely important. The following statements summarize the rules for recording the entries in the Identification Division.

1. The beginning of the Identification Division is marked by the "Division Header Entry" which consists of the name IDENTIFICATION DIVISION. A Division Header entry always begins on a line by itself, must begin in Area A, and must be followed by a period.

2. The Identification Division is made up of "Paragraph Headers". These Paragraph Headers consist of a series of fixed names (PROGRAM-ID, AUTHOR, INSTALLATION, DATE-WRITTEN, DATE-COMPILED, and SECURITY). Paragraph Headers must begin in Area A and be followed by a period and a space.

3. The words or sentences following the Paragraph Headers must be contained within Area B.

4. The Program Name following PROGRAM-ID must consist of alphabetic and numeric characters, one of which must be alphabetic. The first eight characters of the Program Name identify the object program.

5. The words following the Paragraph Header entries AUTHOR, INSTALLATION, DATE-WRITTEN, DATE-COMPILED, and SECURITY may be originated at the discretion of the programmer and may contain any characters available on the computer. Coding may not be extended into columns 73-80. The programmer may break off the coding anywhere before column 73 and record the following entries on the next line if they are contained within Area B.

6. Each of the entries in the Identification Division must be terminated by a period.

As can be seen from the example in Figure 3-8, the entries recorded for the sample program in this chapter are used to identify the program and the programmers. Thus, the program name is SUBLIST and it was written by Shelly and Cashman. The program was written on 12/09/76 and compiled on 05/26/77. It should be noted that the date on which a program is to be compiled is many times not known to the programmer when the program is written. In addition, it may be compiled a number of times in order to correct mistakes, make changes to the program, or for other reasons. Therefore, most COBOL compilers will insert the correct compilation date, that is, the date on which the compilation takes place, automatically if the DATE-COMPILED Paragraph Header is included in the Identification Division.

It will also be noted in Figure 3-8 that line number 001020 is blank and that each of the entries following the Paragraph Header entries begins in column 23. Although not required, these entries are recorded in this manner so that the listing will be clear and easy to read. It is extremely important that the program listing be easy to read and one way in which this can be done is to utilize uniform ways of recording information on the coding form. The coding conventions illustrated in Figure 3-8 for the Identification Division will be used throughout this text.

It can also be seen from Figure 3-8 that an asterisk (*) is included in column 7 for lines 001100 through 001150. Whenever an asterisk is included in column 7, the statement is treated **as a comment statement**. A comment statement will appear on the source listing but will not become a part of the machine language instructions generated by the compiler. The comments in the Identification Division appear on the source listing as illustrated below.

EXAMPLE

```
00001   001010 IDENTIFICATION DIVISION.                                          SUBLIST
00002   001020                                                                   SUBLIST
00003   001030 PROGRAM-ID.     SUBLIST.                                          SUBLIST
00004   001040 AUTHOR.         SHELLY AND CASHMAN.                               SUBLIST
00005   001050 INSTALLATION.  ANAHEIM.                                           SUBLIST
00006   001060 DATE-WRITTEN.  12/09/76.                                          SUBLIST
00007   001070 DATE-COMPILED. 05/26/77                                           SUBLIST
00008   001080 SECURITY.       UNCLASSIFIED.                                     SUBLIST
00009   001090                                                                   SUBLIST
00010   001100****************************************************************** SUBLIST
00011   001110*                                                               * SUBLIST
00012   001120*   THIS PROGRAM PRODUCES A LISTING OF PERSONS ON A MAGAZINE    * SUBLIST
00013   001130*   SUBSCRIPTION LIST.                                          * SUBLIST
00014   001140*                                                               * SUBLIST
00015   001150****************************************************************** SUBLIST
```

Figure 3-9 Example of Comment Statements

Comments are normally used to specify or help clarify the processing which takes place within the program. Any characters available on the computer can appear in the comment statements. When used in the Identification Division, comments are usually used to specify the processing which is to take place within the program. In the sample program, the comments are used to specify that the program produces the Magazine Subscription List.

When coding the Identification Division, the Paragraph Headers (PROGRAM-ID, AUTHOR, etc.) must begin in Area A of the coding form and the words or sentences following the Paragraph Headers must be contained within Area B. They do not, however, have to be on the same line. The example in Figure 3-10 illustrates an alternative method of recording the entries for the Identification Division on the COBOL coding form.

EXAMPLE

SEQUENCE					COBOL STATEMENT												

```
0 0 1 0 1 0  IDENTIFICATION DIVISION.
0 0 1 0 2 0
0 0 1 0 3 0  PROGRAM-ID.
0 0 1 0 4 0       SUBLIST.
0 0 1 0 5 0  AUTHOR.
0 0 1 0 6 0       SHELLY AND CASHMAN.
0 0 1 0 7 0  INSTALLATION.
0 0 1 0 8 0       ANAHEIM.
0 0 1 0 9 0  DATE-WRITTEN.
0 0 1 1 0 0       03/31/77.
0 0 1 1 1 0  DATE-COMPILED.
0 0 1 1 2 0       03/31/77.
0 0 1 1 3 0  SECURITY.
0 0 1 1 4 0       UNCLASSIFIED.
0 0 1 1 5 0
0 0 1 1 6 0 *****************************************************************
0 0 1 1 7 0 *                                                             *
0 0 1 1 8 0 *  THIS PROGRAM PRODUCES A LISTING OF PERSONS ON A MAGAZINE   *
0 0 1 1 9 0 *  SUBSCRIPTION LIST.                                         *
0 0 1 2 0 0 *                                                             *
0 0 1 2 1 0 *****************************************************************
```

Figure 3-10 Identification Division with Entries on Separate Lines

FORMAT NOTATION

Technical reference manuals developed for the COBOL programming language provide a standard format notation for the various elements of COBOL. These generalized descriptions are intended to guide the programmer in writing COBOL programs. The format notation for the Identification Division is illustrated below.

```
IDENTIFICATION DIVISION.

PROGRAM-ID.  program-name.

[AUTHOR.  [comment-entry]  ... ]

[INSTALLATION.  [comment-entry]  ...]

[DATE-WRITTEN.  [comment-entry]  ...]

[DATE-COMPILED.  [comment-entry]  ...]

[SECURITY.  [comment-entry]  ...]
```

Figure 3-11 Format Notation for Identification Division

It is imperative that the COBOL programmer thoroughly understand this system of notation. The basic rules as related to the Identification Division are summarized below.

1. All words printed entirely in capital letters are RESERVED words. These words have preassigned meanings in the COBOL language and are not to be used for any other purpose. In all formats, words written in capital letters selected for use must be duplicated exactly.

2. All underlined reserved words are required unless the portion of the format containing them is itself optional. These are key words. If any such word is missing or is incorrectly spelled, it is considered an error in the program. Reserved words which are not underlined may be included or excluded at the programmer's option, but if they are included, they must be spelled properly.

3. Lower case words in formats represent information that must be supplied by the programmer.

4. Punctuation, except for commas and semi-colons, is essential where it is shown. Commas and semi-colons are optional.

5. Square brackets ([...]) are used to indicate that the enclosed item may be used or omitted, depending on the requirements of the particular program.

By applying the above rules of format notation to the Identification Division, it can be seen that AUTHOR, INSTALLATION, DATE-WRITTEN, DATE-COMPILED, and SECURITY are enclosed in brackets and are optional, that is, these paragraphs are not a required portion of the Identification Division. Note, therefore, that the only required entries in the Identification Division are the Division Header, IDENTIFICATION DIVISION, and the PROGRAM-ID.

SUMMARY - IDENTIFICATION DIVISION

It should be again noted that there are two areas on the COBOL coding sheet, Area A (columns 8-11) and Area B (columns 12-72).

The Division Header, IDENTIFICATION DIVISION, must begin in Area A, and be followed by a period. This entry must appear on a line by itself.

The Paragraph Headers, PROGRAM-ID, AUTHOR, DATE-WRITTEN, DATE-COMPILED, and SECURITY must also begin in Area A and must be followed immediately by a period and then a space. Sentences within a paragraph may start on the same line as the Paragraph Header or on a separate line. Succeeding lines of the paragraph must begin within Area B.

ENVIRONMENT DIVISION

The next division of the COBOL program to be coded is the Environment Division. The Environment Division contains two "Sections", the **CONFIGURATION SECTION** and the **INPUT-OUTPUT SECTION**. The Configuration Section identifies the computer on which the program is to be compiled and executed. The Input-Output Section assigns files to input and output devices and may also specify special input/output techniques.

Configuration Section

The following segment of the COBOL coding form illustrates the suggested entries for the Configuration Section of the Environment Division.

EXAMPLE

```
001190  ENVIRONMENT DIVISION.
001200
002010  CONFIGURATION SECTION.
002020
002030  SOURCE-COMPUTER. IBM-370.
002040  OBJECT-COMPUTER. IBM-370.
```

Figure 3-12 Environment Division - Configuration Section

The Division Header, ENVIRONMENT DIVISION, the Section Header, CONFIGURATION SECTION, and the Paragraph Headers, SOURCE-COMPUTER, OBJECT-COMPUTER, must begin in Area A and be followed by a period. There must always be at least one blank space following a period. The entries following Source-Computer and Object-Computer must be contained within Area B.

The SOURCE-COMPUTER paragraph specifies the computer on which the COBOL compiler is to be run to prepare the Object Program. The OBJECT-COMPUTER paragraph identifies the computer on which the Object Program is to be run to process the data. In the sample program, the computer on which the programs are to be compiled and executed is an IBM System/370. Therefore, the term IBM-370 is specified for both SOURCE-COMPUTER and OBJECT-COMPUTER. It should be noted that these entries are treated strictly as comments and, therefore, have no value except for documentation purposes. Each manufacturer has specific entries which may be placed in these paragraphs, depending upon the model of the computer being used and other manufacturer-dependent specifications.

The COBOL format notation for the Configuration Section is illustrated below.

```
ENVIRONMENT DIVISION.

CONFIGURATION SECTION.

SOURCE-COMPUTER.    computer-name

OBJECT-COMPUTER.    computer-name
```

Figure 3-13 Configuration Section - Format Notation

In the format notation illustrated in Figure 3-13, it can be seen that the terms CONFIGURATION SECTION, SOURCE-COMPUTER, and OBJECT-COMPUTER must be included as shown and be followed by the computer-name, which describes the source and object computers.

Input-Output Section

The INPUT-OUTPUT SECTION of the Environment Division contains the FILE-CONTROL paragraph. The File-Control paragraph is used to name the files to be processed and associate those files with the input/output devices being used. In the sample program, the Subscription Input File (a punched card file) and the Subscription Report File (a printed report) must be defined. The Subscription Input File is to be read using the IBM 2540 Card Reader and the Subscription Report File is to be printed on the IBM 1403 Printer. It should be noted that the use of these particular devices is incidental to the solution of the problem and any type of card reader and printer from any manufacturer could be used.

The following example illustrates the entries used in the sample program for the Input-Output Section of the Environment Division.

EXAMPLE

```
002060    INPUT-OUTPUT SECTION.
002070
002080    FILE-CONTROL.
002090        SELECT SUBSCRIPTION-INPUT-FILE
002100            ASSIGN TO SYS007-UR-2540R-S.
002110        SELECT SUBSCRIPTION-REPORT-FILE
002120            ASSIGN TO SYS013-UR-1403-S.
```

Figure 3-14 Input-Output Section

The general format of the Select Statement within the File-Control paragraph is illustrated in Figure 3-15.

```
SELECT [OPTIONAL]  file-name

    ASSIGN TO implementor-name-1  [, implementor-name-2] ...

    [; RESERVE integer-1  [ AREA  ]]
                          [ AREAS ]

    [; ORGANIZATION IS SEQUENTIAL]

    [; ACCESS MODE IS SEQUENTIAL]

    [; FILE STATUS IS data-name-1] .
```

Figure 3-15 Format Notation - Select Clause

Note from the format notation illustrated in Figure 3-15 that the Select and Assign Clauses are required and the remaining clauses are optional, that is, they are enclosed within brackets ([...]). In the sample program, only the Select Clause and the Assign Clause are required.

Thus, the only entry required in the sample program for the Input-Output Section is the File-Control paragraph, consisting of the Select Clause and the Assign Clause. The Select Clause is used to name each file within the program and the Assign Clause is used to assign a file to an external device on the computer system. The Select and Assign Clauses used for the card input file in the sample program are illustrated below.

EXAMPLE

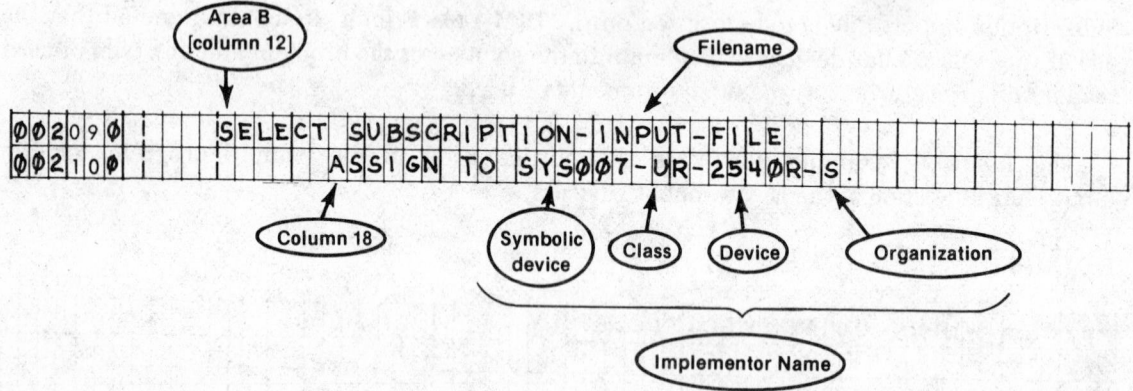

Figure 3-16 Select Clause and Assign Clause

The Select clause must begin with the word SELECT and be followed by a "file-name." A file-name should be assigned that is descriptive of the file being processed. The "file-name" is a name originated by the programmer and may be composed of a combination of not more than 30 characters chosen from the following set of 37 characters:

>   0 through 9 (numeric digits)
>   A through Z (alphabetic letters)
>   - (hyphen)

A file-name must contain at least one alphabetic character. The name must not begin or end with a hyphen but a hyphen may be contained within the name. The end of a file-name is detected by the COBOL compiler by the space at the end of the name. Therefore, no blanks are permitted within the name. The name of each file must be unique within the program.

Note in Figure 3-16 that the name assigned to the Subscription List Card File is SUBSCRIPTION-INPUT-FILE. It should be noted that this name was chosen because it was descriptive of the file to be processed.

The Assign Clause within the Select Clause is used to relate the file to a particular input/output device. In the example in Figure 3-16 it can be seen that the words ASSIGN TO begin the Assign Clause. The word ASSIGN is required in the clause and the word TO may be used at the option of the programmer. It is not required (see Figure 3-15).

It should be noted that although the COBOL language is designed to be used on any piece of computer hardware regardless of the manufacturer, there are several areas within the COBOL program where the entries to be used depend upon the COBOL compiler being used. One of these areas is the Assign Clause used in the Select Clause. It will be noted in Figure 3-15 that the entry to be used with the Assign Clause is "implementor-name-1." This means that the value to be placed in the Assign Clause is defined by the implementor of the COBOL compiler, and can change based upon the implementor. In the example of the sample program in Figure 3-16, the implementor is the IBM Disk Operating System COBOL compiler and these entries will be explained below. The entries required for other COBOL compilers can be found in the reference manuals for the particular manufacturer.

For the IBM DOS COBOL Compiler, the implementor-name consists of the Symbolic Device entry, the Class entry, the Device entry, and the Organization entry. The Symbolic Device is a name which must begin with the letters of the alphabet SYS. It is used by the Disk Operating System to associate a particular device with the file which is defined within the program. It should be noted that this entry is not normally required with other COBOL compilers. In the example in Figure 3-16 it can be seen that the Symbolic Device SYS007 is used because this is the name which is associated with the proper card reader by the operating system. It should be noted that this entry may vary from one DOS system to another.

The Class entry is used to specify the device class. The entry "UR" is used for a card reader and stands for Unit-Record. Card readers and printers are always defined as Unit-Record devices and must have the class entry "UR."

The Device entry specifies the type of device which is to be used for the file. There are a number of different entries which can be used, based upon the type of device to be used. In the sample program, an IBM 2540 Card Reader is used. Therefore, the entry specified in the program is 2540R, which indicates that the card file is to be read from an IBM 2540 Card Reader.

The Organization entry is used to indicate the file organization. In the example, it can be seen the entry is the letter of the alphabet "S," which indicates a sequential organization. All files which utilize unit-record devices must be organized in a sequential manner.

It should also be noted in Figure 3-16 that the Select Clause (line 090) for the SUBSCRIPTION-INPUT-FILE is continued on line 100. This continued line must begin within Area B. In the example, the "ASSIGN TO..." line was indented six spaces to begin in column 18, for readability. In all sample programs within this text, any continuing lines will be indented six spaces. It should be noted, however, that the continued line could begin in column 12 or any column within Area B. In addition, it is not required that the Assign Clause be placed on a separate line. It could have been placed on the same line as the Select Clause, with one blank between the last letter of the file-name and the word ASSIGN.

The Select and Assign Clauses for the SUBSCRIPTION-REPORT-FILE are illustrated in Figure 3-17.

EXAMPLE

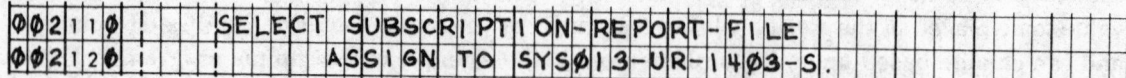

Figure 3-17 Select Clause for Report File

As can be seen from the example in Figure 3-17, the same format is used for the printer output file as is used for the card input file. The sentence must always start with the word SELECT. The file-name used for the printer output file is SUBSCRIPTION-REPORT-FILE which, again, is a name which denotes the file which it names.

The Symbolic Device entry specifies that the device to be used for the file will be assigned to the symbolic name SYS013 by the Disk Operating System. As noted previously, a printer is always a unit-record class of device and, therefore, the UR entry is specified for the Class entry.

The type of printer to be used for the report is an IBM 1403 so the value 1403 is entered for the Device entry to indicate to the COBOL compiler that the file is to be printed using a 1403 printer. The organization on a printer is always sequential (S). As has been noted, the entries for compilers and computers other than IBM may differ from the entries described because they are implementor-defined.

The Select and Assign clauses are used to give a name to a file and to indicate the type of hardware which is to be used for the file. It remains, however, to indicate further attributes of the file such as the length of the records in the file and the formats of the records which are utilized in the file processing. These definitions are made in the Data Division of the COBOL program.

DATA DIVISION

The Data Division of a COBOL source program describes the files to be processed by the program. The Data division is subdivided into sections. In the sample program introduced in this chapter, the File Section and the Working-Storage Section of the Data Division are used.

File Section

The File Section describes the content and organization of the files to be processed. In addition to describing the files to be processed, Record Description entries are required which describe the individual fields contained in a data record of a file.

The first segment of the File Section of the Data Division used in the sample program consists of the entries illustrated below.

EXAMPLE

```
002140 DATA DIVISION.
002150
002160 FILE SECTION.
002170
002180 FD  SUBSCRIPTION-INPUT-FILE
002190         RECORD CONTAINS 80 CHARACTERS
002200         LABEL RECORDS ARE OMITTED
003010         DATA RECORD IS SUBSCRIPTION-INPUT-RECORD.
```

Figure 3-18 Data Division - File Section Entries

The entries illustrated in Figure 3-18 are used to provide a general description of the contents and organization of the records contained in the file. The format of the entries used in the sample problem in the File Section of the Data Division are illustrated below.

```
DATA DIVISION.

[FILE SECTION.

[FD  file-name

    [; RECORD CONTAINS [integer-3 TO]  integer-4 CHARACTERS]

    ; LABEL  {RECORD IS  }  {STANDARD}
             {RECORDS ARE}  {OMITTED }

    [; DATA  {RECORD IS  }  data-name-3  [, data-name-4]  ...]
             {RECORDS ARE}

[record-description-entry]  ...  ]  ...
```

Figure 3-19 Format Notation - File Section

Note from the format notation in Figure 3-19 that the Division Header, DATA DIVISION is a required statement, that is, it is not enclosed in brackets, and must be spelled as shown. It must appear on a line by itself.

As can be seen also, the entire File Section is optional, that is, it is enclosed within brackets. The File Section is optional only if there are no files to be processed by the program. This occurs infrequently in business application programming, and in all programs within this text, the File Section will be required because files are to be processed. The words FILE SECTION are required if a File Section is to be used and must appear on a separate line with the correct spelling. It will be noted from Figure 3-18 that both DATA DIVISION and FILE SECTION begin in column 8 of the coding form. The requirement is that they begin in Area A. In all programs in this text, they will begin in column 8. Note also that the DATA DIVISION and FILE SECTION entries are separated by a blank line. Although this is not required, it is suggested that it be done in order to increase the readability of the source listing.

The FD level indicator (File Description) describes each data file (for example, the card input file) to be processed by the program. The name following the FD must be the file-name used in the Select Clause of the File-Control paragraph (see Figure 3-16). The FD entry must begin in Area A and the file-name must begin in Area B.

EXAMPLE

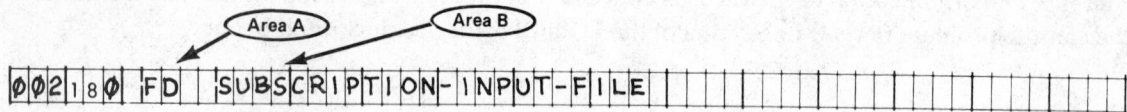

Figure 3-20 FD Entry

Note from the example in Figure 3-20 that the letters FD must begin in Area A and the file-name must begin in Area B. Although any columns within Area A may be used for the FD level indicator, all sample programs will use column 8. In the same manner, the file-name may begin in any column within Area B. In the sample programs, the file-name always begins in column 12.

RECORD CONTAINS Clause

Following the FD level indicator is the **Record Contains** Clause. The Record Contains Clause is used to specify the number of characters in a logical record. The entry from the sample program is illustrated below.

EXAMPLE

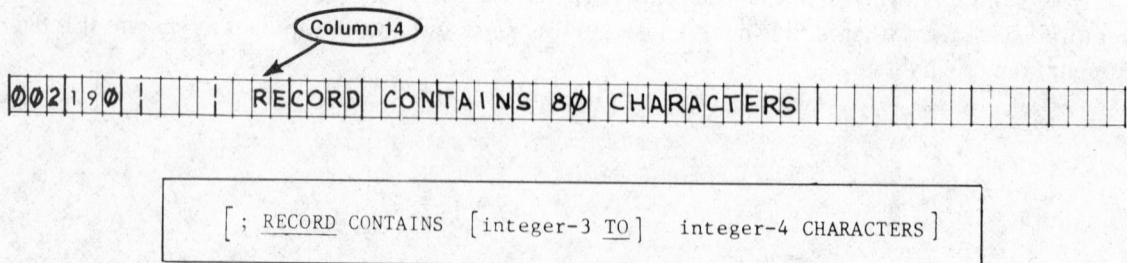

Figure 3-21 RECORD CONTAINS Clause

The Record Contains Clause must begin in Area B. In the example, it begins in column 14 for readability. Integer-3 and Integer-4 in the format notation are used to specify minimum and maximum record sizes respectively if there are records in the file with variable lengths. In the sample program, the records are fixed-length, that is, all of the records in the file have the same length. Therefore, only a single value is specified. In the example, the entry RECORD CONTAINS 80 CHARACTERS is used because a punched card contains eighty characters.

It should be noted that the Record Contains clause is not required (note the brackets in the format notation). It is suggested, however, that the entry be included for documentation purposes. Record lengths are determined by the compiler regardless of whether or not the clause is specified.

LABEL RECORDS Clause

The **Label Records** Clause specifies the presence of standard or non-standard labels on a file, or the absence of labels. Labels are used when processing files stored on magnetic tape or disk. They are not used when processing punched card files. An example of the entry used in the sample program is illustrated below.

EXAMPLE

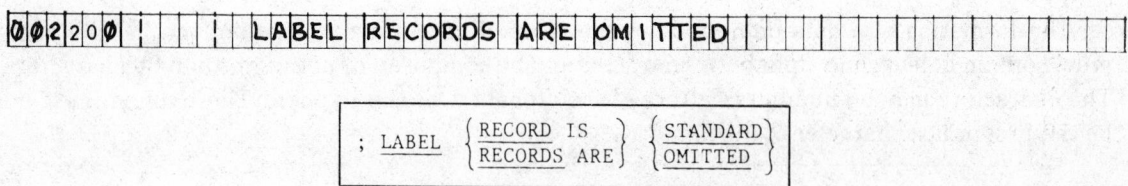

Figure 3-22 LABEL RECORDS Clause

Note from the format notation illustrated in Figure 3-22 that the Label Records Clause is required in the FD Statement (no brackets). Therefore, whenever a file is being defined with the FD Statement in the File Section of the Data Division, the Label Records Clause must be included. In the example, the word OMITTED is used because there are no labels which are used with card files. Whenever a file is assigned to a unit record device (such as a card reader or printer), the OMITTED option must be specified.

DATA RECORD Clause

The **Data Record** Clause specifies the name of the logical records within a file. The Data Record Clause used in the sample program is illustrated in Figure 3-23.

EXAMPLE

```
003010 !     !   DATA RECORD IS SUBSCRIPTION-INPUT-RECORD.
```

```
[ ; DATA { RECORD IS  } data-name-3 [ , data-name-4 ] ... ]
         { RECORDS ARE }
```

Figure 3-23 DATA RECORD Clause

Note from the format illustrated in Figure 3-23 that the Data Record Clause is not required (brackets around it). Again, however, it is suggested that the clause be included in the source program for documentation purposes.

The entry for "data-name-3..." in the Data Record Clause is for the purpose of assigning a symbolic name to the individual records (cards) of a file. In the sample problem, the entry DATA RECORD IS SUBSCRIPTION-INPUT-RECORD is specified. Thus, the name SUBSCRIPTION-INPUT-RECORD may be used in subsequent sections of the program to reference the individual cards to be processed. It should be noted that more than one type of record may be contained within a single file, and the "data-name-4", etc. entries are used to give names to all of the different types of records which may be found in a file.

The formation of a data-name follows the rules of data-name formation, that is, the name must contain at least one alphabetic character and be composed of not more than 30 characters. The characters may be numbers, letters of the alphabet, or the hyphen. The hyphen must not be the first or last character of the name.

It should be noted that a period follows the data-name. This is because this is the last entry in the FD Statement. As was mentioned previously, the use of the period is critical when writing COBOL programs. Therefore, strict attention must be paid to the format notation and the examples given in the text so that punctuation errors are not made.

At this point, in the COBOL program, the programmer has assigned a symbolic name to the entire file, and a symbolic name for each record within the file.

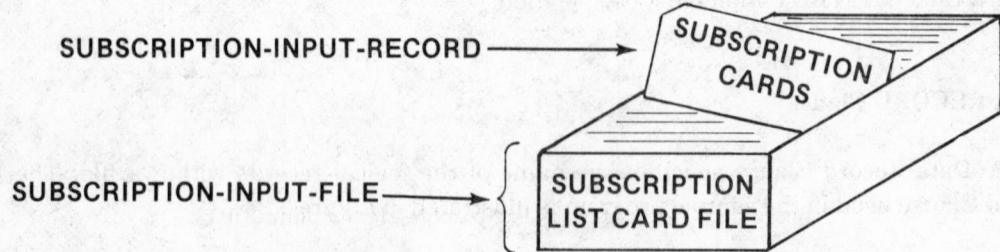

Figure 3-24 Illustration of File and Records within a File

RECORD DESCRIPTION

After the file has been described by the Record Contains, Label Records Are, and Data Record Is Clauses, the individual records within the file are described. The following segment of the COBOL program developed in this chapter illustrates the entries to describe the individual records (cards) to be processed.

EXAMPLE

```
002140 DATA DIVISION.
002150
002160 FILE SECTION.
002170
002180 FD  SUBSCRIPTION-INPUT-FILE
002190       RECORD CONTAINS 80 CHARACTERS
002200       LABEL RECORDS ARE OMITTED
003010       DATA RECORD IS SUBSCRIPTION-INPUT-RECORD.
003020 01  SUBSCRIPTION-INPUT-RECORD.
003030     05  NAME-INPUT                      PICTURE X(25).
003040     05  ADDRESS-INPUT                   PICTURE X(25).
003050     05  CITY-STATE-INPUT                PICTURE X(20).
003060     05  EXPIRATION-DATE-INPUT           PICTURE X(8).
003070     05  FILLER                          PICTURE XX.
```

Figure 3-25 Record Description Entries

A Record Description entry specifies the characteristics of each item in a data record. Every item must be described as a separate entry in the same order in which the item appears in the record. Each Record Description entry in the sample program consists of a Level-Number, a Data-Name, and a Picture Clause.

The general format of the Record Description entry used in the sample program is illustrated below.

$$
\text{level-number}\ \left\{ \begin{array}{l} \text{data-name-1} \\ \underline{\text{FILLER}} \end{array} \right\}
$$

$$
\left[;\ \left\{ \begin{array}{l} \underline{\text{PICTURE}} \\ \underline{\text{PIC}} \end{array} \right\}\ \text{IS character-string} \right]
$$

Figure 3-26 Format Notation-Record Description Entry

LEVEL NUMBERS

Level Numbers are used to show how data items are related to each other. Level number 01 is used to specify a logical record. Thus, an individual card (logical record) is identified by an 01 level number. In the sample program, the individual logical record of the SUBSCRIPTION-INPUT-FILE is identified by the entry "01 SUBSCRIPTION-INPUT-RECORD."

EXAMPLE

```
003010           DATA RECORD IS SUBSCRIPTION-INPUT-RECORD.
003020    01   SUBSCRIPTION-INPUT-RECORD.
```

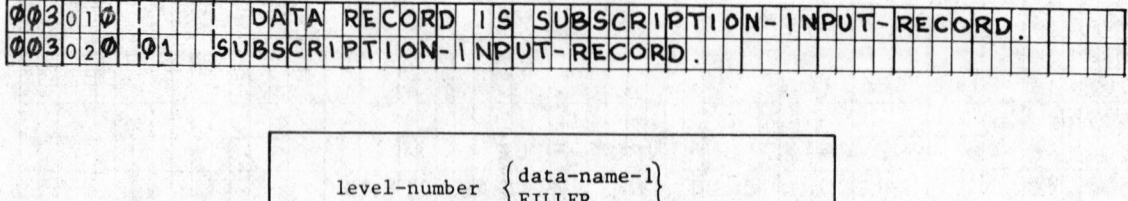

Figure 3-27 Record Description Entry

Note in the example in Figure 3-27 that the level number 01 is specified in Area A and the data-name SUBSCRIPTION-INPUT-RECORD is specified in Area B. All 01 level numbers must be specified in Area A.

Subordinate data items (fields) that constitute a logical record are grouped in a hierarchy, and identified with level numbers 02 through 49. Thus, fields within the record are identified by additional level numbers. In the sample program level number 05 is used to identify the fields within a record. Any number higher than 01 could have been selected. Identifying the fields within a record with a level number of 05 allows further subdivision of the record if required at some future time.

The following example illustrates the entries to describe the fields within the "SUBSCRIPTION-INPUT-RECORD."

EXAMPLE

```
003020    01   SUBSCRIPTION-INPUT-RECORD.
003030         05   NAME-INPUT                      PICTURE X(25).
003040         05   ADDRESS-INPUT                   PICTURE X(25).
003050         05   CITY-STATE-INPUT                PICTURE X(20).
003060         05   EXPIRATION-DATE-INPUT           PICTURE X(8).
003070         05   FILLER                          PICTURE XX.
```

Figure 3-28 Entries to Describe Fields Within a Record

The entries on lines 030, 040, 050, 060, and 070 in Figure 3-28 are used to describe the fields within the record referenced by the symbolic name "SUBSCRIPTION-INPUT-RECORD."

When describing the fields within a record, a data-name or the COBOL word FILLER must be specified following the level number. The data-name selected may contain up to 30 characters. The construction of the name follows the same rules as those for the formation of file-names. Note in the example in Figure 3-28 that the data-names NAME-INPUT, ADDRESS-INPUT, CITY-STATE-INPUT, and EXPIRATION-DATE-INPUT have been selected to reference the corresponding fields on the input record to be processed. These names have been chosen because they represent the content of each field within the record. Whenever data-names are used, they should always indicate the contents of the field—this is mandatory in order to make the program as readable as possible.

Note also that the suffix "INPUT" is used on all data-names to indicate that the names refer to fields in the input record. Whenever data-names are used to describe fields within an input or output record, a suffix should be used to indicate the source of the field.

If some of the characters in a record are not used in the processing steps of a program, then the data description of these characters need not include a data-name. Instead, the COBOL word FILLER is written after the level number. Note the use of the word FILLER in the illustration below to reference the unused two characters at the end of the input record. Note also that the data-names for each field are indented two spaces following the level 05 entry. This indention is designed to improve the readability of the source program.

EXAMPLE

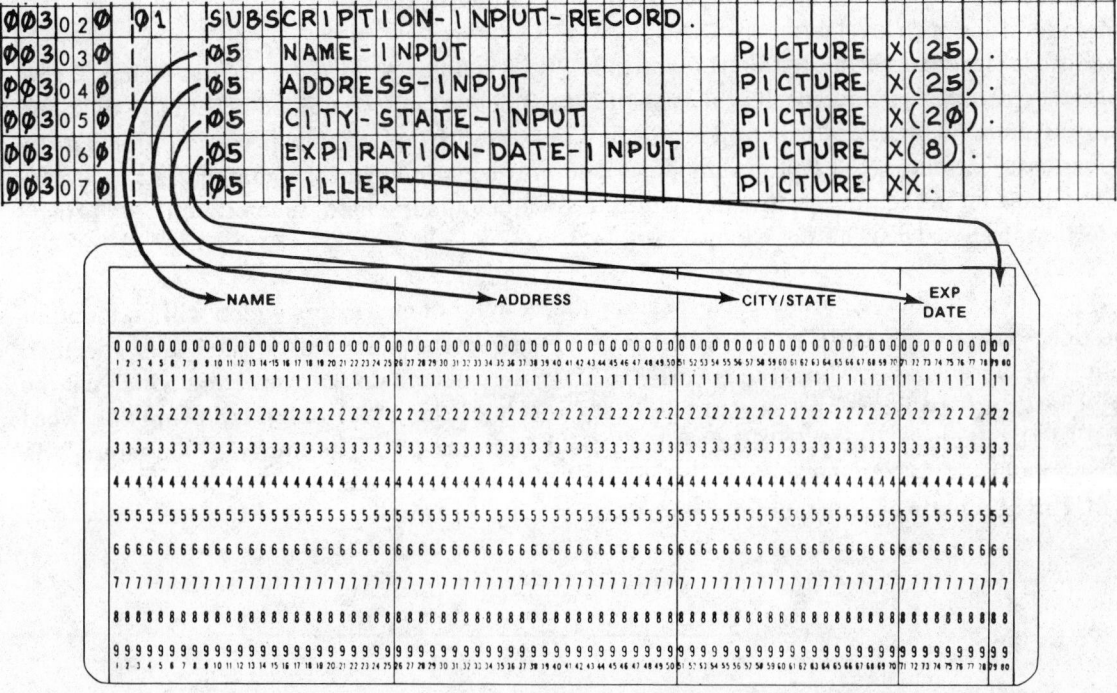

Figure 3-29 Illustration of Card Format and Record Description Entries

The subdivisions of a record that are not themselves subdivided are called **Elementary Items**. Thus, from the example in Figure 3-29, the fields with the data-names NAME-INPUT, ADDRESS-INPUT, CITY-STATE-INPUT, and EXPIRATION-DATE-INPUT are called Elementary Items. Data items which are subdivided are called **Group Items**. Thus, the record name SUBSCRIPTION-INPUT-RECORD is a Group Item.

PICTURE Clause

With each Elementary Item (identified by level-number 05 in the sample program) there must be an associated **Picture** Clause. The Picture Clause specifies a detailed description of an elementary level data item. This description indicates the number of characters in the data item and also the type of character, such as letters of the alphabet only; letters of the alphabet, numbers, and/or special symbols; or numbers only. The Picture Clauses used for the fields in the input record in the sample program are illustrated below.

EXAMPLE

PICTURE Clauses

```
ØØ302Ø  Ø1  SUBSCRIPTION-INPUT-RECORD.
ØØ303Ø      Ø5  NAME-INPUT                 PICTURE X(25).
ØØ304Ø      Ø5  ADDRESS-INPUT              PICTURE X(25).
ØØ305Ø      Ø5  CITY-STATE-INPUT           PICTURE X(2Ø).
ØØ306Ø      Ø5  EXPIRATION-DATE-INPUT      PICTURE X(8).
ØØ307Ø      Ø5  FILLER                     PICTURE XX.
```

```
[ ; {PICTURE}  IS character-string ]
    {PIC    }
```

Figure 3-30 Example of PICTURE Clause

Note in the example above that the word PICTURE is followed by a "character string." This character string is used to specify the type of data which is to be contained within the field and also the number of characters which are in the field. In the sample program, the data is alphanumeric, that is, the fields being described may contain any of the characters which may be available on the computer. In order to define an alphanumeric field, the notation "X" is used following the word PICTURE.

The value within the parentheses specifies the number of characters which will be found in the field. The NAME-INPUT field will contain 25 characters, since this is the value specified within the parentheses. Thus, the NAME-INPUT field will contain 25 characters which can be any characters available on the computer as a result of the X(25) entry following the word PICTURE. Similarly, the ADDRESS-INPUT field contains 25 alphanumeric characters, the CITY-STATE-INPUT field contains 20 alphanumeric characters, and the EXPIRATION-DATE-INPUT field contains 8 alphanumeric characters.

It will be noted that these field sizes correspond to the input card format, as illustrated below.

EXAMPLE

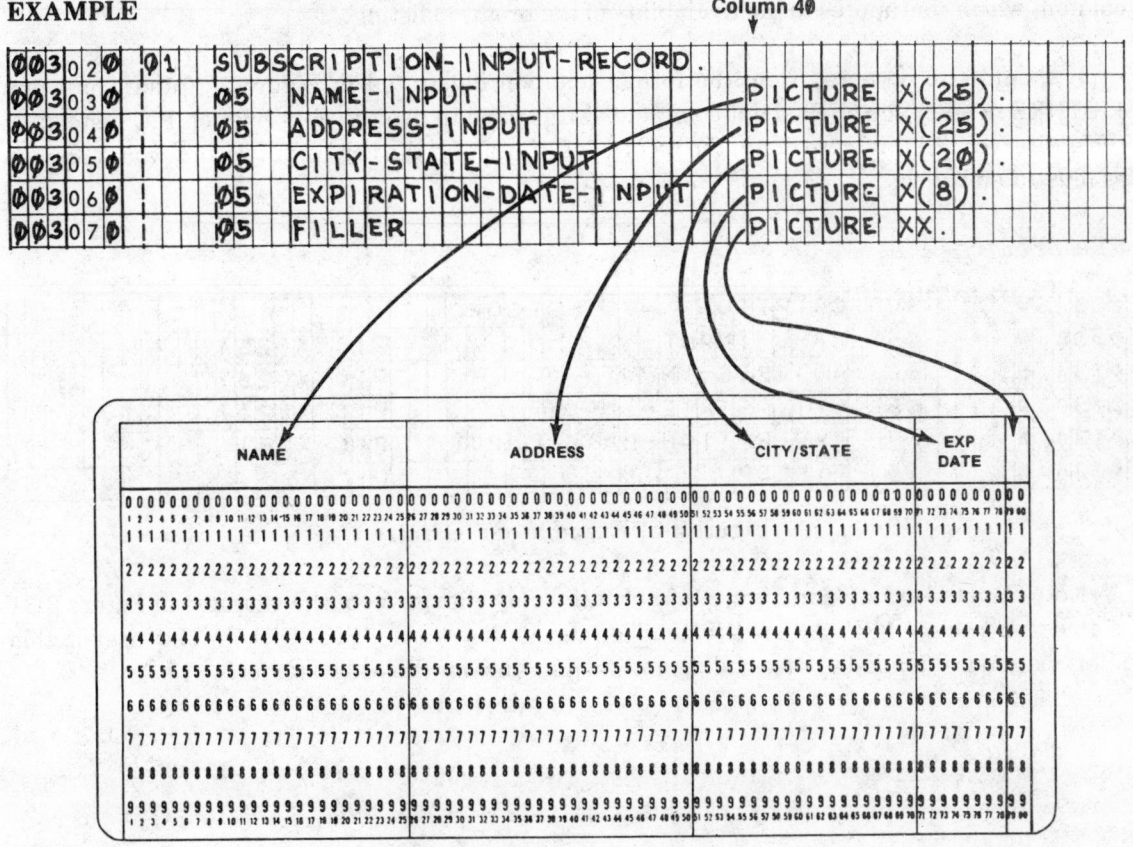

Figure 3-31 PICTURE Clause and Input Card

As can be seen from Figure 3-31, the field sizes as specified in the Picture Clause correspond to the sizes of the fields in the input record. In addition, the fields are specified on the coding form in the same sequence in which they are found on the input card. Thus, the Name field is first, followed by the Address, City/State and Expiration Date fields.

It should be noted that instead of specifying the 25 within the parentheses for NAME-INPUT and ADDRESS-INPUT, 25 separate X's could be written to indicate the number of characters in the field. The use of the parentheses provides a convenient method for representing the number of occurences of the X and greatly reduces the amount of writing required. When, however, the number of positions in a field is small, then an X can be written for each position in the field. For example, the final entry to describe the input record consists of a FILLER followed by PICTURE XX. This entry indicates that the FILLER field consists of two characters (columns 79-80 in the input record). The nomenclature X(2) is identical and could be used instead, however.

In the sample program, the word PICTURE begins in column 40 of the coding form. Although the word could have begun after one blank space following the data-name, it is recorded on column 40 so that all Picture Clauses for the program will begin in the same column, which contributes to the readability of the program listing.

It should also be noted from the format notation illustrated in Figure 3-30 that the word PICTURE need not be spelled out completely. It is valid to use the abbreviation PIC instead of the entire word. If this were done, the record description for the card input record would appear as illustrated below.

EXAMPLE

003020	01	SUBSCRIPTION-INPUT-RECORD.		
003030		05	NAME-INPUT	PIC X(25).
003040		05	ADDRESS-INPUT	PIC X(25).
003050		05	CITY-STATE-INPUT	PIC X(20).
003060		05	EXPIRATION-DATE-INPUT	PIC X(8).
003070		05	FILLER	PIC XX.

Figure 3-32 Example of PIC Entry

Note from the example in Figure 3-32 that the only change from the example in Figure 3-31 is that the value "PIC" is used instead of the entire word "PICTURE". The use of this abbreviation is intended to save coding and writing time for the programmer.

DEFINITION OF REPORT FILE

The next entry in the sample program is used to define the Report File and the Report Line that is to be used in the program.

EXAMPLE

```
0030900  FD  SUBSCRIPTION-REPORT-FILE
0031000          RECORD CONTAINS 133 CHARACTERS
0031100          LABEL RECORDS ARE OMITTED
0031200          DATA RECORD IS SUBSCRIPTION-REPORT-LINE.
0031300  01  SUBSCRIPTION-REPORT-LINE.
0031400      05  CARRIAGE-CONTROL              PICTURE X.
0031500      05  EXPIRATION-DATE-REPORT        PICTURE X(8).
0031600      05  FILLER                        PICTURE X(5).
0031700      05  NAME-REPORT                   PICTURE X(25).
0031800      05  FILLER                        PICTURE X(5).
0031900      05  ADDRESS-REPORT                PICTURE X(25).
0032000      05  FILLER                        PICTURE X(5).
0040100      05  CITY-STATE-REPORT             PICTURE X(20).
0040200      05  FILLER                        PICTURE X(39).
```

Figure 3-33 File and Record Definition for Print File

As with the card input file, the printer output file is defined through the use of the FD Statement. The name following the FD level indicator must be the same as the name specified in the Select Clause of the File-Control paragraph (see Figure 3-17). Thus, the name used is SUBSCRIPTION-REPORT-FILE. The remaining entries for the printer file are quite similar to the entries for the card file.

The Record Contains Clause indicates that the record is to contain 133 characters. The maximum number of print positions available on the IBM 1403 printer used in the sample program is 132. One additional position is specified to allow for a special carriage control character which is specified as the first character in the definition of the print line and is used by the program to control single spacing, double spacing, etc. The carriage control character is not printed when the line is printed on the report. Thus, 132 print positions plus 1 additional position required for carriage control functions equals the "133" specified in the Record Contains Clause.

The Label Records Are Clause is included next. Whenever unit-record devices such as card readers and printers are used for a file, there are no labels. Therefore, LABEL RECORDS ARE OMITTED must be included in the FD Statement.

The Data Record Is Clause is the last clause of the FD Statement. This clause is used to specify the name of the print line which is to be printed. Here, the name of the print line is SUBSCRIPTION-REPORT-LINE. Note the period following the Data Record Is Clause to indicate the end of the FD Statement.

The print line must then be defined as specified on the printer spacing chart. Like the card input file, the 01 Level Number is used for the name of the entire record. Here, the name chosen is SUBSCRIPTION-REPORT-LINE; which must be the same name as specified in the Data Record Is Clause.

The 05 Level Numbers below the entry for the SUBSCRIPTION-REPORT-LINE are used to describe the format of the output line (see Figure 3-34). The first position of the output line consists of a one position field (PICTURE X) called CARRIAGE-CONTROL. As was noted, the first position of the output line will contain a special code that controls the functions of single, double, or triple spacing, or skipping from one page to the next when printing a line. It should be noted that although this character is not referenced in the program, it is given the name CARRIAGE-CONTROL for clarity purposes. This single character, which is not printed, must always be present in the definition of a print line.

Following the one position CARRIAGE-CONTROL field is the 05 Level Number with the related data-name EXPIRATION-DATE-REPORT. This entry describes where the Expiration Date is to be printed on the report line. The Expiration Date will be printed in the first 8 positions of the report line (it should be remembered that the first position for the carriage control character is not printed). Note that the suffix REPORT is appended to the name EXPIRATION-DATE to identify the field as a part of the report line. The entry following EXPIRATION-DATE-REPORT consists of FILLER with a PICTURE X(5). This entry indicates that there are to be five unused positions following the EXPIRATION-DATE-REPORT field.

The remaining entries describe where the Name, Address, and City/State fields are to be printed on the output report. The diagram in Figure 3-34 illustrates the entries for the SUBSCRIPTION-REPORT-LINE and the relationship of the PICTURE Clauses and the printed report.

EXAMPLE

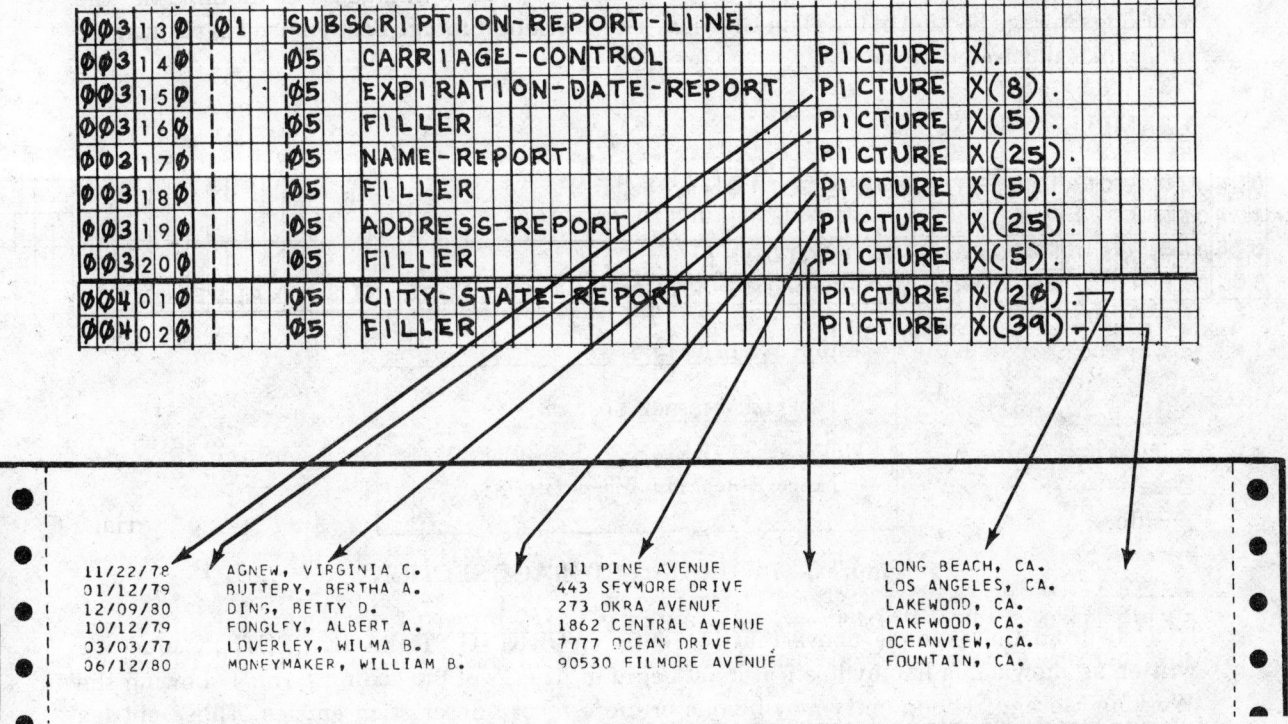

Figure 3-34 Record Description Entries for Subscription-Report-Line and Related Output

Note from the example in Figure 3-34 that each of the 132 positions which are to be used on the output listing, as well as the position for the carriage control character, must be specified as Elementary Items within the Group Item SUBSCRIPTION-REPORT-LINE. As has been noted, a group item is any item which is further subdivided, such as SUBSCRIPTION-REPORT-LINE.

WORKING-STORAGE SECTION

The File Section of the Data Division is used to describe the content and organization of the files to be processed within the program. However, the only data which can be described within the File Section is the data which is found in the records to be processed, such as the card input record and the printer output record.

In many programs, such as the sample program in this chapter, data other than that found in the input and output records must be defined for use. This data is defined in the Working-Storage Section of the Data Division. The Working-Storage Section used in the sample program is illustrated below.

EXAMPLE

```
004040  WORKING-STORAGE SECTION.
004050
004060  01   PROGRAM-INDICATORS.
004070       05   ARE-THERE-MORE-RECORDS  PICTURE X(3) VALUE 'YES'.
```

```
┌ WORKING-STORAGE SECTION.
│ ⎡ 77-level-description-entry ⎤
│ ⎣ record-description-entry   ⎦ ...
```

Figure 3-35 WORKING-STORAGE SECTION

Note from the example above that the entry WORKING-STORAGE SECTION must be written as shown on a line by itself. It must begin in Area A of the coding form. Following the Working-Storage Section entry may be one or more record-description entries. These entries follow the same rules as discussed for record-description entries in the File Section. They consist of a level number plus a data name for Group Items; and a level number, a data-name, and a picture for Elementary Items.

In the example in Figure 3-35, it can be seen that the first entry in the Working-Storage Section is "01 PROGRAM-INDICATORS." The 01 Level Number is used to indicate that the group item is being defined. The data-name, which is chosen by the programmer, reflects the fact that the elementary items within the group are to be used as indicators. An indicator is a field within a program which can have one value to indicate one condition and another value to indicate another condition. For example, if the indicator field contains the value "yes", it could mean that there are more input cards to process; if the indicator field contains the value "no", it could indicate that there are no more input cards to process.

The elementary item within the group item is defined using level number 05. The elementary item will act as the indicator. The data-name chosen by the programmer is ARE-THERE-MORE-RECORDS. This data-name is chosen to reflect the question which will be answered by the indicator. In this instance, the question which the indicator will answer by the value stored in the indicator field is "Are there more records?".

The field will be three characters in length as designated by the entry PICTURE X(3). Whenever a field is used as an indicator, it is usually necessary to give the field an initial value; that is, set the three characters in the field to a given value which has meaning within the program and which can be tested within the program. In the sample program, the value "YES" in the indicator field ARE-THERE-MORE-RECORDS will indicate that there are more records to process. The value "NO" in the field ARE-THERE-MORE-RECORDS is used to indicate there are no more input records left to process. Therefore, prior to the beginning of the execution of the program, the indicator field should contain the value "YES" to indicate that there are input cards to process.

In order to give a field an initial value, that is, a value which it will have when the execution of the program begins, the VALUE Clause is used. The format of the VALUE Clause is illustrated below.

EXAMPLE

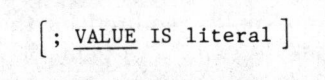

Figure 3-36 Format of VALUE Clause

As can be seen from the format notation above, the word VALUE is required and the word IS is an optional word. Following the words VALUE IS, a "literal" is specified. A literal is the actual value which will be contained in the field at the beginning of the execution of the program.

When the Picture Clause describes an alphanumeric field, that is, when Picture X is used, then the literal specified must be enclosed within single apostrophes as illustrated in Figure 3-35. The literal specified must be the same length or a lesser length than the field length, that is, the literal in the example must be three characters or less. As a result of the VALUE Clause, the ARE-THERE-MORE-RECORDS field will contain the value "YES" when program execution begins, as illustrated below.

EXAMPLE

| 0 0 4 | 0 6 0 | 0 1 | PROGRAM-INDICATORS . |
| 0 0 4 | 0 7 0 | | 0 5 | ARE-THERE-MORE-RECORDS | PICTURE X(3) | VALUE 'YES' . |

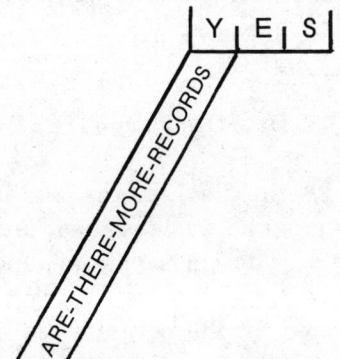

Figure 3-37 Example of VALUE Clause

Note in the example above that as a result of the VALUE Clause, the value "YES" is placed in the field ARE-THERE-MORE-RECORDS. This value will be in the field at the beginning of the execution of the program and will remain there until it is changed by an instruction within the program.

DATA DESIGN

It will be recalled that prior to beginning the coding of the program, the files, records, and fields required for the program were specified (see Figure 3-4). As the coding of the Data Division progressed, the programmer would be referencing these specifications and coding the program from them. At the conclusion of the coding of the Data Division, the programmer should review the files, records, and fields required for the program to ensure that they are contained in the program. The files, records, and fields required for the sample program and the resulting Data Division are illustrated below.

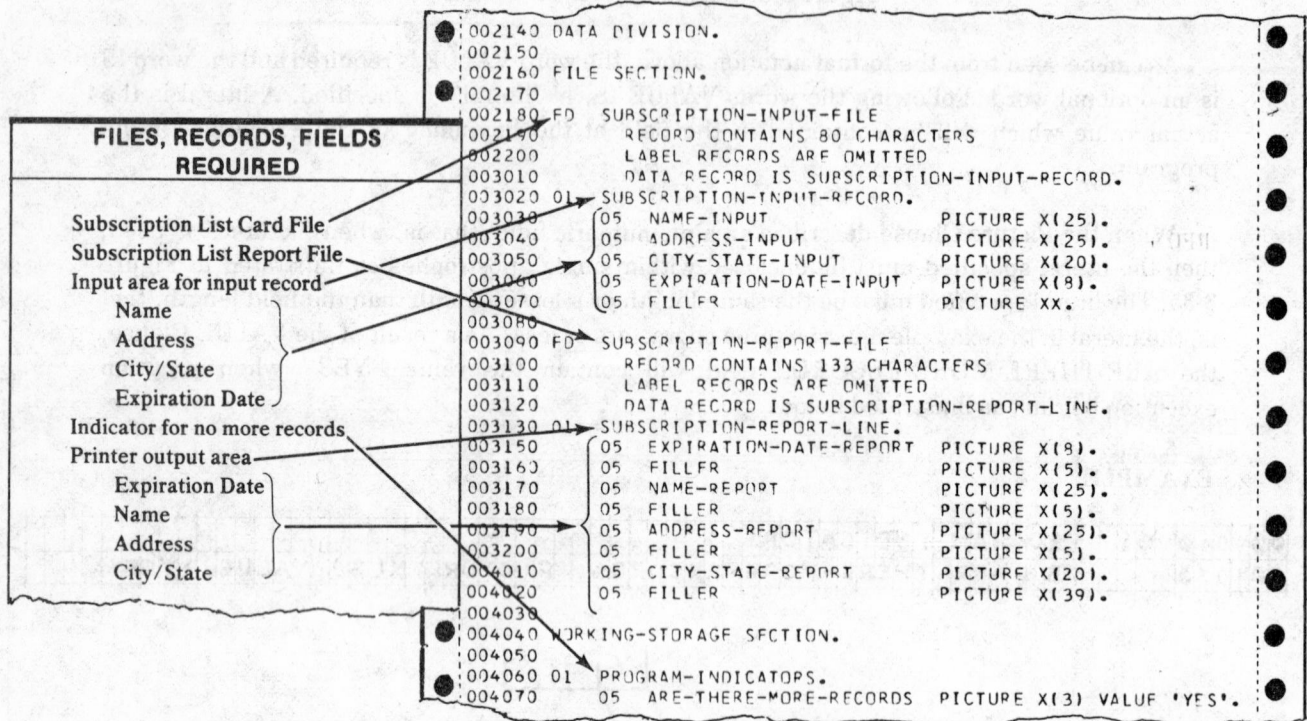

Figure 3-38 Data Design and Data Division

As can be seen from Figure 3-38, the files, records, and fields which are required for the program, as determined when the program was designed, are defined in the Data Division of the sample program. Thus, the program design is quite an important phase in the programming of the problem because it is from the design that the program itself will be coded. Since all of the files, records, and fields required for the program are defined, the coding of the Data Division is completed and the coding of the Procedure Division can begin.

PROCEDURE DIVISION

The Procedure Division of a COBOL program specifies those procedures necessary to solve a given problem. These steps (computations, logical decisions, input/output, etc) are expressed in meaningful statements, similar to English, which employ the concept of verbs to denote actions, and statements and sentences to describe procedures. The Procedure Division is coded directly from the pseudocode which was developed in the program design phase of the program development cycle. The pseudocode and Procedure Division for the sample program are illustrated below.

EXAMPLE

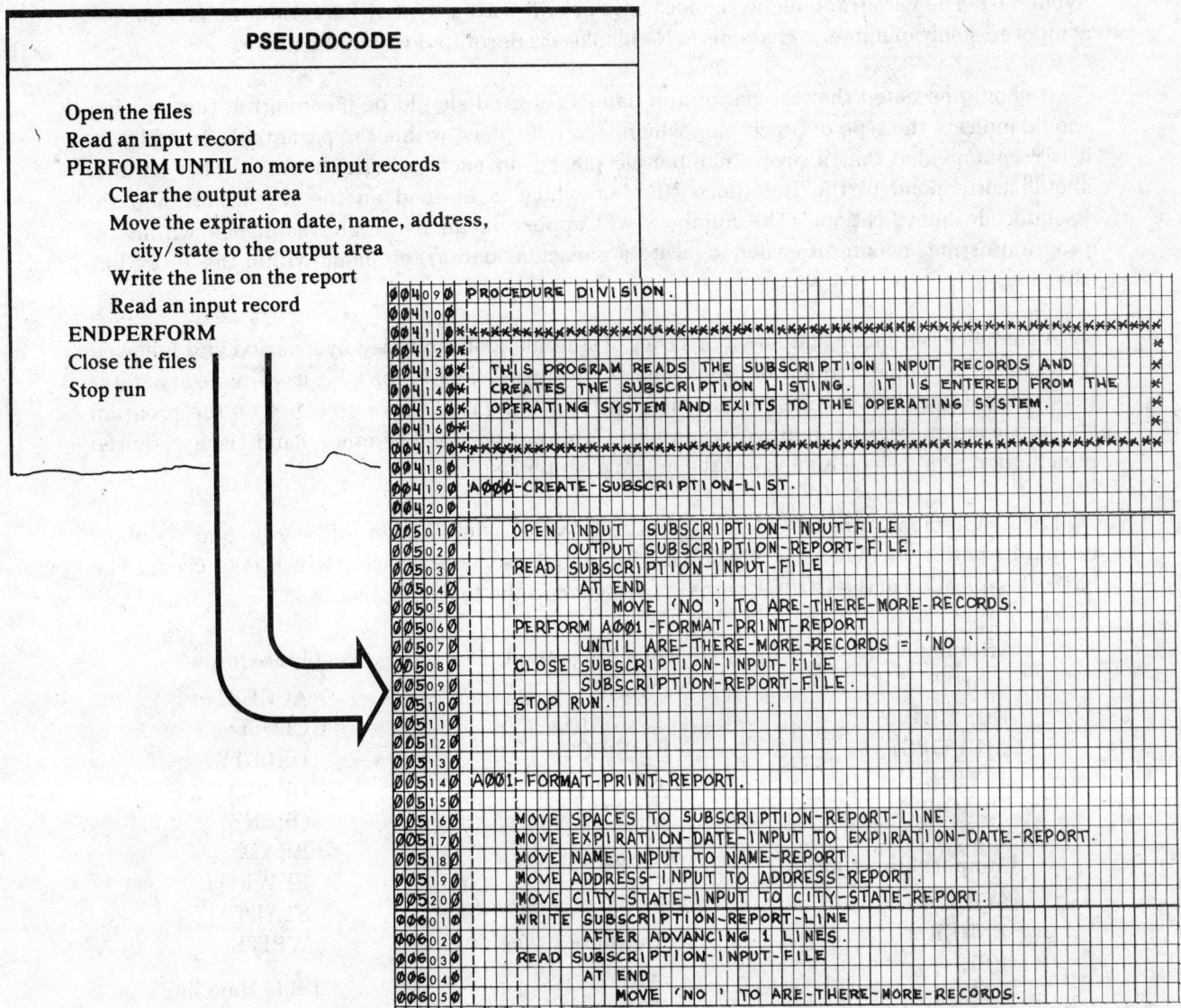

PSEUDOCODE

Open the files
Read an input record
PERFORM UNTIL no more input records
    Clear the output area
    Move the expiration date, name, address,
        city/state to the output area
    Write the line on the report
    Read an input record
ENDPERFORM
Close the files
Stop run

```
004090  PROCEDURE DIVISION.
004100
004110 ***************************************************************
004120 *
004130 *    THIS PROGRAM READS THE SUBSCRIPTION INPUT RECORDS AND    *
004140 *    CREATES THE SUBSCRIPTION LISTING.  IT IS ENTERED FROM THE *
004150 *    OPERATING SYSTEM AND EXITS TO THE OPERATING SYSTEM.       *
004160 *
004170 ***************************************************************
004180
004190  A000-CREATE-SUBSCRIPTION-LIST.
004200
005010      OPEN INPUT  SUBSCRIPTION-INPUT-FILE
005020           OUTPUT SUBSCRIPTION-REPORT-FILE.
005030      READ SUBSCRIPTION-INPUT-FILE
005040          AT END
005050              MOVE 'NO ' TO ARE-THERE-MORE-RECORDS.
005060      PERFORM A001-FORMAT-PRINT-REPORT
005070          UNTIL ARE-THERE-MORE-RECORDS = 'NO '.
005080      CLOSE SUBSCRIPTION-INPUT-FILE
005090            SUBSCRIPTION-REPORT-FILE.
005100      STOP RUN.
005110
005120
005130
005140  A001-FORMAT-PRINT-REPORT.
005150
005160      MOVE SPACES TO SUBSCRIPTION-REPORT-LINE.
005170      MOVE EXPIRATION-DATE-INPUT TO EXPIRATION-DATE-REPORT.
005180      MOVE NAME-INPUT TO NAME-REPORT.
005190      MOVE ADDRESS-INPUT TO ADDRESS-REPORT.
005200      MOVE CITY-STATE-INPUT TO CITY-STATE-REPORT.
006010      WRITE SUBSCRIPTION-REPORT-LINE
006020          AFTER ADVANCING 1 LINES.
006030      READ SUBSCRIPTION-INPUT-FILE
006040          AT END
006050              MOVE 'NO ' TO ARE-THERE-MORE-RECORDS.
```

Figure 3-39 Pseudocode and Procedure Division

Note from Figure 3-39 that the Division Header, PROCEDURE DIVISION, begins in Area A (column 8) and is on a line by itself, followed by a period. The basic structure of the Procedure Division consists of Paragraphs, containing a series of Sentences.

Paragraphs are logical entities consisting of one or more sentences. Each paragraph must begin with a paragraph name, which must begin in Area A. The sample program has two paragraphs—the A000-CREATE-SUBSCRIPTION-LIST paragraph and the A001-FORMAT-PRINT-REPORT paragraph. A paragraph ends at the next paragraph name or at the end of the Procedure Division.

The paragraph name, also called a procedure name, may be composed of not more than 30 characters, and may consist of the digits 0-9, the letters of the alphabet A through Z, or the hyphen (-). The paragraph name cannot begin or end with a hypen. Paragraph names may be composed solely of numeric characters. No blanks are permitted within the name.

It should be noted that the paragraph names selected should be meaningful; that is, they should indicate the type of processing which is to take place within the paragraph. In addition, it is recommended that a prefix number be placed on each paragraph name. This number should correspond to the Reference Number which is defined on the IPO Chart and the Pseudocode Specifications. The numbers will appear in an ascending sequence within the program listing, making it easier to locate a particular paragraph name within the Procedure Division.

A sentence is a single statement or series of statements terminated by a period and followed by a space. A single comma or semicolon or the word THEN may be used as a separator between statements. Commas, semicolons, or the word THEN have no effect on the program and are used merely to improve readability. The period, on the other hand, is a required punctuation symbol which indicates the end of a sentence.

Each statement consists of a syntactically valid combination of words and symbols beginning with a COBOL verb. A COBOL verb indicates the processing which is to occur. The basic classification of the COBOL verbs is presented in the following list.

Arithmetic	Data Movement	Input-Output
ADD	MOVE	ACCEPT
SUBTRACT	EXAMINE	CLOSE
MULTIPLY	INSPECT	DELETE
DIVIDE	STRING	DISPLAY
COMPUTE	UNSTRING	OPEN
		READ
Compiler Directing	**Ending**	REWRITE
COPY	STOP	START
ENTER		WRITE
USE	**Procedure Branching**	
EJECT	ALTER	**Table Handling**
	CALL	
Conditional	EXIT	SEARCH
IF	GO TO	SET
	PERFORM	

COMMENTS

It can be seen in Figure 3-39 that following the Division Header PROCEDURE DIVISION is a series of comment statements (asterisks in column 7). These comments are used to explain the function of the program. It will be noted that the comments do not say how the function is to be performed, merely what is to take place. In general, comments should be included at the start of a program or program module to explain the function of the module.

In addition, the comments state that the program is entered from and exits to the "operating system". The operating system is a series of programs which allow for the continuous operation of a computer and programs are always given control from the operating system; and when they are complete, they relinquish control back to the operating system. Comments which explain the function of a program or of a module within a program should normally identify where control is received from and where control is relinquished to at the conclusion of the processing.

OPEN STATEMENT

The first statement in the A000-CREATE-SUBSCRIPTION-LIST paragraph is the Open Statement, as illustrated below.

EXAMPLE

```
004190 A000-CREATE-SUBSCRIPTION-LIST.
004200
005010     OPEN INPUT SUBSCRIPTION-INPUT-FILE
005020          OUTPUT SUBSCRIPTION-REPORT-FILE.
```

```
      OPEN  ⎧ INPUT file-name-1  [, file-name-2] ...  ⎫
            ⎨ OUTPUT file-name-3 [, file-name-4] ...  ⎬ ...
            ⎩ I-O file-name-5    [, file-name-6] ...  ⎭
```

Figure 3-40 Example of OPEN Statement

The Open Statement initiates the processing of files and must be executed prior to any other input/output statement for a file. The Open statement, by itself, does not make an input record available for processing; a Read statement must be executed in order to obtain the first data-record. For an output file, an Open statement makes available an area for development of the first output record.

In the general format of the Open Statement illustrated in Figure 3-40, it can be seen that the word INPUT must precede the file-name of the input file to be opened and the word OUTPUT must precede the file-name of the output file to be opened. Thus, in the example in Figure 3-40, the OPEN verb is followed by the word INPUT and then the file-name of the card input file, SUBSCRIPTION-INPUT-FILE. Since there is only one input file, the word OUTPUT is specified next, followed by the name of the printer output file, SUBSCRIPTION-REPORT-FILE. Note that the OPEN verb need be specified only one time in order to open both the card file and the printer file. In addition, the input file and the output file are specified on different lines of the coding form and are vertically aligned. This is to aid in the readability of the program and has no consequence concerning the Open Statement itself. The termination of the Open Sentence is indicated by the period and blank space following the name of the output file.

READ STATEMENT

The next statement in the sample program is the Read Statement.

EXAMPLE

```
004190  A000-CREATE-SUBSCRIPTION-LIST.
004200
005010      OPEN INPUT  SUBSCRIPTION-INPUT-FILE
005020           OUTPUT SUBSCRIPTION-REPORT-FILE.
005030      READ SUBSCRIPTION-INPUT-FILE
005040           AT END
005050           MOVE 'NO' TO ARE-THERE-MORE-RECORDS.
```

```
READ file-name RECORD [INTO identifier] [; AT END imperative-statement]
```

Figure 3-41 Example of READ Statement

The function of the Read Statement is to make available a logical record from an input file and to allow the performance of specified operations when end-of-file is detected. End-of-file is normally detected by the presence of an ''end-of-data'' control card. On the System/360 and System/370, a card with the values /* in columns 1 and 2 indicates end-of-data. Other computer systems may have different methods of indicating end-of-data.

When a Read Statement is executed, the next logical record in the file named in the Read Statement becomes available for processing in the input area defined by the associated Record Description entry in the Data Division. The file-name which is specified must be defined by a File Description entry (FD) in the Data Division. Note in the example in Figure 3-41 that the file-name SUBSCRIPTION-INPUT-FILE is specified, since this is the name of the card input file as defined in the Data Division.

The record remains available for processing in the input area until the next Read Statement (or until a Close Statement) is executed for that file.

The At End option is required for files which are accessed sequentially, such as the card input file. The At End portion of the Read Statement is executed when an end-of-file condition is detected, that is, when the end-of-data card is read.

In the example in Figure 3-41, when the end-of-data card is detected, the value "NO " will be moved to the field ARE-THERE-MORE-RECORDS. It will be recalled that the field ARE-THERE-MORE-RECORDS is used as an indicator to specify whether more records are available for processing. It was given the initial value of "YES" through the use of the Value Clause in the Data Division (see Figure 3-37). As long as the ARE-THERE-MORE-RECORDS field contains the value "YES", it indicates there are more input records to process. However, when the value "NO " is moved to the field as a result of the At End portion of the Read Statement, then the indicator specifies that there are no more records in the input file to be processed.

Once the At End portion of the Read Statement has been executed for a file, any subsequent attempt to read from that file or to refer to logical records in that file constitutes an error and the program may be abnormally terminated.

It will be noted from Figure 3-41 that the words AT END are on a separate coding line from the READ verb and file-name, and are indented six spaces. Although this is not required, the convention within the programs in this text, and one that is recommended, is that any statement which must be continued onto the next coding line be indented six spaces from the previous line. In this manner, it is easy to see that the statement has been continued onto the next line.

In addition, it will be noted that the processing following the AT END words will not take place each time an input record is read; it takes place only when the end-of-data card has been read. Therefore, the At End clause is called a conditional clause since it will be executed only under a given condition. Within all programs in this text, those instructions which are to be executed based upon a given condition will be on a separate line from the statement of the condition and will be indented three spaces. Thus, in this example, the condition is "AT END", and the statement which is to be executed on that condition (the Move Statement) is placed on the next coding line and is indented three spaces.

These conventions for writing the statements within the program are again illustrated below.

EXAMPLE

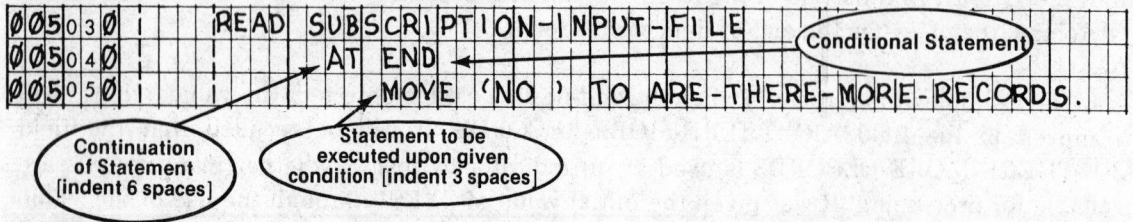

Figure 3-42 Example of Coding Conventions

Note from the example above that the continuation of the Read Statement is indented six spaces and the statement to be executed when the condition is satisfied is indented three spaces. As noted, this spacing convention will be used throughout the text in order to make the program listing more readable, and it is the suggested convention when writing COBOL programs.

PERFORM STATEMENT

The next statement in the sample program is the Perform Statement, which is illustrated in Figure 3-43.

EXAMPLE

```
004190 A000-CREATE-SUBSCRIPTION-LIST.
004200
005010     OPEN INPUT  SUBSCRIPTION-INPUT-FILE
005020          OUTPUT SUBSCRIPTION-REPORT-FILE.
005030     READ SUBSCRIPTION-INPUT-FILE
005040         AT END
005050             MOVE 'NO ' TO ARE-THERE-MORE-RECORDS.
005060     PERFORM A001-FORMAT-PRINT-REPORT
005070         UNTIL ARE-THERE-MORE-RECORDS = 'NO '.
```

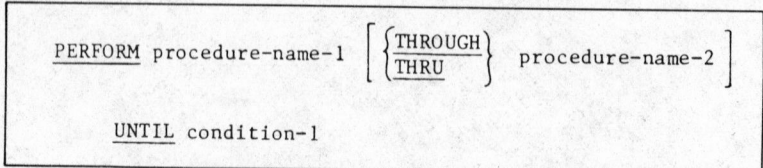

Figure 3-43 Example of PERFORM Statement

The Perform Statement is used to transfer control to the paragraph specified as procedure-name-1 in the format notation. The statements within the paragraph specified as procedure-name-1 will be executed until "condition-1" is true, at which time control will be returned to the statement following the Perform Statement in the program.

In the sample program, the PERFORM Statement works in the following manner:

Step 1: The condition "ARE-THERE-MORE-RECORDS = 'NO '"is checked first, that is, the value in the field ARE-THERE-MORE-RECORDS is compared to the value 'NO '.

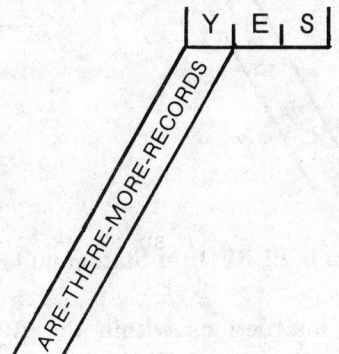

Figure 3-44 Condition is Checked

Note in the example above that the value in the field ARE-THERE-MORE-RECORDS is "YES", which indicates that there are more input records to process. Therefore, it is desired to execute the A001-FORMAT-PRINT-REPORT paragraph, which will format and print the input record.

Step 2: Since the condition is not satisfied, that is, since the field ARE-THERE-MORE-RECORDS does not contain the value 'NO ', the statements in the A001-FORMAT-PRINT-REPORT paragraph will be executed.

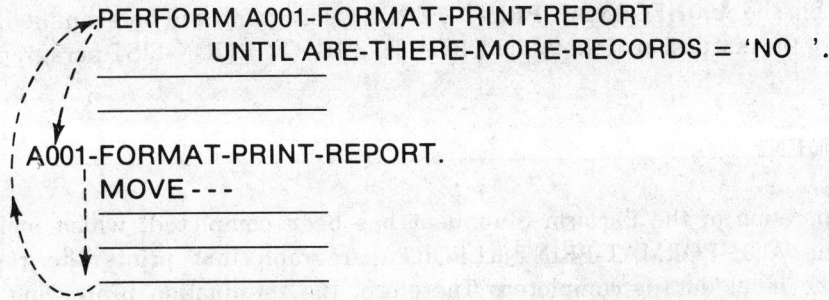

Figure 3-45 Example of Perform Statement Execution

Note in the example above that the PERFORM Statement causes control to be transferred to the A001-FORMAT-PRINT-REPORT paragraph, where all of the statements within that paragraph will be executed.

After the A001-FORMAT-PRINT-REPORT paragraph has been executed one time, the condition specified in the Perform Statement will again be checked.

Step 3: **The condition in the Perform Statement is again checked, that is, the field ARE-THERE-MORE-RECORDS is checked to determine if it contains the value 'NO '.**

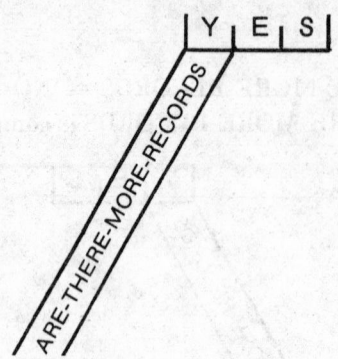

Figure 3-46 Condition in PERFORM Statement is Checked Again

Note in Step 3 that after the instructions within the A001-FORMAT-PRINT-REPORT paragraph have been executed one time, the condition specified in the Perform Statement is again checked. In the example above, the value in the ARE-THERE-MORE-RECORDS field has not changed because the end-of-data card was not found in the input stream. Therefore, the A001-FORMAT-PRINT-REPORT paragraph will be executed again.

This processing will continue until the value 'NO ' is found in the ARE-THERE-MORE-RECORDS field. At that time, the statement following the Perform Statement will be executed. It should be noted that there must be instructions within the A001-FORMAT-PRINT-REPORT paragraph which will change the value in the ARE-THERE-MORE-RECORDS field from 'YES' to 'NO '. If there are not, then this "looping" will never terminate, that is, the value 'NO ' will never be found and the A001-FORMAT-PRINT-REPORT paragraph will be performed endlessly. Therefore, whenever a paragraph is performed until a certain condition occurs, that condition must occur within the performed paragraph so that the loop can be terminated. The instructions within the A001-FORMAT-PRINT-REPORT paragraph will be examined following the completion of the discussion of the A000-CREATE-SUBSCRIPTION-LIST paragraph.

CLOSE STATEMENT

After the operation of the Perform Statement has been completed, which includes the execution of the A001-FORMAT-PRINT-REPORT paragraph that prints the report, the processing of the input data is completed. Therefore, the termination processing must be accomplished. In the sample program, the termination consists of closing the files and stopping the program.

In order to close the files, the Close Statement is used, as illustrated in Figure 3-47.

EXAMPLE

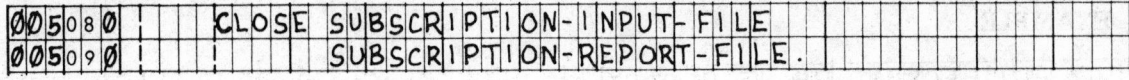

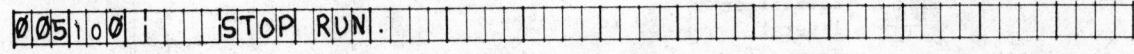

CLOSE file-name-1 [WITH LOCK] [, file-name-2 [WITH LOCK]] ...

Figure 3-47 Example of CLOSE Statement

Note from Figure 3-47 that the Close Statement begins with the CLOSE Verb. It is followed by the file-names of those files to be closed. Prior to terminating the program, it is necessary to close any files which have been previously opened. Therefore, the filenames SUBSCRIPTION-INPUT-FILE and SUBSCRIPTION-OUTPUT-FILE are specified because they are the files which were previously opened (see Figure 3-40). After a file has been closed, it cannot be referenced in a Read or Write Statement unless the file is reopened through the use of the Open Statement.

The optional entries within the brackets (WITH LOCK) are not used for card or printer files.

STOP RUN STATEMENT

In order to terminate the program, the Stop Run Statement is used, as illustrated below.

EXAMPLE

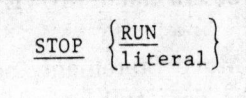

$$\text{STOP} \begin{Bmatrix} \underline{RUN} \\ literal \end{Bmatrix}$$

Figure 3-48 Example of Stop Statement

The Stop Run Statement terminates the execution of the program and returns control to the operating system. It is the last statement executed in a program.

PERFORMED PARAGRAPH

It will be recalled that the processing required to format and print the report is performed (see Figure 3-43). The paragraph which is performed is illustrated below.

EXAMPLE

```
005140  A001-FORMAT-PRINT-REPORT.
005150
005160      MOVE SPACES TO SUBSCRIPTION-REPORT-LINE.
005170      MOVE EXPIRATION-DATE-INPUT TO EXPIRATION-DATE-REPORT.
005180      MOVE NAME-INPUT TO NAME-REPORT.
005190      MOVE ADDRESS-INPUT TO ADDRESS-REPORT.
005200      MOVE CITY-STATE-INPUT TO CITY-STATE-REPORT.
006010      WRITE SUBSCRIPTION-REPORT-LINE
006020          AFTER ADVANCING 1 LINES.
006030      READ SUBSCRIPTION-INPUT-FILE
006040          AT END
006050              MOVE 'NO ' TO ARE-THERE-MORE-RECORDS.
```

Figure 3-49 Performed Paragraph

Note that the performed paragraph, named A001-FORMAT-PRINT-REPORT, consists of Move Statements, a Write Statement, and a Read Statement.

MOVE STATEMENTS

The Move Statement is used to move data from one area of computer storage to another. The format of the Move Statement is illustrated in Figure 3-50.

$$\underline{\text{MOVE}} \begin{Bmatrix} \text{identifier-1} \\ \text{literal} \end{Bmatrix} \underline{\text{TO}} \text{ identifier-2 } [\text{ , identifier-3}] \dots$$

Figure 3-50 Format of MOVE Statement

In the format notation for the Move Statement, note that "identifier-1" refers to the data-name of the field containing the data to be moved. "Identifier-2", "identifer-3", etc. refers to the data-names of the fields to which the data from "identifier-1" will be moved. It should be noted that there must be at least one field which is the "receiving field", that is, the field to which the data is to be moved; but there can be more than one field, if required.

The first Move Statement in Figure 3-49 is used to move spaces (blanks) to the printer output area so that the printer output area will not contain any extraneous data. The operation of this Move Statement is illustrated below.

EXAMPLE

```
005160 !    MOVE SPACES TO SUBSCRIPTION-REPORT-LINE.
```

Before Move   SUBSCRIPTION-REPORT-LINE

```
N Z Q R 1 2 7 0 5 6 │ N I G H T │ M A R T Z Q F F │ B O K T E M Q 7 7 3 │ │ 9 7 ...... 2 Z Q R Z 7 7 8 8 9 3
```

|——————————————————— 133 positions ———————————————————|

After Move

```
│ │ │ │ │ │ │ │ │ │ │ │ │ │ │ │ │ │ │ │ │ │ │ │ │ │ │ │ │ │ │ │ │ │ │ │ ...... │ │ │ │ │ │ │ │ │ │ │
```

|——————————————— 133 printing positions ———————————————|

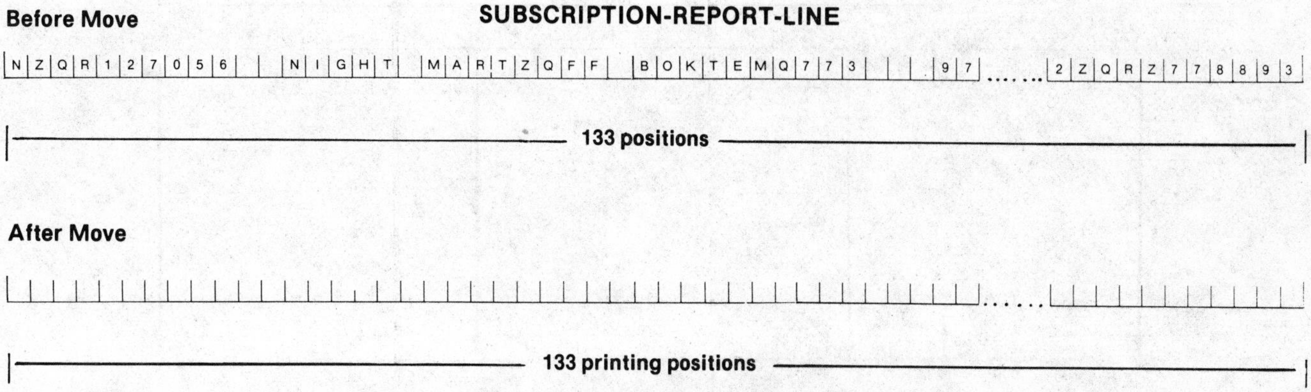

Figure 3-51 Example of Move Spaces Statement

Note in the example above that prior to the execution of the Move Statement, the SUBSCRIPTION-REPORT-LINE area contains meaningless data. The data in the area may originate from data fields previously stored in computer storage or from other sources. This data must not be present when the data to be printed is moved to the printer output area. Thus, the Move Statement to move blanks to the printer output area is required. After the execution of the Move Statement, the SUBSCRIPTION-REPORT-LINE area contains blanks, which is the desired result.

The word SPACES in the example above illustrates the use of a Figurative Constant, that is, a standard COBOL data-name to which a value has been assigned. The figurative constant SPACE or SPACES represents one or more "blanks" or "spaces" when specified in a COBOL program. Therefore, as noted, the effect of the Move Statement in Figure 3-51 is to move blanks to the printer output area.

The next Move Statements are used to move the data in the input area to the printer output area. The Move Statements are illustrated in Figure 3-52.

EXAMPLE

```
005170        MOVE EXPIRATION-DATE-INPUT TO EXPIRATION-DATE-REPORT.
005180        MOVE NAME-INPUT TO NAME-REPORT.
005190        MOVE ADDRESS-INPUT TO ADDRESS-REPORT.
005200        MOVE CITY-STATE-INPUT TO CITY-STATE-REPORT.
```

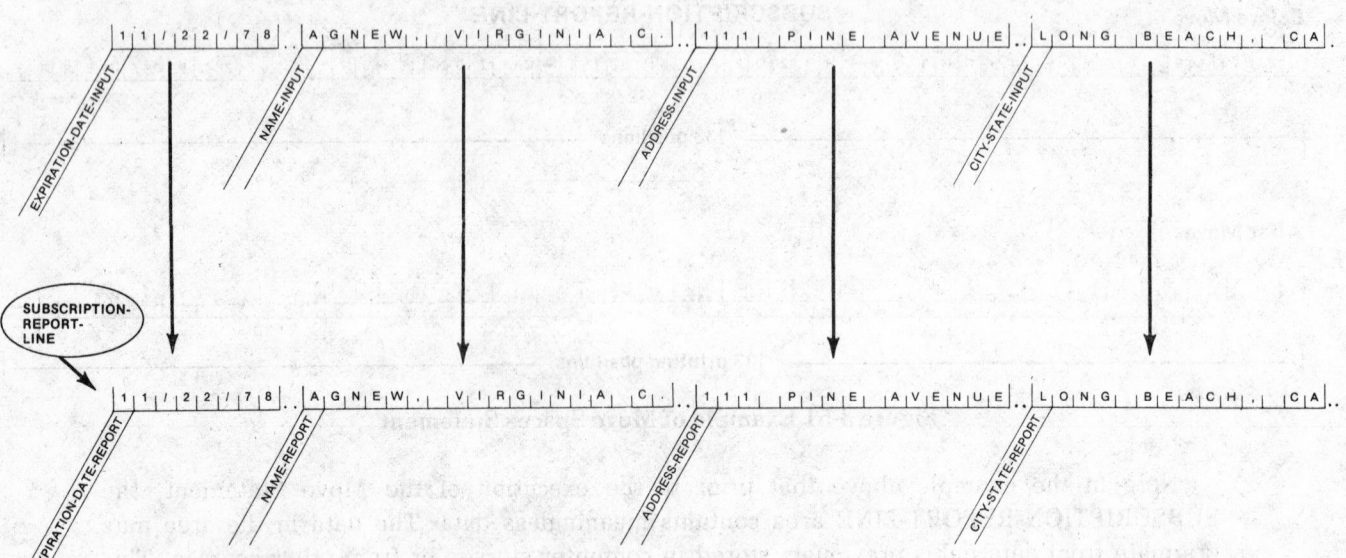

Figure 3-52 Example of Move Statements

Note from the example in Figure 3-52 that the Move Statement is used to move data from the input area to the printer output area. These areas have been previously defined in the Data Division.

MULTIPLE RECEIVING FIELDS

In the previous examples, the data in one sending field has been moved to one receiving field. It is also possible to move the data in one sending field to more than one receiving field using only one Move Statement. This is illustrated below.

EXAMPLE

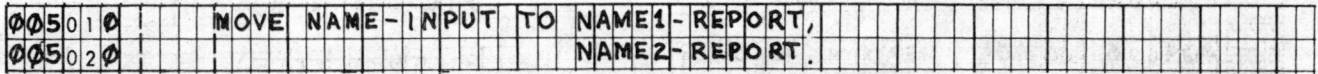

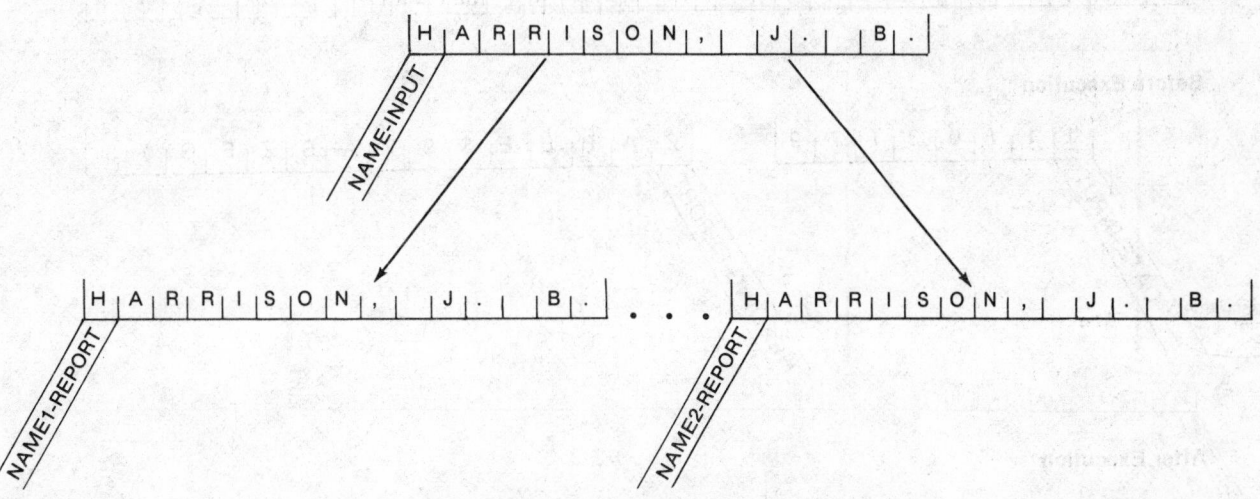

Figure 3-53 Example of Multiple Receiving Fields

Note in the example above that the Move Statement contains one sending field, NAME-INPUT. Two receiving fields are specified—NAME1-REPORT and NAME2-REPORT. Thus, when the Move Statement is executed, the data in NAME-INPUT will be moved to both NAME1-REPORT and NAME2-REPORT. This format of the Move Statement is useful when a single field must be moved to multiple areas within computer storage. It can be seen that the names of the two receiving fields are on separate lines and are separated by a comma. This is done to make the Move Statement more readable and is not required.

DIFFERENT LENGTH FIELDS

In all previous examples, the sending field and the receiving field each have the same length; that is, they contain the same number of characters in their Picture Clauses in the Data Division. For example, the ADDRESS-INPUT field and the ADDRESS-REPORT field are both 25 characters in length. If the fields are of unequal length, however, COBOL will process the fields based upon certain rules.

Receiving Field Longer than Sending Field

If the receiving field is longer than the sending field when moving alphanumeric (Picture X) data, the right portion of the receiving field will be filled with blanks. This is illustrated below.

EXAMPLE

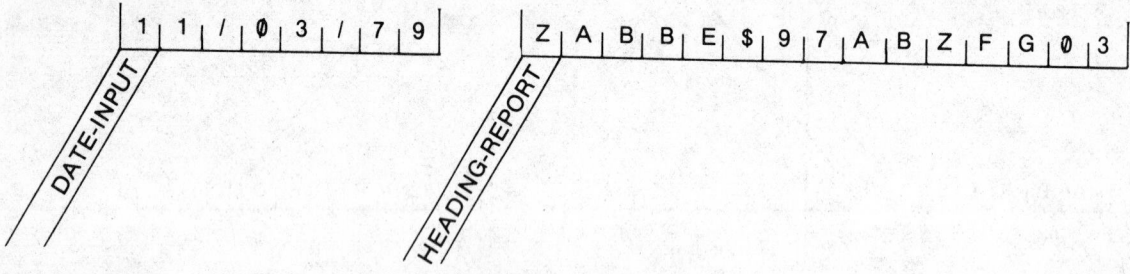

Before Execution

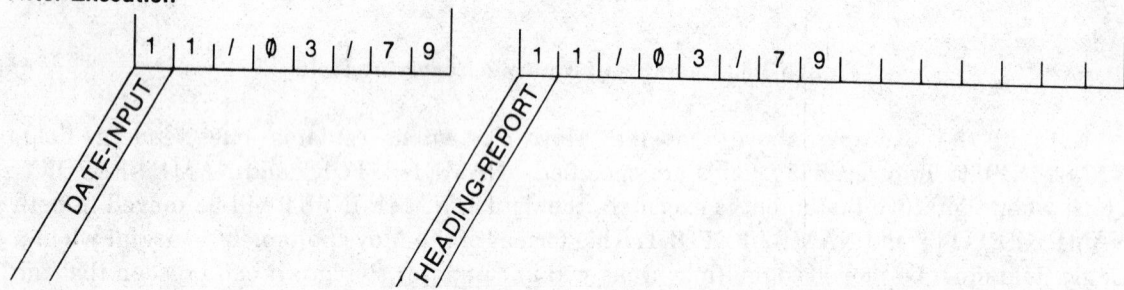

After Execution

Figure 3-54 Example of MOVE Statement

Note in the example above that the HEADING-REPORT field, which is the receiving field, contains 15 characters, and the DATE-INPUT field, which is the sending field, contains 8 characters. When the DATE-INPUT field is moved to the HEADING-REPORT field, the eight characters in the DATE-INPUT field are moved to the leftmost positions in the HEADING-REPORT field and the remaining positions in the receiving field are filled with blanks.

Receiving Field Shorter than Sending Field

If the receiving field is smaller than the sending field, then "truncation" will occur on the right end of the data when it is placed in the receiving field; that is, only the leftmost characters of the sending field will be placed in the receiving field. This is illustrated in Figure 3-55.

EXAMPLE

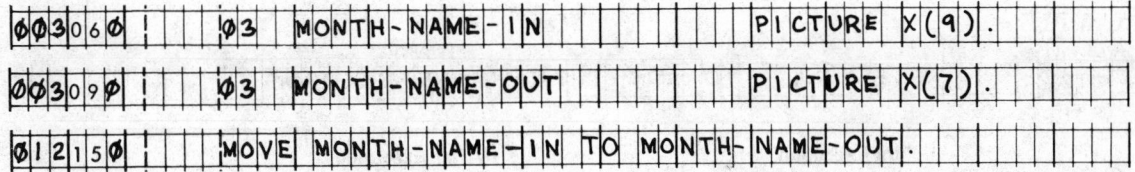

Before Execution

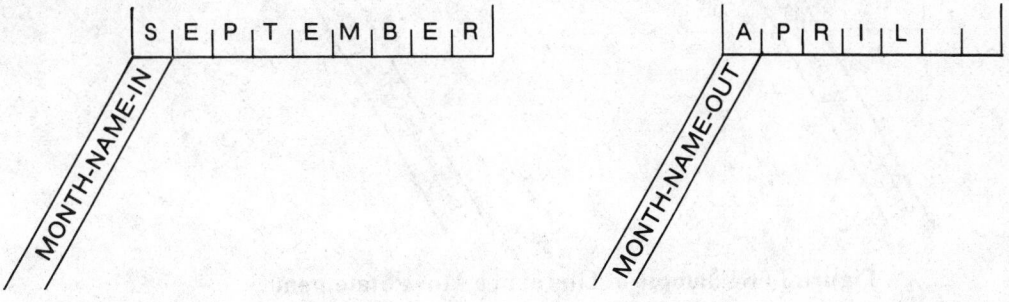

After Execution

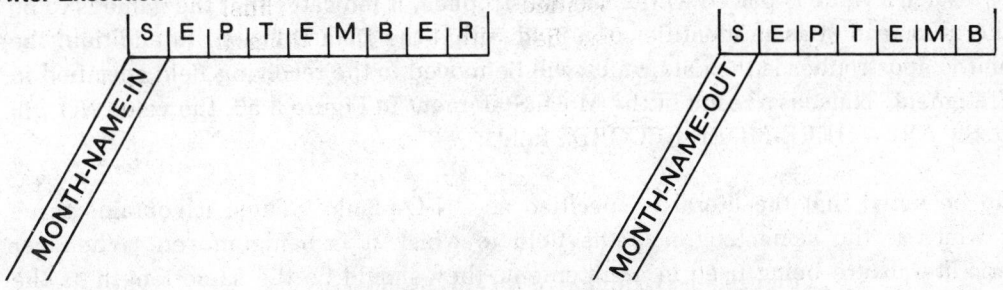

Figure 3-55 Example of MOVE Statement

Note from the example above that when the receiving field (MONTH-NAME-OUT) is shorter than the sending field (MONTH-NAME-IN), the leftmost characters of the sending field are moved to the receiving field until all of the positions within the receiving field are filled, at which time the execution of the Move Statement ceases.

In most cases, the lengths of the two fields involved in a Move Statement will be the same and the programmer should be careful to note those times when they are not equal in order to ensure that the fields are defined properly.

LITERALS

In previous examples, the sending field in the Move Statement was defined in the Data Division. It is also possible to define the data which is to be moved in the Move Statement itself, through the use of a Literal. A literal is set of characters which act as the data to be processed, rather than as an identifier referencing a storage area which contains the data to be processed. The use of an alphanumeric literal in a Move Statement is illustrated below.

EXAMPLE

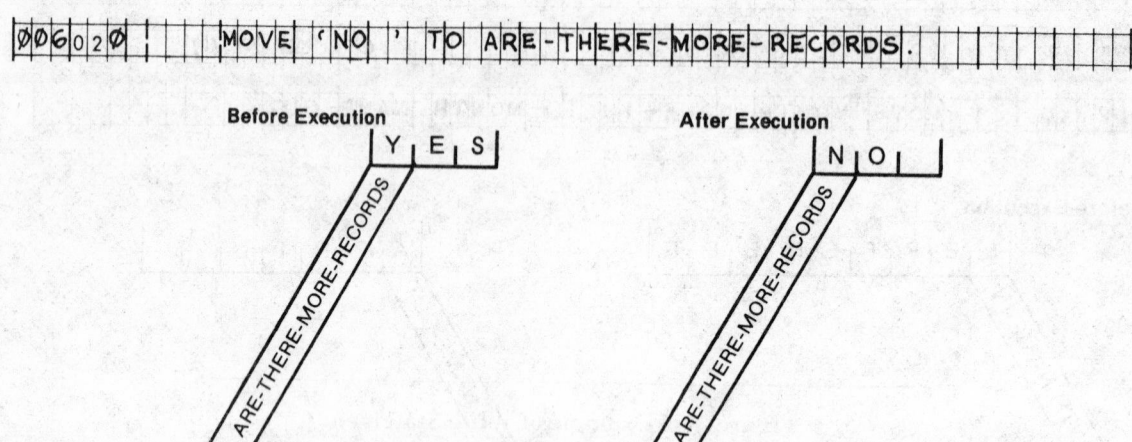

Figure 3-56 Example of Literal in a Move Statement

Note in the Move Statement illustrated above that the value NO is specified within single apostrophes. When a value is placed within the apostrophes, it indicates that the value is to be used as a literal instead of as an identifier of a field within the Data Division. In addition, the value within the apostrophes is the data which will be moved to the receiving field specified in the Move Statement. Thus, as a result of the Move Statement in Figure 3-56, the value NO will be moved to the ARE-THERE-MORE-RECORDS field.

It should be noted that the literal is specified as "N-O-blank." Thus, it contains three characters, which is the same length as the field to which it is being moved. Whenever alphanumeric literals are being used in a statement, they should be the same length as the receiving fields in order to make the object program more efficient. If, for some reason, the literal is not the same length as the receiving field, the rules for different length fields as discussed previously are applied.

WRITE STATEMENT

After the fields have been moved to the printer output area, the Write Statement is used to cause a line to be printed on the printer.

The Write Statement used in the sample program is illustrated below.

EXAMPLE

```
006010    WRITE SUBSCRIPTION-REPORT-LINE
006020        AFTER ADVANCING 1 LINES.
```

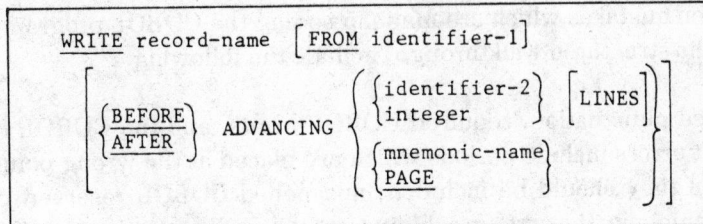

Figure 3-57 Example of Write Statement

The Record-Name entry in the general format refers to the record which is defined in the File Section of the Data Division (see Figure 3-33). In the sample program, this record-name is SUBSCRIPTION-REPORT-LINE, which is used in the Write Statement in the sample program. Note that the "FROM" Clause is not used in the sample program—it is an optional entry.

The Advancing Option is used to control the spacing of the report. It specifies whether the line is to be printed before spacing (BEFORE) or after spacing the printer (AFTER). In the example, the After Advancing option is used, which means that the printer will be spaced and then the line will be printed after the printer is spaced.

The value specified as "integer" in the general format is used to indicate the number of lines to be spaced. Any value from 0 through 99 can be specified. In the example in Figure 3-57, the value 1 is specified (ie, AFTER ADVANCING 1 LINES). Therefore, after the line from the SUBSCRIPTION-REPORT-LINE area is printed, the printer will be spaced one line so that the next line can be printed. The value 2 would be used if double spacing were desired, the value 3 for triple spacing, etc.

It should be noted that when the Advancing Option is used for a file, every Write Statement for records in the same file must contain an Advancing Option. In addition, when the Advancing Option is used, the first character in the output line must be reserved for a carriage control character (see Figure 3-33).

An Open Statement must be executed for the file prior to executing the first Write Statement. After the Write Statement is executed, the logical record named by "record-name" is no longer available for processing.

After the Write Statement is executed and the line is written on the printer, the processing for the record is complete. Therefore, the next statement in the Performed paragraph is a Read Statement which will read the next record to be processed (see Figure 3-49). After the last record has been processed, control will be returned to the "mainline" routine which will Close the Files and Stop the Run.

PROGRAMMING TIPS

A program should compile and execute the first time it is placed on the computer. In order for this to occur, each phase within the program development cycle must be followed exactly. One of the phases within the cycle is the coding of the program. Within the coding of the program, one of the steps which must take place is a structured walkthrough of the code in the program. Common mistakes which are made in coding the COBOL program, and which should be looked for in the structured walkthrough, include the following:

1. All required punctuation, required COBOL words, and the COBOL formatting must be correct. Frequent errors include periods which are placed at the wrong point, or periods which are omitted when they should be included; misspelled COBOL reserved or required words; statements beginning in the wrong columns on the coding form; and omission of required COBOL words.

2. The definitions of the fields in the Data Division must correspond exactly to the program specifications for the data.

3. Data-names should reflect the fields which they are defining.

4. The data-names used must be spelled the same in the Procedure Division as they are in the Data Division.

5. The coding in the Procedure Division must correspond exactly to the logic expressed in the pseudocode.

6. Comments should be used where necessary to explain what is to occur within a program module.

7. Indentation and the physical structure of the program should be according to established standards, and the source program should be easily read. The indentation rules used in this text will be discussed in the appropriate chapters. In all programs in this book, the Data Division and the Procedure Division will begin on new source listing pages. This page skipping can be caused by one of two ways: with some compilers the character slash (/) in column 7 will cause a skip to a new page; with other compilers, the word EJECT written in columns 12-16 on a line by itself will cause the page skipping.

Remember, A PROGRAM SHOULD WORK THE FIRST TIME!! If the steps in the program development cycle are followed closely, and if the program is designed and written with care and concentration, then there is every chance that it will. If any of the steps within the program development cycle are omitted, however, there is every likelihood that it will not.

SAMPLE PROGRAM

The following pages illustrate the Output, Input, IPO Chart, Pseudocode Specifications, Source Listing, and printed output of the sample program to create the Subscription List Report.

OUTPUT

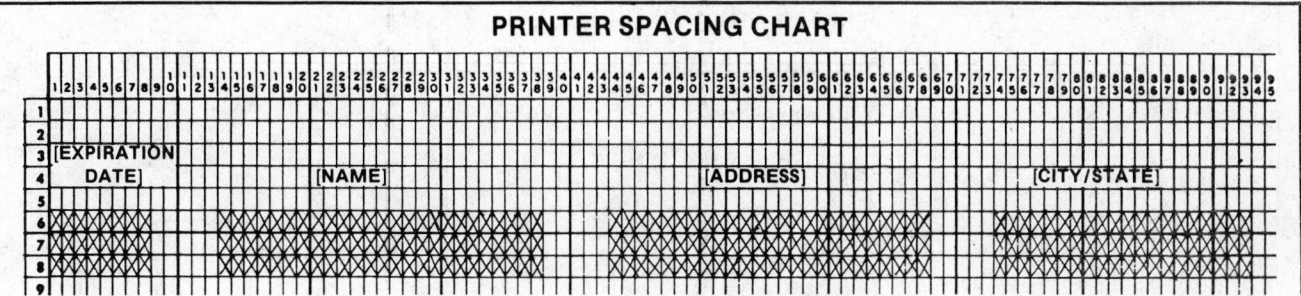

Figure 3-58 Program Output

INPUT

Figure 3-59 Program Input

IPO CHART

PROGRAM: Subscription List Report		PROGRAMMER: Shelly/Cashman		DATE: Dec.8

MODULE NAME: Create Subscription List Report	REF: A000	MODULE FUNCTION: Create Subscription List Report

INPUT	PROCESSING	REF:	OUTPUT
1. Subscription List Card File	1. Initialization		1. Subscription List Report
	2. Obtain the input data		
	3. Format the print line		
	4. Write the report		
	5. Termination		

Figure 3-60 IPO Chart

PSEUDOCODE SPECIFICATIONS

PROGRAM: Subscription List Report	PROGRAMMER: Shelly/Cashman	DATE: Dec 8

MODULE NAME: Create Subscription List Report	REF: A000	MODULE FUNCTION: Create Subscription List Report

PSEUDOCODE	REF:	FILES, RECORDS, FIELDS REQUIRED
Open the files		Subscription list card file
Read an input record		Subscription list report file
PERFORM UNTIL no more input records		Input area for input record
Clear the output area		Name
Move the expiration date, name, address,		Address
city/state to the output area		City/State
Write the line on the report		Expiration date
Read an input record		Indicator for no more records
ENDPERFORM		Printer output area
Close the files		Expiration date
Stop run		Name
		Address
		City/State

Figure 3-61 Logic Design Chart

SOURCE LISTING

```
  1                          IBM DOS AMERICAN NATIONAL STANDARD COBOL          CBF CL3-4              05/26/77

00001    001010 IDENTIFICATION DIVISION.                                            SUBLIST
00002    001020                                                                     SUBLIST
00003    001030 PROGRAM-ID.      SUBLIST.                                           SUBLIST
00004    001040 AUTHOR.          SHELLY AND CASHMAN.                                SUBLIST
00005    001050 INSTALLATION.    ANAHEIM.                                           SUBLIST
00006    001060 DATE-WRITTEN.    12/09/76.                                          SUBLIST
00007    001070 DATE-COMPILED.   05/26/77                                           SUBLIST
00008    001080 SECURITY.        UNCLASSIFIED.                                      SUBLIST
00009    001090                                                                     SUBLIST
00010    001100 *********************************************************            SUBLIST
00011    001110*                                                        *           SUBLIST
00012    001120*   THIS PROGRAM PRODUCES A LISTING OF PERSONS ON A MAGAZINE *       SUBLIST
00013    001130*   SUBSCRIPTION LIST.                                    *           SUBLIST
00014    001140*                                                        *           SUBLIST
00015    001150 *********************************************************            SUBLIST
00016    001160                                                                     SUBLIST
00017    001170                                                                     SUBLIST
00018    001180                                                                     SUBLIST
00019    001190 ENVIRONMENT DIVISION.                                               SUBLIST
00020    001200                                                                     SUBLIST
00021    002010 CONFIGURATION SECTION.                                              SUBLIST
00022    002020                                                                     SUBLIST
00023    002030 SOURCE-COMPUTER. IBM-370.                                           SUBLIST
00024    002040 OBJECT-COMPUTER. IBM-370.                                           SUBLIST
00025    002050                                                                     SUBLIST
00026    002060 INPUT-OUTPUT SECTION.                                               SUBLIST
00027    002070                                                                     SUBLIST
00028    002080 FILE-CONTROL.                                                       SUBLIST
00029    002090     SELECT SUBSCRIPTION-INPUT-FILE                                  SUBLIST
00030    002100          ASSIGN TO SYS007-UR-2540R-S.                               SUBLIST
00031    002110     SELECT SUBSCRIPTION-REPORT-FILE                                 SUBLIST
00032    002120          ASSIGN TO SYS013-UR-1403-S.                                SUBLIST
```

```
  2

00033    002140 DATA DIVISION.                                                      SUBLIST
00034    002150                                                                     SUBLIST
00035    002160 FILE SECTION.                                                       SUBLIST
00036    002170                                                                     SUBLIST
00037    002180 FD  SUBSCRIPTION-INPUT-FILE                                         SUBLIST
00038    002190     RECORD CONTAINS 80 CHARACTERS                                   SUBLIST
00039    002200     LABEL RECORDS ARE OMITTED                                       SUBLIST
00040    003010     DATA RECORD IS SUBSCRIPTION-INPUT-RECORD.                       SUBLIST
00041    003020 01  SUBSCRIPTION-INPUT-RECORD.                                      SUBLIST
00042    003030     05  NAME-INPUT            PICTURE X(25).                        SUBLIST
00043    003040     05  ADDRESS-INPUT         PICTURE X(25).                        SUBLIST
00044    003050     05  CITY-STATE-INPUT      PICTURE X(20).                        SUBLIST
00045    003060     05  EXPIRATION-DATE-INPUT PICTURE X(8).                         SUBLIST
00046    003070     05  FILLER                PICTURE XX.                           SUBLIST
00047    003080                                                                     SUBLIST
00048    003090 FD  SUBSCRIPTION-REPORT-FILE                                        SUBLIST
00049    003100     RECORD CONTAINS 133 CHARACTERS                                  SUBLIST
00050    003110     LABEL RECORDS ARE OMITTED                                       SUBLIST
00051    003120     DATA RECORD IS SUBSCRIPTION-REPORT-LINE.                        SUBLIST
00052    003130 01  SUBSCRIPTION-REPORT-LINE.                                       SUBLIST
00053    003140     05  CARRIAGE-CONTROL       PICTURE X.                           SUBLIST
00054    003150     05  EXPIRATION-DATE-REPORT PICTURE X(8).                        SUBLIST
00055    003160     05  FILLER                 PICTURE X(5).                        SUBLIST
00056    003170     05  NAME-REPORT            PICTURE X(25).                       SUBLIST
00057    003180     05  FILLER                 PICTURE X(5).                        SUBLIST
00058    003190     05  ADDRESS-REPORT         PICTURE X(25).                       SUBLIST
00059    003200     05  FILLER                 PICTURE X(5).                        SUBLIST
00060    004010     05  CITY-STATE-REPORT      PICTURE X(20).                       SUBLIST
00061    004020     05  FILLER                 PICTURE X(39).                       SUBLIST
00062    004030                                                                     SUBLIST
00063    004040 WORKING-STORAGE SECTION.                                            SUBLIST
00064    004050                                                                     SUBLIST
00065    004060 01  PROGRAM-INDICATORS.                                             SUBLIST
00066    004070     05  ARE-THERE-MORE-RECORDS PICTURE X(3) VALUE 'YES'.            SUBLIST
```

Figure 3-62 Source Listing [Part 1 of 2]

```
     3

00067  004090 PROCEDURE DIVISION.                                        SUBLIST
00068  004100                                                            SUBLIST
00069  004110*********************************************************** SUBLIST
00070  004120*                                                         * SUBLIST
00071  004130*   THIS PROGRAM READS THE SUBSCRIPTION INPUT RECORDS AND  * SUBLIST
00072  004140*   CREATES THE SUBSCRIPTION LISTING.  IT IS ENTERED FROM THE * SUBLIST
00073  004150*   OPERATING SYSTEM AND EXITS TO THE OPERATING SYSTEM.    * SUBLIST
00074  004160*                                                         * SUBLIST
00075  004170*********************************************************** SUBLIST
00076  004180                                                            SUBLIST
00077  004190 A000-CREATE-SUBSCRIPTION-LIST.                             SUBLIST
00078  004200                                                            SUBLIST
00079  005010     OPEN INPUT  SUBSCRIPTION-INPUT-FILE                    SUBLIST
00080  005020          OUTPUT SUBSCRIPTION-REPORT-FILE.                  SUBLIST
00081  005030     READ SUBSCRIPTION-INPUT-FILE                           SUBLIST
00082  005040          AT END                                           SUBLIST
00083  005050              MOVE 'NO ' TO ARE-THERE-MORE-RECORDS.        SUBLIST
00084  005060     PERFORM A001-FORMAT-PRINT-REPORT                       SUBLIST
00085  005070          UNTIL ARE-THERE-MORE-RECORDS = 'NO '.            SUBLIST
00086  005080     CLOSE SUBSCRIPTION-INPUT-FILE                          SUBLIST
00087  005090           SUBSCRIPTION-REPORT-FILE.                        SUBLIST
00088  005100     STOP RUN.                                              SUBLIST
00089  005110                                                            SUBLIST
00090  005120                                                            SUBLIST
00091  005130                                                            SUBLIST
00092  005140 A001-FORMAT-PRINT-REPORT.                                  SUBLIST
00093  005150                                                            SUBLIST
00094  005160     MOVE SPACES TO SUBSCRIPTION-REPORT-LINE.               SUBLIST
00095  005170     MOVE EXPIRATION-DATE-INPUT TO EXPIRATION-DATE-REPORT.  SUBLIST
00096  005180     MOVE NAME-INPUT TO NAME-REPORT.                        SUBLIST
00097  005190     MOVE ADDRESS-INPUT TO ADDRESS-REPORT.                  SUBLIST
00098  005200     MOVE CITY-STATE-INPUT TO CITY-STATE-REPORT.            SUBLIST
00099  006010     WRITE SUBSCRIPTION-REPORT-LINE                         SUBLIST
00100  006020           AFTER ADVANCING 1 LINES.                         SUBLIST
00101  006030     READ SUBSCRIPTION-INPUT-FILE                           SUBLIST
00102  006040          AT END                                           SUBLIST
00103  006050              MOVE 'NO ' TO ARE-THERE-MORE-RECORDS.        SUBLIST
```

Figure 3-63 Source Listing [Part 2 of 2]

PRINTED OUTPUT:

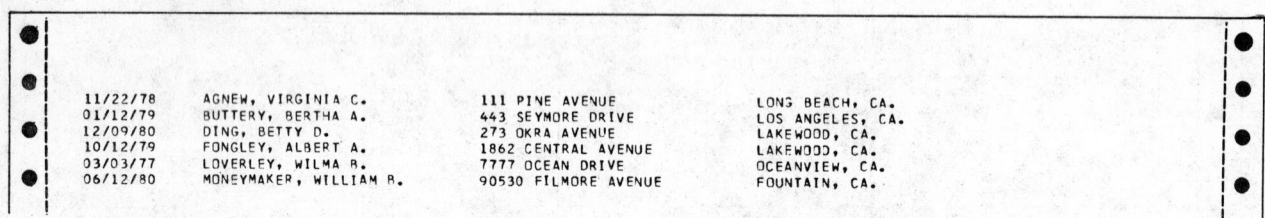

```
11/22/78   AGNEW, VIRGINIA C.      111 PINE AVENUE        LONG BEACH, CA.
01/12/79   BUTTERY, BERTHA A.      443 SEYMORE DRIVE      LOS ANGELES, CA.
12/09/80   DING, BETTY D.          273 OKRA AVENUE        LAKEWOOD, CA.
10/12/79   FONGLEY, ALBERT A.      1862 CENTRAL AVENUE    LAKEWOOD, CA.
03/03/77   LOVERLEY, WILMA R.      7777 OCEAN DRIVE       OCEANVIEW, CA.
06/12/80   MONEYMAKER, WILLIAM R.  90530 FILMORE AVENUE   FOUNTAIN, CA.
```

Figure 3-64 Printed Report

CHAPTER 3

REVIEW QUESTIONS

1. What information should be recorded in the area called Punching Instructions on the COBOL Coding Form?

    Instruction to Key punch operator

2. What is the purpose of the Identification Division?

3. List the Paragraph Headers that make up the Identification Division. What is the only Paragraph Header required in the Identification Division?

    p 3.10

4. What occurs when an asterisk (*) is recorded in column 7 of the COBOL Coding Form?

5. What do square brackets indicate in COBOL format notation?

    may be omitted
    Depending on system

6. What do underlined words in capital letters signify in COBOL format notation?

    required

7. What do lower-case words represent in COBOL format notation?

    programmer's words

8. What is contained in the Configuration Section of a COBOL program?

    Source-comp
    Object-comp

9. What is specified in the File-Control paragraph of the Input-Output Section?

10. What are the rules for the construction of a file-name?

11. What is the purpose of the Data Division? What are two of the sections within the Data Division?

File working storage

12. How are the fields in an input record defined within the Data Division?

13. What is the purpose of Level Numbers in the Data Division? Why is Level Number 05 used to identify the fields in a record?

14. When a field is defined with a Picture X, what characters may be contained within that field?

15. Why is the entry RECORD CONTAINS 133 CHARACTERS used when describing the printed report when the maximum number of print positions is 132?

for carriage control

16. What is the purpose of the Procedure Division?

17. What are the rules for the construction of a paragraph name used within the Procedure Division?

18. Explain the operation of the statement PERFORM A001-FORMAT-PRINT-REPORT UNTIL ARE-THERE-MORE-RECORDS = 'NO '.

CHAPTER 3

DEBUGGING COBOL PROGRAMS

PROBLEM 1

INSTRUCTIONS

The following COBOL program contains an error or errors which have occurred during compilation. Circle each error and record the corrected entries directly on the listing. Explain the error and the method of correction in the space provided on the following page.

```
    1                          IBM DOS AMERICAN NATIONAL STANDARD COBOL        CBF CL3-4        05/20/77

    00001    001010 IDENTIFICATION DIVISION.                                    SUBLIST
    00002    001020                                                             SUBLIST
    00003    001030 PROGRAM-ID.    SUBLIST.                                     SUBLIST
    00004    001040 AUTHOR.        SHELLY AND CASHMAN.                          SUBLIST
    00005    001050 INSTALLATION.  ANAHEIM.                                     SUBLIST
    00006    001060 DATE-WRITTEN.  05/20/77.                                    SUBLIST
    00007    001070 DATE-COMPILED. 05/20/77                                     SUBLIST
    00008    001080 SECURITY.      UNCLASSIFIED.                                SUBLIST
    00009    001090                                                            SUBLIST
    00010    001100***********************************************************  SUBLIST
    00011    001110*                                                         *  SUBLIST
    00012    001120*  THIS PROGRAM PRODUCES A LISTING OF PERSONS ON A MAGAZINE *  SUBLIST
    00013    001130*  SUBSCRIPTION LIST.                                      *  SUBLIST
    00014    001140*                                                         *  SUBLIST
    00015    001150***********************************************************  SUBLIST
    00016    001160                                                            SUBLIST
    00017    001170                                                            SUBLIST
    00018    001180                                                            SUBLIST
    00019    001190 ENVIRONMENT DIVISION.                                      SUBLIST
    00020    001200                                                            SUBLIST
    00021    002010 CONFIGURATION SECTION.                                     SUBLIST
    00022    002020                                                            SUBLIST
    00023    002030 SOURCE-COMPUTER. IBM-370.                                  SUBLIST
    00024    002040 OBJECT-COMPUTER. IBM-370.                                  SUBLIST
    00025    002050                                                            SUBLIST
    00026    002060 INPUT-OUTPUT SECTION.                                      SUBLIST
    00027    002070                                                            SUBLIST
    00028    002080 FILE-CONTROL.                                              SUBLIST
    00029    002090     SELECT SUBSCRIPTION-INPUT-FILE                         SUBLIST
    00030    002100         ASSIGN TO SYS007-UR-2540R-S.                       SUBLIST
    00031    002110     SELECT SUBSCRIPTION-REPORT-FILE                        SUBLIST
    00032    002120         ASSIGN TO SYS013-UR-1403-S.                        SUBLIST


    2

    00033    002140 DATA DIVISION.                                             SUBLIST
    00034    002150                                                            SUBLIST
    00035    002160 FILE SECTION.                                              SUBLIST
    00036    002170                                                            SUBLIST
    00037    002180 FD  SUBSCRIPTION-INPUT-FILE                                SUBLIST
    00038    002190     RECORD CONTAINS 80 CHARACTERS                          SUBLIST
    00039    002200     LABEL RECORDS ARE OMITTED                              SUBLIST
    00040    003010     DATA RECORD IS SUBSCRIPTION-INPUT-RECORD               SUBLIST
    00041    003020 01  SUBSCRIPTION-INPUT-RECORD.                             SUBLIST
    00042    003030     05  NAME-INPUT            PICTURE X(25).               SUBLIST
    00043    003040     05  ADDRESS-INPUT         PICTURE X(25).               SUBLIST
    00044    003050     05  CITY-STATE-INPUT      PICTURE X(20).               SUBLIST
    00045    003060     05  EXPIRATION-DATE-INPUT PICTURE X(8).                SUBLIST
    00046    003070     05  FILLER                PICTURE XX.                  SUBLIST
    00047    003080                                                            SUBLIST
    00048    003090 FD  SUBSCRIPTION-REPORT-FILE                               SUBLIST
    00049    003100     RECORD CONTAINS 133 CHARACTERS                         SUBLIST
    00050    003110     LABEL RECORDS ARE OMITTED                              SUBLIST
    00051    003120     DATA RECORD IS SUBSCRIPTION-REPORT-LINE.               SUBLIST
    00052    003130 01  SUBSCRIPTION-REPORT-LINE.                              SUBLIST
    00053    003140     05  CARRIAGE-CONTROL        PICTURE X.                 SUBLIST
    00054    003150     05  EXPIRATION-DATE-REPORT  PICTURE X(8).              SUBLIST
    00055    003160     05  FILLER                  PICTURE X(5).              SUBLIST
    00056    003170     05  NAME-REPORT             PICTURE X(25).             SUBLIST
    00057    003180     05  FILLER                  PICTURE X(5).              SUBLIST
    00058    003190     05  ADDRESS-REPORT          PICTURE X(25).             SUBLIST
    00059    003200     05  FILLER                  PICTURE X(5).              SUBLIST
    00060    004010     05  CITY-STATE-REPORT       PICTURE X(20).             SUBLIST
    00061    004020     05  FILLER                  PICTURE X(39).             SUBLIST
    00062    004030                                                            SUBLIST
    00063    004040 WORKING-STORAGE SECTION.                                   SUBLIST
    00064    004050                                                            SUBLIST
    00065    004060 01  PROGRAM-INDICATORS.                                    SUBLIST
    00066    004070     05  ARE-THERE-MORE-RECORDS  PICTURE X(3) VALUE 'YES'.  SUBLIST
```

```
      3

00067 004090 PROCEDURE DIVISION.                                          SUBLIST
00068 004100                                                              SUBLIST
00069 004110********************************************************       SUBLIST
00070 004120*                                                       *     SUBLIST
00071 004130*  THIS PROGRAM READS THE SUBSCRIPTION INPUT RECORDS AND      SUBLIST
00072 004140*  CREATES THE SUBSCRIPTION LISTING.  IT IS ENTERED FROM THE  *  SUBLIST
00073 004150*  OPERATING SYSTEM AND EXITS TO THE OPERATING SYSTEM.     *  SUBLIST
00074 004160*                                                       *     SUBLIST
00075 004170********************************************************       SUBLIST
00076 004180                                                              SUBLIST
00077 004190 A000-CREATE-SUBSCRIPTION-LIST.                               SUBLIST
00078 004200                                                              SUBLIST
00079 005010     OPEN INPUT SUBSCRIPTION-INPUT-FILE                       SUBLIST
00080 005020          OUTPUT SUBSCRIPTION-REPORT-FILE.                    SUBLIST
00081 005030     READ SUBSCRIPTION-INPUT-FILE                             SUBLIST
00082 005040          AT END                                             SUBLIST
00083 005050            MOVE 'NO ' TO ARE-THERE-MORE-RECORDS.             SUBLIST
00084 005060     PERFORM 0001-FORMAT-PRINT-REPORT                         SUBLIST
00085 005070          UNTIL ARE-THERE-MORE-RECORDS = 'NO '.               SUBLIST
00086 005080     CLOSE SUBSCRIPTION-INPUT-FILE                            SUBLIST
00087 005090           SUBSCRIPTION-REPORT-FILE.                          SUBLIST
00088 005100 STOP RUN.                                                    SUBLIST
00089 005110                                                              SUBLIST
00090 005120                                                              SUBLIST
00091 005130                                                              SUBLIST
00092 005140 A001-FORMAT-PRINT-REPORT.                                    SUBLIST
00093 005150                                                              SUBLIST
00094 005170     MOVE EXPIRATION-DATE-INPUT TO EXPIRATION-DATE-REPORT.    SUBLIST
00095 005180     MOVE NAME-INPUT TO NAME-REPORT.                          SUBLIST
00096 005190     MOVE ADDRESS-INPUT TO ADDRESS-REPORT                     SUBLIST
00097 005200     MOVE CITY-STATE-INPUT TO CITY-STATE-REPORT.              SUBLIST
00098 006010     WRITE SUBSCRIPTION-REPORT-LINE                           SUBLIST
00099 006020           AFTER ADVANCING 1 LINES.                           SUBLIST
00100 006030     READ SUBSCRIPTION-INPUT-FILE                             SUBLIST
00101 006040          AT END                                             SUBLIST
00102 006050            MOVE 'NO ' TO ARE-THERE-MORE-RECORDS.             SUBLIST
```

```
      5

CARD   ERROR MESSAGE

41     ILA1043I-W    END OF SENTENCE SHOULD PRECEDE 01 . ASSUMED PRESENT.
84     ILA3001I-E    0001-FORMAT-PRINT-REPORT NOT DEFINED. STATEMENT DISCARDED.
88     ILA1087I-W    ' STOP ' SHOULD NOT BEGIN IN AREA A.
95     ILA3001I-E    NAME NOT DEFINED. DISCARDED.
96     ILA3001I-E    ADDRES-REPORT NOT DEFINED. DISCARDED.
102    ILA4001I-C    OUTCOME OF A PRECEDING CONDITION LEADS TO NON-EXISTENT 'NEXT SENTENCE'. 'GOBACK'
                     INSERTED.

ILA0004I- LINK OPTION RESET -- D OR E LEVEL ERROR FOUND
```

EXPLANANTION

_____

_____

_____

_____

_____

_____

CHAPTER 3

DEBUGGING COBOL PROGRAMS

PROBLEM 2

INSTRUCTIONS

The following COBOL program contains an error or errors which occurred during execution. Circle each error and record the corrected entries directly on the listing. Explain the error and method of correction in the space provided below.

```
     1                          IBM DOS AMERICAN NATIONAL STANDARD COBOL        CBF CL3-4        05/20/77

00001   001010 IDENTIFICATION DIVISION.                                    SUBLIST
00002   001020                                                             SUBLIST
00003   001030 PROGRAM-ID.    SUBLIST.                                     SUBLIST
00004   001040 AUTHOR.        SHELLY AND CASHMAN.                          SUBLIST
00005   001050 INSTALLATION.  ANAHEIM.                                     SUBLIST
00006   001060 DATE-WRITTEN.  05/20/77.                                    SUBLIST
00007   001070 DATE-COMPILED. 05/20/77                                     SUBLIST
00008   001080 SECURITY.      UNCLASSIFIED.                                SUBLIST
00009   001090                                                             SUBLIST
00010   001100******************************************************************  SUBLIST
00011   001110*                                                          *  SUBLIST
00012   001120*  THIS PROGRAM PRODUCES A LISTING OF PERSONS ON A MAGAZINE *  SUBLIST
00013   001130*  SUBSCRIPTION LIST.                                      *  SUBLIST
00014   001140*                                                          *  SUBLIST
00015   001150******************************************************************  SUBLIST
00016   001160                                                             SUBLIST
00017   001170                                                             SUBLIST
00018   001180                                                             SUBLIST
00019   001190 ENVIRONMENT DIVISION.                                       SUBLIST
00020   001200                                                             SUBLIST
00021   002010 CONFIGURATION SECTION.                                      SUBLIST
00022   002020                                                             SUBLIST
00023   002030 SOURCE-COMPUTER. IBM-370.                                   SUBLIST
00024   002040 OBJECT-COMPUTER. IBM-370.                                   SUBLIST
00025   002050                                                             SUBLIST
00026   002060 INPUT-OUTPUT SECTION.                                       SUBLIST
00027   002070                                                             SUBLIST
00028   002080 FILE-CONTROL.                                               SUBLIST
00029   002090     SELECT SUBSCRIPTION-INPUT-FILE                          SUBLIST
00030   002100         ASSIGN TO SYS007-UR-2540R-S.                        SUBLIST
00031   002110     SELECT SUBSCRIPTION-REPORT-FILE                         SUBLIST
00032   002120         ASSIGN TO SYS013-UR-1403-S.                         SUBLIST
```

```
     2

00033   002140 DATA DIVISION.                                              SUBLIST
00034   002150                                                             SUBLIST
00035   002160 FILE SECTION.                                               SUBLIST
00036   002170                                                             SUBLIST
00037   002180 FD  SUBSCRIPTION-INPUT-FILE                                 SUBLIST
00038   002190     RECORD CONTAINS 80 CHARACTERS                           SUBLIST
00039   002200     LABEL RECORDS ARE OMITTED                               SUBLIST
00040   003010     DATA RECORD IS SUBSCRIPTION-INPUT-RECORD.               SUBLIST
00041   003020 01  SUBSCRIPTION-INPUT-RECORD.                              SUBLIST
00042   003030     05  NAME-INPUT              PICTURE X(25).              SUBLIST
00043   003040     05  ADDRESS-INPUT           PICTURE X(25).              SUBLIST
00044   003050     05  CITY-STATE-INPUT        PICTURE X(20).              SUBLIST
00045   003060     05  EXPIRATION-DATE-INPUT   PICTURE X(8).               SUBLIST
00046   003070     05  FILLER                  PICTURE XX.                 SUBLIST
00047   003080                                                             SUBLIST
00048   003090 FD  SUBSCRIPTION-REPORT-FILE                                SUBLIST
00049   003100     RECORD CONTAINS 133 CHARACTERS                          SUBLIST
00050   003110     LABEL RECORDS ARE OMITTED                               SUBLIST
00051   003120     DATA RECORD IS SUBSCRIPTION-REPORT-LINE.                SUBLIST
00052   003130 01  SUBSCRIPTION-REPORT-LINE.                               SUBLIST
00053   003150     05  EXPIRATION-DATE-REPORT  PICTURE X(8).               SUBLIST
00054   003160     05  FILLER                  PICTURE X(5).               SUBLIST
00055   003170     05  NAME-REPORT             PICTURE X(25).              SUBLIST
00056   003180     05  FILLER                  PICTURE X(5).               SUBLIST
00057   003190     05  ADDRESS-REPORT          PICTURE X(25).              SUBLIST
00058   003200     05  FILLER                  PICTURE X(5).               SUBLIST
00059   004010     05  CITY-STATE-REPORT       PICTURE X(20).              SUBLIST
00060   004020     05  FILLER                  PICTURE X(39).              SUBLIST
00061   004030                                                             SUBLIST
00062   004040 WORKING-STORAGE SECTION.                                    SUBLIST
00063   004050                                                             SUBLIST
00064   004060 01  PROGRAM-INDICATORS.                                     SUBLIST
00065   004070     05  ARE-THERE-MORE-RECORDS  PICTURE X(3) VALUE 'YES'.   SUBLIST
```

```
  3

00066   004090  PROCEDURE DIVISION.                                              SUBLIST
00067   004100                                                                   SUBLIST
00068   004110*********************************************************          SUBLIST
00069   004120*                                                         *        SUBLIST
00070   004130*    THIS PROGRAM READS THE SUBSCRIPTION INPUT RECORDS AND *        SUBLIST
00071   004140*    CREATES THE SUBSCRIPTION LISTING.  IT IS ENTERED FROM THE *    SUBLIST
00072   004150*    OPERATING SYSTEM AND EXITS TO THE OPERATING SYSTEM.    *        SUBLIST
00073   004160*                                                         *        SUBLIST
00074   004170*********************************************************          SUBLIST
00075   004180                                                                   SUBLIST
00076   004190  A000-CREATE-SUBSCRIPTION-LIST.                                   SUBLIST
00077   004200                                                                   SUBLIST
00078   005010      OPEN INPUT  SUBSCRIPTION-INPUT-FILE                          SUBLIST
00079   005020           OUTPUT SUBSCRIPTION-REPORT-FILE.                        SUBLIST
00080   005030      READ SUBSCRIPTION-INPUT-FILE                                 SUBLIST
00081   005040          AT END                                                   SUBLIST
00082   005050              MOVE 'NO ' TO ARE-THERE-MORE-RECORDS.                SUBLIST
00083   005060      PERFORM A001-FORMAT-PRINT-REPORT                             SUBLIST
00084   005070          UNTIL ARE-THERE-MORE-RECORDS = 'NO '.                   SUBLIST
00085   005080      CLOSE SUBSCRIPTION-INPUT-FILE                                SUBLIST
00086   005090            SUBSCRIPTION-REPORT-FILE.                              SUBLIST
00087   005100      STOP RUN.                                                    SUBLIST
00088   005110                                                                   SUBLIST
00089   005120                                                                   SUBLIST
00090   005130                                                                   SUBLIST
00091   005140  A001-FORMAT-PRINT-REPORT.                                        SUBLIST
00092   005150      move space  to Subscription-Report-Line.                    SUBLIST
00093   005170      MOVE EXPIRATION-DATE-INPUT TO EXPIRATION-DATE-REPORT.        SUBLIST
00094   005180      MOVE NAME-INPUT TO NAME-REPORT.                             SUBLIST
00095   005190      MOVE ADDRESS-INPUT TO ADDRESS-REPORT.                       SUBLIST
00096   005200      MOVE CITY-STATE-INPUT TO CITY-STATE-REPORT.                 SUBLIST
00097   006010      WRITE SUBSCRIPTION-REPORT-LINE                              SUBLIST
00098   006020          AFTER ADVANCING 1 LINES.                               SUBLIST
00099   006030      READ SUBSCRIPTION-INPUT-FILE                                SUBLIST
00100   006040          AT END                                                  SUBLIST
00101   006050              MOVE 'NO ' TO ARE-THERE-MORE-RECORDS.               SUBLIST
```

```
1/22/78GB&  QAGNEW, VIRGINIA C.        O G03111 PINE AVENUE        GO: GLONG BEACH, CA.     0#:GO&4GO&&  Q&'8Q&'MQ&'HQ
1/12/79@WK"=BUTTERY, BERTHA A.         &-8 K443 SEYMORE DRIVE      E-O&QLOS ANGELES, CA.    001N|-CGOO:&_O@E? @/%K"O1&
2/09/80GB&  QDING, BETTY D.            O G03273 OKRA AVENUE        GO: GLAKEWOOD, CA.       0#:GO&4GO&&  Q&'8Q&'MQ&'HQ
O/12/79@WK"=FONGLEY, ALBERT A.         &-8 K1862 CENTRAL AVENUE    E-O&QLAKEWOOD, CA.       001N|-CGOO:&_O@E? @/%K"O1&
3/03/77GB&  QLOVERLEY, WILMA B.        O G037777 OCEAN DRIVE       GO: GOCEANVIEW, CA.      0#:GO&4GO&&  Q&'8Q&'MQ&'HQ
6/12/80@WK"=MONEYMAKER, WILLIAM B.     &-8 K90530 FILMORE AVENUE   E-O&QFOUNTAIN, CA.       001N|-CGOO:&_O@E? @/%K"O1&
```

EXPLANATION

CHAPTER 3

PROGRAMMING ASSIGNMENT 1

INSTRUCTIONS

A Payroll Register is to be prepared. Write the COBOL program to prepare this listing. The IPO Chart and Pseudocode Specifications prepared in Chapter 2 should be used when coding the program. Use Test Data Set 1, contained in Appendix A.

INPUT

Input is to consist of Payroll Cards that contain the Employee Number, the Employee Name, the Department, and the Hours Worked. The format of the Payroll Cards is illustrated below.

OUTPUT

Output is to consist of a Payroll Register listing the Employee Number, the Department Number, the Employee Name, and the Hours Worked. The printer spacing chart for the report is illustrated below.

CHAPTER 3

PROGRAMMING ASSIGNMENT 2 ✓

INSTRUCTIONS

An Inventory Report is to be prepared. Write the COBOL program to prepare the listing. Use the IPO Chart and the Pseudocode Specifications prepared in Chapter 2 when coding the program. Use Test Data Set 1, in Appendix A.

INPUT

Input is to consist of Inventory Cards that contain the Item Number, the Item Description, the Quantity on Hand, the Quantity Sold, and the Store Number. The format of the Inventory Cards is illustrated below.

OUTPUT

The output is a listing of the fields contained in the Inventory Cards and is to contain the Store Number, the Item Number, the Item Description, the Quantity on Hand, and the Quantity Sold. The printer spacing chart is illustrated below. Note that the report is to be double spaced.

CHAPTER 3

PROGRAMMING ASSIGNMENT 3

INSTRUCTIONS

Two listings of a company's customers are to be prepared. Since two listings are required, it has been decided to print each of the fields on the card twice on the same line. Write the COBOL program to prepare the listing. The IPO Chart and the Pseudocode Specifications prepared in Chapter 2 should be used when coding the program. Use Test Data Set 2, in Appendix A.

INPUT

The input is to consist of Customer Name Cards that contain the Customer Number and the Customer Name. The format of the cards is illustrated below.

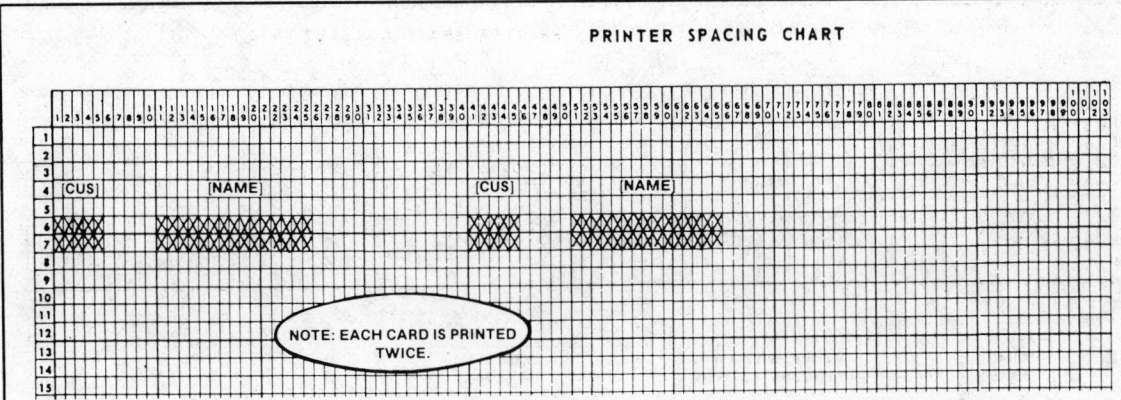

OUTPUT

The output is to consist of two listings of the cards. A printer spacing chart of the report that is to be prepared is illustrated below.

CHAPTER 3

PROGRAMMING ASSIGNMENT 4

INSTRUCTIONS

An Employee Roster is to be prepared listing new employees. Write the COBOL program to prepare the listing. The IPO Chart and the Pseudocode Specifications prepared in Chapter 2 should be used when coding the program. Use Test Data Set 1, in Appendix A.

INPUT

The input to the program is the New Employee Card File. The records in the file contain the Department Number, the Employee Name (Last Name first), and the Social Security Number. The format of the records is illustrated below.

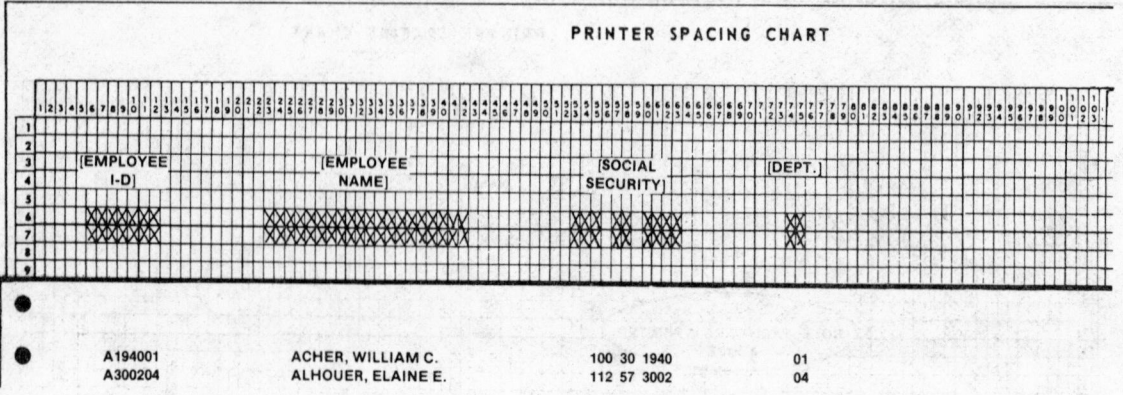

OUTPUT

The output from the program is the Employee Roster, containing the Employee Identification, the Employee Name, the Social Security Number, and the Department. The Employee Identification is generated as follows: The first character is the first letter of the last name of the employee. This is followed by the last four digits of the Social Security Number and the Department Number. Thus, the Identification for employee Acher whose Social Security Number is 100-30-1940 and who works in Department 01 would be A194001. The printer spacing chart for the report is illustrated below.

ADDITION, SUBTRACTION, REPORT EDITING

4

> *One can, in fact, observe a rough law that the less time spent coding, the more successful a programming project will be. 1*

INTRODUCTION

The arithmetic operations of Addition and Subtraction are basic to many business applications. In addition, the editing of numeric data on a printed report is done in virtually all business reports. Editing refers to the process of printing numeric fields with special characters such as the dollar sign, comma, and decimal point; and zero suppression, that is, suppressing the printing of leading non-significant zeros. The sample program developed in this chapter illustrates a basic crossfooting operation in which two fields are added together to give a total. Also, the numeric fields which are printed on the report are edited.

THE PROBLEM

In the sample problem, an Accounting Report is to be created. The format of the report is illustrated below.

OUTPUT

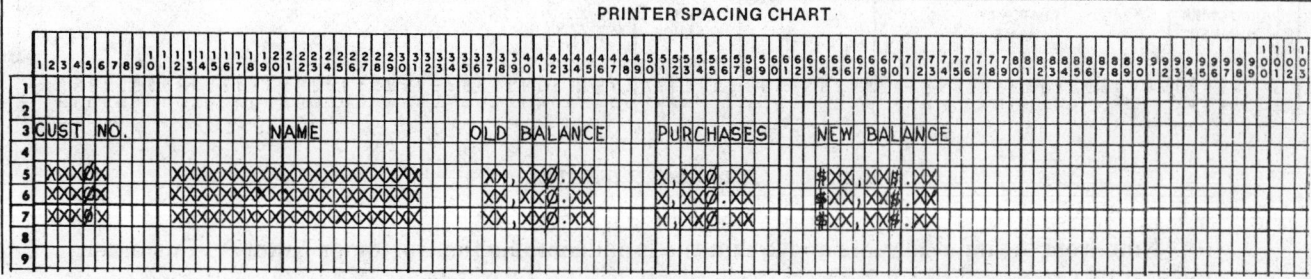

Figure 4-1 Printer Spacing Chart of Output

As can be seen from Figure 4-1, the report contains the Customer Number, the Customer Name, the Old Balance, the Purchases, and the New Balance. The New Balance is obtained by adding the Old Balance and the Purchases. Also, headings are to be printed on the report to identify the values contained in each of the columns on the report.

---

1 Brown, P. J., "Programming and Documenting Software Projects," ACM COMPUTING SURVEYS, Vol. 6, No. 4, December 1974.

It will be noted also that punctuation, such as commas, periods, and dollar signs are included on the report. This is accomplished through the use of report editing, as will be illustrated in this chapter. It can also be seen that the Customer Number, Old Balance, and Purchases have zeros (Ø) within their specification on the printer spacing chart. This is the method used to indicate the zero suppression is to take place. The technique used is illustrated in this chapter.

The input consists of a Customer Account Card File with records containing the Customer Number, Customer Name, Old Balance, and Purchases. The format of the input card is illustrated below.

INPUT

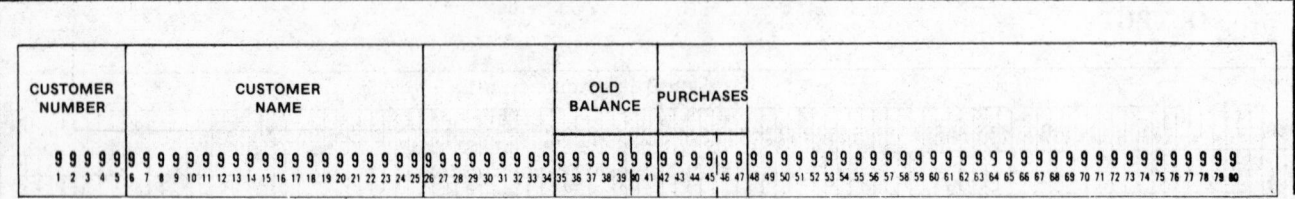

MULTIPLE-CARD LAYOUT FORM

Figure 4-2 INPUT

Note from the input formats above that the input contains the Customer Number, Customer Name, Old Balance, and Purchases. The Old Balance and Purchases fields are dollar amount fields. The dotted lines are used to indicate where the implied decimal points appear in these fields. The decimal point is not actually in the input record but is to be treated within the program as appearing where the dotted lines appear.

PROCESSING

The Programming Specifications for the sample problem are illustrated below.

PROGRAMMING SPECIFICATIONS			
SUBJECT Accounting Report	**DATE** April 11		**PAGE** 1 **OF** 1
TO Programmer	**FROM** Systems Analyst		

A program is to be written to prepare an Accounting Report. The formats for the input card file and the printer spacing chart are included as a part of this narrative. The program should include the following processing:

1. The program should read the input cards and create the Accounting Report as per the format illustrated on the printer spacing chart. The report shall contain the Customer Number, the Customer Name, the Old Balance, the Purchases, and the New Balance.

2. Headings should be printed on the first page to indicate the values contained in the columns on the report.

3. One line is to be printed on the report for each card which is read. The lines are to be single-spaced.

4. The New Balance is calculated by adding the Old Balance and the Purchases.

5. Editing of the data on the report is to occur as illustrated on the printer spacing chart.

6. The program should be written in COBOL.

Figure 4-3 Programming Specifications

As can be seen from Figure 4-3, the requirements for the program processing are specified on the Programming Specifications.

PHASE 1: Review System and Programming Specifications

After these programming specifications are received from the systems analyst, the programmer must review them to ensure that there are no questions concerning the processing which is to take place within the program. Once the programmer is satisfied that the processing is understood, then the second phase of the programming development cycle, the program design, can begin.

PHASE 2: Design the Program

The first step in the program design is to prepare the IPO Chart. The output from the program is the Accounting Report. This should be entered on the IPO Chart as follows:

IPO CHART

PROGRAM: Accounting Report	PROGRAMMER: Shelly/Cashman	DATE: April 11
MODULE NAME: Create Account Report	REF: A000	MODULE FUNCTION: Create Accounting Report

INPUT	PROCESSING	REF:	OUTPUT
			1. Accounting Report

Figure 4-4 Output Entry on IPO Chart

Note from Figure 4-4 that the output to be produced from the program consists of the Accounting Report and this output is entered in the Output portion of the IPO Chart.

The input to the program is the Customer Account Card File. The programmer should enter this on the IPO Chart as follows.

IPO CHART

PROGRAM: Accounting Report	PROGRAMMER: Shelly/Cashman	DATE: April 11
MODULE NAME: Create Account Report	REF: A000	MODULE FUNCTION: Create Accounting Report

INPUT	PROCESSING	REF:	OUTPUT
1. Customer Account Card File			1. Accounting Report

Figure 4-5 Input Specification on IPO Chart

As can be seen from Figure 4-5, the input to the program and the output from the program are specified on the IPO Chart. The programmer must then determine the major processing tasks which are necessary to transform the input to the output.

As was noted previously, the major processing tasks should be listed on the IPO Chart. The major processing tasks for the sample program are illustrated in Figure 4-6.

IPO CHART

PROGRAM: Accounting Report		PROGRAMMER: Shelly/Cashman		DATE: April 11
MODULE NAME: Create Account Report		REF: A000	MODULE FUNCTION: Create Accounting Report	

INPUT	PROCESSING	REF:	OUTPUT
1. Customer Account	1. Initialization		1. Accounting Report
Card File	2. Obtain input data		
	3. Perform calculations		
	4. Format print line		
	5. Write the report		
	6. Termination		

Figure 4-6 IPO Chart with Major Processing Tasks

As with most programs, the sample program requires initialization processing. The input records must also be obtained for processing. As noted previously, there are calculations which must be performed within this program. Therefore, one of the processing steps which must be accomplished is "Perform calculations." It can be seen that the details concerning the calculations are not specified on the IPO Chart. These details are left until the development of the pseudocode.

The print line must be formatted and the report written also, so these processing steps are specified on the IPO Chart. The final step is the termination processing which must be accomplished. It should be noted that these major processing steps are not necessarily specified in the same sequence in which they will take place within the program. This is because the major processing tasks on the IPO Chart are used to specify WHAT is to take place within the program, not HOW and WHEN.

After the major processing tasks have been specified, the programmer would review each step to determine if they are of such a size so as to cause the module to be more than 50 statements, or to be so complex as to require a further decomposition of the module. In the sample program, none of the major processing tasks is large enough or complex enough to require further decomposition; so the IPO Chart for the program is complete.

After the IPO Chart is completed, the programmer would normally review the entries with the systems analyst and perhaps the user of the system to ensure that a viable solution has been developed for the problem.

PSEUDOCODE

After the processing on the IPO Chart has been approved, the programmer will design the logic to implement the processing required for the program. As noted previously, the tool used is pseudocode. The pseudocode for the sample program is illustrated in Figure 4-7.

PSEUDOCODE SPECIFICATIONS

PROGRAM: Accounting Report	PROGRAMMER: Shelly/Cashman	DATE: April 13
MODULE NAME: Create Account Report	REF: A000 MODULE FUNCTION:	Create Accounting Report

PSEUDOCODE	REF:	FILES, RECORDS, FIELDS REQUIRED

Open the files
Write the heading line
Set space control for double spacing
Read an input record
PERFORM UNTIL no more data
    Clear the printer line
    Move the customer number, customer name,
      old balance and purchases to output area
    Calculate new balance = old balance + purchases
      and place in the output area
    Write a line on the report
    Set space control for single spacing
    Read an input record
ENDPERFORM
Close the files
Stop run		

Figure 4-7 Pseudocode for Sample Program

Note from the example above that the pseudocode developed for this application follows the same general pattern as that for the application in Chapter 2 and Chapter 3. First, the files are opened in order to ready them for processing.

After the files are opened, the heading on the report is printed because the heading must be printed prior to printing any of the detail lines. After the heading is printed, the spacing for the report must be set to double spacing, since there will be double spacing following the heading line (see Figure 4-1). The technique to accomplish this will be illustrated later in this chapter.

After the heading has been printed and the spacing set, the first input record is read. The routine to format and print the report is then performed until there is no more input data, at which time the files will be closed and the program terminated.

Within the routine which formats and prints the report, the printer output area is cleared with blanks and then the data from the input record (Customer Number, Customer Name, Old Balance, and Purchases) is moved from the input area to the printer output area. The New Balance is then calculated by adding the Old Balance to the Purchases, and this New Balance is placed in the output area.

After the report line is formatted, it is written and the spacing is set for single spacing so that the remainder of the report will be single spaced, as specified on the printer spacing chart (see Figure 4-1). The next record to be processed is then read.

After the pseudocode is completed, a structured walkthrough would normally be conducted in order to ensure that the logic expressed in the pseudocode is correct and will accomplish the desired processing.

DEFINITION OF FILES, RECORDS, AND FIELDS

As in the program in Chapter 3, the files, records, and fields required for the program will be specified from the pseudocode developed to solve the problem. The entries on the Pseudocode Specifications for the program in this chapter are illustrated in Figure 4-8.

PSEUDOCODE SPECIFICATIONS

PROGRAM: Accounting Report	PROGRAMMER: Shelly/Cashman	DATE: April 13
MODULE NAME: Create Account Report	REF: A000 MODULE FUNCTION:	Create Accounting Report

PSEUDOCODE	REF:	FILES, RECORDS, FIELDS REQUIRED

Open the files
Write the heading line
Set space control for double spacing
Read an input record
PERFORM UNTIL no more data
   Clear the printer line
   Move the customer number, customer name,
     old balance and purchases to output area
   Calculate new balance = old balance + purchases
     and place in the output area
   Write a line on the report
   Set space control for single spacing
   Read an input record
ENDPERFORM
Close the files
Stop run
		Customer account card file
		Accounting report file
		Heading line
		Printer spacing field
		Double space control character
		Input record area
		  Customer number
		  Customer name
		  Old balance
		  Purchases
		End-of-data indicator
		Printer output line
		  Customer number
		  Customer name
		  Old balance
		  Purchases
		  New balance
		  Single space control character

Figure 4-8 Files, Records, and Fields Required for Program

As in Chapter 2 and Chapter 3, the files, records, and fields required for the program are determined from the processing which is to take place as specified in the pseudocode for the program. The Customer Account Card File is the input file for the program and the Accounting Report File is the printed report file. Since headings are to be printed on the report, a heading line containing the values to be printed in the heading must be defined.

As was noted previously, the report is to be double spaced after the heading is printed, but the remainder of the report is to be single spaced. Therefore, there must be a field which is to contain the control character which will designate whether single or double spacing is to occur. In addition, the control character to cause the double spacing must also be defined within the program.

In order to read the input record, an input area must be defined. Within the input area are fields for the Customer Number, Customer Name, Old Balance, and Purchases. As in the previous program, there must be an end-of-data indicator which is used to indicate that all of the data in the input file has been read. In order to clear the printer line, the printer output area must be defined. Within the printer output area are the fields for the Customer Number, Customer Name, Old Balance, Purchases, and New Balance. Since the report is to be single spaced, the control character to cause single spacing must be defined.

Once the pseudocode and the files, records, and fields for the program have been defined, the programmer may begin coding the program. Much of the coding required for the sample program will be similar to that used in the previous program and will not be discussed in detail in this chapter. The following paragraphs discuss the new elements of the COBOL language required for this sample program.

DEFINITION OF NUMERIC DATA

In Chapter 3, the data which was defined for the input card was specified as alphanumeric data, that is, the Picture X clause was used. When data is to be used in arithmetic operations, such as addition or subtraction, or is to be edited on a report, the data must be defined as Numeric Data. In order to define data as numeric, the Picture 9 clause must be used, where the "9" indicates that the data to be stored in the field will be numeric.

In addition, when fields represent amounts expressed in terms of dollars and cents, the Compiler must be informed of the effective location of the decimal points in order to perform the arithmetic and editing operations properly. In most applications, the decimal points are not actually punched on a card. Therefore, the COBOL Compiler allows the programmer to specify where the implied decimal point is located through the use of the character "V" within a Picture clause.

In the sample program, the input record contains an Old Balance field and a Purchases field. Both of these fields are recorded on the card in terms of dollars and cents. Thus, the assumed decimal point is two positions to the left of the units position in each field. The example in Figure 4-9 is an illustration of the format of the input card and the corresponding entries in the File Section of the Data Division used to define the card input file and the associated input record.

EXAMPLE

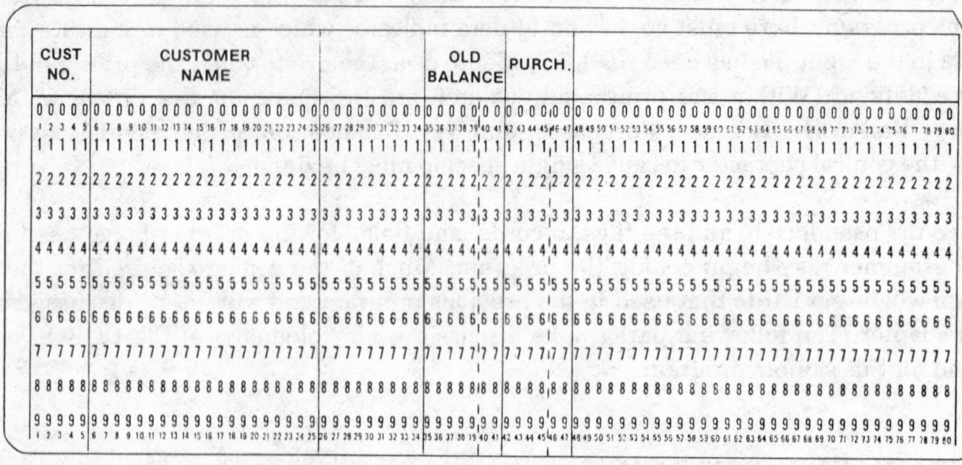

CUST NO.	CUSTOMER NAME	OLD BALANCE	PURCH.	

Sequence		CONT.	A	B	COBOL Statement
(PAGE)	(SERIAL)				

```
003010   FILE SECTION.
003020
003030   FD  ACCOUNT-INPUT-FILE
003040       RECORD CONTAINS 80 CHARACTERS
003050       LABEL RECORDS ARE OMITTED
003060       DATA RECORD IS ACCOUNT-INPUT-RECORD.
003070   01  ACCOUNT-INPUT-RECORD.
003080       05  CUSTOMER-NUMBER-INPUT      PIC 9(5).
003090       05  CUSTOMER-NAME-INPUT        PIC X(20).
003100       05  FILLER                     PIC X(9).
003110       05  OLD-BALANCE-INPUT          PIC 9(5)V99.
003120       05  PURCHASES-INPUT            PIC 9(4)V99.
003130       05  FILLER                     PIC X(33).
```

Figure 4-9 Definition of Numeric Fields

Note in Figure 4-9 that the Picture for the OLD-BALANCE-INPUT field is expressed as "PIC 9(5)V99" and the Picture for the PURCHASES-INPUT field is specified as "PIC 9(4)V99". The "9" in the Picture indicates that the fields are to be treated as Numeric fields and that they may be involved in arithmetic operations and editing. The "V" in the Picture specifies the position of the assumed decimal point. It should again be noted that storage is not reserved for the "V" and that the "V" is used merely to provide the Compiler with the information concerning the decimal alignment of numeric items involved in computations.

Since the Customer Number is to be zero suppressed on the report (see Figure 4-1), it must also be defined as a numeric field. Thus, the Picture specified is "PIC 9(5)". Even though there are no decimal positions in the Customer Number (it is treated as a whole number), it must be specified as numeric since it will be edited on the report.

Note also from Figure 4-9 that the FILLER field defined on coding line 003100 contains the Picture entry PIC X(9). It should be emphasized again that the value within the parentheses indicates the number of characters in the field being defined. Thus, this Picture Clause states that there will be nine alphanumeric characters in the Filler field. The "9" within the parentheses has no relationship to the nine which specifies a numeric field for the Old Balance field and the Purchases field.

ADD STATEMENT

The Add Statement as used in the sample program to determine the New Balance is illustrated below.

EXAMPLE

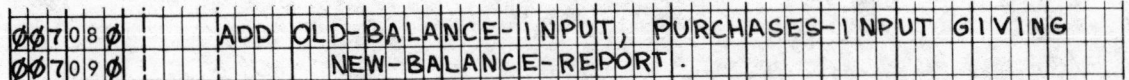

Figure 4-10 Example of ADD Statement

In the example above, the value in the OLD-BALANCE-INPUT field is added to the value in the PURCHASES-INPUT field and the answer is stored in the NEW-BALANCE-REPORT field. The format notation for the Add Statement used in the sample program is illustrated below.

```
ADD  {identifier-1}  ,  {identifier-2}  [, identifier-3]  ...
     {literal-1   }     {literal-2   }  [, literal-3   ]

     GIVING identifier-m [ROUNDED] [, identifier-n [ROUNDED]] ...

     [; ON SIZE ERROR imperative-statement]
```

Figure 4-11 Add Statement - Format Notation

The word ADD is the first word in the Add Statement. It must begin in Area B on the coding form. The values in those fields specified as identifier-1, identifier-2, identifier-3...are added together and the result is placed in the field identified by identifier-m. The word GIVING following all of the fields to be added and preceeding the field where the sum is to be stored is required. It will also be noted that more than one field can follow the word GIVING. Thus, as a result of the Add Statement, the values in two or more fields can be added together and the sum placed in one or more fields. The comma between identifiers is used merely for ease of readability and is not required.

When the Add Statement is executed with the GIVING option, the answer is first developed in a work area set up by the Compiler and then moved to the area referenced by identifier-m following the word GIVING. The following example illustrates this operation.

EXAMPLE

```
ØØ7Ø8Ø         ADD OLD-BALANCE-INPUT, PURCHASES-INPUT GIVING
ØØ7Ø9Ø             NEW-BALANCE-REPORT.
```

Step 1: When the Add Statement is executed, the two fields are added and the answer is stored in a work area.

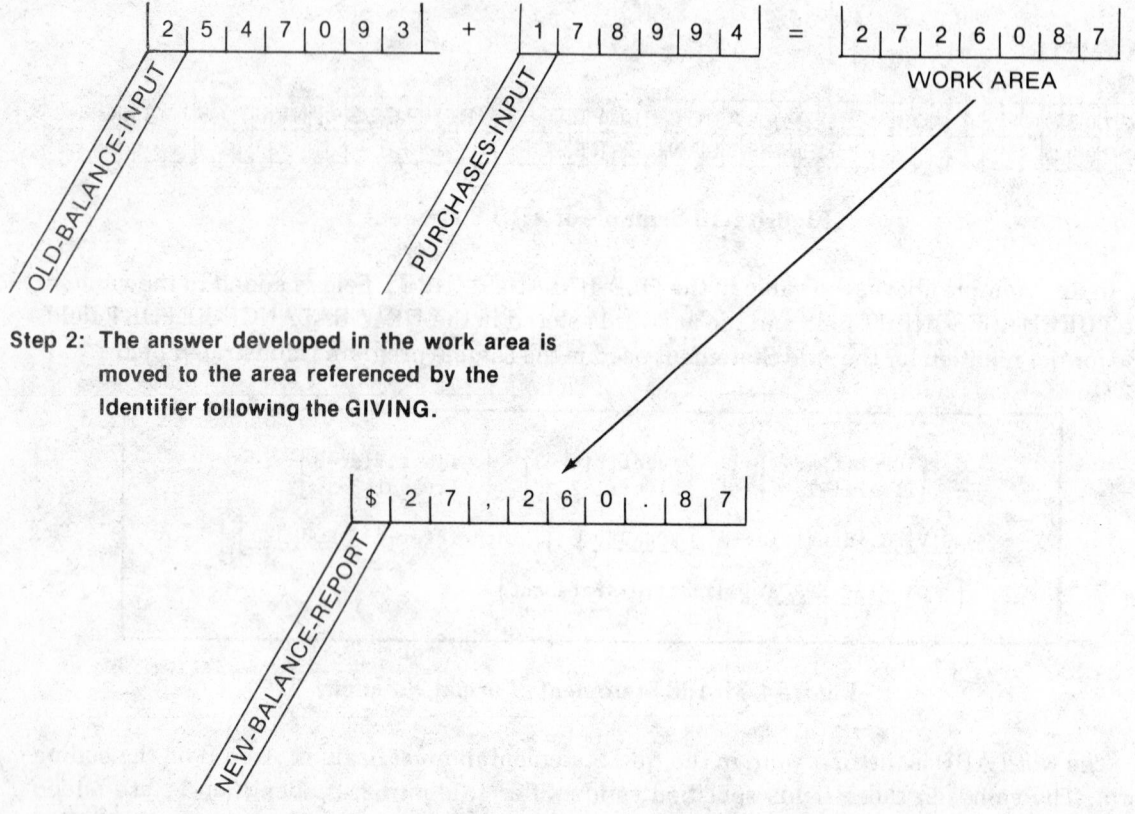

Step 2: The answer developed in the work area is moved to the area referenced by the Identifier following the GIVING.

Figure 4-12 Operation of the Add Statement

Note from the example in Figure 4-12 that the answer to the Addition operation is first placed in a work area and then it is moved to the field specified following the word GIVING. In the example, the answer is edited with a dollar sign, comma, and decimal point when it is placed in the NEW-BALANCE-REPORT field. The technique for editing this field will be explained later in this chapter. It should again be noted that the operation of placing the sum in the work area and then moving it to the result field takes place as a result of specifying the Add Statement with the Giving option.

As noted, there may be more than one field specified following the word GIVING in the Add Statement. The following example illustrates an operation in which the values in three different fields are added together and placed in two result fields.

EXAMPLE

Figure 4-13 Example of Multiple Fields with Add Statement

Note in the example above that the fields SALES1-INPUT, SALES2-INPUT, and SALES3-INPUT would be added together and the sum would be stored in both the FIRST3-SALES-OUTPUT field and the FIRST3-SALES-REPORT field.

When the Add Statement is executed, the fields specified by identifier-1, identifier-2, etc. are not altered. In addition, each of these identifiers must refer to an elementary numeric field. They cannot refer to an alphanumeric field (Picture X) nor to a group item. The total number of digits in all of the fields to be added cannot exceed 18.

ADD STATEMENT - LITERALS

In the general format in Figure 4-11, it will be noted that a numeric literal may be used as a part of the Add Statement. A numeric literal is a number which may be used in an arithmetic statement rather than an identifier. The following example illustrates the use of a numeric literal.

EXAMPLE

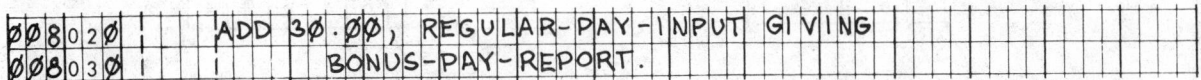

Figure 4-14 Example of Add Statement with Numeric Literal

In the example above, the contents of the area referenced by REGULAR-PAY-INPUT and the value 30.00 are added together and the answer is stored in the area referenced by BONUS-PAY-REPORT.

A numeric literal must contain at least one and not more than 18 digits, and may consist of the digits 0 through 9, the plus or minus sign, and the decimal point. If a numeric literal is unsigned, it is assumed positive. A decimal point may appear anywhere within the literal except as the rightmost character. If a numeric literal does not contain a decimal point, it is assumed to be a whole number.

ADD STATEMENT - "TO" OPTION

The Add Statement may also be written using the TO option. The following example illustrates the use of this option.

EXAMPLE

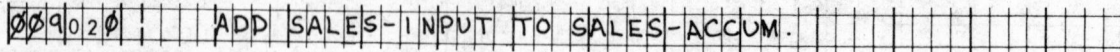

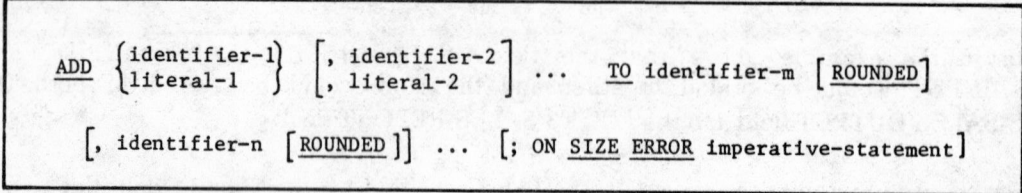

$$
\underline{ADD} \left\{ \begin{array}{l} \text{identifier-1} \\ \text{literal-1} \end{array} \right\} \left[\begin{array}{l} \text{, identifier-2} \\ \text{, literal-2} \end{array} \right] \dots \underline{TO} \text{ identifier-m } \left[\underline{ROUNDED} \right]
$$

$$
\left[\text{, identifier-n } \left[\underline{ROUNDED} \right] \right] \dots \left[\text{; ON } \underline{SIZE} \ \underline{ERROR} \text{ imperative-statement} \right]
$$

Before Execution

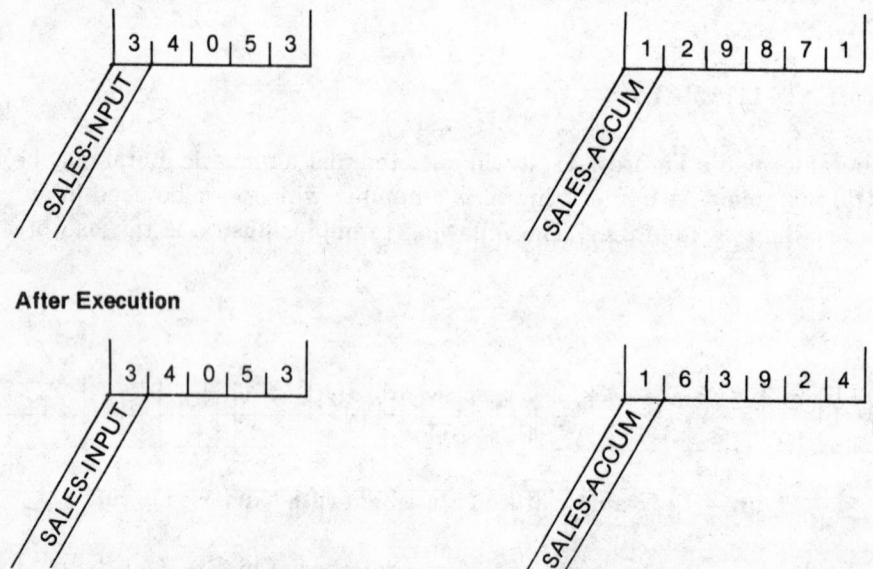

After Execution

Figure 4-15 Example of Add Statement with TO Option

When the TO option is used in an Add Statement, the values in the fields specified by identifier-1, identifier-2,..., and identifier-m are added together and the sum is placed in the field specified as identifier-m. Thus, in the example above, the value in the SALES-INPUT field (34053) is added to the value in the SALES-ACCUM field (129871) and the result (163924) is stored in the SALES-ACCUM field.

It will be noted from the general format that more than one field can be specified as the receiving field, that is, the field where the answer will be stored. This is illustrated in Figure 4-16.

EXAMPLE

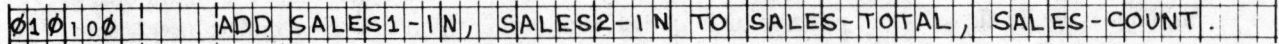

Before Execution

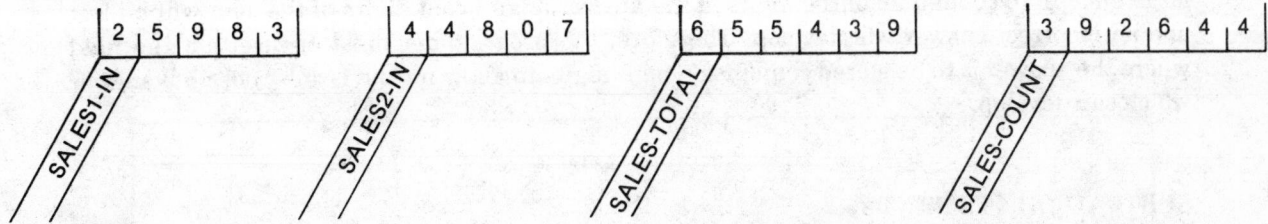

After Execution

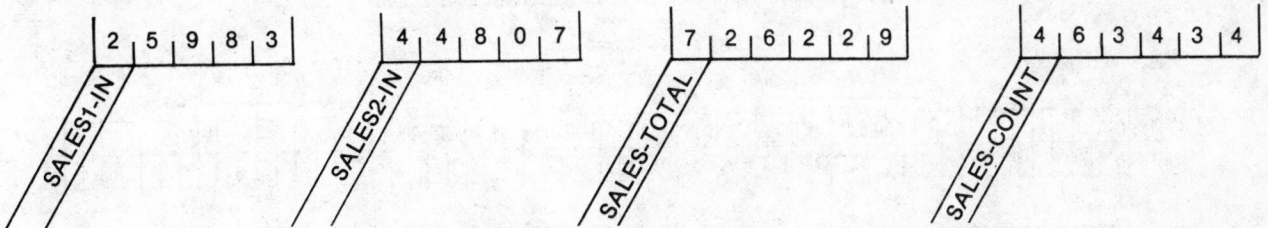

Figure 4-16 Example of Multiple Identifiers with Add Statement

In the example above, the value in SALES1-IN (25983) and SALES2-IN (44807) are added together and this sum is then added to the value in SALES-TOTAL (655439). The result (726229) is then stored in the SALES-TOTAL field. In the same manner, the values in SALES1-IN and SALES2-IN are added to the value in SALES-COUNT (392644) and the result (463434) is stored in the SALES-COUNT field.

A numeric literal may also be used in the Add Statement when using the TO option. The following example illustrates the use of a numeric literal in the Add Statement using the TO option.

EXAMPLE

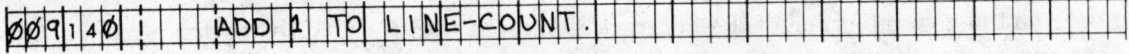

Figure 4-17 Example of Add Statement with Numeric Literal

In the example above, the number 1 is added to the value in the LINE-COUNT field and the answer is stored in the LINE-COUNT field. The Add Statement with the TO option is frequently used with literals when a field must be incremented by a fixed value, such as when counting the number of lines printed on a report.

With all formats of the Add Statement, fields are aligned according to the decimal point within each field. Also, all quantities are added algebraically, which means that the result of the add operation could be either positive or negative, depending upon the signs and values within the fields or literals to be added.

If the size of the area which is to contain the sum after the calculations are performed is not large enough to contain all of the digits in the answer, significant digits of the sum will be lost and an incorrect answer will develop. Therefore, the programmer must ensure that the field where the answer is to be stored contains enough digits to allow for the largest possible answer which can develop.

SUBTRACT STATEMENT

The Subtract Statement subtracts one, or a sum of two or more, numeric data items from a specified item and sets the value of one or more data items equal to the difference.

The following example illustrates the use of the Subtract Statement.

EXAMPLE

```
006030        SUBTRACT COST-INPUT FROM SALES-INPUT GIVING
006040           PROFIT-REPORT.
```

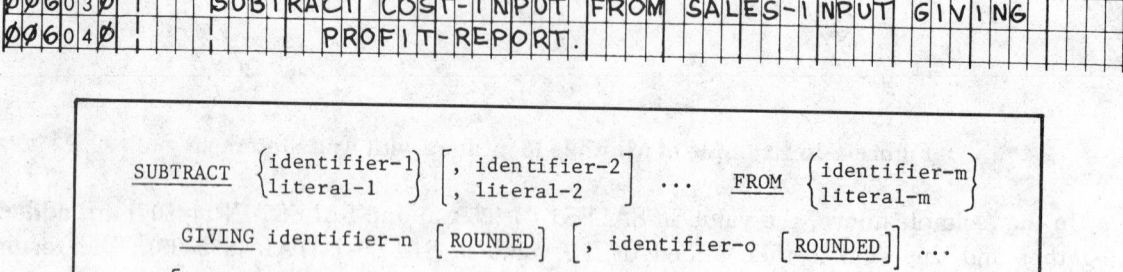

Figure 4-18 Example of Subtract Statement

In the example above, the value in the field COST-INPUT will be subtracted from the value in the field SALES-INPUT and the answer will be stored in the field PROFIT-REPORT. Note that the GIVING option works for the Subtract Statement in the same manner as for the Add Statement.

From the general format of the Subtract Statement with the GIVING option it can be seen that one or more fields can be accumulated prior to being subtracted from the value in the identifier-m field. Also, the answer can be stored in more than one field since identifier-n, identifier-o, ... can be specified following the word GIVING.

The use of two or more fields before the word FROM and following the word GIVING is illustrated below.

EXAMPLE

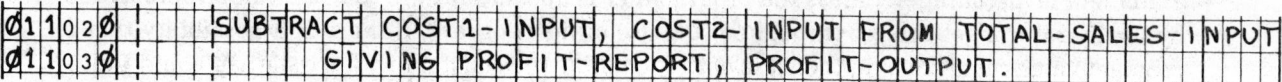

Figure 4-19 Example of Multiple Operands with Subtract Statement

In the example above, the values in the fields COST1-INPUT and COST2-INPUT would be added together and the sum of these values would be subtracted from the TOTAL-SALES-INPUT field. The answer would be stored in the PROFIT-REPORT field and the PROFIT-OUTPUT field. It should be noted that all of this processing takes place as a result of the Subtract Statement and the programmer need not be concerned with the intermediate results which would be produced by this processing.

The GIVING option is not required by the Subtract Statement. An example of the Subtract Statement without the GIVING option is illustrated in Figure 4-20.

EXAMPLE

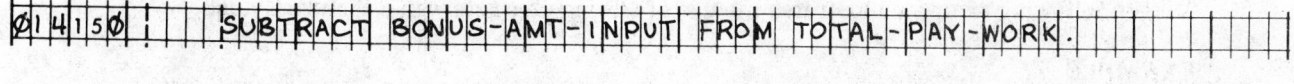

Figure 4-20 Example of Subtract Statement

In the example in Figure 4-20, the value in the field BONUS-AMT-INPUT would be subtracted from the value in the field TOTAL-PAY-WORK and the answer would be stored in the TOTAL-PAY-WORK field. Thus, after the subtraction operation is completed, the original value in the TOTAL-PAY-WORK field will no longer be available—it is replaced by the answer from the subtraction operation.

Literals can also be used in the Subtract Statement, as illustrated below.

EXAMPLE

Figure 4-21 Example of Literal in Subtract Statement

The effect of the Subtract Statement in Figure 4-21 is to subtract the value 5.00 from the OVERTIME-PAY-WORK field and store the answer in the same field.

It should be noted that the use of literals in both the Add Statement and the Subtract Statement is discouraged unless the programmer is absolutely sure that the value represented by the literal will not change throughout the use of the program. If there is a possibility that a constant value could change, then it is better to define the constant with a data-name and Value Clause in the Data Division. This is because it is easier to make changes to data in the Data Division than it is to search the Procedure Division for all of the literals which must be changed. Therefore, literals should be used with discrimination by the programmer and only when a value is very unlikely to be changed later in the life of the program.

EDITING

Business reports normally require some form of report editing. Editing consists of suppressing leading zeros in numeric fields and inserting punctuation within a field in order to make it more legible on the report. Editing is easily accomplished in COBOL through the use of special editing characters. To edit a field with a dollar sign, comma, and decimal point, the dollar sign, comma, and decimal point are inserted in the Picture Clause as they are to appear when the field is printed.

The following example illustrates the use of editing characters in a Picture Clause.

EXAMPLE

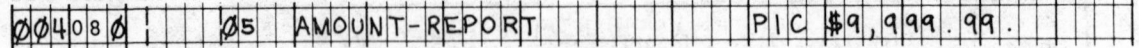

Figure 4-22 Example of Report Editing

When the program is executed, the data from the source field, when moved to the AMOUNT-REPORT field, is edited according to the format established in the Picture Clause.

The following chart illustrates data as it appears in storage, a related Picture Clause, and the printed output that would result.

DATA IN STORAGE	PICTURE	PRINTED OUTPUT
132550	PICTURE $9,999.99	$1,325.50

*The " ∧ " indicates the location of the assumed decimal point

Figure 4-23 Picture Clause and Related Printed Output

As can be seen from Figure 4-23, the printed output contains the dollar sign, comma, and period which are placed in the output in the same positions as they are contained in the Picture Clause.

ZERO SUPPRESSION

An important editing function which must be performed constantly in business applications is Zero Suppression. Zero suppression is the process of replacing leading, non-significant zeros in a numeric field with blanks or other chosen characters. To zero suppress a field with blanks, the letter "Z" is placed in the Picture Clause in each position which is to be zero suppressed. The example in Figure 4-24 illustrates zero suppression.

EXAMPLE

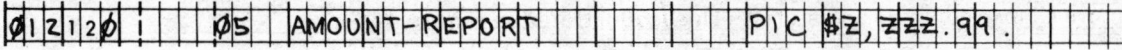

DATA IN STORAGE	PICTURE	PRINTED OUTPUT
032595	PICTURE $Z,ZZZ.99	$ 325.95

Figure 4-24 Example of Zero Suppression

Note in the example above that the leading zero in the data in storage is replaced by a blank when it is zero suppressed. The methods of causing the report editing illustrated in Figure 4-23 and 4-24 are discussed in detail in the following paragraphs.

Zero Suppression - Blank Fill

The letter of the alphabet "Z" in the Picture Clause represents numeric digits that are to be suppressed, that is, made blank, when they are zero. The only characters which can precede the "Z" in a Picture Clause are the dollar sign, minus sign, plus sign, or comma. A "Z" in a Picture Clause indicates that the leading zeros in the indicated positions are to be replaced with spaces. The following examples illustrate the use of the "Z" in a Picture Clause.

EXAMPLES: Zero Suppression - Blank Fill

DATA IN STORAGE	PICTURE	PRINTED OUTPUT
12595	PICTURE ZZZ99	12595
00123	PICTURE ZZZ99	123
00005	PICTURE ZZZ99	05
00000	PICTURE ZZZZZ	[blank]
00409	PICTURE ZZZZZ	409

Figure 4-25 Examples of Zero Suppression

Note in the examples in Figure 4-25 that leading zeros are changed to blanks if the corresponding position in the Picture Clause contains a ''Z''. If the corresponding position in the Picture Clause contains a ''9'', the zero is printed. After the first significant digit is printed, all following zeros are printed.

Zero Suppression - Asterisk Fill

The asterisk (*) can also be used in zero suppression. When the asterisk is specified in the Picture Clause, leading zeros are changed to asterisks if the corresponding position in the Picture Clause contains an asterisk. This is illustrated in Figure 4-26.

EXAMPLES: Zero Suppression - Asterisk Fill

DATA IN STORAGE	PICTURE	PRINTED OUTPUT
12345	PICTURE ***99	12345
00123	PICTURE ***99	**123
00100	PICTURE ***99	**100
00000	PICTURE ***99	***00
00000	PICTURE *****	*****

Figure 4-26 Example of Zero Suppression with Asterisk Fill

The use of asterisks in zero suppression is usually limited to cases where blanks are not desirable in front of dollar figures, such as on a payroll check.

INSERTION CHARACTERS

The use of insertion characters will cause the character specified in the Picture Clause to be placed in the corresponding position of the field when data is moved to that field. When insertion characters are used, the Picture must be large enough to hold both the data and the insertion characters. The dollar sign, comma, and decimal point can be used only when the data in the field is numeric.

The appearance of a single symbol ''$'' in a Picture Clause indicates that a dollar sign is to be inserted at the position occupied by the symbol. Several consecutive repetitions of the symbol ''$'' indicates that the data is to be edited with a floating dollar sign, that is, a dollar sign which is to print to the left of and adjacent to the first significant character.

When the comma is used in the Picture Clause, a comma will be inserted in the same place as it appears in the Picture. If the zero to the left of the comma has been suppressed, then the comma will not be inserted in the position where it appears; rather, the comma will be replaced by the character which is replacing the zeros in the zero suppression operation.

When the decimal appears in a Picture Clause, a period will be inserted at the position occupied by the decimal in the Picture. The data in the field to be moved to the edited Picture will be aligned so that the assumed decimal point, as indicated by the character "V", corresponds to the actual decimal point. The decimal can appear in the Picture Clause only one time. The following examples illustrate the use of the dollar sign, comma, and decimal point in the Picture Clause.

EXAMPLES: Character Insertion, Zero Suppression

DATA IN STORAGE	PICTURE	PRINTED OUTPUT
000125	PICTURE $Z,ZZZ.99	$ 1.25
000000	PICTURE $Z,ZZZ.99	$ .00
000325	PICTURE $$,$$$.99	$3.25
000000	PICTURE $$,$$$.99	$.00
000550	PICTURE $*,***.99	$****5.50
000005	PICTURE $*,***.99	$*****.05
1250	PICTURE $$,$$9.99	$0.12
1234	PICTURE $Z,ZZZ.99	$1,234.00

Figure 4-27 Examples of Insertion of Dollar Sign, Comma, and Decimal Point

MINUS SIGNS

Minus signs (-) can be used at either end of the Picture Clause. Data moved from any field that does not have a processing sign is considered positive. When the minus sign appears at either end of the Picture Clause, the minus sign will be printed in the position in which it is placed, when the data is negative. When the data is positive, a space is inserted. This is illustrated in Figure 4-28.

EXAMPLES: Minus Sign

DATA IN STORAGE	PICTURE	PRINTED OUTPUT
4500	PICTURE -9999	4500
-4500	PICTURE -9999	-4500
4500	PICTURE 9999-	4500
-4500	PICTURE 9999-	4500-

Figure 4-28 Example of Minus Signs

The minus sign can also be floated from the left-hand end of the Picture by placing the minus symbol in each leading numeric position to be suppressed. Each leading zero is replaced with a space, and either a space or a minus sign is placed in the position of the last suppressed zero. The use of a floating minus sign is illustrated below.

EXAMPLES: Floating Minus Sign

DATA IN STORAGE	PICTURE	PRINTED OUTPUT
12345	PICTURE ----99	12345
00034	PICTURE ----99	34
00000	PICTURE ----99	00
-12345	PICTURE ----99	-12345
-00045	PICTURE ----99	-45
-00006	PICTURE ----99	-06

Figure 4-29 Examples of Floating Minus Sign

Note from the examples above that, as with all editing, there must be enough room in the Picture Clause to store the data which is being moved to the Picture. The data in storage contains five digits in the example. Therefore, the Picture Clause contains space for these five digits plus the minus sign. Whenever data is to be edited, there must always be room in the Picture for all of the digits in order for editing to take place properly.

PLUS SIGN

When the plus sign (+) appears at either end of a Picture Clause, the sign of the data will be indicated in the position where the plus sign appears. If the data is positive, a "+" is inserted; if the data is negative, a "-" is inserted. This is shown below.

EXAMPLES: Plus Sign

DATA IN STORAGE	PICTURE	PRINTED OUTPUT
12	PICTURE + 99	+ 12
-12	PICTURE + 99	-12
-12	PICTURE 99 +	12-
12	PICTURE 99 +	12 +

Figure 4-30 Example of Plus Sign

The plus sign can be floated in the same way as the minus sign.

CREDIT AND DEBIT SYMBOLS

When the CR symbol appears at the right-hand end of a Picture Clause, the sign of the data being edited will be indicated in the character positions occupied by the symbol. If the data is positive, two blanks are inserted; if the data is negative, the letters CR are inserted.

EXAMPLES: CR [Credit]

DATA IN STORAGE	PICTURE	PRINTED OUTPUT
12345	PICTURE $***.99CR	$123.45
-12345	PICTURE $***.99CR	$123.45CR
-012345	PICTURE $$,$$$.99 CR	$123.45 CR
-004560	PICTURE $$,$$$.99CR	$45.60CR

Figure 4-31 Examples of CR Symbol

When the letters DB appear at the right-hand end of the Picture Clause and the data to be edited is negative, the letters DB will appear in the positions in which they are placed; if the data is positive, two blanks are inserted.

EXAMPLES: DB [Debit]

DATA IN STORAGE	PICTURE	PRINTED OUTPUT
001256	PICTURE $Z,ZZZ.99DB	$ 12.56
001256	PICTURE $*,***.99DB	$***12.56
-001256	PICTURE $*,***.99DB	$***12.56DB
-001256	PICTURE $*,***.99 DB	$***12.56 DB
-001256	PICTURE $$,$$$.99 DB	$12.56 DB

Figure 4-32 Examples of DB Symbol

Note from the examples of the CR and DB symbols that a space can be included in the Picture Clause following the specifications for the data to be edited and before either the CR or DB symbols. This allows the symbols to be separated from the actual data which is edited and is many times used for a more clear report. The CR and DB symbols can only be used on the right end of the Picture Clause.

"P" SYMBOL

If the assumed decimal point location is not within the field, the symbol P is used to indicate each scaling position beyond either end of the data in storage. In effect, each P represents an implied position.

EXAMPLES: P [Implied Position]

DATA IN STORAGE	PICTURE	PRINTED OUTPUT
123	PICTURE 999PPP	123000.
123	PICTURE PP999	.00123

Figure 4-33 Examples of "P" Symbol

BLANK, ZERO [0], AND STROKE [/]

In all of the previous examples of editing, the data to be edited must be numeric; that is, it must be defined with a Picture 9 Clause and it must contain actual numeric data. The Blank, Zero (0), and Stroke (/) insertion characters can be used with either numeric fields (Picture 9) or alphanumeric fields (Picture X). When used, these characters are inserted in the field in the positions in which they appear within the Picture Clause. The following examples illustrate the use of these editing characters.

EXAMPLES:

Blank

DATA IN STORAGE	PICTURE	PRINTED OUTPUT
00000	PICTURE 99B999	00 000
060978	PICTURE 99B99B99	06 09 78
ABCDEF	PICTURE XXBXXXBX	AB CDE F

Zero Symbol

DATA IN STORAGE	PICTURE	PRINTED OUTPUT
125	PICTURE 99900	12500
125	PICTURE 00999	00125
125	PICTURE XXX0	1250
125	PICTURE 000XXX	000125

Stroke

DATA IN STORAGE	PICTURE	PRINTED OUTPUT
082977	PICTURE 99/99/99	08/29/77
ABCDEF	PICTURE X/XXX/X/X	A/BCD/E/F
007563	PICTURE Z/ZZZ/ZZ	75/63

Figure 4-34 Examples of Blank, Zero, and Stroke

MOVE STATEMENT

The previous chapter explained the basic operation of the Move Statement with alphanumeric data. This statement is used to move data from one area of storage to another.

When the field from which the data is to be moved and the field or fields to receive the data are numeric by definition (Picture with 9's or editing characters), then the data is aligned by the actual or assumed decimal. If the fields are of unequal length, then truncation or extension will occur on one or both ends of the data when it is moved to the receiving field.

When data is moved from one area to another, the field is edited according to the editing characters specified in the receiving field. The following examples illustrate the operation of the Move Statement when numeric data is being moved and edited.

EXAMPLE 1: Fields contain the same number of numeric digits to the left of and right of the decimal point.

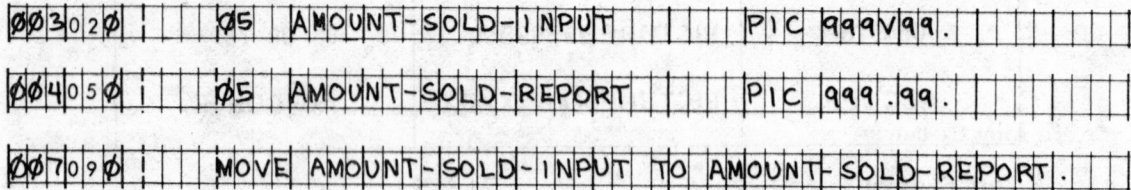

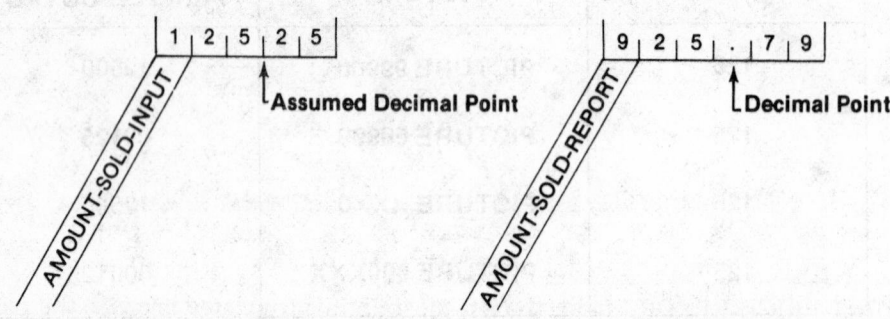

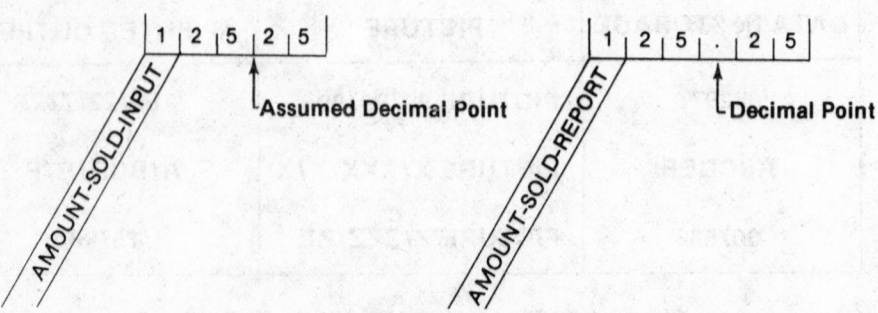

Figure 4-35 Example of Editing

In this example, the data in AMOUNT-SOLD-INPUT is moved to AMOUNT-SOLD-REPORT, and the data in AMOUNT-SOLD-INPUT is aligned in AMOUNT-SOLD-REPORT on the basis of the assumed and actual decimal points specified in the Picture Clauses.

EXAMPLE 2: Receiving field contains fewer digits to the left of the decimal point than the sending field.

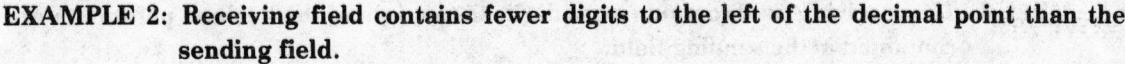

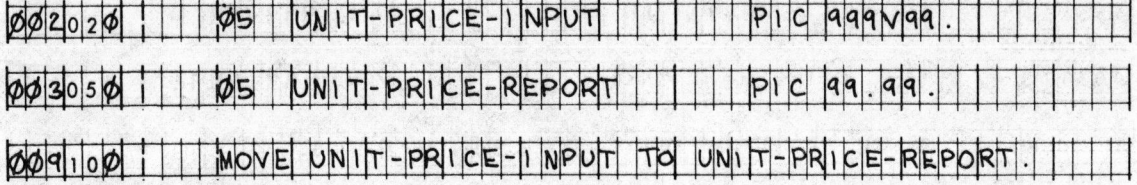

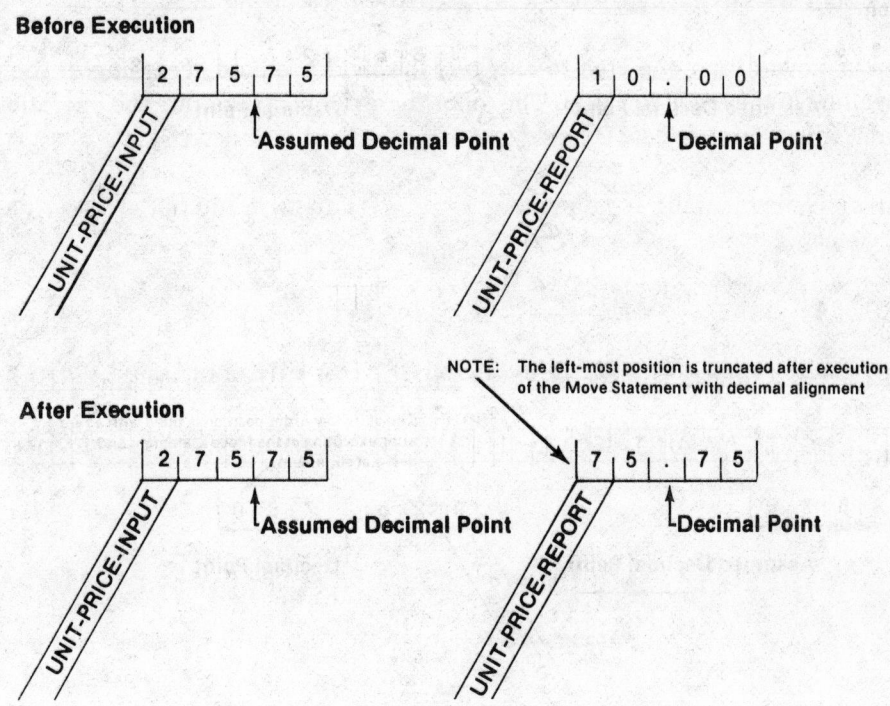

Figure 4-36 Example of Truncation when Editing

Note in the example above that when the data is moved from the UNIT-PRICE-INPUT field to the UNIT-PRICE-REPORT field, the left-most digit is truncated because the receiving field, UNIT-PRICE-REPORT, does not contain space for the left-most digit. It should be noted that the same thing will occur if there is not room for digits to the right of the decimal point. Any digits for which there is not room will be truncated.

EXAMPLE 3: **The receiving field contains more digits to the right of the decimal point than are contained in the sending field.**

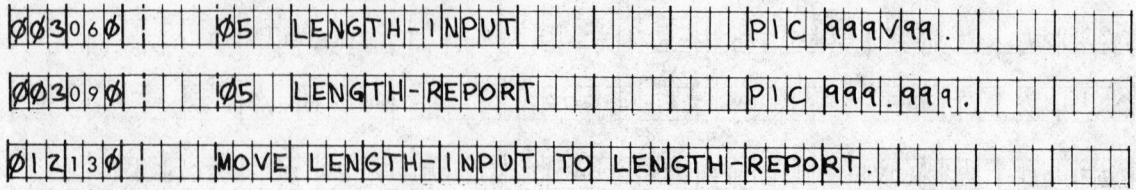

Before Execution

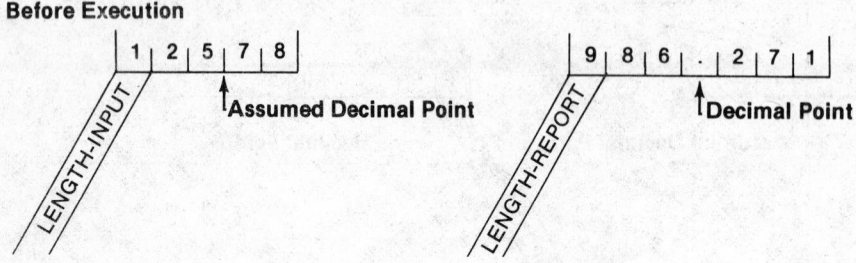

NOTE: The extra low-order position is filled with a zero after execution of the Move Statement and decimal alignment.

After Execution

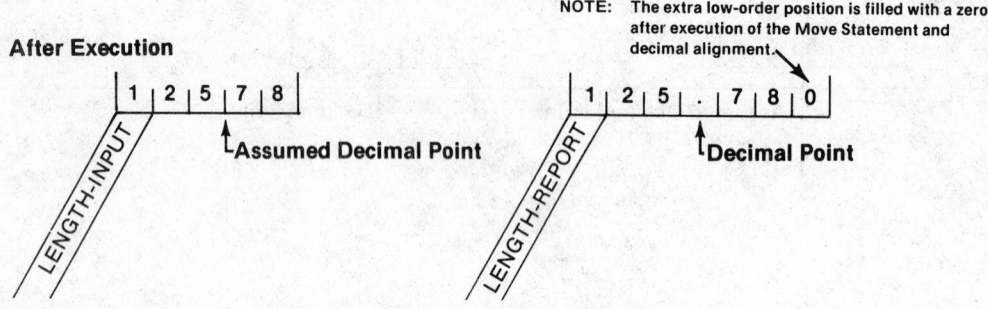

Figure 4-37 Example of Zero-Fill in Larger Fields

Note from the example in Figure 4-37 that when the receiving field contains more positions than there are digits in the sending field, then the receiving field is "zero-filled," that is, zeros are placed in the extra positions. In the example, the extra positions are to the right of the decimal point. The same processing would occur if the extra positions were to the left of the decimal point; that is, the extra high-order positions would be filled with zeros.

REPORT HEADINGS

The program in this chapter is to print headings on the first page of the report. The headings which are printed are illustrated in the printer spacing chart and printout below.

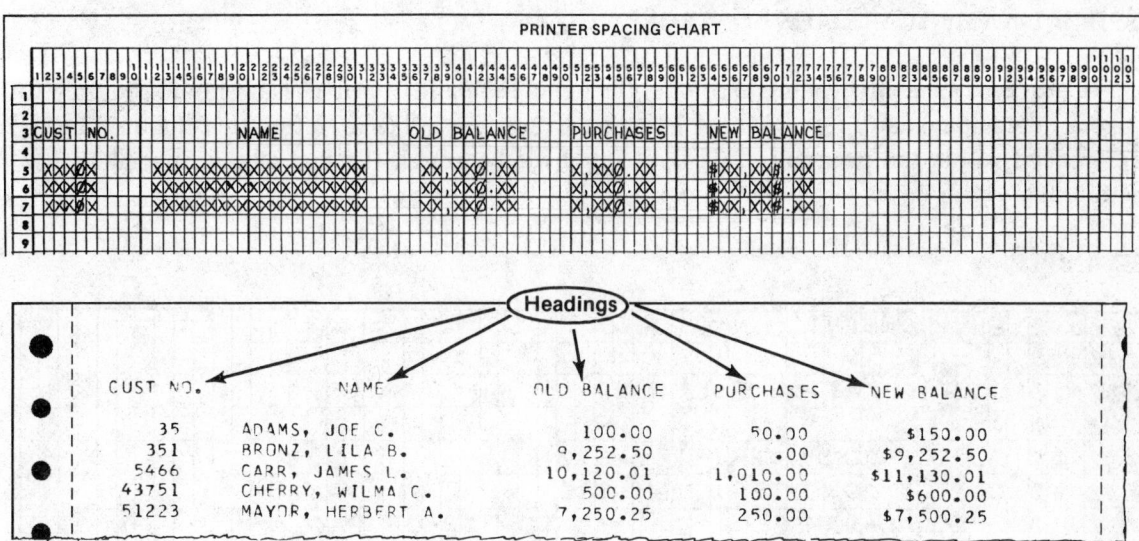

Figure 4-38 Example of Report Headings

Note from the example above that the headings are printed at the top of the page. On a Computer printer, the top of the page is identified by a carriage control tape which is mounted on the printer and contains punches in "channels" on the tape to identify the top of the page. This is illustrated in Figure 4-40.

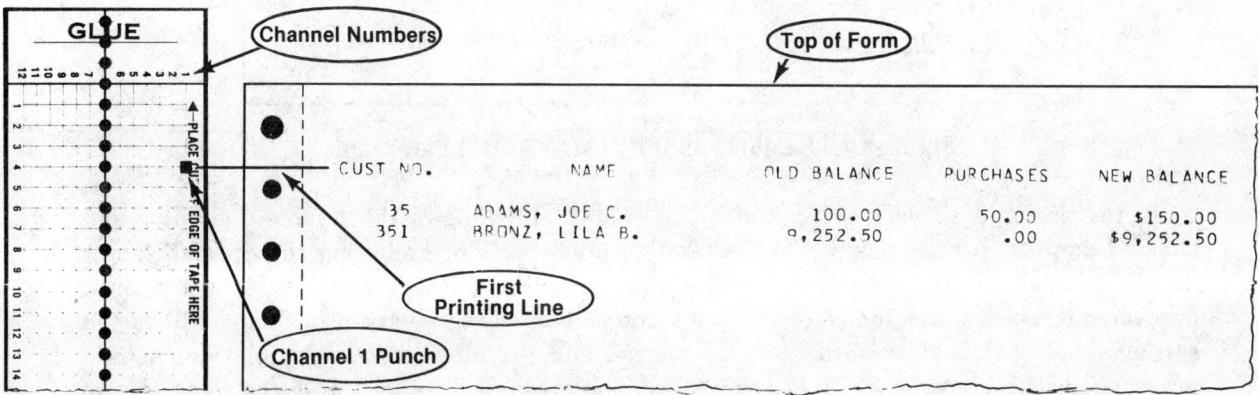

Figure 4-39 Example of Carriage Control Tape

Note in Figure 4-39 that a punch in Channel 1 of the carriage control tape signifies the first line on a page where printing is to begin. In most installations, Channel 1 is used to signify top-of-forms.

SPECIAL-NAMES CARRIAGE CONTROL

In order to cause the heading to print at the top of the page, it is necessary in the program to give a "mnemonic-name" to Channel 1 in the carriage control tape so that this channel can be referenced within the program. This is accomplished through the use of the Special-Names paragraph within the Environment Division, as illustrated below.

EXAMPLE

```
ØØ201Ø ENVIRONMENT DIVISION.
ØØ202Ø
ØØ203Ø CONFIGURATION SECTION.
ØØ204Ø
ØØ205Ø SOURCE-COMPUTER.  IBM-37Ø.
ØØ206Ø OBJECT-COMPUTER.  IBM-37Ø.
ØØ207Ø SPECIAL-NAMES.    CØ1 IS TO-TOP-OF-PAGE.
```

```
ENVIRONMENT DIVISION.

CONFIGURATION SECTION.

SOURCE-COMPUTER.   computer-name

OBJECT-COMPUTER.   computer-name

[ SPECIAL-NAMES.  [, implementor-name IS mnemonic-name ]]
```

Figure 4-40 Example of SPECIAL-NAMES Paragraph

In the example above, the Special-Names paragraph follows the Source-Computer and Object-Computer paragraphs within the Configuration Section. Following the Special-Names paragraph name is the sentence "C01 IS TO-TOP-OF-PAGE." The "C01" is a special implementor-name which indicates that a mnemonic-name is to be given to Channel 01 in the carriage control tape. The word "IS" is required and the mnemonic-name following it is a programmer-chosen name which is a symbolic name given to Channel 1 in the carriage control tape. In the sample program, the name chosen is "TO-TOP-OF-PAGE."

It is possible that other punches within the carriage control tape must be used to indicate where lines are to be printed on the report. When this is necessary, the desired punch must be defined with a mnemonic-name. Thus, if Channel 11 in the carriage control tape were to be used, the entry "C11 IS . . ." would be included in the Special-Names paragraph to give a symbolic name to Channel 11. There are 12 channels in the carriage control tape. As noted, however, the punch in Channel 1 is normally used for the first printing line.

DEFINITION OF THE HEADING LINE

In addition to giving the punch in the carriage control tape a mnemonic-name, it is necessary to define, in the Working-Storage Section of the Data Division, the heading line to be printed. The entries used in the sample program to define the heading line are illustrated below.

EXAMPLE

```
004190  01   REPORT-HEADINGS.
004200       05   CARRIAGE-CONTROL              PIC X.
005010       05   FILLER                        PIC X(8)   VALUE 'CUST NO.'.
005020       05   FILLER                        PIC X(11)  VALUE SPACES.
005030       05   FILLER                        PIC X(4)   VALUE 'NAME'.
005040       05   FILLER                        PIC X(12)  VALUE SPACES.
005050       05   FILLER                        PIC X(11)  VALUE 'OLD BALANCE'.
005060       05   FILLER                        PIC X(4)   VALUE SPACES.
005070       05   FILLER                        PIC X(9)   VALUE 'PURCHASES'.
005080       05   FILLER                        PIC X(4)   VALUE SPACES.
005090       05   FILLER                        PIC X(11)  VALUE 'NEW BALANCE'.
005100       05   FILLER                        PIC X(58)  VALUE SPACES.
```

Figure 4-41 Definition of Header Line

Note in the example above that the group item 01 REPORT-HEADINGS is used to give a name to the entire heading line. Each elementary item within the heading has FILLER as the data-name since none of the elementary items will be referenced within the program.

The Pictures for each of the FILLER fields are alphanumeric and indicate the length of each of the entries. These lengths correspond to the format of the heading line (see Figure 4-38). The Value Clauses are used to give the values to each of the fields. As can be seen, the values specified correspond to the entries for the heading line. The VALUE SPACES clause specifies that the entire field as defined by the Picture Clause is to contain spaces. Thus, with the column headings and the intervening spaces specified in a manner which corresponds to the format of the heading line, the heading line to be printed on the report is defined.

WRITING THE HEADING LINE

As with other lines on the report, the Write Statement is used to write the heading line. The Write Statement used in the sample program is illustrated below.

EXAMPLE

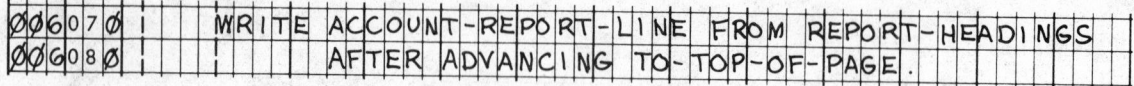

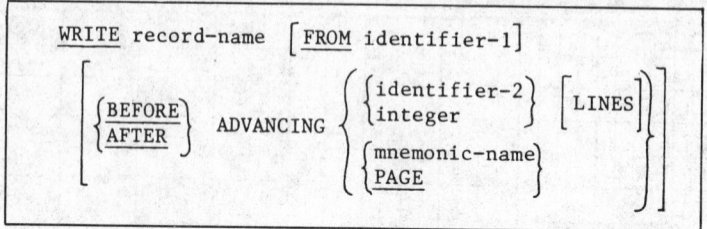

Figure 4-42 Example of Write Statement to Print Headings

In the example in Figure 4-42, ACCOUNT-REPORT-LINE is the data-name used to define the printer output area in the File Section of the Data Division. In addition, the FROM Option is used with the Write Statement used to write the heading. When the From Option is used, the data in identifier-1, in this case REPORT-HEADINGS, is moved to the record-name specified, ACCOUNT-REPORT-LINE. The line is then written. Thus, as a result of the Write Statement in Figure 4-42, the headings defined in REPORT-HEADINGS (see Figure 4-41) will be printed on the report.

Note also that the After Advancing option is used and the mnemonic-name TO-TOP-OF-PAGE is specified. As a result of this After Advancing clause, the printer will be skipped to Channel 1 in the carriage control tape before printing the line, since TO-TOP-OF-PAGE is the same as Channel 1 in the carriage control tape (see Figure 4-40).

Thus, as a result of the Write Statement in Figure 4-42, the printer will be skipped to Channel 1 in the carriage control tape, which is the first line to be printed on the page, and then the headings will be printed on the report.

VARIABLE LINE SPACING

It will be recalled that after the heading is printed on the report, the report is to be double-spaced; but all of the remaining lines on the report are to be single-spaced. This is illustrated below.

EXAMPLE

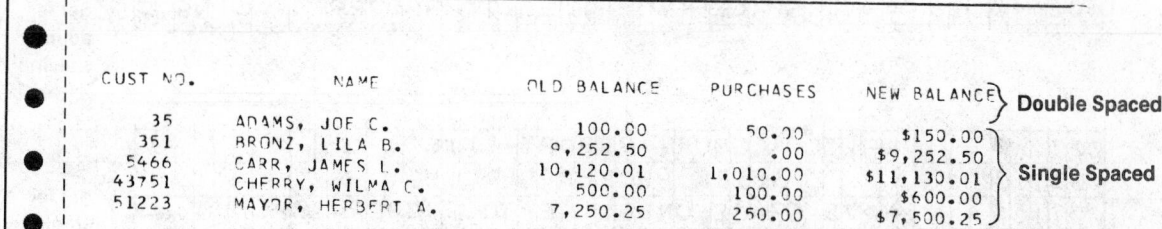

Figure 4-43 Example of Spacing on Report

Note from Figure 4-43 that the first detail line for Adams, Joe C. is double-spaced but the remaining detail lines are single-spaced. In order for this to occur, a field must be defined which will contain a character used to indicate what spacing should occur. In addition, the program must have fields which contain the specific spacing control characters. The definition of these fields is illustrated below.

EXAMPLE

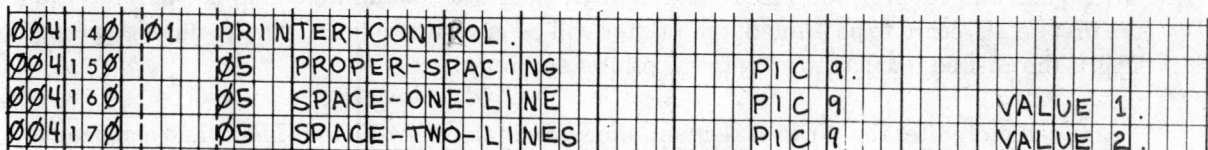

Figure 4-44 Printer Control Values

The PROPER-SPACING field is the field which will contain the control character which will indicate the spacing that is to occur in the writing of the report. It must be defined as a numeric field (Picture 9). If it contains the value 1, then the report will be single-spaced. If it contains the value 2, then the report will be double-spaced. The SPACE-ONE-LINE field contains the constant value 1 (as a result of the VALUE 1 Clause) which will be moved to the PROPER-SPACING field to cause single-spacing. The SPACE-TWO-LINES field contains the value 2 which will be moved to the PROPER-SPACING field when double-spacing is required. It will be noted in the example in Figure 4-44 that the values to be contained in the fields (1 and 2) are not contained within single quotes as has been done previously (see Figure 4-41). This is because when the Value Clause is used with numeric fields (Picture 9), the values are not placed in single quotes. Only when the fields are alphanumeric (Picture X) are the quotes required.

The values must be moved to the PROPER-SPACING field prior to the Write Statement so that the spacing will take place properly. The sequence which is followed in the program is illustrated below.

EXAMPLE

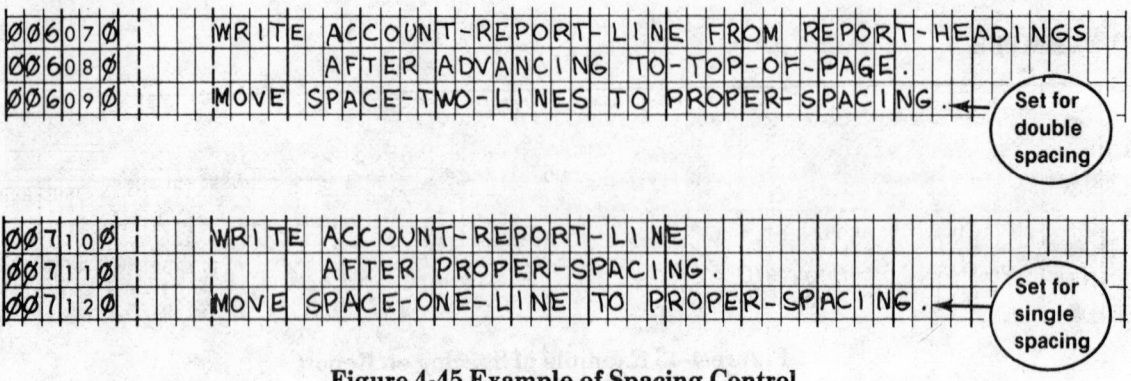

Figure 4-45 Example of Spacing Control

Note from Figure 4-45 that immediately after the headings are written (lines 006070 and 006080), the value in the SPACE-TWO-LINES field is moved to the PROPER-SPACING field. As will be recalled from Figure 4-44, the value in the SPACE-TWO-LINES field is 2. Thus, the value 2 is stored in the PROPER-SPACING field.

When the Write Statement to print the detail record is encountered for the first time (line 007100 and line 007110), the PROPER-SPACING field will contain the value 2. Therefore, for the first detail record to be printed, the printer will be spaced two lines, that is, double-spaced. This is the desired result according to the printer spacing chart.

Immediately after the Write Statement, the value in the SPACE-ONE-LINE field is moved to the PROPER-SPACING field. The SPACE-ONE-LINE field contains the value 1 (see Figure 4-44). Therefore, after the first Write Statement for a detail line, the PROPER-SPACING field contains the value 1.

Since the remaining detail records will be written by the Write Statement on lines 007100 and 007110, all of the records will be single spaced. This is the desired result. It should be noted that spacing on the report can be varied at any time by placing the proper value in the spacing control field. The maximum number of lines which can be spaced is 99. In the sample program, only double and single spacing are used.

SAMPLE PROGRAM

The sample program in this chapter creates an Accounting Report by processing the Customer Account Card File. The output, input, IPO Chart, Pseudocode Specifications, Source Listing, and printer output of the program are illustrated on the following pages.

OUTPUT

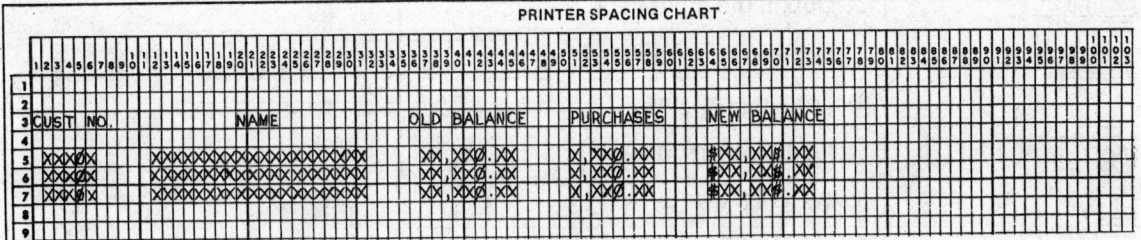

Figure 4-46 Printer Spacing Chart

INPUT

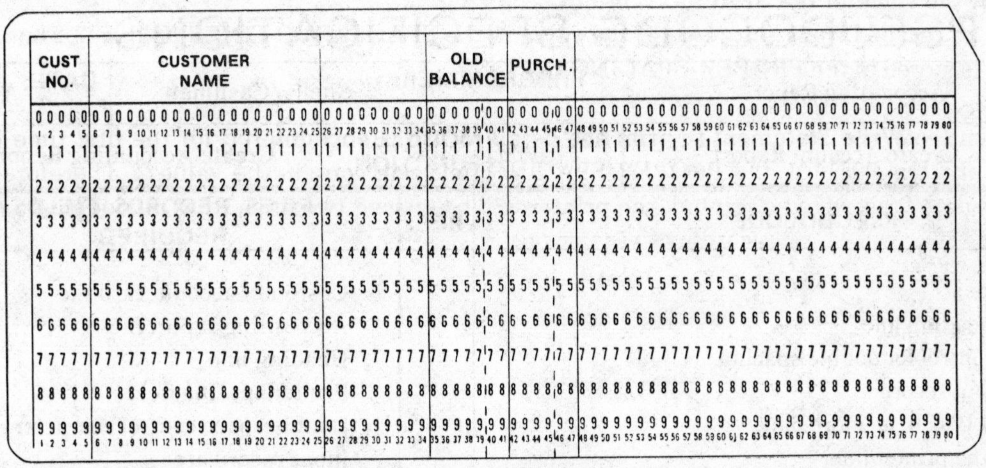

Figure 4-47 Input

IPO CHART

PROGRAM: Accounting Report	PROGRAMMER: Shelly/Cashman		DATE: April 11
MODULE NAME: Create Account Report	REF: A000	MODULE FUNCTION: Create Accounting Report	

INPUT	PROCESSING	REF:	OUTPUT
1. Customer Account	1. Initialization		1. Accounting Report
Card File	2. Obtain the input data		
	3. Perform calculations		
	4. Format print line		
	5. Write the report		
	6. Termination		

Figure 4-48 IPO Chart

PSEUDOCODE SPECIFICATIONS

PROGRAM: Accounting Report	PROGRAMMER: Shelly/Cashman		DATE: April 13
MODULE NAME: Create Account Report	REF: A000	MODULE FUNCTION: Create Accounting Report	

PSEUDOCODE	REF:	FILES, RECORDS, FIELDS REQUIRED

Open the files
Write the heading line
Set space control for double spacing
Read an input record
PERFORM UNTIL no more data
    Clear the printer line
    Move the customer number, customer name,
      old balance and purchases to output area
    Calculate new balance = old balance + purchases
      and place in the output area
    Write a line on the report
    Set space control for single spacing
    Read an input record
ENDPERFORM
Close the files
Stop run
		Customer account card file
		Accounting report file
		Heading line
		Printer spacing field
		Double space control character
		Input record area
		    Customer number
		    Customer name
		    Old balance
		    Purchases
		End-of-data indicator
		Printer output line
		    Customer number
		    Customer name
		    Old balance
		    Purchases
		    New balance
		Single space control character

Figure 4-49 Pseudocode Specifications

Source Listing

```
                         IBM DOS AMERICAN NATIONAL STANDARD COBOL        CBF CL3-4        05/26/77

00001   001010 IDENTIFICATION DIVISION.                                    ACCTREPT
00002   001020                                                            ACCTREPT
00003   001030 PROGRAM-ID.    ACCTREPT.                                    ACCTREPT
00004   001040 AUTHOR.        SHELLY AND CASHMAN.                          ACCTREPT
00005   001050 INSTALLATION.  ANAHEIM.                                     ACCTREPT
00006   001060 DATE-WRITTEN.  05/26/77                                     ACCTREPT
00007   001070 DATE-COMPILED. 05/26/77                                     ACCTREPT
00008   001080 SECURITY.      UNCLASSIFIED.                                ACCTREPT
00009   001090                                                            ACCTREPT
00010   001100************************************************************* ACCTREPT
00011   001110*                                                         *  ACCTREPT
00012   001120*  THIS PROGRAM PRODUCES AN ACCOUNTING REPORT, LISTING THE NEW * ACCTREPT
00013   001130*  BALANCE IN EACH CUSTOMER ACCOUNT.  NEW BALANCE IS CALCULATED* ACCTREPT
00014   001140*  BY ADDING PURCHASES TO THE CUSTOMER'S OLD BALANCE.      *  ACCTREPT
00015   001150*                                                         *  ACCTREPT
00016   001160*************************************************************  ACCTREPT
00017   001170                                                            ACCTREPT
00018   001180                                                            ACCTREPT
00019   001190                                                            ACCTREPT
00020   001200 ENVIRONMENT DIVISION.                                       ACCTREPT
00021   002010                                                            ACCTREPT
00022   002020 CONFIGURATION SECTION.                                      ACCTREPT
00023   002030                                                            ACCTREPT
00024   002040 SOURCE-COMPUTER. IBM-370.                                   ACCTREPT
00025   002050 OBJECT-COMPUTER. IBM-370.                                   ACCTREPT
00026   002060 SPECIAL-NAMES.   C01 IS TO-TOP-OF-PAGE.                     ACCTREPT
00027   002070                                                            ACCTREPT
00028   002080 INPUT-OUTPUT SECTION.                                       ACCTREPT
00029   002090                                                            ACCTREPT
00030   002100 FILE-CONTROL.                                               ACCTREPT
00031   002110     SELECT ACCOUNT-INPUT-FILE                               ACCTREPT
00032   002120         ASSIGN TO SYS007-UR-2540R-S.                        ACCTREPT
00033   002130     SELECT ACCOUNT-REPORT-FILE                              ACCTREPT
00034   002140         ASSIGN TO SYS013-UR-1403-S.                         ACCTREPT
```

```
      2

00035   002160 DATA DIVISION.                                              ACCTREPT
00036   002170                                                            ACCTREPT
00037   002180 FILE SECTION.                                               ACCTREPT
00038   002190                                                            ACCTREPT
00039   002200 FD  ACCOUNT-INPUT-FILE                                      ACCTREPT
00040   002210     RECORD CONTAINS 80 CHARACTERS                           ACCTREPT
00041   003010     LABEL RECORDS ARE OMITTED                               ACCTREPT
00042   003020     DATA RECORD IS ACCOUNT-INPUT-RECORD.                    ACCTREPT
00043   003030 01  ACCOUNT-INPUT-RECORD.                                   ACCTREPT
00044   003040     05  CUSTOMER-NUMBER-INPUT    PIC 9(5).                  ACCTREPT
00045   003050     05  CUSTOMER-NAME-INPUT      PIC X(20).                 ACCTREPT
00046   003060     05  FILLER                   PIC X(9).                  ACCTREPT
00047   003070     05  OLD-BALANCE-INPUT        PIC 9(5)V99.               ACCTREPT
00048   003080     05  PURCHASES-INPUT          PIC 9(4)V99.               ACCTREPT
00049   003090     05  FILLER                   PIC X(33).                 ACCTREPT
00050   003100                                                            ACCTREPT
00051   003110 FD  ACCOUNT-REPORT-FILE                                     ACCTREPT
00052   003120     RECORD CONTAINS 133 CHARACTERS                          ACCTREPT
00053   003130     LABEL RECORDS ARE OMITTED                               ACCTREPT
00054   003140     DATA RECORD IS ACCOUNT-REPORT-LINE.                     ACCTREPT
00055   003150 01  ACCOUNT-REPORT-LINE.                                    ACCTREPT
00056   003160     05  CARRIAGE-CONTROL         PIC X.                     ACCTREPT
00057   003170     05  FILLER                   PIC X.                     ACCTREPT
00058   003180     05  CUSTOMER-NUMBER-REPORT   PIC ZZZZ9.                 ACCTREPT
00059   003190     05  FILLER                   PIC X(5).                  ACCTREPT
00060   003200     05  CUSTOMER-NAME-REPORT     PIC X(20).                 ACCTREPT
00061   004010     05  FILLER                   PIC X(5).                  ACCTREPT
00062   004020     05  OLD-BALANCE-REPORT       PIC ZZ,ZZZ.99.             ACCTREPT
00063   004030     05  FILLER                   PIC X(5).                  ACCTREPT
00064   004040     05  PURCHASES-REPORT         PIC Z,ZZZ.99.              ACCTREPT
00065   004050     05  FILLER                   PIC X(5).                  ACCTREPT
00066   004060     05  NEW-BALANCE-REPORT       PIC $$$,$$$.99.            ACCTREPT
00067   004070     05  FILLER                   PIC X(59).                 ACCTREPT
00068   004080                                                            ACCTREPT
00069   004090 WORKING-STORAGE SECTION.                                    ACCTREPT
00070   004100                                                            ACCTREPT
00071   004110 01  PROGRAM-INDICATORS.                                     ACCTREPT
00072   004120     05  ARE-THERE-MORE-RECORDS   PIC X(3)     VALUE 'YES'.  ACCTREPT
00073   004130                                                            ACCTREPT
00074   004140 01  PRINTER-CONTROL.                                        ACCTREPT
00075   004150     05  PROPER-SPACING           PIC 9.                     ACCTREPT
00076   004160     05  SPACE-ONE-LINE           PIC 9        VALUE 1.      ACCTREPT
00077   004170     05  SPACE-TWO-LINES          PIC 9        VALUE 2.      ACCTREPT
00078   004180                                                            ACCTREPT
00079   004190 01  REPORT-HEADING.                                         ACCTREPT
00080   004200     05  CARRIAGE-CONTROL         PIC X.                     ACCTREPT
00081   005010     05  FILLER                   PIC X(8)  VALUE 'CUST NO.'. ACCTREPT
00082   005020     05  FILLER                   PIC X(11) VALUE SPACES.    ACCTREPT
00083   005030     05  FILLER                   PIC X(4)  VALUE 'NAME'.    ACCTREPT
00084   005040     05  FILLER                   PIC X(12) VALUE SPACES.    ACCTREPT
00085   005050     05  FILLER                   PIC X(11) VALUE 'OLD BALANCE'. ACCTREPT
00086   005060     05  FILLER                   PIC X(4)  VALUE SPACES.    ACCTREPT
00087   005070     05  FILLER                   PIC X(9)  VALUE 'PURCHASES'. ACCTREPT
00088   005080     05  FILLER                   PIC X(4)  VALUE SPACES.    ACCTREPT
00089   005090     05  FILLER                   PIC X(11) VALUE 'NEW BALANCE'. ACCTREPT
00090   005100     05  FILLER                   PIC X(58) VALUE SPACES.    ACCTREPT
```

Figure 4-50 Source Listing [Part 1 of 2]

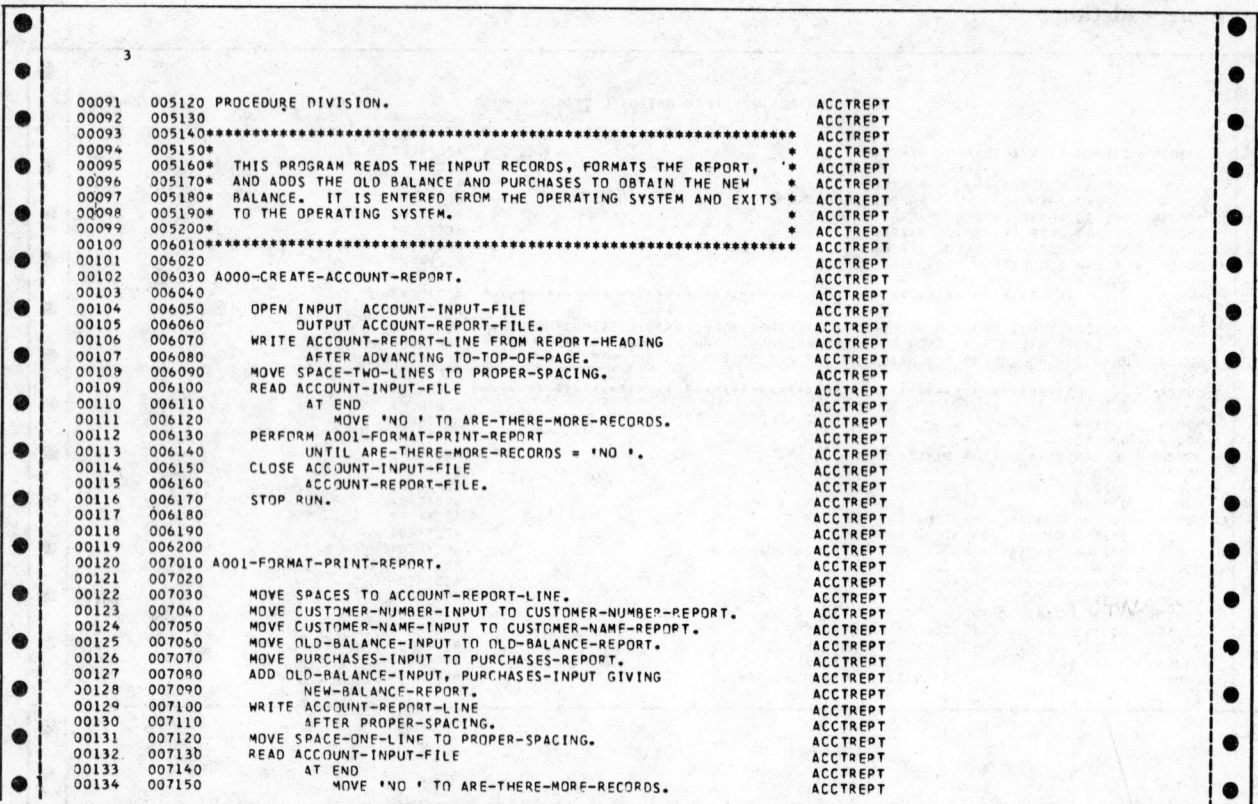

```
      3
00091  005120 PROCEDURE DIVISION.                                              ACCTREPT
00092  005130                                                                  ACCTREPT
00093  005140************************************************************      ACCTREPT
00094  005150*                                                          *      ACCTREPT
00095  005160*  THIS PROGRAM READS THE INPUT RECORDS, FORMATS THE REPORT, '*   ACCTREPT
00096  005170*  AND ADDS THE OLD BALANCE AND PURCHASES TO OBTAIN THE NEW  *    ACCTREPT
00097  005180*  BALANCE.  IT IS ENTERED FROM THE OPERATING SYSTEM AND EXITS *  ACCTREPT
00098  005190*  TO THE OPERATING SYSTEM.                                  *    ACCTREPT
00099  005200*                                                          *      ACCTREPT
00100  006010************************************************************      ACCTREPT
00101  006020                                                                  ACCTREPT
00102  006030 A000-CREATE-ACCOUNT-REPORT.                                      ACCTREPT
00103  006040                                                                  ACCTREPT
00104  006050     OPEN INPUT  ACCOUNT-INPUT-FILE                               ACCTREPT
00105  006060          OUTPUT ACCOUNT-REPORT-FILE.                             ACCTREPT
00106  006070     WRITE ACCOUNT-REPORT-LINE FROM REPORT-HEADING                ACCTREPT
00107  006080          AFTER ADVANCING TO-TOP-OF-PAGE.                         ACCTREPT
00109  006090     MOVE SPACE-TWO-LINES TO PROPER-SPACING.                      ACCTREPT
00109  006100     READ ACCOUNT-INPUT-FILE                                      ACCTREPT
00110  006110          AT END                                                  ACCTREPT
00111  006120               MOVE 'NO ' TO ARE-THERE-MORE-RECORDS.              ACCTREPT
00112  006130     PERFORM A001-FORMAT-PRINT-REPORT                             ACCTREPT
00113  006140          UNTIL ARE-THERE-MORE-RECORDS = 'NO '.                   ACCTREPT
00114  006150     CLOSE ACCOUNT-INPUT-FILE                                     ACCTREPT
00115  006160          ACCOUNT-REPORT-FILE.                                    ACCTREPT
00116  006170     STOP RUN.                                                    ACCTREPT
00117  006180                                                                  ACCTREPT
00118  006190                                                                  ACCTREPT
00119  006200                                                                  ACCTREPT
00120  007010 A001-FORMAT-PRINT-REPORT.                                        ACCTREPT
00121  007020                                                                  ACCTREPT
00122  007030     MOVE SPACES TO ACCOUNT-REPORT-LINE.                          ACCTREPT
00123  007040     MOVE CUSTOMER-NUMBER-INPUT TO CUSTOMER-NUMBER-REPORT.        ACCTREPT
00124  007050     MOVE CUSTOMER-NAME-INPUT TO CUSTOMER-NAME-REPORT.            ACCTREPT
00125  007060     MOVE OLD-BALANCE-INPUT TO OLD-BALANCE-REPORT.                ACCTREPT
00126  007070     MOVE PURCHASES-INPUT TO PURCHASES-REPORT.                    ACCTREPT
00127  007080     ADD OLD-BALANCE-INPUT, PURCHASES-INPUT GIVING                ACCTREPT
00128  007090          NEW-BALANCE-REPORT.                                     ACCTREPT
00129  007100     WRITE ACCOUNT-REPORT-LINE                                    ACCTREPT
00130  007110          AFTER PROPER-SPACING.                                   ACCTREPT
00131  007120     MOVE SPACE-ONE-LINE TO PROPER-SPACING.                       ACCTREPT
00132  007130     READ ACCOUNT-INPUT-FILE                                      ACCTREPT
00133  007140          AT END                                                  ACCTREPT
00134  007150               MOVE 'NO ' TO ARE-THERE-MORE-RECORDS.              ACCTREPT
```

Figure 4-51 Source Listing [Part 2 of 2]

OUTPUT

```
CUST NO.        NAME          OLD BALANCE   PURCHASES    NEW BALANCE

   35     ADAMS, JOE C.          100.00        50.00       $150.00
  351     BRONZ, LILA B.       9,252.50          .00     $9,252.50
 5466     CARR, JAMES L.      10,120.01     1,010.00    $11,130.01
43751     CHERRY, WILMA C.       500.00       100.00       $600.00
51223     MAYOR, HERBERT A.    7,250.25       250.00     $7,500.25
```

Figure 4-52 Program Output

CHAPTER 4

REVIEW QUESTIONS

1. When is a Picture Clause with 9's required in a COBOL program?

2. What is the purpose of a "V" in a Picture Clause?

3. Write the COBOL Statement to add the fields REGULAR-EARNINGS-INPUT and OVERTIME-EARNINGS-INPUT, storing the answer in TOTAL-EARNINGS-REPORT.

4. Write the COBOL Statement to add the fields QTR1-INPUT, QTR2-INPUT, and QTR3-INPUT, storing the answer in TOTAL-REPORT.

5. Write the COBOL Statement to add the field SALES-BONUS-INPUT and 5.00, storing the answer in TOTAL-COMMISSION.

6. Explain the rules for construction of a numeric literal.

7. Write the COBOL Statement to add the field NEW-BALANCE to the field NEW-BALANCE-ACCUM, storing the answer in the field NEW-BALANCE-ACCUM.

8. Write the COBOL Statement to subtract the field SALES-RETURNS-INPUT from the field SALES-INPUT, storing the answer in NET-SALES.

9. Write the COBOL Statement to subtract the numeric literal 10.00 from DEDUCTIONS-WORK, storing the answer in DEDUCTIONS-WORK.

10. Write the Picture Clause to cause a six digit field to be printed with a fixed dollar sign, a comma, and a decimal point. The field is to be zero suppressed up to the decimal point. There are to be two positions to the right of the decimal point in the edited field.

11. Write the Picture Clause to cause a six digit field to be printed with a floating dollar sign, a comma, and a decimal point. The field is to be zero suppressed up to the decimal point. There are to be two positions to the right of the decimal point in the edited field.

12. Explain the operation of the Move Statement when the sending and receiving fields are defined as numeric (Picture 9's).

13. What determines where the first printing line occurs on a report?

14. Explain the entries in the SPECIAL-NAMES Paragraph as related to the printing of report headings.

CHAPTER 4

DEBUGGING COBOL PROGRAMS

PROBLEM 1

INSTRUCTIONS

The following COBOL program contains an error or errors which have occurred during compilation. Circle each error and record the corrected entries directly on the listing. Explain the error and method of correction in the space provided on page 4.42

```
    1                    IBM DOS AMERICAN NATIONAL STANDARD COBOL       CBF CL3-4        05/20/77

00001   001010 IDENTIFICATION DIVISION.                                    ACCTREPT
00002   001020                                                             ACCTREPT
00003   001030 PROGRAM-ID.    ACCTREPT.                                    ACCTREPT
00004   001040 AUTHOR.        SHELLY AND CASHMAN.                          ACCTREPT
00005   001050 INSTALLATION.  ANAHEIM.                                     ACCTREPT
00006   001060 DATE-WRITTEN.  05/20/77.                                    ACCTREPT
00007   001070 DATE-COMPILED. 05/20/77                                     ACCTREPT
00008   001080 SECURITY.      UNCLASSIFIED.                                ACCTREPT
00009   001090                                                            ACCTREPT
00010   001100*************************************************************** ACCTREPT
00011   001110*                                                          * ACCTREPT
00012   001120*   THIS PROGRAM PRODUCES AN ACCOUNTING REPORT, LISTING THE NEW * ACCTREPT
00013   001130*   BALANCE IN EACH CUSTOMER ACCOUNT.  NEW BALANCE IS CALCULATED* ACCTREPT
00014   001140*   BY ADDING PURCHASES TO THE CUSTOMER'S OLD BALANCE.     * ACCTREPT
00015   001150*                                                          * ACCTREPT
00016   001160*************************************************************** ACCTREPT
00017   001170                                                            ACCTREPT
00018   001180                                                            ACCTREPT
00019   001190                                                            ACCTREPT
00020   001200 ENVIRONMENT DIVISION.                                       ACCTREPT
00021   002010                                                            ACCTREPT
00022   002020 CONFIGURATION SECTION.                                      ACCTREPT
00023   002030                                                            ACCTREPT
00024   002040 SOURCE-COMPUTER. IBM-370.                                   ACCTREPT
00025   002050 OBJECT-COMPUTER. IBM-370.                                   ACCTREPT
00026   002060 SPECIAL-NAMES.   C01 IS TO-TOP-OF-PAGE.                     ACCTREPT
00027   002070                                                            ACCTREPT
00028   002080 INPUT-OUTPUT SECTION.                                       ACCTREPT
00029   002090                                                            ACCTREPT
00030   002100 FILE-CONTROL.                                               ACCTREPT
00031   002110     SELECT ACCOUNT-INPUT-FILE                               ACCTREPT
00032   002120.        ASSIGN TO SYS007-UR-2540R-S.                        ACCTREPT
00033   002130     SELECT ACCOUNT-REPORT-FILE                              ACCTREPT
00034   002140        ASSIGN TO SYS013-UR-1403-S.                          ACCTREPT
```

```
    2

00035   002160 DATA DIVISION.                                              ACCTREPT
00036   002170                                                            ACCTREPT
00037   002180 FILE SECTION.                                               ACCTREPT
00038   002190                                                            ACCTREPT
00039   002200 FD  ACCOUNT-INPUT-FILE                                      ACCTREPT
00040   002210     RECORD CONTAINS 80 CHARACTERS                           ACCTREPT
00041   003010     LABEL RECORDS ARE OMITTED                               ACCTREPT
00042   003020     DATA RECORD IS ACCOUNT-INPUT-RECORD.                    ACCTREPT
00043   003030 01  ACCOUNT-INPUT-RECORD.                                   ACCTREPT
00044   003040     05  CUSTOMER-NUMBER-INPUT   PIC 9(5).                   ACCTREPT
00045   003050     05  CUSTOMER-NAME-INPUT     PIC X(20).                  ACCTREPT
00046   003060     05  FILLER                  PIC X(9).                   ACCTREPT
00047   003070     05  OLD-BALANCE-INPUT       PIC 9(5)V99.                ACCTREPT
00048   003080     05  PURCHASES-INPUT         PIC 9(4)V99.                ACCTREPT
00049   003090     05  FILLER                  PIC X(33).                  ACCTREPT
00050   003100                                                            ACCTREPT
00051   003110 FD  ACCOUNT-REPORT-FILE                                     ACCTREPT
00052   003120     RECORD CONTAINS 133 CHARACTERS                          ACCTREPT
00053   003130     LABEL RECORDS ARE OMITTED                               ACCTREPT
00054   003140     DATA RECORD IS ACCOUNT-REPORT-LINE.                     ACCTREPT
00055   003150 01  ACCOUNT-REPORT-LINE.                                    ACCTREPT
00056   003160     05  CARRIAGE-CONTROL        PIC X.                      ACCTREPT
00057   003170     05  FILLER                  PIC X.                      ACCTREPT
00058   003180     05  CUSTOMER-NUMBER-REPORT  PIC ZZZZ9.                  ACCTREPT
00059   003190     05  FILLER                  PIC X(5).                   ACCTREPT
00060   003200     05  CUSTOMER-NAME-REPORT    PIC X(20).                  ACCTREPT
00061   004010     05  FILLER                  PIC X(5).                   ACCTREPT
00062   004020     05  OLD-BALANCE-REPORT      PIC ZZ,ZZZ.99.              ACCTREPT
00063   004030     05  FILLER                  PIC X(5).                   ACCTREPT
00064   004040     05  PURCHASES-REPORT        PIC Z,ZZZ.99.               ACCTREPT
00065   004050     05  FILLER                  PIC X(5).                   ACCTREPT
00066   004060     05  NEW-BALANCE-REPORT      PIC $$,$$$.99.              ACCTREPT
00067   004070     05  FILLER                  PIC X(59).                  ACCTREPT
00068   004080                                                            ACCTREPT
```

```
   3
00069  004090  WORKING-STORAGE SECTION.                                    ACCTREPT
00070  004100                                                              ACCTREPT
00071  004110  01  PROGRAM-INDICATORS.                                     ACCTREPT
00072  004120      05  ARE-THERE-MORE-RECORDS  PIC X(3)      VALUE YES.    ACCTREPT
00073  004130                                                              ACCTREPT
00074  004140  01  PRINTER-CONTROL.                                        ACCTREPT
00075  004150      05  PROPER-SPACING          PIC 9.                      ACCTREPT
00076  004160      05  SPACE-ONE-LINE          PIC 9        VALUE 1.       ACCTREPT
00077  004170      05  SPACE-TWO-LINES         PIC 9        VALUE 2.       ACCTREPT
00078  004180                                                              ACCTREPT
00079  004190  01  REPORT-HEADINGS.                                        ACCTREPT
00080  004200      05  CARRIAGE-CONTROL        PIC X.                      ACCTREPT
00081  005010      05  FILLER                  PIC X(8)     VALUE 'CUST NO.'. ACCTREPT
00082  005020      05  FILLER                  PIC X(11)    VALUE SPACES.  ACCTREPT
00083  005030      05  FILLER                  PIC X(4)     VALUE 'NAME'.  ACCTREPT
00084  005040      05  FILLER                  PIC X(12)    VALUE SPACES.  ACCTREPT
00085  005050      05  FILLER                  PIC X(11)    VALUE 'OLD BALANCE'.ACCTREPT
00086  005060      05  FILLER                  PIC X(4)     VALUE SPACES.  ACCTREPT
00087  005070      05  FILLER                  PIC X(9)     VALUE 'PURCHASES'. ACCTREPT
00088  005080      05  FILLER                  PIC X(4)     VALUE SPACES.  ACCTREPT
00089  005090      05  FILLER                  PIC X(11)    VALUE 'NEW BALANCE'.ACCTREPT
00090  005100      05  FILLER                  PIC X(58)    VALUE SPACES.  ACCTREPT
```

```
   4
00091  005120  PROCEDURE DIVISION.                                         ACCTREPT
00092  005130                                                              ACCTREPT
00093  005140*********************************************************************ACCTREPT
00094  005150*                                                          *  ACCTREPT
00095  005160*  THIS PROGRAM READS THE INPUT RECORDS, FORMATS THE REPORT, * ACCTREPT
00096  005170*  AND ADDS THE OLD BALANCE AND PURCHASES TO OBTAIN THE NEW * ACCTREPT
00097  005180*  BALANCE.  IT IS ENTERED FROM THE OPERATING SYSTEM AND EXITS * ACCTREPT
00098  005190*  TO THE OPERATING SYSTEM.                                 *  ACCTREPT
00099  005200*                                                          *  ACCTREPT
00100  006010*********************************************************************ACCTREPT
00101  006020                                                              ACCTREPT
00102  006030  A000-CREATE-ACCOUNT-REPORT.                                 ACCTREPT
00103  006040                                                              ACCTREPT
00104  006050      OPEN INPUT  ACCOUNT-INPUT-FILE                          ACCTREPT
00105  006060           OUTPUT ACCOUNT-REPORT-FILE.                        ACCTREPT
00106  006070      WRITE REPORT-HEADINGS                                   ACCTREPT
00107  006080          AFTER ADVANCING TO-TOP-OF-PAGE.                     ACCTREPT
00108  006090      MOVE SPACE-TWO-LINES TO PROPER-SPACING.                 ACCTREPT
00109  006100      READ ACCOUNT-INPUT-FILE                                 ACCTREPT
00110  006110          AT END                                             ACCTREPT
00111  006120              MOVE 'NO ' TO ARE-THERE-MORE-RECORDS.           ACCTREPT
00112  006130      PERFORM A001-FORMAT-PRINT-REPORT                        ACCTREPT
00113  006140          UNTIL ARE-THERE-MORE-RECORDS = 'NO '.               ACCTREPT
00114  006150      CLOSE ACCOUNT-INPUT-FILE                                ACCTREPT
00115  006160            ACCOUNT-REPORT-FILE.                              ACCTREPT
00116  006170      STOP RUN.                                               ACCTREPT
00117  006180                                                              ACCTREPT
00118  006190                                                              ACCTREPT
00119  006200                                                              ACCTREPT
00120  007010  A001-FORMAT-PRINT-REPORT.                                   ACCTREPT
00121  007020                                                              ACCTREPT
00122  007030      MOVE SPACES TO ACCOUNT-REPORT-LINE.                     ACCTREPT
00123  007040      MOVE CUSTOMER-NUMBER-INPUT TO CUSTOMER-NUMBER-REPORT.   ACCTREPT
00124  007050      MOVE CUSTOMER-NAME-INPUT TO CUSTOMER-NAME-REPORT.       ACCTREPT
00125  007060      MOVE OLD-BALANCE-INPUT TO OLD-BALANCE-REPORT.           ACCTREPT
00126  007070      MOVE PURCHASES-INPUT TO PURCHASES-REPORT.               ACCTREPT
00127  007080      ADD OLD-BALANCE-INPUT TO PURCHASES-INPUT GIVING         ACCTREPT
00128  007090          NEW-BALANCE-REPORT.                                 ACCTREPT
00129  007100      WRITE ACCOUNT-REPORT-LINE                               ACCTREPT
00130  007110          AFTER PROPER-SPACING.                               ACCTREPT
00131  007120      MOVE SPACE-ONE-LINE TO PROPER-SPACING.                  ACCTREPT
00132  007130      READ ACCOUNT-INPUT-FILE                                 ACCTREPT
00133  007140          AT END                                             ACCTREPT
00134  007150              MOVE 'NO ' TO ARE-THERE-MORE-RECORDS.           ACCTREPT
```

```
   6

CARD   ERROR MESSAGE

 33    ILA2146I-W    RECORD CONTAINS DISAGREES WITH COMPUTED MAXIMUM. USING COMPUTED MAXIMUM.
 72    ILA1017I-E    YES INVALID IN VALUE CLAUSE. SKIPPING TO NEXT CLAUSE.
106    ILA4050I-E    SYNTAX REQUIRES RECORD-NAME . FOUND DNM=2-363 . STATEMENT DISCARDED.
106    ILA3001I-E    TO-TOP-OF-PAGE NOT DEFINED.
127    ILA4008I-W    SUPERFLUOUS TO FOUND IN ADD STATEMENT. IGNORED.
127    ILA5011I-W    HIGH ORDER TRUNCATION MIGHT OCCUR.
134    ILA4072I-W    EXIT FROM PERFORMED PROCEDURE ASSUMED BEFORE PROCEDURE-NAME .

ILA0004I- LINK OPTION RESET -- D OR E LEVEL ERROR FOUND
```

EXPLANATION

_____

_____

_____

_____

CHAPTER 4

DEBUGGING COBOL PROGRAMS

PROBLEM 2

INSTRUCTIONS

The following COBOL program contains an error or errors which occur during execution. Circle each error and record the corrected entries directly on the listing. Explain the error and method of correction in the space provided on page 4.44.

```
        1                          IBM DOS AMERICAN NATIONAL STANDARD COBOL        CBF CL3-4        05/20/77

   00001    001010 IDENTIFICATION DIVISION.                                         ACCTREPT
   00002    001020                                                                  ACCTREPT
   00003    001030 PROGRAM-ID.      ACCTREPT.                                       ACCTREPT
   00004    001040 AUTHOR.          SHELLY AND CASHMAN.                             ACCTREPT
   00005    001050 INSTALLATION.    ANAHEIM.                                        ACCTREPT
   00006    001060 DATE-WRITTEN.    05/20/77.                                       ACCTREPT
   00007    001070 DATE-COMPILED.   05/20/77                                        ACCTREPT
   00008    001080 SECURITY.        UNCLASSIFIED.                                   ACCTREPT
   00009    001090                                                                  ACCTREPT
   00010    001100***********************************************************       ACCTREPT
   00011    001110*                                                         *       ACCTREPT
   00012    001120*  THIS PROGRAM PRODUCES AN ACCOUNTING REPORT, LISTING THE NEW *  ACCTREPT
   00013    001130*  BALANCE IN EACH CUSTOMER ACCOUNT.  NEW BALANCE IS CALCULATED* ACCTREPT
   00014    001140*  BY ADDING PURCHASES TO THE CUSTOMER'S OLD BALANCE.        *    ACCTREPT
   00015    001150*                                                         *       ACCTREPT
   00016    001160***********************************************************       ACCTREPT
   00017    001170                                                                  ACCTREPT
   00018    001180                                                                  ACCTREPT
   00019    001190                                                                  ACCTREPT
   00020    001200 ENVIRONMENT DIVISION.                                            ACCTREPT
   00021    002010                                                                  ACCTREPT
   00022    002020 CONFIGURATION SECTION.                                           ACCTREPT
   00023    002030                                                                  ACCTREPT
   00024    002040 SOURCE-COMPUTER. IBM-370.                                        ACCTREPT
   00025    002050 OBJECT-COMPUTER. IBM-370.                                        ACCTREPT
   00026    002060 SPECIAL-NAMES.   C01 IS TO-TOP-OF-PAGE.                          ACCTREPT
   00027    002070                                                                  ACCTREPT
   00028    002080 INPUT-OUTPUT SECTION.                                            ACCTREPT
   00029    002090                                                                  ACCTREPT
   00030    002100 FILE-CONTROL.                                                    ACCTREPT
   00031    002110     SELECT ACCOUNT-INPUT-FILE                                    ACCTREPT
   00032    002120         ASSIGN TO SYS007-UR-2540R-S.                             ACCTREPT
   00033    002130     SELECT ACCOUNT-REPORT-FILE                                   ACCTREPT
   00034    002140         ASSIGN TO SYS013-UR-1403-S.                              ACCTREPT


        2

   00035    002160 DATA DIVISION.                                                   ACCTREPT
   00036    002170                                                                  ACCTREPT
   00037    002180 FILE SECTION.                                                    ACCTREPT
   00038    002190                                                                  ACCTREPT
   00039    002200 FD  ACCOUNT-INPUT-FILE                                           ACCTREPT
   00040    002210     RECORD CONTAINS 80 CHARACTERS                                ACCTREPT
   00041    003010     LABEL RECORDS ARE OMITTED                                    ACCTREPT
   00042    003020     DATA RECORD IS ACCOUNT-INPUT-RECORD.                         ACCTREPT
   00043    003030 01  ACCOUNT-INPUT-RECORD.                                        ACCTREPT
   00044    003040     05  CUSTOMER-NUMBER-INPUT   PIC 9(5).                        ACCTREPT
   00045    003050     05  CUSTOMER-NAME-INPUT     PIC X(20).                       ACCTREPT
   00046    003060     05  FILLER                  PIC X(9).                        ACCTREPT
   00047    003070     05  OLD-BALANCE-INPUT       PIC 9(5)V99.                     ACCTREPT
   00048    003080     05  PURCHASES-INPUT         PIC 9(4)V99.                     ACCTREPT
   00049    003090     05  FILLER                  PIC X(33).                       ACCTREPT
   00050    003100                                                                  ACCTREPT
   00051    003110 FD  ACCOUNT-REPORT-FILE                                          ACCTREPT
   00052    003120     RECORD CONTAINS 133 CHARACTERS                               ACCTREPT
   00053    003130     LABEL RECORDS ARE OMITTED                                    ACCTREPT
   00054    003140     DATA RECORD IS ACCOUNT-REPORT-LINE.                          ACCTREPT
   00055    003150 01  ACCOUNT-REPORT-LINE.                                         ACCTREPT
   00056    003160     05  CARRIAGE-CONTROL        PIC X.                           ACCTREPT
   00057    003170     05  FILLER                  PIC X.                           ACCTREPT
   00058    003180     05  CUSTOMER-NUMBER-REPORT  PIC ZZZZ9.                       ACCTREPT
   00059    003190     05  FILLER                  PIC X(5).                        ACCTREPT
   00060    003200     05  CUSTOMER-NAME-REPORT    PIC X(20).                       ACCTREPT
   00061    004010     05  FILLER                  PIC X(5).                        ACCTREPT
   00062    004020     05  OLD-BALANCE-REPORT      PIC ZZ,ZZZV99.                   ACCTREPT
   00063    004030     05  FILLER                  PIC X(5).                        ACCTREPT
   00064    004040     05  PURCHASES-REPORT        PIC Z,ZZZV99.                    ACCTREPT
   00065    004050     05  FILLER                  PIC X(5).                        ACCTREPT
   00066    004060     05  NEW-BALANCE-REPORT      PIC $$$,$$$V99.                  ACCTREPT
   00067    004070     05  FILLER                  PIC X(59).                       ACCTREPT
   00068    004080                                                                  ACCTREPT
```

```
      3
   00069   004090 WORKING-STORAGE SECTION.                              ACCTREPT
   00070   004100                                                       ACCTREPT
   00071   004110 01  PROGRAM-INDICATORS.                               ACCTREPT
   00072   004120     05  ARE-THERE-MORE-RECORDS  PIC X(3)   VALUE 'YES'. ACCTREPT
   00073   004130                                                       ACCTREPT
   00074   004140 01  PRINTER-CONTROL.                                  ACCTREPT
   00075   004150     05  PROPER-SPACING          PIC 9.               ACCTREPT
   00076   004160     05  SPACE-ONE-LINE          PIC 9.     VALUE 1.  ACCTREPT
   00077   004170     05  SPACE-TWO-LINES         PIC 9.     VALUE 2.  ACCTREPT
   00078   004180                                                       ACCTREPT
   00079   004190 01  REPORT-HEADINGS.                                  ACCTREPT
   00080   004200     05  CARRIAGE-CONTROL        PIC X.               ACCTREPT
   00081   005010     05  FILLER                  PIC X(8)   VALUE 'CUST NO.'. ACCTREPT
   00082   005020     05  FILLER                  PIC X(11)  VALUE SPACES.    ACCTREPT
   00083   005030     05  FILLER                  PIC X(4)   VALUE 'NAME'.    ACCTREPT
   00084   005040     05  FILLER                  PIC X(12)  VALUE SPACES.    ACCTREPT
   00085   005050     05  FILLER                  PIC X(11)  VALUE 'OLD BALANCE'. ACCTREPT
   00086   005060     05  FILLER                  PIC X(4)   VALUE SPACES.    ACCTREPT
   00087   005070     05  FILLER                  PIC X(9)   VALUE 'PURCHASES'. ACCTREPT
   00088   005080     05  FILLER                  PIC X(4)   VALUE SPACES.    ACCTREPT
   00089   005090     05  FILLER                  PIC X(11)  VALUE 'NEW BALANCE'. ACCTREPT
   00090   005100     05  FILLER                  PIC X(58)  VALUE SPACES.    ACCTREPT
```

```
      4
   00091   005120 PROCEDURE DIVISION.                                   ACCTREPT
   00092   005130                                                       ACCTREPT
   00093   005140**********************************************************  ACCTREPT
   00094   005150*                                                       *  ACCTREPT
   00095   005160*  THIS PROGRAM READS THE INPUT RECORDS, FORMATS THE REPORT, * ACCTREPT
   00096   005170*  AND ADDS THE OLD BALANCE AND PURCHASES TO OBTAIN THE NEW  * ACCTREPT
   00097   005180*  BALANCE.  IT IS ENTERED FROM THE OPERATING SYSTEM AND EXITS * ACCTREPT
   00098   005190*  TO THE OPERATING SYSTEM.                            *  ACCTREPT
   00099   005200*                                                       *  ACCTREPT
   00100   006010**********************************************************  ACCTREPT
   00101   006020                                                       ACCTREPT
   00102   006030 A000-CREATE-ACCOUNT-REPORT.                           ACCTREPT
   00103   006040                                                       ACCTREPT
   00104   006050     OPEN INPUT  ACCOUNT-INPUT-FILE                    ACCTREPT
   00105   006060          OUTPUT ACCOUNT-REPORT-FILE.                  ACCTREPT
   00106   006070     WRITE ACCOUNT-REPORT-LINE FROM REPORT-HEADINGS    ACCTREPT
   00107   006080         AFTER ADVANCING TO-TOP-OF-PAGE.               ACCTREPT
   00108   006090     MOVE SPACE-TWO-LINES TO PROPER-SPACING.           ACCTREPT
   00109   006100     READ ACCOUNT-INPUT-FILE                           ACCTREPT
   00110   006110         AT END                                        ACCTREPT
   00111   006120             MOVE 'NO ' TO ARE-THERE-MORE-RECORDS.     ACCTREPT
   00112   006130     PERFORM A001-FORMAT-PRINT-REPORT                  ACCTREPT
   00113   006140         UNTIL ARE-THERE-MORE-RECORDS = 'NO '.         ACCTREPT
   00114   006150     CLOSE ACCOUNT-INPUT-FILE                          ACCTREPT
   00115   006160           ACCOUNT-REPORT-FILE.                        ACCTREPT
   00116   006170     STOP RUN.                                         ACCTREPT
   00117   006180                                                       ACCTREPT
   00118   006190                                                       ACCTREPT
   00119   006200                                                       ACCTREPT
   00120   007010 A001-FORMAT-PRINT-REPORT.                             ACCTREPT
   00121   007020                                                       ACCTREPT
   00122   007030     MOVE SPACES TO ACCOUNT-REPORT-LINE.               ACCTREPT
   00123   007040     MOVE CUSTOMER-NUMBER-INPUT TO CUSTOMER-NUMBER-REPORT. ACCTREPT
   00124   007050     MOVE CUSTOMER-NAME-INPUT TO CUSTOMER-NAME-REPORT. ACCTREPT
   00125   007060     MOVE OLD-BALANCE-INPUT TO OLD-BALANCE-REPORT.     ACCTREPT
   00126   007070     MOVE PURCHASES-INPUT TO PURCHASES-REPORT.         ACCTREPT
   00127   007080     ADD OLD-BALANCE-INPUT, PURCHASES-INPUT GIVING     ACCTREPT
   00128   007090         NEW-BALANCE-REPORT.                           ACCTREPT
   00129   007100     WRITE ACCOUNT-REPORT-LINE                         ACCTREPT
   00130   007110         AFTER PROPER-SPACING.                         ACCTREPT
   00131   007120     MOVE SPACE-ONE-LINE TO PROPER-SPACING.            ACCTREPT
   00132   007130     READ ACCOUNT-INPUT-FILE                           ACCTREPT
   00133   007140         AT END                                        ACCTREPT
   00134   007150             MOVE 'NO ' TO ARE-THERE-MORE-RECORDS.     ACCTREPT
```

```
      6

   CARD    ERROR MESSAGE

    33     ILA2146I-W    RECORD CONTAINS DISAGREES WITH COMPUTED MAXIMUM. USING COMPUTED MAXIMUM.
   127     ILA5011I-W    HIGH ORDER TRUNCATION MIGHT OCCUR.
   134     ILA4072I-W    EXIT FROM PERFORMED PROCEDURE ASSUMED BEFORE PROCEDURE-NAME .
```

CUST NO.	NAME	OLD BALANCE	PURCHASES	NEW BALANCE
35	ADAMS, JOE C.	10000	5000	$15000
351	BRONZ, LILA B.	9,25250	00	$9,25250
5466	CARR, JAMES L.	10,12001	1,01000	$11,13001
43751	CHERRY, WILMA C.	50000	10000	$60000
51223	MAYOR, HERBERT A.	7,25025	25000	$7,50025

EXPLANATION

_____

_____

_____

CHAPTER 4

PROGRAMMING ASSIGNMENT 1

INSTRUCTIONS

A Payroll Register is to be prepared. Design and write the COBOL program to produce the required report. An IPO Chart and Pseudocode Specifications should be used when designing the program. Use Test Data Set 1, in Appendix A.

INPUT

Input is to consist of Payroll Cards that contain the Employee Number, the Employee Name, Regular Earnings, and Overtime Earnings. The format of the Payroll Card is illustrated below.

OUTPUT

Output is to consist of a Payroll Register. Total Earnings are to be calculated by adding Regular Earnings and Overtime Earnings. Regular Earnings and Overtime Earnings are to be zero suppressed. Total Earnings is to be printed with a floating dollar sign. The printer spacing chart for the report is illustrated below.

CHAPTER 4

PROGRAMMING ASSIGNMENT 2

INSTRUCTIONS

A Sales Analysis Report is to be prepared. Design and write the COBOL program to produce the required report. An IPO Chart and Pseudocode Specifications should be used when designing the program. Use Test Data Set 1 in Appendix A.

INPUT

Input is to consist of Sales Cards that contain an Item Number, Item Description, Sales Amount and Sales Returns. The format of the Sales Card is illustrated below.

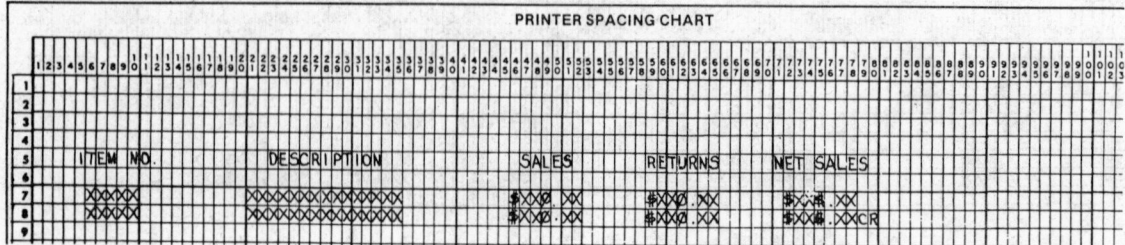

OUTPUT

Output is to consist of a Sales Analysis Report containing Net Sales. Net Sales is calculated by subtracting the Sales Returns from the Sales Amount. The Sales Amount and Sales Returns fields are to be printed with a fixed dollar sign. The Net Sales field is to be printed with a floating dollar sign. If the calculated Net Sales is negative, a credit symbol (CR) is to be printed. The printer spacing chart is illustrated below.

CHAPTER 4

PROGRAMMING ASSIGNMENT 3

INSTRUCTIONS

A Sales Report is to be prepared. Design and write the COBOL program to produce the required report. An IPO Chart and Pseudocode Specifications should be used when designing the program. Use Test Data Set 1 contained in Appendix A.

INPUT

Input is to consist of Sales Cards containing the sales for January, February, March and April. The format of the Sales Cards is illustrated below.

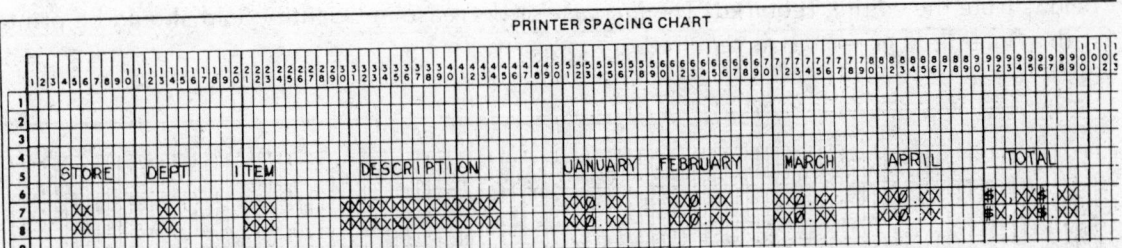

OUTPUT

Output is to consist of a Sales Report for the first four months of this year; that is, the total sales for January, February, March, and April are to be accumulated and printed. The Total Sales field is to be edited with a floating dollar sign. The printer spacing chart is illustrated below.

CHAPTER 4

PROGRAMMING ASSIGNMENT 4

INSTRUCTIONS

A Comparative Sales Report is to be prepared. Design and write the COBOL program to produce the required report. An IPO Chart and Pseudocode Specifications should be used when designing the program. Use Test Data Set 1, in Appendix A.

INPUT

Input is to consist of Sales Cards containing the Item Number, the Description, Quantity Sold Last Year, Quantity Sold This Year, the Sales Amount Last Year, and the Sales Amount This Year. The format of the Sales Cards is illustrated below.

OUTPUT

Output is to consist of a Comparative Sales Report. The Quantity Sold Last Year is to be subtracted from the Quantity Sold This Year to obtain the increase or decrease in the Quantity Sold. Also, the Sales Amount Last Year is to be subtracted from the Sales Amount This Year to obtain the increase or decrease in the Amount Sold. The printer spacing chart is illustrated below. Note the editing required. The increase or decrease in Quantity Sold should be printed with a floating + or − sign as required.

MULTIPLY; DIVIDE; COMPUTE

5

> *Readability is the best single criterion of program quality: If a program is easy to read it is probably a good program; if it is hard to read, it probably isn't good.* [1]

INTRODUCTION

In the previous chapter, the Addition and Subtraction operations were introduced. The Multiplication and Division operations are also important tools when programming business applications. In addition, many arithmetic operations which are performed in business applications require that the answers be stored in intermediate storage areas so that they can be used in subsequent calculations.

In order to illustrate these concepts, the sample program in this chapter will produce a Loan Report. The format of the report is illustrated in Figure 5-1.

ACCOUNT NUMBER	NAME	LOAN AMOUNT	INTEREST RATE	INTEREST AMOUNT	TOTAL AMOUNT	NO OF PMTS	MONTHLY PAYMENT
11993	AHERS, ROSCOE R.	2,000.00	18%	360.00	2,360.00	12	$ 196.67
111213	BACKER, OTTO A.	10,000.00	18%	1,800.00	11,800.00	20	$ 590.00
185431	MENLO, SEYMOUR D.	500.00	18%	90.00	590.00	12	$ 49.17
522121	HUNTER, JESSE C.	6,000.54	18%	1,080.10	7,080.64	36	$ 196.68
777255	JAWLEY, SUSAN C.	12,300.00	18%	2,214.00	14,514.00	60	$ 241.90

Figure 5-1 Loan Report

Note from Figure 5-1 that the report contains an Account Number, Name, Loan Amount, Interest Rate, Interest Amount, Total Amount, Number of Payments, and Monthly Payment.

---

1 Kernighan, B. W. and Plauger, P. J., *SOFTWARE TOOLS*, Addison-Wesley Publishing Company, 1976

The input required to prepare the Loan Report is a Loan Report Card File. The format of the Loan Cards is illustrated below.

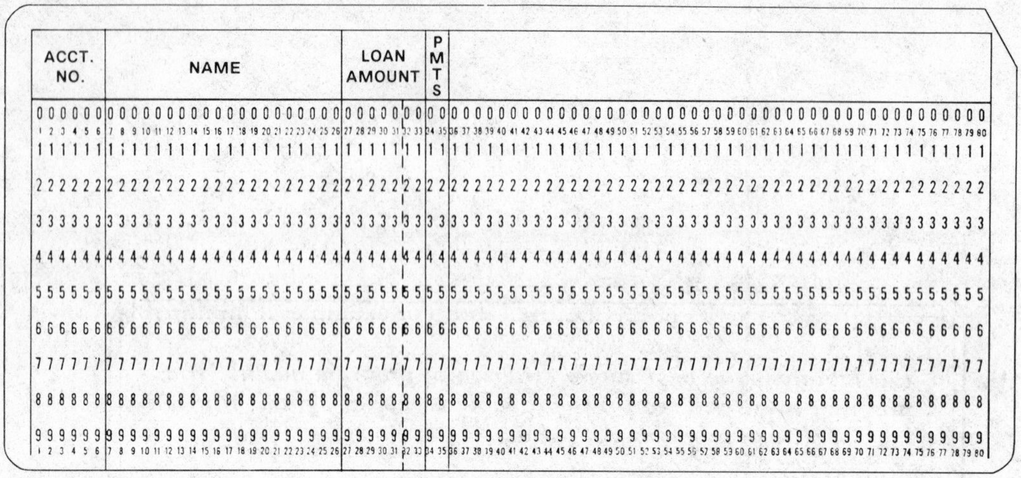

Figure 5-2 Input

From the card illustrated above, it can be seen that the input record contains the Account Number, the Name, the Loan Amount, and the Number of Payments.

From the report and the input it can be seen that the Interest Amount must be calculated by multiplying the Loan Amount by the Interest Rate. The Total Amount must then be calculated by adding the Interest Amount to the Loan Amount. The Monthly Payment is determined by dividing the Total Amount by the Number of Payments.

Thus, addition, multiplication, and division must be performed to produce the required output.

MULTIPLICATION

When performing multiplication operations, it is important for the programmer to understand the procedure for determining the maximum size answer that may develop as a result of the multiplication operation; and it is also important to understand the method of rounding answers.

Determining Maximum Size Answers

In performing any multiplication operation, manually or with a computer, the maximum size of the answer that may develop can be determined by adding the number of digits in the multiplier to the number of digits in the multiplicand. For example, if multiplying a seven digit Loan Amount field by a two digit Interest Rate field, the maximum size of the answer that may develop is nine digits in length. This is illustrated below.

EXAMPLE

```
     99,999.99  LOAN AMOUNT [Multiplicand]
          .99   INTEREST RATE [Multiplier]
     89999991
     89999991
     98,999.9901  [Maximum size answer - 9 digits in length]
```

Figure 5-3 Example of Multiplication

Note from Figure 5-3 that even when the largest possible numbers for the Loan Amount and the Interest Rate are multiplied together, the most digits which can be in the answer (9) is the sum of the number of digits in the multiplicand (7) plus the number of digits in the multiplier (2).

It should be noted also that the number of positions to the right of the decimal point in the answer of a multiplication operation is the sum of the number of digits to the right of the decimal point in the multiplicand plus the number of digits to the right of the decimal point in the multiplier. Thus, in the example in Figure 5-3 the number of digits to the right of the decimal point in the answer is four, since there are two digits to the right of the decimal point in the Loan Amount and two in the Interest Rate.

It is important that the programmer understand these basic concepts of arithmetic in order to properly perform multiplication operations using the computer.

Rounding

In programming for business applications involving decimal positions in the answer, it is frequently desirable to round off the answer. For example, if the answer in a problem is developed as 987.768, it may be desirable to round the answer to 987.77 so that the answer can be expressed in terms of dollars and cents. If the answer to the problem is 987.763, then after rounding the value used for dollars and cents would be 987.76. Note in the preceeding examples that if the low order position is less than 5, the amount is not rounded upward; if the low order position is 5 or more, the amount is rounded upward.

When programming in COBOL, rounding is accomplished by the use of the "ROUNDED" option, which is available with all arithmetic statements.

MULTIPLY STATEMENT

When multiplying in COBOL, the Multiply Statement is used. The Multiply Statement to multiply a Loan Amount by an Interest Rate to obtain the Interest Amount is illustrated below.

EXAMPLE

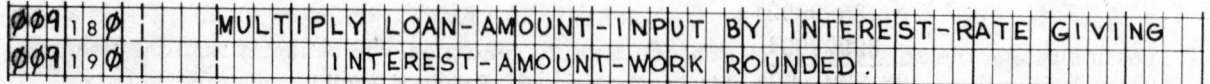

```
Ø Ø 9  1 8 Ø       MULTIPLY LOAN-AMOUNT-INPUT BY INTEREST-RATE GIVING
Ø Ø 9  1 9 Ø              INTEREST-AMOUNT-WORK ROUNDED.
```

```
MULTIPLY  {identifier-1}  BY  {identifier-2}  GIVING identifier-3  [ROUNDED]
          {literal-1   }      {literal-2   }

          [, identifier-4  [ROUNDED]]  ...  [; ON SIZE ERROR imperative-statement]
```

Figure 5-4 Example of Multiply Statement

The Multiply Statement begins with the word MULTIPLY, which is required. When the Giving option is used, as in the example, the value in the identifier-1 field is multiplied by the value in the identifier-2 field and the answer is stored in the identifier-3, identifier-4, . . . fields which follow the word GIVING. Thus, in the example, the value in the field LOAN-AMOUNT-INPUT would be multiplied by the value in the field INTEREST-RATE and the answer would be stored in the INTEREST-AMOUNT-WORK field.

It will be noted also from the general format that literals can be used for the first and second operands.

The word ROUNDED is used following identifier-3 (INTEREST-AMOUNT-WORK) to indicate that the answer to the multiplication operation should be rounded prior to being placed in the field. Rounding takes place as was discussed previously. It should be noted that if the word ROUNDED is not specified in the Multiply Statement, truncation will occur on those digits for which there is not room in the identifier-3 Picture Clause. The results after both rounding and truncation are illustrated in Figure 5-5.

Calculated Result	Item to Receive Calculated Result		
	PICTURE	Value After Rounding	Value After Truncating
12.36	99V9	12ᵢ4	12ᵢ3
8.432	9V9	8ᵢ4	8ᵢ4
35.6	99V9	35ᵢ6	35ᵢ6
65.6	99V	66ᵢ	65ᵢ
.0055	V999	ᵢ006	ᵢ005

ᵢ = Assumed Decimal Point

Figure 5-5 Example of Rounding and Truncation

It should be noted that in most business application programs, rounding is performed instead of truncation. Therefore, as a general rule, whenever it is possible that an answer will develop with more digits to the right of the decimal place than will be contained in the final answer, rounding should be specified in the Multiply Statement.

The ON SIZE ERROR entry in the Multiply Statement is utilized when there is the possibility that the answer as a result of the Multiply Statement will be larger than the field in which the answer is to be stored. Its use will be explained in detail in a later chapter.

As with the Add Statement and the Subtract Statement, the GIVING option is not required with the Multiply Statement. The following example illustrates the Multiply Statement without the GIVING option.

EXAMPLE

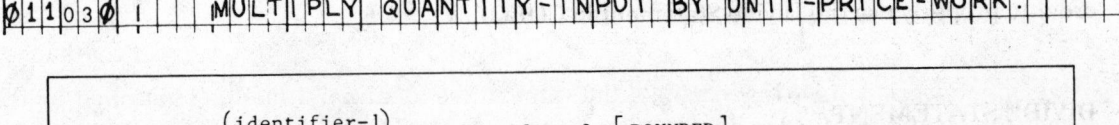

```
MULTIPLY  {identifier-1}  BY identifier-2 [ROUNDED]
          {literal-1   }

         [, identifier-3 [ROUNDED]] ... [; ON SIZE ERROR imperative-statement]
```

Figure 5-6 Example of Multiply Statement

Note in Figure 5-6 that the Multiply Statement is used without the GIVING option. When this form of the Multiply Statement is used, the value in the identifier-1 field or literal-1 is multiplied by the value in identifier-2 and the answer is stored in identifier-2. Thus, in the example, the value in QUANTITY-INPUT is multiplied by the value in UNIT-PRICE-WORK and the answer is stored in UNIT-PRICE-WORK. Note that identifier-3, . . . can be specified if desired; it would be treated the same as identifier-2. Note also that a literal cannot be specified for identifier-2, identifier-3, . . .,but a literal can be used in place of identifier-1.

DIVISION

When division is performed, the programmer must be aware of the sizes of the fields being used so that the quotient field and the remainder field can be properly defined. In a division operation, the maximum number of digits which may be found in the answer is equal to the number of digits in the Dividend. This is illustrated in the following example.

EXAMPLE

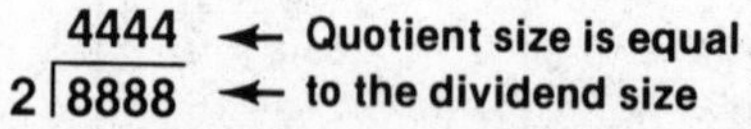

$$\begin{array}{r} 4444 \\ 2\overline{)8888} \end{array}$$ ← Quotient size is equal to the dividend size

Figure 5-7 Example of Division Operation

Note in the example above that the quotient size, that is, the number of digits in the answer to the division operation, is equal to the size of the dividend.

The largest remainder which can be generated in a division operation is equal to the number of digits in the divisor. This is illustrated below.

EXAMPLE

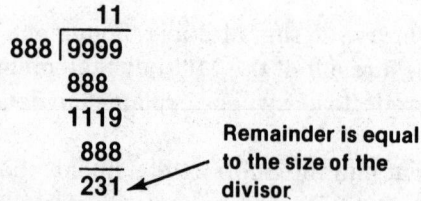

Figure 5-8 Example of Size of Remainder

Note from Figure 5-8 that the remainder contains the same number of digits as the divisor. It is important that the programmer understand these functions of the division operation in order to properly use the Divide Statement in COBOL.

DIVIDE STATEMENT

In order to cause division to occur, the Divide Statement is used in COBOL. An example of the Divide Statement is contained in Figure 5-9.

EXAMPLE 1

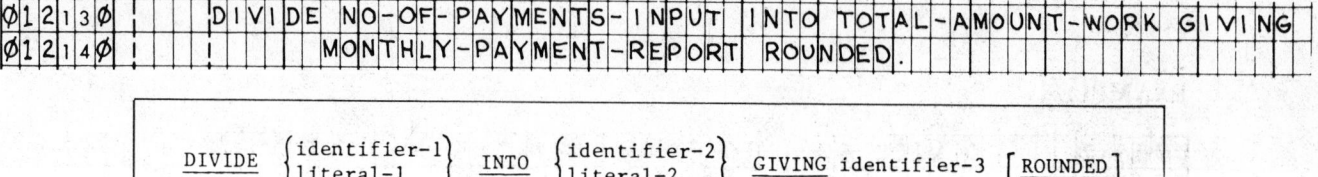

EXAMPLE 2

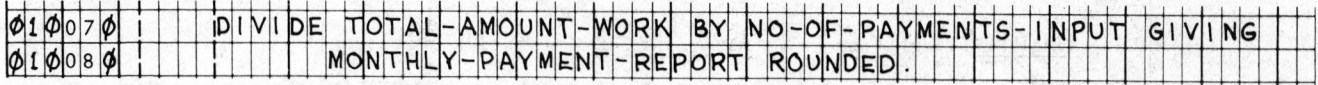

Figure 5-9 Example of Divide Statement

In the examples above it can be seen that the Divide Statement with the Giving option can be specified in two formats. In Example 1, the value in identifier-1 is divided **into** the value in identifier-2 and the answer to the division operation is stored in identifier-3, identifier-4, . . . Thus, the value in NO-OF-PAYMENTS-INPUT is divided **into** the value in TOTAL-AMOUNT-WORK and the answer is stored in MONTHLY-PAYMENT-REPORT.

In Example 2, the value in identifier-1 is divided **by** the value in identifier-2 and the answer is stored in identifier-3, identifier-4, . . . Therefore, in Example 2, the value in TOTAL-AMOUNT-WORK will be divided **by** the value in NO-OF-PAYMENTS-INPUT and the answer will be stored in MONTHLY-PAYMENT-REPORT. Thus, as can be seen, the two Divide Statements in Example 1 and Example 2 are equivalent to one another, that is, the value in MONTHLY-PAYMENT-REPORT after the division operation will be the same for both formats of the Divide Statement.

The Rounded option can be specified for either format of the Divide Statement. It operates in the same manner as the rounding which takes place in the Multiply Statement. The ON SIZE ERROR entry in the Divide Statement can be used when there is a possibility that the answer to the division operation will be too large for the field defined for it; or if the divisor of the division operation may be zero, which is not allowed. A detailed explanation of the use of the On Size Error option is contained in a later chapter.

As was noted previously, a remainder may develop as a result of the division operation. If the program is to process the remainder, one of the two formats illustrated below should be used.

EXAMPLE 1

```
ØØ8Ø3Ø        DIVIDE 6Ø INTO TOTAL-MINUTES-INPUT GIVING
ØØ8Ø4Ø            HOURS-REPORT
ØØ8Ø5Ø            REMAINDER MINUTES-REPORT.
```

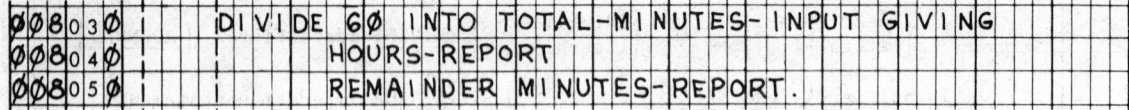

EXAMPLE 2

```
ØØ91ØØ        DIVIDE TOTAL-MINUTES-INPUT BY 6Ø GIVING
ØØ911Ø            HOURS-REPORT
ØØ912Ø            REMAINDER MINUTES-REPORT.
```

Figure 5-10 Example of Remainder Option in Divide Statement

As can be seen, the formats of the Divide Statement when the remainder is to be retained are basically the same as when the remainder is not kept. There are several differences. First, the word REMAINDER is required, followed by the data-name of the field into which the remainder will be placed. Thus, in both of the examples above, the remainder after the division takes place will be stored in the field MINUTES-REPORT.

Another difference is that only one field (identifier-3) may be specified following the word GIVING instead of multiple fields, as when the Remainder option is not used (see Figure 5-9).

The Divide Statement can also be written without the Giving option, as illustrated in Figure 5-11.

EXAMPLE

```
009100    DIVIDE 12 INTO QUANTITY-ORDERED-INPUT,
009110              AMOUNT-RECEIVED-INPUT.
```

```
DIVIDE  { identifier-1 }  INTO identifier-2 [ ROUNDED ]
        { literal-1    }

        [ , identifier-3 [ ROUNDED ] ] ...  [ ; ON SIZE ERROR imperative-statement ]
```

Figure 5-11 Example of Divide Statement

In the example above, the value in identifier-1 is divided into the value in identifier-2, identifier-3, . . . and the answer is stored in identifier-2, identifier-3, etc. Thus, the value 12 will be divided into the value in the QUANTITY-ORDERED-INPUT field and the answer will be stored in the QUANTITY-ORDERED-INPUT field. Similarly, the value 12 will be divided into the value in the field AMOUNT-RECEIVED-INPUT and the answer will be stored in the field AMOUNT-RECEIVED-INPUT. The Rounded option may be specified if required for the application.

COMPUTE STATEMENT

Although not utilized in the sample program in this chapter, in some applications it is necessary to perform a series of arithmetic calculations. With the Compute Verb, the programmer can use arithmetic expressions to specify one or a series of arithmetic operations. The following example illustrates the use of the Compute Statement.

EXAMPLE

```
011020    COMPUTE PROFIT-REPORT = SALES-INPUT - COST-INPUT.
```

```
COMPUTE identifier-1 [ ROUNDED ] [ , identifier-2 [ ROUNDED ] ] ...

        = arithmetic-expression [ ; ON SIZE ERROR imperative-statement ]
```

Figure 5-12 Example of Compute Statement

In the Compute Statement, the arithmetic expression on the right side of the equal sign (=) is evaluated and then the answer is stored in identifier-1, identifier-2, . . . on the left side of the equal sign. Thus, in the example above, the value in the COST-INPUT field will be subtracted from the value in the SALES-INPUT field and the answer will be stored in the PROFIT-REPORT field.

In the Compute Statement, identifier-1, identifier-2, . . . must be defined as numeric items or edited numeric items. The arithmetic expressions on the right side of the equal sign may consist of literals, identifiers, and arithmetic operators. The arithmetic operators which may be specified in the Compute Statement are specified below.

Operator	Arithmetic Operation
+	Addition
—	Subtraction
*	Multiplication
/	Division
**	Exponentiation

Figure 5-13 Arithmetic Operators

The following examples illustrate the use of the arithmetic operators in the Compute Statement. Note the space before and after the equal sign, and before and after each of the arithmetic operators. An arithmetic operator must always be preceeded by and followed by a space.

EXAMPLE 1: Addition

```
008110    COMPUTE TOTAL-PARTS-MSTR = QTY-ON-HAND-IN + QTY-ON-ORDER-IN.
```

Figure 5-14 Example of Addition Arithmetic Operator

In Example 1, the value in the field QTY-ON-HAND-IN is added to the value in the field QTY-ON-ORDER-IN and the answer is stored in the TOTAL-PARTS-MSTR field.

EXAMPLE 2: Subtraction

```
009030    COMPUTE QTY-ON-HAND-OUT = TOTAL-PARTS-IN - QTY-ON-ORDER-IN.
```

Figure 5-15 Example of Subtraction Arithmetic Operator

In Example 2, the value in the QTY-ON-ORDER-IN field is subtracted from the value in the TOTAL-PARTS-IN field and the answer is stored in the QTY-ON-HAND-OUT field.

EXAMPLE 3: Multiplication

```
Ø1208Ø     COMPUTE TOTAL-PAY-REPORT = RATE-MSTR * HOURS-INPUT.
```

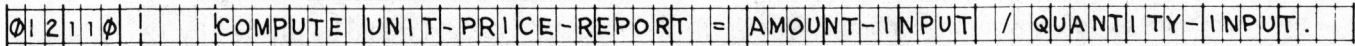

Figure 5-16 Example of Multiplication Arithmetic Operator

In Example 3, the value in the RATE-MSTR field is multiplied by the value in the HOURS-INPUT field and the answer is stored in the TOTAL-PAY-REPORT field.

EXAMPLE 4: Division

```
Ø1211Ø     COMPUTE UNIT-PRICE-REPORT = AMOUNT-INPUT / QUANTITY-INPUT.
```

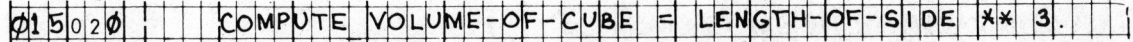

Figure 5-17 Example of Division Arithmetic Operator

In the example in Figure 5-17, the value in the AMOUNT-INPUT field is divided by the value in the QUANTITY-INPUT field and the answer is stored in the UNIT-PRICE-REPORT field.

EXAMPLE 5: Exponentiation

Exponentiation means raising to a power. The value A^3 is the same as A * A * A. The following example illustrates exponentiation in a Compute Statement.

```
Ø1502Ø     COMPUTE VOLUME-OF-CUBE = LENGTH-OF-SIDE ** 3.
```

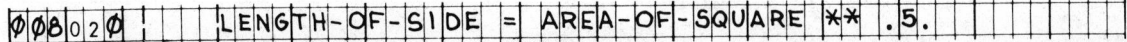

Figure 5-18 Example of Exponentiation Operator

Note from Figure 5-18 that a double asterisk (**) is used to indicate that a value is to be raised to a certain power. In the example, the value in the field LENGTH-OF-SIDE will be raised to the third power. The answer will be stored in the field VOLUME-OF-CUBE.

EXAMPLE 6: Exponentiation

Exponentiation can also be used to determine the square root of a value, since $\sqrt{X}$ is the same as $X^{1/2}$. This is illustrated below.

```
ØØ802Ø     LENGTH-OF-SIDE = AREA-OF-SQUARE ** .5.
```

Figure 5-19 Example of Exponentiation Operator

In Example 6, the value in the field AREA-OF-SQUARE is raised to the one-half power, which is the same as taking square root of the value. The answer is stored in the LENGTH-OF-SIDE field.

EXAMPLE 7: Numeric Literals

Numeric literals may be specified within the arithmetic expression used in the Compute Statement. They cannot, however, be used on the left side of the equal sign in a Compute Statement (see Figure 5-12). An example of a numeric literal in an arthmetic expression is illustrated below.

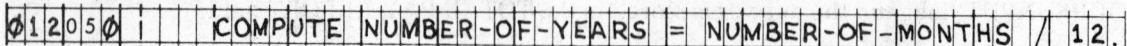

Ø12Ø5Ø   COMPUTE NUMBER-OF-YEARS = NUMBER-OF-MONTHS / 12.

Figure 5-20 Example of Numeric Literal in Arithmetic Expression

In the example above, the value in the NUMBER-OF-MONTHS field would be divided by 12 and the answer stored in the NUMBER-OF-YEARS field.

EXAMPLE 8: Rounded Option

The rounded option can be used to cause the answer to be rounded prior to being placed in the field to the left of the equal sign.

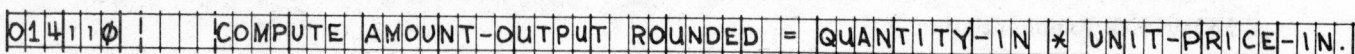

Ø141Ø   COMPUTE AMOUNT-OUTPUT ROUNDED = QUANTITY-IN * UNIT-PRICE-IN.

Figure 5-21 Example of Rounded Option with Compute Statement

EVALUATING ARITHMETIC EXPRESSIONS

The way in which the arithmetic expressions which appear in a Compute Statement are evaluated may be specified through the use of parentheses. This may be necessary when the expression might be ambiguous. For example, in the expression A * B + C, does the programmer mean (A * B) + C or does he mean A * (B + C)? In COBOL, the programmer may use pairs of parentheses in order to describe exactly the way in which a computation is to be performed.

If parentheses are NOT written to specify the order of computation, the COBOL compiler will generate instructions to evaluate an arithmetic expression using the following rules:

1. All exponentiation is performed first.

2. Then, multiplication and division are performed.

3. Finally, addition and subtraction are performed.

4. In each of the three above steps, computation starts at the left of the expression and proceeds to the right. Thus, A * B / C is computed as (A * B) / C, and A / B * C is computed as (A / B) * C.

If parentheses are present, computation begins with the innermost set and proceeds to the outermost set. Items grouped within parentheses will be evaluated in accordance with the above rules, and the result will then be treated as if the parentheses were removed.

The following examples illustrate the use of the Compute Statement to compute the Overtime Earnings of an employee. The Overtime Earnings are calculated by subtracting 40 from the Hours Worked in order to determine the Overtime Hours. The Overtime Hours are then multiplied by 1.5 to determine the hours which will be used to calculate the Overtime Pay. The Overtime Hours are then multiplied by the Pay Rate to determine the Overtime Pay. Example 1 illustrates an incorrect method for writing the Compute Statement to perform these calculations; Example 2 illustrates the correct method.

EXAMPLE 1: Incorrect Method

```
Ø18150        COMPUTE OVERTIME-EARNINGS-WORK =
Ø18160            HOURS-INPUT - 40 * 1.5 * PAY-RATE-INPUT.
```

Figure 5-22 Example of Incorrect Arithmetic Expression

In the example in Figure 5-22, there are no parentheses in the arithmetic expression to the right of the equal sign. Therefore, the evaluation of the arithmetic expression will proceed according to the priorities indicated previously. The value 40 will be multiplied by 1.5 and the result of this multiplication operation will be multiplied by the value in the field PAY-RATE-INPUT. This answer will then be subtracted from the value in the field HOURS-INPUT.

Suppose that the HOURS-INPUT field contains the value 44 and the PAY-RATE-INPUT field contains the value 4.00. The value placed in OVERTIME-EARNINGS-WORK would be minus 196. Clearly, this is incorrect. The correct method for expressing the computations to be performed in the arithmetic expression is illustrated in Figure 5-23.

EXAMPLE 2: Correct Method

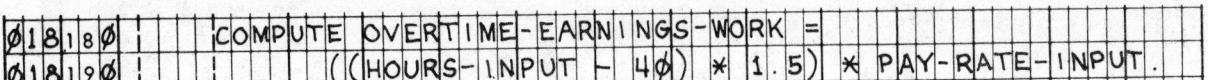
```
Ø18180        COMPUTE OVERTIME-EARNINGS-WORK =
Ø18190            ((HOURS-INPUT - 40) * 1.5) * PAY-RATE-INPUT.
```

Figure 5-23 Example of Correct Arithmetic Expression

In the example above, parentheses are used to specify the sequence of operations which should take place within the arithmetic expression. As noted previously, the expressions within the innermost parentheses are evaluated first. Thus, the first operation to occur above is that the value 40 is subtracted from the value in the HOURS-INPUT field. Next, the result of this subtraction operation will be multiplied by the value 1.5. This result will in turn be multiplied by the value in the PAY-RATE-INPUT field. Thus, if the same values as above are used, the result of the (HOURS-INPUT - 40) operation will be 4. This value is then multiplied by 1.5, yielding an answer of 6. The value in PAY-RATE-INPUT (4.00) is then multiplied by 6, giving an Overtime Earnings of 24.00, the correct answer.

The Compute Statement is a valuable programming tool when complex arithmetic expressions must be evaluated. The programmer, however, must take care when writing the arithmetic expression to ensure that the correct computations will take place.

SAMPLE PROGRAM

Many of the techniques previously explained are utilized in the sample program in this chapter. To illustrate the basic programming techniques involving multiplication and division, a Loan Report is to be created from a Loan Card Input File. The printer spacing chart for the Loan Report is illustrated below.

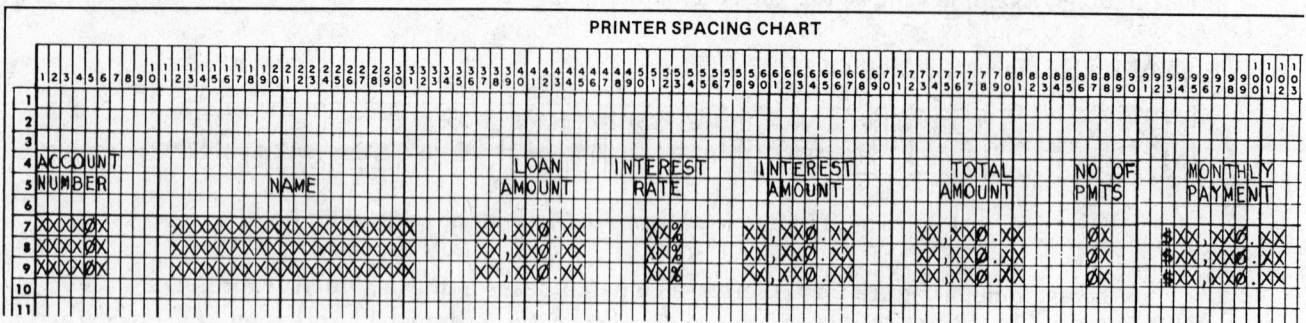

Figure 5-24 Printer Spacing Chart

It should again be pointed out that the Loan Report contains the Account Number, the Name, the Loan Amount, the Interest Rate, the Interest Amount, the Total Amount, the Number of Payments, and the Monthly Payment. Note that the column headings require two lines to identify each field on the report; and that editing is to be performed on the Account Number, the dollar amounts, the Interest Rate, and the Number of Payments. Note also that the percent sign (%) is to be printed as a constant adjacent to the Interest Rate on the report.

The input consists of Loan Cards, containing the Account Number, the Name, the Loan Amount, and the Number of Payments. The format of the input cards is illustrated below.

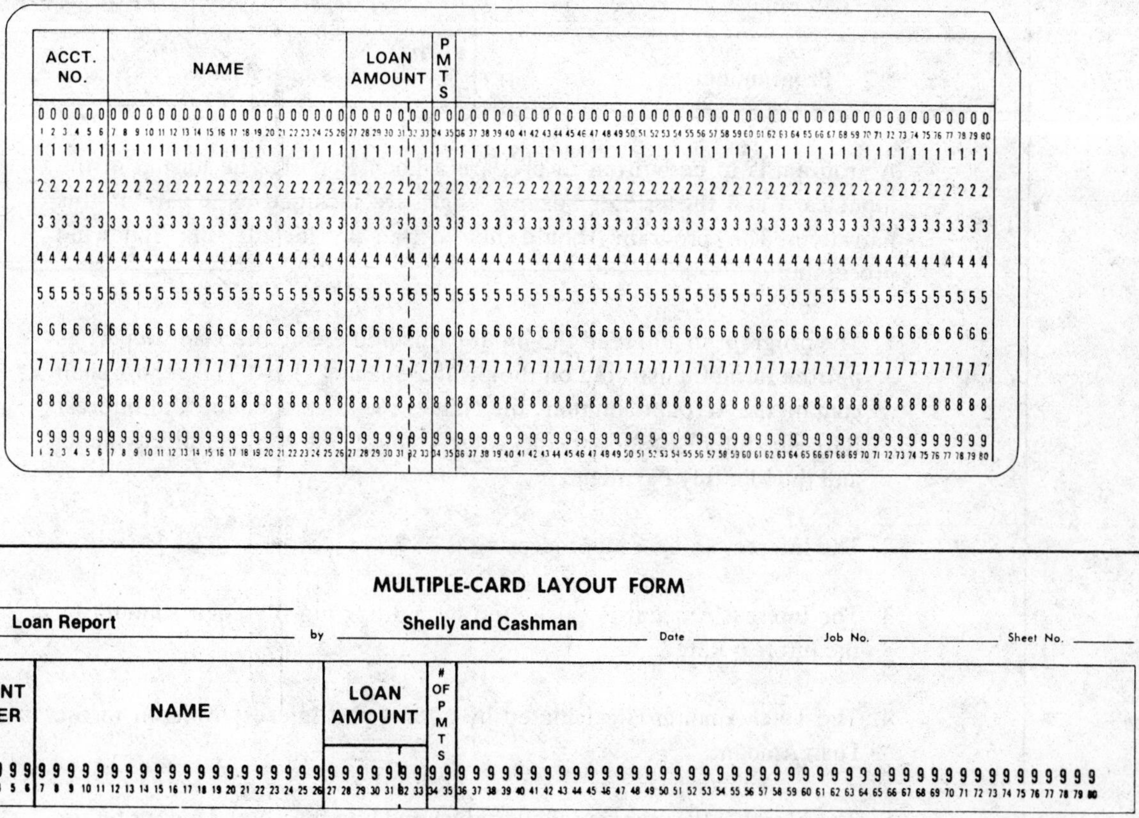

Figure 5-25 Input

The detailed Programming Specifications are illustrated on the following page. Particular attention should be paid to the calculations that are to be performed to produce the required report.

PROGRAMMING SPECIFICATIONS			
SUBJECT Loan Report	**DATE** April 9		**PAGE** 1 OF 1
TO Programmer	**FROM** Systems Analyst		

A program is to be written to prepare a Loan Report. The format of the input card and the printer spacing chart are included as a part of this narrative. The program should be written to include the following processing:

1. The program should read the input cards and create the Loan Report as per the format illustrated on the printer spacing chart. The report shall contain the Account Number, the Name, the Loan Amount, the Interest Rate, the Interest Amount, the Total Amount, the Number of Payments and the Monthly Payment.

2. The Interest Rate for all processing is 18%.

3. The Interest Amount is calculated by multiplying the Loan Amount by the Interest Rate.

4. The Total Amount is calculated by adding the Interest Amount to the Loan Amount.

5. The Monthly Payment is calculated by dividing the Total Amount by the Number of Payments.

6. One line is to be printed on the report for each card which is read.

7. The program should be written in COBOL.

Figure 5-26 Programming Specifications

As in previous programs, the programmer must analyze the programming specifications together with the format of the input records and the printing spacing chart in order to determine the processing which must take place to transform the input to the output.

It is important that the programmer understand the processing which must take place on each individual record prior to specifying what must occur within the program to transform the input to output. The diagrams on the following pages illustrate the steps which must occur in order to process an input record.

The first processing step that occurs involves reading the input record into the input area and moving the fields from the input area to the output area. These operations are illustrated below.

EXAMPLE

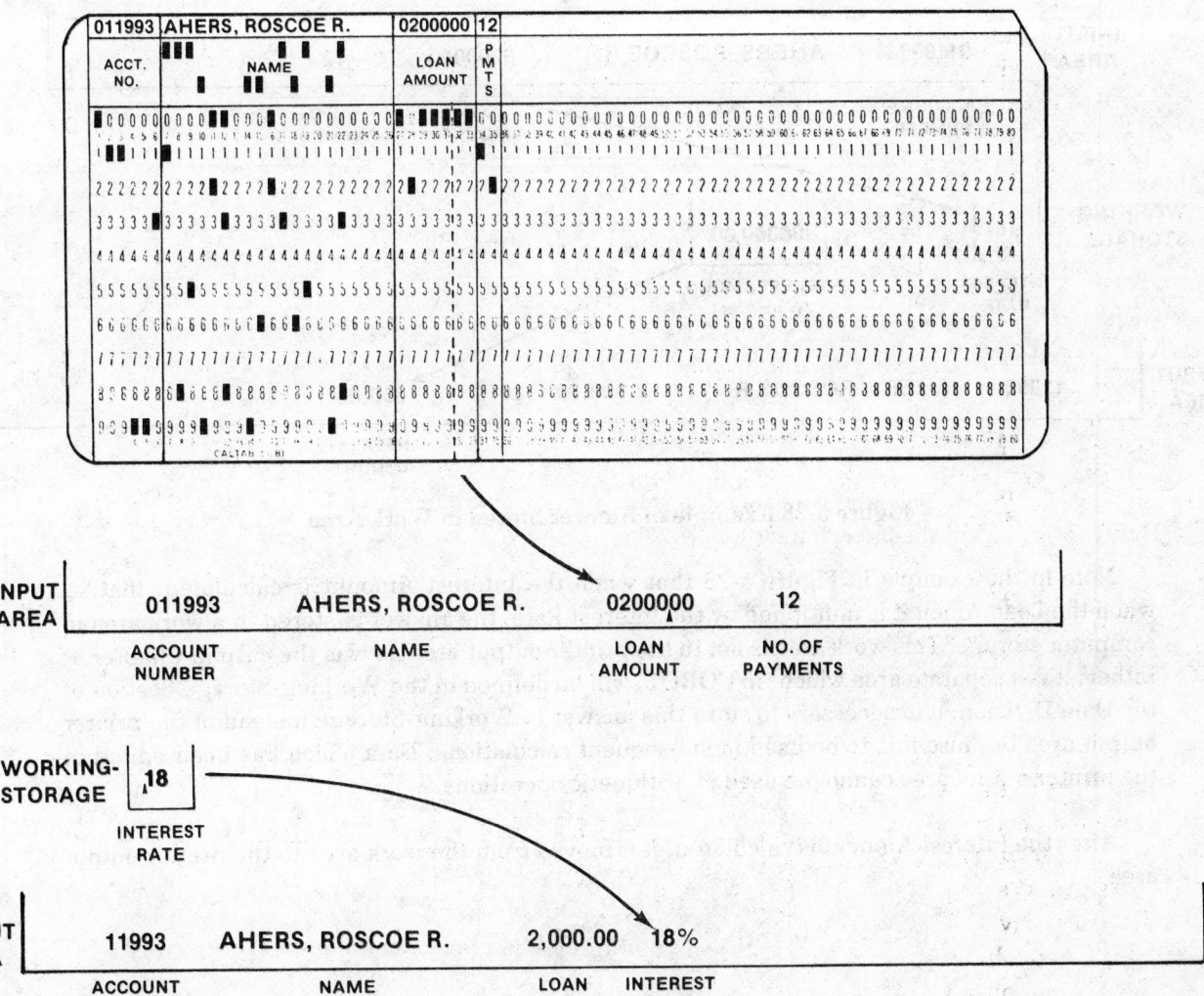

Figure 5-27 Output Area after Moves

Note from Figure 5-27 that the input card is read into the input area. After it is read into the input area, the Account Number, Name, Loan Amount, Interest Rate and Percent Sign are moved to the output area. The Account Number, Name and Loan Amount are contained in the input card. The Interest Rate must be defined within the program (in COBOL, it would be defined in Working-Storage). The Percent Sign will be an alphanumeric literal in the program.

After the data is moved to the output area the next step is to calculate the Interest Amount by multiplying the Loan Amount by the Interest Rate. The Interest Amount is then moved to the output area. This processing is illustrated below.

EXAMPLE

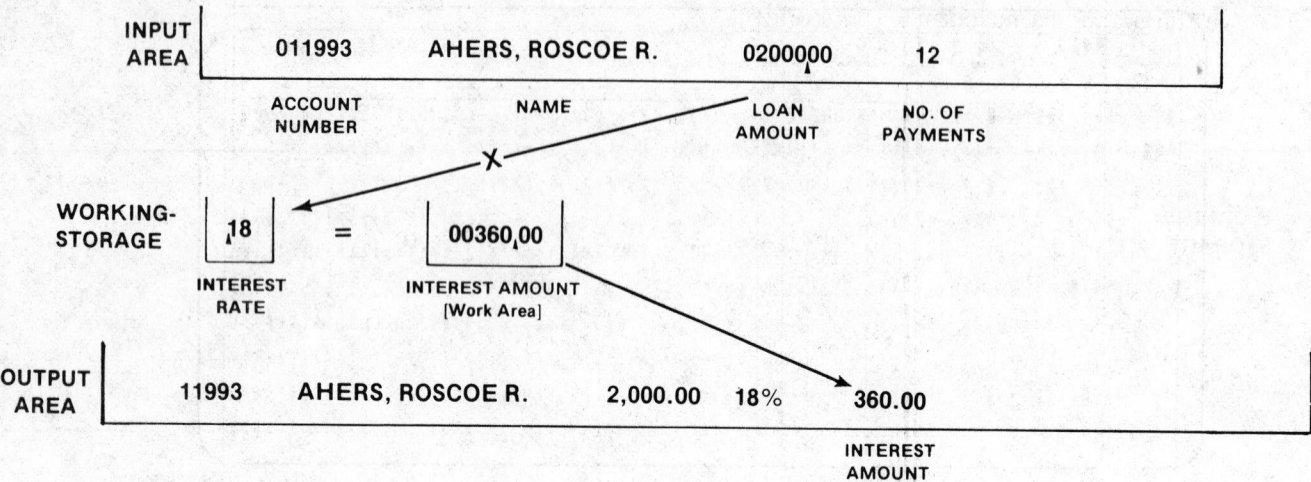

Figure 5-28 Example of Answer Stored in Work Area

Note in the example in Figure 5-28 that when the Interest Amount is calculated, that is, when the Loan Amount is multiplied by the Interest Rate, the answer is stored in a work area in computer storage. This work area is not in the printer output area as was the case in Chapter 4; rather, it is a separate area which, in COBOL, will be defined in the Working-Storage Section of the Data Division. It is necessary to store this answer in Working-Storage instead of the printer output area because it is to be used in subsequent calculations. Data which has been edited in the printer output area cannot be used in arithmetic operations.

After the Interest Amount is calculated, it is moved from the work area to the printer output area.

The next steps involve the calculation of the Total Amount by adding the Interest Amount and the Loan Amount, moving the Total Amount to the output area, and moving the Number of Payments to the output area. These steps are illustrated below.

EXAMPLE

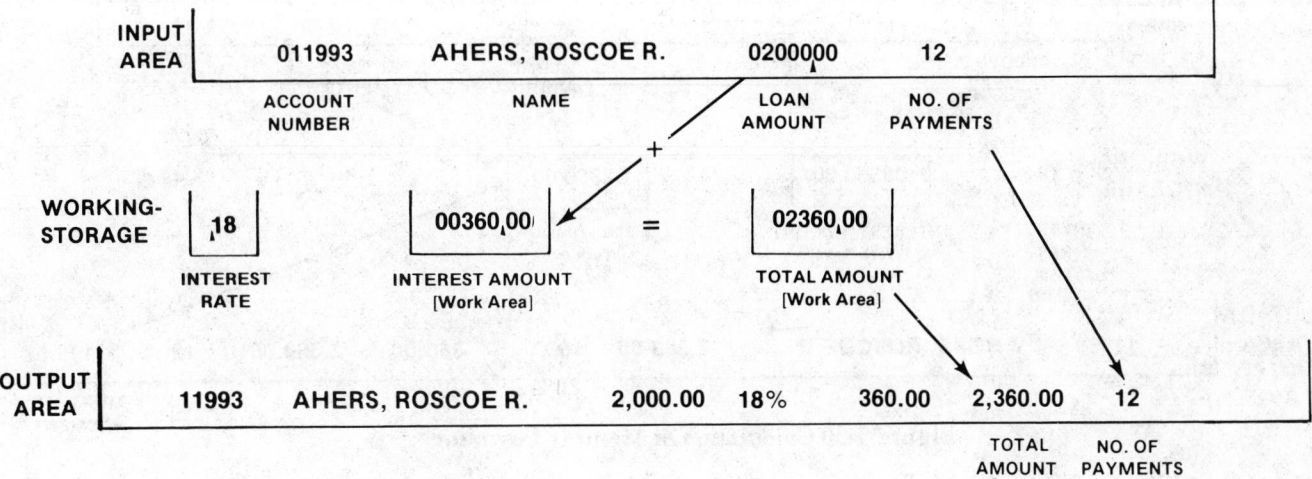

Figure 5-29 Calculation of Total Amount

Note in the example above that the Loan Amount is added to the Interest Amount to obtain the Total Amount. The Loan Amount is stored in the input area since it was read from the input card. The Interest Amount is in a work area since it was calculated (see Figure 5-28). The Total Amount will also be stored in a work area since it will be used in another calculation. After the Total Amount is calculated and stored in a work area, it is moved to the output area. The Number of Payments field is also moved to the output area.

The calculation of the Monthly Payment occurs next. The Monthly Payment is obtained by dividing the Total Amount by the Number of Payments, as illustrated in the example below.

EXAMPLE

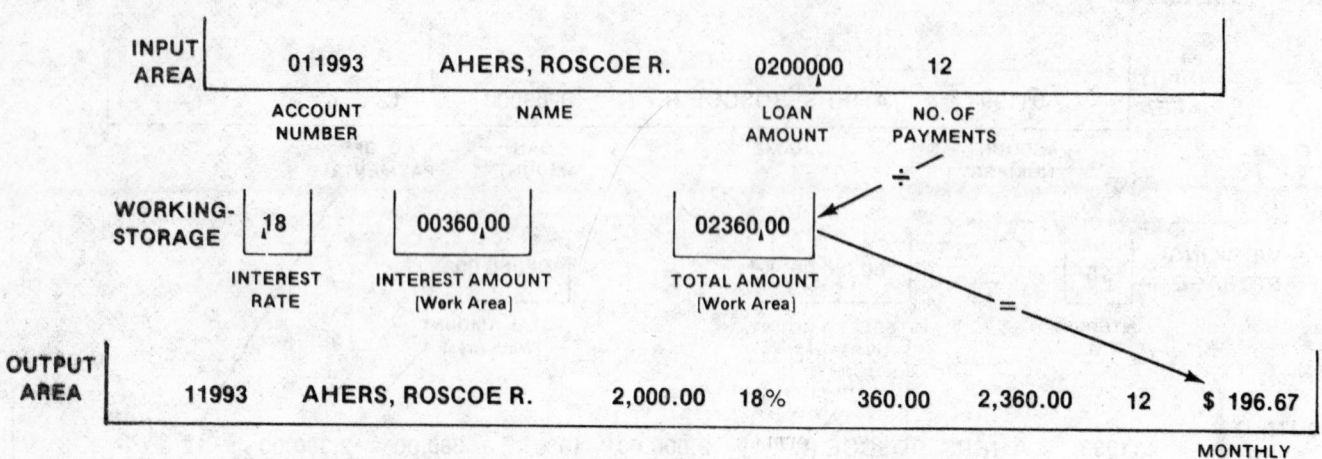

Figure 5-30 Calculation of Monthly Payment

Note in Figure 5-30 that the Monthly Payment is calculated by dividing the Total Amount, which is stored in a work area, by the Number of Payments, which is stored in the input area. The answer is placed directly in the output area; it need not be placed in a work area because there are no further calculations which must be performed on it. Thus, as can be seen, if the answer to a calculation is to be used in subsequent calculations, then it should be stored in a work area; if it is not to be used in subsequent calculations, it can be placed directly in the output area.

After the calculations are completed, the line is printed on the report, and another input record is read. This processing will continue until there are no more input records to process, at which time processing will be terminated.

PROGRAM DESIGN

After the output, input, and Programming Specifications are analyzed, and the programmer thoroughly understands the processing that is to occur, the programmer can then begin the design of the program by developing the IPO Chart and the Pseudocode Specifications. The IPO Chart for the sample program is illustrated below.

IPO CHART

PROGRAM: Loan Report		PROGRAMMER: Shelly/Cashman		DATE: April 10
MODULE NAME: Create Loan Report		REF: A000	MODULE FUNCTION: Create the Loan Report	

INPUT	PROCESSING	REF:	OUTPUT
1. Loan Report Card File	1. Initialization		1. Loan Report
	2. Obtain input data		
	3. Format print line		
	4. Perform calculations		
	5. Write the report		
	6. Termination		

Figure 5-31 IPO Chart for Loan Report Program

Note from Figure 5-31 that the processing which must be accomplished to transform the input to the output is basically the same as was seen in Chapter 4. The operations necessary to carry out this processing, however, are somewhat more involved. For example, the calculations involve a multiplication and division operation, rather than a simple add operation. In examining the processing which is required there is nothing which is of such magnitude so as to cause the Create Loan Report module to be exceedingly large, that is, greater than 50 statements and the processing is relatively straight-forward; therefore, there is no requirement that this module be decomposed into lower level modules.

After the IPO Chart has been completed and reviewed for correctness and completeness, the programmer should prepare the Pseudocode Specifications by specifying the pseudocode required to solve the problem and identifying the files, records, and fields required for the program. The Pseudocode Specifications for the sample program are illustrated in Figure 5-32.

PSEUDOCODE SPECIFICATIONS

PROGRAM: Loan Report **PROGRAMMER:** Shelly/Cashman **DATE:** April 10

MODULE NAME: Create Loan Report **REF:** A000 **MODULE FUNCTION:** Create the Loan Report

PSEUDOCODE	REF:	FILES, RECORDS, FIELDS REQUIRED

Open the files
Write the two heading lines
Set space control for double spacing
Read an input record
PERFORM UNTIL no more records
  Clear the printer line
  Move account number, name, loan amount,
    interest rate and % sign to output area
  Calculate interest amount = loan amount x rate
  Move interest amount to output area
  Calculate total amount = loan amount
    + interest amount
  Move total amount to output area
  Move number of payments to output area
  Calculate monthly payments = total amount/# of pmts
    and place in output area
  Write a line on the report
  Set space control for single spacing
  Read an input record
ENDPERFORM
Close the files
Stop run
		Loan report card file
		Loan report file
		Heading lines
		Printer spacing field
		Double space control character
		Input record area
		  Account number
		  Name
		  Loan amount
		  Number of payments
		No more records indicator
		Printer output area
		  Account number
		  Name
		  Loan amount
		  Interest rate
		  Interest amount
		  Total amount
		  Number of payments
		  Monthly payments
		Interest rate
		% sign
		Interest amount work area
		Total amount work area
		Single space control character

Figure 5-32 Pseudocode Specifications

Note that the Pseudocode Specifications contain the pseudocode and a definition of the files, records, and fields required. As can be seen, the pseudocode reflects a detailed description of the steps required in the solution of the problem.

CODING THE PROGRAM

After the Pseudocode Specifications have been completed, and a structured walkthrough conducted to review the design of the program, the program may be coded. The Identification Division and the Environment Division for the sample program are very similar to previous programs. The File Section of the Data Division is illustrated below.

Data Division - File Section

```
002010  DATA DIVISION.
002020
002030  FILE SECTION.
002040
002050  FD  LOAN-INPUT-FILE
002060          RECORD CONTAINS 80 CHARACTERS
002070          LABEL RECORDS ARE OMITTED
002080          DATA RECORD IS LOAN-INPUT-RECORD.
002090  01  LOAN-INPUT-RECORD.
002100      05  ACCOUNT-NUMBER-INPUT          PIC 9(6).
002110      05  NAME-INPUT                    PIC X(20).
002120      05  LOAN-AMOUNT-INPUT             PIC 9(5)V99.
002130      05  NO-OF-PAYMENTS-INPUT          PIC 99.
002140      05  FILLER                        PIC X(45).
002150
002160  FD  LOAN-REPORT-FILE
002170          RECORD CONTAINS 133 CHARACTERS
002180          LABEL RECORDS ARE OMITTED
002190          DATA RECORD IS LOAN-REPORT-LINE.
002200  01  LOAN-REPORT-LINE.
003010      05  CARRIAGE-CONTROL              PIC X.
003020      05  ACCOUNT-NUMBER-REPORT         PIC ZZZZZ9.
003030      05  FILLER                        PIC X(5).
003040      05  NAME-REPORT                   PIC X(20).
003050      05  FILLER                        PIC X(5).
003060      05  LOAN-AMOUNT-REPORT            PIC ZZ,ZZZ.99.
003070      05  FILLER                        PIC X(5).
003080      05  INTEREST-RATE-REPORT          PIC V99.
003090      05  PERCENT-SIGN-REPORT           PIC X.
003100      05  FILLER                        PIC X(5).
003110      05  INTEREST-AMOUNT-REPORT        PIC ZZ,ZZZ.99.
003120      05  FILLER                        PIC X(5).
003130      05  TOTAL-AMOUNT-REPORT           PIC ZZ,ZZZ.99.
003140      05  FILLER                        PIC X(5).
003150      05  NO-OF-PAYMENTS-REPORT         PIC Z9.
003160      05  FILLER                        PIC X(4).
003170      05  MONTHLY-PAYMENT-REPORT        PIC $ZZ,ZZZ.99.
003180      05  FILLER                        PIC X(30).
```

Figure 5-33 File Section of Data Division

Note that the File Section of the Data Division describes the files being processed, and defines the format of the input records and output report.

Working-Storage Section

The Working-Storage Section of the Data Division contains several new entries, including the use of a condition name, the use of program constants, and the use of work areas for the intermediate storage of answers resulting from arithmetic operations. These entries are illustrated below.

EXAMPLE

```
005010 WORKING-STORAGE SECTION.
005020
005030 01  PROGRAM-INDICATORS.
005040     05  ARE-THERE-MORE-RECORDS    PIC XXX        VALUE 'YES'.
005050     88  THERE-ARE-NO-MORE-RECORDS                VALUE 'NO '.
        (Condition Name)
005060
005070 01  WORK-AREAS.
005080     05  INTEREST-AMOUNT-WORK      PIC S9(5)V99 USAGE IS COMP-3.
005090     05  TOTAL-AMOUNT-WORK         PIC S9(5)V99 USAGE IS COMP-3.
005100
005110 01  PROGRAM-CONSTANTS.
005120     05  INTEREST-RATE-CONSTANT    PIC V99        VALUE .18
005130                                                USAGE IS COMP-3.
```

Figure 5-34 Working-Storage Section of Data Division

Condition Names

The first entry in the Working-Storage Section is "01 PROGRAM-INDICATORS." This group item contains both an 05 level entry (ARE-THERE-MORE-RECORDS) and an 88 level entry (THERE-ARE-NO-MORE-RECORDS). The 88 level entry is used to establish a Condition Name. The use of condition names is explained in the following paragraphs.

In previous programs in Chapter 3 and Chapter 4, the Until Clause within the Perform Statement to cause a loop contained a condition which had to be satisfied in order for the loop to be stopped. This is illustrated below.

EXAMPLE

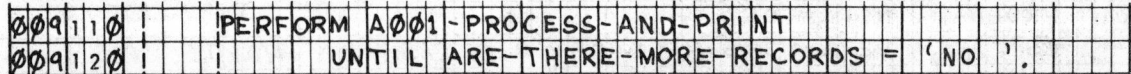

Figure 5-35 Example of Perform Statement

In the Perform Statement above, the A001-PROCESS-AND-PRINT paragraph will be performed until such time as the field ARE-THERE-MORE-RECORDS contains the value "NO ". When the field does contain this value, the loop will be terminated.

Although the statement in Figure 5-35 executes properly, the use of a condition name can make the statement more clear in terms of reading the program. A condition name is merely a name given to a value which appears within a field. Thus, in the example above, the condition name THERE-ARE-NO-MORE-RECORDS could be given to the value "NO " in the ARE-THERE-MORE-RECORDS field. The Perform Statement could then be written as illustrated in Figure 5-36.

EXAMPLE

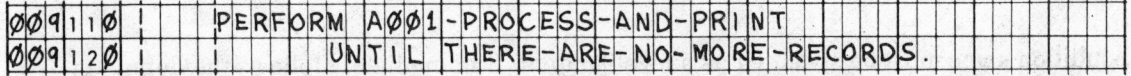

Figure 5-36 Example of Condition Name in Perform Statement

The Perform Statement in Figure 5-36 will work exactly the same as the Perform Statement in Figure 5-35 provided the condition name THERE-ARE-NO-MORE-RECORDS is equated to the value "NO " being in the field ARE-THERE-MORE-RECORDS. Note from the use of the condition name that the exact reason for ceasing the looping is specified; that is, it is to be terminated when there are no more records. This is clearer than specifying the equal condition as in Figure 5-35 and condition names should normally be used when a value in the field can be equated to a condition name.

In order to define a condition name, an 88 level number is used. The entry in the Data Division to define the condition name THERE-ARE-NO-MORE-RECORDS is illustrated in Figure 5-37.

EXAMPLE

```
005030 01  PROGRAM-INDICATORS.
005040     05  ARE-THERE-MORE-RECORDS   PIC XXX        VALUE 'YES'.
005050         88  THERE-ARE-NO-MORE-RECORDS           VALUE 'NO '.
```

$$88 \quad \text{condition-name;} \quad \left\{ \begin{array}{l} \underline{\text{VALUE}} \text{ IS} \\ \underline{\text{VALUES}} \text{ ARE} \end{array} \right\} \quad \text{literal-1} \quad \left[\left\{ \begin{array}{l} \underline{\text{THROUGH}} \\ \underline{\text{THRU}} \end{array} \right\} \quad \text{literal-2} \right]$$

$$\left[\text{, literal-3} \quad \left[\left\{ \begin{array}{l} \underline{\text{THROUGH}} \\ \underline{\text{THRU}} \end{array} \right\} \quad \text{literal-4} \right] \right] \text{...} \quad \text{.}$$

Figure 5-37 Example of Condition Name

Note in the example above that the group item (PROGRAM-INDICATORS) and the elementary item (ARE-THERE-MORE-RECORDS) are defined in exactly the same manner as in previous programs. In addition, however, a level-88 item is defined. This is the condition name.

A condition name must be specified as a level-88 item. It immediately follows the definition of the field to which it applies. Thus, in the example, it must immediately follow the ARE-THERE-MORE-RECORDS field. The condition name entry must contain two parts—the condition name itself and the value which is to be associated with the condition name. In the example, the condition name is THERE-ARE-NO-MORE-RECORDS. The value to be associated with this condition name is indicated through the use of the Value Clause. Thus, the clause VALUE 'NO ' must be included to indicate that when the ARE-THERE-MORE-RECORDS field contains the value "NO ", then the condition name will be true. Specifying the condition name is the same as specifying a statement in which the value in the identifier (ARE-THERE-MORE-RECORDS) is compared to the value "NO ".

Thus, in the Perform Statement in Figure 5-36, specifying the condition name is the same as the Perform Statement in Figure 5-35 where the value in the field ARE-THERE-MORE-RECORDS is compared to the value "NO ". So long as the field does not contain the value "NO ", the condition tested through the use of the condition name will be considered false. When the field contains the value "NO ", then the condition tested by the condition name is considered true, and whatever processing is supposed to take place when the condition is true will occur. When the Until Clause is used in the Perform Statement, the loop is terminated when the condition is true.

DEFINITION OF WORK AREAS IN WORKING-STORAGE

As noted previously, two work areas are required for the sample program—one in which to store the Interest Amount and one in which to store the Total Amount. When coding the program in COBOL, these work areas are defined in the Working-Storage Section of the Data Division. The two work areas defined in the sample program are illustrated in Figure 5-38.

EXAMPLE

```
005010   WORKING-STORAGE SECTION.
005020
005030   01  PROGRAM-INDICATORS.
005040       05  ARE-THERE-MORE-RECORDS      PIC XXX        VALUE 'YES'.
005050           88  THERE-ARE-NO-MORE-RECORDS              VALUE 'NO '.
005060
005070   01  WORK-AREAS.
005080       05  INTEREST-AMOUNT-WORK        PIC S9(5)V99   USAGE IS COMP-3.
005090       05  TOTAL-AMOUNT-WORK           PIC S9(5)V99   USAGE IS COMP-3.
005100
005110   01  PROGRAM-CONSTANTS.
005120       05  INTEREST-RATE-CONSTANT      PIC V99        VALUE .18
005130                                                      USAGE IS COMP-3.
```

(Work Area → points to lines 005080 and 005090)

Figure 5-38 Example of Working-Storage Entries for Work Areas

Note in the example above that the group item, WORK-AREAS, is used to designate that the elementary items following it are to be used as work areas. The level numbers and data-names are utilized as has been seen in previous examples. There are, however, two new entries in specifying the attributes of the fields: the Sign, and the Usage Clause.

Sign

The character "S" is used in the Picture Clause to indicate the presence of an operational sign. If used, it must be the leftmost character of the Picture Clause. When the "S" is included with a Picture Clause for numeric data, any data which is stored in the field as a result of a Move Statement or an arithmetic statement (Add, Subtract, Multiply, Divide, Compute) will contain the algebraic sign of the result of the operation. If the letter "S" is not included in the Picture Clause, then the absolute value of the result will be placed in the field, regardless of the sign generated from the arithmetic operation.

Therefore, whenever there is the possibility that the answer developed from an arithmetic operation will be negative, the "S" should always be included in the Picture Clause. In addition, however, the programmer should normally include the "S" in any Picture into which an answer from an arithmetic operation is to be placed or a numeric value moved unless absolute values are always desired. If the "S" is not included, additional code is generated by the Compiler to ensure that data in the field is treated as an absolute value; and this coding is generally unnecessary. Therefore, unless absolute values are required for a numeric field, the "S" should always be included on any numeric field which will contain an answer to an arithmetic operation or to which a numeric value will be moved.

Usage Clause

The Usage Clause is used to describe the form in which data is to be stored in the Data Division. In the example in Figure 5-38, the clause "USAGE IS COMP-3" is used. This clause will cause the areas referenced by INTEREST-AMOUNT-WORK and TOTAL-AMOUNT-WORK to be stored in the Computational-3 format.

If an area is reserved in the Data Division without specifying Computational-3 or Comp-3, the area is set up in the Display format. The following example illustrates how the amount 0023600 would be stored in the INTEREST-AMOUNT-WORK field if Usage is Comp-3 is not specified in the Picture Clause.

EXAMPLE

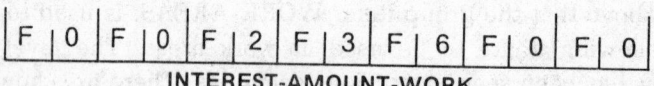

INTEREST-AMOUNT-WORK

NOTE: The format shown is that used by computers using the Extended Binary Coded Decimal Interchange Code [EBCDIC].

Figure 5-39 INTEREST-AMOUNT-WORK Field in Display Format

Note from Figure 5-39 that seven bytes of storage are reserved for the field and one byte or position in storage is used for each digit in the field. In the example, each digit is preceeded by an "F". The "F" is a hexadecimal representation of the high order bits of the byte containing the digit. Thus, the number "0" is represented interally as "F0", the number 2 as "F2", etc. The entire number 0023600 is stored internally as F0F0F2F3F6F0F0.

When the field is converted to a Computational-3 format, however, all of the sign positions ("F") of the bytes are dropped, except for the low-order sign, which is the sign for the field. The hexadecimal "F" is a valid plus sign. This is illustrated in Figure 5-40.

EXAMPLE

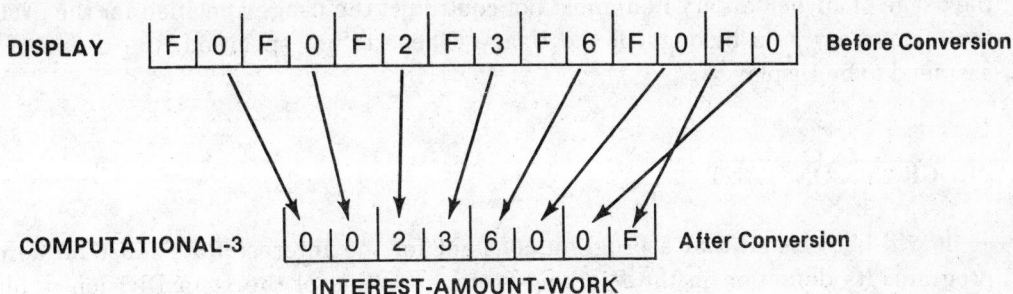

Figure 5-40 INTEREST-AMOUNT-WORK Field in Computational-3 Format

As can be seen, when numeric data is converted from the Display format to the Computational-3 format, the sign in the low-order position of the Display field is placed in the rightmost four bits of the Computational-3 field, and then only the numeric portion of the bytes is placed in the Computational-3 field. Thus, numeric data which requires seven bytes in the Display format requires only four bytes in the Computational-3 format. It should be noted that the Computational-3 format is not found on all computers. It is found, however, on many computers used for business applications such as the IBM System/360 and the IBM System/370.

The general format of the Usage Clause is illustrated below.

FORMAT NOTATION

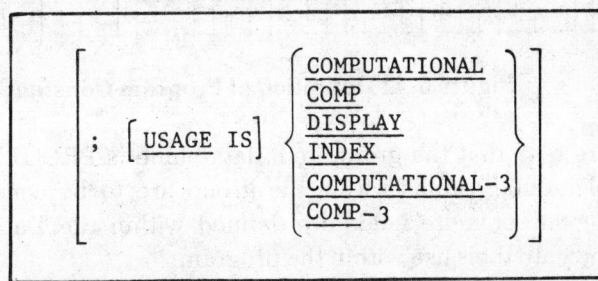

Figure 5-41 General Format of Usage Clause

Note from the general format illustrated in Figure 5-41 that the word USAGE is required in the Usage Clause. The word IS is optional. The COMPUTATIONAL or COMP option specifies that the numeric data is to be stored in a binary format. The DISPLAY option indicates that the data is to be stored in the Display format.

The INDEX option specifies that the field is a special field used in table look-up operations. The use of this option will be explained in a later chapter. As noted previously, the COMPUTATIONAL-3 or COMP-3 option specifies that the data will be stored in the "internal decimal" format.

The Usage Clause may be written either at the group level or the elementary level. At the group level, it applies to each elementary item within the group. If it is used at the group level, the usage of an elementary item must not contradict the usage specified for the group to which the elementary item belongs. If the Usage Clause is not specified, the usage of an item is assumed to be Display.

PROGRAM CONSTANT

It will be recalled that a program constant for the Interest Rate must be defined in the program. Its definition in the Working-Storage Section of the Data Division is illustrated in Figure 5-42.

EXAMPLE

```
005010  WORKING-STORAGE SECTION.
005020
005030  01   PROGRAM-INDICATORS.
005040       05   ARE-THERE-MORE-RECORDS      PIC XXX         VALUE 'YES'.
005050            88   THERE-ARE-NO-MORE-RECORDS              VALUE 'NO '.
005060
005070  01   WORK-AREAS.
005080       05   INTEREST-AMOUNT-WORK        PIC S9(5)V99    USAGE IS COMP-3.
005090       05   TOTAL-AMOUNT-WORK           PIC S9(5)V99    USAGE IS COMP-3.
005100
005110  01   PROGRAM-CONSTANTS.
005        05   INTEREST-RATE-CONSTANT      PIC V99         VALUE .18
005                                                         USAGE IS COMP-3.
```
(Program Constant)

Figure 5-42 Definition of Program Constant

Note from Figure 5-42 that the group item data-name is PROGRAM-CONSTANTS, which indicates that all elementary items within the group are to be constants for use within the program. Whenever one or more fields are defined within the Data Division, a group item should be used to indicate their use within the program.

The INTEREST-RATE-CONSTANT field has a Picture Clause of PIC V99. This indicates that it consists of two numeric digits, both of which are to the right of the decimal point. This is the desired result since the Interest Rate is a percentage, not a whole number.

The Value Clause is used to place a value in the field. In the example, the value specified is ".18". The use of the decimal point in the value is to inform the Compiler of the location of the decimal point. The decimal point will not be contained in the value which is stored in computer storage. The Usage Clause is used to specify that the numeric data is to be stored in the Computational-3 format. Thus, as a result of the entries in Figure 5-42, the following constant would be developed in Working-Storage.

EXAMPLE

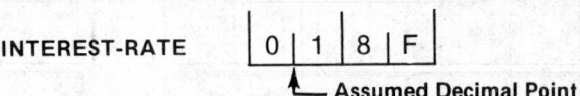

Figure 5-43 Representation of INTEREST-RATE in Computer Storage

As can be seen from Figure 5-43, the Interest Rate is stored in the Computational-3 format. The assumed decimal point is to the left of the "1", as indicated by the "V" in the Picture Clause in Figure 5-42. It will be noted that the value in the field actually contains three digits, even though only two digits are specified in the Picture Clause. This is because a Computational-3 field can never contain an even number of digits; it will always contain an odd number of digits even if an even number of digits are specified in the Picture Clause. When an even number of digits are specified in the Picture Clause, the high-order digit in the Computational-3 field will always be zero.

Whenever numeric constants or numeric work areas are defined in a COBOL program, they should be defined as Computational-3 fields because many computers require numeric data to be in the Computational-3 format before arithmetic or editing operations can be performed. If the programmer does not define these areas as Computational-3 fields in the Working-Storage Section of the Data Division, the Compiler will generate instructions to convert the data in the fields to a Computational-3 format prior to performing arithmetic or editing operations. To prevent these unnecessary instructions from being generated, the numeric fields in Working-Storage should normally be defined as Computational-3.

PRINTER CONTROL AND HEADING LINES

Following the definition of the work areas and the program constants are the entries for printer spacing control and the headings. These entries are illustrated in Figure 5-44.

EXAMPLE

```
005130 01 PRINTER-CONTROL.
005140    05 PROPER-SPACING         PIC 9.
005150    05 SPACE-ONE-LINE         PIC 9           VALUE 1.
005160    05 SPACE-TWO-LINES        PIC 9           VALUE 2.
005170
005180 01 HEADING-LINES.
005190    05 FIRST-HEADING-LINE.
005200       10 CARRIAGE-CONTROL    PIC X.
006010       10 FILLER              PIC X(7)         VALUE 'ACCOUNT'.
006020       10 FILLER              PIC X(32)        VALUE SPACES.
006030       10 FILLER              PIC X(4)         VALUE 'LOAN'.
006040       10 FILLER              PIC X(4)         VALUE SPACES.
006050       10 FILLER              PIC X(8)         VALUE 'INTEREST'.
006060       10 FILLER              PIC X(4)         VALUE SPACES.
006070       10 FILLER              PIC X(8)         VALUE 'INTEREST'.
006080       10 FILLER              PIC X(8)         VALUE SPACES.
006090       10 FILLER              PIC X(5)         VALUE 'TOTAL'.
006100       10 FILLER              PIC X(5)         VALUE SPACES.
006110       10 FILLER              PIC X(5)         VALUE 'NO OF'.
006120       10 FILLER              PIC X(4)         VALUE SPACES.
006130       10 FILLER              PIC X(7)         VALUE 'MONTHLY'.
006140       10 FILLER              PIC X(31)        VALUE SPACES.
006150    05 SECOND-HEADING-LINE.
006160       10 CARRIAGE-CONTROL    PIC X.
006170       10 FILLER              PIC X(6)         VALUE 'NUMBER'.
006180       10 FILLER              PIC X(13)        VALUE SPACES.
006190       10 FILLER              PIC X(4)         VALUE 'NAME'.
006200       10 FILLER              PIC X(15)        VALUE SPACES.
007010       10 FILLER              PIC X(6)         VALUE 'AMOUNT'.
007020       10 FILLER              PIC X(5)         VALUE SPACES.
007030       10 FILLER              PIC X(4)         VALUE 'RATE'.
007040       10 FILLER              PIC X(7)         VALUE SPACES.
007050       10 FILLER              PIC X(6)         VALUE 'AMOUNT'.
007060       10 FILLER              PIC X(8)         VALUE SPACES.
007070       10 FILLER              PIC X(6)         VALUE 'AMOUNT'.
007080       10 FILLER              PIC X(5)         VALUE SPACES.
007090       10 FILLER              PIC X(4)         VALUE 'PMTS'.
007100       10 FILLER              PIC X(5)         VALUE SPACES.
007110       10 FILLER              PIC X(7)         VALUE 'PAYMENT'.
007120       10 FILLER              PIC X(31)        VALUE SPACES.
```

Figure 5-44 Printer Control and Headings

As can be seen from Figure 5-44, the printer spacing control fields are the same as have been used previously. It will be recalled from the sample report that two lines are required for the printing of the heading. Note in the coding above that these two lines are defined by two separate 05 level entries, followed by the level 10 elementary entries which describe the contents of each line.

PROCEDURE DIVISION

The first section of the Procedure Division is illustrated below. In this section, the files are opened; the heading lines are printed; and then the main line processing is entered, causing the first record to be read and further processing to take place.

EXAMPLE

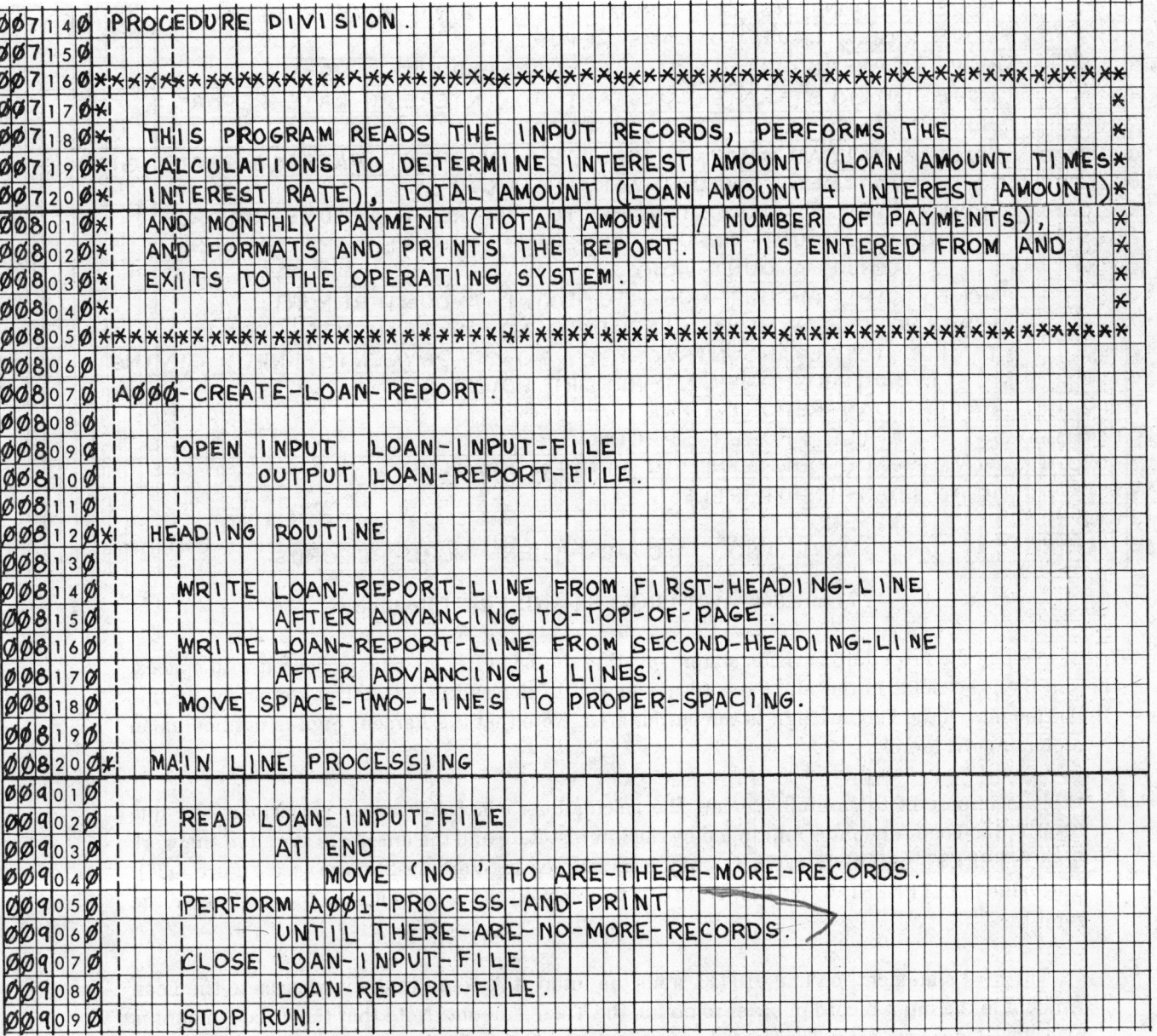

```
007140  PROCEDURE DIVISION.
007150
007160 ***********************************************************************
007170 *                                                                     *
007180 *  THIS PROGRAM READS THE INPUT RECORDS, PERFORMS THE                  *
007190 *  CALCULATIONS TO DETERMINE INTEREST AMOUNT (LOAN AMOUNT TIMES*
007200 *  INTEREST RATE), TOTAL AMOUNT (LOAN AMOUNT + INTEREST AMOUNT)*
008010 *  AND MONTHLY PAYMENT (TOTAL AMOUNT / NUMBER OF PAYMENTS),      *
008020 *  AND FORMATS AND PRINTS THE REPORT. IT IS ENTERED FROM AND     *
008030 *  EXITS TO THE OPERATING SYSTEM.                                *
008040 *                                                                     *
008050 ***********************************************************************
008060
008070  A000-CREATE-LOAN-REPORT.
008080
008090      OPEN INPUT  LOAN-INPUT-FILE
008100           OUTPUT LOAN-REPORT-FILE.
008110
008120 *    HEADING ROUTINE
008130
008140      WRITE LOAN-REPORT-LINE FROM FIRST-HEADING-LINE
008150          AFTER ADVANCING TO-TOP-OF-PAGE.
008160      WRITE LOAN-REPORT-LINE FROM SECOND-HEADING-LINE
008170          AFTER ADVANCING 1 LINES.
008180      MOVE SPACE-TWO-LINES TO PROPER-SPACING.
008190
008200 *    MAIN LINE PROCESSING
009010
009020      READ LOAN-INPUT-FILE
009030          AT END
009040              MOVE 'NO ' TO ARE-THERE-MORE-RECORDS.
009050      PERFORM A001-PROCESS-AND-PRINT
009060          UNTIL THERE-ARE-NO-MORE-RECORDS.
009070      CLOSE LOAN-INPUT-FILE
009080            LOAN-REPORT-FILE.
009090      STOP RUN.
```

Figure 5-45 A000-CREATE-LOAN-REPORT Routine

The asterisks on lines 008120 and 008200, followed by the entries HEADING ROUTINE and MAIN ROUTINE, are merely comments to separate the various routines within the module for ease of reading.

The A001-PROCESS-AND-PRINT routine contains the detail processing which is required to produce the report.

EXAMPLE

```
009130  A001-PROCESS-AND-PRINT.
009140  |
009150  |     MOVE SPACES TO LOAN-REPORT-LINE.
009160  |     MOVE ACCOUNT-NUMBER-INPUT TO ACCOUNT-NUMBER-REPORT.
009170  |     MOVE NAME-INPUT TO NAME-REPORT.
009180  |     MOVE LOAN-AMOUNT-INPUT TO LOAN-AMOUNT-REPORT.
009190  |     MOVE INTEREST-RATE-CONSTANT TO INTEREST-RATE-REPORT.
009200  |     MOVE '%' TO PERCENT-SIGN-REPORT.
010010  |     MULTIPLY LOAN-AMOUNT-INPUT BY INTEREST-RATE-CONSTANT GIVING
010020  |         INTEREST-AMOUNT-WORK ROUNDED.
010030  |     MOVE INTEREST-AMOUNT-WORK TO INTEREST-AMOUNT-REPORT.
010040  |     ADD LOAN-AMOUNT-INPUT, INTEREST-AMOUNT-WORK GIVING
010050  |         TOTAL-AMOUNT-WORK.
010060  |     MOVE TOTAL-AMOUNT-WORK TO TOTAL-AMOUNT-REPORT.
010070  |     MOVE NO-OF-PAYMENTS-INPUT TO NO-OF-PAYMENTS-REPORT.
010080  |     DIVIDE TOTAL-AMOUNT-WORK BY NO-OF-PAYMENTS-INPUT GIVING
010090  |         MONTHLY-PAYMENT-REPORT ROUNDED.
010100  |     WRITE LOAN-REPORT-LINE
010110  |         AFTER PROPER-SPACING.
010120  |     MOVE SPACE-ONE-LINE TO PROPER-SPACING.
010130  |     READ LOAN-INPUT-FILE
010140  |         AT END
010150  |             MOVE 'NO ' TO ARE-THERE-MORE-RECORDS.
```

Figure 5-46 A001-PROCESS-AND-PRINT Routine

Note in the Procedure Division statements that the Loan Report Line is cleared with spaces, and then the fields in the input record are moved to the output area. The statement on line 009200 moves the Percent Sign to the output area. Note that the Percent Sign is defined as an alphanumeric literal.

It is important to carefully review the calculations which are being performed. On line 010010, the Loan Amount is multiplied by the Interest Rate and the answer is stored in the work area INTEREST-AMOUNT-WORK, which was defined in Working-Storage (see Figure 5-38). The value in INTEREST-AMOUNT-WORK is then moved to the output area for printing on the report.

The next statement, on line 010040, adds the Interest Amount in the work area to the Loan Amount in the input record in order to obtain the Total Amount. Note that the Total Amount is also stored in a work area. The Total Amount in the work area is then moved to the output area.

The Number of Payments are moved from the input record to the output area and then, on line 010080, the Total Amount in the work area is divided by the Number of Payments, giving the Monthly Payment. A line is then printed, spacing is set, and another record is read for processing.

The following pages contain the complete source listing for the COBOL program to prepare the Loan Report.

Source Listing

```
       1                              IBM DOS AMERICAN NATIONAL STANDARD COBOL              CBF CL3-4          05/18/77

   00001    001010 IDENTIFICATION DIVISION.                                          LOANREPT
   00002    001020                                                                   LOANREPT
   00003    001030 PROGRAM-ID.    LOANREPT.                                          LOANREPT
   00004    001040 AUTHOP.        SHELLY AND CASHMAN.                                LOANREPT
   00005    001050 INSTALLATION.  ANAHEIM.                                           LOANREPT
   00006    001060 DATE-WRITTEN.  05/18/77.                                          LOANREPT
   00007    001070 DATE-COMPILED. 05/18/77                                           LOANREPT
   00008    001080 SECURITY.      UNCLASSIFIED.                                      LOANREPT
   00009    001090 .                                                                 LOANREPT
   00010    001100********************************************************************* LOANREPT
   00011    001110*                                                                 * LOANREPT
   00012    001120*   THIS PROGRAM PREPARES A LOAN REPORT CALCULATING CUSTOMER      * LOANREPT
   00013    001130*   MONTHLY PAYMENTS.  THE LOAN AMOUNT IS MULTIPLIED BY THE       * LOANREPT
   00014    001140*   INTEREST RATE TO OBTAIN THE INTEREST AMOUNT.  THE INTEREST    * LOANREPT
   00015    001150*   AMOUNT IS ADDED TO THE LOAN AMOUNT TO OBTAIN THE TOTAL        * LOANREPT
   00016    001160*   AMOUNT DUE, AND THE TOTAL AMOUNT DUE IS THEN DIVIDED BY       * LOANREPT
   00017    001170*   THE NUMBER OF PAYMENTS TO DETERMINE THE MONTHLY PAYMENTS.     * LOANREPT
   00018    001180*                                                                 * LOANREPT
   00019    001190********************************************************************* LOANREPT
   00020    001200                                                                   LOANREPT
   00021    002010                                                                   LOANREPT
   00022    002020                                                                   LOANREPT
   00023    002030 ENVIRONMENT DIVISION.                                             LOANREPT
   00024    002040                                                                   LOANREPT
   00025    002050 CONFIGURATION SECTION.                                            LOANREPT
   00026    002060                                                                   LOANREPT
   00027    002070 SOURCE-COMPUTER. IBM-370.                                         LOANREPT
   00028    002080 OBJECT-COMPUTER. IBM-370.                                         LOANREPT
   00029    002090 SPECIAL-NAMES.   C01 IS TO-TOP-OF-PAGE.                           LOANREPT
   00030    002100                                                                   LOANREPT
   00031    002110 INPUT-OUTPUT SECTION.                                             LOANREPT
   00032    002120                                                                   LOANREPT
   00033    002130 FILE-CONTROL.                                                     LOANREPT
   00034    002140     SELECT LOAN-INPUT-FILE                                        LOANREPT
   00035    002150         ASSIGN TO SYS007-UR-2540R-S.                              LOANREPT
   00036    002160     SELECT LOAN-REPORT-FILE                                       LOANREPT
   00037    002170         ASSIGN TO SYS013-UR-1403-S.                               LOANREPT
```

```
       2

   00038    002190 DATA DIVISION.                                                    LOANREPT
   00039    002200                                                                   LOANREPT
   00040    003010 FILE SECTION.                                                     LOANREPT
   00041    003020                                                                   LOANREPT
   00042    003030 FD  LOAN-INPUT-FILE                                              LOANREPT
   00043    003040     RECORD CONTAINS 80 CHARACTERS                                 LOANREPT
   00044    003050     LABEL RECORDS ARE OMITTED                                     LOANREPT
   00045    003060     DATA RECORD IS LOAN-INPUT-RECORD.                             LOANREPT
   00046    003070 01  LOAN-INPUT-RECORD.                                            LOANREPT
   00047    003080     05  ACCOUNT-NUMBER-INPUT    PIC 9(6).                         LOANREPT
   00048    003090     05  NAME-INPUT              PIC X(20).                        LOANREPT
   00049    003100     05  LOAN-AMOUNT-INPUT       PIC 9(5)V99.                      LOANREPT
   00050    003110     05  NO-OF-PAYMENTS-INPUT    PIC 99.                           LOANREPT
   00051    003120     05  FILLER                  PIC X(45).                        LOANREPT
   00052    003130                                                                   LOANREPT
   00053    003140 FD  LOAN-REPORT-FILE                                             LOANREPT
   00054    003150     RECORD CONTAINS 133 CHARACTERS                                LOANREPT
   00055    003160     LABEL RECORDS ARE OMITTED                                     LOANREPT
   00056    003170     DATA RECORD IS LOAN-REPORT-LINE.                             LOANREPT
   00057    003180 01  LOAN-REPORT-LINE.                                             LOANREPT
   00058    003190     05  CARRIAGE-CONTROL        PIC X.                            LOANREPT
   00059    003200     05  ACCOUNT-NUMBER-REPORT   PIC ZZZZZ9.                       LOANREPT
   00060    004010     05  FILLER                  PIC X(5).                         LOANREPT
   00061    004020     05  NAME-REPORT             PIC X(20).                        LOANREPT
   00062    004030     05  FILLER                  PIC X(5).                         LOANREPT
   00063    004040     05  LOAN-AMOUNT-REPORT      PIC ZZ,ZZZ.99.                    LOANREPT
   00064    004050     05  FILLER                  PIC X(5).                         LOANREPT
   00065    004060     05  INTEREST-RATE-REPORT    PIC V99.                          LOANREPT
   00066    004069     05  PERCENT-SIGN-REPORT     PIC X.                            LOANREPT
   00067    004070     05  FILLER                  PIC X(5).                         LOANREPT
   00068    004080     05  INTEREST-AMOUNT-REPORT  PIC ZZ,ZZZ.99.                    LOANREPT
   00069    004090     05  FILLER                  PIC X(5).                         LOANREPT
   00070    004100     05  TOTAL-AMOUNT-REPORT     PIC ZZ,ZZZ.99.                    LOANREPT
   00071    004110     05  FILLER                  PIC X(5).                         LOANREPT
   00072    004120     05  NO-OF-PAYMENTS-REPORT   PIC Z9.                           LOANREPT
   00073    004130     05  FILLER                  PIC X(4).                         LOANREPT
   00074    004140     05  MONTHLY-PAYMENT-REPORT  PIC $ZZ,ZZZ.99.                   LOANREPT
   00075    004150     05  FILLER                  PIC X(30).                        LOANREPT
   00076    004160                                                                   LOANREPT
   00077    004170 WORKING-STORAGE SECTION.                                          LOANREPT
   00078    004180                                                                   LOANREPT
   00079    004190 01  PROGRAM-INDICATORS.                                           LOANREPT
   00080    005010     05  ARE-THERE-MORE-RECORDS  PIC XXX      VALUE 'YES'.         LOANREPT
   00081    005020         88  THERE-ARE-NO-MORE-RECORDS        VALUE 'NO '.         LOANREPT
   00082    005030                                                                   LOANREPT
   00083    005040 01  WORK-AREAS.                                                   LOANREPT
   00084    005050     05  INTEREST-AMOUNT-WORK    PIC S9(5)V99 USAGE IS COMP-3.     LOANREPT
   00085    005060     05  TOTAL-AMOUNT-WORK       PIC S9(5)V99 USAGE IS COMP-3.     LOANREPT
   00086    005070                                                                   LOANREPT
   00087    005080 01  PROGRAM-CONSTANTS.                                            LOANREPT
   00088    005090     05  INTEREST-RATE-CONSTANT  PIC V99      VALUE .18            LOANREPT
   00089    005110                                              USAGE IS COMP-3.     LOANREPT
   00090    005120                                                                   LOANREPT
   00091    005130 01  PRINTER-CONTROL.                                              LOANREPT
   00092    005140     05  PROPER-SPACING          PIC 9.                            LOANREPT
   00093    005150     05  SPACE-ONE-LINE          PIC 9        VALUE 1.             LOANREPT
   00094    005160     05  SPACE-TWO-LINES         PIC 9        VALUE 2.             LOANREPT
```

Figure 5-47 Source Listing [Part 1 of 2]

```
      3

00095   005170                                                          LOANREPT
00096   005180 01   HEADING-LINES.                                      LOANREPT
00097   005190    05   FIRST-HEADING-LINE.                              LOANREPT
00098   005200       10   CARRIAGE-CONTROL      PIC X.                  LOANREPT
00099   006010       10   FILLER                PIC X(7)   VALUE 'ACCOUNT'.   LOANREPT
00100   006020       10   FILLER                PIC X(32)  VALUE SPACES.      LOANREPT
00101   006030       10   FILLER                PIC X(4)   VALUE 'LOAN'.      LOANREPT
00102   006040       10   FILLER                PIC X(4)   VALUE SPACES.      LOANREPT
00103   006050       10   FILLER                PIC X(8)   VALUE 'INTEREST'.  LOANREPT
00104   006060       10   FILLER                PIC X(4)   VALUE SPACES.      LOANREPT
00105   006070       10   FILLER                PIC X(8)   VALUE 'INTEREST'.  LOANREPT
00106   006080       10   FILLER                PIC X(8)   VALUE SPACES.      LOANREPT
00107   006090       10   FILLER                PIC X(5)   VALUE 'TOTAL'.     LOANREPT
00108   006100       10   FILLER                PIC X(5)   VALUE SPACES.      LOANREPT
00109   006110       10   FILLER                PIC X(5)   VALUE 'NO OF'.     LOANREPT
00110   006120       10   FILLER                PIC X(4)   VALUE SPACES.      LOANREPT
00111   006130       10   FILLER                PIC X(7)   VALUE 'MONTHLY'.   LOANREPT
00112   006140       10   FILLER                PIC X(31)  VALUE SPACES.      LOANREPT
00113   006150    05   SECOND-HEADING-LINE.                             LOANREPT
00114   006160       10   CARRIAGE-CONTROL      PIC X.                  LOANREPT
00115   006170       10   FILLER                PIC X(6)   VALUE 'NUMBER'.    LOANREPT
00116   006180       10   FILLER                PIC X(13)  VALUE SPACES.      LOANREPT
00117   006190       10   FILLER                PIC X(4)   VALUE 'NAME'.      LOANREPT
00118   006200       10   FILLER                PIC X(15)  VALUE SPACES.      LOANREPT
00119   007010       10   FILLER                PIC X(6)   VALUE 'AMOUNT'.    LOANREPT
00120   007020       10   FILLER                PIC X(5)   VALUE SPACES.      LOANREPT
00121   007030       10   FILLER                PIC X(4)   VALUE 'RATE'.      LOANREPT
00122   007040       10   FILLER                PIC X(7)   VALUE SPACES.      LOANREPT
00123   007050       10   FILLER                PIC X(6)   VALUE 'AMOUNT'.    LOANREPT
00124   007060       10   FILLER                PIC X(8)   VALUE SPACES.      LOANREPT
00125   007070       10   FILLER                PIC X(6)   VALUE 'AMOUNT'.    LOANREPT
00126   007080       10   FILLER                PIC X(5)   VALUE SPACES.      LOANREPT
00127   007090       10   FILLER                PIC X(4)   VALUE 'PMTS'.      LOANREPT
00128   007100       10   FILLER                PIC X(5)   VALUE SPACES.      LOANREPT
00129   007110       10   FILLER                PIC X(7)   VALUE 'PAYMENT'.   LOANREPT
00130   007120       10   FILLER                PIC X(31)  VALUE SPACES.      LOANREPT


      4

00131   007140 PROCEDURE DIVISION.                                     LOANREPT
00132   007150                                                          LOANREPT
00133   007160*****************************************************************  LOANREPT
00134   007170*                                                      *  LOANREPT
00135   007180*   THIS PROGRAM READS THE INPUT RECORDS, PERFORMS THE  *  LOANREPT
00136   007190*   CALCULATIONS TO DETERMINE INTEREST AMOUNT (LOAN AMOUNT TIMES*  LOANREPT
00137   007200*   INTEREST RATE), TOTAL AMOUNT (LOAN AMOUNT + INTEREST AMOUNT)*  LOANREPT
00138   008010*   AND MONTHLY PAYMENT (TOTAL AMOUNT / NUMBER OF PAYMENTS),  *  LOANREPT
00139   008020*   AND FORMATS AND PRINTS THE REPORT.  IT IS ENTERED FROM AND  *  LOANREPT
00140   008030*   EXITS TO THE OPERATING SYSTEM.                     *  LOANREPT
00141   008040*                                                      *  LOANREPT
00142   008050*****************************************************************  LOANREPT
00143   008060                                                          LOANREPT
00144   008070 A000-CREATE-LOAN-REPORT.                                 LOANREPT
00145   008080                                                          LOANREPT
00146   008090    OPEN INPUT  LOAN-INPUT-FILE                           LOANREPT
00147   008100         OUTPUT LOAN-REPORT-FILE.                         LOANREPT
00148   008110                                                          LOANREPT
00149   008120*  HEADING ROUTINE                                        LOANREPT
00150   008130                                                          LOANREPT
00151   008140    WRITE LOAN-REPORT-LINE FROM FIRST-HEADING-LINE        LOANREPT
00152   008150         AFTER ADVANCING TO-TOP-OF-PAGE.                  LOANREPT
00153   008160    WRITE LOAN-REPORT-LINE FROM SECOND-HEADING-LINE       LOANREPT
00154   008170         AFTER ADVANCING 1 LINES.                         LOANREPT
00155   008180    MOVE SPACE-TWO-LINES TO PROPER-SPACING.               LOANREPT
00156   008190                                                          LOANREPT
00157   008200*  MAIN LINE PROCESSING                                   LOANREPT
00158   009010                                                          LOANREPT
00159   009020    READ LOAN-INPUT-FILE                                  LOANREPT
00160   009030         AT END                                           LOANREPT
00161   009040            MOVE 'NO ' TO ARE-THERE-MORE-RECORDS.         LOANREPT
00162   009050    PERFORM A001-PROCESS-AND-PRINT                        LOANREPT
00163   009060         UNTIL THERE-ARE-NO-MORE-RECORDS.                 LOANREPT
00164   009070    CLOSE LOAN-INPUT-FILE                                 LOANREPT
00165   009080          LOAN-REPORT-FILE.                               LOANREPT
00166   009090    STOP RUN.                                             LOANREPT
00167   009100                                                          LOANREPT
00168   009110                                                          LOANREPT
00169   009120                                                          LOANREPT
00170   009130 A001-PROCESS-AND-PRINT.                                  LOANREPT
00171   009140                                                          LOANREPT
00172   009150    MOVE SPACES TO LOAN-REPORT-LINE.                      LOANREPT
00173   009160    MOVE ACCOUNT-NUMBER-INPUT TO ACCOUNT-NUMBER-REPORT.   LOANREPT
00174   009170    MOVE NAME-INPUT TO NAME-REPORT.                       LOANREPT
00175   009180    MOVE LOAN-AMOUNT-INPUT TO LOAN-AMOUNT-REPORT.         LOANREPT
00176   009190    MOVE INTEREST-RATE-CONSTANT TO INTEREST-RATE-REPORT.  LOANREPT
00177   009200    MOVE '%' TO PERCENT-SIGN-REPORT.                      LOANREPT
00178   009210    MULTIPLY LOAN-AMOUNT-INPUT BY INTEREST-RATE-CONSTANT GIVING  LOANREPT
00179   010010         INTEREST-AMOUNT-WORK ROUNDED.                    LOANREPT
00180   010020    MOVE INTEREST-AMOUNT-WORK TO INTEREST-AMOUNT-REPORT.  LOANREPT
00181   010030    ADD LOAN-AMOUNT-INPUT, INTEREST-AMOUNT-WORK GIVING    LOANREPT
00182   010040         TOTAL-AMOUNT-WORK.                               LOANREPT
00183   010050    MOVE TOTAL-AMOUNT-WORK TO TOTAL-AMOUNT-REPORT.        LOANREPT
00184   010060    MOVE NO-OF-PAYMENTS-INPUT TO NO-OF-PAYMENTS-REPORT.   LOANREPT
00185   010070    DIVIDE TOTAL-AMOUNT-WORK BY NO-OF-PAYMENTS-INPUT GIVING  LOANREPT
00186   010080         MONTHLY-PAYMENT-REPORT ROUNDED.                  LOANREPT
00187   010090    WRITE LOAN-REPORT-LINE                                LOANREPT
00188   010100         AFTER PROPER-SPACING.                            LOANREPT
00189   010110    MOVE SPACE-ONE-LINE TO PROPER-SPACING.                LOANREPT
00190   010120    READ LOAN-INPUT-FILE                                  LOANREPT
00191   010130         AT END                                           LOANREPT
00192   010140            MOVE 'NO ' TO ARE-THERE-MORE-RECORDS.         LOANREPT
```

Figure 5-48 Source Listing [Part 2 of 2]

CHAPTER 5

REVIEW QUESTIONS

1. What is the rule for determining the maximum size answer that may develop when performing a multiplication operation?

2. Write the COBOL statement to multiply the value in the field HOURS-INPUT by the value in the field RATE-INPUT, storing the answer in GROSS-PAY-WORK.

3. Write the COBOL statement to multiply the value in the field TOTAL-DUE-INPUT by the value in the field TAX-WORK, storing the answer in TAX-WORK.

4. In a division operation, if the divisor contains 2 digits and the dividend contains 4 digits, what is the maximum size answer that can develop? What is the basic rule for determining the size of an answer in a division operation?

5. In a division operation, if the divisor contains 2 digits and the dividend contains 4 digits, what is the maximum size remainder that can develop? What is the basic rule for determining the size of a remainder in a division operation?

6. Write the COBOL statement to divide the value in the field UNITS-PRODUCED-INPUT by the value in the field DAYS-WORKED-INPUT, storing the answer in AVERAGE-WORK.

7. Write the COBOL statement to divide the value in the field MONTHS-WORKED-INPUT into the value in the field YEARLY-SALARY-INPUT, storing the answer into MONTHLY-SALARY-WORK.

8. Write the COBOL statement to divide the value in the field DAILY-PRODUCTION-INPUT by 8, storing the answer in HOURLY-PRODUCTION-WORK. Any remainder is to be stored in the field EXCESS-UNITS-WORK.

9. Write the COBOL statement to divide the values in the fields SALES-AMOUNT1-WORK and SALES-AMOUNT2-WORK by UNIT-COST-WORK, storing the respective answers developed in SALES-AMOUNT1-WORK and SALES-AMOUNT2-WORK.

10. Using the COMPUTE verb, write the COBOL statement to add the values in the fields YTD-SALES-INPUT, and CURRENT-SALES-INPUT, and then subtract the value in the field SALES-RETURNS-INPUT. The answer is to be stored in the NET-SALES-REPORT field.

11. Using the COMPUTE verb, write the COBOL statement to add the values in the fields QUARTER-ONE-IN, QUARTER-TWO-IN, QUARTER-THREE-IN, and QUARTER-FOUR-IN and divide by 4, storing the answer in QUARTER-AVERAGE-REPORT.

12. Briefly summarize the rules for evaluating arithmetic expressions.

13. What is the advantage in using "Condition Names" in a program?

14. What does an "S" signify in a Picture Clause? When should an "S" be used in a Picture Clause?

15. Briefly explain the purpose of the Clause USAGE IS COMPUTATIONAL-3.

CHAPTER 5

DEBUGGING COBOL PROGRAMS

PROBLEM 1

INSTRUCTIONS

The following COBOL program contains an error or errors which occur during compilation. Circle each error and record the corrected entries on the listing. Explain the error and method of correction in the space provided.

```
     1                              IBM DOS AMERICAN NATIONAL STANDARD COBOL        CBF CL3-4        05/23/77

00001   001010 IDENTIFICATION DIVISION.                                    LOANREPT
00002   001020                                                             LOANREPT
00003   001030 PROGRAM-ID.     LOANREPT.                                   LOANREPT
00004   001040 AUTHOR.         SHELLY AND CASHMAN.                         LOANREPT
00005   001050 INSTALLATION.   ANAHEIM.                                    LOANREPT
00006   001060 DATE-WRITTEN.   05/18/77.                                   LOANREPT
00007   001070 DATE-COMPILED. 05/23/77                                     LOANREPT
00008   001080 SECURITY.       UNCLASSIFIED.                               LOANREPT
00009   001090                                                             LOANREPT
00010   001100*********************************************************** LOANREPT
00011   001110*                                                          * LOANREPT
00012   001120*   THIS PROGRAM PREPARES A LOAN REPORT CALCULATING CUSTOMER * LOANREPT
00013   001130*   MONTHLY PAYMENTS.  THE LOAN AMOUNT IS MULTIPLIED BY THE  * LOANREPT
00014   001140*   INTEREST RATE TO OBTAIN THE INTEREST AMOUNT.  THE INTEREST * LOANREPT
00015   001150*   AMOUNT IS ADDED TO THE LOAN AMOUNT TO OBTAIN THE TOTAL  * LOANREPT
00016   001160*   AMOUNT DUE, AND THE TOTAL AMOUNT DUE IS THEN DIVIDED BY * LOANREPT
00017   001170*   THE NUMBER OF PAYMENTS TO DETERMINE THE MONTHLY PAYMENTS. * LOANREPT
00018   001180*                                                          * LOANREPT
00019   001190*********************************************************** LOANREPT
00020   001200                                                             LOANREPT
00021   002010                                                             LOANREPT
00022   002020                                                             LOANREPT
00023   002030 ENVIROMENT DIVISION.                                        LOANREPT
00024   002040                                                             LOANREPT
00025   002050 CONFIGURATION SECTION.                                      LOANREPT
00026   002060                                                             LOANREPT
00027   002070 SOURCE-COMPUTER. IBM-370.                                   LOANREPT
00028   002080 OBJECT-COMPUTER. IBM-370.                                   LOANREPT
00029   002090 SPECIAL-NAMES.   C01 IS TO-TOP-OF-PAGE.                     LOANREPT
00030   002100                                                             LOANREPT
00031   002110 INPUT-OUTPUT SECTION.                                       LOANREPT
00032   002120                                                             LOANREPT
00033   002130 FILE-CONTROL.                                               LOANREPT
00034   002140     SELECT LOAN-INPUT-FILE                                  LOANREPT
00035   002150         ASSIGN TO SYS007-UR-2540R-S.                        LOANREPT
00036   002160     SELECT LOAN-REPORT-FILE                                 LOANREPT
00037   002170         ASSIGN TO SYS013-UR-1403-S.                         LOANREPT
```

```
    2
00038   002190 DATA DIVISION.                                              LOANREPT
00039   002200                                                            LOANREPT
00040   003010 FILE SECTION.                                               LOANREPT
00041   003020                                                            LOANREPT
00042   003030 FD  LOAN-INPUT-FILE                                         LOANREPT
00043   003040     RECORD CONTAINS 80 CHARACTERS                           LOANREPT
00044   003050     LABEL RECORDS ARE OMITTED                               LOANREPT
00045   003060     DATA RECORD IS LOAN-INPUT-RECORD.                       LOANREPT
00046   003070 01  LOAN-INPUT-RECORD.                                      LOANREPT
00047   003080     05  ACCOUNT-NUMBER-INPUT     PIC X(6).                  LOANREPT
00048   003090     05  NAME-INPUT               PIC X(20).                 LOANREPT
00049   003100     05  LOAN-AMOUNT-INPUT        PIC 9(5)V99.               LOANREPT
00050   003110     05  NO-OF-PAYMENTS-INPUT     PIC 99.                    LOANREPT
00051   003120     05  FILLER                   PIC X(45).                 LOANREPT
00052   003130                                                            LOANREPT
00053   003140 FD  LOAN-REPORT-FILE                                        LOANREPT
00054   003150     RECORD CONTAINS 133 CHARACTERS                          LOANREPT
00055   003160     LABEL RECORDS ARE OMITTED                               LOANREPT
00056   003170     DATA RECORD IS LOAN-REPORT-LINE.                        LOANREPT
00057   003180 01  LOAN-REPORT-LINE.                                       LOANREPT
00058   003190     05  CARRIAGE-CONTROL         PIC X.                     LOANREPT
00059   003200     05  ACCOUNT-NUMBER-REPORT    PIC ZZZZZ9.                LOANREPT
00060   004010     05  FILLER                   PIC X(5).                  LOANREPT
00061   004020     05  NAME-REPORT              PIC X(20).                 LOANREPT
00062   004030     05  FILLER                   PIC X(5).                  LOANREPT
00063   004040     05  LOAN-AMOUNT-REPORT       PIC ZZ,ZZZ.99.             LOANREPT
00064   004050     05  FILLER                   PIC X(5).                  LOANREPT
00065   004060     05  INTEREST-RATE-REPORT     PIC V99.                   LOANREPT
00066   004069     05  PERCENT-SIGN-REPORT      PIC X.                     LOANREPT
00067   004070     05  FILLER                   PIC X(5).                  LOANREPT
00068   004080     05  INTEREST-AMOUNT-REPORT   PIC ZZ,ZZZ.99.             LOANREPT
00069   004090     05  FILLER                   PIC X(5).                  LOANREPT
00070   004100     05  TOTAL-AMOUNT-REPORT      PIC ZZ,ZZZ.99.             LOANREPT
00071   004110     05  FILLER                   PIC X(5).                  LOANREPT
00072   004120     05  NO-OF-PAYMENTS-REPORT    PIC Z9.                    LOANREPT
00073   004130     05  FILLER                   PIC X(4).                  LOANREPT
00074   004140     05  MONTHLY-PAYMENT-REPORT   PIC $ZZ,ZZZ.99.            LOANREPT
00075   004150     05  FILLER                   PIC X(30).                 LOANREPT
00076   004160                                                            LOANREPT
00077   004170 WORKING-STORAGE SECTION.                                    LOANREPT
00078   004180                                                            LOANREPT
00079   004190 01  PROGRAM-INDICATORS.                                     LOANREPT
00080   005010     05  ARE-THERE-MORE-RECORDS   PIC XXX    VALUE 'YES'.    LOANREPT
00081   005020     88  THERE-ARE-NO-MORE-RECORDS           VALUE 'NO '.    LOANREPT
00082   005030                                                            LOANREPT
00083   005040 01  WORK-AREAS.                                             LOANREPT
00084   005050     05  INTEREST-AMOUNT-WORK  PIC S9(5)V99 USAGE IS COMP-3. LOANREPT
00085   005060     05  TOTAL-AMOUNT-WORK     PIC S9(5)V99 USAGE IS COMP-3. LOANREPT
00086   005070                                                            LOANREPT
00087   005080 01  PROGRAM-CONSTANTS.                                      LOANREPT
00088   005090     05  INTEREST-RATE-CONSTANT PIC V99     VALUE .18.       LOANREPT
00089   005110                                           USAGE IS COMP-3.  LOANREPT
00090   005120                                                            LOANREPT
00091   005130 01  PRINTER-CONTROL.                                        LOANREPT
00092   005140     05  PROPER-SPACING           PIC 9.                     LOANREPT
00093   005150     05  SPACE-ONE-LINE           PIC 9      VALUE 1.        LOANREPT
00094   005160     05  SPACE-TWO-LINES          PIC 9      VALUE 2.        LOANREPT

    3
00095   005170                                                            LOANREPT
00096   005180 01  HEADING-LINES.                                          LOANREPT
00097   005190     05  FIRST-HEADING-LINE.                                 LOANREPT
00098   005200         10  CARRIAGE-CONTROL     PIC X.                     LOANREPT
00099   006010         10  FILLER               PIC X(7)  VALUE 'ACCOUNT'. LOANREPT
00100   006020         10  FILLER               PIC X(32) VALUE SPACES.    LOANREPT
00101   006030         10  FILLER               PIC X(4)  VALUE 'LOAN'.    LOANREPT
00102   006040         10  FILLER               PIC X(4)  VALUE SPACES.    LOANREPT
00103   006050         10  FILLER               PIC X(8)  VALUE 'INTEREST'.LOANREPT
00104   006060         10  FILLER               PIC X(4)  VALUE SPACES.    LOANREPT
00105   006070         10  FILLER               PIC X(8)  VALUE 'INTEREST'.LOANREPT
00106   006080         10  FILLER               PIC X(8)  VALUE SPACES.    LOANREPT
00107   006090         10  FILLER               PIC X(5)  VALUE 'TOTAL'.   LOANREPT
00108   006100         10  FILLER               PIC X(5)  VALUE SPACES.    LOANREPT
00109   006110         10  FILLER               PIC X(5)  VALUE 'NO OF'.   LOANREPT
00110   006120         10  FILLER               PIC X(4)  VALUE SPACES.    LOANREPT
00111   006130         10  FILLER               PIC X(7)  VALUE 'MONTHLY'. LOANREPT
00112   006140         10  FILLER               PIC X(31) VALUE SPACES.    LOANREPT
00113   006150     05  SECOND-HEADING-LINE.                                LOANREPT
00114   006160         10  CARRIAGE-CONTROL     PIC X.                     LOANREPT
00115   006170         10  FILLER               PIC X(6)  VALUE 'NUMBER'.  LOANREPT
00116   006180         10  FILLER               PIC X(13) VALUE SPACES.    LOANREPT
00117   006190         10  FILLER               PIC X(4)  VALUE 'NAME'.    LOANREPT
00118   006200         10  FILLER               PIC X(15) VALUE SPACES.    LOANREPT
00119   007010         10  FILLER               PIC X(6)  VALUE 'AMOUNT'.  LOANREPT
00120   007020         10  FILLER               PIC X(5)  VALUE SPACES.    LOANREPT
00121   007030         10  FILLER               PIC X(4)  VALUE 'RATE'.    LOANREPT
00122   007040         10  FILLER               PIC X(7)  VALUE SPACES.    LOANREPT
00123   007050         10  FILLER               PIC X(6)  VALUE 'AMOUNT'.  LOANREPT
00124   007060         10  FILLER               PIC X(8)  VALUE SPACES.    LOANREPT
00125   007070         10  FILLER               PIC X(6)  VALUE 'AMOUNT'.  LOANREPT
00126   007080         10  FILLER               PIC X(5)  VALUE SPACES.    LOANREPT
00127   007090         10  FILLER               PIC X(5)  VALUE 'PMTS'.    LOANREPT
00128   007100         10  FILLER               PIC X(5)  VALUE SPACES.    LOANREPT
00129   007110         10  FILLER               PIC X(7)  VALUE 'PAYMENT'. LOANREPT
00130   007120         10  FILLER               PIC X(31) VALUE SPACES.    LOANREPT
```

```
      4
  00131  007140 PROCEDURE DIVISION.                                          LOANREPT
  00132  007150                                                              LOANREPT
  00133  007160**********************************************************    LOANREPT
  00134  007170*                                                        *    LOANREPT
  00135  007180*  THIS PROGRAM READS THE INPUT RECORDS, PERFORMS THE    *    LOANREPT
  00136  007190*  CALCULATIONS TO DETERMINE INTEREST AMOUNT (LOAN AMOUNT TIMES*  LOANREPT
  00137  007200*  INTEREST RATE), TOTAL AMOUNT (LOAN AMOUNT + INTEREST AMOUNT)*  LOANREPT
  00138  008010*  AND MONTHLY PAYMENT (TOTAL AMOUNT / NUMBER OF PAYMENTS),  *  LOANREPT
  00139  008020*  AND FORMATS AND PRINTS THE REPORT.  IT IS ENTERED FROM AND *  LOANREPT
  00140  008030*  EXITS TO THE OPERATING SYSTEM.                         *    LOANREPT
  00141  008040*                                                        *    LOANREPT
  00142  008050**********************************************************    LOANREPT
  00143  008060                                                              LOANREPT
  00144  008070 A000-CREATE-LOAN-REPORT.                                     LOANREPT
  00145  008080                                                              LOANREPT
  00146  008090     OPEN INPUT  LOAN-INPUT-FILE                              LOANREPT
  00147  008100          OUTPUT LOAN-REPORT-FILE.                            LOANREPT
  00148  008110                                                              LOANREPT
  00149  008120* HEADING ROUTINE                                            LOANREPT
  00150  008130                                                              LOANREPT
  00151  008140     WRITE LOAN-REPORT-LINE FROM FIRST-HEADING-LINE           LOANREPT
  00152  008150          AFTER ADVANCING TO-TOP-OF-PAGE.                     LOANREPT
  00153  008160     WRITE LOAN-REPORT-LINE FROM SECOND-HEADING-LINE          LOANREPT
  00154  008170          AFTER ADVANCING 1 LINES.                            LOANREPT
  00155  008180     MOVE SPACE-TWO-LINES TO PROPER-SPACING.                  LOANREPT
  00156  008190                                                              LOANREPT
  00157  008200* MAIN LINE PROCESSING                                       LOANREPT
  00158  009010                                                              LOANREPT
  00159  009020     READ LOAN-INPUT-FILE                                     LOANREPT
  00160  009030          AT END                                              LOANREPT
  00161  009040               MOVE 'NO ' TO ARE-THERE-MORE-RECORDS.          LOANREPT
  00162  009050     PERFORM A001-PROCESS-AND-PRINT                           LOANREPT
  00163  009060          UNTIL THERE-ARE-NO-MORE-RECORDS.                    LOANREPT
  00164  009070     CLOSE LOAN-INPUT-FILE                                    LOANREPT
  00165  009080           LOAN-REPORT-FILE.                                  LOANREPT
  00166  009090     STOP RUN.                                                LOANREPT
  00167  009100                                                              LOANREPT
  00168  009110                                                              LOANREPT
  00169  009120 A001-PROCESS-AND-PRINT.                                      LOANREPT
  00170  009130                                                              LOANREPT
  00171  009140                                                              LOANREPT
  00172  009150     MOVE SPACES TO LOAN-REPORT-LINE.                         LOANREPT
  00173  009160     MOVE ACCOUNT-NUMBER-INPUT TO ACCOUNT-NUMBER-REPORT.      LOANREPT
  00174  009170     MOVE NAME-INPUT TO NAME-REPORT.                          LOANREPT
  00175  009180     MOVE LOAN-AMOUNT-INPUT TO LOAN-AMOUNT-REPORT.            LOANREPT
  00176  009190     MOVE INTEREST-RATE-CONSTANT TO INTEREST-RATE-REPORT.     LOANREPT
  00177  009200     MOVE '%' TO PERCENT-SIGN-REPORT.                         LOANREPT
  00178  009210     MULTIPLY LOAN-AMOUNT-INPUT, INTEREST-RATE-CONSTANT GIVING  LOANREPT
  00179  010010          INTEREST-AMOUNT-WORK ROUNDED.                       LOANREPT
  00180  010020     MOVE INTEREST-AMOUNT-WORK TO INTEREST-AMOUNT-REPORT.     LOANREPT
  00181  010030     ADD LOAN-AMOUNT-INPUT, INTEREST-AMOUNT-WORK GIVING       LOANREPT
  00182  010040          TOTAL-AMOUNT-WORK.                                  LOANREPT
  00183  010050     MOVE TOTAL-AMOUNT-WORK TO TOTAL-AMOUNT-REPORT.           LOANREPT
  00184  010060     MOVE NO-OF-PAYMENTS-INPUT TO NO-OF-PAYMENTS-REPORT.      LOANREPT
  00185  010070     DIVIDE TOTAL-AMOUNT-REPORT BY NO-OF-PAYMENTS-INPUT GIVING  LOANREPT
  00186  010080          MONTHLY-PAYMENT-REPORT ROUNDED.                     LOANREPT
  00187  010090     WRITE LOAN-REPORT-LINE                                   LOANREPT
  00188  010100          AFTER PROPER-SPACING.                               LOANREPT
  00189  010110     MOVE SPACE-ONE-LINE TO PROPER-SPACING.                   LOANREPT
  00190  010120     READ LOAN-INPUT-FILE                                     LOANREPT
  00191  010130          AT END                                             LOANREPT
  00192  010140               MOVE 'NO ' TO ARE-THERE-MORE-RECORDS.          LOANREPT
```

```
      7

  CARD   ERROR MESSAGE

   23    ILA1087I-W    ' ENVIROMENT ' SHOULD NOT BEGIN IN AREA A.
   38    ILA1026I-W    FOUND DATA . EXPECTING ENVIRONMENT.  ALL ENV. DIV. STATEMENTS IGNORED.
   45    ILA1056I-E    FILE-NAME NOT DEFINED IN A SELECT. DESCRIPTION IGNORED.
   56    ILA1056I-E    FILE-NAME NOT DEFINED IN A SELECT. DESCRIPTION IGNORED.
   89    ILA1004I-E    INVALID WORD USAGE . SKIPPING TO NEXT RECOGNIZABLE WORD.
  146    ILA3001I-E    LOAN-INPUT-FILE NOT DEFINED. DELETING TILL LEGAL ELEMENT FOUND.
  146    ILA3001I-E    LOAN-REPORT-FILE NOT DEFINED. DELETING TILL LEGAL ELEMENT FOUND.
  146    ILA4002I-E    OPEN STATEMENT INCOMPLETE. STATEMENT DISCARDED.
  151    ILA4050I-E    SYNTAX REQUIRES RECORD-NAME . FOUND DNM=1-244 . STATEMENT DISCARDED.
  151    ILA3001I-E    TO-TOP-OF-PAGE NOT DEFINED.
  153    ILA4050I-E    SYNTAX REQUIRES RECORD-NAME . FOUND DNM=1-244 . STATEMENT DISCARDED.
  159    ILA3001I-E    LOAN-INPUT-FILE NOT DEFINED. STATEMENT DISCARDED.
  164    ILA3001I-E    LOAN-INPUT-FILE NOT DEFINED. DELETING TILL LEGAL ELEMENT FOUND.
  164    ILA3001I-E    LOAN-REPORT-FILE NOT DEFINED.
  164    ILA4002I-E    CLOSE STATEMENT INCOMPLETE. STATEMENT DISCARDED.
  178    ILA4007I-C    BY MISSING OR MISPLACED IN MULTIPLY STATEMENT. ASSUMED IN REQUIRED POSITION.
  185    ILA4019I-E    DNM=2-112  (NE) MAY NOT BE USED AS ARITHMETIC OPERAND IN DIVIDE STATEMENT.
                       ARBITRARILY SUBSTITUTING TALLY .
  187    ILA4050I-E    SYNTAX REQUIRES RECORD-NAME . FOUND DNM=1-244 . STATEMENT DISCARDED.
  190    ILA3001I-E    LOAN-INPUT-FILE NOT DEFINED. STATEMENT DISCARDED.

  ILA0004I- LINK OPTION RESET -- D OR E LEVEL ERROR FOUND
```

EXPLANATION:

_____

_____

_____

CHAPTER 5

DEBUGGING COBOL PROGRAMS

PROBLEM 2

INSTRUCTIONS

The following COBOL program contains an error or errors which occur during execution. Circle each error and record the corrected entries directly on the listing. Explain the error and method of correction in the space provided.

```
     1                        IBM DOS AMERICAN NATIONAL STANDARD COBOL          C8F CL3-4        05/23/77

00001   001010 IDENTIFICATION DIVISION.                                   LOANREPT
00002   001020                                                            LOANREPT
00003   001030 PROGRAM-ID.     LOANREPT.                                  LOANREPT
00004   001040 AUTHOR.         SHELLY AND CASHMAN.                        LOANREPT
00005   001050 INSTALLATION.   ANAHEIM.                                   LOANREPT
00006   001060 DATE-WRITTEN.   05/18/77.                                  LOANREPT
00007   001070 DATE-COMPILED. 05/23/77                                    LOANREPT
00008   001080 SECURITY.       UNCLASSIFIED.                              LOANREPT
00009   001090                                                            LOANREPT
00010   001100************************************************************ LOANREPT
00011   001110*                                                         * LOANREPT
00012   001120*    THIS PROGRAM PREPARES A LOAN REPORT CALCULATING CUSTOMER * LOANREPT
00013   001130*    MONTHLY PAYMENTS.  THE LOAN AMOUNT IS MULTIPLIED BY THE  * LOANREPT
00014   001140*    INTEREST RATE TO OBTAIN THE INTEREST AMOUNT.  THE INTEREST * LOANREPT
00015   001150*    AMOUNT IS ADDED TO THE LOAN AMOUNT TO OBTAIN THE TOTAL  * LOANREPT
00016   001160*    AMOUNT DUE, AND THE TOTAL AMOUNT DUE IS THEN DIVIDED BY  * LOANREPT
00017   001170*    THE NUMBER OF PAYMENTS TO DETERMINE THE MONTHLY PAYMENTS. * LOANREPT
00018   001180*                                                         * LOANREPT
00019   001190************************************************************ LOANREPT
00020   001200                                                            LOANREPT
00021   002010                                                            LOANREPT
00022   002020                                                            LOANREPT
00023   002030 ENVIRONMENT DIVISION.                                      LOANREPT
00024   002040                                                            LOANREPT
00025   002050 CONFIGURATION SECTION.                                     LOANREPT
00026   002060                                                            LOANREPT
00027   002070 SOURCE-COMPUTER. IBM-370.                                  LOANREPT
00028   002080 OBJECT-COMPUTER. IBM-370.                                  LOANREPT
00029   002090 SPECIAL-NAMES.   C01 IS TO-TOP-OF-PAGE.                    LOANREPT
00030   002100                                                            LOANREPT
00031   002110 INPUT-OUTPUT SECTION.                                      LOANREPT
00032   002120                                                            LOANREPT
00033   002130 FILE-CONTROL.                                              LOANREPT
00034   002140     SELECT LOAN-INPUT-FILE                                 LOANREPT
00035   002150         ASSIGN TO SYS007-UR-2540R-S.                       LOANREPT
00036   002160     SELECT LOAN-REPORT-FILE                                LOANREPT
00037   002170         ASSIGN TO SYS013-UR-1403-S.                        LOANREPT
```

```
        2
00038  002190 DATA DIVISION.                                                    LOANREPT
00039  002200                                                                   LOANREPT
00040  003010 FILE SECTION.                                                     LOANREPT
00041  003020                                                                   LOANREPT
00042  003030 FD  LOAN-INPUT-FILE                                              LOANREPT
00043  003040        RECORD CONTAINS 80 CHARACTERS                              LOANREPT
00044  003050        LABEL RECORDS ARE OMITTED                                  LOANREPT
00045  003060        DATA RECORD IS LOAN-INPUT-RECORD.                          LOANREPT
00046  003070 01  LOAN-INPUT-RECORD.                                            LOANREPT
00047  003080     05  ACCOUNT-NUMBER-INPUT     PIC 9(6).                        LOANREPT
00048  003090     05  NAME-INPUT               PIC X(20).                       LOANREPT
00049  003100     05  LOAN-AMOUNT-INPUT        PIC 9(5)V99.                     LOANREPT
00050  003110     05  NO-OF-PAYMENTS-INPUT     PIC 99.                          LOANREPT
00051  003120     05  FILLER                   PIC X(45).                       LOANREPT
00052  003130                                                                   LOANREPT
00053  003140 FD  LOAN-REPORT-FILE                                             LOANREPT
00054  003150        RECORD CONTAINS 133 CHARACTERS                             LOANREPT
00055  003160        LABEL RECORDS ARE OMITTED                                  LOANREPT
00056  003170        DATA RECORD IS LOAN-REPORT-LINE.                           LOANREPT
00057  003180 01  LOAN-REPORT-LINE.                                             LOANREPT
00058  003190     05  CARRIAGE-CONTROL         PIC X.                           LOANREPT
00059  003200     05  ACCOUNT-NUMBER-REPORT    PIC ZZZZZ9.                      LOANREPT
00060  004010     05  FILLER                   PIC X(5).                        LOANREPT
00061  004020     05  NAME-REPORT              PIC X(20).                       LOANREPT
00062  004030     05  FILLER                   PIC X(5).                        LOANREPT
00063  004040     05  LOAN-AMOUNT-REPORT       PIC ZZ,ZZZ.99.                   LOANREPT
00064  004050     05  FILLER                   PIC X(5).                        LOANREPT
00065  004060     05  INTEREST-RATE-REPORT     PIC V99.                         LOANREPT
00066  004069     05  PERCENT-SIGN-REPORT      PIC X.                           LOANREPT
00067  004070     05  FILLER                   PIC X(5).                        LOANREPT
00068  004080     05  INTEREST-AMOUNT-REPORT   PIC ZZ,ZZZ.99.                   LOANREPT
00069  004090     05  FILLER                   PIC X(5).                        LOANREPT
00070  004100     05  TOTAL-AMOUNT-REPORT      PIC ZZ,ZZZ.99.                   LOANREPT
00071  004110     05  FILLER                   PIC X(5).                        LOANREPT
00072  004120     05  NO-OF-PAYMENTS-REPORT    PIC Z9.                          LOANREPT
00073  004130     05  FILLER                   PIC X(4).                        LOANREPT
00074  004140     05  MONTHLY-PAYMENT-REPORT   PIC $ZZ,ZZZ.99.                  LOANREPT
00075  004150     05  FILLER                   PIC X(30).                       LOANREPT
00076  004160                                                                   LOANREPT
00077  004170 WORKING-STORAGE SECTION.                                          LOANREPT
00078  004180                                                                   LOANREPT
00079  004190 01  PROGRAM-INDICATORS.                                           LOANREPT
00080  005010     05  ARE-THERE-MORE-RECORDS PIC XXX     VALUE 'YES'.           LOANREPT
00081  005020         88  THERE-ARE-NO-MORE-RECORDS      VALUE 'NO '.           LOANREPT
00082  005030                                                                   LOANREPT
00083  005040 01  WORK-AREAS.                                                   LOANREPT
00084  005050     05  INTEREST-AMOUNT-WORK    PIC S9(5)V99 USAGE IS COMP-3.     LOANREPT
00085  005060     05  TOTAL-AMOUNT-WORK       PIC S9(5)V99 USAGE IS COMP-3.     LOANREPT
00086  005070                                                                   LOANREPT
00087  005080 01  PROGRAM-CONSTANTS.                                            LOANREPT
00088  005090     05  INTEREST-RATE-CONSTANT  PIC 99       VALUE .18            LOANREPT
00089  005110                                              USAGE IS COMP-3.     LOANREPT
00090  005120                                                                   LOANREPT
00091  005130 01  PRINTER-CONTROL.                                              LOANREPT
00092  005140     05  PROPER-SPACING          PIC 9.                           LOANREPT
00093  005150     05  SPACE-ONE-LINE          PIC 9        VALUE 1.             LOANREPT
00094  005160     05  SPACE-TWO-LINES         PIC 9        VALUE 2.             LOANREPT

        3
00095  005170                                                                   LOANREPT
00096  005180 01  HEADING-LINES.                                                LOANREPT
00097  005190     05  FIRST-HEADING-LINE.                                       LOANREPT
00098  005200         10  CARRIAGE-CONTROL    PIC X.                           LOANREPT
00099  006010         10  FILLER              PIC X(7)    VALUE 'ACCOUNT'.      LOANREPT
00100  005020         10  FILLER              PIC X(32)   VALUE SPACES.         LOANREPT
00101  006030         10  FILLER              PIC X(4)    VALUE 'LOAN'.         LOANREPT
00102  006040         10  FILLER              PIC X(4)    VALUE SPACES.         LOANREPT
00103  006050         10  FILLER              PIC X(8)    VALUE 'INTEREST'.     LOANREPT
00104  006060         10  FILLER              PIC X(4)    VALUE SPACES.         LOANREPT
00105  006070         10  FILLER              PIC X(8)    VALUE 'INTEREST'.     LOANREPT
00106  006080         10  FILLER              PIC X(8)    VALUE SPACES.         LOANREPT
00107  006090         10  FILLER              PIC X(5)    VALUE 'TOTAL'.        LOANREPT
00108  006100         10  FILLER              PIC X(5)    VALUE SPACES.         LOANREPT
00109  006110         10  FILLER              PIC X(5)    VALUE 'NO OF'.        LOANREPT
00110  006120         10  FILLER              PIC X(4)    VALUE SPACES.         LOANREPT
00111  006130         10  FILLER              PIC X(7)    VALUE 'MONTHLY'.      LOANREPT
00112  006140         10  FILLER              PIC X(31)   VALUE SPACES.         LOANREPT
00113  006150     05  SECOND-HEADING-LINE.                                      LOANREPT
00114  006160         10  CARRIAGE-CONTROL    PIC X.                           LOANREPT
00115  006170         10  FILLER              PIC X(6)    VALUE 'NUMBER'.       LOANREPT
00116  006180         10  FILLER              PIC X(13)   VALUE SPACES.         LOANREPT
00117  006190         10  FILLER              PIC X(4)    VALUE 'NAME'.         LOANREPT
00118  006200         10  FILLER              PIC X(15)   VALUE SPACES.         LOANREPT
00119  007010         10  FILLER              PIC X(6)    VALUE 'AMOUNT'.       LOANREPT
00120  007020         10  FILLER              PIC X(5)    VALUE SPACES.         LOANREPT
00121  007030         10  FILLER              PIC X(4)    VALUE 'RATE'.         LOANREPT
00122  007040         10  FILLER              PIC X(7)    VALUE SPACES.         LOANREPT
00123  007050         10  FILLER              PIC X(6)    VALUE 'AMOUNT'.       LOANREPT
00124  007060         10  FILLER              PIC X(8)    VALUE SPACES.         LOANREPT
00125  007070         10  FILLER              PIC X(6)    VALUE 'AMOUNT'.       LOANREPT
00126  007080         10  FILLER              PIC X(5)    VALUE SPACES.         LOANREPT
00127  007090         10  FILLER              PIC X(4)    VALUE 'PMTS'.         LOANREPT
00128  007100         10  FILLER              PIC X(5)    VALUE SPACES.         LOANREPT
00129  007110         10  FILLER              PIC X(7)    VALUE 'PAYMENT'.      LOANREPT
00130  007120         10  FILLER              PIC X(31)   VALUE SPACES.         LOANREPT
```

```
      4
00131   007140 PROCEDURE DIVISION.                                    LOANREPT
00132   007150                                                        LOANREPT
00133   007160*************************************************************  LOANREPT
00134   007170*                                                    *  LOANREPT
00135   007180*  THIS PROGRAM READS THE INPUT RECORDS, PERFORMS THE *  LOANREPT
00136   007190*  CALCULATIONS TO DETERMINE INTEREST AMOUNT (LOAN AMOUNT TIMES*  LOANREPT
00137   007200*  INTEREST RATE), TOTAL AMOUNT (LOAN AMOUNT + INTEREST AMOUNT)*  LOANREPT
00138   008010*  AND MONTHLY PAYMENT (TOTAL AMOUNT / NUMBER OF PAYMENTS), *  LOANREPT
00139   008020*  AND FORMATS AND PRINTS THE REPORT.  IT IS ENTERED FROM AND *  LOANREPT
00140   008030*  EXITS TO THE OPERATING SYSTEM.                      *  LOANREPT
00141   008040*                                                    *  LOANREPT
00142   008050*************************************************************  LOANREPT
00143   008060                                                        LOANREPT
00144   008070 A000-CREATE-LOAN-REPORT.                               LOANREPT
00145   008080                                                        LOANREPT
00146   008090     OPEN INPUT  LOAN-INPUT-FILE                        LOANREPT
00147   008100         OUTPUT LOAN-REPORT-FILE.                       LOANREPT
00148   008110                                                        LOANREPT
00149   008120* HEADING ROUTINE                                       LOANREPT
00150   008130                                                        LOANREPT
00151   008140     WRITE LOAN-REPORT-LINE FROM FIRST-HEADING-LINE     LOANREPT
00152   008150         AFTER ADVANCING TO-TOP-OF-PAGE.                LOANREPT
00153   008160     WRITE LOAN-REPORT-LINE FROM SECOND-HEADING-LINE    LOANREPT
00154   008170         AFTER ADVANCING 1 LINES.                       LOANREPT
00155   008180     MOVE SPACE-TWO-LINES TO PROPER-SPACING.            LOANREPT
00156   008190                                                        LOANREPT
00157   008200* MAIN LINE PROCESSING                                  LOANREPT
00158   009010                                                        LOANREPT
00159   009020     READ LOAN-INPUT-FILE                               LOANREPT
00160   009030         AT END                                         LOANREPT
00161   009040             MOVE 'NO ' TO ARE-THERE-MORE-RECORDS.      LOANREPT
00162   009050     PERFORM A001-PROCESS-AND-PRINT                     LOANREPT
00163   009060         UNTIL THERE-ARE-NO-MORE-RECORDS.               LOANREPT
00164   009070     CLOSE LOAN-INPUT-FILE                              LOANREPT
00165   009080           LOAN-REPORT-FILE.                            LOANREPT
00166   009090     STOP RUN.                                          LOANREPT
00167   009100                                                        LOANREPT
00168   009110                                                        LOANREPT
00169   009120                                                        LOANREPT
00170   009130 A001-PROCESS-AND-PRINT.                                LOANREPT
00171   009140                                                        LOANREPT
00172   009150     MOVE SPACES TO LOAN-REPORT-LINE.                   LOANREPT
00173   009160     MOVE ACCOUNT-NUMBER-INPUT TO ACCOUNT-NUMBER-REPORT. LOANREPT
00174   009170     MOVE NAME-INPUT TO NAME-REPORT.                    LOANREPT
00175   009180     MOVE LOAN-AMOUNT-INPUT TO LOAN-AMOUNT-REPORT.      LOANREPT
00176   009190     MOVE INTEREST-RATE-CONSTANT TO INTEREST-RATE-REPORT. LOANREPT
00177   009200     MOVE '%' TO PERCENT-SIGN-REPORT.                   LOANREPT
00178   009210     MULTIPLY LOAN-AMOUNT-INPUT BY INTEREST-RATE-CONSTANT GIVING LOANREPT
00179   010010         INTEREST-AMOUNT-WORK ROUNDED.                  LOANREPT
00180   010020     MOVE INTEREST-AMOUNT-WORK TO INTEREST-AMOUNT-REPORT. LOANREPT
00181   010030     ADD LOAN-AMOUNT-INPUT, INTEREST-AMOUNT-WORK GIVING LOANREPT
00182   010040         TOTAL-AMOUNT-WORK.                             LOANREPT
00183   010050     MOVE TOTAL-AMOUNT-WORK TO TOTAL-AMOUNT-REPORT.     LOANREPT
00184   010060     MOVE NO-OF-PAYMENTS-INPUT TO NO-OF-PAYMENTS-REPORT. LOANREPT
00185   010070     DIVIDE TOTAL-AMOUNT-WORK BY NO-OF-PAYMENTS-INPUT GIVING LOANREPT
00186   010080         MONTHLY-PAYMENT-REPORT ROUNDED.                LOANREPT
00187   010090     WRITE LOAN-REPORT-LINE                             LOANREPT
00188   010100         AFTER PROPER-SPACING.                          LOANREPT
00189   010110     MOVE SPACE-ONE-LINE TO PROPER-SPACING.             LOANREPT
00190   010120     READ LOAN-INPUT-FILE                               LOANREPT
00191   010130         AT END                                         LOANREPT
00192   010140             MOVE 'NO ' TO ARE-THERE-MORE-RECORDS.      LOANREPT
```

```
      7

   CARD    ERROR MESSAGE

    88     ILA2129I-C     VALUE CLAUSE LITERAL DOES NOT CONFORM TO PICTURE. CHANGED TO ZERO.
   192     ILA4072I-W     EXIT FROM PERFORMED PROCEDURE ASSUMED BEFORE PROCEDURE-NAME .
```

ACCOUNT NUMBER	NAME	LOAN AMOUNT	INTEREST RATE	INTEREST AMOUNT	TOTAL AMOUNT	NO OF PMTS	MONTHLY PAYMENT
11993	AHERS, ROSCOE R.	2,000.00	00%	.00	2,000.00	12	$ 166.67
111213	BACKER, OTTO A.	10,000.00	00%	.00	10,000.00	20	$ 500.00
185431	MENLO, SEYMOUR D.	500.00	00%	.00	500.00	12	$ 41.67
622121	HUNTER, JESSE C.	6,000.54	00%	.00	6,000.54	36	$ 166.68
777255	JAWLEY, SUSAN C.	12,300.00	00%	.00	12,300.00	60	$ 205.00

EXPLANATION:

_____

_____

_____

_____

CHAPTER 5

PROGRAMMING ASSIGNMENT 1

INSTRUCTIONS

An Accounts Receivable Report is to be prepared. Design and write the COBOL program to prepare the required report. An IPO Chart and Pseudocode Specifications should be used when designing the program. Use Test Data Set 1, contained in Appendix A.

INPUT

Input is to consist of Accounts Receivable Cards containing the Customer Number, the Customer Name, and the Sales Amount. The format of the cards is illustrated below.

OUTPUT

Output is to consist of an Accounts Receivable Report containing the Customer Number, Customer Name, Sales Amount, Sales Tax Percent (6%), Tax Amount, and Amount Due. The Tax Amount is calculated by multiplying the Sales Amount by 6%. The Amount Due is obtained by adding the Sales Amount and the Tax Amount. The printer spacing chart for the report is illustrated below.

CHAPTER 5

PROGRAMMING ASSIGNMENT 2

INSTRUCTIONS

A Sales Report is to be prepared. Design and write the COBOL program to prepare the required report. An IPO Chart and Pseudocode Specifications should be used when designing the report. Use Test Data Set 1, contained in Appendix A.

INPUT

Input is to consist of Sales Cards containing the Salesman Number, Salesman Name, the Months Employed, the Previous Sales, and the Current Sales. The format of the card is illustrated below.

OUTPUT

Output is to consist of a Sales Report listing the Salesman Number, the Salesman Name, the Previous Sales, the Current Sales, the Total Sales, the Months Employed, and the Monthly Sales Average. Total Sales is to be calculated by adding the Previous Sales and the Current Sales. The Monthly Sales Average is to be calculated by dividing the Total Sales by the Months Employed. The printer spacing chart for the report is illustrated below.

CHAPTER 5

PROGRAMMING ASSIGNMENT 3

INSTRUCTIONS

A Pricing Report is to be prepared. Design and write the COBOL program to prepare the required report. An IPO Chart and Pseudocode Specifications should be used when designing the program. Use Test Data Set 1, contained in Appendix A.

INPUT

The input to the program consists of Pricing Cards which contain the Product Number, the Quantity Produced, the Description, the Total Cost, and the Markup Percentage. The format of the input record is illustrated below.

OUTPUT

The output is the Pricing Report containing the Product Number, Description, Quantity, Total Cost, Unit Cost, Markup Percentage, and Unit Price. The Unit Cost is determined by dividing the Total Cost by the Quantity. The Unit Price is calculated by multiplying the Unit Cost by the Markup Percentage and then adding the result to the Unit Cost. For example, an item with a Unit Cost of 10.00, and a markup percentage of 150% would have a Unit Price of $25.00.

CHAPTER 5

PROGRAMMING ASSIGNMENT 4

INSTRUCTIONS

A Stock Summary Report is to be prepared. Write the COBOL program to produce the required report. An IPO Chart and Pseudocode Specifications should be used when designing the program. Use Test Data Set 2 in Appendix A.

INPUT

Input is to consist of a punched card file, with each record containing the Number of Shares of Stock purchased and sold, the Dividends Paid per Share, the Company Name, the Price per Share when purchased, and the Price per Share when sold. It should be noted that the number of shares purchased is the same as the number of shares sold, that is, if 20 shares were purchased, 20 shares were sold. The format of the input record is illustrated below.

OUTPUT

The output of the program is the Stock Summary Report. It contains the Company Name, the Number of Shares Purchased and Sold, the Purchase Price per Share, the Total Purchase Price, the Dividends per Share, the Total Dividends received, the Selling Price per Share, the Total Selling Price, the Amount of Gain or Loss, and the Percentage of Gain or Loss. The format of the report is illustrated on page 5.49.

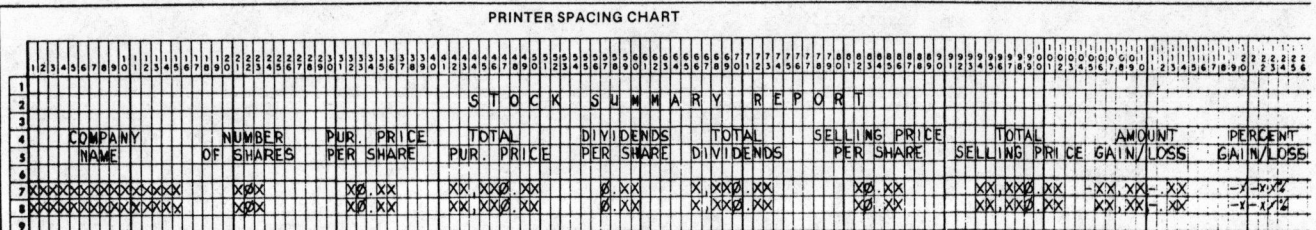

The following calculations must be performed in the program.

1. Multiply the Purchase Price per Share by the Number of Shares to obtain the Total Purchase Price.

2. Multiply the Number of Shares by the Dividends per Share to obtain the Total Dividends.

3. Multiply the Number of Shares by the Selling Price per Share to obtain the Total Selling Price.

4. Add the Total Selling Price and the Total Dividends to obtain the Total Income derived from the shares of stock (Total Income is not contained on the report).

5. Subtract the Total Purchase Price of the stock from the Total Income derived from the shares of stock to obtain the Gain or Loss on the sale of the stock.

6. Divide the Gain or Loss on the Stock (the answer in step 5) by the Total Purchase Price of the stock to obtain the Percentage of Gain or Loss.

COMPARING; FINAL TOTALS

6

> *. . .your real opportunity to know you have written a correct program is to never find the first error in it, no matter how much it is inspected, tested, and used.* [1]

INTRODUCTION

In Chapter 1 it was pointed out that three basic control structures can be used to express the logic of any program—the SEQUENCE, the IF-THEN-ELSE, and the DO WHILE. This chapter will be used to explain the IF-THEN-ELSE structure.

The IF-THEN-ELSE structure is a conditional statement and specifies that certain events are to take place only upon given conditions. This is illustrated in the diagram below.

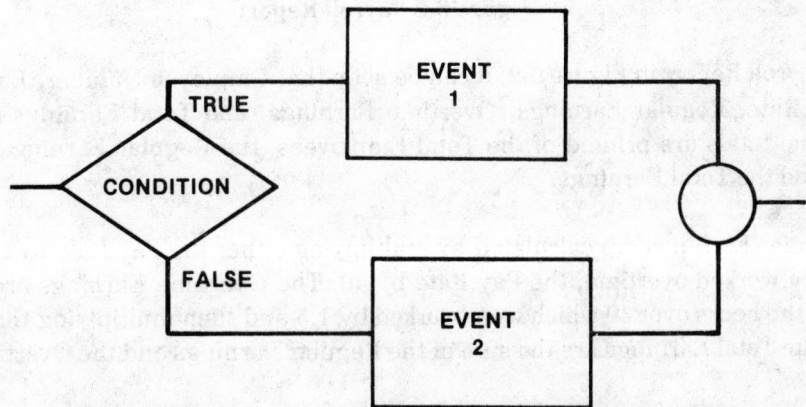

Figure 6-1 Example of IF-THEN-ELSE Structure

1 H. D. Mills, *HOW TO WRITE CORRECT PROGRAMS AND KNOW IT, IBM Federal Systems Division, IBM, February 1973.*

As can be seen from Figure 6-1, Event 1 will occur if the Condition tested is true, and Event 2 will take place if the Condition is false. The real power of a computer in solving problems is in its ability to take alternative courses of action, as indicated in the IF-THEN-ELSE structure, based upon conditions which can be tested within the program. This ability is normally implemented through the use of instructions which compare values stored in computer storage, and take action based upon the relationship of these values to one another; that is, whether they are equal or not equal, or whether one is greater than or less than another. In this chapter, the IF Statement, which is used in COBOL to compare two values and which implements the IF-THEN-ELSE structure, will be explained.

When values are computed in a business program, in many applications it is necessary to accumulate final totals; that is, totals which reflect the accumulated values of a field or fields. The techniques for accumulating final totals are also illustrated in this chapter.

SAMPLE PROBLEM

In order to illustrate Comparing and Final Totals, the problem in this chapter is to create a Payroll Report. A sample of the report is illustrated below.

```
                        P A Y R O L L    R E P O R T
   EMP.           EMPLOYEE                    PAY      REGULAR     OVERTIME       TOTAL
    NO.             NAME          HOURS        RATE    EARNINGS    EARNINGS      EARNINGS

   1005     ABBOTT, CHARLES         40        3.00     120.00        .00        120.00
   1009     ANCHOR, WILLIAM B.      41        3.00     120.00       4.50        124.50
   2714     BRADLEY, CYNTHIA C.     39        3.00     117.00        .00        117.00
   2881     CANA, CARY K.           50        4.50     180.00      67.50        247.50
   2995     DOGER, MARY L.          20        3.50      70.00        .00         70.00
   3015     SEGERSTROM, JUDY M.     26        4.00     104.00        .00        104.00

   TOTAL EMPLOYEES    6            FINAL TOTALS   $711.00      $72.00        $783.00
```

Figure 6-2 Payroll Report

In the Payroll Report in Figure 6-2, it can be seen that Employee Number, Employee Name, Hours, Pay Rate, Regular Earnings, Overtime Earnings, and Total Earnings are printed. In addition, final totals are printed of the Total Employees, the Regular Earnings, the Overtime Earnings, and the Total Earnings.

The Regular Earnings are calculated by multiplying either the Pay Rate by the Hours or, if the employee worked overtime, the Pay Rate by 40. The Overtime Earnings are calculated by multiplying the hours over 40 which were worked by 1.5 and then multiplying that result by the Pay Rate. The Total Earnings are the sum of the Regular Earnings and the Overtime Earnings.

INPUT

   The input to the program is the Payroll Card File. The format of the Payroll Cards in this file is illustrated in Figure 6-3.

INPUT

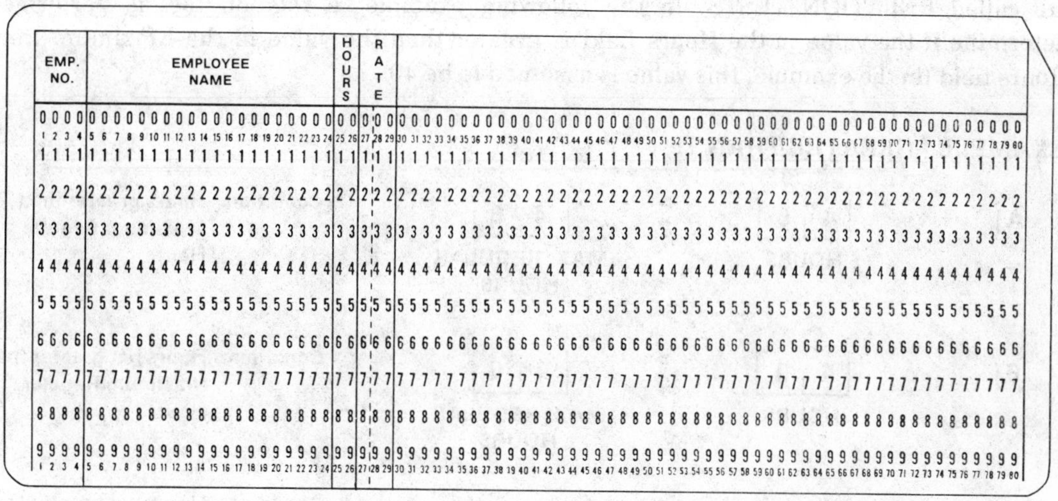

Figure 6-3 Input Record

   Note from Figure 6-3 that the input record contains the Employee Number, the Employee Name, the Hours, and the Pay Rate.

   To determine if an employee is to receive Overtime Pay, the Hours field on the input card must be compared to the constant 40. If an employee works over 40 hours, Overtime Pay is to be calculated. If an employee works 40 hours or less, only Regular Pay is calculated.

   The paragraphs on the following pages explain the basic concepts of comparing which are required for an understanding of the solution to this problem.

CONCEPTS OF COMPARING

There are three major comparing operations which can be performed on data in computer storage: a comparision can be made to determine if the data in one field is greater than the data in another field, whether the data in one field is less than the data in another field, or whether the data in one field is equal to the data in another field. These types of comparing operations are called RELATION TESTS. In the following example, a relation test is performed to determine if the value in the Hours field is greater than the value in the Maximum Regular Hours field (in the example, this value is assumed to be 40).

EXAMPLE - GREATER THAN Test

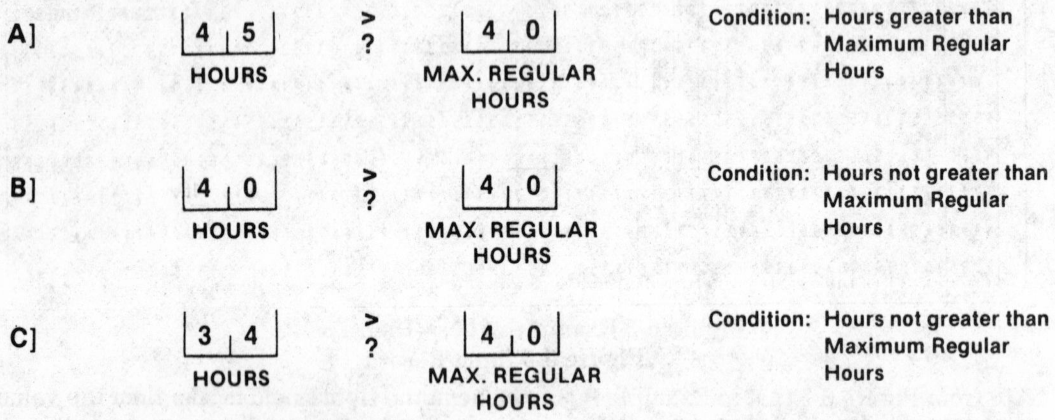

A] | 4 | 5 | > | 4 | 0 | Condition: Hours greater than
            HOURS   ?   MAX. REGULAR   Maximum Regular
                                          HOURS   Hours

B] | 4 | 0 | > | 4 | 0 | Condition: Hours not greater than
            HOURS   ?   MAX. REGULAR   Maximum Regular
                                          HOURS   Hours

C] | 3 | 4 | > | 4 | 0 | Condition: Hours not greater than
            HOURS   ?   MAX. REGULAR   Maximum Regular
                                          HOURS   Hours

Note: The symbol > means greater than

Figure 6-4 Example of Greater Than Test

In Example A, the value in the Hours field is 45 and the value in the Maximum Regular Hours field is 40. Therefore, the value in the Hours field is greater than the value in the Maximum Regular Hours field. In Example B, both fields contain the value 40. Therefore, the value in the Hours field is not greater than the value in the Maximum Regular Hours field. In Example C, the value 34 in the Hours field is clearly not greater than the value in the Maximum Regular Hours field.

A second test which can be performed on data stored in computer storage is to determine if one value is less than another value. This is illustrated below.

EXAMPLE - LESS THAN Test

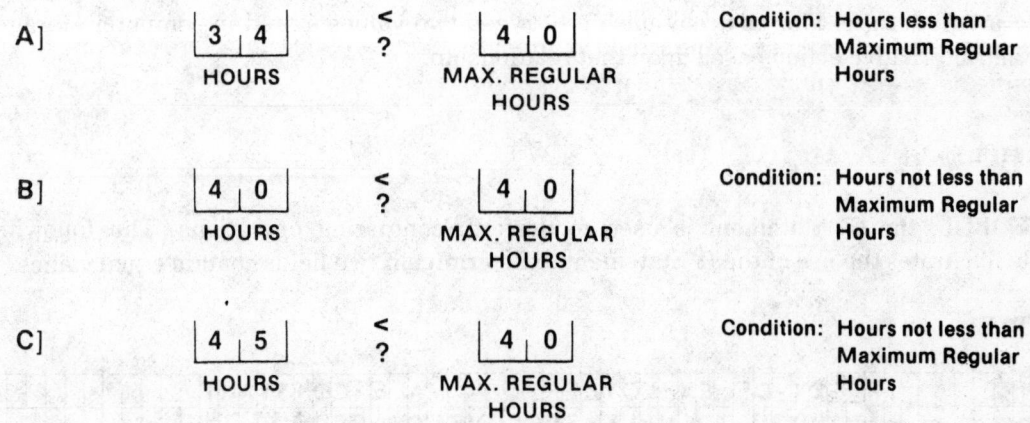

Note: The symbol < means less than

Figure 6-5 Example of Less Than Test

Note from Figure 6-5 that in Example A, the value in the Hours field is less than the value in the Maximum Regular Hours field. In Example B, the value in the Hours field is not less than the value in the Maximum Regular Hours field; nor is it less in Example C.

The third test which can be performed is the equal test, which is illustrated in Figure 6-6.

EXAMPLE - EQUAL Test

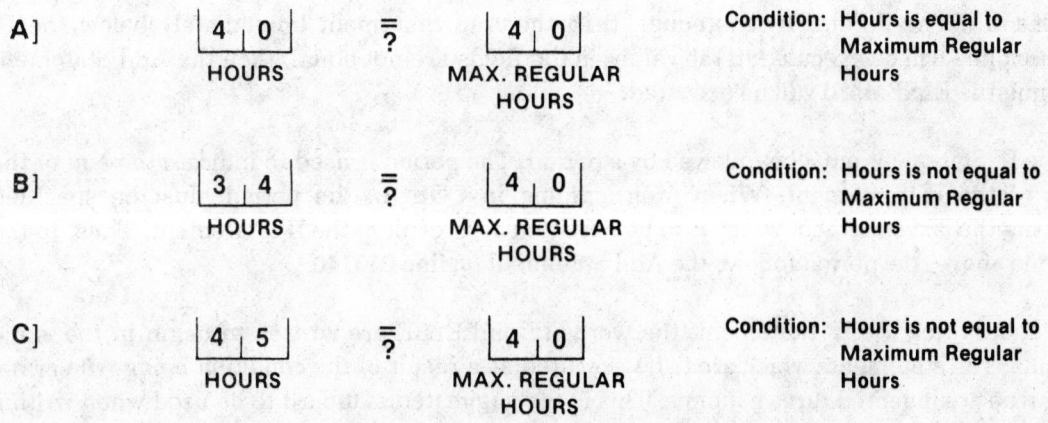

Figure 6-6 Example of Equal Test

As can be seen from Figure 6-6, in Example A both fields contain the value 40 and are therefore considered equal. In Example B and Example C, the values are not equal.

It should be noted also that it is possible to test for conditions of NOT GREATER THAN, NOT LESS THAN, and NOT EQUAL, as well as those illustrated previously. Thus, it is possible within a program to test for any relationship between two values stored in computer storage, and to take alternative action based upon that relationship.

IF STATEMENT

In COBOL, the IF Statement is used to perform comparing operations. The following example illustrates the use of the IF Statement to determine if two fields contain equal values.

EXAMPLE

```
012110        IF SEX-OF-EMPLOYEE-IN = MALE-CONSTANT
012120           ADD 1 TO MALE-EMPLOYEES-ACCUM
013130        ELSE
013140           ADD 1 TO FEMALE-EMPLOYEES-ACCUM.
```

```
IF condition;  { statement-1  }  { ; ELSE statement-2      }
               { NEXT SENTENCE }  { ; ELSE NEXT SENTENCE    }
```

Figure 6-7 Example of IF Statement

Note from the format illustrated in Figure 6-7 that the IF Statement begins with the word IF. It is followed by a condition which is to be tested. In the example, the condition tested is whether the value in the field SEX-OF-EMPLOYEE-IN is equal to the value in the MALE-CONSTANT field. If it is equal, then the Add Statement immediately below the IF condition line will be executed; if the values in the fields are not equal, then the Add Statement following the ELSE word will be executed.

The IF Statement must be followed by a period. The period is used to indicate the end of the effect of the IF Statement. When programming in COBOL, the period must be specified following the last statement which is to be executed as a result of the IF Statement. Thus, in the example above, the period follows the Add Statement on line 013140.

When writing the IF Statement, the words IF and ELSE are written to begin in the same columns. The statements which are to be executed as a result of the condition being true or not being true are indented three columns. This is the suggested standard to be used when writing the IF Statement, although it is not required in order for the IF Statement to function properly.

More than one statement can be specified following the IF or the ELSE words. The following example illustrates an IF Statement containing several statements following the IF and several statements following the ELSE.

EXAMPLE

```
Ø14020    IF SEX-OF-EMPLOYEE-INPUT = MALE-CONSTANT
Ø14030       PERFORM CØ3Ø-PROCESS-MALE-EMPLOYEE
Ø14040       ADD 1 TO MALE-EMPLOYEES-ACCUM
Ø14050    ELSE
Ø14060       PERFORM CØ4Ø-PROCESS-FEMALE-EMPLOYEE
Ø14070       ADD 1 TO FEMALE-EMPLOYEE-ACCUM.
Ø14080    MOVE SEX-OF-EMPLOYEE-INPUT TO SEX-OF-EMPLOYEE-REPORT.
```

Figure 6-8 Example of Multiple Statements

It should be noted that after execution of the IF Statement, the statement following the period at the end of the IF Statement is executed. Thus, in the example above, after the IF Statement has been executed, that is, after the condition has been evaluated and the appropriate processing has occured, the Move Statement on line 014080 will be executed. It will be executed regardless of the condition which is found in the IF Statement because it follows the period which terminates the IF Statement. As can be seen, the period is quite important when using the IF Statement. The following example illustrates a common error in the placement of the period within the IF Statement.

EXAMPLE

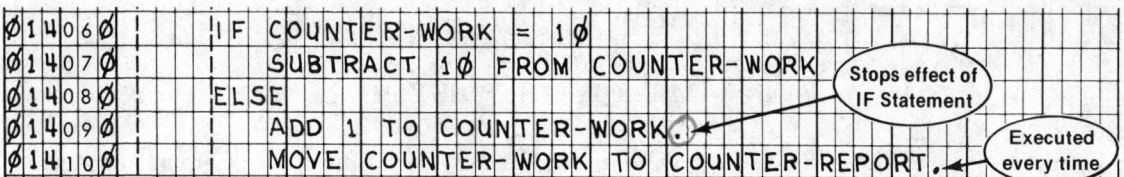

```
Ø14060    IF COUNTER-WORK = 1Ø
Ø14070       SUBTRACT 1Ø FROM COUNTER-WORK          Stops effect of
Ø14080    ELSE                                       IF Statement
Ø14090       ADD 1 TO COUNTER-WORK.
Ø14100    MOVE COUNTER-WORK TO COUNTER-REPORT.      Executed
                                                     every time
```

Figure 6-9 Example of Misplaced Period

In the example above, if the value in COUNTER-WORK is equal to 10, then 10 is subtracted from the field. If it is not equal to 10, then what is supposed to occur is that 1 is added to COUNTER-WORK and the value in the field is moved to the COUNTER-REPORT field. Instead, since the period follows the Add Statement, the Move Statement moving the contents of COUNTER-WORK to COUNTER-REPORT will be executed every time this IF Statement is encountered, regardless of whether the value in COUNTER-WORK is equal to 10. This is not what was intended by the programmer but it is what will occur. Therefore, it can be seen that it is very important, when writing COBOL code, to place the periods where they are supposed to be.

The entry NEXT SENTENCE can be placed in an IF Statement to indicate that the next sentence in the program is to be executed upon a given condition. The next sentence is the COBOL statement following the period in the IF Statement. This is illustrated below.

EXAMPLE

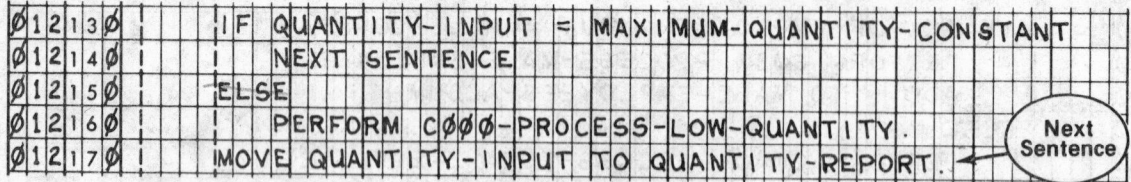

Figure 6-10 Example of NEXT SENTENCE Entry

In the example above, if the value in the QUANTITY-INPUT field is equal to the value in the MAXIMUM-QUANTITY-CONSTANT field, the statement following the period in the IF Statement (line 012170) is executed. In most instances, the NEXT SENTENCE entry will not be used in coding COBOL programs.

It should be noted also that the ELSE Clause in an IF Statement is not required. If it is omitted and the condition is true, the processing specified following the condition will be executed. If the condition is not true, then the next sentence will be executed. This is illustrated in Figure 6-11.

EXAMPLE

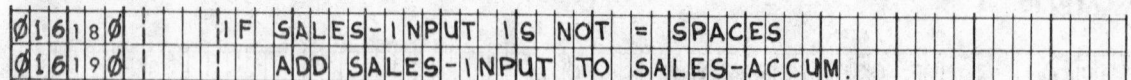

Figure 6-11 Example of No ELSE Entry

In the example in Figure 6-11, if the value in the SALES-INPUT field is not equal to spaces, then the value will be added to the SALES-ACCUM field. If the field is equal to spaces, then the statement following the IF Statement, that is, the statement following the period, will be executed.

It is important that the programmer thoroughly understand the use of the IF Statement because it is often used when programming in COBOL and, if used improperly, can be the source of errors which are difficult to uncover when the program is being tested and debugged.

RELATION TEST

In Figure 6-7 it can be seen that the IF Statement is used to test a "condition". One type of condition which can be tested is a relation test, where the values in two different fields are compared to one another. The general format of the relation condition is shown below.

Relation Condition

```
┌                      ┐ ┌                     ┐          ┌                         ┐
│ identifier-1         │ │ IS [NOT] GREATER THAN │          │ identifier-2            │
│ literal-1            │ │ IS [NOT] LESS THAN    │          │ literal-2               │
│ arithmetic-expression-1 │ IS [NOT] EQUAL TO    │          │ arithmetic-expression-2 │
│ index-name-1         │ │ IS [NOT] >           │          │ index-name-2            │
│                      │ │ IS [NOT] <           │          │                         │
└                      ┘ │ IS [NOT] =           │          └                         ┘
                         └                     ┘
```

Figure 6-12 Format of Relation Condition

In the example above it can be seen that the values in an identifier, a literal, an arithmetic-expression, or an index-name can be compared to determine if one is greater than, less than, equal to, not greater than, not less than, or not equal to the other. Either the words or the symbols may be used to express the relation being tested; it is suggested that the words be used except when testing for an equal condition.

The following examples illustrate the use of identifiers, literals, and arithmetic-expressions in IF Statements.

EXAMPLE 1: Identifiers

EXAMPLE 2: Literal

EXAMPLE 3: Arithmetic Expression

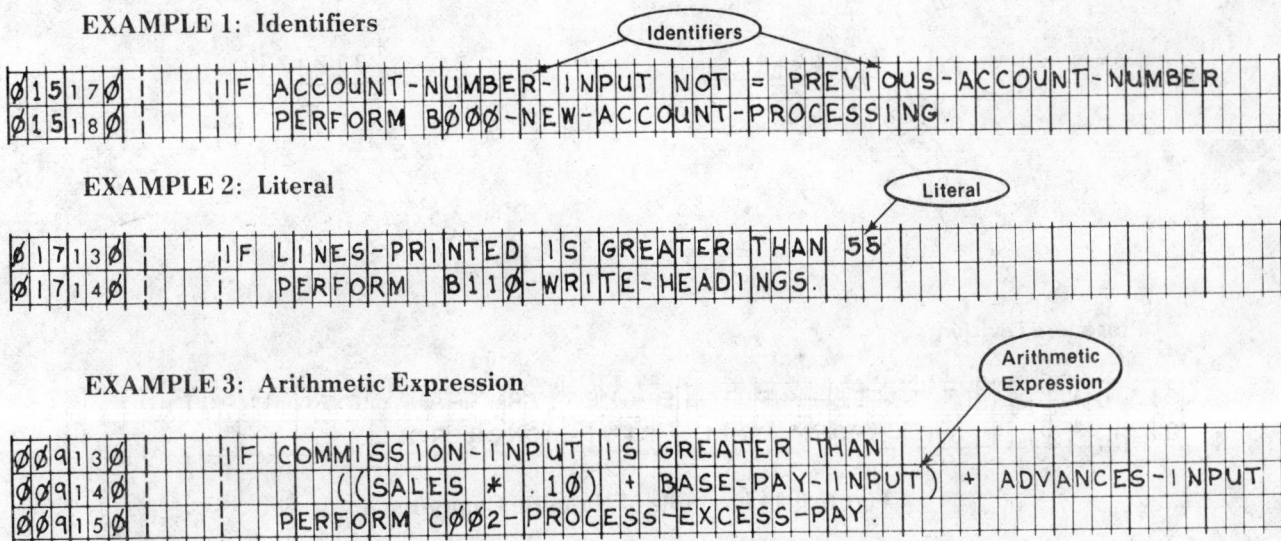

Figure 6-13 Example of Data Types in IF Statements

Note in the examples in Figure 6-13 that identifiers, literals, and arithmetic expressions may be used in an IF Statement when using a relation test. The arithmetic expression is evaluated using the same rules as the Compute Statement. The resulting answer is then compared to identifier-1, literal-1, or arithmetic-expression-1.

COMPARISON OF NUMERIC ITEMS [PICTURE 9]

For numeric items, a relation test determines if the value of one of the items is less than, equal to, or greater than the other, regardless of the length of the items. When both items are numeric, the comparison is based directly on their algebraic values. Length differences are ignored. For example, 07.6000 is considered to be equal to 0007.60. If no decimal points are indicated, the values are considered whole numbers. For example, 076000 would be considered 76,000 and 000760 would be considered 760.

Since zero is considered a unique value, neither positive nor negative, items with zero values are considered equal regardless of length, decimal points, and signs.

The following example illustrates the comparison of numeric items.

EXAMPLE

Data Division

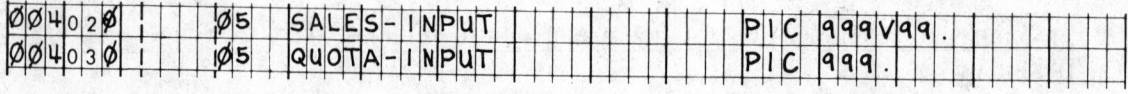

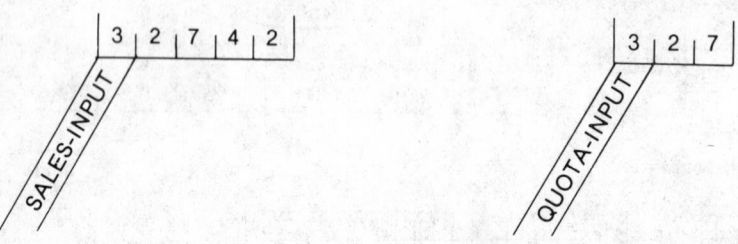

Procedure Division

```
013120       IF SALES-INPUT IS GREATER THAN QUOTA-INPUT
013130           PERFORM B001-PRINT-HONOR-ROLL.
```

Figure 6-14 Example of Numeric Comparison

In the example in Figure 6-14, the condition tested would be evaluated as true, that is, the SALES-INPUT would be greater than the QUOTA-INPUT. This is because the QUOTA-INPUT field will be extended with zeros in the two positions to the right of the decimal point and then be compared. Thus, the values compared would be 327.42 to 327.00.

It should be noted that when comparing fields defined as numeric (Picture 9), the fields must contain valid plus or minus signs. As the sign of the field is considered in a numeric compare, any value other than a valid sign in the sign position may result in the abnormal termination of the program. It should also be noted that, on many computers, numeric data must be in the Computational-3 format prior to being compared. Therefore, if possible, any numeric fields which are to be compared should be defined as Computational-3 fields. If they are not, such as when the numeric fields are contained in card input records, the COBOL compiler will generate instructions to internally convert the data prior to the comparison operation.

COMPARISON OF ALPHANUMERIC DATA [PICTURE X]

For fields defined as alphanumeric (Picture X), a comparison results in the determination that the value in one of the fields is greater than, less than, or equal to the other with respect to the binary collating sequence of characters in the character set of the computer.

If alphanumeric fields are of the same length, the comparison proceeds by comparing characters in each of the fields being referenced, starting from the high-order positions and continuing until either a pair of unequal characters is found or until the characters in the low-order position have been compared.

The following example illustrates the comparison of alphanumeric fields.

EXAMPLE

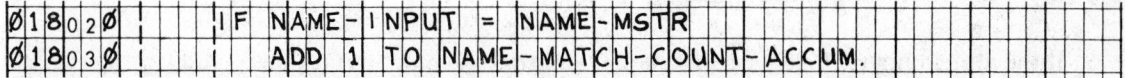

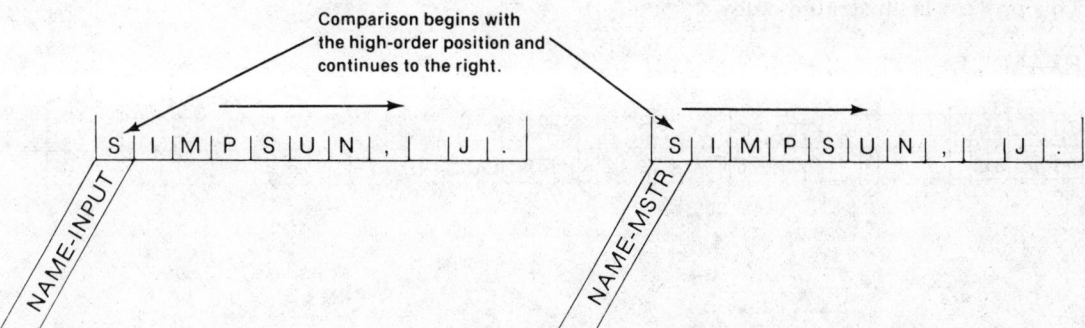

Figure 6-15 Example of Alphanumeric Comparison

Note in the example in Figure 6-15 that the comparison begins with the leftmost character in the field and proceeds to the right. In this example, the data in the fields is equal. Therefore, from the coding illustrated, the value 1 would be added to the NAME-MATCH-COUNT-ACCUM field.

When an unequal condition occurs with alphanumeric fields, the first pair of unequal characters encountered is compared for relative position in the collating sequence. The item containing the character that is positioned higher in the collating sequence is the greater item. The following example illustrates the comparison of alphanumeric data in which an unequal condition results.

EXAMPLE

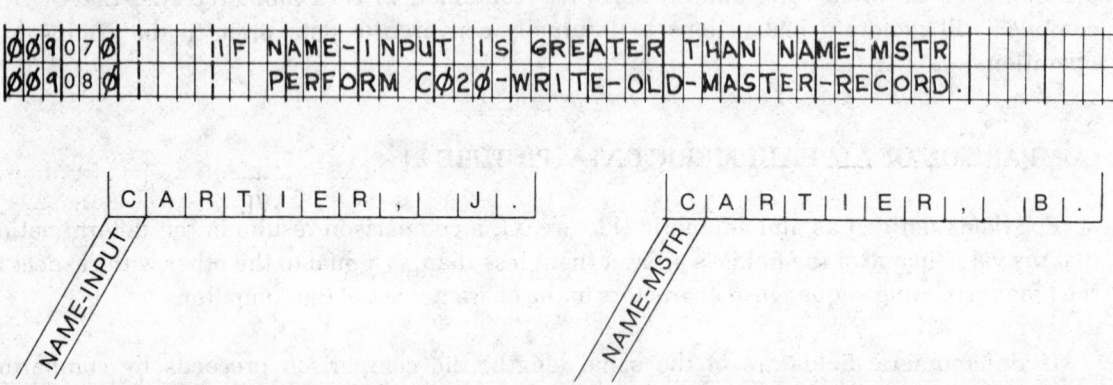

Figure 6-16 Example of Unequal Alphanumeric Comparison

In the example in Figure 6-16, the value in the NAME-INPUT field is greater than the value in the NAME-MSTR field because the letter of the alphabet "J" is considered higher than the letter of the alphabet "B". On most computer systems, the letter Z is greater than the letter A, that is, A is the lowest in the alphabet and Z is the highest; and the numbers are considered greater than any letters of the alphabet.

If the alphanumeric fields are of unequal length, the value in the shorter field is "extended" internally with blanks until it is the length of the longer field. The two fields are then compared as illustrated previously. A blank is lower in the collating sequence than any letters or numbers. This process is illustrated below.

EXAMPLE

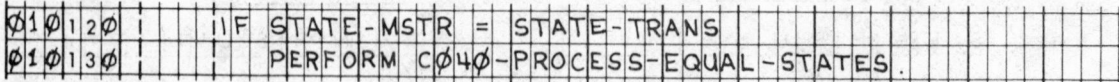

Figure 6-17 Example of Alphanumeric Compare with Different Length Fields

In the example in Figure 6-17, the STATE-MSTR field is two characters in length and the STATE-TRANS field is five characters in length. Therefore, when they are compared, the STATE-MSTR field is extended, internally within computer storage, so that it is the same length as the longer STATE-TRANS field and then the values are compared. As can be seen, even though the first two characters are equal, the STATE-TRANS field contains the values "LIF" in the last three positions while the STATE-MSTR field contains the extended blanks. The value in the STATE-TRANS field is considered greater than the value in the STATE-MSTR field because all letters of the alphabet are greater than blanks in the collating sequence of the computer.

SIGN TEST

The previous examples have illustrated the use of the Relation Test when using the IF Statement. There are several other tests which also may be used. One of these is the Sign Test.

The Sign Test is a type of condition test that may be used with an IF Statement to determine whether the value of an arithmetic-expression is less than zero (NEGATIVE), greater than zero (POSITIVE), or equal to zero (ZERO). The value Zero is considered neither positive nor negative. The following example illustrates the use of the Sign Test.

EXAMPLE

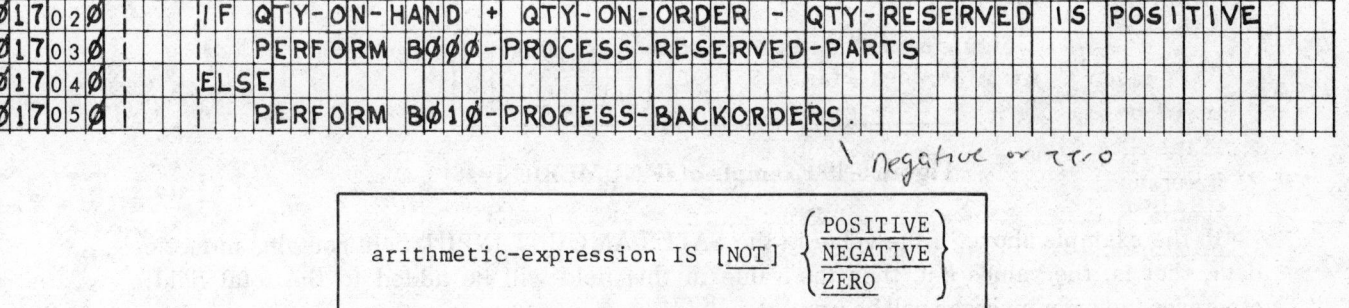

Figure 6-18 Example of Sign Test

Note in Figure 6-18 that the arithmetic expression will be evaluated and then will be checked to determine if the result is positive. If it is positive, then the B000-PROCESS-RESERVED-PARTS module will be performed; if it is not positive, then the B010-PROCESS-BACKORDERS module will be performed.

If the result of an arithmetic expression need not be used in subsequent operations but the sign of the result is important, the Sign Test provides a convenient method of expressing these conditions.

CLASS TEST

Another test which is useful in some applications is the Class Test. When a Class Test is specified, a determination is made as to whether or not a field contains data consisting solely of the following:

1. The characters 0 (zero) through 9 (NUMERIC);

2. The characters A through Z and blank (ALPHABETIC).

The Alphabetic Test may be performed only on elementary alphabetic (Picture A) or alphanumeric (Picture X) fields. The Numeric Test may be performed on elementary alphanumeric fields and numeric (Picture 9) fields which are in the Display format.

The following is an example of the Class Test.

EXAMPLE

```
Ø21Ø2Ø      IF SALES-AMOUNT-INPUT IS NUMERIC
Ø21Ø3Ø         ADD SALES-AMOUNT-INPUT TO SALES-AMOUNT-TOTAL
Ø21Ø4Ø      ELSE
Ø21Ø5Ø         PERFORM BØØ1-PRINT-ERROR-MESSAGES.
```

```
identifier IS [NOT] { NUMERIC
                      ALPHABETIC }
```

Figure 6-19 Example of IF NUMERIC Test

In the example above, if the value in the SALES-AMOUNT-INPUT field contains numeric data, that is, the values 0-9, then the value in this field will be added to the total field; otherwise, an error message will be printed.

There are several rules with regard to the IF NUMERIC Test which should be understood:

1. If the field being tested is defined as an Alphanumeric field (Picture X), then it must contain an absolute sign or it will be considered non-numeric. On the System/360 and System/370, the field must contain a hexadecimal "F" in the zone portion of the low-order byte. The field will be considered non-numeric if it contains the operational signs "C" or "D" in the zone portion of the low-order byte.

2. If the field being tested is a numeric field (Picture 9) without the Sign indication, it is treated the same way as a Picture X field.

3. If the field being tested is defined as a Numeric field with a Sign (Picture S9), then the data may contain an absolute sign or an operational sign and be considered numeric. Thus, on the System/360 and System/370, a sign of "F", "C", or "D" in the zone portion of the low-order byte will be considered a valid sign for numeric data.

The IF NUMERIC Class test is particularly useful in checking input data to ensure that it is valid data.

SAMPLE PROGRAM

The sample program in this chapter creates a Payroll Report. The output, input, and programming specifications are illustrated below and on the following page.

OUTPUT

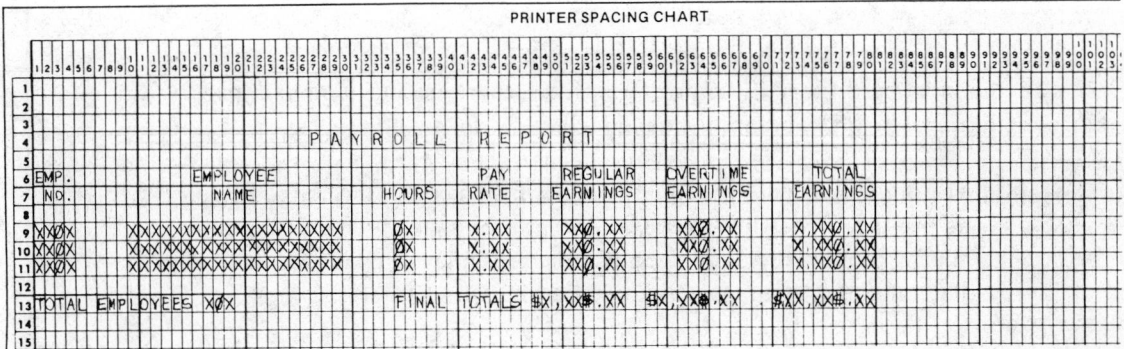

Figure 6-20 Output

INPUT

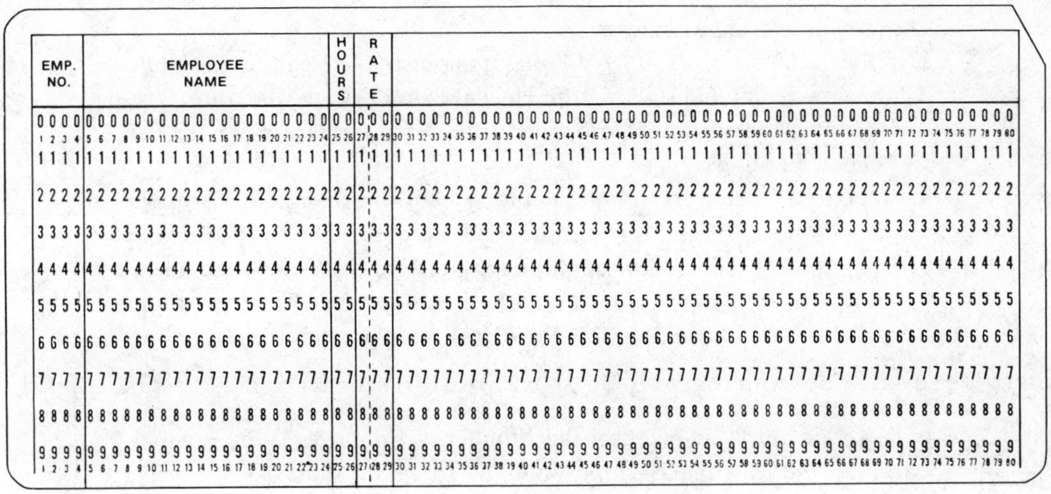

Figure 6-21 Input

PROGRAMMING SPECIFICATIONS			
SUBJECT Payroll Report	**DATE** April 25		**PAGE** 1 OF 1
TO Programmer	**FROM** Systems Analyst		

A program is to be written to prepare a Payroll Report. The format for the input card file and the printer spacing chart are included as a part of this narrative. The program should include the following processing:

1. The program should read the input cards and create the Payroll Report as per the format illustrated on the printer spacing chart. The report should contain the Employee Number, Employee Name, Hours, Pay Rate, Regular Earnings, Overtime Earnings, and Total Earnings.

2. Headings should be printed on the first page to indicate the values contained in the columns of the report.

3. One line is to be printed on the report for each card which is read. The lines are to be single-spaced.

4. The calculations are as follows:
   a. If the employee works forty (40) hours or less, the Regular Earnings are obtained by multiplying the Hours worked by the Pay rate. The Overtime Earnings are zero. The Total Earnings are equal to the Regular Earnings.
   b. If the Employee works more than forty hours, the Regular Earnings are obtained by multiplying the Pay Rate by 40. The Overtime Earnings are obtained by multiplying the Hours greater than 40 by 1.5 and multiplying that result by the Pay Rate. The Total Earnings are obtained by adding the Regular Earnings and the Overtime Earnings.

5. Final Totals are to be taken of the Number of Employees, the Regular Earnings, the Overtime Earnings, and the Total Earnings.

6. Editing of the report is to occur as illustrated on the printer spacing chart.

7. The program should be written in COBOL.

Figure 6-22 Programming Specifications

PROGRAM DESIGN

The first step in the design of the program is to complete the IPO Chart for the module whose function is to Create the Payroll Report. This is illustrated below.

IPO CHART				
PROGRAM: Payroll Report Program		**PROGRAMMER:** Shelly/Cashman		**DATE:** April 26
MODULE NAME: Create Payroll Report		**REF:** A000	**MODULE FUNCTION:** Create the Payroll Report	
INPUT	**PROCESSING**		**REF:**	**OUTPUT**
1. Payroll Card File	1. Initialization			1. Payroll Report
	2. Obtain the input data			
	3. Process the detail records		B000	
	4. Print the final totals		B010	
	5. Termination			

Figure 6-23 IPO Chart

In the IPO Chart above it can be seen that there are five major processing tasks which must take place in order to create the payroll report—these are initialization, obtain the input data, process the detail records, print the final totals, and termination. It will be noted that the tasks of "initialization" and "obtain the input data" are the same as have been used in previous programs.

However, the "process the detail records" task differs from previous programs. It is a more generalized statement of the task to be performed than has been used in previous programs. The reason it is more generalized is that, as can be seen from the programming specifications, the processing which must be accomplished in order to perform the calculations and format the print line is more complex than in previous programs. Since it is more complex, a more generalized statement of the major processing task to be performed should be made. The programmer would then analyze the task to determine if it is of sufficient complexity as to require a separate, lower-level module.

The next major processing task is to "print the final totals." This too differs from previous programs in that the program in this chapter requires not only the detail lines to be printed on the report but also the final total line. Therefore, it is not sufficient to merely state that the report must be written. It is necessary to specify that two major areas must be processed—the detail record processing and the final total processing.

The last major processing task is the termination, which has been seen previously.

After the IPO Chart has been made by the programmer, the major processing tasks must then be analyzed to determine if the module should be decomposed into lower-level modules. As noted previously, this determination is made by analyzing each major processing task with regard to the function which it is to perform and also with regard to the amount of processing which is required in order to accomplish the task. In the IPO Chart in Figure 6-23, the tasks of "initialization" and "obtain the input data" do not require significant processing.

The task of "process the detail records," however, does require significant processing. In addition, it is a well-defined function which must be accomplished in order to transform the input to the output. Therefore, the major processing task of "process the detail records" should be made into a lower-level module. A further review of the IPO Chart reveals that the major processing task of "print the final totals" is a specific, well-defined function which must be performed within the program and it may also contain a significant amount of processing. Thus, the major processing task of "print the final totals" should also be made into a separate, lower-level module also.

When there is more than a single module in a program, a HIERARCHY CHART is drawn to show the relationship between the modules within the program. The following diagram illustrates the hierarchy chart for the sample program.

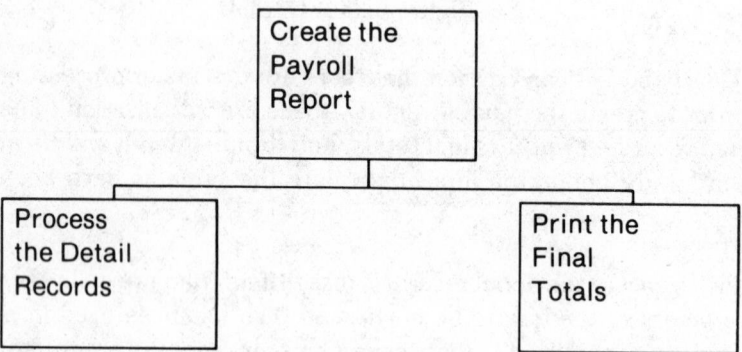

Figure 6-24 Hierarchy Chart

Note from the hierarcy chart in Figure 6-24 that the modules which process the detail records and print the final totals are both under the module whose function is to create the payroll report. In the program, the "Create the Payroll Report" module will cause the "Process the Detail Records" module to be executed, and it will also cause the "Print the Final Totals" module to be executed. However, the two modules "Process the Detail Records" and "Print the Final Totals" will never reference one another, that is, no instructions in the "Process the Detail Records" module will cause any processing in the "Print the Final Totals" module to be executed, and vice versa. Thus, the hierarchy chart not only shows the relationships between modules but also shows which modules control other modules.

After the structure of the modules on the second level of the program has been defined through the use of a hierarchy chart, the next step is to define the major processing tasks for each of the modules on the second level. Thus, an IPO Chart for the module whose function is to process the detail records and an IPO Chart for the module whose function is to print the final totals must be developed by the programmer.

The IPO Chart for the module whose function is to process the detail records is illustrated below.

IPO CHART

PROGRAM: Payroll Report Program		PROGRAMMER: Shelly/Cashman		DATE: April 26
MODULE NAME: Process Detail Records		REF: B000	MODULE FUNCTION: Process the Detail Records	

INPUT	PROCESSING	REF:	OUTPUT
1. Payroll Card Record	1. Format print line		1. Detail Print Line
2. Final Total Accumulators	2. Perform detail calculations		2. Updated Final Total
	a. Calculate regular earnings,		Accumulators
	overtime earnings, total earnings		
	3. Update final totals		
	a. Number of employees, regular		
	earnings, overtime earnings,		
	total earnings		
	4. Write the detail line		

Figure 6-25 IPO Chart for Process the Detail Records

Note from Figure 6-25 that the same form is used for the module whose function is to Process the Detail Records as is used for the module whose function is to Create the Payroll Report. The program name is the same; however, the module name and module function are different since this is a different module.

The output from the module, that is, the information which is produced within the module and is either written on an external device or is passed to another module within the program, is the Detail Print Line and the Updated Final Total Accumulators. The detail print line is printed on the printer and the final total accumulators are used in another module within the program.

The input to the module, that is, the data on which the module is to operate, is the Payroll Card Record and the Final Total Accumulators. The Payroll Record contains the data to be used in formatting the report and performing the required calculations. The Final Total Accumulators are input to the module because they contain data (the accumulated totals) which will be used in calculations within the module. Whenever data is required for calculations within the module, the data should be specified as input to the module.

The major processing tasks which are required to process the detail records are specified on the IPO Chart. Note that they consist of formatting the print line, performing the detail calculations, updating the final totals, and writing the detail line. These are the tasks which are necessary in order to process the detail records.

It will also be noted from the IPO Chart in Figure 6-25 that the reference number (REF) for this module is B000, whereas the reference number for the "create payroll report" module is A000 (see Figure 6-23). The reference number is used to indicate the "hierarchy" of the modules within a program and to illustrate their relationship to one another. The hierarchy chart for the program with the reference numbers included is illustrated below.

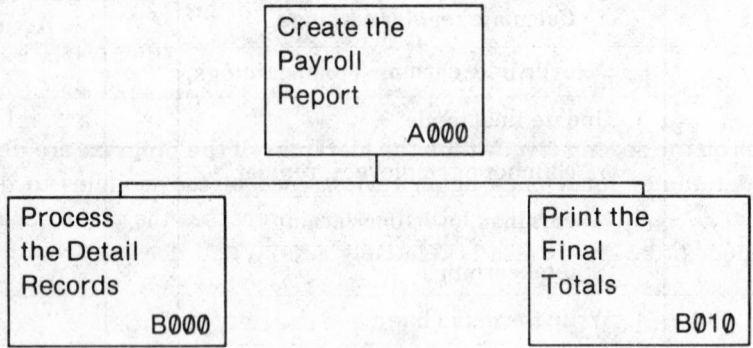

Figure 6-26 Hierarchy Chart with Reference Numbers

Note from Figure 6-26 that reference numbers have been added to the hierarchy chart. The highest level module (Create the Payroll Report) contains the prefix "A" in the reference number. The second level modules contain the prefix "B" in their reference numbers. In this manner, the prefix letter is used to indicate the level on which the particular module is found within the program. The numbers are incremented by 10 (i.e., the first is 000 and the second is 010) so as to give a unique number to each module on a given level.

In order to illustrate on the IPO Chart that processing tasks are going to be accomplished in separate modules, the REF column is used to indicate the reference number of those tasks which are separate modules. Thus, in Figure 6-23 it can be seen that the entry for the task "Process the Detail Records" is B000, and the entry for the task "Print the Final Totals" is B010. In this manner, it is clear which tasks specified on the IPO Chart are going to be accomplished by separate modules within the program. Whenever a task is going to be performed in a separate module, an entry should be made on the IPO Chart to indicate this.

After the IPO Chart for the module whose function is to process the detail records is completed, the programmer would then complete the IPO Chart for the module whose function is to print the final totals. This IPO Chart is illustrated in Figure 6-27.

IPO CHART					
PROGRAM: Payroll Report Program		**PROGRAMMER:** Shelly/Cashman			**DATE:** April 26
MODULE NAME: Print Final Totals		**REF:** B010	**MODULE FUNCTION:** Print the Final Totals		
INPUT	**PROCESSING**		**REF:**	**OUTPUT**	
1. Final Total Accumulators	1. Format final total line			1. Final Total Line	
	2. Print final total line				

Figure 6-27 IPO Chart for Print the Final Totals

As with the previous IPO Charts, the one above contains the standard identification material. Note that the reference number is B010, which is the same as that contained on the hierarchy chart in Figure 6-26. The output from the module is the Final Total Line which is printed on the report. The input to the module are the Final Total Accumulators, which are the fields containing the totals which were accumulated in the module which processed the detail records.

In order to transform the input to the output, the major processing tasks are to format the final total line and to print the final total line.

After the modules on the second level within the hierarchy of the program are defined using IPO Charts, the programmer must once again review each of the modules to determine if further decomposition is required. For the module which processes the detail records (Figure 6-25), each of the major processing tasks is relatively simple and does not require extensive programming to accomplish. Therefore, the decision is that the module need not be decomposed further. An analysis of the module which is to print the final totals yields a similar result. Therefore, the modules for the program have been completely defined. Their relationship to one another is illustrated in Figure 6-28.

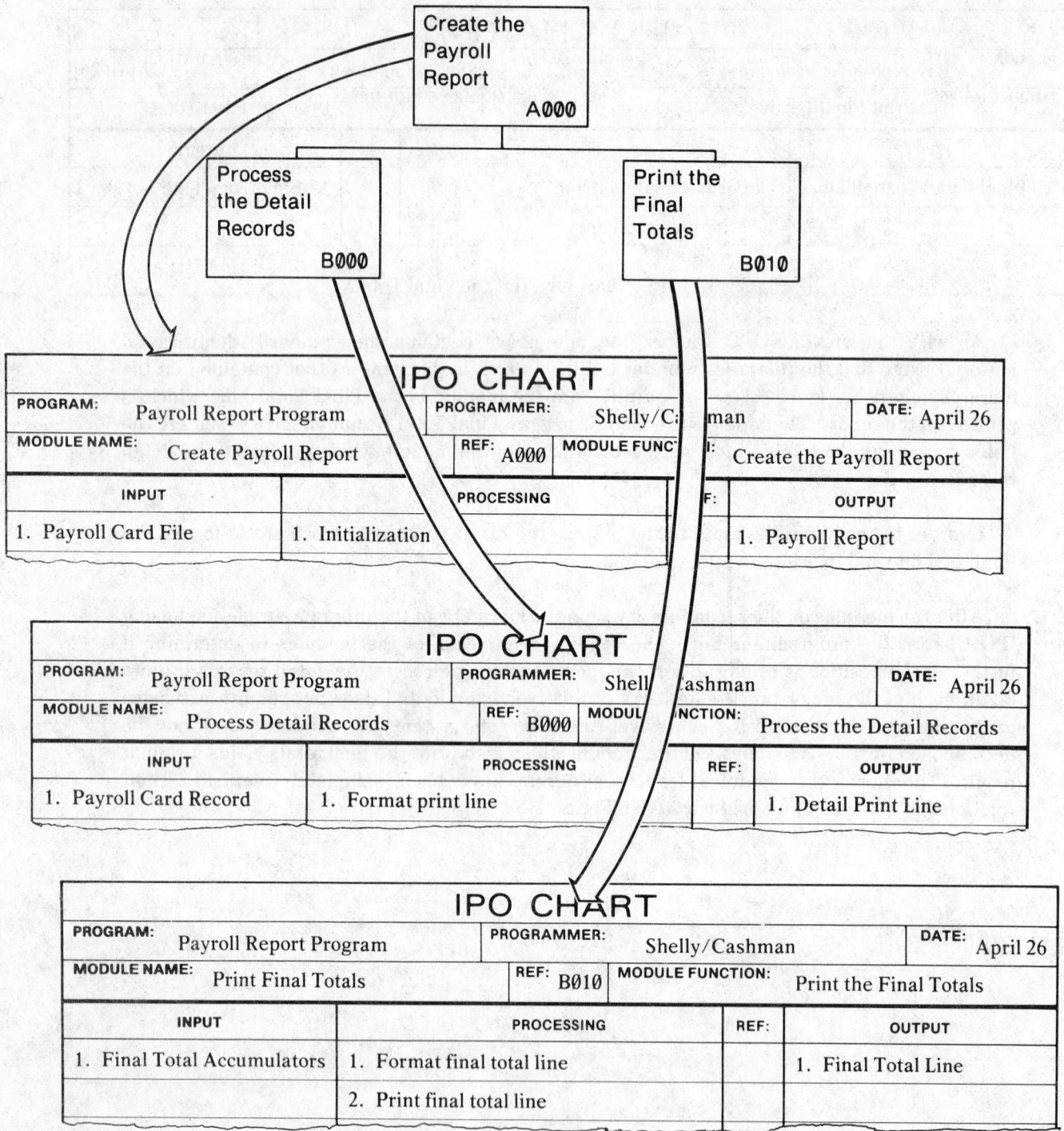

Figure 6-28 Relationship of Hierarchy Chart and IPO Chart

Note from Figure 6-28 that each module in the hierarchy has a corresponding definition on the IPO Chart. Thus, as can be seen, an IPO Chart is prepared for each module within the program.

PSEUDOCODE SPECIFICATIONS

Once the IPO Chart and the related Hierarchy Chart are completed, the programmer must prepare the Pseudocode Specifications, which specify the methods in which the processing defined on the IPO Charts will be implemented. The hierarchy chart, IPO Chart, and Pseudocode Specifications for the "Create Payroll Report" module are illustrated below.

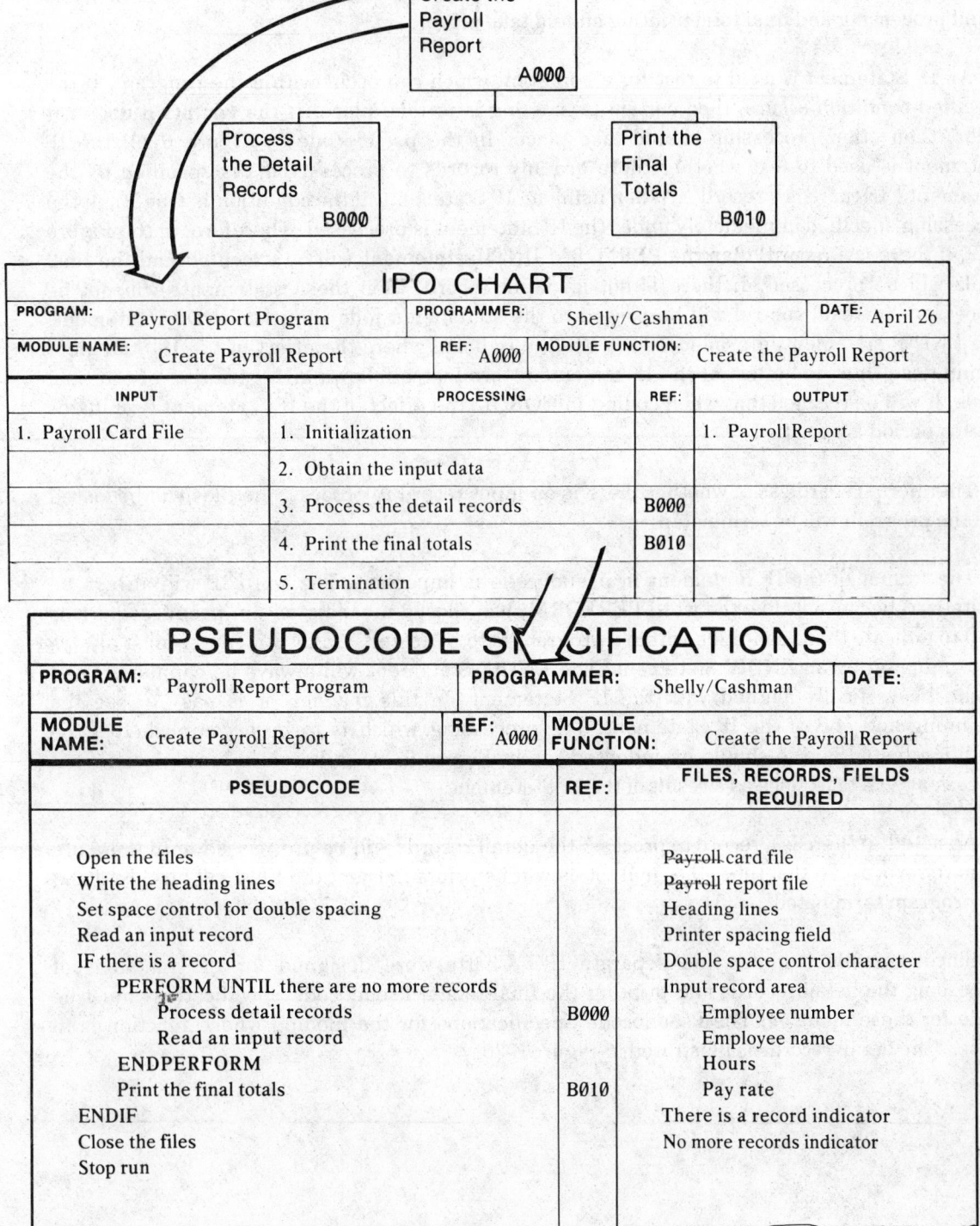

Figure 6-29 Pseudocode Specifications

The first step in the module is to open the files, as has been true in previous programs. The headings are then written on the report and the spacing control is set for double spacing so that the first detail iine on the report will be double spaced. This is the same processing which has occurred previously. The first input record is then read.

In some cases, there may not be any input records at all; although this is unusual, it is a possibility. If there are no input records to process, then the detail processing and the printing of the final totals should not take place. Therefore, an IF Statement is used to determine if the detail processing and final total printing should take place.

An IF Statement is used to test for a condition which can occur within the program. If the specified condition occurs, then certain processing is to take place. If the condition does not occur, then other processing should take place. In the pseudocode in Figure 6-29, the IF Statement is used to test whether there are any records to process. This is specified by the statement ''IF there is a record''. When using an IF Statement, if the condition is true, then the processing specified immediately under the IF Statement is processed. Therefore, in the Figure 6-29, if there is a record, then the PERFORM UNTIL statement will be executed and the final totals will be processed. If there is not an input record, then these statements will not be processed. Instead, control will be passed to the statements following the ENDIF statement. The ENDIF statement in pseudocode is used to indicate where the effect of the IF Statement terminates. Thus, the effect of the IF Statement terminates following the printing of the final totals. It will be recalled that when coding in COBOL, the effect of the IF Statement terminates when a period is specified.

Therefore, regardless of whether there is an input record to process, the files will be closed and the program will be terminated.

The format of the IF Statement in pseudocode is important. The word IF will always be capitalized because it, like the word PERFORM, has special meaning within pseudocode. It is used to indicate that a condition within a program is to be tested. An IF Statement must always be terminated by an ENDIF Statement. The ENDIF Statement will always be capitalized and should be vertically aligned with the IF Statement. In this manner, it is easy to see the beginning and end of the IF Statement. The processing which is to be accomplished if the condition tested is true should be indented, as in Figure 6-29, so it can be easily seen what processing will take place as a result of the IF Statement.

As noted, if there is a record to process, the detail records will be processsed until there are no more records. At that time, the final totals will be printed. Then, the files will be closed and the program terminated.

Since separate modules and separate IPO Charts were designed for the functions of processing the detail records and printing the final totals, Pseudocode Specifications must be made for these modules. The Pseudocode Specifications for the module whose function is to process the detail records is illustrated in Figure 6-30.

```
                          ┌──────────────┐
                          │ Create the   │
                          │ Payroll      │
                          │ Report       │
                          │        A000  │
                          └──────┬───────┘
              ┌──────────────────┴──────────────────┐
     ┌────────┴────────┐                    ┌────────┴────────┐
     │ Process         │                    │ Print the       │
     │ the Detail      │                    │ Final           │
     │ Records         │                    │ Totals          │
     │          B000   │                    │          B010   │
     └─────────────────┘                    └─────────────────┘
```

IPO CHART

PROGRAM: Payroll Report Program	PROGRAMMER: Shelly/Cashman	DATE: April 26

MODULE NAME: Process Detail Records	REF: B000	MODULE FUNCTION: Process the Detail Records

INPUT	PROCESSING	REF:	OUTPUT
1. Payroll Card Record	1. Format print line		1. Detail Print Line
2. Final Total Accumulators	2. Perform detail calculations		2. Updated Final Total
	a. Calculate regular earnings,		Accumulators
	overtime earnings, total earnings		
	3. Update final totals		
	a. Number of employees, regular		
	earnings, overtime earnings,		
	total earnings		
	4. Write the detail line		

PSEUDOCODE SPECIFICATIONS

PROGRAM: Payroll Report Program	PROGRAMMER: Shelly/Cashman	DATE: April 27

MODULE NAME: Process Detail Records	REF: B000	MODULE FUNCTION: Process the Detail Records

PSEUDOCODE	REF:	FILES, RECORDS, FIELDS REQUIRED
Clear the printer line		Printer output area
Move employee number, employee name, hours,		Employee number
and pay rate to output area		Employee name
IF hours > maximum regular hours		Hours
Calculate regular earnings =		Pay rate
pay rate x max. regular hours		Regular earnings
Calculate overtime earnings =		Overtime earnings
((Hours - max. hrs) x 1.5) x pay rate		Total earnings
Calculate total earnings =		Input record area
regular earnings + overtime earnings		Employee number
ELSE		Employee name
Calculate regular earnings =		Hours
pay rate x hours		Pay rate
Set overtime earnings = 0		Maximum regular hours
Set total earnings = regular earnings		Regular earnings work area
ENDIF		Overtime earnings work area
Move regular earnings, overtime earnings,		Total earnings work area
total earnings to output area		Number of employees accumulator
Add 1 to number of employees accumulator		Regular earnings accumulator
Add regular earnings, overtime earnings,		Overtime earnings accumulator
total earnings to final total accumulators		Total earnings accumulator
Write a line on the report		Printer spacing control field
Set space control for single spacing		Single space control character

Figure 6-30 Pseudocode Specifications

The first step in the processing within the module which processes the detail records is to clear the printer line. The next step is to move the Employee Number, Employee Name, Hours, and Pay Rate to the printer output area. Next, the earnings must be calculated.

As noted previously, the relationship checked in order to calculate the earnings is whether the value in the Hours field is greater than the Maximum Regular Hours. This relationship is tested through the use of the IF Statement, which is again illustrated in Figure 6-31.

```
                        PSEUDOCODE

    Clear the printer line
    Move employee number, employee name, hours,
        and pay rate to output area
    IF hours > maximum regular hours
        Calculate regular earnings =
            pay rate x max. regular hours
        Calculate overtime earnings =
            ( (Hours - max. hrs) x 1.5) x pay rate
        Calculate total earnings =
            regular earnings + overtime earnings
    ELSE
        Calculate regular earnings =
            pay rate x hours
        Set overtime earnings = 0
        Set total earnings = regular earnings
    ENDIF
```

Figure 6-31 Example of IF Statement

In the example above it can be seen that the IF Statement specifies "IF hours > maximum regular hours." Thus, the IF Statement is used to determine if the hours worked by an employee are greater than the maximum number of hours for regular pay, that is, whether the employee is entitled to overtime pay. It will be recalled that when the condition stated in the IF Statement is true, then the operations specified immediately below the IF Statement are executed. Therefore, if the Hours are greater than the Maximum Regular Hours, the three calculations immediately following the IF Statement will be executed.

It was noted in the statement of the problem that if the Hours are greater than the Maximum Regular Hours, then Overtime Pay must be calculated. The calculations which must be performed are illustrated below.

EXAMPLE - Assume Hours = 50; Pay Rate = 4.50

1. Calculate Regular Earnings = Pay Rate x Maximum Regular Hours

4	5	0	x	4	0	=	1	8	0	0	0
Pay Rate				Maximum			Regular Earnings				
				Regular Hours							

2. Calculate Overtime Earnings = ((Hours - Max. Regular Hours) x 1.5) x Pay rate

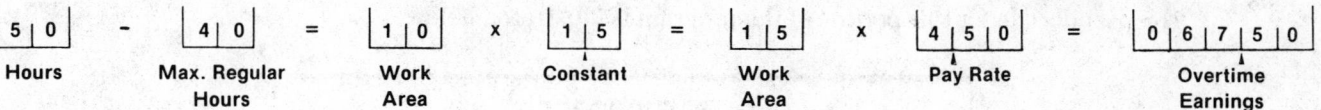

3. Calculate Total Earnings = Regular Earnings + Overtime Earnings

| 1 | 8 | 0 | 0 | 0 | + | 0 | 6 | 7 | 5 | 0 | = | 0 | 2 | 4 | 7 | 5 | 0 |
| Regular Earnings | | | | | | Overtime Earnings | | | | | | Total Earnings | | | | | |

Figure 6-32 Calculations for Overtime Earnings

Note from the examples above that the Regular Earnings, Overtime Earnings, and Total Earnings are calculated when the Hours are greater than the Maximum Regular Hours. This follows the operations which are to be accomplished according to the pseudocode in Figure 6-31.

As previously discussed, in many applications where relations between fields are tested, one set of operations is accomplished when the condition is true and another set of operations is done when the condition is not true. In order to specify those operations to be done when the condition tested is not true, the ELSE Clause is used.

Thus, from Figure 6-31 it can be seen that if the Hours are not greater than the Maximum Regular Hours, the instructions following the ELSE portion of the IF Statement will be executed. These instructions will calculate the Regular Pay (Pay Rate x Hours), set the Overtime Earnings to zero, and set the Total Earnings equal to the Regular Earnings.

The ENDIF word indicates the end of the effect of the IF Statement in pseudocode, that is, it specifies the end of the statements which will be executed within the ELSE Clause of the IF Statement.

After the Regular Earnings, Overtime Earnings, and Total Earnings have been calculated, they are moved to the printer output area. The final total accumulators are then incremented. The pseudocode for this portion of the program is illustrated below.

```
                         PSEUDOCODE

        Move regular earnings, overtime earnings,
             total earnings to output area
        Add 1 to number of employees accumulator
        Add regular earnings, overtime earnings,
             total earnings to final total accumulators
        Write a line on the report
        Set space control for single spacing
```

Figure 6-33 Pseudocode for Accumulating Final Totals

As can be seen from Figure 6-33, after the Regular Earnings, Overtime Earnings, and Total Earnings have been calculated (see Figure 6-31), they are moved to the output area. The value 1 is then added to the Employees Accumulator and the Regular Earnings, Overtime Earnings, and Total Earnings are added to the final total accumulators. This is necessary in order to accumulate the final totals which will be printed at the end of the program. The processing which would take place is illustrated in Figure 6-34.

EXAMPLE

First Record

Before Execution

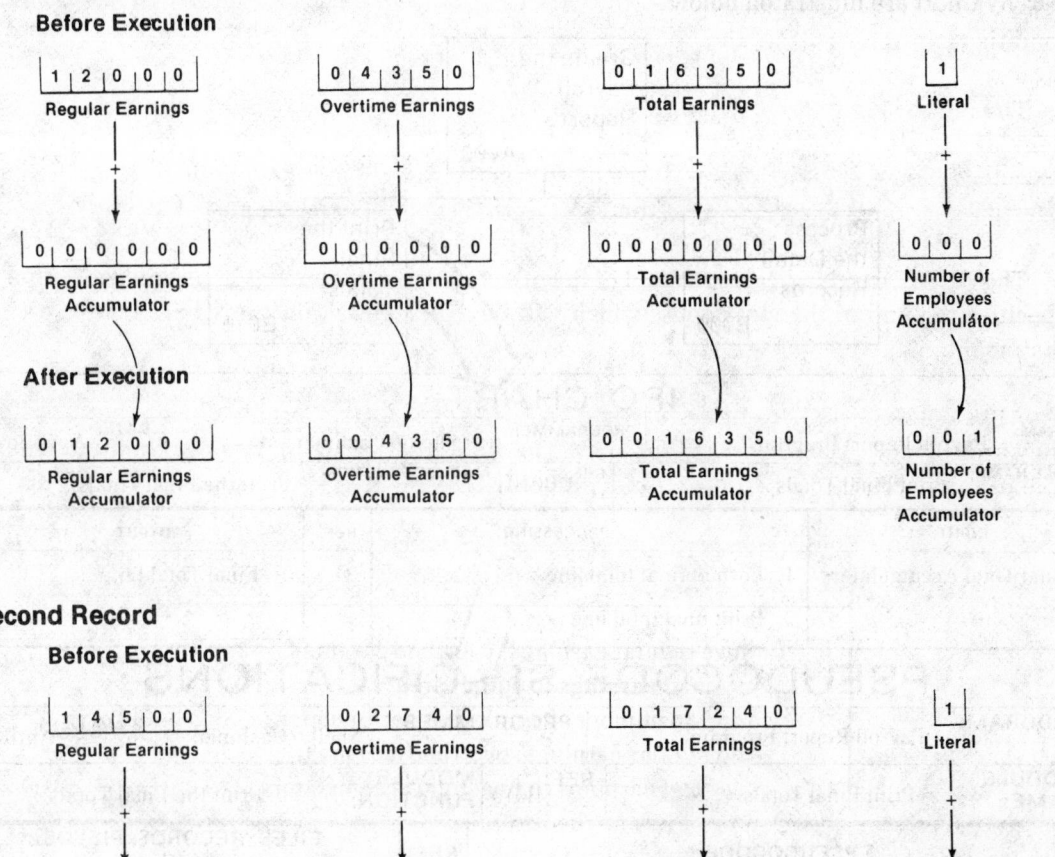

Second Record

Before Execution

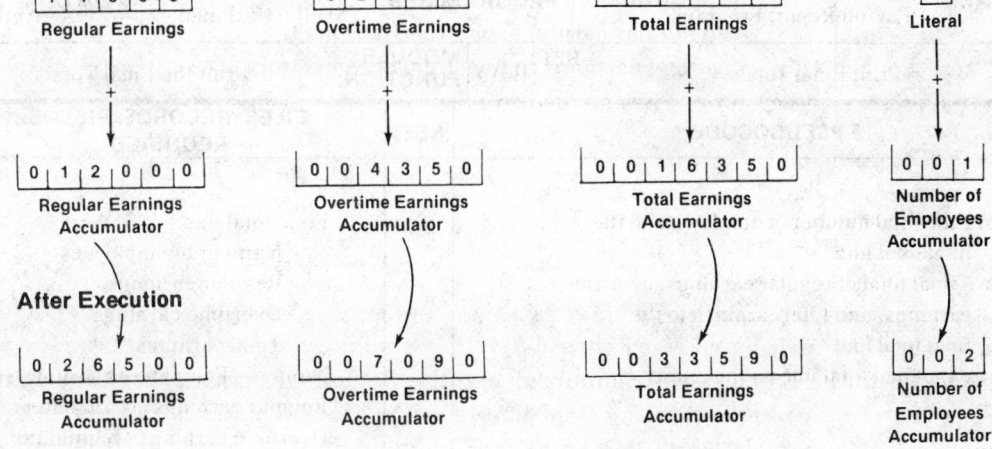

Figure 6-34 Example of Final Total Accumulation

Note in the examples above that the final total accumulators for the Regular Earnings, Overtime Earnings, Total Earnings, and Number of Employees are set to zero prior to the first record being processed. When the first record is processed, the values which are calculated for Regular Earnings, Overtime Earnings, Total Earnings, and Number of Employees are added to these accumulators. When the second record is processed, the same processing occurs. Thus, since the accumulators contain the values from the first record, after the second record is processed they will contain the total values for the first and second records. These totals will be accumulated for each record which is processed.

As will be noted from Figure 6-33, after the final total accumulators have been processed, the detail line is printed on the report, and the spacing is set for single spacing.

The Pseudocode Specifications for the module which prints the final totals must also be prepared by the programmer. The Pseudocode Specifications together with the IPO Chart and Hierarchy Chart are illustrated below.

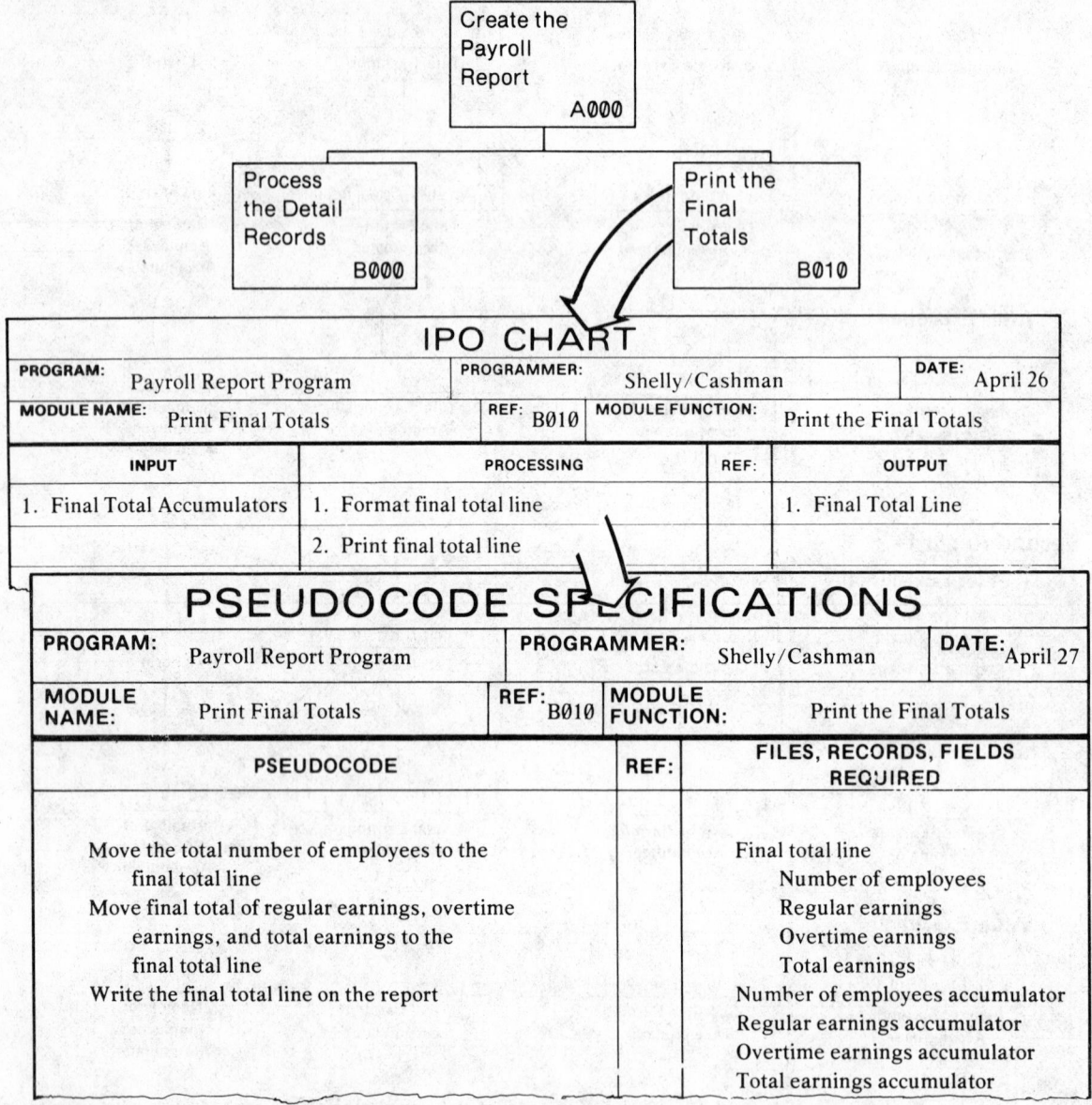

Figure 6-35 Pseudocode Specifications for Final Total Processing

Note from the pseudocode on the Pseudocode Specifications above that the printing of the final totals consists of moving the values in the total accumulators to the final total print line and then printing the final total line.

On all of the Pseudocode Specifications, the Files, Records, and Fields required for processing should also be specified as in the previous programs. When this activity is completed and the pseudocode has been reviewed, then the programmer is ready to begin coding the program.

DATA DIVISION - FILE SECTION

The File Section of the Data Division of the sample program is illustrated below.

EXAMPLE

```
003040  DATA DIVISION.
003050
003060  FILE SECTION.
003070
003080  FD  PAYROLL-INPUT-FILE
003090          RECORD CONTAINS 80 CHARACTERS
003100          LABEL RECORDS ARE OMITTED
003110          DATA RECORD IS PAYROLL-INPUT-RECORD.
003120  01  PAYROLL-INPUT-RECORD.
003130      05  EMPLOYEE-NUMBER-INPUT           PIC 9999.
003140      05  EMPLOYEE-NAME-INPUT             PIC X(20).
003150      05  HOURS-INPUT                     PIC 99.
003160      05  PAY-RATE-INPUT                  PIC 9V99.
003170      05  FILLER                          PIC X(51).
003180
003190  FD  PAYROLL-REPORT-FILE
003200          RECORD CONTAINS 133 CHARACTERS
004010          LABEL RECORDS ARE OMITTED
004020          DATA RECORD IS PAYROLL-REPORT-LINE.
004030  01  PAYROLL-REPORT-LINE.
004040      05  CARRIAGE-CONTROL               PIC X.
004050      05  EMPLOYEE-NUMBER-REPORT         PIC ZZZ9.
004060      05  FILLER                          PIC X(5).
004070      05  EMPLOYEE-NAME-REPORT           PIC X(20).
004080      05  FILLER                          PIC X(5).
004090      05  HOURS-REPORT                    PIC Z9.
004100      05  FILLER                          PIC X(5).
004110      05  PAY-RATE-REPORT                PIC 9.99.
004120      05  FILLER                          PIC X(5).
004130      05  REGULAR-EARNINGS-REPORT        PIC ZZZ.99.
004140      05  FILLER                          PIC X(5).
004150      05  OVERTIME-EARNINGS-REPORT       PIC ZZZ.99.
004160      05  FILLER                          PIC X(5).
004170      05  TOTAL-EARNINGS-REPORT          PIC Z,ZZZ.99.
004180      05  FILLER                          PIC X(52).
```

Figure 6-36 File Section of Data Division

The File Section of the Data Division is used to describe the input and output files and the formats of the input record and report line. This is similar to previous programs.

DEFINITION OF TOTAL ACCUMULATORS

As has been noted, in order to accumulate final totals, areas within storage must be defined in which to store the accumulated values. These areas are defined within the Working-Storage Section of the Data Division. A portion of the Working-Storage Section which includes the total accumulators is illustrated in Figure 6-37.

EXAMPLE

004200	WORKING-STORAGE SECTION.	
005010		
005020	01 PROGRAM-INDICATORS.	
005030	05 ARE-THERE-MORE-RECORDS PIC XXX	VALUE 'YES'.
005040	88 THERE-IS-A-RECORD	VALUE 'YES'.
005050	88 THERE-ARE-NO-MORE-RECORDS	VALUE 'NO '.
005060		
005070	01 PROGRAM-CONSTANTS.	
005080	05 MAX-HRS-FOR-REG-PAY PIC 999	VALUE 40
005090		USAGE IS COMP-3.
005100		
005110	01 WORK-AREAS	USAGE IS COMP-3.
005120	05 REGULAR-EARNINGS-WORK PIC S999V99.	
005130	05 OVERTIME-EARNINGS-WORK PIC S999V99.	
005140	05 TOTAL-EARNINGS-WORK PIC S9(4)V99.	
005150		
005160	01 TOTAL-ACCUMULATORS	USAGE IS COMP-3.
005170	05 REGULAR-EARNINGS-ACCUM PIC S9(4)V99	VALUE ZERO.
005180	05 OVERTIME-EARNINGS-ACCUM PIC S9(4)V99	VALUE ZERO.
005190	05 TOTAL-EARNINGS-ACCUM PIC S9(5)V99	VALUE ZERO.
005200	05 NUMBER-OF-EMPS-ACCUM PIC S999	VALUE ZERO.

Figure 6-37 Definition of Total Accumulators

In the example above it can be seen that the Program Indicators, Program Constants, and Work Areas are defined in the same manner as in previous programs. The group name TOTAL-ACCUMULATORS is used to identify the areas which will be used as final total accumulators. It will be noted that the USAGE IS COMP-3 Clause is used with the group item. When the Usage Clause is used in this manner, each elementary item within the group will be a Computational-3 field. Thus, the REGULAR-EARNINGS-ACCUM field, the OVERTIME-EARNINGS-ACCUM field, etc. will be Computational-3 numeric fields.

In addition, whenever fields are to be used to accumulate values, they should have an initial value of zero. Therefore, the Value Clause is used for the final total accumulators in order to give them an initial value of ZERO. The word ZERO is a Figurative Constant which will cause the value zero to be placed in the field.

The printer control fields and the heading lines are defined in the Working-Storage Section in the same manner as is found in previous programs (these are not shown here).

DEFINING THE FINAL TOTAL LINE

The final total line must be defined in the Working-Storage Section of the Data Division. The coding to define it is illustrated below.

EXAMPLE

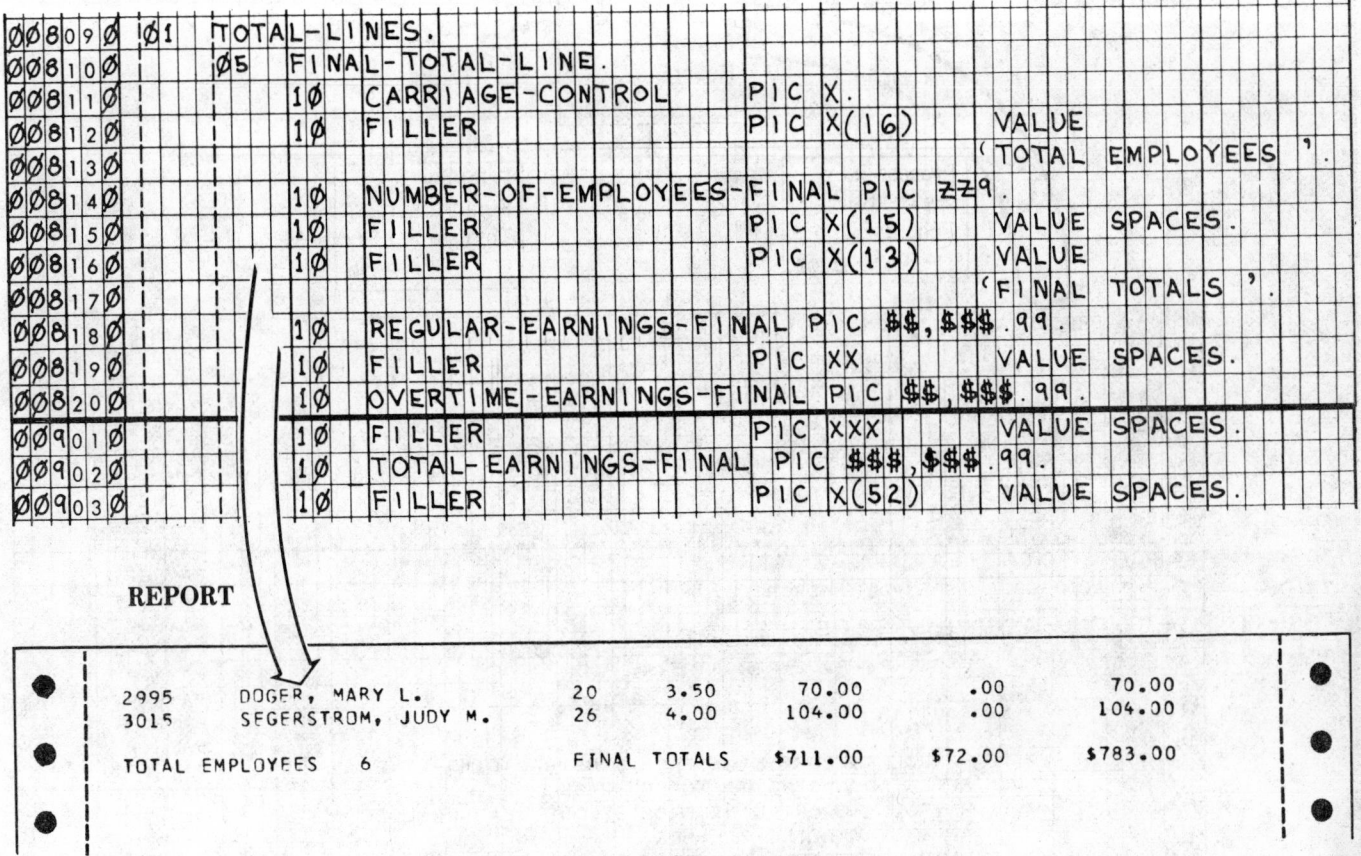

REPORT

```
  2995      DOGER, MARY L.          20    3.50    70.00        .00       70.00
  3015      SEGERSTROM, JUDY M.     26    4.00   104.00        .00      104.00

  TOTAL EMPLOYEES    6              FINAL TOTALS  $711.00    $72.00     $783.00
```

Figure 6-38 Definition of Final Total Line

In Figure 6-38, the entries in Working-Storage are used to define the Final Total Line. The constants "TOTAL EMPLOYEES" and "FINAL TOTALS" are defined, together with the fields which will contain the final totals. It should be noted that the spacing in the definition of the total line should correspond to the format illustrated on the printer spacing chart and that the entire line should be 133 characters in length.

PROCEDURE DIVISION

The A000-CREATE-PAYROLL-REPORT module in the Procedure Division is illustrated below.

EXAMPLE

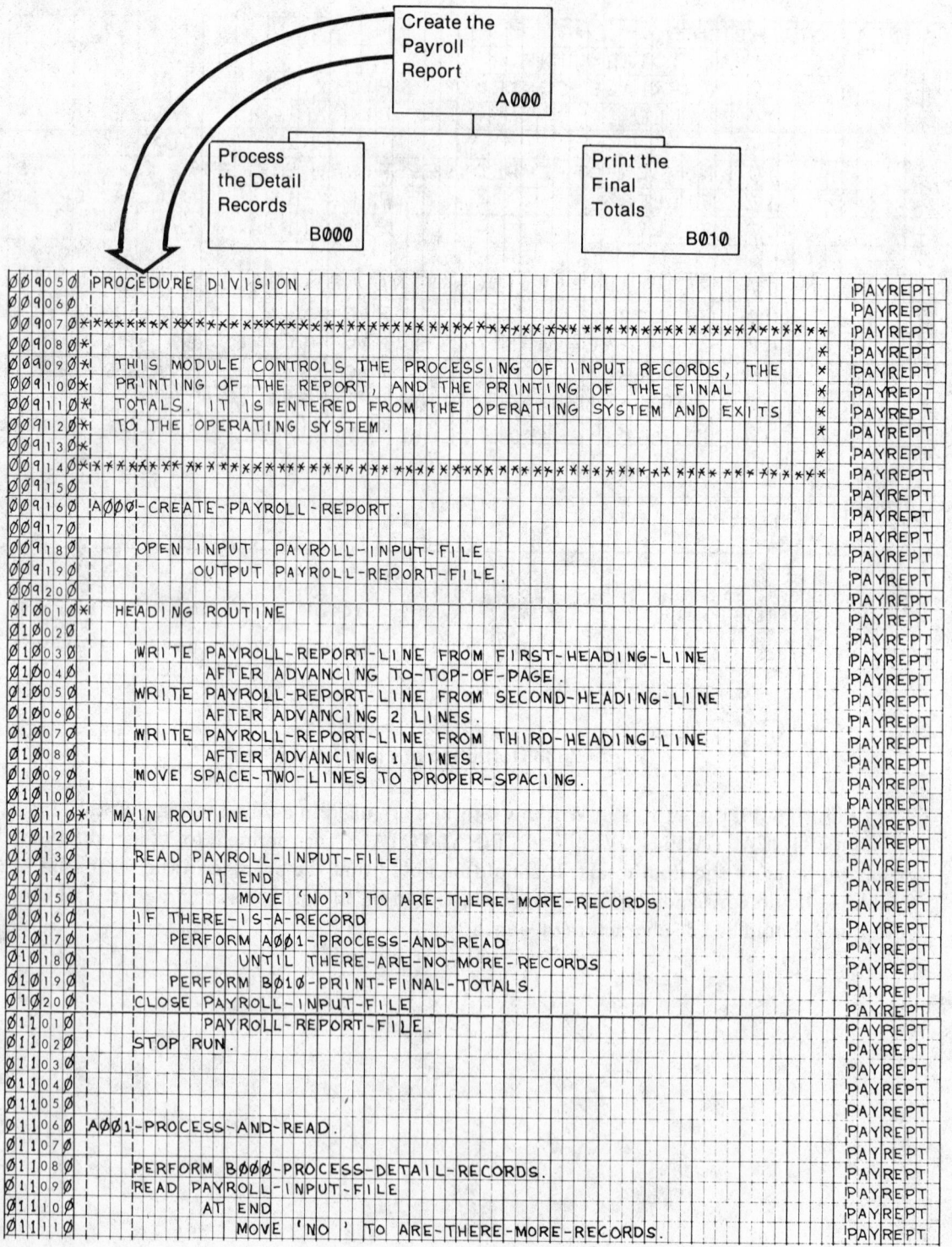

Figure 6-39 A000-CREATE-PAYROLL-REPORT Module

The A000-CREATE-PAYROLL-REPORT module opens the files, writes the report headings, and reads the first input record. If there is a record, the A001-PROCESS-AND-READ module is performed until there are no more input records. The A001-PROCESS-AND-READ module causes the detail record to be processed and then reads another input record. After all of the detail records have been read and processed, the final totals are printed, the files are closed, and the program is terminated.

Condition Names

In the previous chapter it was illustrated how condition names can be used in the Perform Until Statement. They can also be used in an IF Statement. The following example illustrates the use of a condition name in an IF Statement in the sample program.

EXAMPLE

```
004200  WORKING-STORAGE SECTION.
005010
005020  01  PROGRAM-INDICATORS.
005030      05  ARE-THERE-MORE-RECORDS   PIC XXX        VALUE 'YES'.
005040          88  THERE-IS-A-RECORD                   VALUE 'YES'.
005050          88  THERE-ARE-NO-MORE-RECORDS           VALUE 'NO '.

009050  PROCEDURE DIVISION.

010130      READ PAYROLL-INPUT-FILE
010140          AT END
010150              MOVE 'NO ' TO ARE-THERE-MORE-RECORDS.
010160      IF THERE-IS-A-RECORD
010170          PERFORM A001-PROCESS-AND-READ
010180              UNTIL THERE-ARE-NO-MORE-RECORDS
010190          PERFORM B010-PRINT-FINAL-TOTALS.
```

Figure 6-40 Example of Condition Names

Note in Figure 6-40 that two condition names are used for the indicator ARE-THERE-MORE-RECORDS. The first, which is equated to the value "YES" being in the indicator, is THERE-IS-A-RECORD. The second, which is equated to the value "NO ", is THERE-ARE-NO-MORE-RECORDS. In the Procedure Division coding shown, it can be seen that the Read Statement on line 010130 is used to read the first input record. If no input record is read, that is, if there is not one input card in the file, then the value "NO " will be moved to the indicator ARE-THERE-MORE-RECORDS.

If there is an input record, however, the value "YES" will remain in the indicator field. When the IF Statement on line 010160 is tested, the condition THERE-IS-A-RECORD will be true. Therefore, the Perform Statements on lines 010170 and 010190 will be executed. Thus, if an input record is read, the processing for the detail records and final totals will be accomplished; if there is not an input record, then this processing will be bypassed. It will be recalled that this is the processing specified in the pseudocode (see Figure 6-29).

When a detail record is read, it is processed by the B000-PROCESS-DETAIL-RECORDS module, which is illustrated below.

EXAMPLE

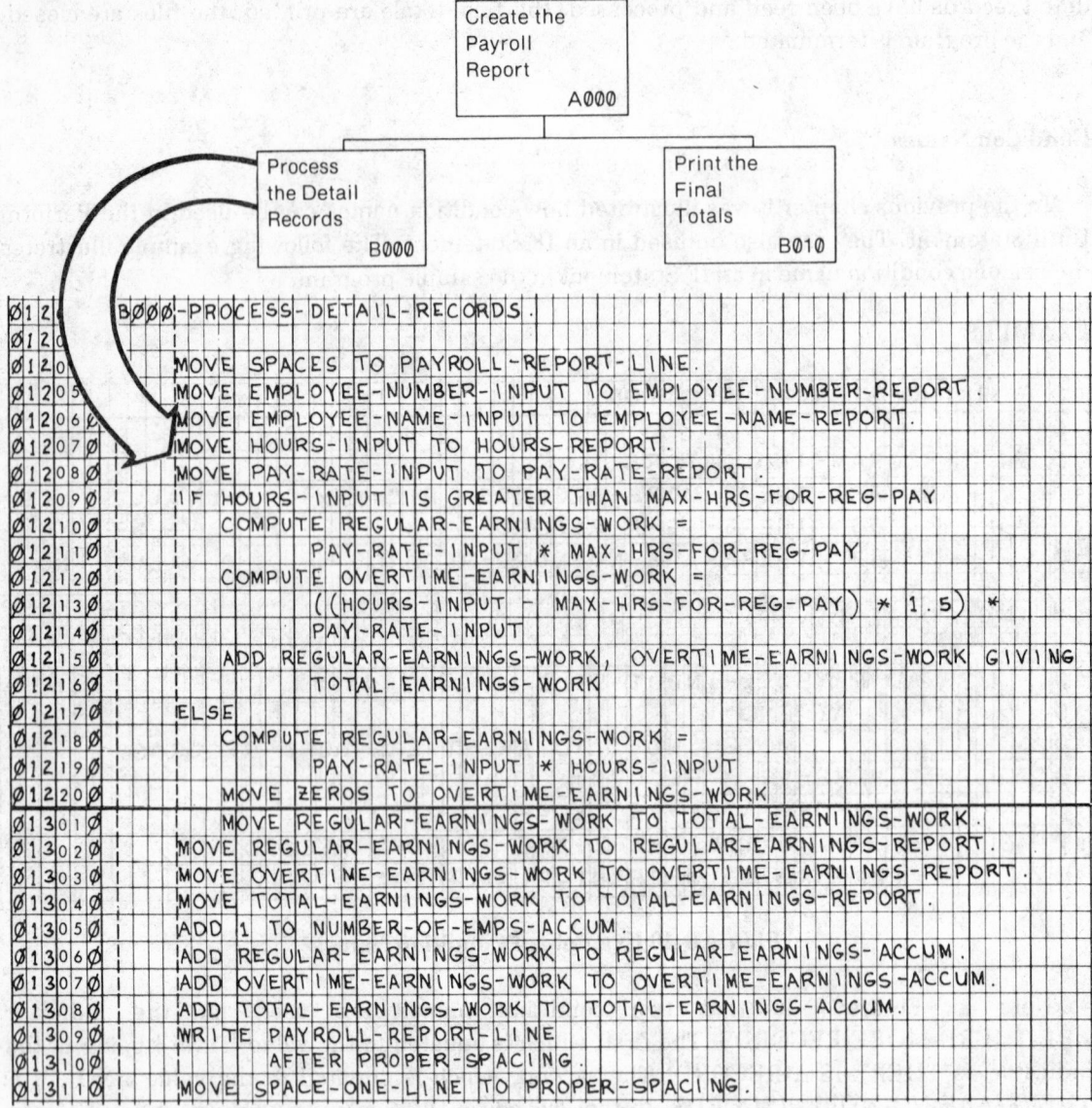

```
Ø12Ø    BØØØ-PROCESS-DETAIL-RECORDS.
Ø12Ø
Ø12Ø        MOVE SPACES TO PAYROLL-REPORT-LINE.
Ø12Ø5       MOVE EMPLOYEE-NUMBER-INPUT TO EMPLOYEE-NUMBER-REPORT.
Ø12Ø6Ø      MOVE EMPLOYEE-NAME-INPUT TO EMPLOYEE-NAME-REPORT.
Ø12Ø7Ø      MOVE HOURS-INPUT TO HOURS-REPORT.
Ø12Ø8Ø      MOVE PAY-RATE-INPUT TO PAY-RATE-REPORT.
Ø12Ø9Ø      IF HOURS-INPUT IS GREATER THAN MAX-HRS-FOR-REG-PAY
Ø121ØØ          COMPUTE REGULAR-EARNINGS-WORK =
Ø12110              PAY-RATE-INPUT * MAX-HRS-FOR-REG-PAY
Ø12120          COMPUTE OVERTIME-EARNINGS-WORK =
Ø12130              ((HOURS-INPUT - MAX-HRS-FOR-REG-PAY) * 1.5) *
Ø12140              PAY-RATE-INPUT
Ø12150          ADD REGULAR-EARNINGS-WORK, OVERTIME-EARNINGS-WORK GIVING
Ø12160              TOTAL-EARNINGS-WORK
Ø12170      ELSE
Ø12180          COMPUTE REGULAR-EARNINGS-WORK =
Ø12190              PAY-RATE-INPUT * HOURS-INPUT
Ø122ØØ          MOVE ZEROS TO OVERTIME-EARNINGS-WORK
Ø13Ø1Ø          MOVE REGULAR-EARNINGS-WORK TO TOTAL-EARNINGS-WORK.
Ø13Ø2Ø      MOVE REGULAR-EARNINGS-WORK TO REGULAR-EARNINGS-REPORT.
Ø13Ø3Ø      MOVE OVERTIME-EARNINGS-WORK TO OVERTIME-EARNINGS-REPORT.
Ø13Ø4Ø      MOVE TOTAL-EARNINGS-WORK TO TOTAL-EARNINGS-REPORT.
Ø13Ø5Ø      ADD 1 TO NUMBER-OF-EMPS-ACCUM.
Ø13Ø6Ø      ADD REGULAR-EARNINGS-WORK TO REGULAR-EARNINGS-ACCUM.
Ø13Ø7Ø      ADD OVERTIME-EARNINGS-WORK TO OVERTIME-EARNINGS-ACCUM.
Ø13Ø8Ø      ADD TOTAL-EARNINGS-WORK TO TOTAL-EARNINGS-ACCUM.
Ø13Ø9Ø      WRITE PAYROLL-REPORT-LINE
Ø131ØØ          AFTER PROPER-SPACING.
Ø13110      MOVE SPACE-ONE-LINE TO PROPER-SPACING.
```

Figure 6-41 B000-PROCESS-DETAIL-RECORDS Module

Note from Figure 6-41 that the COBOL Statements closely follow the pseudocode which was developed for this module (see Figure 6-30). The first portion of the coding clears the printer output area and moves the fields in the input record to the output area.

The earnings are then calculated. If the value in the HOURS-INPUT field is greater than the value in the MAX-HRS-FOR-REG-PAY field, then the Regular Earnings and Overtime Earnings are calculated as illustrated previously. The Regular Earnings and the Overtime Earnings are added together to obtain the Total Earnings. If the value in the HOURS-INPUT field is equal to or less than the value in MAX-HRS-FOR-REG-PAY, the Regular Earnings are calculated, zeros are moved to the Overtime Earnings field, and the Regular Earnings are moved to the Total Earnings.

The earnings are then moved to the output area, the Total Employees Accumulator is incremented by 1, and the earnings are added to the final total accumulators. A line is printed and the space control is set for single spacing. This completes the processing in the B000-PROCESS-DETAIL-RECORDS module.

The B010-PRINT-FINAL-TOTALS module is used to print the final totals on the report. It is illustrated below.

EXAMPLE

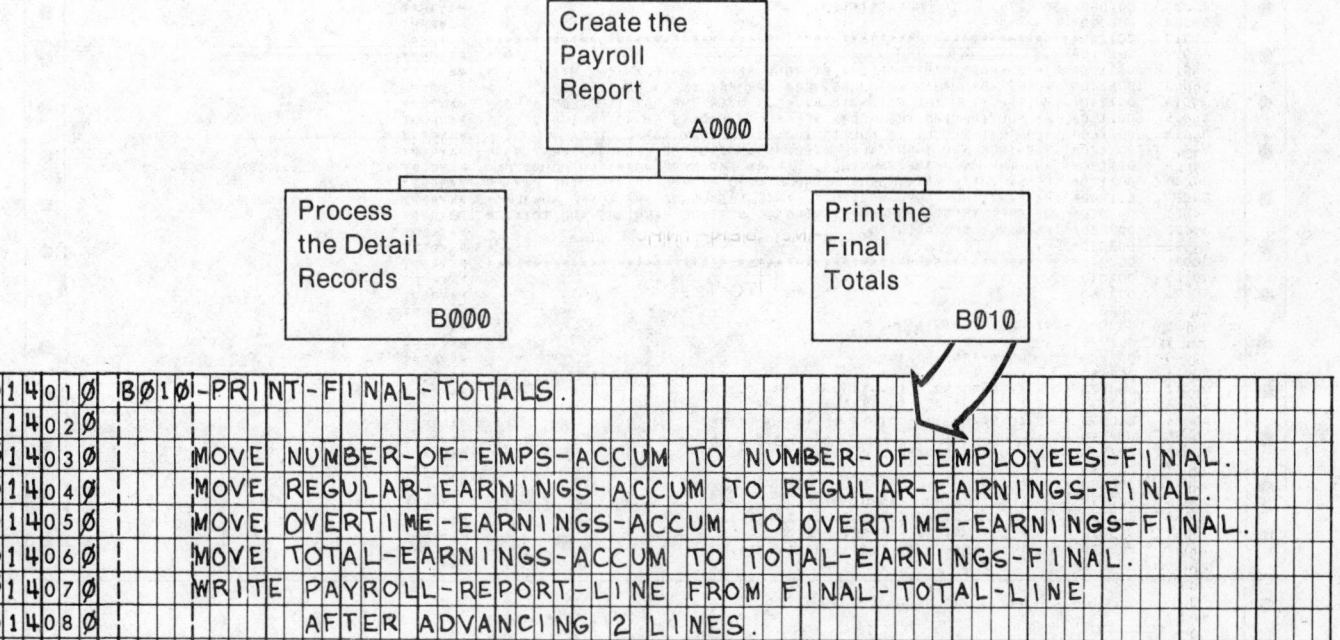

Figure 6-42 B010-PRINT-FINAL-TOTALS Module

As can be seen from Figure 6-42, the values in the total accumulators are moved to the final total line and the line is written on the report. Again, this corresponds to the pseudocode which was developed for this module (see Figure 6-35).

SUMMARY

From the program design and coding of the payroll report program it can be seen that it is extremely important in the earliest design phases to carefully analyze the processing which must occur and the major processing tasks which are necessary; and to decompose each of these major processing tasks into individual modules if there is a significant amount of processing to be accomplished and if each task represents a specific function to be performed within the program. Using this approach, the programmer may concentrate on developing accurate, efficient processing in each individual module rather than trying to consider all aspects of the entire problem at one time.

SOURCE LISTING

The source listing for the sample program is contained on this and the following pages.

```
     1                        IBM DOS AMERICAN NATIONAL STANDARD COBOL        CBF CL3-4          05/26/77

   00001   001010 IDENTIFICATION DIVISION.                                      PAYREPT
   00002   001020                                                               PAYREPT
   00003   001030 PROGRAM-ID.     PAYREPT.                                      PAYREPT
   00004   001040 AUTHOR.             SHELLY AND CASHMAN.                        PAYREPT
   00005   001050 INSTALLATION.   ANAHEIM.                                       PAYREPT
   00006   001060 DATE-WRITTEN.   05/18/77.                                      PAYREPT
   00007   001070 DATE-COMPILED. 05/26/77                                        PAYREPT
   00008   001080 SECURITY.       UNCLASSIFIED.                                  PAYREPT
   00009   001090                                                               PAYREPT
   00010   001100***********************************************************     PAYREPT
   00011   001110*                                                         *     PAYREPT
   00012   001120*   THIS PROGRAM PREPARES A PAYROLL REPORT.  IF AN EMPLOYEE *   PAYREPT
   00013   001130*   WORKS MORE THAN 40 HOURS, REGULAR PAY IS CALCULATED BY  *   PAYREPT
   00014   001140*   MULTIPLYING THE PAY RATE BY 40.  OVERTIME PAY IS CALCULATED * PAYREPT
   00015   001150*   BY MULTIPLYING THE HOURS WORKED IN EXCESS OF 40 BY 1.5  *   PAYREPT
   00016   001160*   AND THAT RESULT IS MULTIPLIED BY THE PAY RATE.  TOTAL   *   PAYREPT
   00017   001170*   EARNINGS ARE THEN CALCULATED BY ADDING THE REGULAR EARNINGS * PAYREPT
   00018   001180*   AND THE OVERTIME EARNINGS.  IF AN EMPLOYEE WORKS 40 HOURS OR* PAYREPT
   00019   001190*   LESS, TOTAL EARNINGS ARE CALCULATED BY MULTIPLYING THE PAY * PAYREPT
   00020   001200*   RATE BY THE HOURS WORKED.  FINAL TOTALS OF THE TOTAL NUMBER * PAYREPT
   00021   002010*   OF EMPLOYEES, REGULAR EARNINGS, OVERTIME EARNINGS AND TOTAL * PAYREPT
   00022   002020*   EARNINGS ARE PRINTED.                                   *   PAYREPT
   00023   002030*                                                          *    PAYREPT
   00024   002040***********************************************************     PAYREPT
   00025   002050                                                               PAYREPT
   00026   002060                                                               PAYREPT
   00027   002070                                                               PAYREPT
   00028   002080 ENVIRONMENT DIVISION.                                          PAYREPT
   00029   002090                                                               PAYREPT
   00030   002100 CONFIGURATION SECTION.                                         PAYREPT
   00031   002110                                                               PAYREPT
   00032   002120 SOURCE-COMPUTER.  IBM-370.                                     PAYREPT
   00033   002130 OBJECT-COMPUTER.  IBM-370.                                     PAYREPT
   00034   002140 SPECIAL-NAMES.    C01 IS TO-TOP-OF-PAGE.                       PAYREPT
   00035   002150                                                               PAYREPT
   00036   002160 INPUT-OUTPUT SECTION.                                          PAYREPT
   00037   002170                                                               PAYREPT
   00038   002180 FILE-CONTROL.                                                  PAYREPT
   00039   002190     SELECT PAYROLL-INPUT-FILE                                  PAYREPT
   00040   002200         ASSIGN TO SYS007-UR-2540R-S.                           PAYREPT
   00041   003010     SELECT PAYROLL-REPORT-FILE                                 PAYREPT
   00042   003020         ASSIGN TO SYS013-UR-1403-S.                            PAYREPT
```

```
     2

   00043   003040 DATA DIVISION.                                                 PAYREPT
   00044   003050                                                               PAYREPT
   00045   003060 FILE SECTION.                                                  PAYREPT
   00046   003070                                                               PAYREPT
   00047   003080 FD  PAYROLL-INPUT-FILE                                         PAYREPT
   00048   003090     RECORD CONTAINS 80 CHARACTERS                              PAYREPT
   00049   003100     LABEL RECORDS ARE OMITTED                                  PAYREPT
   00050   003110     DATA RECORD IS PAYROLL-INPUT-RECORD.                       PAYREPT
   00051   003120 01  PAYROLL-INPUT-RECORD.                                      PAYREPT
   00052   003130     05  EMPLOYEE-NUMBER-INPUT   PIC 9999.                      PAYREPT
   00053   003140     05  EMPLOYEE-NAME-INPUT     PIC X(20).                     PAYREPT
   00054   003150     05  HOURS-INPUT             PIC 99.                        PAYREPT
   00055   003160     05  PAY-RATE-INPUT          PIC 9V99.                      PAYREPT
   00056   003170     05  FILLER                  PIC X(51).                     PAYREPT
   00057   003180                                                               PAYREPT
   00058   003190 FD  PAYROLL-REPORT-FILE                                        PAYREPT
   00059   003200     RECORD CONTAINS 133 CHARACTERS                             PAYREPT
   00060   004010     LABEL RECORDS ARE OMITTED                                  PAYREPT
   00061   004020     DATA RECORD IS PAYROLL-REPORT-LINE.                        PAYREPT
   00062   004030 01  PAYROLL-REPORT-LINE.                                       PAYREPT
   00063   004040     05  CARRIAGE-CONTROL        PIC X.                         PAYREPT
   00064   004050     05  EMPLOYEE-NUMBER-REPORT  PIC ZZZ9.                      PAYREPT
   00065   004060     05  FILLER                  PIC X(5).                      PAYREPT
   00066   004070     05  EMPLOYEE-NAME-REPORT    PIC X(20).                     PAYREPT
   00067   004080     05  FILLER                  PIC X(5).                      PAYREPT
   00068   004090     05  HOURS-REPORT            PIC Z9.                        PAYREPT
   00069   004100     05  FILLER                  PIC X(5).                      PAYREPT
   00070   004110     05  PAY-RATE-REPORT         PIC 9.99.                      PAYREPT
   00071   004120     05  FILLER                  PIC X(5).                      PAYREPT
   00072   004130     05  REGULAR-EARNINGS-REPORT PIC ZZZ.99.                    PAYREPT
   00073   004140     05  FILLER                  PIC X(5).                      PAYREPT
   00074   004150     05  OVERTIME-EARNINGS-REPORT PIC ZZZ.99.                   PAYREPT
   00075   004160     05  FILLER                  PIC X(5).                      PAYREPT
   00076   004170     05  TOTAL-EARNINGS-REPORT   PIC Z,ZZZ.99.                  PAYREPT
   00077   004180     05  FILLER                  PIC X(52).                     PAYREPT
   00078   004190                                                               PAYREPT
```

Figure 6-43 Source Listing [Part 1 of 4]

```
    3
00079   004200 WORKING-STORAGE SECTION.                                  PAYREPT
00080   005010                                                           PAYREPT
00081   005020 01  PROGRAM-INDICATORS.                                   PAYREPT
00082   005030     05  ARE-THERE-MORE-RECORDS  PIC XXX      VALUE 'YES'. PAYREPT
00083   005040         88  THERE-IS-A-RECORD                VALUE 'YES'. PAYREPT
00084   005050         88  THERE-ARE-NO-MORE-RECORDS        VALUE 'NO '. PAYREPT
00085   005060                                                           PAYREPT
00086   005070 01  PROGRAM-CONSTANTS.                                    PAYREPT
00087   005080     05  MAX-HRS-FOR-REG-PAY     PIC 999      VALUE 40     PAYREPT
00088   005090                                             USAGE IS COMP-3. PAYREPT
00089   005100                                                           PAYREPT
00090   005110 01  WORK-AREAS                               USAGE IS COMP-3. PAYREPT
00091   005120     05  REGULAR-EARNINGS-WORK   PIC S999V99. PAYREPT
00092   005130     05  OVERTIME-EARNINGS-WORK  PIC S999V99. PAYREPT
00093   005140     05  TOTAL-EARNINGS-WORK     PIC S9(4)V99. PAYREPT
00094   005150                                                           PAYREPT
00095   005160 01  TOTAL-ACCUMULATORS                       USAGE IS COMP-3. PAYREPT
00096   005170     05  REGULAR-EARNINGS-ACCUM  PIC S9(4)V99 VALUE ZERO.  PAYREPT
00097   005180     05  OVERTIME-EARNINGS-ACCUM PIC S9(4)V99 VALUE ZERO.  PAYREPT
00098   005190     05  TOTAL-EARNINGS-ACCUM    PIC S9(5)V99 VALUE ZERO.  PAYREPT
00099   005200     05  NUMBER-OF-EMPS-ACCUM    PIC S999     VALUE ZERO.  PAYREPT
00100   006010                                                           PAYREPT
00101   006020 01  PRINTER-CONTROL.                                      PAYREPT
00102   006030     05  PROPER-SPACING          PIC 9.                    PAYREPT
00103   006040     05  SPACE-ONE-LINE          PIC 9        VALUE 1.     PAYREPT
00104   006050     05  SPACE-TWO-LINES         PIC 9        VALUE 2.     PAYREPT
00105   006060                                                           PAYREPT
00106   006070 01  HEADING-LINES.                                        PAYREPT
00107   006080     05  FIRST-HEADING-LINE.                               PAYREPT
00108   006090         10  CARRIAGE-CONTROL    PIC X.                    PAYREPT
00109   006100         10  FILLER              PIC X(26)    VALUE SPACES. PAYREPT
00110   006110         10  FILLER              PIC X(13)    VALUE        PAYREPT
00111   006120                                             'P A Y R O L L'. PAYREPT
00112   006130         10  FILLER              PIC XXX      VALUE SPACES. PAYREPT
00113   006140         10  FILLER              PIC X(11)    VALUE        PAYREPT
00114   006150                                             'R E P O R T'. PAYREPT
00115   006160         10  FILLER              PIC X(79)    VALUE SPACES. PAYREPT
00116   006170     05  SECOND-HEADING-LINE.                              PAYREPT
00117   006180         10  CARRIAGE-CONTROL    PIC X.                    PAYREPT
00118   006190         10  FILLER              PIC X(4)     VALUE 'EMP.'. PAYREPT
00119   006200         10  FILLER              PIC X(11)    VALUE SPACES. PAYREPT
00120   007010         10  FILLER              PIC X(8)     VALUE 'EMPLOYEE'. PAYREPT
00121   007020         10  FILLER              PIC X(19)    VALUE SPACES. PAYREPT
00122   007030         10  FILLER              PIC XXX      VALUE 'PAY'. PAYREPT
00123   007040         10  FILLER              PIC X(5)     VALUE SPACES. PAYREPT
00124   007050         10  FILLER              PIC X(7)     VALUE 'REGULAR'. PAYREPT
00125   007060         10  FILLER              PIC XXX      VALUE SPACES. PAYREPT
00126   007070         10  FILLER              PIC X(8)     VALUE 'OVERTIME'. PAYREPT
00127   007080         10  FILLER              PIC X(6)     VALUE SPACES. PAYREPT
00128   007090         10  FILLER              PIC X(5)     VALUE 'TOTAL'. PAYREPT
00129   007100         10  FILLER              PIC X(53)    VALUE SPACES. PAYREPT
00130   007110     05  THIRD-HEADING-LINE.                               PAYREPT
00131   007120         10  CARRIAGE-CONTROL    PIC X        VALUE SPACES. PAYREPT
00132   007130         10  FILLER              PIC X        VALUE SPACES. PAYREPT
00133   007140         10  FILLER              PIC XXX      VALUE 'NO.'. PAYREPT
00134   007150         10  FILLER              PIC X(13)    VALUE SPACES. PAYREPT
00135   007160         10  FILLER              PIC X(4)     VALUE 'NAME'. PAYREPT
00136   007170         10  FILLER              PIC X(12)    VALUE SPACES. PAYREPT
00137   007180         10  FILLER              PIC X(5)     VALUE 'HOURS'. PAYREPT
00138   007190         10  FILLER              PIC XXX      VALUE SPACES. PAYREPT
00139   007200         10  FILLER              PIC XXXX     VALUE 'RATE'. PAYREPT
00140   008010         10  FILLER              PIC XXXX     VALUE SPACES. PAYREPT
00141   008020         10  FILLER              PIC X(8)     VALUE 'EARNINGS'. PAYREPT
00142   008030         10  FILLER              PIC XXX      VALUE SPACES. PAYREPT
00143   008040         10  FILLER              PIC X(8)     VALUE 'EARNINGS'. PAYREPT
00144   008050         10  FILLER              PIC X(4)     VALUE SPACES. PAYREPT
00145   008060         10  FILLER              PIC X(8)     VALUE 'EARNINGS'. PAYREPT
00146   009070         10  FILLER              PIC X(52)    VALUE SPACES. PAYREPT
00147   008080                                                           PAYREPT
00148   008090 01  TOTAL-LINES.                                          PAYREPT
00149   008100     05  FINAL-TOTAL-LINE.                                 PAYREPT
00150   008110         10  CARRIAGE-CONTROL    PIC X.                    PAYREPT
00151   008120         10  FILLER              PIC X(16)    VALUE        PAYREPT
00152   008130                                         'TOTAL EMPLOYEES '. PAYREPT
00153   008140         10  NUMBER-OF-EMPLOYEES-FINAL PIC ZZ9.            PAYREPT
00154   008150         10  FILLER              PIC X(15)    VALUE SPACES. PAYREPT
00155   008160         10  FILLER              PIC X(13)    VALUE        PAYREPT
00156   008170                                         'FINAL TOTALS '. PAYREPT
00157   008180         10  REGULAR-EARNINGS-FINAL PIC $$,$$$.99.         PAYREPT
00158   008190         10  FILLER              PIC XX       VALUE SPACES. PAYREPT
00159   008200         10  OVERTIME-EARNINGS-FINAL PIC $$,$$$.99.        PAYREPT
00160   009010         10  FILLER              PIC XXX      VALUE SPACES. PAYREPT
00161   009020         10  TOTAL-EARNINGS-FINAL PIC $$$,$$$.99.          PAYREPT
00162   009030         10  FILLER              PIC X(52)    VALUE SPACES. PAYREPT
```

Figure 6-44 Source Listing [Part 2 of 4]

```
        4
00163   009050 PROCEDURE DIVISION.                                         PAYREPT
00164   009060                                                             PAYREPT
00165   009070*******************************************************     PAYREPT
00166   009080*                                                      *     PAYREPT
00167   009090*  THIS MODULE CONTROLS THE PROCESSING OF INPUT RECORDS, THE * PAYREPT
00168   009100*  PRINTING OF THE REPORT, AND THE PRINTING OF THE FINAL   * PAYREPT
00169   009110*  TOTALS. IT IS ENTERED FROM THE OPERATING SYSTEM AND EXITS * PAYREPT
00170   009120*  TO THE OPERATING SYSTEM.                               * PAYREPT
00171   009130*                                                      *     PAYREPT
00172   009140*******************************************************     PAYREPT
00173   009150                                                             PAYREPT
00174   009160 A000-CREATE-PAYROLL-REPORT.                                 PAYREPT
00175   009170                                                             PAYREPT
00176   009180     OPEN INPUT  PAYROLL-INPUT-FILE                          PAYREPT
00177   009190          OUTPUT PAYROLL-REPORT-FILE.                        PAYREPT
00178   009200                                                             PAYREPT
00179   010010*  HEADING ROUTINE                                           PAYREPT
00180   010020                                                             PAYREPT
00181   010030     WRITE PAYROLL-REPORT-LINE FROM FIRST-HEADING-LINE       PAYREPT
00182   010040          AFTER ADVANCING TO-TOP-OF-PAGE.                    PAYREPT
00183   010050     WRITE PAYROLL-REPORT-LINE FROM SECOND-HEADING-LINE      PAYREPT
00184   010060          AFTER ADVANCING 2 LINES.                          PAYREPT
00185   010070     WRITE PAYROLL-REPORT-LINE FROM THIRD-HEADING-LINE       PAYREPT
00186   010080          AFTER ADVANCING 1 LINES.                          PAYREPT
00187   010090     MOVE SPACE-TWO-LINES TO PROPER-SPACING.                 PAYREPT
00188   010100                                                             PAYREPT
00189   010110*  MAIN ROUTINE                                              PAYREPT
00190   010120                                                             PAYREPT
00191   010130     READ PAYROLL-INPUT-FILE                                 PAYREPT
00192   010140          AT END                                            PAYREPT
00193   010150              MOVE 'NO ' TO ARE-THERE-MORE-RECORDS.          PAYREPT
00194   010160     IF THERE-IS-A-RECORD                                    PAYREPT
00195   010170        PERFORM A001-PROCESS-AND-READ                        PAYREPT
00196   010180            UNTIL THERE-ARE-NO-MORE-RECORDS                  PAYREPT
00197   010190        PERFORM B010-PRINT-FINAL-TOTALS.                     PAYREPT
00198   010200     CLOSE PAYROLL-INPUT-FILE                                PAYREPT
00199   011010           PAYROLL-REPORT-FILE.                              PAYREPT
00200   011020     STOP RUN.                                               PAYREPT
00201   011030                                                             PAYREPT
00202   011040                                                             PAYREPT
00203   011050                                                             PAYREPT
00204   011060 A001-PROCESS-AND-READ.                                      PAYREPT
00205   011070                                                             PAYREPT
00206   011080     PERFORM B000-PROCESS-DETAIL-RECORDS.                    PAYREPT
00207   011090     READ PAYROLL-INPUT-FILE                                 PAYREPT
00208   011100          AT END                                            PAYREPT
00209   011110              MOVE 'NO ' TO ARE-THERE-MORE-RECORDS.          PAYREPT
```

Figure 6-45 Source Listing [Part 3 of 4]

```
   5
00210   011130*********************************************************   PAYREPT
00211   011140*                                                      *   PAYREPT
00212   011150*  THIS MODULE FORMATS THE REPORT, CALCULATES REGULAR PAY AND  *   PAYREPT
00213   011160*  OVERTIME PAY, ACCUMULATES THE FINAL TOTALS, AND PRINTS THE  *   PAYREPT
00214   011170*  DETAIL LINE.  IT IS ENTERED FROM AND EXITS TO THE   *   PAYREPT
00215   011180*  A001-PROCESS-AND-READ MODULE.                       *   PAYREPT
00216   011190*                                                      *   PAYREPT
00217   011200*********************************************************   PAYREPT
00218   012010                                                           PAYREPT
00219   012020 B000-PROCESS-DETAIL-RECORDS.                              PAYREPT
00220   012030                                                           PAYREPT
00221   012040     MOVE SPACES TO PAYROLL-REPORT-LINE.                   PAYREPT
00222   012050     MOVE EMPLOYEE-NUMBER-INPUT TO EMPLOYEE-NUMBER-REPORT. PAYREPT
00223   012060     MOVE EMPLOYEE-NAME-INPUT TO EMPLOYEE-NAME-REPORT.     PAYREPT
00224   012070     MOVE HOURS-INPUT TO HOURS-REPORT.                     PAYREPT
00225   012080     MOVE PAY-RATE-INPUT TO PAY-RATE-REPORT.              PAYREPT
00226   012090     IF HOURS-INPUT IS GREATER THAN MAX-HRS-FOR-REG-PAY    PAYREPT
00227   012100         COMPUTE REGULAR-EARNINGS-WORK =                   PAYREPT
00228   012110             PAY-RATE-INPUT * MAX-HRS-FOR-REG-PAY          PAYREPT
00229   012120         COMPUTE OVERTIME-EARNINGS-WORK =                  PAYREPT
00230   012130             ((HOURS-INPUT - MAX-HRS-FOR-REG-PAY) * 1.5) * PAYREPT
00231   012140             PAY-RATE-INPUT                               PAYREPT
00232   012150         ADD REGULAR-EARNINGS-WORK, OVERTIME-EARNINGS-WORK GIVING  PAYREPT
00233   012160             TOTAL-EARNINGS-WORK                          PAYREPT
00234   012170     ELSE                                                 PAYREPT
00235   012180         COMPUTE REGULAR-EARNINGS-WORK =                  PAYREPT
00236   012190             PAY-RATE-INPUT * HOURS-INPUT                 PAYREPT
00237   012200         MOVE ZEROS TO OVERTIME-EARNINGS-WORK            PAYREPT
00238   012210         MOVE REGULAR-EARNINGS-WORK TO TOTAL-EARNINGS-WORK.  PAYREPT
00239   013010     MOVE REGULAR-EARNINGS-WORK TO REGULAR-EARNINGS-REPORT.  PAYREPT
00240   013020     MOVE OVERTIME-EARNINGS-WORK TO OVERTIME-EARNINGS-REPORT.  PAYREPT
00241   013030     MOVE TOTAL-EARNINGS-WORK TO TOTAL-EARNINGS-REPORT.    PAYREPT
00242   013040     ADD 1 TO NUMBER-OF-EMPS-ACCUM.                       PAYREPT
00243   013050     ADD REGULAR-EARNINGS-WORK TO REGULAR-EARNINGS-ACCUM. PAYREPT
00244   013060     ADD OVERTIME-EARNINGS-WORK TO OVERTIME-EARNINGS-ACCUM.  PAYREPT
00245   013070     ADD TOTAL-EARNINGS-WORK TO TOTAL-EARNINGS-ACCUM.     PAYREPT
00246   013080     WRITE PAYROLL-REPORT-LINE                            PAYREPT
00247   013090         AFTER PROPER-SPACING.                           PAYREPT
00248   013100     MOVE SPACE-ONE-LINE TO PROPER-SPACING.              PAYREPT
```

```
   6
00249   013120*********************************************************   PAYREPT
00250   013130*                                                      *   PAYREPT
00251   013140*  THIS MODULE PRINTS THE FINAL TOTALS. IT IS ENTERED FROM AND  *   PAYREPT
00252   013150*  EXITS TO THE A000-CREATE-PAYROLL-REPORT MODULE.     *   PAYREPT
00253   013160*                                                      *   PAYREPT
00254   013170*********************************************************   PAYREPT
00255   013180                                                           PAYREPT
00256   013190 B010-PRINT-FINAL-TOTALS.                                  PAYREPT
00257   013200                                                           PAYREPT
00258   014010     MOVE NUMBER-OF-EMPS-ACCUM TO NUMBER-OF-EMPLOYEES-FINAL.  PAYREPT
00259   014020     MOVE REGULAR-EARNINGS-ACCUM TO REGULAR-EARNINGS-FINAL.  PAYREPT
00260   014030     MOVE OVERTIME-EARNINGS-ACCUM TO OVERTIME-EARNINGS-FINAL.  PAYREPT
00261   014040     MOVE TOTAL-EARNINGS-ACCUM TO TOTAL-EARNINGS-FINAL.    PAYREPT
00262   014050     WRITE PAYROLL-REPORT-LINE FROM FINAL-TOTAL-LINE      PAYREPT
00263   014060         AFTER ADVANCING 2 LINES.                        PAYREPT
```

Figure 6-46 Source Listing [Part 4 of 4]

CHAPTER 6

REVIEW QUESTIONS

1. Write the IF statement to determine if the value in the field referenced by SHIFTCODE is equal to the value in the field referenced by DAY-CONSTANT. If the values are equal, add 1 to DAY-SHIFT-ACCUM. If the fields are not equal, add 1 to NIGHT-SHIFT-ACCUM.

2. Explain the use of the period in an IF Statement.

3. In the coding illustrated below there is a period following the sentence on line 014070. What would be the effect on the logic of the IF statement if the period were removed?

```
014020        IF SEX-OF-EMPLOYEE-INPUT = MALE-CONSTANT
014030            PERFORM C030-PROCESS-MALE-EMPLOYEE
014040            ADD 1 TO MALE-EMPLOYEES-ACCUM
014050        ELSE
014060            PERFORM C040-PROCESS-FEMALE-EMPLOYEE
014070            ADD 1 TO FEMALE-EMPLOYEE-ACCUM.
014080        MOVE SEX-OF-EMPLOYEE-INPUT TO SEX-OF-EMPLOYEE-REPORT.
```

4. In the coding illustrated below when will the statement on line 014100, MOVE COUNTER-WORK to COUNTER-REPORT be executed?

```
014060        IF COUNTER-WORK = 10
014070            SUBTRACT 10 FROM COUNTER-WORK
014080        ELSE
014090            ADD 1 TO COUNTER-WORK.
014100        MOVE COUNTER-WORK TO COUNTER-REPORT.
```

5. Explain the use of the entry NEXT SENTENCE in an IF statement.

6. In the example below what occurs when SALES-INPUT is equal to spaces?

```
Ø16 18Ø      IF SALES-INPUT IS NOT = SPACES
Ø16 19Ø         ADD SALES-INPUT TO SALES-ACCUM.
```

7. List the types of Relation Tests that may be performed when using an IF statement.

8. Explain how a numeric comparison takes place, that is, comparing fields defined with a Picture 9.

9. Explain how comparing takes place for alphanumeric fields, that is, fields defined with a Picture X.

10. What is meant by a ''Sign Test''? Write an IF statement using Sign Test.

11. What is meant by a ''Class test''? Write an IF statement using a Class Test.

CHAPTER 6

DEBUGGING COBOL PROGRAMS

PROBLEM 1

INSTRUCTIONS

The following COBOL program contains an error or errors which occurred during execution. Circle each error and record the corrected entries directly on the listing. Explain the error and method of correction in the space provided below.

```
     1                      IBM DOS AMERICAN NATIONAL STANDARD COBOL      CBF CL3-4         06/27/77

  00001   001010 IDENTIFICATION DIVISION.                                      PAYREPT
  00002   001020                                                               PAYREPT
  00003   001030 PROGRAM-ID.    PAYREPT.                                        PAYREPT
  00004   001040 AUTHOR.        SHELLY AND CASHMAN.                             PAYREPT
  00005   001050 INSTALLATION.  ANAHEIM.                                        PAYREPT
  00006   001060 DATE-WRITTEN.  05/18/77.                                       PAYREPT
  00007   001070 DATE-COMPILED. 06/27/77                                        PAYREPT
  00008   001080 SECURITY.      UNCLASSIFIED.                                   PAYREPT
  00009   001090                                                               PAYREPT
  00010   001100***************************************************************  PAYREPT
  00011   001110*                                                            *  PAYREPT
  00012   001120*  THIS PROGRAM PREPARES A PAYROLL REPORT.  IF AN EMPLOYEE   *  PAYREPT
  00013   001130*  WORKS MORE THAN 40 HOURS, REGULAR PAY IS CALCULATED BY    *  PAYREPT
  00014   001140*  MULTIPLYING THE PAY RATE BY 40.  OVERTIME PAY IS CALCULATED *  PAYREPT
  00015   001150*  BY MULTIPLYING THE HOURS WORKED IN EXCESS OF 40 BY 1.5    *  PAYREPT
  00016   001160*  AND THAT RESULT IS MULTIPLIED BY THE PAY RATE.  TOTAL     *  PAYREPT
  00017   001170*  EARNINGS ARE THEN CALCULATED BY ADDING THE REGULAR EARNINGS *  PAYREPT
  00018   001180*  AND THE OVERTIME EARNINGS.  IF AN EMPLOYEE WORKS 40 HOURS OR* PAYREPT
  00019   001190*  LESS, TOTAL EARNINGS ARE CALCULATED BY MULTIPLYING THE PAY *  PAYREPT
  00020   001200*  RATE BY THE HOURS WORKED.  FINAL TOTALS OF THE TOTAL NUMBER * PAYREPT
  00021   002010*  OF EMPLOYEES, REGULAR EARNINGS, OVERTIME EARNINGS AND TOTAL* PAYREPT
  00022   002020*  EARNINGS ARE PRINTED.                                      *  PAYREPT
  00023   002030*                                                               PAYREPT
  00024   002040***************************************************************  PAYREPT
  00025   002050                                                               PAYREPT
  00026   002060                                                               PAYREPT
  00027   002070                                                               PAYREPT
  00028   002080 ENVIRONMENT DIVISION.                                         PAYREPT
  00029   002090                                                               PAYREPT
  00030   002100 CONFIGURATION SECTION.                                        PAYREPT
  00031   002110                                                               PAYREPT
  00032   002120 SOURCE-COMPUTER.  IBM-370.                                    PAYREPT
  00033   002130 OBJECT-COMPUTER.  IBM-370.                                    PAYREPT
  00034   002140 SPECIAL-NAMES.    C01 IS TO-TOP-OF-PAGE.                       PAYREPT
  00035   002150                                                               PAYREPT
  00036   002160 INPUT-OUTPUT SECTION.                                         PAYREPT
  00037   002170                                                               PAYREPT
  00038   002180 FILE-CONTROL.                                                 PAYREPT
  00039   002190     SELECT PAYROLL-INPUT-FILE                                 PAYREPT
  00040   002200         ASSIGN TO SYS007-UR-2540R-S.                          PAYREPT
  00041   003010     SELECT PAYROLL-REPORT-FILE                                PAYREPT
  00042   003020         ASSIGN TO SYS013-UR-1403-S.                           PAYREPT
```

```
     2

  00043   003040 DATA DIVISION.                                                PAYREPT
  00044   003050                                                               PAYREPT
  00045   003060 FILE SECTION.                                                 PAYREPT
  00046   003070                                                               PAYREPT
  00047   003080 FD  PAYROLL-INPUT-FILE                                        PAYREPT
  00048   003090     RECORD CONTAINS 80 CHARACTERS                             PAYREPT
  00049   003100     LABEL RECORDS ARE OMITTED                                 PAYREPT
  00050   003110     DATA RECORD IS PAYROLL-INPUT-RECORD.                      PAYREPT
  00051   003120 01  PAYROLL-INPUT-RECORD.                                     PAYREPT
  00052   003130     05  EMPLOYEE-NUMBER-INPUT   PIC 9999.                     PAYREPT
  00053   003140     05  EMPLOYEE-NAME-INPUT     PIC X(20).                    PAYREPT
  00054   003150     05  HOURS-INPUT             PIC 99.                       PAYREPT
  00055   003160     05  PAY-RATE-INPUT          PIC 9V99.                     PAYREPT
  00056   003170     05  FILLER                  PIC X(51).                    PAYREPT
  00057   003180                                                               PAYREPT
  00058   003190 FD  PAYROLL-REPORT-FILE                                       PAYREPT
  00059   003200     RECORD CONTAINS 133 CHARACTERS                            PAYREPT
  00060   004010     LABEL RECORDS ARE OMITTED                                 PAYREPT
  00061   004020     DATA RECORD IS PAYROLL-REPORT-LINE.                       PAYREPT
  00062   004030 01  PAYROLL-REPORT-LINE.                                      PAYREPT
  00063   004040     05  CARRIAGE-CONTROL        PIC X.                        PAYREPT
  00064   004050     05  EMPLOYEE-NUMBER-REPORT  PIC ZZZ9.                     PAYREPT
  00065   004060     05  FILLER                  PIC X(5).                     PAYREPT
  00066   004070     05  EMPLOYEE-NAME-REPORT    PIC X(20).                    PAYREPT
  00067   004080     05  FILLER                  PIC X(5).                     PAYREPT
  00068   004090     05  HOURS-REPORT            PIC Z9.                       PAYREPT
  00069   004100     05  FILLER                  PIC X(5).                     PAYREPT
  00070   004110     05  PAY-RATE-REPORT         PIC 9.99.                     PAYREPT
  00071   004120     05  FILLER                  PIC X(5).                     PAYREPT
  00072   004130     05  REGULAR-EARNINGS-REPORT PIC ZZZ.99.                   PAYREPT
  00073   004140     05  FILLER                  PIC X(5).                     PAYREPT
  00074   004150     05  OVERTIME-EARNINGS-REPORT PIC ZZZ.99.                  PAYREPT
  00075   004160     05  FILLER                  PIC X(5).                     PAYREPT
  00076   004170     05  TOTAL-EARNINGS-REPORT   PIC Z,ZZZ.99.                 PAYREPT
  00077   004180     05  FILLER                  PIC X(52).                    PAYREPT
  00078   004190                                                               PAYREPT
```

```
      3.
00079  004200 WORKING-STORAGE SECTION.                              PAYREPT
00080  005010                                                       PAYREPT
00081  005020 01  PROGRAM-INDICATORS.                               PAYREPT
00082  005030     05  ARE-THERE-MORE-RECORDS  PIC XXX    VALUE 'YES'.   PAYREPT
00083  005040         88  THERE-IS-A-RECORD              VALUE 'YES'.   PAYREPT
00084  005050         88  THERE-ARE-NO-MORE-RECORDS      VALUE 'NO '.   PAYREPT
00085  005060                                                       PAYREPT
00086  005070 01  PROGRAM-CONSTANTS.                                PAYREPT
00087  005080     05  MAX-HRS-FOR-REG-PAY     PIC 999    VALUE 40   PAYREPT
00088  005090                                           USAGE IS COMP-3.  PAYREPT
00089  005100                                                       PAYREPT
00090  005110 01  WORK-AREAS                            USAGE IS COMP-3.  PAYREPT
00091  005120     05  REGULAR-EARNINGS-WORK   PIC S999V99.          PAYREPT
00092  005130     05  OVERTIME-EARNINGS-WORK  PIC S999V99.          PAYREPT
00093  005140     05  TOTAL-EARNINGS-WORK     PIC S9(4)V99.         PAYREPT
00094  005150                                                       PAYREPT
00095  005160 01  TOTAL-ACCUMULATORS                    USAGE IS COMP-3.  PAYREPT
00096  005170     05  REGULAR-EARNINGS-ACCUM  PIC S9(4)V99 VALUE ZERO.  PAYREPT
00097  005180     05  OVERTIME-EARNINGS-ACCUM PIC S9(4)V99 VALUE ZERO.  PAYREPT
00098  005190     05  TOTAL-EARNINGS-ACCUM    PIC S9(5)V99 VALUE ZERO.  PAYREPT
00099  005200     05  NUMBER-OF-EMPS-ACCUM    PIC S999   VALUE ZERO.  PAYREPT
00100  006010                                                       PAYREPT
00101  006020 01  PRINTER-CONTROL.                                  PAYREPT
00102  006030     05  PROPER-SPACING          PIC 9.                PAYREPT
00103  006040     05  SPACE-ONE-LINE          PIC 9      VALUE 1.   PAYREPT
00104  006050     05  SPACE-TWO-LINES         PIC 9      VALUE 2.   PAYREPT
00105  006060                                                       PAYREPT
00106  006070 01  HEADING-LINES.                                    PAYREPT
00107  006080     05  FIRST-HEADING-LINE.                           PAYREPT
00108  006090         10  CARRIAGE-CONTROL    PIC X.                PAYREPT
00109  005100         10  FILLER              PIC X(26)  VALUE SPACES.  PAYREPT
00110  006110         10  FILLER              PIC X(13)  VALUE      PAYREPT
00111  006120                                            'P A Y R O L L'.  PAYREPT
00112  006130         10  FILLER              PIC XXX    VALUE SPACES.  PAYREPT
00113  006140         10  FILLER              PIC X(11)  VALUE      PAYREPT
00114  006150                                            'R E P O R T'.  PAYREPT
00115  006160         10  FILLER              PIC X(79)  VALUE SPACES.  PAYREPT
00116  006170     05  SECOND-HEADING-LINE.                          PAYREPT
00117  006180         10  CARRIAGE-CONTROL    PIC X.                PAYREPT
00118  006190         10  FILLER              PIC X(4)   VALUE 'EMP.'.  PAYREPT
00119  006200         10  FILLER              PIC X(11)  VALUE SPACES.  PAYREPT
00120  007010         10  FILLER              PIC X(8)   VALUE 'EMPLOYEE'.  PAYREPT
00121  007020         10  FILLER              PIC X(19)  VALUE SPACES.  PAYREPT
00122  007030         10  FILLER              PIC XXX    VALUE 'PAY'.  PAYREPT
00123  007040         10  FILLER              PIC X(5)   VALUE SPACES.  PAYREPT
00124  007050         10  FILLER              PIC X(7)   VALUE 'REGULAR'.  PAYREPT
00125  007060         10  FILLER              PIC XXX    VALUE SPACES.  PAYREPT
00126  007070         10  FILLER              PIC X(8)   VALUE 'OVERTIME'.  PAYREPT
00127  007080         10  FILLER              PIC X(6)   VALUE SPACES.  PAYREPT
00128  007090         10  FILLER              PIC X(5)   VALUE 'TOTAL'.  PAYREPT
00129  007100         10  FILLER              PIC X(53)  VALUE SPACES.  PAYREPT
00130  007110     05  THIRD-HEADING-LINE.                           PAYREPT
00131  007120         10  CARRIAGE-CONTROL    PIC X.                PAYREPT
00132  007130         10  FILLER              PIC X      VALUE SPACES.  PAYREPT
00133  007140         10  FILLER              PIC XXX    VALUE 'NO.'.  PAYREPT
00134  007150         10  FILLER              PIC X(13)  VALUE SPACES.  PAYREPT
00135  007160         10  FILLER              PIC X(4)   VALUE 'NAME'.  PAYREPT
00136  007170         10  FILLER              PIC X(12)  VALUE SPACES.  PAYREPT
00137  007180         10  FILLER              PIC X(5)   VALUE 'HOURS'.  PAYREPT
00138  007190         10  FILLER              PIC XXX    VALUE SPACES.  PAYREPT
00139  007200         10  FILLER              PIC XXXX   VALUE 'RATE'.  PAYREPT
00140  008010         10  FILLER              PIC XXXX   VALUE SPACES.  PAYREPT
00141  008020         10  FILLER              PIC X(8)   VALUE 'EARNINGS'.  PAYREPT
00142  008030         10  FILLER              PIC XXX    VALUE SPACES.  PAYREPT
00143  008040         10  FILLER              PIC X(8)   VALUE 'EARNINGS'.  PAYREPT
00144  008050         10  FILLER              PIC X(4)   VALUE SPACES.  PAYREPT
00145  008060         10  FILLER              PIC X(8)   VALUE 'EARNINGS'.  PAYREPT
00146  008070         10  FILLER              PIC X(52)  VALUE SPACES.  PAYREPT
00147  008080                                                       PAYREPT
00148  008090 01  TOTAL-LINES.                                      PAYREPT
00149  008100     05  FINAL-TOTAL-LINE.                             PAYREPT
00150  008110         10  CARRIAGE-CONTROL    PIC X.                PAYREPT
00151  008120         10  FILLER              PIC X(16)  VALUE      PAYREPT
00152  008130                                            'TOTAL EMPLOYEES '.  PAYREPT
00153  008140         10  NUMBER-OF-EMPLOYEES-FINAL PIC ZZ9.        PAYREPT
00154  008150         10  FILLER              PIC X(15)  VALUE SPACES.  PAYREPT
00155  008160         10  FILLER              PIC X(13)  VALUE      PAYREPT
00156  008170                                            'FINAL TOTALS '.  PAYREPT
00157  008180         10  REGULAR-EARNINGS-FINAL PIC $$,$$$.99.     PAYREPT
00158  008190         10  FILLER              PIC XX     VALUE SPACES.  PAYREPT
00159  008200         10  OVERTIME-EARNINGS-FINAL PIC $$,$$$.99.    PAYREPT
00160  009010         10  FILLER              PIC XXX    VALUE SPACES.  PAYREPT
00161  009020         10  TOTAL-EARNINGS-FINAL PIC $$$,$$$.99.      PAYREPT
00162  009030         10  FILLER              PIC X(52)  VALUE SPACES.  PAYREPT
```

```
     4
00163    009050 PROCEDURE DIVISION.                                           PAYREPT
00164    009060                                                              PAYREPT
00165    009070*******************************************************************  PAYREPT
00166    009080*                                                        *  PAYREPT
00167    009090*   THIS MODULE CONTROLS THE PROCESSING OF INPUT RECORDS, THE     *  PAYREPT
00168    009100*   PRINTING OF THE REPORT, AND THE PRINTING OF THE FINAL         *  PAYREPT
00169    009110*   TOTALS. IT IS ENTERED FROM THE OPERATING SYSTEM AND EXITS     *  PAYREPT
00170    009120*   TO THE OPERATING SYSTEM.                                      *  PAYREPT
00171    009130*                                                        *  PAYREPT
00172    009140*******************************************************************  PAYREPT
00173    009150                                                              PAYREPT
00174    009160 A000-CREATE-PAYROLL-REPORT.                                   PAYREPT
00175    009170                                                              PAYREPT
00176    009180      OPEN INPUT  PAYROLL-INPUT-FILE                           PAYREPT
00177    009190           OUTPUT PAYROLL-REPORT-FILE.                         PAYREPT
00178    009200                                                              PAYREPT
00179    010010*  HEADING ROUTINE                                            PAYREPT
00180    010020                                                              PAYREPT
00181    010030      WRITE PAYROLL-REPORT-LINE FROM FIRST-HEADING-LINE        PAYREPT
00182    010040           AFTER ADVANCING TO-TOP-OF-PAGE.                     PAYREPT
00183    010050      WRITE PAYROLL-REPORT-LINE FROM SECOND-HEADING-LINE       PAYREPT
00184    010060           AFTER ADVANCING 2 LINES.                           PAYREPT
00185    010070      WRITE PAYROLL-REPORT-LINE FROM THIRD-HEADING-LINE        PAYREPT
00186    010080           AFTER ADVANCING 1 LINES.                           PAYREPT
00187    010090      MOVE SPACE-TWO-LINES TO PROPER-SPACING.                  PAYREPT
00188    010100                                                              PAYREPT
00189    010110*  MAIN ROUTINE                                               PAYREPT
00190    010120                                                              PAYREPT
00191    010130      READ PAYROLL-INPUT-FILE                                 PAYREPT
00192    010140           AT END                                            PAYREPT
00193    010150                MOVE 'NO ' TO ARE-THERE-MORE-RECORDS.          PAYREPT
00194    010160      IF THERE-IS-A-RECORD                                    PAYREPT
00195    010170           PERFORM A001-PROCESS-AND-READ                      PAYREPT
00196    010180                UNTIL THERE-ARE-NO-MORE-RECORDS               PAYREPT
00197    010190      PERFORM B010-PRINT-FINAL-TOTALS.                        PAYREPT
00198    010200      CLOSE PAYROLL-INPUT-FILE                                PAYREPT
00199    011010            PAYROLL-REPORT-FILE.                              PAYREPT
00200    011020      STOP RUN.                                               PAYREPT
00201    011030                                                              PAYREPT
00202    011040                                                              PAYREPT
00203    011050                                                              PAYREPT
00204    011060 A001-PROCESS-AND-READ.                                       PAYREPT
00205    011070                                                              PAYREPT
00206    011080      PERFORM B000-PROCESS-DETAIL-RECORDS.                    PAYREPT
00207    011090      READ PAYROLL-INPUT-FILE                                 PAYREPT
00208    011100           AT END                                            PAYREPT
00209    011110                MOVE 'NO ' TO ARE-THERE-MORE-RECORDS.          PAYREPT
```

```
      5
   00210  011130******************************************************* PAYREPT
   00211  011140*                                                     * PAYREPT
   00212  011150*  THIS MODULE FORMATS THE REPORT, CALCULATES REGULAR PAY AND * PAYREPT
   00213  011160*  OVERTIME PAY, ACCUMULATES THE FINAL TOTALS, AND PRINTS THE * PAYREPT
   00214  011170*  DETAIL LINE.  IT IS ENTERED FROM AND EXITS TO THE  * PAYREPT
   00215  011180*  A001-PROCESS-AND-READ MODULE.                      * PAYREPT
   00216  011190*                                                     * PAYREPT
   00217  011200******************************************************* PAYREPT
   00218  012010                                                        PAYREPT
   00219  012020 B000-PROCESS-DETAIL-RECORDS.                           PAYREPT
   00220  012030                                                        PAYREPT
   00221  012040     MOVE SPACES TO PAYROLL-REPORT-LINE.                PAYREPT
   00222  012050     MOVE EMPLOYEE-NUMBER-INPUT TO EMPLOYEE-NUMBER-REPORT. PAYREPT
   00223  012060     MOVE EMPLOYEE-NAME-INPUT TO EMPLOYEE-NAME-REPORT.  PAYREPT
   00224  012070     MOVE HOURS-INPUT TO HOURS-REPORT.                 PAYREPT
   00225  012080     MOVE PAY-RATE-INPUT TO PAY-RATE-REPORT.           PAYREPT
   00226  012090     IF HOURS-INPUT IS GREATER THAN MAX-HRS-FOR-REG-PAY PAYREPT
   00227  012100        COMPUTE REGULAR-EARNINGS-WORK =                PAYREPT
   00228  012110           PAY-RATE-INPUT * MAX-HRS-FOR-REG-PAY        PAYREPT
   00229  012120        COMPUTE OVERTIME-EARNINGS-WORK =               PAYREPT
   00230  012130           ((HOURS-INPUT - MAX-HRS-FOR-REG-PAY) * 1.5) * PAYREPT
   00231  012140           PAY-RATE-INPUT                             PAYREPT
   00232  012150        ADD REGULAR-EARNINGS-WORK, OVERTIME-EARNINGS-WORK GIVING PAYREPT
   00233  012160           TOTAL-EARNINGS-WORK                        PAYREPT
   00234  012170     ELSE                                             PAYREPT
   00235  012180        COMPUTE REGULAR-EARNINGS-WORK =               PAYREPT
   00236  012190           PAY-RATE-INPUT * HOURS-INPUT               PAYREPT
   00237  012200        MOVE ZEROS TO OVERTIME-EARNINGS-WORK          PAYREPT
   00238  012210        MOVE REGULAR-EARNINGS-WORK TO TOTAL-EARNINGS-WORK PAYREPT
   00239  013010     MOVE REGULAR-EARNINGS-WORK TO REGULAR-EARNINGS-REPORT. PAYREPT
   00240  013020     MOVE OVERTIME-EARNINGS-WORK TO OVERTIME-EARNINGS-REPORT. PAYREPT
   00241  013030     MOVE TOTAL-EARNINGS-WORK TO TOTAL-EARNINGS-REPORT. PAYREPT
   00242  013040     ADD 1 TO NUMBER-OF-EMPS-ACCUM.                    PAYREPT
   00243  013050     ADD REGULAR-EARNINGS-WORK TO REGULAR-EARNINGS-ACCUM. PAYREPT
   00244  013060     ADD OVERTIME-EARNINGS-WORK TO OVERTIME-EARNINGS-ACCUM. PAYREPT
   00245  013070     ADD TOTAL-EARNINGS-WORK TO TOTAL-EARNINGS-ACCUM.  PAYREPT
   00246  013080     WRITE PAYROLL-REPORT-LINE                         PAYREPT
   00247  013090        AFTER PROPER-SPACING.                          PAYREPT
   00248  013100     MOVE SPACE-ONE-LINE TO PROPER-SPACING.            PAYREPT

      6
   00249  013120******************************************************* PAYREPT
   00250  013130*                                                     * PAYREPT
   00251  013140*  THIS MODULE PRINTS THE FINAL TOTALS. IT IS ENTERED FROM AND * PAYREPT
   00252  013150*  EXITS TO THE A000-CREATE-PAYROLL-REPORT MODULE.    * PAYREPT
   00253  013160*                                                     * PAYREPT
   00254  013170******************************************************* PAYREPT
   00255  013180                                                        PAYREPT
   00256  013190 B010-PRINT-FINAL-TOTALS.                               PAYREPT
   00257  013200                                                        PAYREPT
   00258  014010     MOVE NUMBER-OF-EMPS-ACCUM TO NUMBER-OF-EMPLOYEES-FINAL. PAYREPT
   00259  014020     MOVE REGULAR-EARNINGS-ACCUM TO REGULAR-EARNINGS-FINAL. PAYREPT
   00260  014030     MOVE OVERTIME-EARNINGS-ACCUM TO OVERTIME-EARNINGS-FINAL. PAYREPT
   00261  014040     MOVE TOTAL-EARNINGS-ACCUM TO TOTAL-EARNINGS-FINAL. PAYREPT
   00262  014050     WRITE PAYROLL-REPORT-LINE FROM FINAL-TOTAL-LINE   PAYREPT
   00263  014060        AFTER ADVANCING 2 LINES.                       PAYREPT

      8
   CARD   ERROR MESSAGE

   153   ILA1043I-W    END OF SENTENCE SHOULD PRECEDE 10 . ASSUMED PRESENT.
   209   ILA4072I-W    EXIT FROM PERFORMED PROCEDURE ASSUMED BEFORE PROCEDURE-NAME .
```

```
                    P A Y R O L L   R E P O R T

   EMP.      EMPLOYEE              PAY     REGULAR   OVERTIME    TOTAL
   NO.        NAME        HOURS    RATE    EARNINGS  EARNINGS   EARNINGS

   1005   ABBOTT, CHARLES      40   3.00    120.00      .00      120.00
   1009   ANCHOR, WILLIAM B.   41   3.00               4.50      124.50
   2714   BRADLEY, CYNTHIA C.  39   3.00    117.00      .00      117.00
   2891   CANA, CARY K.        50   4.50              67.50      247.50
   2995   DOGER, MARY L.       20   3.50     70.00      .00       70.00
   3015   SEGERSTROM, JUDY M.  26   4.00    104.00      .00      104.00

   TOTAL EMPLOYEES   6      FINAL TOTALS  $711.00   $72.00     $783.00
```

EXPLANATION

CHAPTER 6

PROGRAMMING ASSIGNMENT 1

INSTRUCTIONS

An Accounts Receivable Register is to be prepared. Design and write the COBOL program to produce the required report. An IPO Chart and pseudocode should be used when designing the program. Use Test Data, Set 2, in Appendix A.

INPUT

Input is to consist of Accounts Receivable Cards that contain the Customer Number, the Customer Name, and the Amount of Purchase. The format of the cards is illustrated below.

OUTPUT

Output is to consist of an Accounts Receivable Register. If the Purchased Amount is $100.00 or more, a 10% discount is given. For Purchases less than $100.00, a 7% discount is given. The report is to contain the Customer Number, the Customer Name, the Amount Purchased, the Discount Rate, the Discount Amount, and the Net Amount. The Discount Amount is obtained by multiplying the Amount Purchased by the Discount Rate (7% or 10%). The Net Amount is calculated by subtracting the Discount Amount from the Amount Purchased. Final totals are to be taken of the Amount Purchased, the Discount Amount, and the Net Amount. The format of the report is illustrated below.

CHAPTER 6

PROGRAMMING ASSIGNMENT 2

INSTRUCTIONS

A Sales Commission Report is to be prepared. Design and write the COBOL program to produce the required report. An IPO Chart and pseudocode should be used when designing the program. Use Test Data Set 1 in Appendix A.

INPUT

Input is to consist of Sales Summary Cards containing the Salesman Number, the Salesman Name, and the Amount of Sales. The format of the cards is illustrated below.

OUTPUT

Output is to consist of a Sales Commission Report. For sales equal to or less than $500.00, a 3% commission is paid. For all amounts sold in excess of $500.00, a 5% commission is paid. For example, if a salesman sold $510.00, the salesman would receive a 3% commission on $500.00 and a 5% commission on $10.00. In addition, if a salesman has sales greater than $500.00, the message "OVER QUOTA" is to be printed on the report. The format of the report is illustrated below.

CHAPTER 6

PROGRAMMING ASSIGNMENT 3

INSTRUCTIONS

An Incentive Payroll Report is to be prepared. Design and write the COBOL program to produce the required report. An IPO Chart and pseudocode should be used when designing the program. Use Test Data Set 1 in Appendix A.

INPUT

Input consists of Employee Production Cards containing the Employee Number, Employee Name, Guaranteed Pay, and Units Produced. The format of the cards is illustrated below.

OUTPUT

Output is to consist of an Incentive Payroll Report. Incentive pay is calculated on the basis of the number of units manufactured. $1.80 per unit manufactured is paid for all units manufactured up to and including the first 50 units. For all units manufactured in excess of 50, $2.10 per unit manufactured is paid. Thus, if an employee manufactured 60 units, the pay would be $90.00 (50 x 1.80) for the first fifty units and $21.00 (10 x 2.10) for the next ten units, for a total pay of $111.00.

All employees eligibile for incentive pay are guaranteed a minimum pay, regardless of the number of units manufactured. However, employees do not receive both incentive pay and the guaranteed pay—they receive the higher of the two. Therefore, if the incentive pay is greater than the guaranteed pay, which is contained in the input record, the employee will receive the incentive pay. Otherwise, the employee receives the guaranteed pay. The format of the report is illustrated on page 6.51

Comparing; Final Totals — 6.51

```
                          PRINTER SPACING CHART

        INCENTIVE PAYROLL REPORT
EMPLOYEE        EMPLOYEE        UNITS        AMOUNT OF PAY
NUMBER          NAME           PRODUCED    GUARANTEE - INCENTIVE

XØX     XXXXXXXXXXXXXXXXXXXX    ØX                    XXØ.XX
XØX     XXXXXXXXXXXXXXXXXXXX    ØX          XX.XX

                        FINAL TOTALS $X,XX$.XX    $X,XX$.XX

TOTAL EMPLOYEES XØX

TOTAL EMPLOYEES RECEIVING GUARANTEE XØX

TOTAL EMPLOYEES RECEIVING INCENTIVE XØX
```

Note from the format illustrated above that if an employee receives the guaranteed pay, this amount is to appear under the column GUARANTEE. If an employee receives incentive pay this amount appears under the column INCENTIVE. After all input records have been processed, final totals are to be printed as illustrated.

CHAPTER 6

PROGRAMMING ASSIGNMENT 4

INSTRUCTIONS

A Sales Commission Report and a Report of Outstanding Salesmen are to be prepared. Design and write the COBOL program to produce the required reports. An IPO Chart and pseudocode should be used when designing the program. Use Test Data Set 1 in Appendix A.

INPUT

Input consists of Sales Cards containing the Store Number, the Salesman Name, Jewelry Sales, and Cosmetics Sales. The format of the cards is illustrated below.

OUTPUT

Output is to consist of a Sales Commission Report and a Report of Outstanding Salesmen. The formats of these two reports are illustrated below.

For the Sales Commission Report, the commission for jewelry sales is calculated as follows: For the first $1,500.00 of sales, the commission is 10%. For sales over $1,500.00, the commission is 15% of the amount of sales over $1,500.00. The total jewelry commission for a salesman is calculated by adding the commission for $1,500.00 and less and the commission for sales over $1,500.00. For example, if a Salesman has $1,700.00 in jewelry sales, the commission would be $150.00 (10% x 1,500.00) plus $30.00 (15% x 200.00) for a total commission of $180.00.

For cosmetics, a commission of 10% is paid for the first $100.00 of sales and a 15% commission is paid for those sales above $100.00. The total commission is determined in the same manner as the jewelry commission. For example, if a salesman had sales of $600.00 for cosmetics, the commission would be $10.00 (10% x 100.00) plus $75.00 (15% x 500.00) for a total cosmetic commission of $85.00.

After all of the records have been processed, the final totals are to be printed as illustrated on the Sales Commission Report. The Outstanding Salesmen Report is then to be produced on a separate page. This report is to contain the salesman with the highest sales of cosmetics and the salesman with the highest sales in jewelry. It is to be double spaced as illustrated.

NESTED IF STATEMENTS

7

INTRODUCTION

In the previous chapter, the IF Statement was illustrated. It was shown how the IF Statement can be used in three contexts: the Relation Test, the Sign Test, and the Class Test. In many applications, a single IF Statement or a single condition within the IF Statement will not be sufficient to test the condition required; therefore, two or more IF Statements can be utilized to form a combined condition in which each condition to be tested is separated from the other conditions by the logical operators AND or OR. In addition, one or more IF Statements may be contained within the initial IF Statement. This is called a "nested" IF Statement. This chapter will explain these more involved uses of the IF Statement.

In previous programs, headings have been printed on the first page of the report but no provision has been made to print headings on subsequent pages of the report. In this chapter, the processing necessary to cause headings to print on each page of the report will also be discussed.

SAMPLE PROGRAM

In order to illustrate the use of a Nested IF Statement and the printing of headings on each page of the report, the sample program in this chapter will produce a Personnel Report. A sample of the report is illustrated in Figure 7-1.

```
07/05/77                    PERSONNEL REPORT                    PAGE   1

    DATE            EMPLOYEE         YEARS
  EMPLOYED            NAME          EMPLOYED   EDUCATION      CLASSIFICATION

    04 25 76    JONES, ARLAN C.        1      GRADUATE       PROGRAMMER
    04 25 75    LOVERLY, ARBIE J.      2      GRADUATE       PROGRAMMER
    04 25 74    MANLY, CECLIA A.       3      GRADUATE       SENIOR PROGRAMMER
    03 02 73    HAMM, JAMES C.         4      GRADUATE       SENIOR PROGRAMMER
    04 25 76    OSSIE, JULIE C.        1      NON-GRADUATE   JUNIOR PROGRAMMER
    04 25 75    PRINZ, JIM C.          2      NON-GRADUATE   JUNIOR PROGRAMMER
    04 25 74    RADEN, THOMAS G.       3      NON-GRADUATE   JUNIOR PROGRAMMER
    01 12 73    SAMS, SALLY U.         4      NON-GRADUATE   PROGRAMMER

  SENIOR PROGRAMMERS   2
  PROGRAMMERS          3
  JUNIOR PROGRAMMERS   3
```

Figure 7-1 Example of the Personnel Report

---

1 H. D. Mills, *HOW TO WRITE CORRECT PROGRAMS AND KNOW IT*, IBM Federal Systems Division, IBM, February 1973.

As can be seen from Figure 7-1, the heading on the report contains the Date and the Page Number as well as the other headings. The report itself contains the Date Employed, the Employee Name, the Years Employed, the Education of the employee, and the Classification of the employee. The input to create this report is illustrated below.

INPUT

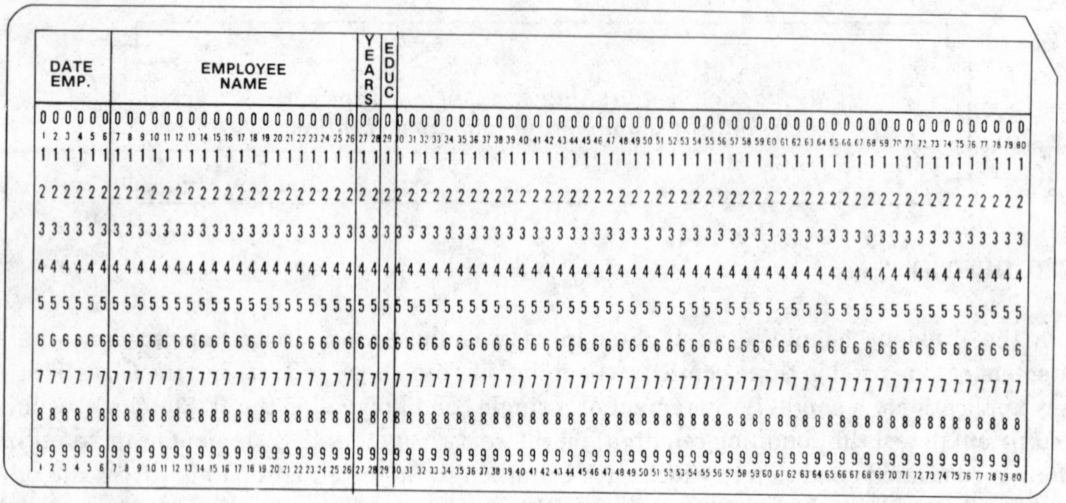

Figure 7-2 Input

Note from Figure 7-2 that the input record contains the Date Employed, the Employee Name, the Years Employed, and the Education of the employee. The classification which is printed on the report is determined in the following manner: If the employee is a college graduate (the value ''G'' in column 29) and has worked for the company more than two years, the classification is Senior Programmer; if the employee is a college graduate with two years or less employment, the classification is Programmer; if the employee is not a college graduate (''N'' in column 29), and has worked for more than three years, the classification is Programmer; if the employee is not a college graduate and has worked for three years or less, the classification is Junior Programmer.

In order to properly process the conditions specified, Nested IF's are required. The use of Nested IF's is explained on the following pages.

NESTED IF STATEMENTS

It will be recalled that the IF Statement is used to test a condition. If the condition is true, then one set of statements is executed; if it is not true, then another set of statements is executed. This general format is illustrated below.

EXAMPLE

```
IF condition
      Execute statements if condition is true
ELSE
      Execute statements if condition is not true
```

Figure 7-3 General Format of IF Statement

A COBOL coding example of this general format is illustrated in Figure 7-4.

EXAMPLE

```
015010          IF EDUCATION-INPUT = 'G'
015020  Executed {MOVE GRADUATE-CONSTANT TO EDUCATION-REPORT
          If
015030  True    {ADD 1 TO GRADUATES-ACCUM
015040          ELSE
015050  Executed {MOVE NON-GRADUATE-CONSTANT TO EDUCATION-REPORT
          If Not
015060  True    {ADD 1 TO NON-GRADUATES-ACCUM.
```

Figure 7-4 Example of IF Statement

In the example above, if the value "G" is contained in the EDUCATION-INPUT field, then the value in GRADUATE-CONSTANT is moved to EDUCATION-REPORT and the value 1 is added to GRADUATES-ACCUM. If a "G" is not contained in EDUCATION-INPUT, then the value in NON-GRADUATE-CONSTANT is moved to EDUCATION-REPORT and the value 1 is added to the NON-GRADUATES-ACCUM field.

It should be noted in Figure 7-4 that a Move Statement and an Add Statement are executed if the condition is true and a Move Statement and an Add Statement are executed if the condition is not true. There is nothing, however, which says that instead of a Move or Add Statement, one of the statements which can be executed if a condition is true or not true is another IF Statement. When one or more IF Statements are contained within the initial IF Statement, the entire statement is called a Nested IF Statement. In order to illustrate the overall structure of a Nested IF Statement, the example in Figure 7-5 is shown. It should be noted that the purpose of this example is to show the overall structure of the Nested IF Statement, and it is not necessary at this time to perform a detailed analysis of each line of code in the example.

EXAMPLE

```
012010        IF EDUCATION-INPUT = 'G'
012020           MOVE GRADUATE-CONSTANT TO EDUCATION-REPORT
012030           IF YEARS-EMPLOYED-INPUT IS GREATER THAN TWO-YRS-CONSTANT
012040              MOVE SENIOR-PROG-CONSTANT TO CLASSIFICATION-REPORT
012050              ADD 1 TO SENIOR-PROGRAMMER-ACCUM
012060           ELSE
012070              MOVE PROGRAMMER-CONSTANT TO CLASSIFICATION-REPORT
012080              ADD 1 TO PROGRAMMER-ACCUM
012090        ELSE
012100           MOVE NON-GRADUATE-CONSTANT TO EDUCATION-REPORT
012110           IF YEARS-EMPLOYED-INPUT IS GREATER THAN THREE-YRS-CONSTANT
012120              MOVE PROGRAMMER-CONSTANT TO CLASSIFICATION-REPORT
012130              ADD 1 TO PROGRAMMER-ACCUM
012140           ELSE
012150              MOVE JUNIOR-PROG-CONSTANT TO CLASSIFICATION-REPORT
012160              ADD 1 TO JUNIOR-PROGRAMMER-ACCUM.
```

Lines 012010–012080 marked "Executed If True"; lines 012090–012160 marked "Executed If Not True".

Figure 7-5 Example of NESTED IF

Note in Figure 7-5 that the statements to be executed if there is a "G" in EDUCATION-INPUT are the Move Statement and the IF Statement. If there is not a "G" in EDUCATION-INPUT, a Move Statement and an IF Statement are also executed. It must be noted that the "inner" IF Statements which will be executed when the condition is true and when the condition is not true are merely statements, like the Add Statement in Figure 7-4, which will be executed when the condition is true or not true. The fact that an IF Statement will be executed as a result of a condition being true or not true does not change the way in which the IF Statement works, nor does it have any other effect on the program; it is merely another statement to be executed.

If each of the "inner" IF Statements is analyzed as individual IF-ELSE Statements, the structure and logic of the Nested IF Statement becomes relatively easy to understand. Thus, the IF Statements which will be executed upon a given condition are themselves evaluated in the same way as all IF Statements. This is illustrated in Figure 7-6.

EXAMPLE

```
012020        IF EDUCATION-INPUT = 'G'
012030            MOVE GRADUATE-CONSTANT TO EDUCATION-REPORT
012040            IF YEARS-EMPLOYED-INPUT IS GREATER THAN TWO-YRS-CONSTANT
012050  Executed     MOVE SENIOR-PROG-CONSTANT TO CLASSIFICATION-REPORT
012060  If    {
         True         ADD 1 TO SENIOR-PROGRAMMER-ACCUM
012070            ELSE
012080  Executed     MOVE PROGRAMMER-CONSTANT TO CLASSIFICATION-REPORT
         If Not {
012090   True         ADD 1 TO PROGRAMMER-ACCUM
012100        ELSE
012110            MOVE NON-GRADUATE-CONSTANT TO EDUCATION-REPORT
012120            IF YEARS-EMPLOYED-INPUT IS GREATER THAN THREE-YRS-CONSTANT
012130  Executed     MOVE PROGRAMMER-CONSTANT TO CLASSIFICATION-REPORT
012140  If    {
         True         ADD 1 TO PROGRAMMER-ACCUM
012150            ELSE
012160  Executed     MOVE JUNIOR-PROG-CONSTANT TO CLASSIFICATION-REPORT
         If Not {
012170   True         ADD 1 TO JUNIOR-PROGRAMMER-ACCUM.
012180        MOVE NAME-INPUT TO NAME-REPORT.
```

Figure 7-6 Example of Nested IFs

Note from Figure 7-6 that the "inner" IF Statements, which are executed as a result of a prior condition being true or not true, are evaluated in the same manner as IF Statements which are not a part of Nested IF Statements; that is, the statements immediately following the IF Statement are executed if the condition is true and the statements following the ELSE word are executed if the condition is not true.

It is important to note that after statements have been executed as a result of the conditions found in the Nested IF Statement, the next sentence in the program is executed, that is, the next sentence following the period in the Nested IF Statement. Thus, in the Figure 7-6, if the value "G" is found in the EDUCATION-INPUT field and if the years employed is greater than 2, then the statements on line 012050 and 012060 will be executed. After they are executed, the word ELSE is encountered; therefore, there are no more statements to be executed as a result of the condition being true. Thus, the remaining statements within the Nested IF Statement are bypassed and the statement on line 012180, which follows the period for the Nested IF Statement, will be executed. The same is true for all of the other conditions which are tested within the Nested IF Statement. When the statements have been executed as a result of the condition's being true or not true, the statement following the period in the Nested IF Statement is executed.

Nested IF Statements may be used in a variety of forms. The following examples illustrate some of the uses of Nested IF Statements.

EXAMPLE 1: Nested IF Statement

```
Ø14 1 1 Ø              ⌠  IF  SALESMAN-TYPE-INPUT = 'C'
Ø14 1 2   Nested  ⌠    │    IF  SALES-INPUT  IS  GREATER  THAN  SALES-QUOTA-CONSTANT
Ø14 1 3   IF      │Inner│        MOVE  OVER-QUOTA-CONSTANT  TO  QUOTA-MESSAGE-REPORT
Ø14 1 4   Stmt    │IF   │ ELSE
Ø14 1 5 Ø         │Stmt ⌡        MOVE  UNDER-QUOTA-CONSTANT  TO  QUOTA-MESSAGE-REPORT.
```

Figure 7-7 Example of Nested IF Statement

In the example above, the first condition tested is whether the value in the SALESMAN-TYPE-INPUT field is equal to "C". If it is, then the value in the SALES-INPUT field is checked to determine if it is greater than the Sales Quota. If the Sales are greater than the Sales Quota, then the Over Quota message is moved to the printer output area; if it is not, then the Under Quota message is moved to the output area.

It will be noted in Figure 7-7 that there is no ELSE Clause for the first IF Statement. Thus, if the SALESMAN-TYPE-INPUT field does not contain the value "C", no further processing will be done by the Nested IF Statement and the statement following line 014150 would be executed.

Example 2, in Figure 7-8, illustrates a Nested If Statement in which both IF Statements contain a related ELSE Clause.

EXAMPLE 2: Nested IF Statement

```
Ø13 1 4 Ø              ⌠  IF  HOURLY-EMPLOYEE
Ø13 1 5 Ø      Inner ⌠ │    IF  HOURS-INPUT  IS  GREATER  THAN  4Ø
Ø13 1 6  Nested IF  │   │        PERFORM  CØØ1-CALCULATE-OVERTIME-PAY
Ø13 1 7  IF    Stmt │   │ ELSE
Ø13 1 8  Stmt       ⌡   │        PERFORM  CØØ2-CALCULATE-REGULAR-PAY
Ø13 1 9 Ø              │ ELSE
Ø13 2 0 Ø             ⌡      PERFORM  CØØ3-CALCULATE-SALARIED-PAY.
```

Figure 7-8 Example of Nested IF Statement

In the example in Figure 7-8, it can be seen that an inner IF Statement (line 013150) is executed if the first condition tested is true, that is, if the employee is an hourly employee. If the employee is an hourly employee, the HOURS-INPUT field is tested to determine if the hours are greater than 40. If the value in HOURS-INPUT is greater than 40, then overtime pay is calculated; if the value in HOURS-INPUT is less than or equal to 40, then regular pay is calculated.

If the employee is not an hourly employee, then the Perform Statement on line 013200 is used to calculate the pay for a salaried employee.

Example 3 illustrates a Nested IF Statement in which the inner IF Statement follows the ELSE portion of the first IF Statement.

EXAMPLE 3: Nested IF Statement

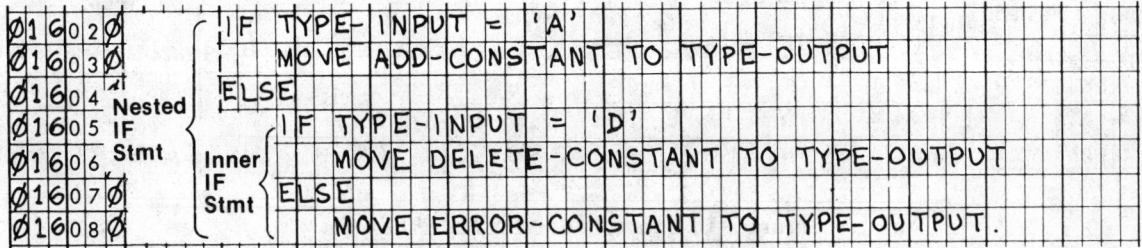

Figure 7-9 Example of Nested IF Statement

In the example in Figure 7-9, if the value in the TYPE-INPUT field is equal to ''A'', then the value in the ADD-CONSTANT field is moved to the TYPE-OUTPUT field. If the value in TYPE-INPUT is not equal to ''A'', then the ELSE Portion of the IF Statement is executed. There, the value in the TYPE-INPUT field is compared to ''D''. If it is equal, then the value in DELETE-CONSTANT is moved to the TYPE-OUTPUT field. If the value is not equal to ''D'', then the value in ERROR-CONSTANT is moved to the output area.

Thus, in the example in Figure 7-9, it can be seen that the inner IF Statement need not be specified after the first IF Statement but may also be specified only after the ELSE associated with the first IF Statement. The determination of where the second IF Statement should be placed in the Nested IF Statement is made from the requirements of the logic of the program.

In some applications, there may be a requirement to test for certain conditions; but unless those conditions occur, no processing is to be done. In these cases, the NEXT SENTENCE Statement is useful. To illustrate this, assume the following conditions must be tested:

1. If the Address field and the City/State field both contain spaces, normal processing is to occur.

2. If the Address field contains spaces but the City/State field contains data, an error message is to be printed.

3. If the Address field contains data but the City/State field contains spaces, an error message is to be printed.

4. If the Address field and the City/State field both contain data, normal processing is to occur.

In summary, both fields must contain spaces or both fields must contain data in order for normal processing to occur. If one of the fields contains data and the other field is blank, an error message is to be printed. The Nested IF Statement to process these conditions is illustrated in Example 4, in Figure 7-10.

EXAMPLE 4: Nested IF Statement

```
015110    IF ADDRESS-INPUT = SPACES
015120        IF CITY-STATE-INPUT = SPACES
015130            NEXT SENTENCE
015140        ELSE
015150            MOVE ERROR-MESSAGE-CONSTANT TO MESSAGE-REPORT
015160    ELSE
015170        IF CITY-STATE-INPUT = SPACES
015180            MOVE ERROR-MESSAGE-CONSTANT TO MESSAGE-REPORT.
```

Figure 7-10 Example of NEXT SENTENCE

From the coding in Figure 7-10, it can be seen that the ADDRESS-INPUT field is first checked for spaces. If the ADDRESS-INPUT field contains spaces, then the CITY-STATE-INPUT field is checked for spaces. If the CITY-STATE-INPUT field contains spaces, NEXT SENTENCE is specified. This will cause the remaining statements in the IF Statement to be bypassed, and the statement following line 015180 would be executed. If, however, the Address field contains spaces but the City-State field does not contain spaces (the field contains data), then an error message is moved to the output area.

The ELSE portion (line 015160) of the first IF statement is executed when the Address field does not contain spaces (the field contains data). When this occurs and the City-State field contains spaces, then an error message is written. Lastly, if neither the Address field nor the City-State field contains spaces (both fields contain data), the statement following line 015180 would be executed, providing for normal processing.

Nested IF Statements are not restricted to two levels. The following example illustrates a Nested IF Statement with three levels.

EXAMPLE 5: Nested IF Statement

```
021020    IF CHECK-DATE-IN IS GREATER THAN DISCOUNT-DATE-IN
021030        IF CHECK-DATE-IN IS GREATER THAN DUE-DATE-IN
021040            IF CHECK-DATE-IN IS GREATER THAN PENALTY-DATE-IN
021050                PERFORM C010-PROCESS-PENALTY-PMT
021060            ELSE
021070                PERFORM C020-PROCESS-LATE-PMT
021080        ELSE
021090            PERFORM C030-PROCESS-NORMAL-PMT
021100    ELSE
021110        PERFORM C040-PROCESS-DISCOUNT-PMT.
```

Figure 7-11 Example of Three-Level Nested IF Statement

In the example in Figure 7-11, an Accounts Payable application is illustrated. The Check Date is the date on which the debt is to be paid. If the debt is paid on or before the Discount Date, the company can take a discount on the debt. If the debt is paid on or before the Due Date, then the normal payment procedures are followed. If the debt is paid after the Due Date but before a Penalty Date, then it is processed as a late payment. If the debt is paid after the Penalty Date, then a penalty must be paid as well as the debt.

In Figure 7-11 it can be seen that the first IF Statement on line 021020 determines if the Check Date is greater than the Discount Date. If it is, then a discount cannot be taken. If it is not greater than the Discount Date, then the ELSE Clause on lines 021100 and 021110 will be executed and a discount will be taken. If a discount cannot be taken, the next question to answer is whether the payment, as indicated by the Check Date, is late. Thus, on line 021030 the IF Statment tests if the Check Date is greater than the Due Date. If it is, it indicates that the payment is late. If it is not, the ELSE Clause on lines 021080 and 021090 is executed and the normal payment is made.

If the Check Date is greater than the Due Date, then the next question to be asked is whether the Check Date is greater than the Penalty Date. If it is, then a penalty payment must be made. If not, then it is merely a late payment. Thus, on line 021040, the IF Statement tests if the Check Date is greater than the Penalty Date. If it is, then the penalty payment will be processed by the Perform Statement on line 021050; otherwise, the late payment will be processed (line 021070).

It is quite important in the previous explanation of Figure 7-11 to realize how the analysis of the Nested IF Statement took place. The first IF Statement within the group is analyzed. If the condition tested is true, then the statement immediately following the IF Statement is analyzed. In the example, this is another IF Statement; but it should be noted that it could be any permissible COBOL statement. If the condition tested is not true, then the processing following the Else Clause is analyzed. Again, it can be any allowable COBOL statement; in the example, it is a Perform Statement. It is critical to realize that the first IF Statement operates just as if there were no other IF Statements in the entire sentence. It is only when the processing which is to take place if the condition is true is analyzed that another IF Statement is found.

When inner IF Statement #1 is found, then it too is analyzed just as if it were the only IF Statement in the sentence. If the condition tested is true, then the statements immediately following the IF Statement are executed. If the condition is not true, then the statements following the ELSE Clause are executed. Again, the IF Statement is treated as though it were a single IF Statement instead of an IF Statement contained within a Nested IF Statement. Inner IF Statement #2 is treated the same way. Thus, even though an inner IF Statement will be executed only upon a particular condition, it still should be analyzed as if it were the only IF Statement in the sentence. In this manner, the reader will not become confused in trying to remember all of the possible conditions which must occur in order to have a statement executed.

WHEN IS A NESTED IF STATEMENT REQUIRED

When designing a program, the programmer must be aware of when a Nested IF Statement is required. Although every condition under which a Nested IF Statement is used cannot be covered, two general rules can be applied to determine if a Nested IF Statement is required:

Rule 1:

If a given condition must be tested only when a previous condition has been tested, AND alternative actions are required for one or more of the conditions [that is, an Else Clause is required]; then a Nested IF Statement must be used.

The following example illustrates the application of this rule.

EXAMPLE - Rule 1

```
Ø2ØØ7Ø        IF HOURLY-EMPLOYEE
Ø2ØØ8Ø           IF HOURS-WORKED IS GREATER THAN 4Ø
Ø2ØØ9Ø              PERFORM CØ1Ø-CALCULATE-REG-AND-OVT-PAY
Ø2Ø1ØØ           ELSE
Ø2Ø11Ø              PERFORM CØ2Ø-CALCULATE-REG-PAY
Ø2Ø12Ø        ELSE
Ø2Ø13Ø           PERFORM CØ3Ø-CALCULATE-SALARY-PAY.
```

Figure 7-12 Example of Nested IF Rule 1

Note in the example above that testing for the condition of whether the Hours Worked are greater than 40 is to take place only if the employee is an Hourly Employee. Thus, the first part of the rule stating that a condition is to be tested only when a previous condition has been tested is satisfied. In addition, both of the conditions tested (Hourly Employee and Hours greater than 40) require alternative actions, that is, actions which will take place when they are true and actions which will take place when they are not true. This is indicated by the ELSE Clauses. Therefore, the second portion of the rule is satisfied and the Nested IF Statement should be used.

Rule 2:

If a given condition must be tested only when a previous condition has been tested, AND one or more statements are to be executed before the second condition is tested; then a Nested IF Statement should be used.

The example in Figure 7-13 illustrates the application of Rule 2.

EXAMPLE - Rule 2

```
Ø13Ø2Ø        IF COMMISSION-SALESMAN
Ø13Ø3Ø           MOVE COMMISSION-CONSTANT TO COMMISSION-REPORT
Ø13Ø4Ø           IF SALES-INPUT IS GREATER THAN COMMISSION-SALES-QUOTA
Ø13Ø5Ø              MOVE OVER-QUOTA-CONSTANT TO QUOTA-MESSAGE-REPORT.
```

Figure 7-13 Example of Nested IF Rule 2

In the example in Figure 7-13, the first condition tested is whether the salesman is a Commission Salesman. If not, then the test for the Sales being greater than the Commission Sales Quota has no meaning; therefore, the first part of the rule is satisfied. If the salesman is a Commission Salesman, then the value in COMMISSION-CONSTANT is to be moved to the report output area regardless of whether the Sales are greater than the Quota. Thus, the second part of the rule which states that one or more statements are to be executed before the second condition is tested is satisfied. Therefore, the Nested IF Statement should be used.

HOW TO WRITE A NESTED IF STATEMENT

Even when a programmer recognizes that a Nested IF Statement is required, based upon the general rules given previously, it is necessary that the Nested IF Statement be written properly, based upon the programming specifications. In some cases, the Nested IF Statement can be a straightforward interpretation of the programming specifications, while in other cases the programmer will be required to conduct some logical reasoning in order to place the IF Statements in the proper sequence. The following example illustrates the programming specifications given for a problem and the step-by-step reasoning which the programmer must perform.

EXAMPLE 1: Programming Specifications

1. If the sales to a customer are greater than $2,000.00 and the customer is entitled to a discount, the discount percentage is 18%.
2. If the sales to a customer are equal to or less than $2,000.00 and the customer is entitled to a discount, the discount percentage is 12%.
3. The customer is entitled to a discount if the value "D" is found in column 32 of the input record.
4. If the customer is not entitled to a discount, the message "NO DISCOUNT" should be printed on the report.

The first step for the programmer is to determine if this is a statement of a problem which requires a Nested IF Statement. As can be seen, if the customer is entitled to a discount, then a determination must be made as to the percentage of discount. Therefore, there is a condition which will be tested based upon the results of a previous condition. Next, if the customer is entitled to a discount, one set of actions will be taken; while if there is no discount allowed, another set of actions will be taken. Therefore, alternative actions will be taken based upon a given condition. This satisfies Rule 1 on page 7.10. Thus, a Nested IF Statement is required.

The next step is to determine the method in which the Nested IF Statement is to be written. The programmer must examine all of the conditions to be tested and determine the most "inclusive" condition, that is, the one which must be true or not true before any of the other conditions can be logically tested. In the programming specifications for this example, the most inclusive test is whether the customer is entitled to a discount. If the customer is entitled to a discount, then the test must be made on the sales amount to determine the correct discount percentage. If the customer is not entitled to a discount, then there is no reason to check the sales amount. The IF Statement to test whether the customer is entitled to a discount is illustrated in Figure 7-14.

Step 1: Write most inclusive IF Statement

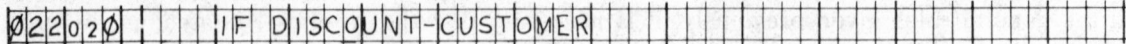

Figure 7-14 First Step in Writing Nested IF Statement

As was noted, the most inclusive test is whether the customer is entitled to a discount. Through the use of the condition name DISCOUNT-CUSTOMER, this test is the first performed in the Nested IF Statement.

After the most inclusive IF Statement is written, the programmer must again analyze the programming specifications to determine what action is to take place if the condition is true. In the programming specifications on page 7.11, item #1 and item #2 both state "and the customer is entitled to a discount." Thus, these items describe the actions to be taken when the customer is to receive a discount.

Item #1 specifies what is to occur if the sales are greater than $2,000.00. Item #2 specifies what is to occur if the sales are equal to or less than $2,000.00. Thus, it can be seen that a determination must be made as to whether the Sales are greater than $2,000.00 or are equal to or less than $2,000.00. The IF Statement to make this determination is illustrated in Figure 7-15.

Step 2: Write first statement of what to do when condition is true.

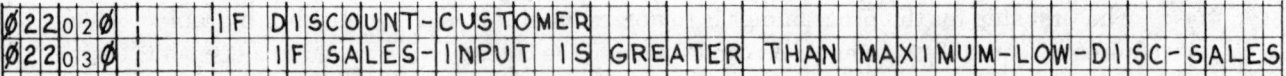

Figure 7-15 Second Step in Writing Nested IF Statement

In step 2, the value in the SALES-INPUT field is compared to the value in the MAXIMUM-LOW-DISC-SALES field, which would be 2000.00. This IF Statement would determine whether the customer was entitled to the higher discount of 18%. It will be recalled from the programming specifications that if the sales are greater than $2,000.00, the customer receives an 18% discount while if they are less than or equal to $2,000.00, the customer receives a 12% discount.

The programmer must now go through the same process as before, that is, it must be determined what processing is to take place if the sales for the customer are greater than $2,000.00. As noted, when this is the case, the customer is entitled to an 18% discount. Therefore, the next statement which must be written is one which will calculate the discount amount using a discount rate of 18%. This is illustrated in Figure 7-16.

Step 3: Write the first statement of what to do when the condition is true.

```
022020      IF DISCOUNT-CUSTOMER
022030         IF SALES-INPUT IS GREATER THAN MAXIMUM-LOW-DISC-SALES
022040            COMPUTE DISCOUNT-AMT-REPORT = SALES-INPUT * HIGH-PCT
```

Figure 7-16 Third Step in Writing Nested IF Statement

In the third step above, it can be seen that a Compute Statement is used to calculate the Discount Amount by mulitplying the value in the SALES-INPUT field by the value in the HIGH-PCT field, which would be 18%. After this statement is written, the programmer must examine the programming specifications to determine if there is any other processing which must be accomplished if the sales are greater than $2,000.00. After examining the programming specifications on page 7.11, it should be clear that there is no further processing to be performed.

The next step is to examine the specifications to determine what should take place when the sales are equal to or less than the value stored in the MAXIMUM-LOW-DISC-SALES field (2,000.00). As can be seen from the specifications, the discount amount is be calculated as 12% of the Sales Amount. This calculation is illustrated below.

Step 4: Write the statement of what to do when the condition is not true.

```
022020      IF DISCOUNT-CUSTOMER
022030         IF SALES-INPUT IS GREATER THAN MAXIMUM-LOW-DISC-SALES
022040            COMPUTE DISCOUNT-AMT-REPORT = SALES-INPUT * HIGH-PCT
022050         ELSE
022060            COMPUTE DISCOUNT-AMT-REPORT = SALES-INPUT * LOW-PCT
```

Figure 7-17 Fourth Step in Writing Nested IF Statement

Note in Figure 7-17 that the ELSE Clause is used to indicate the processing to take place if the Sales are not greater than $2,000.00. As noted previously, the Discount Amount is calculated by multiplying the Sales by 12% (the value in LOW-PCT).

At this point, all processing which is to occur when a customer is entitled to a discount has been completed. Therefore, the programmer must examine the programming specifications to determine what is to occur if the customer is not entitled to a discount. From item #4 on page 7.11, it can be seen that the constant value "NO DISCOUNT" is to be moved to the printer output area. The coding for this processing is illustrated in Figure 7-18.

Step 5: Write the statement to process customers who do not receive a discount.

```
022020        IF DISCOUNT-CUSTOMER
022030           IF SALES-INPUT IS GREATER THAN MAXIMUM-LOW-DISC-SALES
022040              COMPUTE DISCOUNT-AMT-REPORT = SALES-INPUT * HIGH-PCT
022050           ELSE
022060              COMPUTE DISCOUNT-AMT-REPORT = SALES-INPUT * LOW-PCT
022070        ELSE
022080           MOVE NO-DISCOUNT-CONSTANT TO MESSAGE-REPORT.
```

Figure 7-18 Fifth Step in Writing Nested IF Statement

As can be seen from Figure 7-18, the ELSE Clause is used to specify what is to occur if the customer is not entitled to a discount. In the example, the value in the field NO-DISCOUNT-CONSTANT (which would be "NO DISCOUNT") would be moved to the MESSAGE-REPORT field. The programmer would continue to examine the programming specifications to determine if any other processing is to occur when the customer is not entitled to a discount. Since there is no further processing to occur, a period is written and the Nested IF Statement is complete.

Analysis of Nested IF Problems

In the problem presented on page 7.11, it was noted that the most "inclusive" condition, that is, the condition which must be tested before any others, was whether the customer was entitled to a discount. It is extremely important that the programmer recognize the condition which must be tested before others; because if this is not done, the Nested IF Statement may become longer and more complex than necessary and, in fact, may lead to an incorrect statement of the conditions to be tested. In order to illustrate this, the following Nested IF Statement tests whether the Sales are greater than $2,000.00 prior to testing whether a discount is to be allowed.

EXAMPLE - INCORRECT SEQUENCE OF TESTS

```
023020        IF SALES-INPUT IS GREATER THAN MAXIMUM-LOW-DISC-SALES
023030           IF DISCOUNT-CUSTOMER
023040              COMPUTE DISCOUNT-AMT-REPORT = SALES-INPUT * HIGH-PCT
023050           ELSE
023060              MOVE NO-DISCOUNT-CONSTANT TO MESSAGE-REPORT
023070        ELSE
023080           IF DISCOUNT-CUSTOMER
023090              COMPUTE DISCOUNT-AMT-REPORT = SALES-INPUT * LOW-PCT
023100           ELSE
023110              MOVE NO-DISCOUNT-CONSTANT TO MESSAGE-REPORT.
```

Figure 7-19 Example of Incorrect Sequence of Tests

Note in the example in Figure 7-19 that the value in the SALES-INPUT field is compared to the value in the MAXIMUM-LOW-DISC-SALES field; that is, the Sales are compared to the value 2,000.00. If the Sales are greater than 2,000.00, then a test is performed to determine if the customer is entitled to a discount (line 023030). The appropriate processing is then performed.

If the value in the Sales field is not greater than 2,000.00, then a test is again performed to determine if the customer is entitled to a discount (line 023080). Thus, the test for a discount customer must be performed twice—once when the Sales are greater than 2,000.00 and once when the Sales are less than or equal to 2,000.00. This duplication of testing is unnecessary, as is illustrated in Figure 7-18, where the eligibility for a discount is checked first. Note that the Nested IF Statement in Figure 7-18 is more simple than the one in Figure 7-19 and duplicate code is eliminated.

It is extremely important that the programmer be able to determine the first condition to be tested when designing the Nested IF Statement. A **guideline** to determining the proper sequence is to ask the question, "Is there any reason to test this condition if the results of another condition are not known?". If the answer to the question is "no", then the condition being examined should be specified only after the other condition whose results must be known is specified in the Nested IF Statement.

For example, there is no reason to determine the value in the SALES-INPUT field prior to determining whether the customer is entitled to a discount, because if the customer is not entitled to a discount, the value in the Sales field does not matter. Therefore, for the sample problem, the Nested IF Statement in Figure 7-18 is the proper way to solve the problem, while the Nested IF Statement in Figure 7-19 represents a poor way to solve the problem.

If the step-by-step approach together with a careful analysis of the programming specifications is followed when writing Nested IF Statements, the programmer will experience little difficulty in structuring the IF Statements properly. If, on the other hand, the programmer attempts to envision all possible conditions and writes the statement in other than a careful step-by-step process, it is likely that errors will be made.

SPECIAL NESTED IF CONDITIONS

Condition 1

There are several conditions which logically require Nested IF Statements of the kind illustrated previously but which cannot be written as shown previously because of limitations in the COBOL language. Consider the following programming specifications:

1. The Total Salary for all salesmen in a company is to be accumulated and printed on a report. If the salesman is a commission salesman and his sales are greater than the sales quota, then his commission is 10% of his sales; if the sales of a commission salesman are not greater than the sales quota, the commission is 8% of his sales. If the salesman is not on commission, his salary is equal to the salary specified in the input record. The Total Salary for all the salesmen is calculated by accumulating either the commission or the salary.

As can be seen from the programming specifications, this processing should be handled by a Nested IF Statement because one condition (over sales quota) is to be tested only if another condition (commission salesman) is true; and there are alternative actions to perform based upon both conditions.

In order to write the Nested IF Statement required to process the specifications, the programmer would normally proceed as illustrated previously. Using that technique, the following Nested IF Statement, WHICH IS INCORRECT, would be developed.

EXAMPLE - INCORRECT NESTED IF STATEMENT

```
013080        IF COMMISSION-SALESMAN
013090           IF SALES-INPUT IS GREATER THAN COMMISSION-QUOTA-CONSTANT
013100              COMPUTE COMMISSION-WORK = SALES-INPUT * .10
013110           ELSE
013120              COMPUTE COMMISSION-WORK = SALES-INPUT * .08
013130           ADD COMMISSION-WORK TO TOTAL-SALESMAN-SALARY-ACCUM
013140        ELSE
013150           ADD SALARY-INPUT TO TOTAL-SALESMAN-SALARY-ACCUM.
```

Figure 7-20 Example of Incorrect Nested IF Statement

Note from Figure 7-20 that the sequence of statements logically satisfies the programming specifications, that is, if it is a commission salesman and if the sales are greater than the quota, then the commission is computed as 10% of the sales; else, the commission is computed as 8% of the sales. After the commission is computed, it is added to the total salesman salary. If the salesman is not on commission, then the salary from the input record is added to the total salesman salary.

The reason this Nested IF Statement is incorrect is the Add Statement on line 013130. Although it is intended that this Add Statement will add the calculated commission regardless of whether the sales were over the quota or under the quota, in fact, it will add the commission only if the sales were not greater than the quota. This is because it follows the Else Clause for the IF Statement which determines if Sales are greater than the quota. It MUST be noted that any statement following an Else Clause will be executed only when the condition tested is not true. In addition, all statements within the Else Clause, which is terminated by either another Else Statement or a period, will be executed when the condition is not true. Thus, as a result of the Else Clause on line 013110 above, the two statements on lines 013120 and 013130 are executed when the condition tested on line 013090 is false.

There are two methods in which to solve this difficulty imposed by the Nested IF Statement. The first method is illustrated in Figure 7-21.

EXAMPLE - METHOD 1

```
Ø13080    IF COMMISSION-SALESMAN
Ø13090        IF SALES-INPUT IS GREATER THAN COMMISSION-QUOTA-CONSTANT
Ø13100            COMPUTE COMMISSION-WORK = SALES-INPUT * .1Ø
Ø13110            ADD COMMISSION-WORK TO TOTAL-SALESMAN-SALARY-ACCUM
Ø13120        ELSE
Ø13130            COMPUTE COMMISSION-WORK = SALES-INPUT * .Ø8
Ø13140            ADD COMMISSION-WORK TO TOTAL-SALESMAN-SALARY-ACCUM
Ø13150    ELSE
Ø13160        ADD SALARY-INPUT TO TOTAL-SALESMAN-SALARY-ACCUM.
```

Figure 7-21 Example of One Method to Solve Else Problem

Note in the example above that the statement to Add the calculated commission which is stored in the COMMISSION-WORK field is duplicated on line 013110 and line 013140. Therefore, regardless of whether the Sales are greater than the quota or whether they are not greater than the quota, the computed commission will still be added to the Salary Accumulator. This method of duplicating code will many times be used when there are only a few instructions which must be duplicated. If, however, there are many instructions which would have to be duplicated, the method illustrated in Figure 7-22 is normally used.

EXAMPLE - METHOD 2

```
Ø13020    IF COMMISSION-SALESMAN
Ø13030        PERFORM BØØ1-CHECK-SALES
Ø13040        ADD COMMISSION-WORK TO TOTAL-SALESMAN-SALARY-ACCUM
Ø13050    ELSE
Ø13060        ADD SALARY-INPUT TO TOTAL-SALESMAN-SALARY-ACCUM.
Ø13070
Ø13080
Ø13090
Ø13100 BØØ1-CHECK-SALES.
Ø13110
Ø13120    IF SALES-INPUT IS GREATER THAN COMMISSION-QUOTA-CONSTANT
Ø13130        COMPUTE COMMISSION-WORK = SALES-INPUT * .1Ø
Ø13140    ELSE
Ø13150        COMPUTE COMMISSION-WORK = SALES-INPUT * .Ø8.
```

Figure 7-22 Example of Second Method to Solve Else Problem

Note in the example above that the first IF Statement on line 013020 determines if the salesman is a commission salesman. If so, the paragraph B001-CHECK-SALES is performed. This paragraph consists of the IF Statement to determine if the sales are greater than the sales quota and the Compute Statements to calculate the commission when they are greater and when they are not greater.

After the commission has been calculated, control will return to the Add Statement on line 013040, which will add the commission to the accumulated salary. Note that the addition of the commission to the accumulated salary is not dependent upon any condition other than the fact that the salesman is a commission salesman. The IF Statement and related ELSE Clause to determine the commission percentage is placed in the performed paragraph.

Thus, the difficulty which was encountered in Figure 7-20 can be overcome through either of the techniques illustrated. If more than a few statements must be duplicated, it is normally a good practice to use the technique illustrated in Figure 7-22.

Condition 2

Another condition which must be handled properly is illustrated by the following programming specifications.

1. If the sales for a salesman are above the sales quota, the above quota message is to be moved to the printer output area. If the sales are above the sales quota and the employee has been employed for more than two years, then the bonus amount should be added to the commission. If the sales are not above the sales quota, then the below quota message should be moved to the printer output area.

As can be seen, this statement of a problem should be handled with a Nested IF Statement since the employment period of a salesman is to be checked only if the sales are above the sales quota; and an alternative action is required for the first condition (sales greater than sales quota) to be tested. The following Nested IF Statement is an INCORRECT METHOD to solve the problem.

EXAMPLE - INCORRECT METHOD

```
023020      IF SALES-INPUT IS GREATER THAN SALES-QUOTA-CONSTANT
023030          MOVE ABOVE-QUOTA-MESSAGE TO MESSAGE-REPORT
023040          IF YEARS-EMPLOYED-INPUT IS GREATER THAN TWO-YEARS-CONSTANT
023050              ADD BONUS-AMOUNT-CONSTANT TO COMMISSION-WORK
023060      ELSE
023070          MOVE BELOW-QUOTA-MESSAGE TO MESSAGE-REPORT.
```

Figure 7-23 Example of Incorrect Use of Nested IF Statement

In the example above, the sales are compared to the sales quota on line 023020. If the sales are greater than the sales quota, the above quota message is moved to the report output area; the years employed are then checked to determine if the employee has worked more than two years. If so, the bonus amount is added to the commission.

The error in the Nested IF Statement then occurs on line 023060. The Else Clause is intended by the programmer to pertain to the IF Statement on line 023020; instead, it pertains to the IF Statement on line 023040. Therefore, as a result of the Nested IF Statement in Figure 7-23, if the sales are not greater than the sales quota, nothing will take place.

In addition, if the years employed are less than or equal to two years when the sales are greater than the quota, a below quota message will be printed, which is not the proper processing.

The reason that the Else Clause on line 023060 pertains to the IF Statement on line 023040 is that IF Statements and Else Clauses are matched with one another. This is illustrated in the following diagram.

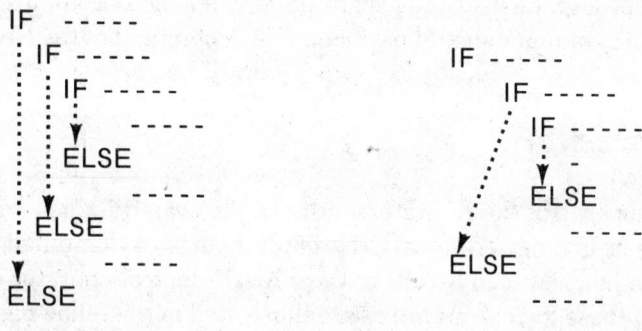

Figure 7-24 Example of Matched IF . . . ELSE Statements

Note from Figure 7-24 that each of the IF Statements is matched by an Else Clause. The rule is that in a Nested IF Statement, the first Else Clause corresponds to the innermost IF Statement. The second Else Clause corresponds to the next innermost IF Statement, and so on. Indentation has no effect whatsoever on the Nested IF Statement.

Therefore, as can be seen from Figure 7-23, the Else Clause on line 023060 applies to the innermost IF Statement, which is the one on line 023040. This is not the intended result. In order to obtain the intended result, it is necessary that the innermost IF Statement, on line 023040, have a corresponding Else Clause. Since nothing is to take place if the Sales are greater than the Quota but the salesman is employed two years or less, the NEXT SENTENCE Clause should be used. The correct Nested IF Statement to solve the problem posed on page 7.18 is illustrated below.

EXAMPLE - CORRECT METHOD

```
023020    IF SALES-INPUT IS GREATER THAN SALES-QUOTA-CONSTANT
023030       MOVE ABOVE-QUOTA-MESSAGE TO MESSAGE-REPORT
023040       IF YEARS-EMPLOYED-INPUT IS GREATER THAN TWO-YEARS-CONSTANT
023050          ADD BONUS-AMOUNT-CONSTANT TO COMMISSION-WORK
023060       ELSE
023070          NEXT SENTENCE
023080    ELSE
023090       MOVE BELOW-QUOTA-MESSAGE TO MESSAGE-REPORT.
```

Figure 7-25 Example of Correct Nested IF Statement

In the example in Figure 7-25 it can be seen that the Else Clause on line 023060 corresponds to the IF Statement on line 023040 and the Else Clause on line 023080 corresponds to the IF Statement on line 023020. Thus, as is required, each IF Statement has a matching Else Clause. The IF Statement in Figure 7-25 will properly execute the processing specified on page 7.18.

SUMMARY

The Nested IF Statement is an extremely important tool when programming in COBOL or any other language. Through its use, the programmer can specify complex logic in a clear and precise manner. The programmer should have complete command of the Nested IF Statement.

COMBINED IF STATEMENTS

The previous discussions of the IF Statement have illustrated its use when testing a single condition either alone or in a nested format. Through the use of Combined IF Statements, two or more conditions can be combined by either the ''AND'' logical operator or the ''OR'' logical operator. Examples of these logical operators are illustrated in the following paragraphs.

AND Logical Operator

The word AND is used to mean ''both'' when two or more conditions are specified in an IF Statement. The use of the ''AND'' logical operator is illustrated in Figure 7-26.

EXAMPLE

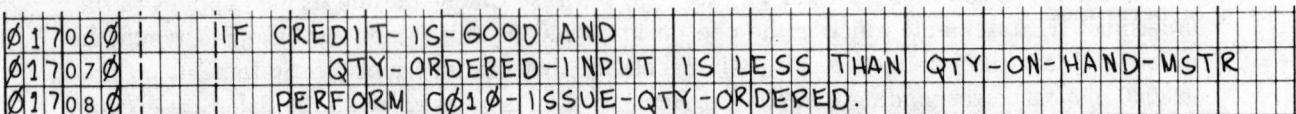

```
017060        IF CREDIT-IS-GOOD AND
017070           QTY-ORDERED-INPUT IS LESS THAN QTY-ON-HAND-MSTR
017080           PERFORM C010-ISSUE-QTY-ORDERED.
```

Figure 7-26 Example of AND Logical Operator

In the example above two conditions are checked—whether the credit is good and whether the quantity ordered is less than the quantity on hand. If BOTH of these conditions are true, then the C010-ISSUE-QTY-ORDERED module will be performed. Note that when the word AND is used, it means both conditions must be true. If either of the conditions is not true, then the Else portion of the IF Statement will be executed; or, if there is no Else Clause, as in the example in Figure 7-26, the next sentence in the program will be executed.

It should be noted that the word IF need not be repeated; that is, the word IF is the first word of the statement and then the conditions are specified, separated by the word AND.

It is important to understand that when the program specifications indicate that BOTH conditions must be true before any processing is to take place, the logical operator AND should be used in the IF Statement instead of a Nested IF Statement. A Nested IF Statement is appropriate only where the testing of one condition is dependent upon the results of another condition and alternative processing is to take place based upon the results of the testing of only one condition.

OR Logical Operator

Two or more conditions can be combined with the logical operator OR to indicate that if EITHER or BOTH of the conditions are true, then the conditions tested are considered true. The use of the OR logical operator is illustrated in Figure 7-27.

EXAMPLE

```
Ø18Ø2Ø        IF PART-NUMBER-INPUT IS NUMERIC OR
Ø18Ø3Ø           PART-NUMBER-INPUT = SPACES
Ø18Ø4Ø           PERFORM CØ4Ø-EDIT-NUMERIC-FIELDS
Ø18Ø5Ø        ELSE
Ø18Ø6Ø           PERFORM CØ5Ø-PROCESS-BAD-PART-NO.
```

Figure 7-27 Example of OR Logical Operator

In the example in Figure 7-27, two conditions are tested. The first is if the part number contains numeric data and the second is whether the part number field contains spaces. If EITHER of these conditions is true, then the entire IF Statement is considered true and the C040-EDIT-NUMERIC-FIELDS module will be performed. If both of the conditions are not true, that is, if the part number field contains neither numeric data nor spaces, then the conditions tested are considered not true and the C050-PROCESS-BAD-PART-NO module will be performed.

Again, it must be noted that when the word OR is used to combine two conditions, it means if EITHER or BOTH of the conditions tested is true, then the entire IF Statement is considered true.

COMPLEX IF STATEMENTS

When two or more combined IF Statements are themselves put together, a complex IF Statement is the result. The following example illustrates the programming specifications and related complex IF Statement to solve the problem.

EXAMPLE

Specifications: If the employee classification of an employee is less
than grade 06 or greater than 15 and this employee is
not a member of the union, then notification of the
non-union member should take place.

```
Ø19Ø5Ø        IF (EMPLOYEE-CLASSIFICATION-INPUT IS LESS THAN '06' OR
Ø19Ø6Ø           GREATER THAN '15') AND
Ø19Ø7Ø           EMPLOYEE-IS-NOT-UNION-MEMBER
Ø19Ø8Ø        PERFORM CØØØ-NOTIFY-NON-UNION-MEMBER.
```

Figure 7-28 Example of Complex IF Statement

Note from the programming specifications in Figure 7-28 that there are two conditions, both of which have to be true, in order for a non-union member to be notified. First, the employee classification must be less than 06 or greater than 15. If it is, then the first part of the two-part condition is satisfied. If it is not, then the two-part condition cannot be satisfied.

The second part of the condition is that the employee not be a union member. If both the first part and the second part of the two-part condition are true, then the non-union member will be notified.

In the IF Statement in Figure 7-28 which is used to solve this problem, parentheses are used to indicate the order in which the conditions are to be evaluated. From the use of the parentheses, the order of evaluation will be as follows:

> 1 - EMPLOYEE-CLASSIFICATION-INPUT IS LESS THAN '06' OR
>   GREATER THAN '15'
>   —AND—
> 2 - EMPLOYEE-IS-NOT-UNION-MEMBER

The reason that the first statement above is evaluated first and as a single unit is because of the parentheses around the statement. Whenever parentheses are placed around conditions within a complex IF Statement, these conditions are evaluated as a single unit, giving a true or not true indication. Thus, #1 above will be evaluated as to whether it is true or not true even though the word OR is present. Number 2 above would also be evaluated as to its being true or not true. If both #1 AND #2 above are true, then the entire IF Statement will be considered true, since the word AND is used to join them. If either #1 or #2 is not true, then the entire IF Statement will be considered not true.

Parentheses are not required in complex IF Statements. If they are not used, then the order of evaluation is as follows:

1. AND and its surrounding conditions are evaluated first, starting at
   the left of the expression and proceeding to the right.

2. OR and its surrounding conditions are then evaluated, also working
   from left to right.

The difference between using and not using parentheses is illustrated in the following examples.

EXAMPLE 1 - With Parentheses

```
019020        IF (EMPLOYEE-IS-A-SALESMAN OR
019030            EMPLOYEE-IS-SALES-MGR) AND
019040            SALARY-DRAW-INPUT IS LESS THAN COMMISSION-INPUT
019050        PERFORM C010-PROCESS-COMMISSION-PMT.
```

Evaluation: 1 - EMPLOYEE-IS-A-SALESMAN OR
                 EMPLOYEE-IS-SALES-MGR
                 —AND—
             2 - SALARY-DRAW-INPUT IS LESS THAN
                 COMMISSION-INPUT

EXAMPLE 2 - Without Parentheses

```
019120        IF EMPLOYEE-IS-A-SALESMAN OR
019130            EMPLOYEE-IS-SALES-MGR AND
019140            SALARY-DRAW-INPUT IS LESS THAN COMMISSION-INPUT
019150        PERFORM C010-PROCESS-COMMISSION-PMT.
```

Evaluation: 1 - EMPLOYEE-IS-A-SALESMAN
                 —OR—
             2 - EMPLOYEE-IS-SALES-MGR AND
                 SALARY-DRAW-INPUT IS LESS THAN
                 COMMISSION-INPUT

Figure 7-29 Example of Effect of Parentheses

In the examples above, it can be seen that the IF Statement is evaluated differently, depending upon whether parentheses are used. In Example 1, with parentheses, note that the phrase within the parentheses is evaluated as a single condition and both (EMPLOYEE-IS-A-SALESMAN OR EMPLOYEE-IS-SALES-MGR) **AND** SALARY-DRAW-INPUT IS LESS THAN COMMISSION-INPUT must be true in order for the If Statement to be true. In Example 2, without parentheses, the rules as specified previously are followed. Thus, the conditions separated by the word AND are evaulated as a single unit; that is, EMPLOYEE-IS-SALES-MGR **AND** SALARY-DRAW-INPUT IS LESS THAN COMMISSION-INPUT is evaluated as a single condition, and the first condition EMPLOYEE-IS-A-SALESMAN is evaluated in an OR (either or both) relationship with the two conditions joined by the word AND. In Example 2, if the employee is a salesman, the C010-PROCESS-COMMISSION-PMT module would be executed.

Thus, an entirely different result will occur, depending upon whether or not parentheses are used. It is strongly suggested that whenever complex IF Statements are to be used, parentheses be specified in the coding whether they are needed or not; that is, even if the way COBOL analyzes the conditions without parentheses is correct, it is still a good idea, for clarity and ease of reading, to include the parentheses. In this manner, the reader has no doubts as to the order of evaluation of the conditions specified.

SAMPLE PROBLEM

As noted previously, the sample program in this chapter will create a Personnel Report. The printer spacing chart for the report to be produced is illustrated in Figure 7-30.

OUTPUT

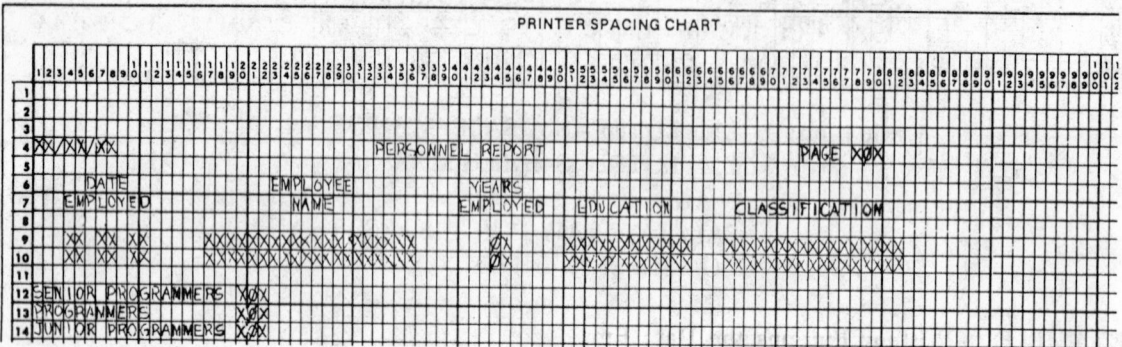

Figure 7-30 Program Output

The input to the program is a file of Personnel Cards. The format of the input cards is illustrated in Figure 7-31.

INPUT

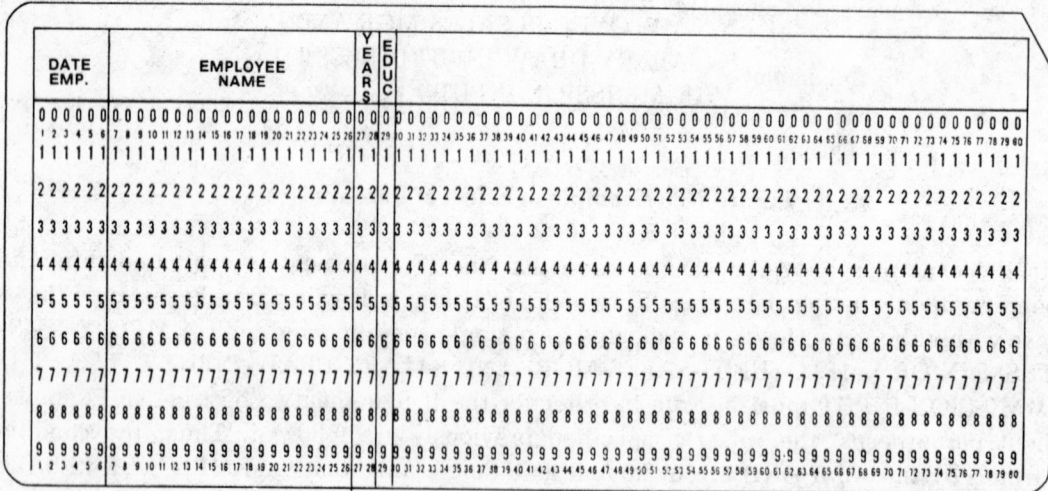

Figure 7-31 Program Input

The Programming Specifications for the sample problem are illustrated below.

PROGRAMMING SPECIFICATIONS		
SUBJECT Personnel Report	**DATE** May 17	**PAGE** 1 OF 1
TO Programmer	**FROM** Systems Analyst	

A program is to be written to prepare a Personnel Report. The formats for the input card file and printer spacing chart are included as a part of this narrative. The program should include the following processing:

1. The program should read the input cards and create the Personnel Report as per the format illustrated on the printer spacing chart. The report contains the Date Employed, the Employee Name, the Years Employed, the Education, and the Classification. Final Totals should be printed for the number of senior programmers, the number of programmers, and the number of junior programmers.

2. If the Education field in the input record contains the value "G", then the Education on the report should be "GRADUATE". If the Education field in the input record contains the value "N", then the Education on the report should be "NON-GRADUATE".

3. If the employee is a graduate and has been employed longer than two years, then the classification is SENIOR PROGRAMMER. If the employee is a graduate and has been employed two years or less, then the classification is PROGRAMMER.

4. If the employee is a non-graduate and has been employed longer than three years, then the classification is PROGRAMMER. If the employee is a non-graduate and has been employed three years or less, the classification is JUNIOR PROGRAMMER.

5. Final totals should be taken for the number of Senior Programmers, the number of Programmers, and the number of Junior Programmers.

6. Headings are to be printed on the top of each new page of the report. The report is to have 55 detail lines per page. The page number should begin at 1, and be incremented by 1 for each new page.

7. The program should be written in COBOL.

Figure 7-32 Programming Specifications

PROGRAM DESIGN

After thoroughly analyzing the programming specifications, the programmer would set about to design the program. The first step is to develop the IPO Charts for the program. The IPO Chart for the module to create the personnel report is illustrated below.

IPO CHART				
PROGRAM: Personnel Report		**PROGRAMMER:** Shelly/Cashman		**DATE:** May 17
MODULE NAME: Create Personnel Report	**REF:** A000	**MODULE FUNCTION:** Create the Personnel Report		
INPUT	**PROCESSING**		**REF:**	**OUTPUT**
1. Personnel Input File	1. Initialization			1. Personnel Report
	2. Obtain the input data			
	3. Process the detail records		B000	
	4. Print the final totals		B010	
	5. Termination			

Figure 7-33 IPO Chart for Create the Personnel Report Module

As in previous programs, it can be seen in Figure 7-33 that the major processing tasks of the module whose function is to create the personnel report are specified, together with the input to the module and the output from the module. After the major processing tasks are listed, each of them is analyzed to determine if they represent a specific function to be performed and are of sufficient size and/or complexity to justify another module. In this program, the major processing tasks of "Process the detail records" and "Print the final totals" each define specific tasks to be accomplished and are potentially of such size and difficulty to justify separate modules.

Once this determination is made, the hierarchy chart for the first and second levels is drawn, as illustrated in Figure 7-34.

Hierarchy Chart

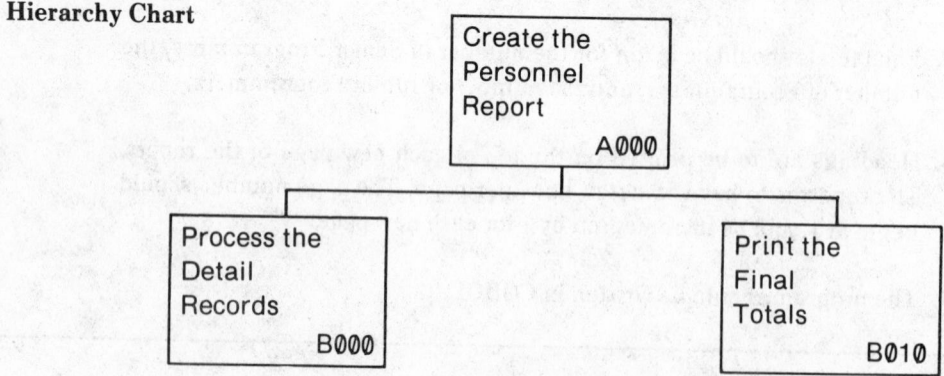

Figure 7-34 First and Second Levels of Hierarchy Chart

After drawing the Hierarchy Chart, the programmer should design the IPO Charts for the modules identified on the Hierarchy Chart. The IPO Charts for the "Process the Detail Records" module and the "Print the Final Totals" module are illustrated below.

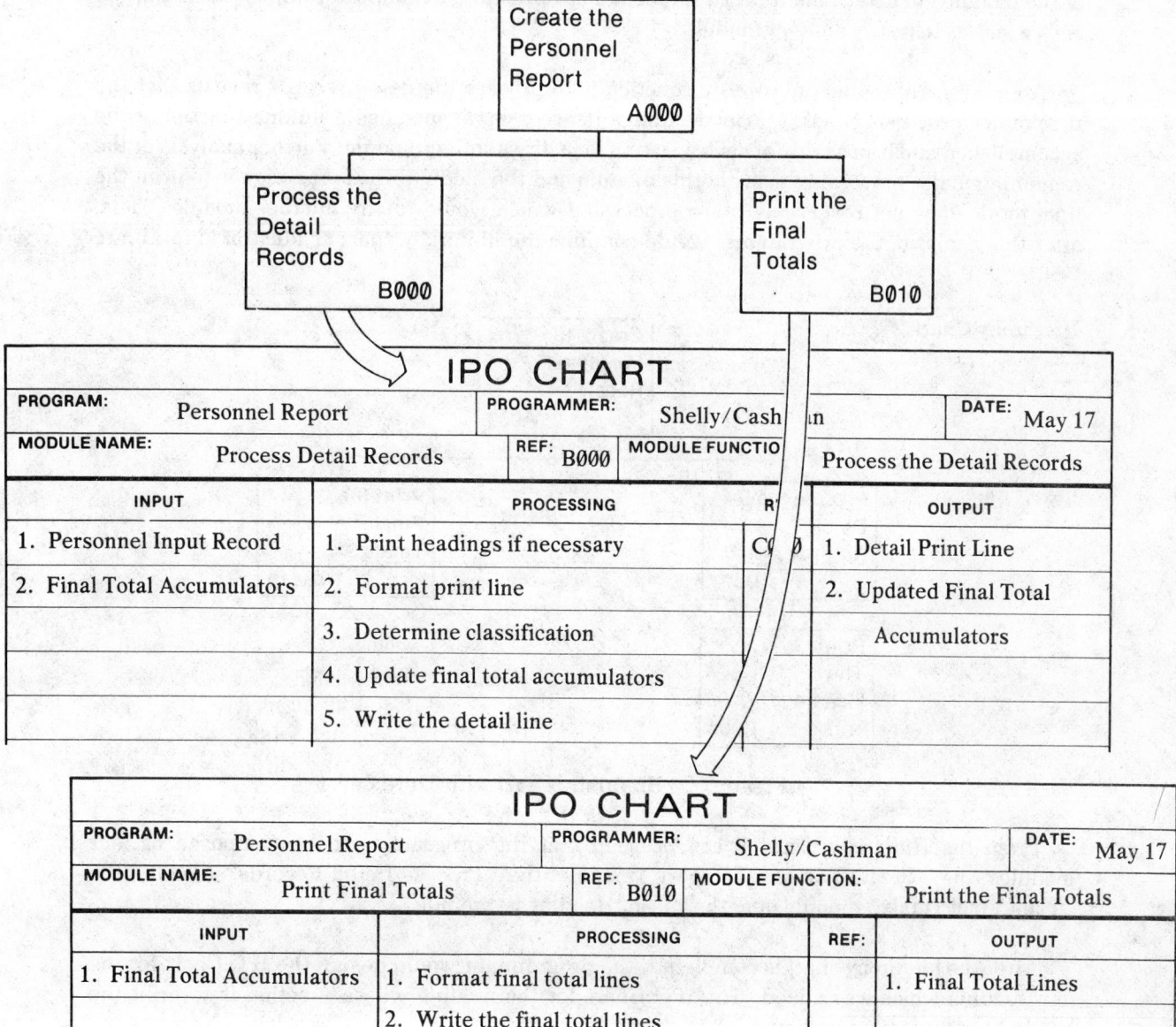

Figure 7-35 IPO Charts for Second Level Modules

Note from Figure 7-35 that the major processing tasks, together with the input and the output, are listed for the two modules on the second level of the hierarchy chart. When the IPO Charts are complete, the programmer would again analyze the major processing tasks in each of the modules to determine if they represent a specific function to be accomplished and are of such a size as to justify another module.

An analysis of the module whose function is to process the detail records reveals that the first major processing task, "Print headings if necessary" specifies a unique function to be accomplished and is probably of such a size as to justify another module. Further analysis of the remaining major processing tasks in this module and the module whose function is to print the final totals does not reveal any other processing which would justify another module. Thus, after this analysis, the programmer would continue the hierarchy chart as illustrated in Figure 7-36.

Hierarchy Chart

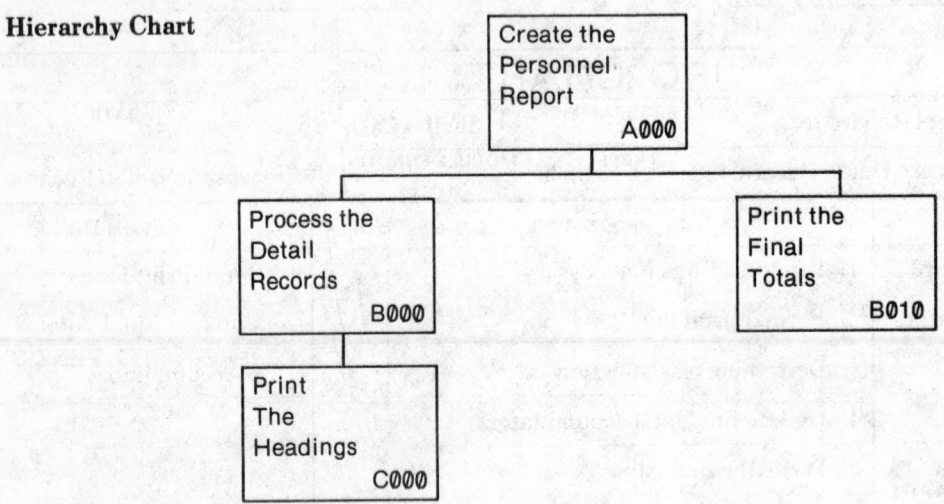

Figure 7-36 Hierarchy Chart with Third Level

From the Hierarchy Chart it can be seen that the program is to be composed of four modules, the "Create Personnel Report" module, the "Process Detail Records" module, the "Print Final Totals" module, and the "Print Headings" module.

After the hierarchy chart is completed, the programmer would design the IPO Chart for the new module which was added. The IPO Chart for the module whose function is to print the headings is illustrated in Figure 7-37.

IPO CHART

PROGRAM: Personnel Report	PROGRAMMER: Shelly/Cashman	DATE: May 17
MODULE NAME: Print Headings	REF: C000	MODULE FUNCTION: Print the Headings on the Report

INPUT	PROCESSING	REF:	OUTPUT
1. Heading Lines	1. Format heading lines		1. Heading Lines on
	2. Print the heading lines		the Report

Figure 7-37 IPO Chart for Third Level Module

An analysis of the IPO Chart for the module to print the headings reveals there are no major processing tasks which appear to require another module. Therefore, the programmer would review the design of the program as specified on the IPO Charts and the Hierarchy Chart and then proceed to the next step, that of designing the logic on the Pseudocode Specifications.

Pseudocode Specifications

The pseudocode for each of the modules is prepared on the Pseudocode Specifications. In general, the pseudocode is prepared for the modules in top-down fashion; that is, the logic for the highest level module is designed first, and then the logic for the modules on the second level is designed, and so on. In this manner, any problems which may arise in the method of solving the problem will be detected early in the design process, instead of late, after many of the lower level modules have already been designed. Thus, in the sample program, the first module for which to design the logic is the module whose function is to ''create the personnel report.'' The Pseudocode Specifications for this module are illustrated in Figure 7-38.

PSEUDOCODE SPECIFICATIONS

PROGRAM: Personnel Report	PROGRAMMER: Shelly/Cashman	DATE: May 17

MODULE NAME: Create Personnel Report	REF: A000	MODULE FUNCTION: Create the Personnel Report

PSEUDOCODE	REF:	FILES, RECORDS, FIELDS REQUIRED
Open the files		Personnel input file
Read an input record		Personnel report file
IF there is a record		Input area for input record
PERFORM UNTIL no more input records		Date employed
Process detail records	B000	Employee name
Read an input record		Years employed
ENDPERFORM		Education
Print the final totals	B010	Indicator for there is a record
ENDIF		Indicator for no more records
Close the files		
Stop run		

Figure 7-38 Pseudocode for Highest Level Module

Note in Figure 7-38 that the logic for the module which creates the Personnel Report is basically the same as was seen for the highest level module in Chapter 6. One major difference is that there are no headings written from this module. The headings will be produced from the module whose function is to write the headings.

It should be noted also from Figure 7-38 that the Reference Numbers for the modules which are called from the "Create Personnel Report" module are contained in the center REF: column to indicate the fact that lower level modules are to be called to perform the function specified in the pseudocode. In this manner, the programmer is able to follow the processing which will take place within the program by following the reference numbers.

After the top level module is designed and reviewed, the next level of modules would be designed. The Pseudocode Specifications for the module whose function is to process the detail records is illustrated in Figure 7-39.

PSEUDOCODE SPECIFICATIONS

PROGRAM: Personnel Report	PROGRAMMER: Shelly/Cashman	DATE: May 17

MODULE NAME: Process Detail Records	REF: B000	MODULE FUNCTION: Process the Detail Records

PSEUDOCODE	REF:	FILES, RECORDS, FIELDS REQUIRED

IF number of lines printed is = or > page size or first page
   Print the headings
ENDIF
Clear printer area
Move date employed, name, and years
      employed to the output area
IF employee is a graduate
   Move 'graduate' to output area
   IF years employed > 2
      Move 'senior programmer' to output area
      Add 1 to senior programmer accumulator
   ELSE
      Move 'programmer' to output area
      Add 1 to programmer accumulator
   ENDIF
ELSE
   Move 'non-graduate' to output area
   IF years employed >3
      Move 'programmer' to output area
      Add 1 to programmer accumulator
   ELSE
      Move 'junior programmer' to output area
      Add 1 to junior programmer accumulator
   ENDIF
ENDIF
Write the line on the report
Add 1 to lines printed
Set spacing to single spacing
	C000	Number of lines printed counter
		Page size constant
		First page indicator
		Printer output area
		   Date employed
		   Employee name
		   Years employed
		   Education
		   Classification
		'Graduate' constant
		Two-year constant
		'Senior programmer' constant
		Senior programmer accumulator
		'Programmer' constant
		Programmer accumulator
		'Non-graduate' constant
		Three-year constant
		'Junior programmer' constant
		Junior programmer accumulator
		Spacing control area
		Single spacing constant
		Input area for input record
		   Date employed
		   Employee name
		   Years employed
		   Education

Figure 7-39 Pseudocode for Detail Record Module

The first IF Statement in the module illustrated in Figure 7-39 is used to determine when the headings should be printed on the report. There are two conditions when they should be printed—first, when the first page of the report is to be printed and second, when the number of lines actually printed on the page are equal to or greater than the number of lines that are supposed to be printed on the page. Thus, the IF Statement in Figure 7-39 checks if the number of lines printed are equal to or greater than the page size, or if the first page is to be printed. If either of these conditions is true, then the headings will be printed. Note that because of this checking, a field for the number of lines printed, the page size constant, and a first page indicator must be defined in the program. The method for defining these fields and values will be illustrated later in this chapter.

After the headings are printed when required, the printer area is cleared to spaces and values from the input record are moved to the output area. The nested IF Statement is then encountered. It will be noted that the first condition is whether the employee is a graduate. If the condition is true, that is, the employee is a graduate, then the constant GRADUATE is moved to the printer output area. An IF Statement is then used to determine if the employee has been employed more than two years. Note that this is a nested IF Statement. If the employee has been employed more than two years, then the constant SENIOR PROGRAMMER is moved to the output area and the final total accumulator for senior programmers is incremented by 1.

If the employee has not been employed more than two years, then the constant PROGRAMMER is moved to the output area and the final total accumulator for programmers is incremented by 1. Following the Else Clause of the imbedded IF Statement is the ENDIF word. As will be recalled from Chapter 6, whenever the effect of an IF Statement is completed, the ENDIF word should be used to indicate that the statements following it are not dependent upon the condition tested in the IF Statement.

After the ENDIF word is the Else Clause for the first IF Statement. Following the Else Clause are the operations which are to take place if the employee is not a graduate. The NON-GRADUATE constant is moved to the output area and then it is determined if the employee has been employed more than three years. If so, the classification is PROGRAMMER and the programmer accumulator is incremented by 1; if not, the classification is JUNIOR PROGRAMMER and the junior programmer accumulator is incremented by 1. The imbedded IF Statement which checked for the years employed is ended with the ENDIF word and then the IF Statement which checked if the employee was a graduate is ended with an ENDIF word. Thus, the Nested IF Statement is completed. It is important to understand how a Nested IF Statement is expressed in pseudocode because, as indicated previously, the Nested IF Statement is an important tool in the programmer's repertoire.

After the Nested IF Statement, the line is written on the report. The number of lines printed is then incremented by 1. This is necessary because the manner in which page overflow is detected is by the number of lines which have been printed on a page. Therefore, after each line is printed on the report, the count must be incremented to reflect this. The spacing is then set for single spacing and the processing of the detail record is complete.

The other module on the second level of the Hierarchy Chart is the module whose function is to print the final totals. The pseudocode for this module is illustrated on the Pseudocode Specifications below.

PSEUDOCODE SPECIFICATIONS

PROGRAM: Personnel Report **PROGRAMMER:** Shelly/Cashman **DATE:** May 17

MODULE NAME: Print Final Totals **REF:** B010 **MODULE FUNCTION:** Print the Final Totals

PSEUDOCODE	REF:	FILES, RECORDS, FIELDS REQUIRED
Move senior programmer total to the total line		Senior programmer accumulator
Write the senior programmer total		Senior programmer total line
Move the programmer total to the total line		Programmer accumulator
Write the programmer total		Programmer total line
Move the junior programmer total to the total line		Junior programmer accumulator
Write the junior programmer total		Junior programmer total line

Figure 7-40 Pseudocode for Final Total Module

Note from the pseudocode in Figure 7-40 that the processing in the final total module consists of moving the final totals to the final total lines and printing the final totals.

Once the pseudocode for the second level modules has been designed, the programmer would begin the design of the modules on the third level. As will be recalled from the Hierarchy Chart (see Figure 7-36), the only module on the third level is the module whose function is to print the headings. The Pseudocode Specifications for this module are illustrated in Figure 7-41.

PSEUDOCODE SPECIFICATIONS

PROGRAM: Personnel Report **PROGRAMMER:** Shelly/Cashman **DATE:** May 17

MODULE NAME: Print Headings **REF:** C000 **MODULE FUNCTION:** Print the Headings on the Report

PSEUDOCODE	REF:	FILES, RECORDS, FIELDS REQUIRED
Move the page count to the heading line		Page count counter
Move the current date to the heading line		Current date
Write the first heading line		First heading line
Write the second heading line		Second heading line
Write the third heading line		Third heading line
Add 1 to the page count		Number of lines printed counter
Reset lines printed counter to zero		Spacing control area
Set spacing for double spacing		Double spacing constant

Figure 7-41 Pseudocode for Heading Module

The first step in writing the headings is to move the page count and the current date to the heading line. The page count begins at one and is incremented by one for each page which is written on the report. The current date is stored in computer storage by the operating system and is moved to the heading line. The technique for accomplishing this in COBOL is illustrated later in this chapter.

After the first heading line is formatted, the three heading lines are printed on the report. The page count is then incremented by one so that the next time the page number is printed, it will be the proper value. The counter for the number of lines is then reset to zero. This is necessary because when each new page is started, the lines will be counted on that page. If the counter were not reset, there would be no way to determine that page overflow had occurred. The spacing for double spacing is then set so that the first line on the new page will be double spaced.

It is important that the programmer understand the relationships of the modules which have just been defined. The Hierarchy Chart and related Pseudocode Specifications are illustrated in Figure 7-42.

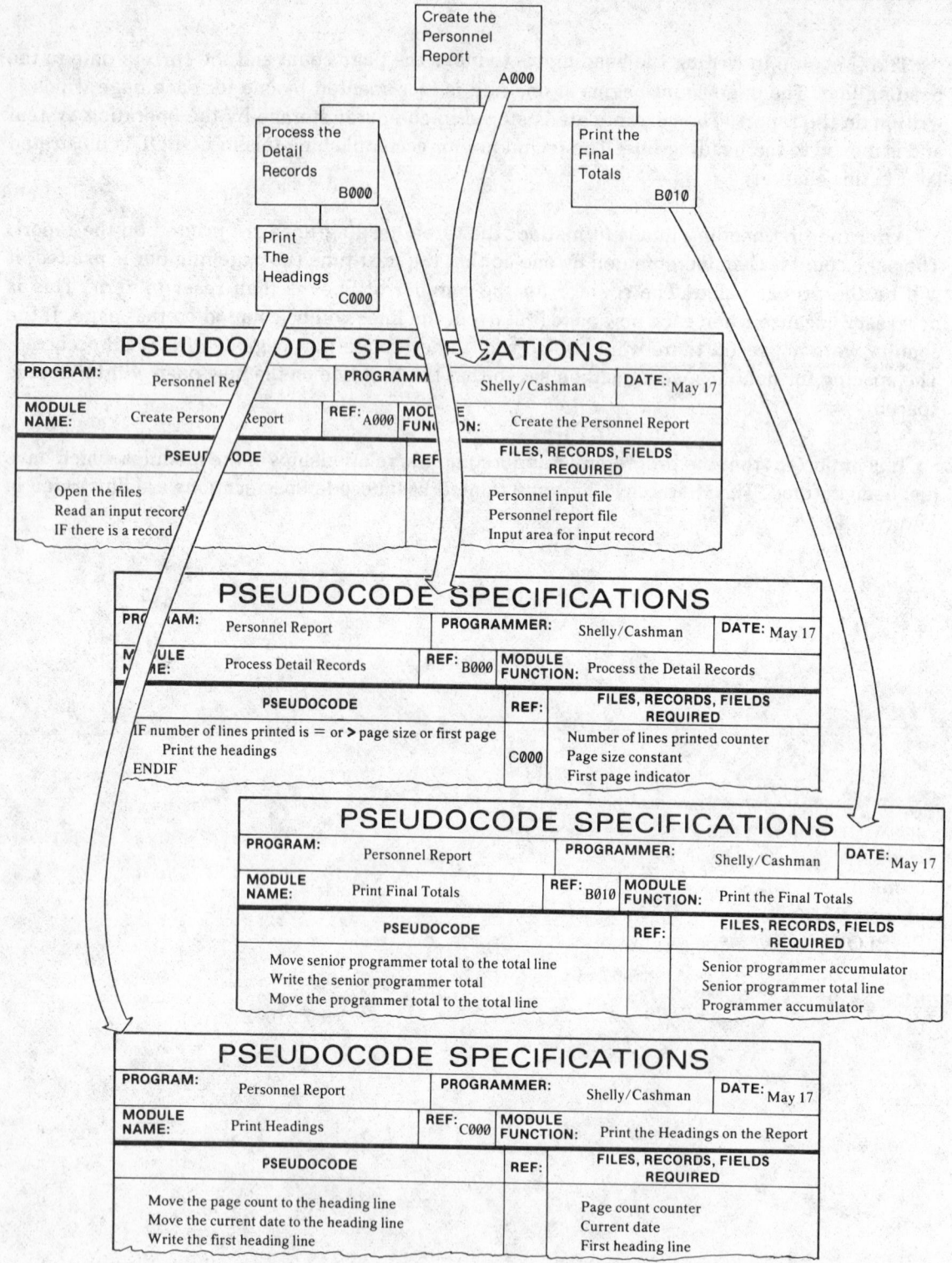

Figure 7-42 Relationship of Modules

Note from Figure 7-42 that Pseudocode Specifications have been prepared for each module which was designed in the Hierarchy Chart through the use of the IPO Charts. After the pseudocode has been prepared, it should be very carefully reviewed in a structured walkthrough. After there is a consensus that the program structure and the logic as expressed in the pseudocode is correct, the programmer can begin the program coding.

DATA DIVISION

Input Record

In previous programs it has been seen how a condition name can be used in the Working-Storage Section of the Data Division. A condition name can also be used in the File Section when defining an input record. The use of a condition name to indicate whether an employee is a graduate or non-graduate in the sample program is illustrated below.

EXAMPLE

```
003100 FD  PERSONNEL-INPUT-FILE
003110         RECORD CONTAINS 80 CHARACTERS
003120         LABEL RECORDS ARE OMITTED
003130         DATA RECORD IS PERSONNEL-INPUT-RECORD.
003140 01  PERSONNEL-INPUT-RECORD.
003150     05  DATE-EMPLOYED-INPUT          PIC X(6).
003160     05  NAME-INPUT                   PIC X(20).
003170     05  YEARS-EMPLOYED-INPUT         PIC 99.
003180     05  EDUCATION-INPUT              PIC X.
003190         88  EMPLOYEE-IS-NOT-A-GRADUATE        VALUE 'N'.
003200         88  EMPLOYEE-IS-A-GRADUATE            VALUE 'G'.
004020     05  FILLER                       PIC X(51).
```

Figure 7-43 Definition of Input File

In the coding illustrated above, the Personnel Input File is defined together with the input area to be used for the Personnel Input Record. The field which is to contain the code indicating whether the employee is a graduate or a non-graduate is called EDUCATION-INPUT. Immediately following the definition of the field are the condition names which are used to identify if the employee is a graduate or non-graduate. On line 003190, the condition name EMPLOYEE-IS-NOT-A-GRADUATE is given to the value "N" appearing in the field. Thus, the condition tested by the condition name will be true if the value "N" is contained in the EDUCATION-INPUT field. Similarly, on line 003200, the condition name EMPLOYEE-IS-A-GRADUATE is given to the value "G" appearing in the field. These condition names can be tested within the Procedure Division to determine the education of the employee.

Printer Control

As noted previously, the page count, the page size, and the number of lines printed are required fields in order to print headings on each page. These fields, together with the spacing control fields which have appeared in previous programs, are illustrated in Figure 7-44.

EXAMPLE

```
006120 01  PRINTER-CONTROL.
006130     05  PROPER-SPACING          PIC 9.
006140     05  SPACE-ONE-LINE          PIC 9       VALUE 1.
006150     05  SPACE-TWO-LINES         PIC 9       VALUE 2.
006160     05  PAGE-COUNT              PIC S999    VALUE +1
006170                                             USAGE IS COMP-3.
006180         88  FIRST-PAGE                      VALUE +1.
006190     05  PAGE-SIZE               PIC 999     VALUE 55
006200                                             USAGE IS COMP-3.
007010     05  LINES-PRINTED           PIC S999    VALUE ZERO
007020                                             USAGE IS COMP-3.
```

Figure 7-44 Definition of Printer Control Fields

Note in the Printer Control group illustrated above that the first three fields for printer spacing control are the same as have been seen in previous programs. The three additional fields, PAGE-COUNT, PAGE-SIZE, and LINES-PRINTED, are required in order to print headings on each page of the report.

The PAGE-COUNT field is used to count the number of pages in the report and to supply the Page Number to be printed on the report. It will be noted that it is given the initial value of +1. It is given this value because the first page on the report will be numbered 1. The plus sign is used because the numeric field is specified as a signed field (PIC S999). It is defined as a Computational-3 field because it will be used in an arithmetic operation when the page number is incremented.

The condition name FIRST-PAGE is used to indicate that the first page of the report is to be printed. It will be recalled in the processing of the detail record (see Figure 7-39) that a test will be made to determine if the first page of the report is to be printed. This condition name is used to test that condition. If the PAGE-COUNT field contains the value +1, then the first page on the report has not yet been printed and the module to print the headings will be invoked to print the headings on the first page.

The PAGE-SIZE field is a constant field which is used to determine if a complete page has been printed. It is given the value 55, which is the number of detail lines which will be printed on each page of the report. When the line count is equal to or greater than this value, then a new page will be begun on the report. It will be noted that the value 55 is chosen by the programmer, and may be any value which is required for the particular report.

The LINES-PRINTED field is used to accumulate a count of the number of lines which have been printed on a page of the report. It is given the initial value zero. As each line is printed on the page, the value 1 will be added to this field. Prior to printing a detail line, the value in this field is checked against the Page Size. If it is equal to or greater than the page size, then headings will be printed.

Defining the Heading Line

The first heading line on the report to be prepared contains the date and the page number (see Figure 7-30). These fields must be defined in the heading line. The definition of the heading line for the sample program is illustrated below.

EXAMPLE

```
007040    01  HEADING-LINES.
007050        05  FIRST-HEADING-LINE.
007060            10  CARRIAGE-CONTROL        PIC X.
007070            10  DATE-HEADING            PIC X(8).
007080            10  FILLER                  PIC X(24)    VALUE SPACES.
007090            10  FILLER                  PIC X(16)    VALUE
007100                                                     'PERSONNEL REPORT'.
007110            10  FILLER                  PIC X(24)    VALUE SPACES.
007120            10  FILLER                  PIC X(5)     VALUE 'PAGE '.
007130            10  PAGE-NUMBER-HEADING     PIC ZZ9.
007140            10  FILLER                  PIC X(52)    VALUE SPACES.
```

Figure 7-45 Definition of Heading Line

In the coding above, note on line 007070 that the field DATE-HEADING is defined for the date which will be printed in the heading. It is eight characters in length because the date will be stored in the MM/DD/YY format.

The page number will be moved to the PAGE-NUMBER-HEADING field each time a new heading is printed. Note that the field will zero-suppress the page number.

PROCEDURE DIVISION

The module which processes the detail records contains the coding to determine when headings should be printed and also the Nested IF Statements necessary to implement the logic illustrated in the Pseudocode Specifications (see Figure 7-38). The coding for the module which processes the detail records is illustrated in Figure 7-46.

EXAMPLE

```
012060 B000-PROCESS-DETAIL-RECORDS.
012070
012080     IF LINES-PRINTED IS EQUAL TO PAGE-SIZE OR
012090        IS GREATER THAN (PAGE-SIZE OR
012100        FIRST-PAGE)
012110         PERFORM C000-PRINT-HEADINGS.
012120     MOVE SPACES TO PERSONNEL-REPORT-LINE.
012130     MOVE DATE-EMPLOYED-INPUT TO DATE-EMPLOYED-REPORT.
012140     MOVE NAME-INPUT TO NAME-REPORT.
012150     MOVE YEARS-EMPLOYED-INPUT TO YEARS-EMPLOYED-REPORT.
012160     IF EMPLOYEE-IS-A-GRADUATE
012170         MOVE GRADUATE-CONSTANT TO EDUCATION-REPORT
012180         IF YEARS-EMPLOYED-INPUT IS GREATER THAN TWO-YRS-CONSTANT
012190             MOVE SENIOR-PROG-CONSTANT TO CLASSIFICATION-REPORT
012200             ADD 1 TO SENIOR-PROGRAMMER-ACCUM
013010         ELSE
013020             MOVE PROGRAMMER-CONSTANT TO CLASSIFICATION-REPORT
013030             ADD 1 TO PROGRAMMER-ACCUM
013040     ELSE
013050         MOVE NON-GRADUATE-CONSTANT TO EDUCATION-REPORT
013060         IF YEARS-EMPLOYED-INPUT IS GREATER THAN THREE-YRS-CONSTANT
013070             MOVE PROGRAMMER-CONSTANT TO CLASSIFICATION-REPORT
013080             ADD 1 TO PROGRAMMER-ACCUM
013090         ELSE
013100             MOVE JUNIOR-PROG-CONSTANT TO CLASSIFICATION-REPORT
013110             ADD 1 TO JUNIOR-PROGRAMMER-ACCUM.
013120     WRITE PERSONNEL-REPORT-LINE
013130         AFTER PROPER-SPACING.
013140     ADD 1 TO LINES-PRINTED.
013150     MOVE SPACE-ONE-LINE TO PROPER-SPACING.
```

Figure 7-46 Detail Processing Module

In the example above, the coding on lines 012080, 012090, and 012100, check for the conditions upon which the headings will be printed on the report. Note that on line 012080 the number of lines which have been printed on the page are compared to the page size and if the number of lines printed are equal to or greater than the number of lines to be printed on the page, the heading module will be performed. The reason that the ''equal to or greater than'' condition is specified instead of just ''equal to'' is that in some programs, for example, where intermediate totals are printed, more than the number of lines specified in the page size may be printed. If the greater than test were not included, page overflow would not occur. Therefore, as a matter of convention, it is suggested that whenever page overflow is checked for, the test should be ''equal to or greater than.''

The Nested IF Statement on lines 012160 through 013110 is used to check the education and classification and follows the rules which were discussed previously for Nested IF Statements.

The Add Statement on line 013140 increments the line counter by one. It must always be remembered by the programmer that whenever page overflow is to be checked by counting the number of lines printed on a page, a statement must be included to increment the line counter by the number of lines which were printed. In the example, the report is single spaced, so the line counter is incremented by one. If the report is to be double spaced, the line counter should be incremented by 2 each time a line is printed.

The module which actually prints the headings on the report is illustrated below.

EXAMPLE

```
Ø15040  CØØØ-PRINT-HEADINGS.
Ø15050
Ø15060      MOVE PAGE-COUNT TO PAGE-NUMBER-HEADING.
Ø15070      MOVE CURRENT-DATE TO DATE-HEADING.
Ø15080      WRITE PERSONNEL-REPORT-LINE FROM FIRST-HEADING-LINE
Ø15090          AFTER ADVANCING TO-TOP-OF-PAGE.
Ø15100      WRITE PERSONNEL-REPORT-LINE FROM SECOND-HEADING-LINE
Ø15110          AFTER ADVANCING 2 LINES.
Ø15120      WRITE PERSONNEL-REPORT-LINE FROM THIRD-HEADING-LINE
Ø15130          AFTER ADVANCING 1 LINES.
Ø15140      ADD 1 TO PAGE-COUNT.
Ø15150      MOVE ZERO TO LINES-PRINTED.
Ø15160      MOVE SPACE-TWO-LINES TO PROPER-SPACING.
```

Figure 7-47 Example of Heading Module

Note on line 015060 that the value in the PAGE-COUNT field is moved to the PAGE-NUMBER-HEADING field. This places the page number in the heading.

On line 015070, the value in a field named CURRENT-DATE is moved to the DATE-HEADING field. The data-name CURRENT-DATE is a special data name available with many COBOL compilers which references the date stored in computer storage as a part of the operating system. This field cannot be defined within the COBOL program. Whenever the data-name CURRENT-DATE is referenced, it refers to an eight character field with the date stored in the format MM/DD/YY.

After the headings are printed, the page count is incremented by one and the number of lines printed counter (LINES-PRINTED) is set to zero. This is done so that the number of lines printed on the page will be counted properly. The spacing is then set for double spacing and the module is completed.

SAMPLE PROGRAM

The sample program prepares a Personnel Report. The output, input, and source listing of the sample program are illustrated on the following pages.

OUTPUT

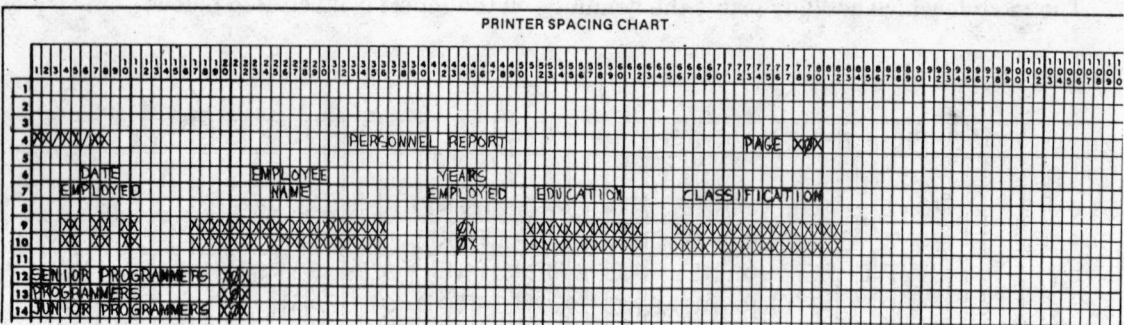

Figure 7-48 Personnel Report

INPUT

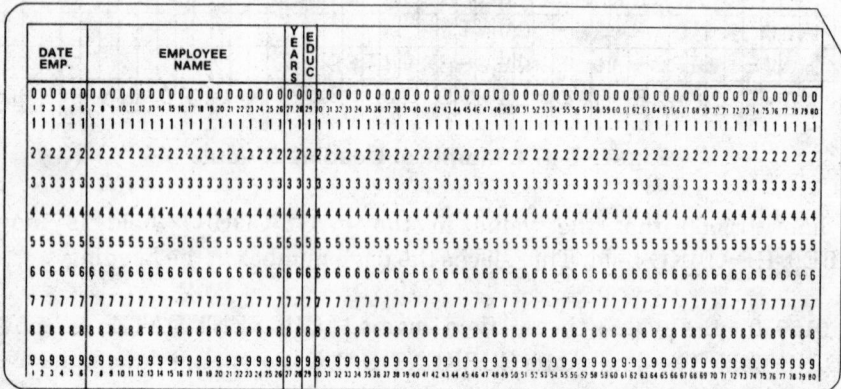

Figure 7-49 Input

Source Listing

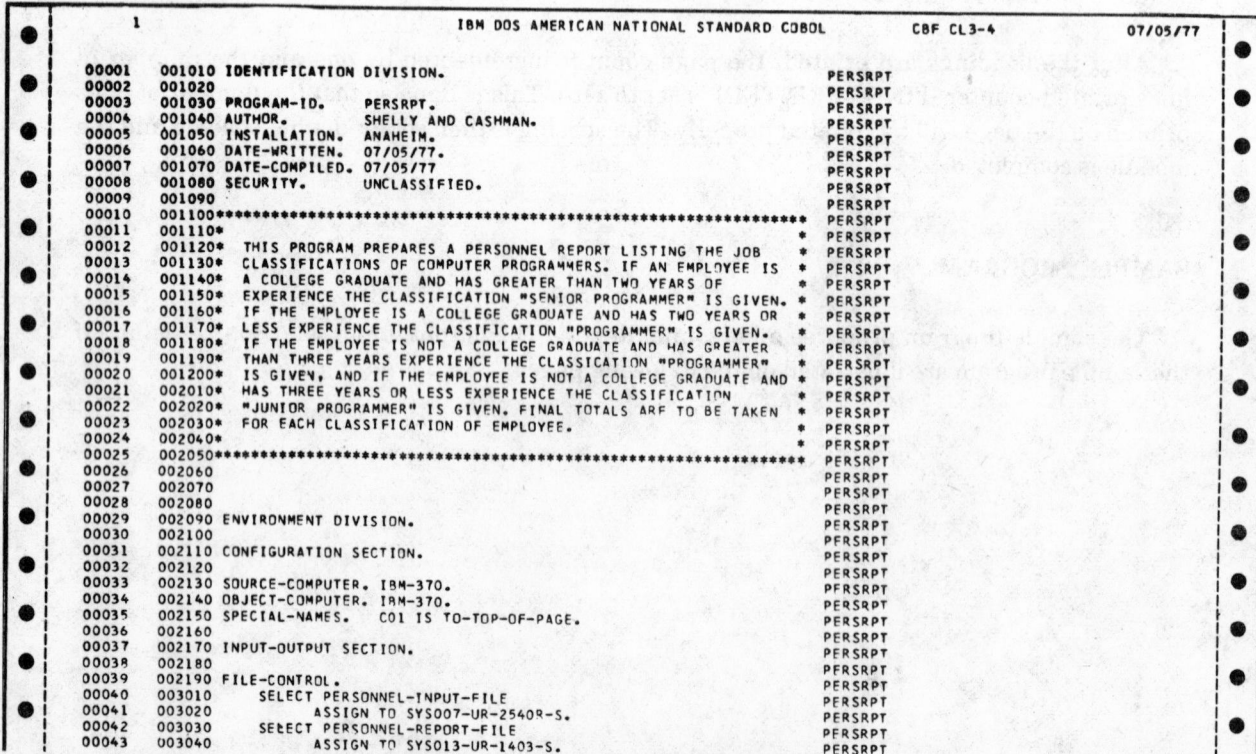

Figure 7-50 Source Listing [Part 1 of 4]

```
 2

00044  003060 DATA DIVISION.                                      PERSRPT
00045  003070                                                     PERSRPT
00046  003080 FILE SECTION.                                       PERSRPT
00047  003090                                                     PERSRPT
00048  003100 FD  PERSONNEL-INPUT-FILE                            PERSRPT
00049  003110     RECORD CONTAINS 80 CHARACTERS                   PERSRPT
00050  003120     LABEL RECORDS ARE OMITTED                       PERSRPT
00051  003130     DATA RECORD IS PERSONNEL-INPUT-RECORD.          PERSRPT
00052  003140 01  PERSONNEL-INPUT-RECORD.                         PERSRPT
00053  003150     05  DATE-EMPLOYED-INPUT      PIC X(6).          PERSRPT
00054  003160     05  NAME-INPUT               PIC X(20).         PERSRPT
00055  003170     05  YEARS-EMPLOYED-INPUT     PIC 99.            PERSRPT
00056  003180     05  EDUCATION-INPUT          PIC X.             PERSRPT
00057  003190         88  EMPLOYEE-IS-NOT-A-GRADUATE    VALUE 'N'. PERSRPT
00058  003200         88  EMPLOYEE-IS-A-GRADUATE        VALUE 'G'. PERSRPT
00059  004020     05  FILLER                   PIC X(51).         PERSRPT
00060  004030                                                     PERSRPT
00061  004040 FD  PERSONNEL-REPORT-FILE                           PERSRPT
00062  004050     RECORD CONTAINS 133 CHARACTERS                  PERSRPT
00063  004060     LABEL RECORDS ARE OMITTED                       PERSRPT
00064  004070     DATA RECORD IS PERSONNEL-REPORT-LINE.           PERSRPT
00065  004080 01  PERSONNEL-REPORT-LINE.                          PERSRPT
00066  004090     05  CARRIAGE-CONTROL         PIC X.             PERSRPT
00067  004100     05  FILLER                   PIC XXX.           PERSRPT
00068  004110     05  DATE-EMPLOYED-REPORT     PIC XXBXXBXX.      PERSRPT
00069  004120     05  FILLER                   PIC X(5).          PERSRPT
00070  004130     05  NAME-REPORT              PIC X(20).         PERSRPT
00071  004140     05  FILLER                   PIC X(7).          PERSRPT
00072  004150     05  YEARS-EMPLOYED-REPORT    PIC Z9.            PERSRPT
00073  004160     05  FILLER                   PIC X(5).          PERSRPT
00074  004170     05  EDUCATION-REPORT         PIC X(12).         PERSRPT
00075  004180     05  FILLER                   PIC XXX.           PERSRPT
00076  004190     05  CLASSIFICATION-REPORT    PIC X(17).         PERSRPT
00077  004200     05  FILLER                   PIC X(50).         PERSRPT
00078  005010                                                     PERSRPT
00079  005020 WORKING-STORAGE SECTION.                            PERSRPT
00080  005030                                                     PERSRPT
00081  005040 01  PROGRAM-INDICATORS.                             PERSRPT
00082  005050     05  ARE-THERE-MORE-RECORDS  PIC XXX   VALUE 'YES'. PERSRPT
00083  005060         88  THERE-IS-A-RECORD         VALUE 'YES'.  PERSRPT
00084  005070         88  THERE-ARE-NO-MORE-RECORDS VALUE 'NO '.  PERSRPT
00085  005080                                                     PERSRPT
00086  005090 01  PROGRAM-CONSTANTS.                              PERSRPT
00087  005100     05  PRINT-CONSTANTS.                            PERSRPT
00088  005110         10  GRADUATE-CONSTANT PIC X(12)   VALUE     PERSRPT
00089  005120             'GRADUATE    '.                         PERSRPT
00090  005130         10  NON-GRADUATE-CONSTANT PIC X(12) VALUE   PERSRPT
00091  005140             'NON-GRADUATE'.                         PERSRPT
00092  005150         10  SENIOR-PROG-CONSTANT PIC X(17) VALUE    PERSRPT
00093  005160             'SENIOR PROGRAMMER'.                    PERSRPT
00094  005170         10  PROGRAMMER-CONSTANT PIC X(17) VALUE     PERSRPT
00095  005180             'PROGRAMMER       '.                    PERSRPT
00096  005190         10  JUNIOR-PROG-CONSTANT PIC X(17) VALUE    PERSRPT
00097  005200             'JUNIOR PROGRAMMER'.                    PERSRPT
00098  006010     05  COMPARE-CONSTANTS.                          PERSRPT
00099  006020         10  TWO-YRS-CONSTANT    PIC 999  VALUE 2    PERSRPT
00100  006030             USAGE IS COMP-3.                        PERSRPT
00101  006040         10  THREE-YRS-CONSTANT  PIC 999  VALUE 3    PERSRPT
00102  006050             USAGE IS COMP-3.                        PERSRPT
00103  006060                                  USAGE IS COMP-3.   PERSRPT
00104  006070 01  TOTAL-ACCUMULATORS                              PERSRPT
00105  006080     05  SENIOR-PROGRAMMER-ACCUM PIC S999  VALUE ZERO. PERSRPT
00106  005090     05  PROGRAMMER-ACCUM        PIC S999  VALUE ZERO. PERSRPT
00107  006100     05  JUNIOR-PROGRAMMER-ACCUM PIC S999  VALUE ZERO. PERSRPT
00108  006110                                                     PERSRPT
00109  006120 01  PRINTER-CONTROL.                                PERSRPT
00110  006130     05  PROPER-SPACING          PIC 9.              PERSRPT
00111  006140     05  SPACE-ONE-LINE          PIC 9     VALUE 1.  PERSRPT
00112  006150     05  SPACE-TWO-LINES         PIC 9     VALUE 2.  PERSRPT
00113  006160     05  PAGE-COUNT              PIC S999  VALUE +1  PERSRPT
00114  006170                                 USAGE IS COMP-3.    PERSRPT
00115  006180         88  FIRST-PAGE                    VALUE +1. PERSRPT
00116  006190     05  PAGE-SIZE               PIC 999   VALUE 55  PERSRPT
00117  006200                                 USAGE IS COMP-3.    PERSRPT
00118  007010     05  LINES-PRINTED           PIC S999  VALUE ZERO PERSRPT
00119  007020                                 USAGE IS COMP-3.    PERSRPT
00120  007030                                                     PERSRPT
00121  007040 01  HEADING-LINES.                                  PERSRPT
00122  007050     05  FIRST-HEADING-LINE.                         PERSRPT
00123  007060         10  CARRIAGE-CONTROL    PIC X.              PERSRPT
00124  007070         10  DATE-HEADING        PIC X(8).           PERSRPT
00125  007080         10  FILLER              PIC X(24) VALUE SPACES. PERSRPT
00126  007090         10  FILLER              PIC X(16)           PERSRPT
00127  007100             'PERSONNEL REPORT'.                     PERSRPT
00128  007110         10  FILLER              PIC X(24) VALUE SPACES. PERSRPT
00129  007120         10  FILLER              PIC X(5)  VALUE 'PAGE '. PERSRPT
00130  007130         10  PAGE-NUMBER-HEADING PIC ZZ9.            PERSRPT
00131  007140         10  FILLER              PIC X(52) VALUE SPACES. PERSRPT
00132  007150     05  SECOND-HEADING-LINE.                        PERSRPT
00133  007160         10  CARRIAGE-CONTROL    PIC X.              PERSRPT
00134  007170         10  FILLER              PIC X(5)  VALUE SPACES. PERSRPT
00135  007180         10  FILLER              PIC X(4)  VALUE 'DATE'. PERSRPT
00136  007190         10  FILLER              PIC X(13) VALUE SPACES. PERSRPT
00137  007200         10  FILLER              PIC X(8)  VALUE 'EMPLOYEE'. PERSRPT
00138  008010         10  FILLER              PIC X(11) VALUE SPACES. PERSRPT
00139  008020         10  FILLER              PIC X(5)  VALUE 'YEARS'. PERSRPT
00140  008030         10  FILLER              PIC X(86) VALUE SPACES. PERSRPT
```

Figure 7-51 Source Listing [Part 2 of 4]

```
  3
00141  008040     05  THIRD-HEADING-LINE.                                PERSRPT
00142  008050         10  CARRIAGE-CONTROL    PIC X.                      PERSRPT
00143  008060         10  FILLER              PIC X(3)     VALUE SPACES.  PERSRPT
00144  008070         10  FILLER              PIC X(8)     VALUE 'EMPLOYED'. PERSRPT
00145  008080         10  FILLER              PIC X(13)    VALUE SPACES.  PERSRPT
00146  008090         10  FILLER              PIC X(4)     VALUE 'NAME'.  PERSRPT
00147  008100         10  FILLER              PIC X(12)    VALUE SPACES.  PERSRPT
00148  008110         10  FILLER              PIC X(8)     VALUE 'EMPLOYED'. PERSRPT
00149  008120         10  FILLER              PIC XXX      VALUE SPACES.  PERSRPT
00150  008130         10  FILLER              PIC X(9)     VALUE 'EDUCATION'. PERSRPT
00151  008140         10  FILLER              PIC X(6)     VALUE SPACES.  PERSRPT
00152  008150         10  FILLER              PIC X(14)    VALUE         PERSRPT
00153  008160                                              'CLASSIFICATION'. PERSRPT
00154  008170         10  FILLER              PIC X(52)    VALUE SPACES.  PERSRPT
00155  008180                                                            PERSRPT
00156  008190  01  TOTAL-LINES.                                          PERSRPT
00157  008200     05  FIRST-TOTAL-LINE.                                  PERSRPT
00158  009010         10  CARRIAGE-CONTROL    PIC X.                     PERSRPT
00159  009020         10  FILLER              PIC X(18)    VALUE         PERSRPT
00160  009030                                              'SENIOR PROGRAMMERS'. PERSRPT
00161  009040         10  FILLER              PIC X        VALUE SPACE.  PERSRPT
00162  009050         10  SENIOR-PROGRAMMER-TOTAL PIC ZZ9.               PERSRPT
00163  009060         10  FILLER              PIC X(110)   VALUE SPACES. PERSRPT
00164  009070     05  SECOND-TOTAL-LINE.                                 PERSRPT
00165  009080         10  CARRIAGE-CONTROL    PIC X.                     PERSRPT
00166  009090         10  FILLER              PIC X(18)    VALUE 'PROGRAMMERS'. PERSRPT
00167  009100         10  FILLER              PIC X        VALUE SPACE.  PERSRPT
00168  009110         10  PROGRAMMER-TOTAL    PIC ZZ9.                   PERSRPT
00169  009120         10  FILLER              PIC X(110)   VALUE SPACES. PERSRPT
00170  009130     05  THIRD-TOTAL-LINE.                                  PERSRPT
00171  009140         10  CARRIAGE-CONTROL    PIC X.                     PERSRPT
00172  009150         10  FILLER              PIC X(18)    VALUE         PERSRPT
00173  009160                                              'JUNIOR PROGRAMMERS'. PERSRPT
00174  009170         10  FILLER              PIC X        VALUE SPACE.  PERSRPT
00175  009180         10  JUNIOR-PROGRAMMER-TOTAL PIC ZZ9.               PERSRPT
00176  009190         10  FILLER              PIC X(110)   VALUE SPACES. PERSRPT
```

```
  4
00177  010010  PROCEDURE DIVISION.                                       PERSRPT
00178  010020                                                            PERSRPT
00179  010030  ******************************************************** PERSRPT
00180  010040  *                                                      * PERSRPT
00181  010050  *  THIS MODULE CONTROLS THE PROCESSING OF THE INPUT RECORDS, * PERSRPT
00182  010060  *  THE PRINTING OF THE REPORT, AND THE PRINTING OF THE FINAL * PERSRPT
00183  010070  *  TOTALS. IT IS ENTERED FROM THE OPERATING SYSTEM AND EXITS * PERSRPT
00184  010080  *  TO THE OPERATING SYSTEM.                             * PERSRPT
00185  010090  *                                                      * PERSRPT
00186  010100  ******************************************************** PERSRPT
00187  010110                                                            PERSRPT
00188  010120  A000-CREATE-PERSONNEL-REPORT.                            PERSRPT
00189  010130                                                            PERSRPT
00190  010140      OPEN INPUT  PERSONNEL-INPUT-FILE                     PERSRPT
00191  010150           OUTPUT PERSONNEL-REPORT-FILE.                   PERSRPT
00192  010160      READ PERSONNEL-INPUT-FILE                            PERSRPT
00193  010170          AT END                                           PERSRPT
00194  010180              MOVE 'NO ' TO ARE-THERE-MORE-RECORDS.        PERSRPT
00195  010190      IF THERE-IS-A-RECORD                                 PERSRPT
00196  010200          PERFORM A001-PROCESS-AND-READ                    PERSRPT
00197  011010              UNTIL THERE-ARE-NO-MORE-RECORDS              PERSRPT
00198  011020          PERFORM B010-PRINT-FINAL-TOTALS.                 PERSRPT
00199  011030      CLOSE PERSONNEL-INPUT-FILE                           PERSRPT
00200  011040            PERSONNEL-REPORT-FILE.                         PERSRPT
00201  011050      STOP RUN.                                            PERSRPT
00202  011060                                                            PERSRPT
00203  011070                                                            PERSRPT
00204  011080                                                            PERSRPT
00205  011090  A001-PROCESS-AND-READ.                                   PERSRPT
00206  011100                                                            PERSRPT
00207  011110      PERFORM B000-PROCESS-DETAIL-RECORDS.                 PERSRPT
00208  011120      READ PERSONNEL-INPUT-FILE                            PERSRPT
00209  011130          AT END                                           PERSRPT
00210  011140              MOVE 'NO ' TO ARE-THERE-MORE-RECORDS.        PERSRPT
```

Figure 7-52 Source Listing [Part 3 of 4]

```
    5
00211  011160********************************************************  PERSRPT
00212  011170*                                                      *  PERSRPT
00213  011180*  THIS MODULE CONTROLS THE PRINTING OF THE REPORT HEADING,  *  PERSRPT
00214  011190*  FORMATS THE REPORT, DETERMINES EDUCATION AND EMPLOYEE   *  PERSRPT
00215  011200*  CLASSIFICATION, AND ACCUMULATES TOTAL NUMBER OF EMPLOYEES IN*  PERSRPT
00216  012010*  EACH CLASSIFICATION.  IT IS ENTERED FROM AND EXITS TO THE  *  PERSRPT
00217  012020*  A000-CREATE-PERSONNEL-REPORT MODULE.                  *  PERSRPT
00218  012030*                                                      *  PERSRPT
00219  012040********************************************************  PERSRPT
00220  012050                                                          PERSRPT
00221  012060 B000-PROCESS-DETAIL-RECORDS.                            PERSRPT
00222  012070                                                          PERSRPT
00223  012080    IF LINES-PRINTED IS EQUAL TO PAGE-SIZE OR            PERSRPT
00224  012090       IS GREATER THAN PAGE-SIZE OR                      PERSRPT
00225  012100       FIRST-PAGE                                        PERSRPT
00226  012110       PERFORM C000-PRINT-HEADINGS.                      PERSRPT
00227  012120    MOVE SPACES TO PERSONNEL-REPORT-LINE.                PERSRPT
00228  012130    MOVE DATE-EMPLOYED-INPUT TO DATE-EMPLOYED-REPORT.    PERSRPT
00229  012140    MOVE NAME-INPUT TO NAME-REPORT.                      PERSRPT
00230  012150    MOVE YEARS-EMPLOYED-INPUT TO YEARS-EMPLOYED-REPORT.  PERSRPT
00231  012160    IF EMPLOYEE-IS-A-GRADUATE                            PERSRPT
00232  012170       MOVE GRADUATE-CONSTANT TO EDUCATION-REPORT        PERSRPT
00233  012180       IF YEARS-EMPLOYED-INPUT IS GREATER THAN TWO-YRS-CONSTANT  PERSRPT
00234  012190          MOVE SENIOR-PROG-CONSTANT TO CLASSIFICATION-REPORT  PERSRPT
00235  012200          ADD 1 TO SENIOR-PROGRAMMER-ACCUM              PERSRPT
00236  013010       ELSE                                             PERSRPT
00237  013020          MOVE PROGRAMMER-CONSTANT TO CLASSIFICATION-REPORT  PERSRPT
00238  013030          ADD 1 TO PROGRAMMER-ACCUM                     PERSRPT
00239  013040    ELSE                                                PERSRPT
00240  013050       MOVE NON-GRADUATE-CONSTANT TO EDUCATION-REPORT   PERSRPT
00241  013060       IF YEARS-EMPLOYED-INPUT IS GREATER THAN THREE-YRS-CONSTANT PERSRPT
00242  013070          MOVE PROGRAMMER-CONSTANT TO CLASSIFICATION-REPORT  PERSRPT
00243  013080          ADD 1 TO PROGRAMMER-ACCUM                     PERSRPT
00244  013090       ELSE                                             PERSRPT
00245  013100          MOVE JUNIOR-PROG-CONSTANT TO CLASSIFICATION-REPORT  PERSRPT
00246  013110          ADD 1 TO JUNIOR-PROGRAMMER-ACCUM.            PERSRPT
00247  013120    WRITE PERSONNEL-REPORT-LINE                         PERSRPT
00248  013130       AFTER PROPER-SPACING.                            PERSRPT
00249  013140    ADD 1 TO LINES-PRINTED.                             PERSRPT
00250  013150    MOVE SPACE-ONE-LINE TO PROPER-SPACING.              PERSRPT

    6
00251  013170********************************************************  PERSRPT
00252  013180*                                                      *  PERSRPT
00253  013190*  THIS MODULE PRINTS THE FINAL TOTALS. IT IS ENTERED FROM  *  PERSRPT
00254  013200*  AND EXITS TO THE A000-CREATE-PERSONNEL-REPORT MODULE.  *  PERSRPT
00255  014010*                                                      *  PERSRPT
00256  014020********************************************************  PERSRPT
00257  014030                                                          PERSRPT
00258  014040 B010-PRINT-FINAL-TOTALS.                               PERSRPT
00259  014050                                                          PERSRPT
00260  014060    MOVE SENIOR-PROGRAMMER-ACCUM TO SENIOR-PROGRAMMER-TOTAL.  PERSRPT
00261  014070    WRITE PERSONNEL-REPORT-LINE FROM FIRST-TOTAL-LINE   PERSRPT
00262  014080       AFTER ADVANCING 2 LINES.                         PERSRPT
00263  014090    MOVE PROGRAMMER-ACCUM TO PROGRAMMER-TOTAL.          PERSRPT
00264  014100    WRITE PERSONNEL-REPORT-LINE FROM SECOND-TOTAL-LINE  PERSRPT
00265  014110       AFTER ADVANCING 1 LINES.                         PERSRPT
00266  014120    MOVE JUNIOR-PROGRAMMER-ACCUM TO JUNIOR-PROGRAMMER-TOTAL.  PERSRPT
00267  014130    WRITE PERSONNEL-REPORT-LINE FROM THIRD-TOTAL-LINE   PERSRPT
00268  014140       AFTER ADVANCING 1 LINES.                         PERSRPT

    7
00269  014160********************************************************  PERSRPT
00270  014170*                                                      *  PERSRPT
00271  014180*  THIS MODULE PRINTS THE HEADINGS ON THE REPORT.  IT IS  *  PERSRPT
00272  014190*  ENTERED FROM AND EXITS TO THE B000-PROCESS-DETAIL-RECORDS  *  PERSRPT
00273  014200*  MODULE.                                             *  PERSRPT
00274  015010*                                                      *  PERSRPT
00275  015020********************************************************  PERSRPT
00276  015030                                                          PERSRPT
00277  015040 C000-PRINT-HEADINGS.                                   PERSRPT
00278  015050                                                          PERSRPT
00279  015060    MOVE PAGE-COUNT TO PAGE-NUMBER-HEADING.             PERSRPT
00280  015070    MOVE CURRENT-DATE TO DATE-HEADING.                  PERSRPT
00281  015080    WRITE PERSONNEL-REPORT-LINE FROM FIRST-HEADING-LINE  PERSRPT
00282  015090       AFTER ADVANCING TO-TOP-OF-PAGE.                  PERSRPT
00283  015100    WRITE PERSONNEL-REPORT-LINE FROM SECOND-HEADING-LINE  PERSRPT
00284  015110       AFTER ADVANCING 2 LINES.                         PERSRPT
00285  015120    WRITE PERSONNEL-REPORT-LINE FROM THIRD-HEADING-LINE  PERSRPT
00286  015130       AFTER ADVANCING 1 LINES.                         PERSRPT
00287  015140    ADD 1 TO PAGE-COUNT.                                PERSRPT
00288  015150    MOVE ZERO TO LINES-PRINTED.                         PERSRPT
00289  015160    MOVE SPACE-TWO-LINES TO PROPER-SPACING.             PERSRPT
```

Figure 7-53 Source Listing [Part 4 of 4]

CHAPTER 7

REVIEW QUESTIONS

1. What is meant by the term ''Nested IF Statements''?

2. Write the Nested IF Statement to perform the following:
   If the employee is a NEW-HIRE and production is greater than the MINIMUM-PRODUCTION, move BONUS-CONSTANT to MESSAGE-REPORT. If the employee is a NEW-HIRE and production is equal to or less than the MINIMUM-PRODUCTION, move NO-BONUS-CONSTANT to MESSAGE-REPORT. If the employee is not a NEW-HIRE, no special processing is to occur.

   If Emp equal New-Hire and prod is greater than min
   move Bon to mes-RP
   Else If Emp equal New-Hire and prod is equal to or is less than min move.

3. Write the Nested IF Statement to perform the following:
   If SINGLE, add ''1'' to SINGLE-ACCUMULATOR. IF MARRIED, add ''1'' to MARRIED-ACCUMULATOR, otherwise add ''1'' to DIVORCED-ACCUMULATOR.

   If Stn-in = Sen-Con
   add 1 to Sen-acc
   Else
   If married-in = mar-con
   add 1 to mar-accum
   Else add 1 to DW-accum.

4. Write the Nested IF Statement to perform the following:
   If an individual is MALE and age is OVER-25, multiply INSURANCE-AMOUNT by GOOD-RISK-RATE, storing the answer in AMOUNT-DUE. If the individual is a MALE and age is not OVER-25, multiply INSURANCE-AMOUNT by STANDARD-RATE, storing the answer in AMOUNT-DUE. If the individual is not MALE, multiply INSURANCE-AMOUNT by FEMALE-RATE, storing the answer in AMOUNT-DUE.

5. Design and write the Nested IF Statement to perform the following functions. Use Pseudocode Specifications and COBOL coding forms.

> If the employee works on the NIGHT-SHIFT, the field PAY-RATE is to be multiplied by 6%, storing the answer in PAY-INCREASE.
>
> If the employee works on the DAY-SHIFT, is a member of the UNION, and MONTHS-EMPLOYED is greater than 12, then the field PAY-RATE is to be multiplied by 6%, with the answer stored in PAY-INCREASE.
>
> If the employee works on the DAY-SHIFT, is a member of the UNION, and MONTHS-EMPLOYED is equal to or less than 12, then the field PAY-RATE is to be multiplied by 5%, with the answer stored in PAY-INCREASE.
>
> If the employee works on the DAY-SHIFT, is not a member of the UNION, and MONTHS-EMPLOYED is greater than 12, then the field PAY-RATE is to be multiplied by 5%, with the answer stored in PAY-INCREASE.
>
> If the employee works on the DAY-SHIFT, is not a member of the UNION, and MONTHS-EMPLOYED is equal to or less than 12, then the field PAY-RATE is to be multiplied by 4%, with the answer stored in PAY-INCREASE.

6. Design and write the Nested IF Statement to perform the following functions. Use Pseudocode Specifications and COBOL coding forms.

> IF the CUSTOMER-NUMBER-TRANS is equal to the CUSTOMER-NUMBER-MSTR and the QUANTITY-SOLD is less than or equal to the QUANTITY-ON-HAND, an invoice should be prepared; if the customer numbers are equal but the QUANTITY-SOLD is greater than the QUANTITY-ON-HAND, an invoice with the notation "backorder" should be prepared. The module to prepare a regular invoice is called C004-PREPARE-INVOICE and the module to prepare a backorder invoice is called C006-PREPARE-BACKORDER-INVOICE. In either case, if the customer numbers are equal, a record from the TRANSACTION-FILE should be read after the above processing is completed.
>
> If the CUSTOMER-NUMBER-TRANS is greater than the CUSTOMER-NUMBER-MSTR a master record should be read from the MASTER-FILE. If the CUSTOMER-NUMBER-TRANS is less than the CUSTOMER-NUMBER-MSTR, a record should be read from the TRANSACTION-FILE.

7. Design and write the Nested IF Statement to perform the following functions. Use Pseudocode Specifications and COBOL coding forms.

> If the company is in the FORTUNE-500 and is ISSUING-STOCK, then perform the D052-STOCK-PURCHASE module. If the company is in the FORTUNE-500 but is not ISSUING-STOCK, no further processing is necessary. If the company is not in the FORTUNE-500, but the PRICE-EARNINGS-RATIO-IS-GOOD and the company is ISSUING-STOCK, perform the D052-STOCK-PURCHASE module. If the PRICE-EARNINGS-RATIO-IS-GOOD but the company is not ISSUING-STOCK, perform the D053-STOCKS-TO-WATCH module.

8. Design and write the Nested IF Statement to perform the following functions. Use Pseudocode Specifications and COBOL coding forms.

> If a customer has PREFERRED-CREDIT-RATING and AMOUNT-PURCHASED-INPUT is less than $1,500.00, move the message "YOU HAVE REMAINING CREDIT WITH US" to INVOICE-MESSAGE-REPORT. If a customer has a PREFERRED-CREDIT-RATING and the AMOUNT-PURCHASED-INPUT is equal to or greater than $1,500.00, move the message "RETAIN YOUR PREFERRED STATUS — NET 45 DAYS" to INVOICE-MESSAGE-REPORT unless the AMOUNT-PURCHASED-INPUT is greater than $5,000.00. If it is, move the message "RETAIN YOUR PREFERRED STATUS — NET 20 DAYS" to INVOICE-MESSAGE-REPORT.

> If the customer has an ACCEPTABLE-CREDIT-RATING and the AMOUNT-PURCHASED-INPUT is less than or equal to $500.00, move the message "NET 30 DAYS" to INVOICE-MESSAGE-REPORT. IF the AMOUNT-PURCHASED-INPUT is greater than $500.00 but less than $1,500.00, move the message "NET 15 DAYS" to INVOICE-MESSAGE-REPORT. If the AMOUNT-PURCHASED-INPUT is equal to or greater than $1,500.00, move the message "PLEASE CONTACT CREDIT OFFICE" to INVOICE-MESSAGE-REPORT.

> If there is NO-CREDIT-RATING the message "PLEASE CONTACT CREDIT OFFICE" should be moved to INVOICE-MESSAGE-REPORT.

> In all cases except when a customer with an ACCEPTABLE-CREDIT-RATING has an AMOUNT-PURCHASED-INPUT equal to or greater than $1,500.00 or when there is NO-CREDIT-RATING, move the message "THANK YOU FOR YOUR BUSINESS" to COURTESY-MESSAGE-REPORT. Write the invoice for all customers by performing the D020-WRITE-INVOICE module.

CHAPTER 7

DEBUGGING COBOL PROGRAMS

PROBLEM 1

INSTRUCTIONS

The following COBOL program contains an error or errors which have occurred during execution. Circle each error and record the corrected entries directly on the listing. Explain the error and method of correction in the space provided.

```
                               IBM DOS AMERICAN NATIONAL STANDARD COBOL        CBF CL3-4        07/05/77
    1

00001   001010 IDENTIFICATION DIVISION.                                          PERSRPT
00002   001020                                                                   PERSRPT
00003   001030 PROGRAM-ID.      PERSRPT.                                         PERSRPT
00004   001040 AUTHOR.          SHELLY AND CASHMAN.                              PERSRPT
00005   001050 INSTALLATION.    ANAHEIM.                                         PERSRPT
00006   001060 DATE-WRITTEN.    07/05/77.                                        PERSRPT
00007   001070 DATE-COMPILED.   07/05/77                                         PERSRPT
00008   001080 SECURITY.        UNCLASSIFIED.                                    PERSRPT
00009   001090                                                                   PERSRPT
00010   001100***********************************************************  *     PERSRPT
00011   001110*                                                            *     PERSRPT
00012   001120*   THIS PROGRAM PREPARES A PERSONNEL REPORT LISTING THE JOB *     PERSRPT
00013   001130*   CLASSIFICATIONS OF COMPUTER PROGRAMMERS. IF AN EMPLOYEE IS *   PERSRPT
00014   001140*   A COLLEGE GRADUATE AND HAS GREATER THAN TWO YEARS OF      *     PERSRPT
00015   001150*   EXPERIENCE THE CLASSIFICATION "SENIOR PROGRAMMER" IS GIVEN. * PERSRPT
00016   001160*   IF THE EMPLOYEE IS A COLLEGE GRADUATE AND HAS TWO YEARS OR *   PERSRPT
00017   001170*   LESS EXPERIENCE THE CLASSIFICATION "PROGRAMMER" IS GIVEN. *     PERSRPT
00018   001180*   IF THE EMPLOYEE IS NOT A COLLEGE GRADUATE AND HAS GREATER *     PERSRPT
00019   001190*   THAN THREE YEARS EXPERIENCE THE CLASSICATION "PROGRAMMER" *     PERSRPT
00020   001200*   IS GIVEN, AND IF THE EMPLOYEE IS NOT A COLLEGE GRADUATE AND *  PERSRPT
00021   002010*   HAS THREE YEARS OR LESS EXPERIENCE THE CLASSIFICATION     *     PERSRPT
00022   002020*   "JUNIOR PROGRAMMER" IS GIVEN. FINAL TOTALS ARE TO BE TAKEN *   PERSRPT
00023   002030*   FOR EACH CLASSIFICATION OF EMPLOYEE.                      *     PERSRPT
00024   002040*                                                            *     PERSRPT
00025   002050***********************************************************  *     PERSRPT
00026   002060                                                                   PERSRPT
00027   002070                                                                   PERSRPT
00028   002080                                                                   PERSRPT
00029   002090 ENVIRONMENT DIVISION.                                             PERSRPT
00030   002100                                                                   PERSRPT
00031   002110 CONFIGURATION SECTION.                                            PERSRPT
00032   002120                                                                   PERSRPT
00033   002130 SOURCE-COMPUTER. IBM-370.                                         PERSRPT
00034   002140 OBJECT-COMPUTER. IBM-370.                                         PERSRPT
00035   002150 SPECIAL-NAMES.   C01 IS TO-TOP-OF-PAGE.                           PERSRPT
00036   002160                                                                   PERSRPT
00037   002170 INPUT-OUTPUT SECTION.                                             PERSRPT
00038   002180                                                                   PERSRPT
00039   002190 FILE-CONTROL.                                                     PERSRPT
00040   003010     SELECT PERSONNEL-INPUT-FILE                                   PERSRPT
00041   003020         ASSIGN TO SYS007-UR-2540R-S.                              PERSRPT
00042   003030     SELECT PERSONNEL-REPORT-FILE                                  PERSRPT
00043   003040         ASSIGN TO SYS013-UR-1403-S.                               PERSRPT
```

```
    2

00044   003060 DATA DIVISION.                                                    PERSRPT
00045   003070                                                                   PERSRPT
00046   003080 FILE SECTION.                                                     PERSRPT
00047   003090                                                                   PERSRPT
00048   003100 FD  PERSONNEL-INPUT-FILE                                          PERSRPT
00049   003110     RECORD CONTAINS 80 CHARACTERS                                 PERSRPT
00050   003120     LABEL RECORDS ARE OMITTED                                     PERSRPT
00051   003130     DATA RECORD IS PERSONNEL-INPUT-RECORD.                        PERSRPT
00052   003140 01  PERSONNEL-INPUT-RECORD.                                       PERSRPT
00053   003150     05  DATE-EMPLOYED-INPUT      PIC X(6).                        PERSRPT
00054   003160     05  NAME-INPUT               PIC X(20).                       PERSRPT
00055   003170     05  YEARS-EMPLOYED-INPUT     PIC 99.                          PERSRPT
00056   003180     05  EDUCATION-INPUT          PIC X.                           PERSRPT
00057   003190         88  EMPLOYEE-IS-NOT-A-GRADUATE    VALUE 'N'.              PERSRPT
00058   003200         88  EMPLOYEE-IS-A-GRADUATE        VALUE 'G'.              PERSRPT
00059   004020     05  FILLER                   PIC X(51).                       PERSRPT
00060   004030                                                                   PERSRPT
```

```
3
00061  004040 FD  PERSONNEL-REPORT-FILE                              PERSRPT
00062  004050       RECORD CONTAINS 133 CHARACTERS                   PERSRPT
00063  004060       LABEL RECORDS ARE OMITTED                        PERSRPT
00064  004070       DATA RECORD IS PERSONNEL-REPORT-LINE.            PERSRPT
00065  004080 01  PERSONNEL-REPORT-LINE.                             PERSRPT
00066  004090     05  CARRIAGE-CONTROL       PIC X.                  PERSRPT
00067  004100     05  FILLER                 PIC XXX.                PERSRPT
00068  004110     05  DATE-EMPLOYED-REPORT   PIC XX8XX8XX.           PERSRPT
00069  004120     05  FILLER                 PIC X(5).               PERSRPT
00070  004130     05  NAME-REPORT            PIC X(20).              PERSRPT
00071  004140     05  FILLER                 PIC X(7).               PERSRPT
00072  004150     05  YEARS-EMPLOYED-REPORT  PIC Z9.                 PERSRPT
00073  004160     05  FILLER                 PIC X(5).               PERSRPT
00074  004170     05  EDUCATION-REPORT       PIC X(12).              PERSRPT
00075  004180     05  FILLER                 PIC XXX.                PERSRPT
00076  004190     05  CLASSIFICATION-REPORT  PIC X(17).              PERSRPT
00077  004200     05  FILLER                 PIC X(50).              PERSRPT
00078  005010                                                       PERSRPT
00079  005020 WORKING-STORAGE SECTION.                              PERSRPT
00080  005030                                                       PERSRPT
00081  005040 01  PROGRAM-INDICATORS.                               PERSRPT
00082  005050     05  ARE-THERE-MORE-RECORDS PIC XXX    VALUE 'YES'. PERSRPT
00083  005060         88  THERE-IS-A-RECORD             VALUE 'YES'. PERSRPT
00084  005070         88  THERE-ARE-NO-MORE-RECORDS     VALUE 'NO '. PERSRPT
00085  005080                                                       PERSRPT
00086  005090 01  PROGRAM-CONSTANTS.                                PERSRPT
00087  005100     05  PRINT-CONSTANTS.                              PERSRPT
00088  005110         10  GRADUATE-CONSTANT PIC X(12)  VALUE        PERSRPT
00089  005120                             'GRADUATE    '.           PERSRPT
00090  005130         10  NON-GRADUATE-CONSTANT PIC X(12) VALUE     PERSRPT
00091  005140                             'NON-GRADUATE'.           PERSRPT
00092  005150         10  SENIOR-PROG-CONSTANT PIC X(17) VALUE      PERSRPT
00093  005160                             'SENIOR PROGRAMMER'.      PERSRPT
00094  005170         10  PROGRAMMER-CONSTANT PIC X(17) VALUE       PERSRPT
00095  005180                             'PROGRAMMER       '.      PERSRPT
00096  005190         10  JUNIOR-PROG-CONSTANT PIC X(17) VALUE      PERSRPT
00097  005200                             'JUNIOR PROGRAMMER'.      PERSRPT
00098  006010     05  COMPARE-CONSTANTS.                            PERSRPT
00099  006020         10  TWO-YRS-CONSTANT   PIC 999  VALUE 2       PERSRPT
00100  006030                                         USAGE IS COMP-3. PERSRPT
00101  006040         10  THREE-YRS-CONSTANT PIC 999  VALUE 3       PERSRPT
00102  006050                                         USAGE IS COMP-3. PERSRPT
00103  006060                                                       PERSRPT
00104  006070 01  TOTAL-ACCUMULATORS                  USAGE IS COMP-3. PERSRPT
00105  006080     05  SENIOR-PROGRAMMER-ACCUM PIC S999 VALUE ZERO.  PERSRPT
00106  006090     05  PROGRAMMER-ACCUM        PIC S999 VALUE ZERO.  PERSRPT
00107  006100     05  JUNIOR-PROGRAMMER-ACCUM PIC S999 VALUE ZERO.  PERSRPT
00108  006110                                                       PERSRPT
00109  006120 01  PRINTER-CONTROL.                                  PERSRPT
00110  006130     05  PROPER-SPACING     PIC 9.                     PERSRPT
00111  006140     05  SPACE-ONE-LINE     PIC 9    VALUE 1.          PERSRPT
00112  006150     05  SPACE-TWO-LINES    PIC 9    VALUE 2.          PERSRPT
00113  006160     05  PAGE-COUNT         PIC S999 VALUE +1          PERSRPT
00114  006170                                     USAGE IS COMP-3.  PERSRPT
00115  006180         88  FIRST-PAGE              VALUE +1.         PERSRPT
00116  006190     05  PAGE-SIZE          PIC 999  VALUE 55          PERSRPT
00117  006200                                     USAGE IS COMP-3.  PERSRPT
00118  007010     05  LINES-PRINTED      PIC S999 VALUE ZERO        PERSRPT
00119  007020                                     USAGE IS COMP-3.  PERSRPT
00120  007030                                                       PERSRPT
00121  007040 01  HEADING-LINES.                                    PERSRPT
00122  007050     05  FIRST-HEADING-LINE.                           PERSRPT
00123  007060         10  CARRIAGE-CONTROL   PIC X.                 PERSRPT
00124  007070         10  DATE-HEADING       PIC X(8).              PERSRPT
00125  007080         10  FILLER             PIC X(24) VALUE SPACES. PERSRPT
00126  007090         10  FILLER             PIC X(16) VALUE        PERSRPT
00127  007100                             'PERSONNEL REPORT'.       PERSRPT
00128  007110         10  FILLER             PIC X(24) VALUE SPACES. PERSRPT
00129  007120         10  FILLER             PIC X(5)  VALUE 'PAGE '. PERSRPT
00130  007130         10  PAGE-NUMBER-HEADING PIC ZZ9.              PERSRPT
00131  007140         10  FILLER             PIC X(52) VALUE SPACES. PERSRPT
00132  007150     05  SECOND-HEADING-LINE.                          PERSRPT
00133  007160         10  CARRIAGE-CONTROL   PIC X.                 PERSRPT
00134  007170         10  FILLER             PIC X(5)  VALUE SPACES. PERSRPT
00135  007180         10  FILLER             PIC X(4)  VALUE 'DATE'. PERSRPT
00136  007190         10  FILLER             PIC X(13) VALUE SPACES. PERSRPT
00137  007200         10  FILLER             PIC X(8)  VALUE 'EMPLOYEE'. PERSRPT
00138  008010         10  FILLER             PIC X(11) VALUE SPACES. PERSRPT
00139  008020         10  FILLER             PIC X(5)  VALUE 'YEARS'. PERSRPT
00140  008030         10  FILLER             PIC X(86) VALUE SPACES. PERSRPT
00141  008040     05  THIRD-HEADING-LINE.                           PERSRPT
00142  008050         10  CARRIAGE-CONTROL   PIC X.                 PERSRPT
00143  008060         10  FILLER             PIC X(3)  VALUE SPACES. PERSRPT
00144  008070         10  FILLER             PIC X(8)  VALUE 'EMPLOYED'. PERSRPT
00145  008080         10  FILLER             PIC X(13) VALUE SPACES. PERSRPT
00146  008090         10  FILLER             PIC X(4)  VALUE 'NAME'. PERSRPT
00147  008100         10  FILLER             PIC X(12) VALUE SPACES. PERSRPT
00148  008110         10  FILLER             PIC X(8)  VALUE 'EMPLOYED'. PERSRPT
00149  008120         10  FILLER             PIC XXX   VALUE SPACES. PERSRPT
00150  008130         10  FILLER             PIC X(9)  VALUE 'EDUCATION'. PERSRPT
00151  008140         10  FILLER             PIC X(6)  VALUE SPACES. PERSRPT
00152  008150         10  FILLER             PIC X(14) VALUE        PERSRPT
00153  008160                             'CLASSIFICATION'.         PERSRPT
00154  008170         10  FILLER             PIC X(52) VALUE SPACES. PERSRPT
00155  008180                                                       PERSRPT
00156  008190 01  TOTAL-LINES.                                      PERSRPT
00157  008200     05  FIRST-TOTAL-LINE.                             PERSRPT
```

```
    4
00158   009010        10  CARRIAGE-CONTROL    PIC X.                          PERSRPT
00159   009020        10  FILLER              PIC X(18)    VALUE              PERSRPT
00160   009030                                         'SENIOR PROGRAMMERS'.PERSRPT
00161   009040        10  FILLER              PIC X        VALUE SPACE.       PERSRPT
00162   009050        10  SENIOR-PROGRAMMER-TOTAL PIC ZZ9.                    PERSRPT
00163   009060        10  FILLER              PIC X(110)   VALUE SPACES.      PERSRPT
00164   009070     05  SECOND-TOTAL-LINE.                                     PERSRPT
00165   009080        10  CARRIAGE-CONTROL    PIC X.                          PERSRPT
00166   009090        10  FILLER              PIC X(18)    VALUE 'PROGRAMMERS'.PERSRPT
00167   009100        10  FILLER              PIC X        VALUE SPACE.       PERSRPT
00168   009110        10  PROGRAMMER-TOTAL    PIC ZZ9.                        PERSRPT
00169   009120        10  FILLER              PIC X(110)   VALUE SPACES.      PERSRPT
00170   009130     05  THIRD-TOTAL-LINE.                                      PERSRPT
00171   009140        10  CARRIAGE-CONTROL    PIC X.                          PERSRPT
00172   009150        10  FILLER              PIC X(18)    VALUE              PERSRPT
00173   009160                                         'JUNIOR PROGRAMMERS'.PERSRPT
00174   009170        10  FILLER              PIC X        VALUE SPACE.       PERSRPT
00175   009180        10  JUNIOR-PROGRAMMER-TOTAL PIC ZZ9.                    PERSRPT
00176   009190        10  FILLER              PIC X(110)   VALUE SPACES.      PERSRPT
```

```
    5
00177   010010 PROCEDURE DIVISION.                                            PERSRPT
00178   010020                                                                PERSRPT
00179   010030***********************************************************    PERSRPT
00180   010040*                                                          *    PERSRPT
00181   010050*   THIS MODULE CONTROLS THE PROCESSING OF THE INPUT RECORDS, * PERSRPT
00182   010060*   THE PRINTING OF THE REPORT, AND THE PRINTING OF THE FINAL * PERSRPT
00183   010070*   TOTALS. IT IS ENTERED FROM THE OPERATING SYSTEM AND EXITS * PERSRPT
00184   010080*   TO THE OPERATING SYSTEM.                                  * PERSRPT
00185   010090*                                                          *    PERSRPT
00186   010100***********************************************************    PERSRPT
00187   010110                                                                PERSRPT
00188   010120 A000-CREATE-PERSONNEL-REPORT.                                  PERSRPT
00189   010130                                                                PERSRPT
00190   010140        OPEN INPUT  PERSONNEL-INPUT-FILE                        PERSRPT
00191   010150             OUTPUT PERSONNEL-REPORT-FILE.                      PERSRPT
00192   010160        READ PERSONNEL-INPUT-FILE                              PERSRPT
00193   010170            AT END                                             PERSRPT
00194   010180                MOVE 'NO ' TO ARE-THERE-MORE-RECORDS.          PERSRPT
00195   010190        IF THERE-IS-A-RECORD                                    PERSRPT
00196   010200            PERFORM A001-PROCESS-AND-READ                       PERSRPT
00197   011010                UNTIL THERE-ARE-NO-MORE-RECORDS.                PERSRPT
00198   011020            PERFORM B010-PRINT-FINAL-TOTALS.                    PERSRPT
00199   011030        CLOSE PERSONNEL-INPUT-FILE                              PERSRPT
00200   011040              PERSONNEL-REPORT-FILE.                            PERSRPT
00201   011050        STOP RUN.                                               PERSRPT
00202   011060                                                                PERSRPT
00203   011070                                                                PERSRPT
00204   011080                                                                PERSRPT
00205   011090 A001-PROCESS-AND-READ.                                         PERSRPT
00206   011100                                                                PERSRPT
00207   011110        PERFORM B000-PROCESS-DETAIL-RECORDS.                    PERSRPT
00208   011120        READ PERSONNEL-INPUT-FILE                              PERSRPT
00209   011130            AT END                                             PERSRPT
00210   011140                MOVE 'NO ' TO ARE-THERE-MORE-RECORDS.          PERSRPT
```

```
    6
00211   011160***********************************************************    PERSRPT
00212   011170*                                                          *    PERSRPT
00213   011180*   THIS MODULE CONTROLS THE PRINTING OF THE REPORT HEADING, * PERSRPT
00214   011190*   FORMATS THE REPORT, DETERMINES EDUCATION AND EMPLOYEE    * PERSRPT
00215   011200*   CLASSIFICATION, AND ACCUMULATES TOTAL NUMBER OF EMPLOYEES IN* PERSRPT
00216   012010*   EACH CLASSIFICATION.  IT IS ENTERED FROM AND EXITS TO THE * PERSRPT
00217   012020*   A000-CREATE-PERSONNEL-REPORT MODULE.                      * PERSRPT
00218   012030*                                                          *    PERSRPT
00219   012040***********************************************************    PERSRPT
00220   012050                                                                PERSRPT
00221   012060 B000-PROCESS-DETAIL-RECORDS.                                   PERSRPT
00222   012070                                                                PERSRPT
00223   012080        IF LINES-PRINTED IS EQUAL TO PAGE-SIZE OR               PERSRPT
00224   012090             IS GREATER THAN PAGE-SIZE OR                       PERSRPT
00225   012100             FIRST-PAGE                                         PERSRPT
00226   012110        PERFORM C000-PRINT-HEADINGS                             PERSRPT
00227   012120        MOVE SPACES TO PERSONNEL-REPORT-LINE.                   PERSRPT
00228   012130        MOVE DATE-EMPLOYED-INPUT TO DATE-EMPLOYED-REPORT.       PERSRPT
00229   012140        MOVE NAME-INPUT TO NAME-REPORT.                         PERSRPT
00230   012150        MOVE YEARS-EMPLOYED-INPUT TO YEARS-EMPLOYED-REPORT.     PERSRPT
00231   012160        IF EMPLOYEE-IS-A-GRADUATE                               PERSRPT
00232   012170            MOVE GRADUATE-CONSTANT TO EDUCATION-REPORT          PERSRPT
00233   012180            IF YEARS-EMPLOYED-INPUT IS GREATER THAN TWO-YRS-CONSTANT PERSRPT
00234   012190                MOVE SENIOR-PROG-CONSTANT TO CLASSIFICATION-REPORT PERSRPT
00235   012200                ADD 1 TO SENIOR-PROGRAMMER-ACCUM                PERSRPT
00236   013010            ELSE                                                PERSRPT
00237   013020                MOVE PROGRAMMER-CONSTANT TO CLASSIFICATION-REPORT PERSRPT
00238   013030                ADD 1 TO PROGRAMMER-ACCUM                       PERSRPT
00239   013040        ELSE                                                    PERSRPT
00240   013050            MOVE NON-GRADUATE-CONSTANT TO EDUCATION-REPORT      PERSRPT
00241   013060            IF YEARS-EMPLOYED-INPUT IS GREATER THAN THREE-YRS-CONSTANT PERSRPT
00242   013070                MOVE PROGRAMMER-CONSTANT TO CLASSIFICATION-REPORT PERSRPT
00243   013080                ADD 1 TO PROGRAMMER-ACCUM                       PERSRPT
00244   013090            ELSE                                                PERSRPT
00245   013100                MOVE JUNIOR-PROG-CONSTANT TO CLASSIFICATION-REPORT. PERSRPT
00246   013110                ADD 1 TO JUNIOR-PROGRAMMER-ACCUM.               PERSRPT
00247   013120        WRITE PERSONNEL-REPORT-LINE                             PERSRPT
00248   013130            AFTER PROPER-SPACING.                               PERSRPT
00249   013140        ADD 1 TO LINES-PRINTED.                                 PERSRPT
00250   013150        MOVE SPACE-ONE-LINE TO PROPER-SPACING.                  PERSRPT
```

```
        7
00251  013170******************************************************  PERSRPT
00252  013180*                                                    *  PERSRPT
00253  013190*  THIS MODULE PRINTS THE FINAL TOTALS. IT IS ENTERED FROM  *  PERSRPT
00254  013200*  AND EXITS TO THE A000-CREATE-PERSONNEL-REPORT MODULE.    *  PERSRPT
00255  014010*                                                    *  PERSRPT
00256  014020******************************************************  PERSRPT
00257  014030                                                        PERSRPT
00258  014040  B010-PRINT-FINAL-TOTALS.                              PERSRPT
00259  014050                                                        PERSRPT
00260  014060      MOVE SENIOR-PROGRAMMER-ACCUM TO SENIOR-PROGRAMMER-TOTAL.  PERSRPT
00261  014070      WRITE PERSONNEL-REPORT-LINE FROM FIRST-TOTAL-LINE  PERSRPT
00262  014080          AFTER ADVANCING 2 LINES.                      PERSRPT
00263  014090      MOVE PROGRAMMER-ACCUM TO PROGRAMMER-TOTAL.        PERSRPT
00264  014100      WRITE PERSONNEL-REPORT-LINE FROM SECOND-TOTAL-LINE  PERSRPT
00265  014110          AFTER ADVANCING 1 LINES.                      PERSRPT
00266  014120      MOVE JUNIOR-PROGRAMMER-ACCUM TO JUNIOR-PROGRAMMER-TOTAL.  PERSRPT
00267  014130      WRITE PERSONNEL-REPORT-LINE FROM THIRD-TOTAL-LINE  PERSRPT
00268  014140          AFTER ADVANCING 1 LINES.                      PERSRPT
```

```
        8
00269  014160******************************************************  PERSRPT
00270  014170*                                                    *  PERSRPT
00271  014180*  THIS MODULE PRINTS THE HEADINGS ON THE REPORT.  IT IS  *  PERSRPT
00272  014190*  ENTERED FROM AND EXITS TO THE B000-PROCESS-DETAIL-RECORDS  *  PERSRPT
00273  014200*  MODULE.                                            *  PERSRPT
00274  015010*                                                    *  PERSRPT
00275  015020******************************************************  PERSRPT
00276  015030                                                        PERSRPT
00277  015040  C000-PRINT-HEADINGS.                                  PERSRPT
00278  015050                                                        PERSRPT
00279  015060      MOVE PAGE-COUNT TO PAGE-NUMBER-HEADING.           PERSRPT
00280  015070      MOVE CURRENT-DATE TO DATE-HEADING.                PERSRPT
00281  015080      WRITE PERSONNEL-REPORT-LINE FROM FIRST-HEADING-LINE  PERSRPT
00282  015090          AFTER ADVANCING TO-TOP-OF-PAGE.               PERSRPT
00283  015100      WRITE PERSONNEL-REPORT-LINE FROM SECOND-HEADING-LINE  PERSRPT
00284  015110          AFTER ADVANCING 2 LINES.                      PERSRPT
00285  015120      WRITE PERSONNEL-REPORT-LINE FROM THIRD-HEADING-LINE  PERSRPT
00286  015130          AFTER ADVANCING 1 LINES.                      PERSRPT
00287  015140      ADD 1 TO PAGE-COUNT.                              PERSRPT
00288  015150      MOVE ZERO TO LINES-PRINTED.                       PERSRPT
00289  015160      MOVE SPACE-TWO-LINES TO PROPER-SPACING.           PERSRPT
```

```
07/05/77                    PERSONNEL REPORT                    PAGE  1

    DATE              EMPLOYEE         YEARS
  EMPLOYED              NAME         EMPLOYED   EDUCATION       CLASSIFICATION

  04 25 76      JONES, ARLAN C.          1      GRADUATE       PROGRAMMER
  04 25 75      LOVERLY, ABBIE J.    EMP 2YED   GRADUATE       PROGRAMMER
  04 25 74      MANLY, CECLIA A.         3      GRADUATE       SENIOR PROGRAMMER
  03 02 73      HAMM, JAMES C.       EMP 4YED   GRADUATE       SENIOR PROGRAMMER
  04 25 76      OSSIE, JULIE C.          1      NON-GRADUATE   JUNIOR PROGRAMMER
  04 25 75      PRINZ, JIM C.        EMP 2YED   NON-GRADUATE   JUNIOR PROGRAMMER
  04 25 74      RADEN, THOMAS G.         3      NON-GRADUATE   JUNIOR PROGRAMMER
  01 12 73      SAMS, SALLY U.       EMP 4YED   NON-GRADUATE   PROGRAMMER

SENIOR PROGRAMMERS    2
PROGRAMMERS           3
JUNIOR PROGRAMMERS    8
```

EXPLANATION

CHAPTER 7

PROGRAMMING ASSIGNMENT 1

INSTRUCTIONS

An Accounts Receivable Summary Report is to be prepared. Write the COBOL program to prepare the report. An IPO Chart and Pseudocode Specifications should be used when designing the program. Use Test Data Set 2 in Appendix A.

INPUT

Input is to consist of Accounts Receivable Cards that contain the Customer Name, the Quantity Purchased, the Item Number, the Unit Price, and the Discount Code. The format of the cards is illustrated below.

OUTPUT

Output is to consist of an Accounts Receivable Summary Report. The Sales Amount is to be calculated by multiplying the Quantity Purchased by the Unit Price. If there is a Discount Code "D" in card column 80, the customer is to receive a discount. If the Sales Amount is equal to or greater than $500.00, a 20% discount is given. If the Sales Amount is less than $500.00, a 15% discount is given. If there is no Discount Code in card column 80, no discount is given. Net Amount is calculated by subtracting the Discount Amount from the Sales Amount. After all cards have been processed, the Total Number of Customers and the Total Net Amount are to be printed. The maximum number of detail lines on one page is 40 lines.

CHAPTER 7

PROGRAMMING ASSIGNMENT 2

INSTRUCTIONS

A Payroll Register is to be prepared. Write the COBOL program to prepare the report. An IPO Chart and Pseudocode Specifications should be used when designing the program. Use Test Data Set 1 in Appendix A.

INPUT

Input is to consist of Payroll Cards that contain a Pay Code, an Employee Number, an Employee Name, the Rate of Pay, the Hours Worked, and a Weekly Salary Field. A Pay Code of "1" indicates an Hourly Employee. With Hourly Employees, the Weekly Salary field will be blank. A Pay Code of "2" indicates a Salaried Employee. For Salaried Employees, the Rate of Pay field and the Hours Worked field will be blank. The format of the input cards is illustrated below.

INPUT

OUTPUT

Output is to consist of a Payroll Register listing Gross Pay of all employees. If an employee is an Hourly Employee (Pay Code "1") and works 40 hours or less, Gross Pay is calculated by multiplying the Hours Worked by the Pay Rate. If an Employee is an Hourly Employee (Pay Code "1") and works more than 40 hours per week, the hours above 40 are paid at time and one half, that is, 1.5 times the overtime hours. For salaried employees (Pay Code "2"), the Weekly Salary (card columns 61-66 on the input record) is the Gross Pay. Employees are to be identified as Hourly or Salaried employees on the report. After all records have been processed, the total number of Hourly employees, the total number of Salaried Employees and the total Gross Pay is to be printed. The maximum number of detail lines on one page is 40 lines.

CHAPTER 7

PROGRAMMING ASSIGNMENT 3

INSTRUCTIONS

A Salesman Report is to be prepared. Write the COBOL program to prepare the required report. An IPO Chart and Pseudocode Specifications should be used when designing the program. Use Test Data Set 1 in Appendix A.

INPUT

Input consists of Sales Cards containing the Salesman Number, the Salesman Name, the Months Employed, and the Sales Amount. The format of the cards is illustrated below.

OUTPUT

Output is to consist of a Salesman Report listing the commission paid to each salesman.

If a salesman is a trainee, that is, is employed from one to six months, the sales quota is $5,000.00. For trainee salesmen, a 10% Commission is paid if the sales are greater than the $5,000.00 quota. For a trainee salesman with sales equal to or less than $5,000.00, a 6% Commission is paid. The Commission is calculated by multiplying the Sales Amount by the appropriate Commission percentage.

If a salesman is "experienced", that is, has been employed longer than six months, the quota is $10,000.00. For experienced salesmen with sales above the $10,000.00 quota, a 12% Commission is paid. For experienced salesmen with sales equal to or less than $10,000.00, a 7% Commission is paid. The commission is calculated in the same manner as for trainee salesmen.

The format of the output report is illustrated on the following page. Note that the message "ABOVE QUOTA" or "BELOW QUOTA" is to be printed for each salesman. In addition, after all the cards have been processed, totals are to be taken of all trainee salesmen and experienced salesmen above and below quotas. The maximum number of detail lines on one page is 40 lines.

PRINTER SPACING CHART

| | 1 2 3 4 5 6 7 8 9 10 | 11 12 13 14 15 16 17 18 19 20 | 21 22 23 24 25 26 27 28 29 30 | 31 32 33 34 35 36 37 38 39 40 | 41 42 43 44 45 46 47 48 49 50 | 51 52 53 54 55 56 57 58 59 60 | 61 62 63 64 65 66 67 68 69 70 | 71 72 73 74 75 76 77 78 79 80 | 81 82 83 84 85 86 87 88 89 90 | 91 92 93 94 95 96 97 98 99 100 | 101 102 |

Row	Content
1	
2	
3	XX/XX/XX .... SALESMAN REPORT .... PAGE XØX
4	
5	S/M .... SALESMAN .... MON. MONTHLY .... COMM.
6	NO. NAME EMP. SALES PCT. COMMISSION .... MESSAGE
7	
8	XXØX XXXXXXXXXXXXXXXXXXXXXXXX .. ØX .. XX,XXØ.XX .. ØX% .. X,XXØ.XX .. ABOVE QUOTA
9	XXØX XXXXXXXXXXXXXXXXXXXXXXXX ØX XX,XXØ.XX ØX% X,XXØ.XX BELOW QUOTA
10	
11	TRAINEE SALESMEN
12	ABOVE QUOTA ØX
13	BELOW QUOTA ØX
14	
15	EXPERIENCED SALESMEN
16	ABOVE QUOTA ØX
17	BELOW QUOTA ØX
18	
19	

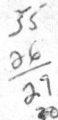

35
26
29
30

CHAPTER 7

PROGRAMMING ASSIGNMENT 4

INSTRUCTIONS

A Property Tax Report is to be prepared. Write the COBOL program to prepare the report. An IPO Chart and Pseudocode Specifications should be used when designing the report. Use Test Data Set 1 in Appendix A.

INPUT

Input is to consist of Property Tax Cards. The card consists of the Property Type field, which indicates the type of property owned (1 = Home; 2 = Commercial Property); the Name of the property owner; the Home Type field (0 = Non-Residence, 1 = Residence); the Commercial Property type (0 = Commercial Land; 1 = Commercial Building); the Tract Parcel Number; and the Assessed Value.

OUTPUT

The output consists of a Property Tax Assessment Report. The printer spacing chart for the report is illustrated below. The maximum number of detail lines on one page is 40 lines.

The processing for the Property Tax Assessment Report is specified below.

1. The yearly quarter for which the report is prepared should be specified in the report heading. If the month in which the report is prepared is January, February, or March, the FIRST quarter should be specified; if the month is April, May, or June, the SECOND quarter should be printed; if the month is July, August, or September, the report is for the THIRD quarter; if the month is October, November, or December, the FOURTH quarter should be specified.

2. The Property Tax is determined in the following manner:
   a. If the property is a home, is used as the primary residence of the owner, and the assessed value is greater than $150,000.00, the tax rate is 2% of the assessed value.
   b. If the property is a home, is used as the primary residence of the owner, and the assessed value is equal to or less than $150,000.00, the tax rate is 1.4%.
   c. If the property is a home, but it is not the primary residence of the owner, and the value is greater than $95,000.00, the tax rate is 2%.
   d. If the property is a home, but it is not a primary residence of the owner, and the value is equal to or less than $95,000.00, the tax rate is 1.4%.
   e. If the property is a commercial building and the value is greater than $200,000.00, the tax rate is 2.5%.
   f. If the property is a commercial building and the value is equal to or less than $200,000.00, the tax rate is 2%.
   g. If the property is commercial land and the value is greater than $60,000.00, the tax rate is 2.5%.
   h. If the property is commercial land and the value is equal to or less than $60,000.00, the tax rate is 2%.

3. Final totals for each category of property are to be printed together with the total tax assessment.

CONTROL BREAKS

8

INTRODUCTION

In the previous COBOL programs illustrated in the text, the data which was read from an input record was formatted in the output area, one or more calculations or comparing operations were performed, and a line was printed. This is commonly called DETAIL PRINTING; that is, detail printing is the printing of one line of information from each input record. In many business applications it is necessary to print intermediate data on the report, such as totals which have been calculated from the input data. The printing of this information normally takes place when a control break occurs.

A CONTROL BREAK occurs during the processing of the records in an input file when the data in a given input field in a record changes from the value found in the field in the previous input record. This is illustrated below.

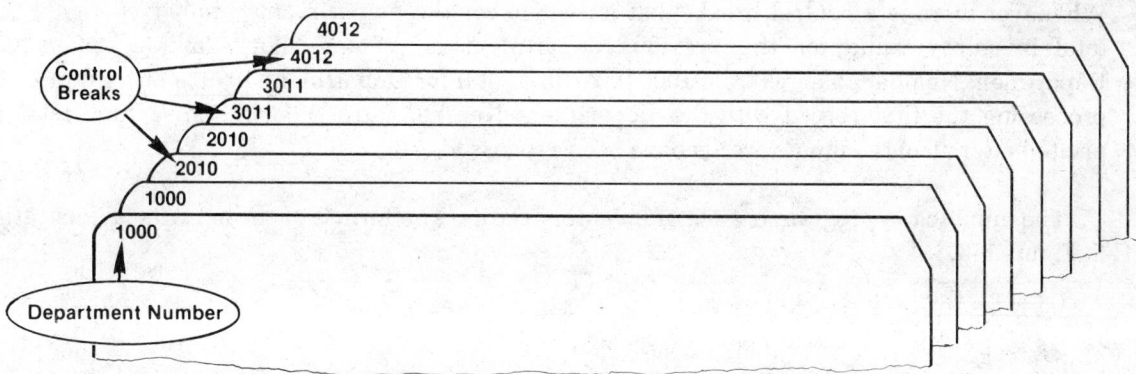

Figure 8-1 Example of Control Break

Note in the example above that a Department Number is contained on each card which is to be read. The first two cards contain Department Number 1000. The third input card, however, contains Department Number 2010. When the third card is read, therefore, a control break is said to occur because the value in the control field, in this case the Department Number, has changed.

---

1 Jackson, Michael A., PRINCIPLES OF PROGRAM DESIGN, Academic Press, 1975

When a control break occurs, it is normally required to perform some type of unique processing, such as taking a total for the department just processed. In order to illustrate the application of control breaks, the sample program in this chapter is designed to produce a Physical Inventory Report. An example of the report is illustrated below.

REPORT

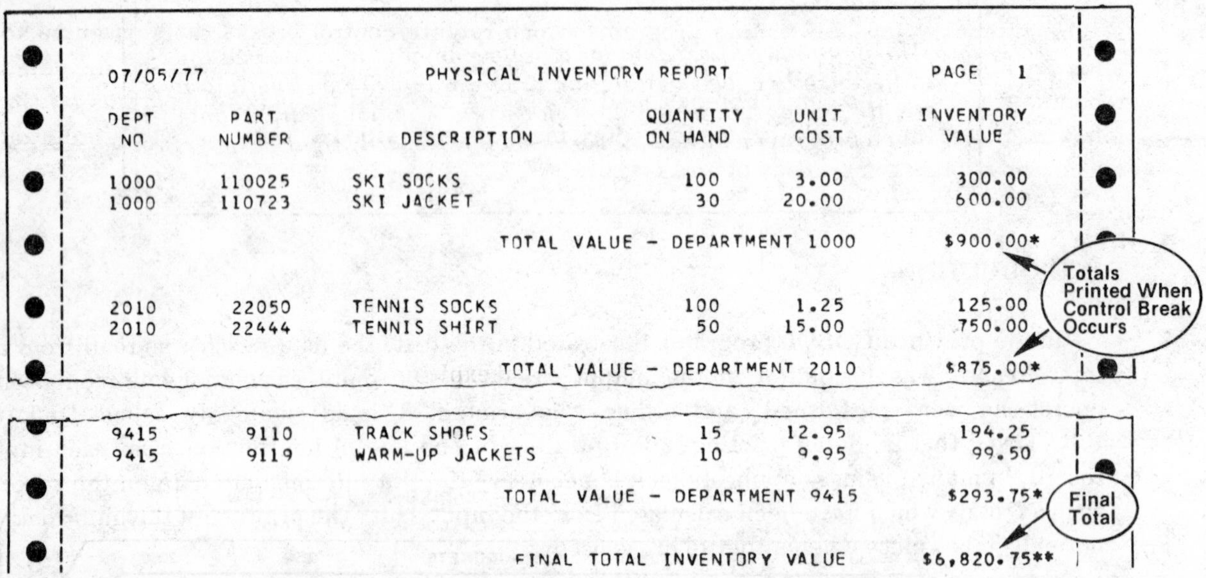

```
07/05/77                    PHYSICAL INVENTORY REPORT                 PAGE    1

DEPT        PART                                    QUANTITY   UNIT      INVENTORY
NO          NUMBER       DESCRIPTION                ON HAND    COST      VALUE

1000        110025       SKI SOCKS                      100    3.00        300.00
1000        110723       SKI JACKET                      30   20.00        600.00

                              TOTAL VALUE - DEPARTMENT 1000         $900.00*

2010        22050        TENNIS SOCKS                   100    1.25        125.00
2010        22444        TENNIS SHIRT                    50   15.00        750.00

                              TOTAL VALUE - DEPARTMENT 2010         $875.00*

9415        9110         TRACK SHOES                     15   12.95        194.25
9415        9119         WARM-UP JACKETS                 10    9.95         99.50

                              TOTAL VALUE - DEPARTMENT 9415         $293.75*

                              FINAL TOTAL INVENTORY VALUE        $6,820.75**
```

Totals Printed When Control Break Occurs

Final Total

Figure 8-2 Example of Report with Control Breaks

Note in the example above that the report contains the Department Number, the Part Number, the Description, the Quantity on Hand, the Unit Cost, and the Inventory Value. Whenever there is a control break, that is, whenever the Department Number changes, the total inventory value for the previous department is printed. For example, when the Department Number changes from 1000 to 2010, a total for Department 1000 is printed prior to processing the first record with the Department Number 2010. In addition, a final total is printed after all of the input records have been processed.

The input to the program is a file of Inventory Cards. The format of these cards is illustrated in Figure 8-3.

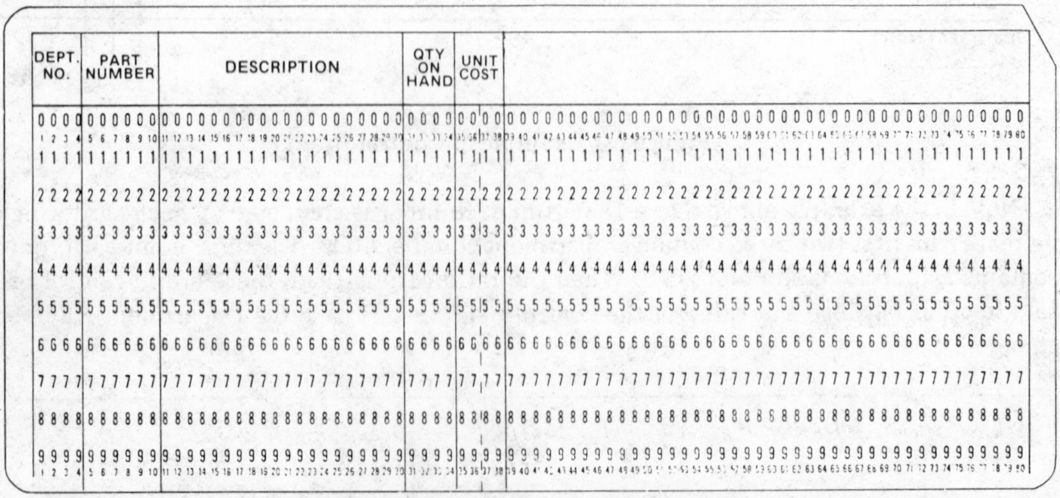

Figure 8-3 Format of Input Records

Note that the input record contains the Department Number, Part Number, Description, Quantity on Hand, and Unit Cost. The control break is taken on the Department Number when processing the records.

CONTROL BREAK PROCESSING

Prior to designing and writing programs which require control breaks, it is essential to understand what takes place when an input record is processed, including processing the detail records, processing the control breaks, and processing the final totals. The diagrams on the following pages illustrate the processing which must be understood in order to create a program which prints totals when a control break occurs.

Initial Processing

Prior to the processing of the first and subsequent detail records, several steps must be accomplished. These are illustrated in Figure 8-4 and explained on page 8.4.

EXAMPLE

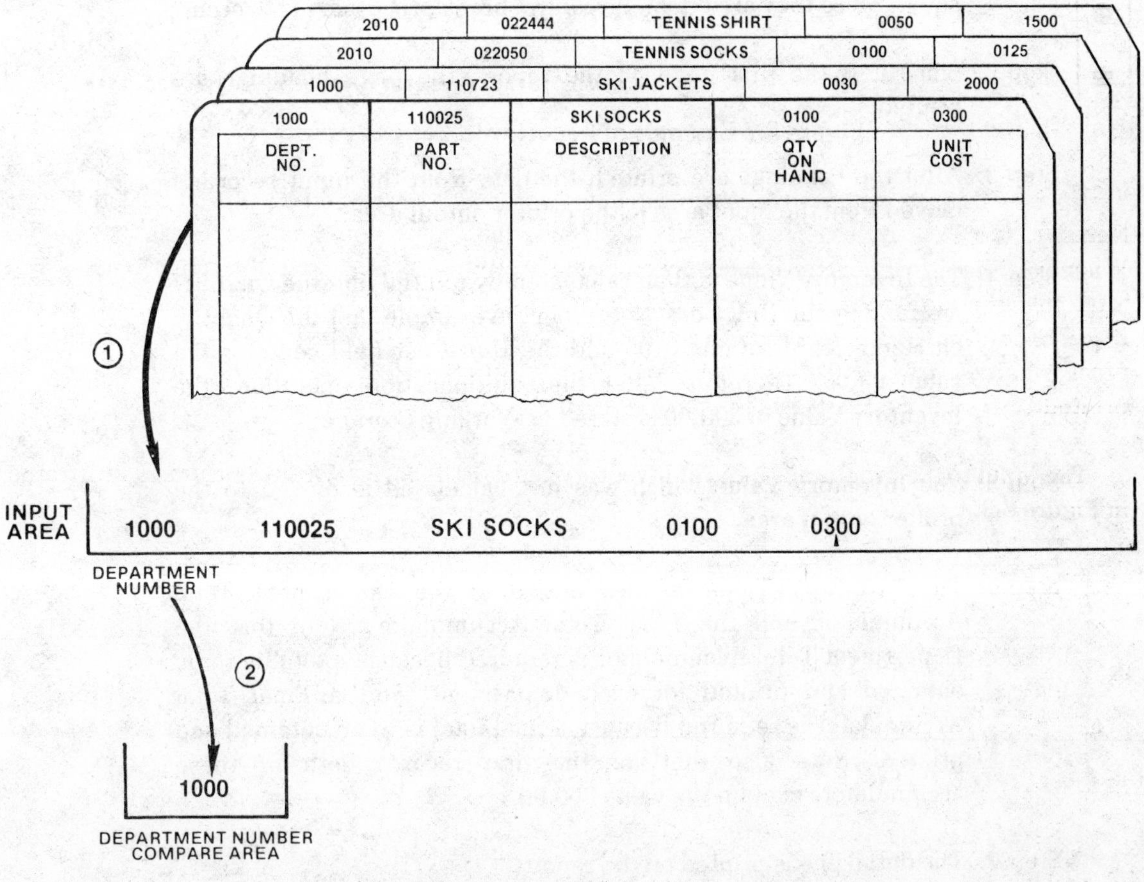

Figure 8-4 Initial Steps in Control Break Processing

The numbered steps accomplish the following processing:

Step 1: The first input record in the file is read into an input area.

Step 2: The Department Number from the first input record is moved to a "Compare Area" in Working Storage. This field will be used to compare the Department Number on subsequent input records to determine if a control break has occured.

Detail Record Processing

After the first detail record is read into the input area and the Department Number is moved to the compare area, the detail record processing will occur. The steps are illustrated in Figure 8-5 and explained below.

Step 1: The Department Number in the record which is in the input area is compared to the Department Number which is in the compare area. Since the Department Number in the compare area was moved from the input area for the first record (see Figure 8-4), they are equal. Since they are equal, no control break processing is to occur.

Step 2: Since it is the first page on the report, the page headings are printed.

Step 3: After the headings are printed, the data from the input record is moved from the input area to the printer output area.

Step 4: The Inventory Value is then calculated by multiplying the Quantity on Hand by the Unit Cost. Note from the example that the Quantity on Hand field contains 0100 and the Unit Cost field contains the value 03.00. Therefore, after the multiplication operation, the Inventory Value of 300.00 is stored in Working Storage.

Step 5: The Inventory Value which was just calculated is moved to the printer output area.

Step 6: The Inventory Value is then added to the Department Total Accumulator and the Final Total Accumulator. Note that the Department Total Accumulator is required because a total is to be obtained and printed for each department; and a Final Total Accumulator is required because a final total is to be obtained and printed. Note also that for the first record, both of these accumulators contain the value 300.00.

Step 7: The detail line is printed on the report.

Detail Processing

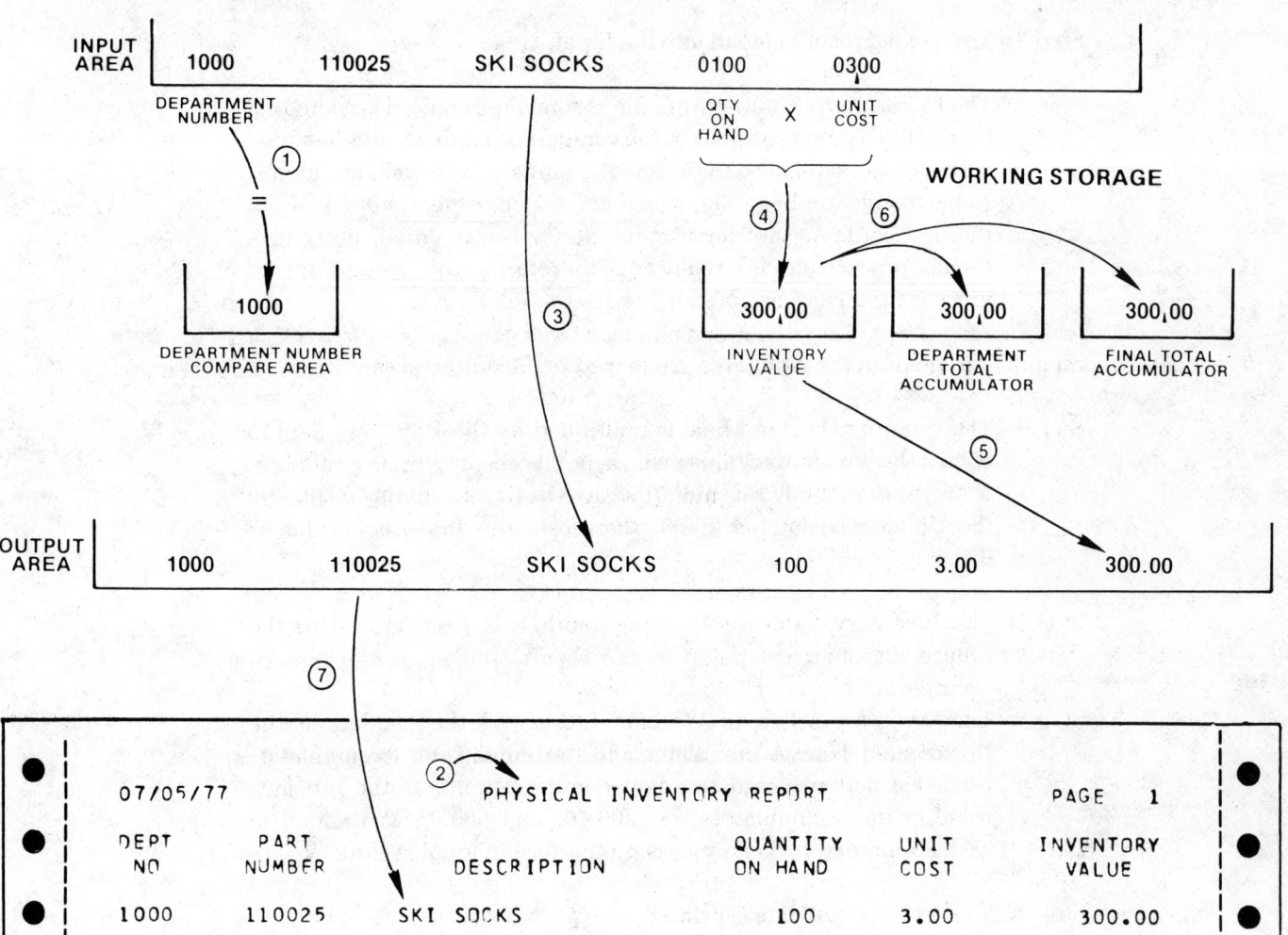

Figure 8-5 Processing of First Detail Record

After the first detail record is processed and printed, the second record is read and the following sequence of operations occurs. See Figure 8-6.

Step 1: The second record is read into the Input Area.

Step 2: The Department Number from the second input record is compared to the Department Number in the compare area. It should be noted in the example that the Department Number in the compare area is Department Number 1000, which is the Department Number from the first card. As the Department Numbers are equal, no control break processing is required; therefore, the detail record processing occurs, as noted in Step 3 through Step 7.

Step 3: The fields in the input area are moved to the output area.

Step 4: The Quantity On Hand field is multiplied by the Unit Cost field to obtain the Inventory Value, which is placed in Working Storage. Note in the example that the Quantity On Hand contains 0030, and the Unit Cost contains 20.00; therefore, the Inventory Value is 600.00.

Step 5: The Inventory Value in Working Storage is then moved to the printer output area.

Step 6: The Inventory Value in Working Storage is then added to the Department Total Accumulator and the Final Total Accumulator. Note that both accumulators now contain 900.00, as the previous value in the accumulators was 300.00, and 600.00 was added to each accumulator when processing the second input record.

Step 7: The second detail line is printed.

As long as there is not a control break, that is, as long as the Department Number on the input card being read is equal to the Department Number in the compare area, then the detail processing steps as described above will take place.

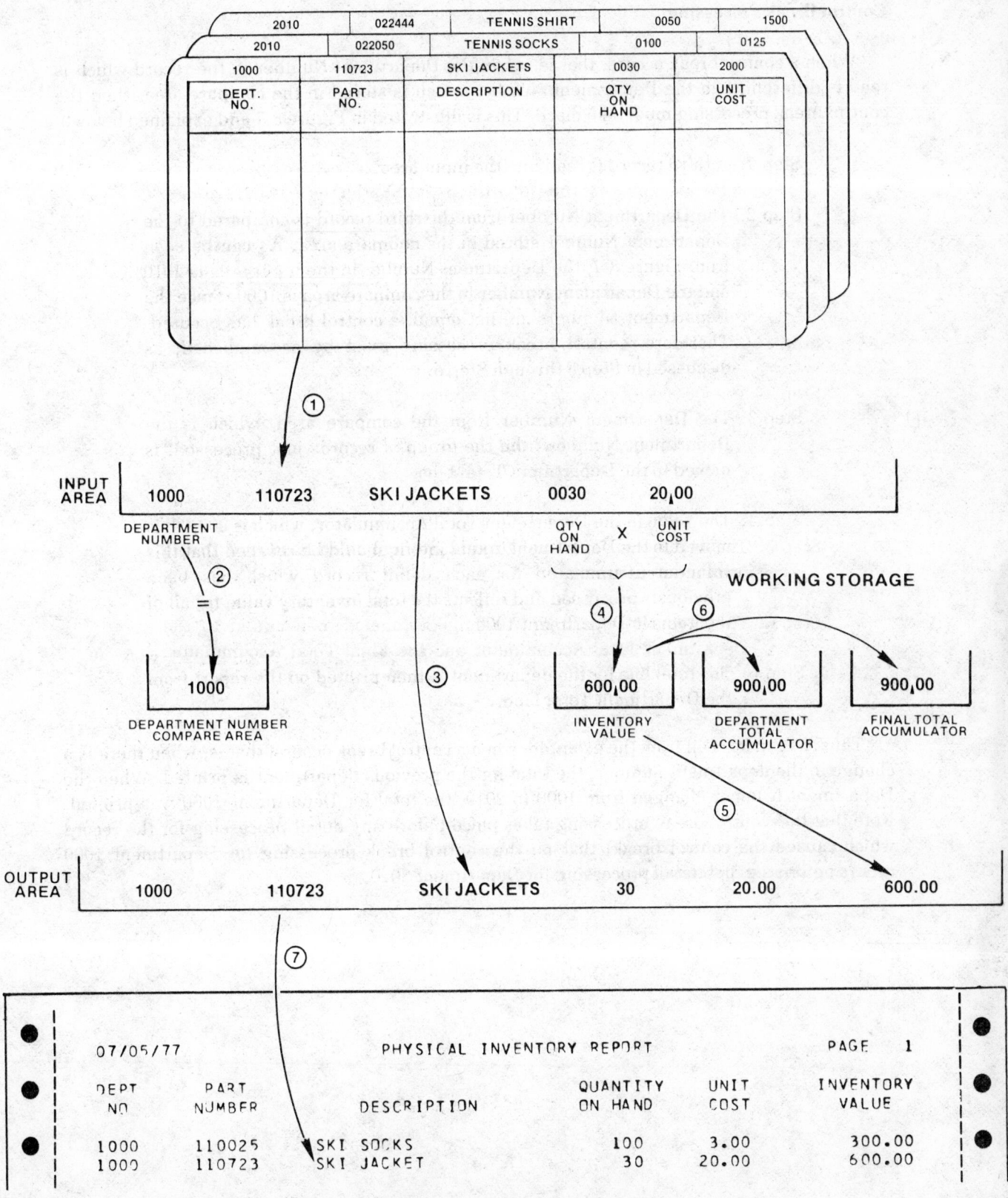

Figure 8-6 Processing the Second Record

Control Break Processing

When a control break occurs, that is, when the Department Number in the record which is read is different than the Department Number which is stored in the compare area, then the control break processing must take place. This is illustrated in Figure 8-7 and explained below.

Step 1: A third record is read into the input area.

Step 2: The Department Number from the third record is compared to the Department Number stored in the compare area. As can be seen from Figure 8-7, the Department Number in the input area is 2010 and the Department Number in the compare area is 1000. Since the Department Numbers are not equal, a control break has occured. Therefore, control break processing must be accomplished, as discussed in Step 3 through Step 5.

Step 3: The Department Number from the compare area, which is the Department Number from the group of records just processed, is moved to the Department Total Line.

Step 4: The value in the Department Total Accumulator, which is 900.00, is moved to the Department Total Line. It should be recalled that this value is accumulated for each detail record which has been previously processed and reflects the total inventory value for all of the items in Department 1000.

Step 5: The total line for the department is then printed on the report from the Department Total Line.

Thus, as can be seen from the example, when a control break occurs, that is, when there is a change in the department number, the total for the previous department is printed. When the Department Number changed from 1000 to 2010, the total for Department 1000 was printed. Note that this control break processing takes place before any detail processing for the record which caused the control break; that is, the control break processing for Department 1000 occurs before the first detail processing for Department 2010.

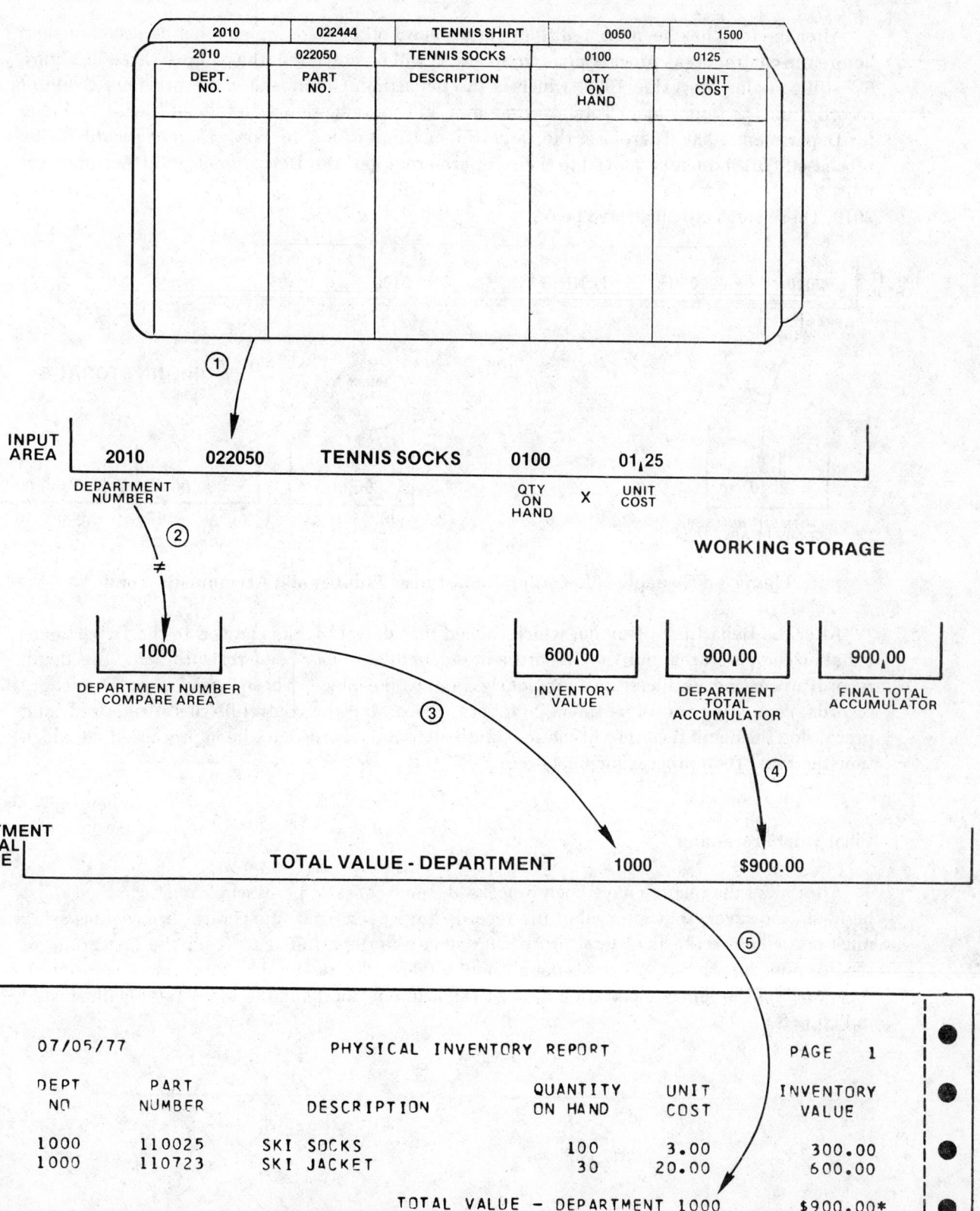

Figure 8-7 Processing Control Break

After the total has been printed, there are several other steps which must be accomplished before the control break processing is complete. It will be noted that the compare area in Figure 8-7 still contains the value 1000, which is the department number for the previous group of records; and the Department Total Accumulator still contains the accumulated Inventory Value for Department 1000. Therefore, the Department Number for the new group of records to be processed (2010) must be moved to the compare area; and the Department Total Accumulator must be reset to zero so that the department total will reflect the total for the new department, 2010. These steps are illustrated below.

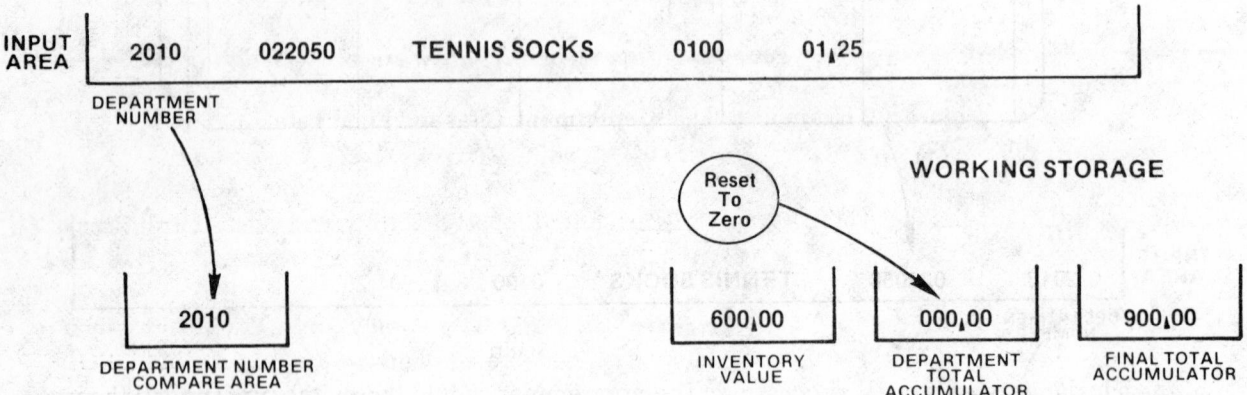

Figure 8-8 Example of Resetting Department Number and Accumulator Total

After the Department Number which caused the control break is moved to the Department Number compare area and the Department Accumulator has been reset to zero, the detail record processing as illustrated previously would take place. These basic steps of reading records, comparing the Department Numbers, processing the control breaks if required, and processing the detail records will continue until all of the records have been processed, at which time the Final Total processing must occur.

Final Total Processing

After all of the records have been processed, the final total processing must occur. It must be noted, however, that after all of the records have been read, the control break processing must occur before the final total processing since the department total for the last group of records must be printed. After this department total is printed, the final totals must be printed. A segment of the report illustrating the last Department Total and the Final Total is illustrated in Figure 8-9.

EXAMPLE - Final Total

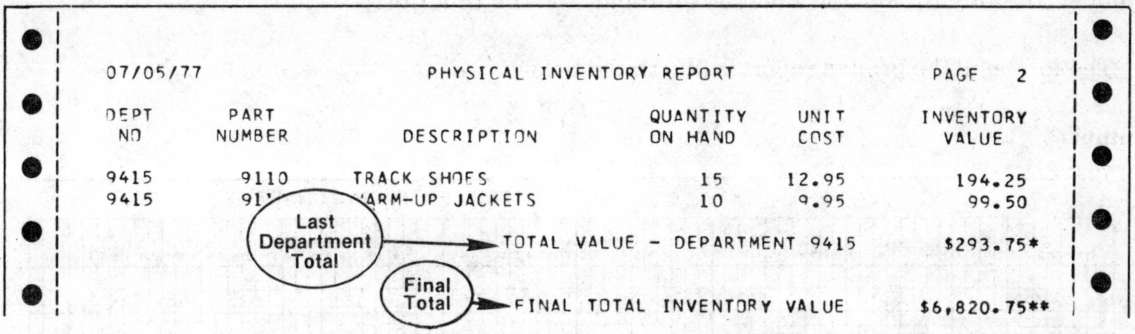

Figure 8-9 Example of Last Department Total and Final Total

Note in the example above that the Department Total for Department Number 9415 is printed and then the Final Total is printed. Thus, after the last record is read, the Control Break processing must be performed first and then the Final Total processing takes place.

It is extremely important to understand the basic steps which are necessary when processing control breaks in order to be able to properly design and code a program in COBOL which includes control break processing. The programmer should thoroughly understand these steps before moving on to the design of the sample program in this chapter.

SAMPLE PROGRAM

To illustrate the design and programming of an application requiring a control break, the problem just described, involving the preparation of a Physical Inventory Report, will be explained. The input to the program is the Inventory Input File. The format of the input records is illustrated in Figure 8-10.

Input

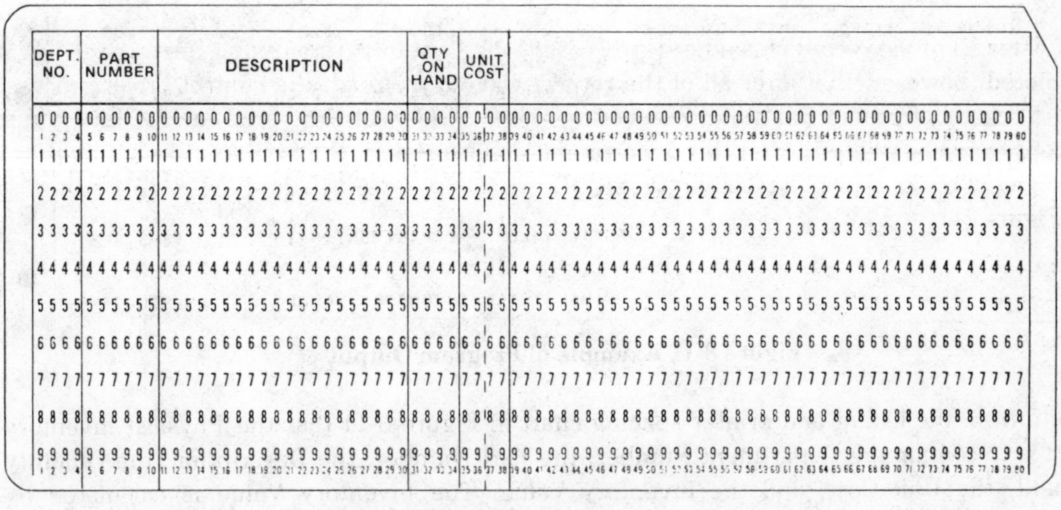

Figure 8-10 Format of Input Record

Note from Figure 8-10 that the input record contains the Department Number, the Part Number, the Description, the Quantity on Hand, and the Unit Cost.

The format of the printed report is illustrated below.

Output

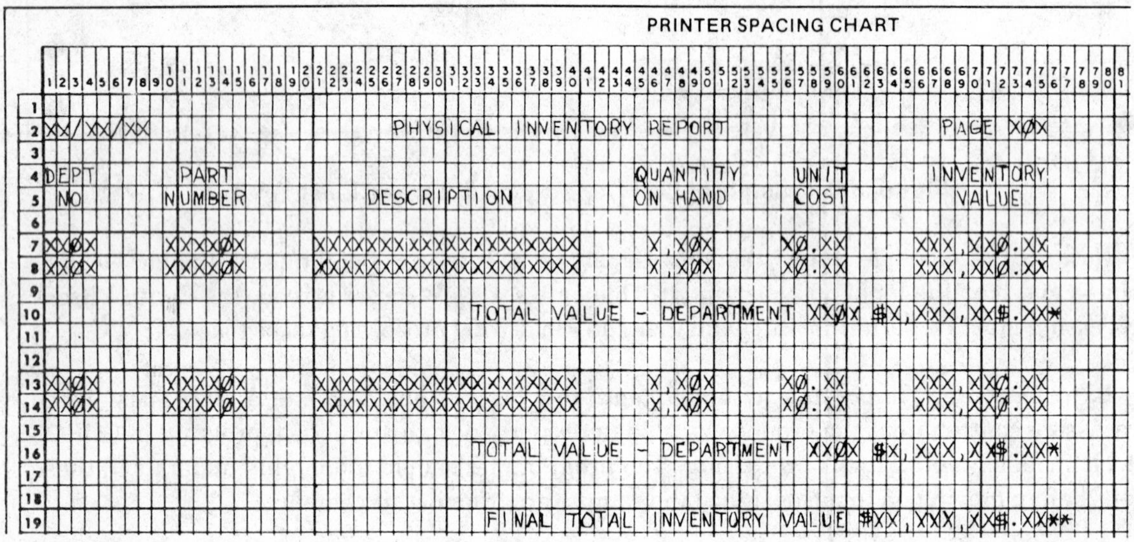


```
07/05/77              PHYSICAL INVENTORY REPORT                    PAGE    1

DEPT      PART                          QUANTITY      UNIT        INVENTORY
 NO      NUMBER       DESCRIPTION        ON HAND      COST          VALUE

1000     110025     SKI SOCKS              100        3.00         300.00
1000     110723     SKI JACKET              30       20.00         600.00

                     TOTAL VALUE - DEPARTMENT 1000                $900.00*

2010      22050     TENNIS SOCKS           100        1.25         125.00
2010      22444     TENNIS SHIPT            50       15.00         750.00

                     TOTAL VALUE - DEPARTMENT 2010                $875.00*

9415       9110     TRACK SHOES             15       12.95         194.25
9415       9119     WARM-UP JACKETS         10        9.95          99.50

                     TOTAL VALUE - DEPARTMENT 9415                $293.75*

                     FINAL TOTAL INVENTORY VALUE                $6,820.75**
```

Figure 8-11 Example of Program Output

Note from the listing and printer spacing chart in Figure 8-11 that the Physical Inventory Report is to contain the Department Number, the Part Number, the Description, the Quantity on Hand, the Unit Cost, and the Inventory Value. The Inventory Value is calculated by multiplying the Quantity on Hand by the Unit Cost. In addition, when there is a change in Department Number, the Inventory Value for the department is to be printed. After all of the input records have been processed, the Final Inventory Value is to be printed.

Programming Specifications

The Programming Specifications for the sample program are illustrated below.

PROGRAMMING SPECIFICATIONS		
SUBJECT Physical Inventory Report	**DATE** June 14	**PAGE** 1 **OF** 1
TO Programmer	**FROM** Systems Analyst	

A program is to be written to prepare a Physical Inventory Report. The formats for the input card file and the printer spacing chart are included as a part of this narrative. The program should include the following processing.

1. The program should read the input cards and create the Physical Inventory Report as per the format illustrated on the printer spacing chart. The report shall contain the Department Number, the Part Number, the Item Description, the Quantity On Hand, the Unit Cost, and the Inventory Value.

2. The Inventory Value is calculated by multiplying the Quantity On Hand by the Unit Cost.

3. Headings should be printed on the first page of the report. The heading is to contain the current date and the page number.

4. Subsequent pages are also to include report and column headings. Fifty-five detail and total lines are to appear on each page before skipping to a new page.

5. One line is to be printed on the report for each card which is read. The lines are to be single spaced.

6. Editing on the report is to occur as illustrated on the printer spacing chart.

7. When there is a change in Department Number, department totals are to be printed. A final total of the Inventory Value is to be printed after all cards have been processed. Spacing for the total lines should correspond to the printer spacing chart.

8. The program is to be written COBOL.

Figure 8-12 Programming Specifications

PROGRAM DESIGN

IPO Chart - Create the Inventory Report

As with previous problems, the programmer must analyze the Programming Specifications, together with the input records and the printer spacing chart, to determine the major processing tasks necessary to transform the input to output. The IPO Chart for the module whose function is to Create the Inventory Report is illustrated below.

IPO CHART				
PROGRAM: Physical Inventory Report		**PROGRAMMER:** Shelly/Cashman		**DATE:** June 17
MODULE NAME: Create Inventory Report	**REF:** A000	**MODULE FUNCTION:** Create the Inventory Report		
INPUT	**PROCESSING**		**REF:**	**OUTPUT**
1. Inventory Input File	1. Initialization			1. Physical Inventory Report
	2. Obtain the input data			
	3. Process detail records		B000	
	4. Process department changes		B010	
	5. Print the final totals		B020	
	6. Termination			

Figure 8-13 IPO Chart - Create Inventory Report

Note from the IPO Chart above that the major processing tasks that are necessary to produce the Physical Inventory Report from the Inventory Input File consist of Initialization, Obtain the input data, Process detail records, Process department changes, Print the final totals, and Termination.

Initialization and obtaining the input data are basically the same functions which have been seen in previous programs. The major processing task of processing the detail records corresponds to the processing which was illustrated previously (see Figure 8-5 and Figure 8-6).

The task of processing the department changes consists of those operations which must be performed when the Department Number in an input record just read is not equal to the Department Number from the previous records. This processing was illustrated in Figure 8-7 and Figure 8-8.

The task of printing the final totals was illustrated in Figure 8-9. The termination processing is the same as in previous programs.

Hierarchy Chart

The next step in the design process is to analyze each of the major processing tasks on the IPO Chart and determine if any of them define a specific function to be performed by the program and are of such a size or complexity as to justify another module.

The Initialization and Obtain the input data tasks are simple tasks to be performed and, as in previous programs, do not justify separate modules. The task of processing the detail records, however, is a specific function which must be accomplished by the program and is of such size and complexity as to require a separate module.

The task of processing department changes also appears to be of such size as to require a separate module. The printing of the final totals also may require some significant processing; thus, it too should be a separate module. The Termination processing is straightforward and simple and would not require another module.

As a result of this analysis of the major processing tasks in the module whose function is to create the Physical Inventory Report, three submodules have been identified. The programmer would then develop the hierarchy chart for the program, as illustrated below.

Hierarchy Chart

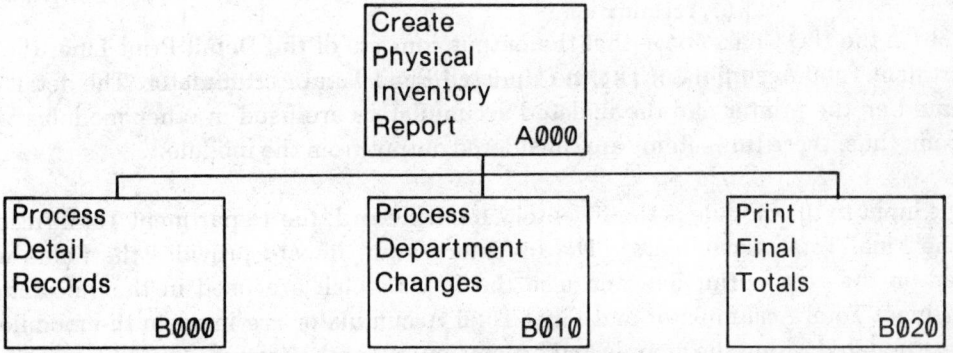

Figure 8-14 Hierarchy Chart

Note in Figure 8-14 that three modules are developed on the second level—a module to process the detail records, a module to process department changes, and a module to print the final totals. The programmer would next design the IPO Charts for each of these new program modules.

IPO Chart - Process the Detail Records

The IPO Chart for the module whose function is to process the detail records is illustrated below.

IPO CHART				
PROGRAM: Physical Inventory Report		**PROGRAMMER:** Shelly/Cashman		**DATE:** June 17
MODULE NAME: Process Detail Record	**REF:** B000	**MODULE FUNCTION:** Process the Detail Records		
INPUT	**PROCESSING**		**REF:**	**OUTPUT**
1. Inventory Input Record	1. Print headings when required		C000	1. Detail Print Line
2. Department Total	2. Format detail line			2. Updated Department
Accumulator	3. Calculate inventory value			Total Accumulator
3. Final Total Accumulator	4. Update accumulators			3. Updated Final
	a. Department totals			Total Accumulator
	b. Final total			
	5. Write the detail line			

Figure 8-15 IPO Chart for Detail Processing Module

Note in the IPO Chart above that the output consists of the Detail Print Line, the Updated Department Total Accumulator and the Updated Final Total Accumulator. The detail print line is printed on the printer and the updated accumulators are used in other modules within the program; thus, these three items are considered output from the module.

The input to the module is the Inventory Input Record, the Department Total Accumulator, and the Final Total Accumulator. The Inventory Input Record provides the fields which are printed on the detail print line and also the fields which are used in the calculations. The Department Total Accumulator and Final Total Accumulator are input to the module because they are updated within the module and become output of the module.

The programmer must then specify the major processing tasks to be accomplished within the module. As with the previous module, the programmer would then analyze each of the major processing tasks specified on the IPO Chart to determine if any of these tasks should be made into lower level modules. The first major processing task is to print the headings when required. As noted in Chapter 7, printing the headings is a well-defined function which normally will require some significant processing. Therefore, it should be made into a lower-level module. The remaining major processing tasks are not large enough nor complex enough to justify any lower-level modules. Therefore, the only lower-level module required from the module whose function is to process the detail records is the module whose function is to print the headings. This would be reflected on the Hierarchy Chart as illustrated in Figure 8-16.

Hierarchy Chart

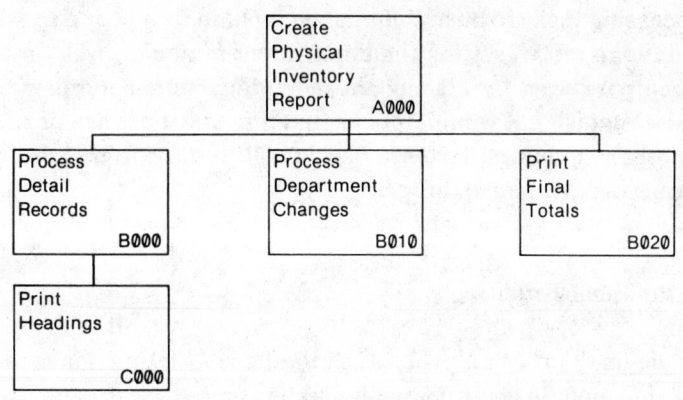

Figure 8-16 Hierarchy Chart

As can be seen from Figure 8-16, the module for printing the headings has been added to the Hierarchy Chart. The programmer would then continue the design of the IPO Charts for the second level modules.

The IPO Chart for the module which processes the department changes is illustrated below.

IPO Chart - Process Department Changes

IPO CHART				
PROGRAM: Physical Inventory Report		**PROGRAMMER:** Shelly/Cashman		**DATE:** June 17
MODULE NAME: Process Dept Change	**REF:** B010	**MODULE FUNCTION:** Process Department Changes		
INPUT	**PROCESSING**	**REF:**	**OUTPUT**	
1. Old Department Number	1. Format department total line		1. Department Total Line	
2. New Department Number	2. Write the department total line		2. Department Total	
3. Department Total	3. Reset department accumulator		Accumulator	
Accumulator	4. Reset department number		3. Department Number	
	compare area		Compare Area	

Figure 8-17 IPO Chart for Process Department Changes Module

Note from the IPO Chart above that the output from the module consists of the Department Total Line, the Department Total Accumulator, and the Department Number Compare Area. The department total line is printed on the report; the Department Total Accumulator is reset and is used in another module for accumulating the department total; and the compare area is reset to the new department number and used in another module. Therefore, these fields constitute the output of the module.

The input to the module to process the department changes are the Old Department Number, the New Department Number, and the Department Total Accumulator. The Old Department Number is printed on the department total line and is, therefore, a required input field to the module. The New Department Number is placed in the Department Compare Area and is required. The Department Total Accumulator contains the value which will be printed on the Department Total Line and this field will also be reset to zero; therefore, it is also required input to the module.

The major processing tasks to be accomplished include formatting the department total line, writing the line on the report, resetting the department total accumulator to zero, and resetting the department compare area by placing the new department number in it. After analyzing these major processing tasks, it would appear that none of them are of such complexity or size so as to justify another module. Therefore, there will be no submodules to the module whose function is to process department changes.

IPO Chart - Print the Final Totals

The third module on the second level is the module whose function is to print the final totals. The IPO Chart for this module is illustrated below.

IPO CHART

PROGRAM: Physical Inventory Report	PROGRAMMER: Shelly/Cashman		DATE: June 18
MODULE NAME: Print Final Totals	REF: B020	MODULE FUNCTION: Print the Final Totals	

INPUT	PROCESSING	REF:	OUTPUT
1. Final Total Accumulator	1. Format total line		1. Final Total Line
	2. Write the final total line		

Figure 8-18 IPO Chart for Print the Final Totals Module

The output from this module is the Final Total Line. The input is the Final Total Accumulator which contains the final total value. The major processing tasks required include formatting the total line and writing the line on the report. Neither of these tasks are large nor complex, so no further decomposition of the module is required.

IPO Chart - Print the Headings

The IPO Chart for the module on the third level of the Hierarchy Chart must now be designed. The IPO Chart for the module whose function is to Print the Headings is illustrated in Figure 8-19.

IPO CHART

PROGRAM: Physical Inventory Report	PROGRAMMER: Shelly/Cashman		DATE: June 18
MODULE NAME: Print Headings	REF: C000	MODULE FUNCTION: Print the Headings	

INPUT	PROCESSING	REF:	OUTPUT
1. Heading Lines	1. Format headings		1. Heading Lines
	2. Write the headings		

Figure 8-19 IPO Chart for Print the Headings Module

Note from the IPO Chart above that the output from the module is the Heading Lines, the input is the Heading Lines, and the major processing tasks to be accomplished are formatting the headings and writing the headings on the report. Neither of the tasks is large nor complex, so no further decomposition is required.

IPO Chart - Summary

The following diagram summarizes the Hierarchy Chart and related IPO Charts for the preparation of the Physical Inventory Report.

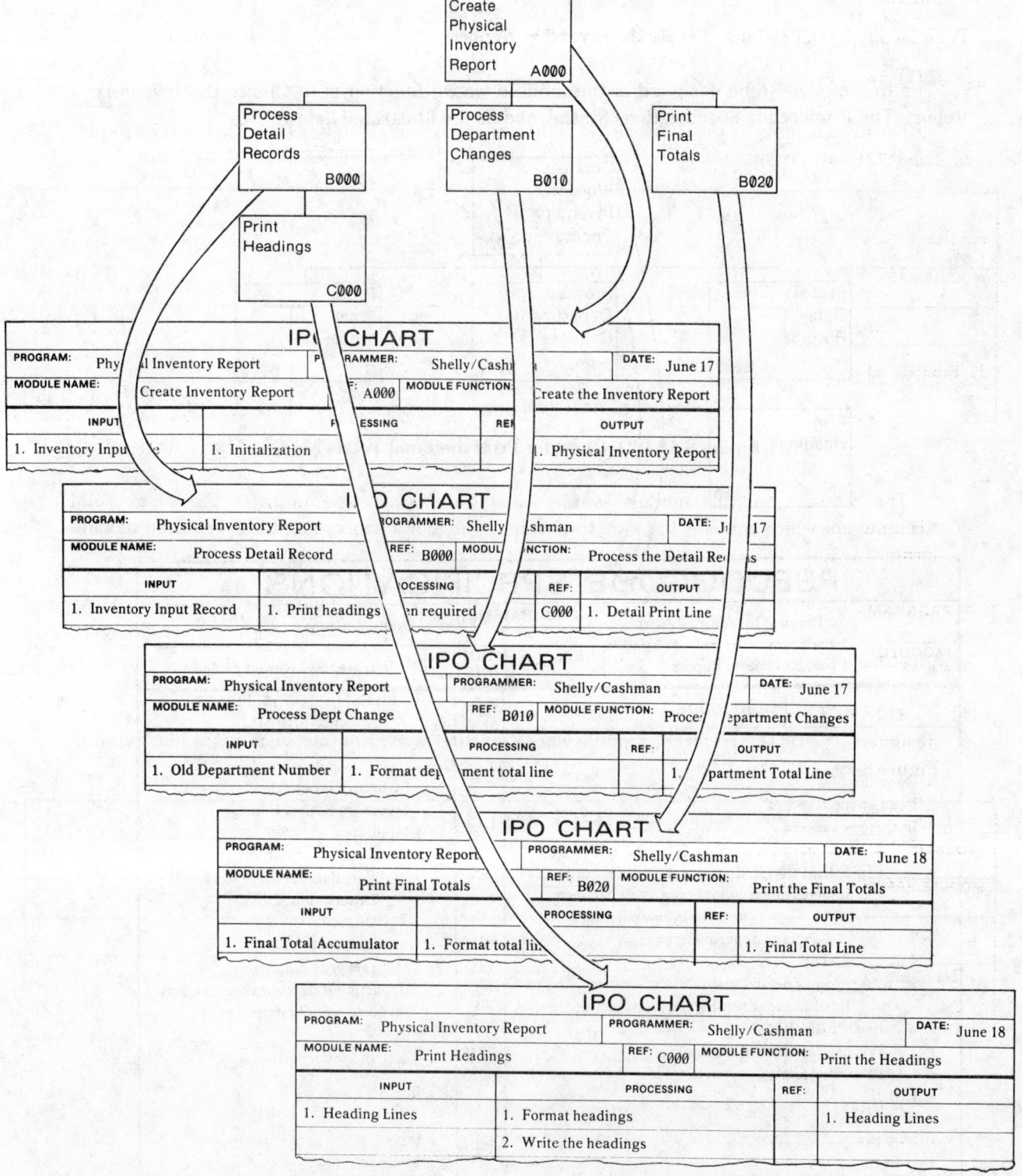

Figure 8-20 Summary of Hierarchy Chart and IPO Charts

As can be seen from Figure 8-20, an IPO Chart is prepared for each module which is a part of the program. Once the IPO Charts are completed and have been reviewed, the programmer may move on to designing the logic for each of the modules through the use of the Pseudocode Specifications.

Pseudocode Specifications - Create the Inventory Report

The first module to be designed is the module whose function is to Create the Inventory Report. The Pseudocode Specifications for the module are illustrated below.

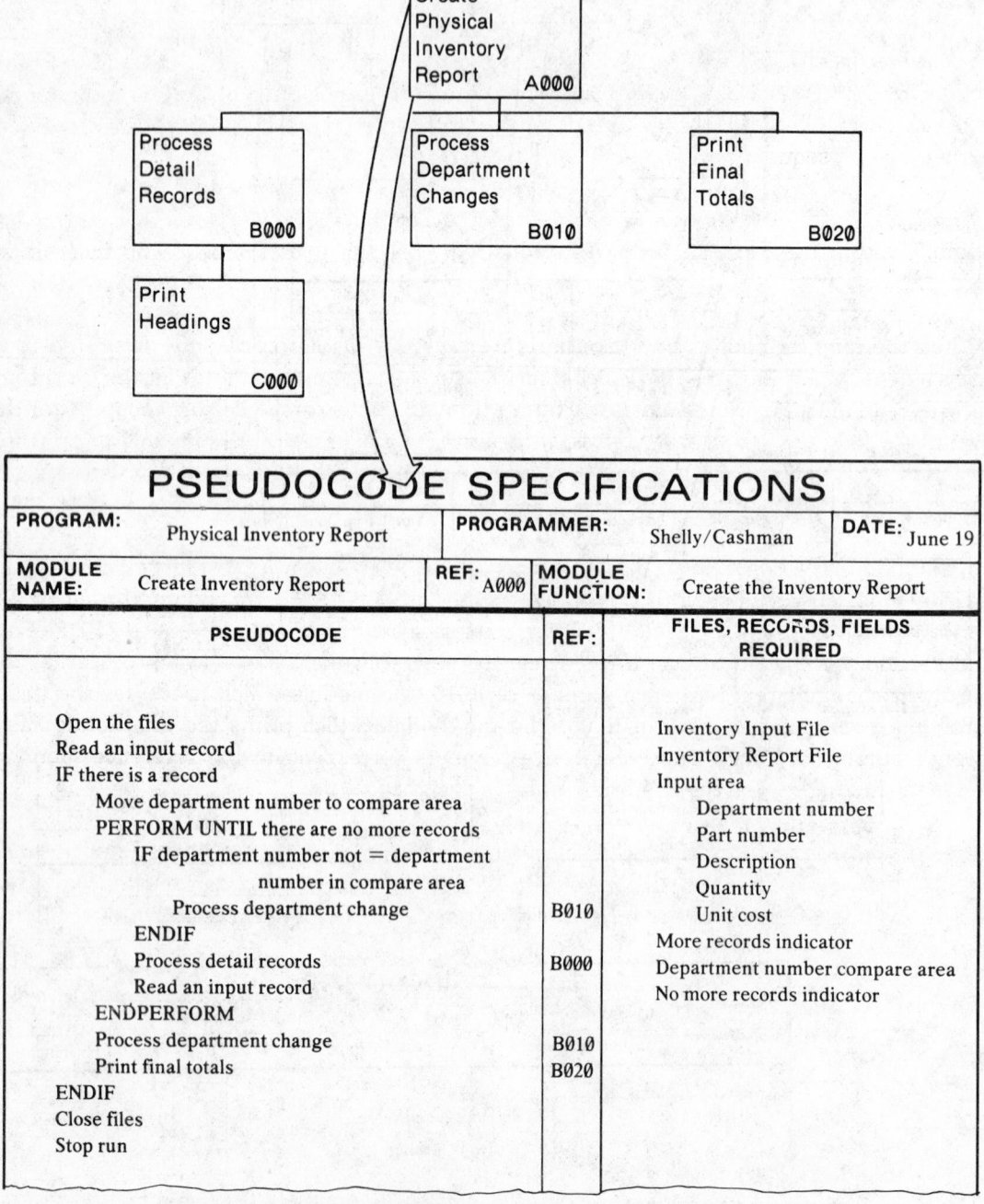

Figure 8-21 Pseudocode for Create Inventory Report Module

The logic expressed in the pseudocode in Figure 8-21 is basically the same as has been seen in previous programs. There are several significant differences, however. If there is an input record, the first action taken is to move the Department Number to the compare area. This initializes the compare area with the Department Number of the first input record (see Figure 8-4 for a detailed drawing of this processing). The Perform Loop is then entered to process the first and remaining input records. The first statement in the loop is to compare the Department Number in the input record with the Department Number in the compare area. If they are not equal, then a control break has occurred and the department change module must be executed. It should be noted that on the first record, they will be equal since the Department Number is moved to the compare area just prior to entering the Perform Loop; subsequent records will be compared each time a new input record is read.

Regardless of whether there is a control break, the detail record will then be processed. Note that the ENDIF word indicates the end of the IF Statement prior to the statement which specifies the detail processing is to be done. The detail processing must be done whether or not there is a control break because the first detail record after the control break must be processed, as well as the subsequent detail records within the same group.

After the detail records are processed, another input record is read. This is the last statement within the Perform Loop. This loop will continue until there are no more input records.

When the loop terminates because there are no more input records, the first step is to process a department change. This is necessary because the department total for the last group of records read must be printed and it will not be through the use of the Perform Loop. After the department total is printed, the final total must be printed. Therefore, the module to print the final totals would be called. The report is then complete; thus, the files are closed and the program is terminated.

In addition to the pseudocode for the module, it should be noted from Figure 8-21 that the Files, Records, and Fields required for the module are specified. In addition, whenever a lower-level module is to be invoked, the module reference number is placed in the REF column of the Pseudocode Specifications. Thus, it can be seen that the module which processes the department change has a reference number of B010, the module which processes the detail records has a reference number of B000, and the module which prints the final totals has a reference number of B020. These reference numbers correspond to the reference numbers given to the modules when the Hierarchy Chart is designed.

After the pseudocode for the top-level module has been designed, the programmer would normally continue the design of the program by writing the pseudocode for the lower-level modules. The pseudocode for the module which processes the detail records is illustrated in Figure 8-22.

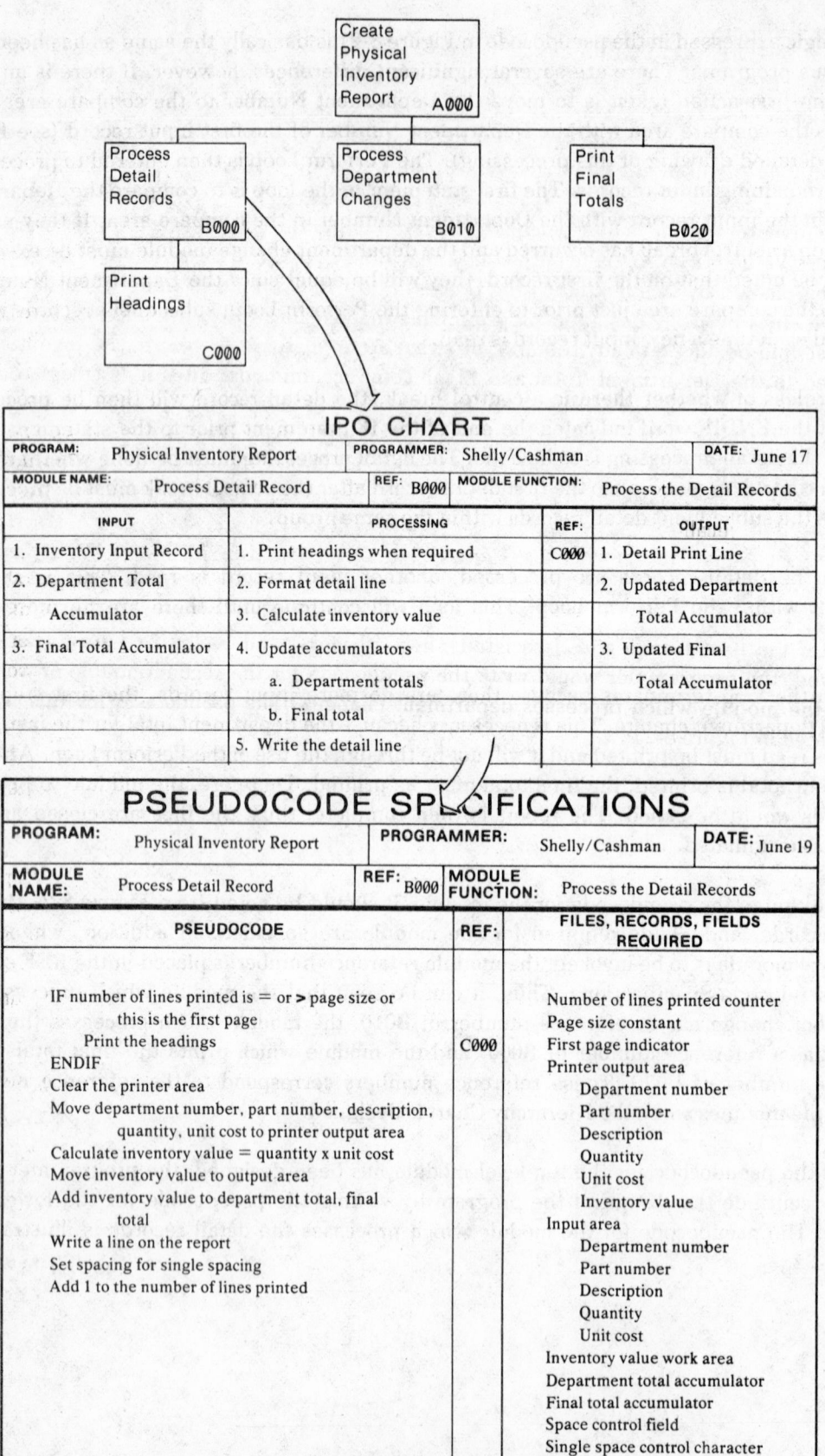

Figure 8-22 Pseudocode Specifications for Detail Processing

Pseudocode Specifications - Process the Detail Records

As in the program in Chapter 7, it can be seen from Figure 8-22 that the first step in processing the detail record is to determine if the headings should be printed. If the number of lines printed on the report is equal to or greater than the page size, or if it is the first page of the report, then the module which prints the headings will be performed. The next step is to clear the printer output area and move the values from the input area to the output area.

The Inventory Value is then calculated by multiplying the Quantity by the Unit Cost, and the Inventory Value is moved to the output area. It should be noted that one of the tasks which must be accomplished by this module is the processing of the Inventory Value which is calculated within it. In a properly designed program, this means that within this module the Inventory Value should be added to any required program accumulators. Therefore, the Inventory Value is added to the Department Total and Final Total accumulators after it is calculated in this module.

After the Inventory Value is added to the accumulators, the detail line is printed on the report, the spacing is set for single spacing, and the number of lines printed is incremented by 1. It should be recalled that whenever headings are to be printed on each page of the report and a line count is used to determine when headings should be printed, the line counter must be incremented by the number of lines which are printed.

After the pseudocode and associated Files, Records, and Fields have been defined and reviewed, the programmer would write the pseudocode for the second module on the second level, the module which processes department changes. The pseudocode for this module is illustrated in Figure 8-23.

Pseudocode Specifications - Process Department Change

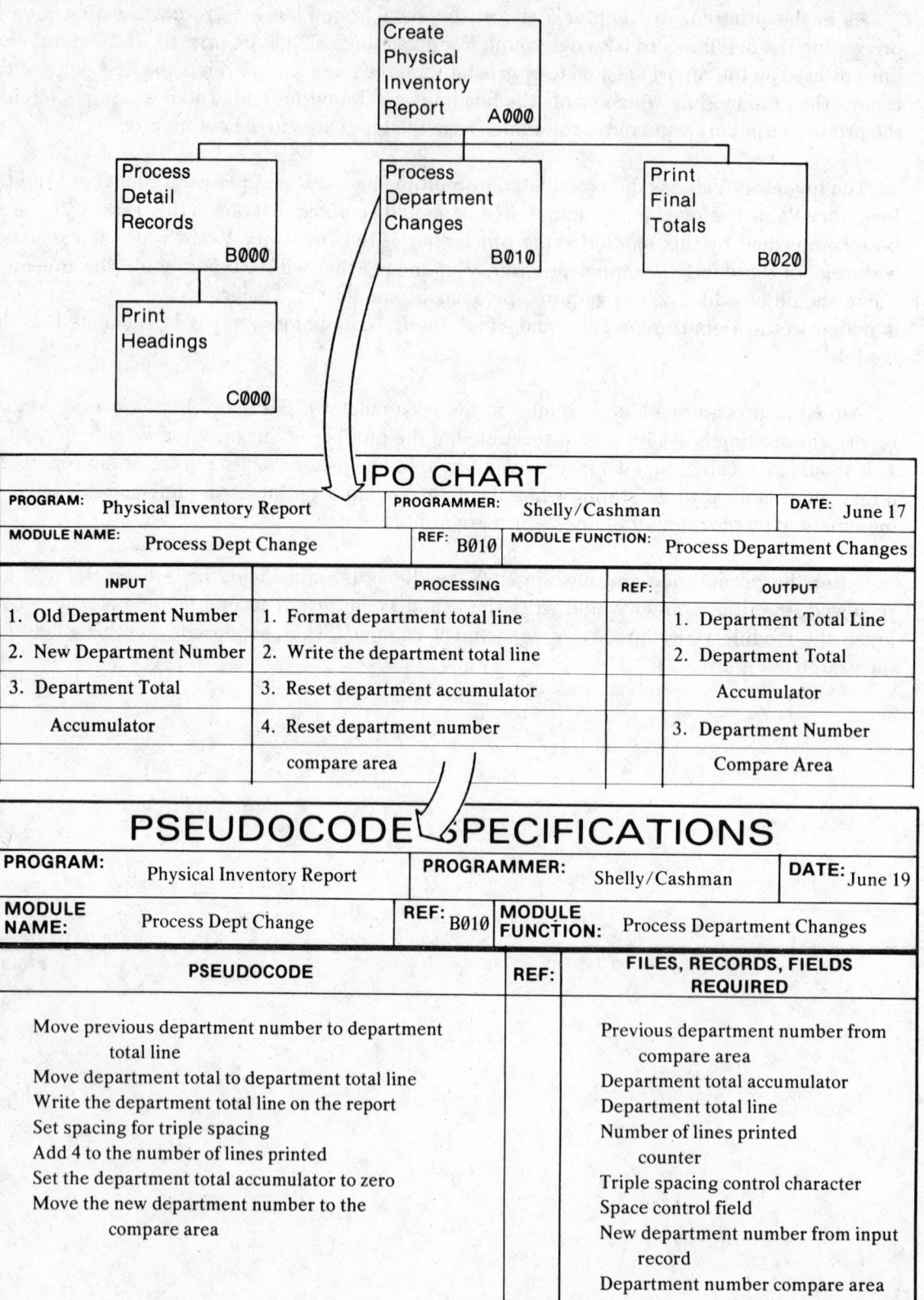

Figure 8-23 Pseudocode Specifications for Processing Department Changes

In Figure 8-23 it can be seen that the first pseudocode entry in the module is to format the Department Total Line by moving the department number and department total to the output line. The Department Total Line is then written on the report. The spacing is then set for triple spacing because there are to be two blank lines between the Department Total Line and the first detail line for the next department (see Figure 8-11). The line counter is then incremented by 4 because the printing of the Department Total Line accounts for four lines on the report—one blank line before the line is printed, the line itself, and two blank lines following the Department Total Line.

The accumulator for the Department Total is then set to zero so that the total for the next department to be processed will begin with zero. The Department Number from the input record which was just read and which caused the control break is moved from the input area to the compare area so that all records with the same department number in subsequent records will not cause a control break. Control is then relinquished by this module back to the module which called it.

The pseudocode for the module which prints the final total would be designed next, as illustrated in Figure 8-24.

Pseudocode Specifications - Print the Final Totals

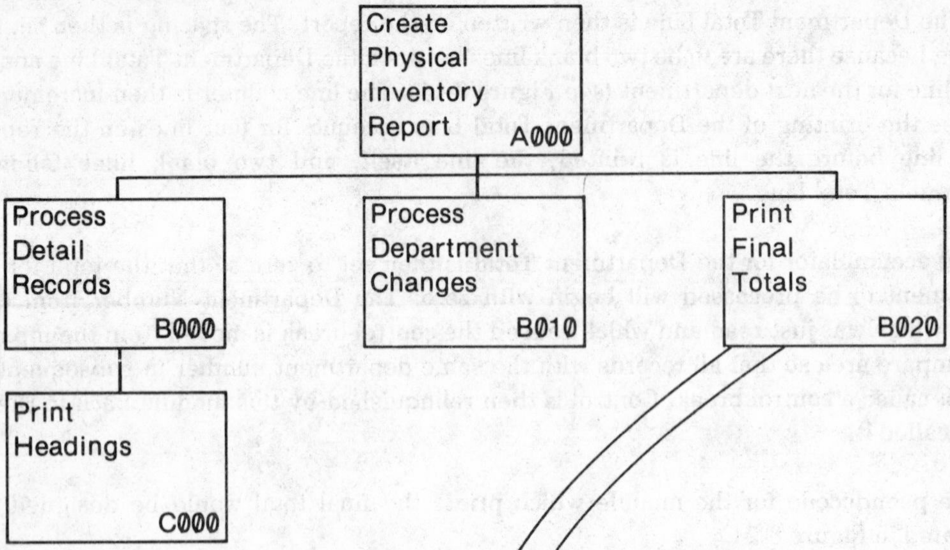

IPO CHART

PROGRAM: Physical Inventory Report		PROGRAMMER: Shelly/Cashman	DATE: June 18
MODULE NAME: Print Final Totals	REF: B020	MODULE FUNCTION: Print the Final Totals	

INPUT	PROCESSING	REF:	OUTPUT
1. Final Total Accumulator	1. Format total line		1. Final Total Line
	2. Write the final total line		

PSEUDOCODE SPECIFICATIONS

PROGRAM: Physical Inventory Report		PROGRAMMER: Shelly/Cashman	DATE: June 20
MODULE NAME: Print Final Totals	REF: B020	MODULE FUNCTION: Print the Final Totals	

PSEUDOCODE	REF:	FILES, RECORDS, FIELDS REQUIRED
Move the final total value to the final total line Write the final total line on the report		Final total accumulator Final total line

Figure 8-24 Pseudocode for Final Total Printing

Note from the pseudocode above that the printing of the final total consists of moving the Final Total Value to the Final Total Line and printing the final total.

Pseudocode Specifications - Print the Headings

The last module to be designed is the module whose function is to print the headings. The pseudocode for this module is illustrated below.

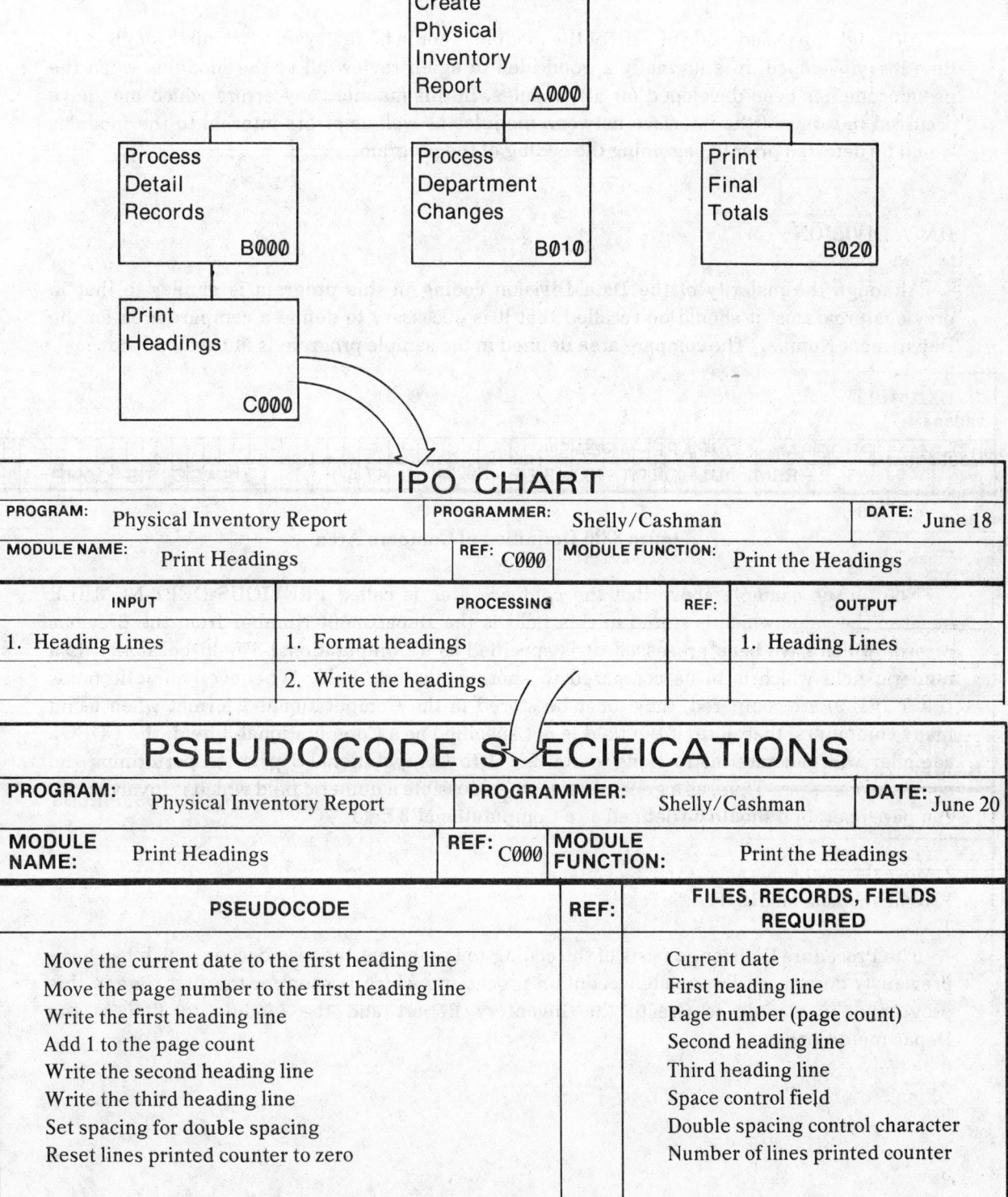

Figure 8-25 Pseudocode for Printing the Headings

The processing in the module whose function is to print the headings is the same as was seen in Chapter 7. The Current Date and Page Number are moved to the first heading line and the line is printed on the report. The Page Count is then incremented by one and the second and third heading lines are printed. The spacing is then set for double spacing and the counter for the number of lines printed on the page is set to zero.

Although the pseudocode of each of the modules should be reviewed in a walkthrough at the time it is developed, it is normally a good idea to again review all of the modules when the pseudocode has been developed for all modules. In this manner, any errors which may have occurred in terms of the interface between modules as well as errors internal to the modules would be detected prior to beginning the coding of the program.

DATA DIVISION

Although the majority of the Data Division coding in this program is similar to that in previous programs, it should be recalled that it is necessary to define a compare area for the Department Number. The compare area defined in the sample program is illustrated below.

EXAMPLE

```
005010 01  PROGRAM-COMPARE-AREAS.
005020     05  PREVIOUS-DEPT-NUMBER      PIC 9(4)      USAGE IS COMP-3.
```

Figure 8-26 Definition of Compare Area

Note in the example above that the compare area is called PREVIOUS-DEPT-NUMBER because the value which is stored in this field is the Department Number from the previous records which have been processed. It is specified as a Computational-3 field because it is a numeric field which is to be compared to another numeric field. Whenever numeric fields (PICTURE 9) are compared, they must be stored in the Computational-3 format when using many computers; therefore, if the field is not specified as a Computational-3 field, the COBOL compiler will generate instructions to convert it to Computational-3 prior to performing the compare operation. Thus, as a general rule, when possible a numeric field which is involved in a compare operation should be defined as a Computational-3 field.

PROCEDURE DIVISION

The Procedure Division consists of the coding to implement the pseudocode which has been previously described. Two modules contain processing which is seen for the first time in this program—the module to Create the Inventory Report and the module to Process the Department Changes.

Module to Create the Inventory Report

The coding for the module whose function is to Create the Inventory Report is illustrated below.

EXAMPLE

```
009190    A000-CREATE-INVENTORY-REPORT.
009200
010010            OPEN INPUT INVENTORY-INPUT-FILE
010020                 OUTPUT INVENTORY-REPORT-FILE.
010030            READ INVENTORY-INPUT-FILE
010040                AT END
010050                    MOVE 'NO ' TO ARE-THERE-MORE-RECORDS.
010060            IF THERE-IS-A-RECORD
010070                MOVE DEPT-NUMBER-INPUT TO PREVIOUS-DEPT-NUMBER
010080                PERFORM A001-COMPARE-AND-PROCESS
010090                    UNTIL THERE-ARE-NO-MORE-RECORDS
010100                PERFORM B010-PROCESS-DEPT-CHANGE
010110                PERFORM B020-PRINT-FINAL-TOTALS.
010120            CLOSE INVENTORY-INPUT-FILE
010130                  INVENTORY-REPORT-FILE.
010140            STOP RUN.
010150
010160
010170
010180    A001-COMPARE-AND-PROCESS.
010190
010200            IF DEPT-NUMBER-INPUT IS NOT = PREVIOUS-DEPT-NUMBER
011010                PERFORM B010-PROCESS-DEPT-CHANGE.
011020            PERFORM B000-PROCESS-DETAIL-RECORD.
011030            READ INVENTORY-INPUT-FILE
011040                AT END
011050                    MOVE 'NO ' TO ARE-THERE-MORE-RECORDS.
```

Figure 8-27 Coding for Create Inventory Report Module

As can be seen from the coding above, the files are opened and the first input record is read. If there is an input record, the Department Number is moved from the input area to the Department compare area. The A001-COMPARE-AND-PROCESS routine is then performed until there are no more input records, at which time the Department Total and Final Totals are printed, the files are closed, and the program is terminated.

In the A001-COMPARE-AND-PROCESS routine, the Department Number in the input record is compared to the Department Number in the compare area (PREVIOUS-DEPT-NUMBER). If they are not equal, then the B010-PROCESS-DEPT-CHANGE module is performed. Regardless of whether the department numbers are equal or not, the detail record processing module (B000-PROCESS-DETAIL-RECORD) is then performed to process the detail record. Another record is then read and, so long as there are more records, the A001-COMPARE-AND-PROCESS routine will be repeated.

Module to Process Department Changes

The module whose function is to process the department changes is illustrated below.

EXAMPLE

```
Ø13Ø8Ø    BØ1Ø-PROCESS-DEPT-CHANGE.
Ø13Ø9Ø
Ø131ØØ        MOVE PREVIOUS-DEPT-NUMBER TO DEPT-NUMBER-TOTAL-LINE.
Ø1311Ø        MOVE DEPT-TOTAL-ACCUM TO DEPT-VALUE-TOTAL-LINE.
Ø1312Ø        WRITE INVENTORY-REPORT-LINE FROM DEPARTMENT-TOTAL-LINE
Ø1313Ø            AFTER ADVANCING 2 LINES.
Ø1314Ø        MOVE SPACE-THREE-LINES TO PROPER-SPACING.
Ø1315Ø        ADD 4 TO LINES-PRINTED.
Ø1316Ø        MOVE ZEROS TO DEPT-TOTAL-ACCUM.
Ø1317Ø        MOVE DEPT-NUMBER-INPUT TO PREVIOUS-DEPT-NUMBER.
```

Figure 8-28 Coding for Process Department Change Module

Note from the coding above that the Department Total Line is formatted with the Department Number and the Department Total and is then written. The spacing is set for triple spacing and the value 4 is added to the line count because the printing of the department total requires four lines. The Department Total Accumulator is then reset to zero and the Department Number from the input record which caused the control break is moved to the compare area. Note that this module follows the pseudocode which was developed in Figure 8-23.

SAMPLE PROGRAM

The following pages contain the Input, Output, and Source Listing of the program to create the Physical Inventory Report.

Input

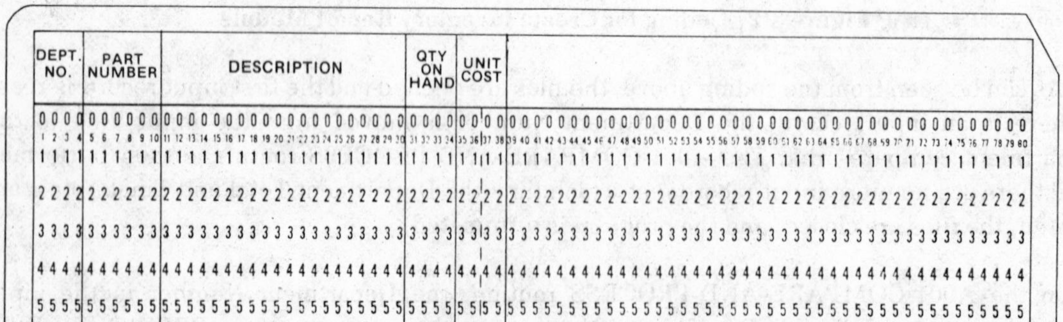

Figure 8-29 Input

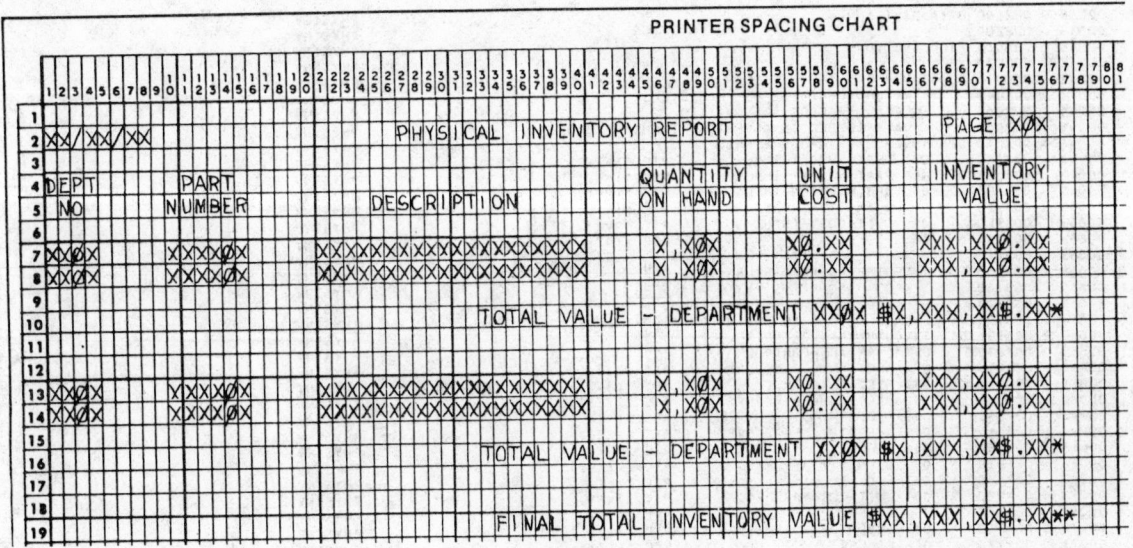

PRINTER SPACING CHART

Figure 8-30 Output

Source Listing

```
                          IBM DOS AMERICAN NATIONAL STANDARD COBOL        CBF CL3-4          07/05/77
      1

00001   001010 IDENTIFICATION DIVISION.                                      PHYSINV
00002   001020                                                               PHYSINV
00003   001030 PROGRAM-ID.      PHYSINV.                                     PHYSINV
00004   001040 AUTHOR.          SHELLY AND CASHMAN.                          PHYSINV
00005   001050 INSTALLATION.    ANAHEIM.                                     PHYSINV
00006   001060 DATE-WRITTEN.    07/05/77.                                    PHYSINV
00007   001070 DATE-COMPILED.   07/05/77                                     PHYSINV
00008   001080 SECURITY.        UNCLASSIFIED.                                PHYSINV
00009   001090                                                              PHYSINV
00010   001100*******************************************************    *  PHYSINV
00011   001110*                                                          *  PHYSINV
00012   001120*  THIS PROGRAM PRODUCES A PHYSICAL INVENTORY REPORT.  FOR EACH*  PHYSINV
00013   001130*  ITEM NUMBER IN INVENTORY THE QUANTITY ON HAND IS MULTIPLIED *  PHYSINV
00014   001140*  BY THE UNIT COST TO OBTAIN THE INVENTORY VALUE.  WHEN THERE *  PHYSINV
00015   001150*  IS A CHANGE IN DEPARTMENT NUMBER A TOTAL IS PRINTED LISTING *  PHYSINV
00016   001160*  THE INVENTORY VALUE FOR THE DEPARTMENT.  AFTER ALL CARDS  *  PHYSINV
00017   001170*  HAVE BEEN PROCESSED A FINAL TOTAL IS PRINTED.             *  PHYSINV
00018   001180*                                                          *  PHYSINV
00019   001190*******************************************************    *  PHYSINV
00020   001200                                                              PHYSINV
00021   002010                                                              PHYSINV
00022   002020                                                              PHYSINV
00023   002030 ENVIRONMENT DIVISION.                                        PHYSINV
00024   002040                                                              PHYSINV
00025   002050 CONFIGURATION SECTION.                                       PHYSINV
00026   002060                                                              PHYSINV
00027   002070 SOURCE-COMPUTER. IBM-370.                                    PHYSINV
00028   002080 OBJECT-COMPUTER. IBM-370.                                    PHYSINV
00029   002090 SPECIAL-NAMES.   C01 IS TO-TOP-OF-PAGE.                      PHYSINV
00030   002100                                                              PHYSINV
00031   002110 INPUT-OUTPUT SECTION.                                        PHYSINV
00032   002120                                                              PHYSINV
00033   002130 FILE-CONTROL.                                                PHYSINV
00034   002140     SELECT INVENTORY-INPUT-FILE                              PHYSINV
00035   002150         ASSIGN TO SYS007-UR-2540R-S.                         PHYSINV
00036   002160     SELECT INVENTORY-REPORT-FILE                             PHYSINV
00037   002170         ASSIGN TO SYS013-UR-1403-S.                          PHYSINV
```

Figure 8-31 Source Listing [Part 1 of 4]

```
      2
00038   002190 DATA DIVISION.                                              PHYSINV
00039   002200                                                             PHYSINV
00040   003010 FILE SECTION.                                               PHYSINV
00041   003020                                                             PHYSINV
00042   003030 FD  INVENTORY-INPUT-FILE                                    PHYSINV
00043   003040       RECORD CONTAINS 80 CHARACTERS                         PHYSINV
00044   003050       LABEL RECORDS ARE OMITTED                             PHYSINV
00045   003060       DATA RECORD IS INVENTORY-INPUT-RECORD.                PHYSINV
00046   003070 01  INVENTORY-INPUT-RECORD.                                 PHYSINV
00047   003080     05   DEPT-NUMBER-INPUT      PIC 9(4).                   PHYSINV
00048   003090     05   PART-NUMBER-INPUT      PIC 9(6).                   PHYSINV
00049   003100     05   DESCRIPTION-INPUT      PIC X(20).                  PHYSINV
00050   003110     05   QUANTITY-INPUT         PIC 9(4).                   PHYSINV
00051   00312D     05   UNIT-COST-INPUT        PIC 99V99.                  PHYSINV
00052   003130     05   FILLER                 PIC X(42).                  PHYSINV
00053   003140                                                             PHYSINV
00054   003150 FD  INVENTORY-REPORT-FILE                                   PHYSINV
00055   003160       RECORD CONTAINS 133 CHARACTERS                       PHYSINV
00056   003170       LABEL RECORDS ARE OMITTED                            PHYSINV
00057   003180       DATA RECORD IS INVENTORY-REPORT-LINE.                PHYSINV
00058   003190 01  INVENTORY-REPORT-LINE.                                  PHYSINV
00059   003200     05   CARRIAGE-CONTROL       PIC X.                      PHYSINV
00060   004010     05   DEPT-NUMBER-REPORT     PIC ZZZ9.                   PHYSINV
00061   004020     05   FILLER                 PIC X(5).                   PHYSINV
00062   004030     05   PART-NUMBER-REPORT     PIC ZZZZZ9.                 PHYSINV
00063   004040     05   FILLER                 PIC X(5).                   PHYSINV
00064   004050     05   DESCRIPTION-REPORT     PIC X(20).                  PHYSINV
00065   004060     05   FILLER                 PIC X(5).                   PHYSINV
00066   004070     05   QUANTITY-REPORT        PIC Z,ZZ9.                  PHYSINV
00067   004080     05   FILLER                 PIC X(5).                   PHYSINV
00068   004090     05   UNIT-COST-REPORT       PIC ZZ.99.                  PHYSINV
00069   004100     05   FILLER                 PIC X(5).                   PHYSINV
00070   004110     05   INVENTORY-VALUE-REPORT PIC ZZZ,ZZZ.99.            PHYSINV
00071   004120     05   FILLER                 PIC X(57).                  PHYSINV
00072   004130                                                             PHYSINV
00073   004140 WORKING-STORAGE SECTION.                                    PHYSINV
00074   004150                                                             PHYSINV
00075   004160 01  PROGRAM-INDICATORS.                                     PHYSINV
00076   004170     05   ARE-THERE-MORE-RECORDS PIC XXX     VALUE 'YES'.   PHYSINV
00077   004180       88  THERE-IS-A-RECORD                 VALUE 'YES'.   PHYSINV
00078   004190       88  THERE-ARE-NO-MORE-RECORDS         VALUE 'NO '.   PHYSINV
00079   004200                                                             PHYSINV
00080   005010 01  PROGRAM-COMPARE-AREAS.                                  PHYSINV
00081   005020     05   PREVIOUS-DEPT-NUMBER   PIC 9(4)    USAGE IS COMP-3. PHYSINV
00082   005030                                                             PHYSINV
00083   005040 01  WORK-AREAS.                                             PHYSINV
00084   005050     05   INVENTORY-VALUE-WORK   PIC S9(6)V99 USAGE IS COMP-3. PHYSINV
00085   005060                                                             PHYSINV
00086   005070 01  TOTAL-ACCUMULATORS                     USAGE IS COMP-3. PHYSINV
00087   005080     05   DEPT-TOTAL-ACCUM       PIC S9(7)V99 VALUE ZERO.   PHYSINV
00088   005090     05   FINAL-TOTAL-ACCUM      PIC S9(8)V99 VALUE ZERO.   PHYSINV
00089   005100                                                             PHYSINV
00090   005110 01  PRINTER-CONTROL.                                        PHYSINV
00091   005120     05   PROPER-SPACING         PIC 9.                      PHYSINV
00092   005130     05   SPACE-ONE-LINE         PIC 9       VALUE 1.        PHYSINV
00093   005140     05   SPACE-TWO-LINES        PIC 9       VALUE 2.        PHYSINV
00094   005150     05   SPACE-THREE-LINES      PIC 9       VALUE 3.        PHYSINV
00095   005160     05   LINES-PRINTED          PIC S999    VALUE ZERO     PHYSINV
00096   005170                                            USAGE IS COMP-3. PHYSINV
00097   005180     05   PAGE-SIZE              PIC 999     VALUE 50        PHYSINV
00098   005190                                            USAGE IS COMP-3. PHYSINV
00099   005200     05   PAGE-COUNT             PIC S999    VALUE +1        PHYSINV
00100   006010                                            USAGE IS COMP-3. PHYSINV
00101   006020       88  FIRST-PAGE                        VALUE +1.       PHYSINV
00102   006030                                                             PHYSINV
00103   006040 01  REPORT-HEADINGS.                                        PHYSINV
00104   006050     05   FIRST-HEADING-LINE.                                PHYSINV
00105   006060       10   CARRIAGE-CONTROL     PIC X.                      PHYSINV
00106   006070       10   DATE-HEADING         PIC X(8).                   PHYSINV
00107   006080       10   FILLER               PIC X(18)   VALUE SPACES.  PHYSINV
00108   006090       10   FILLER               PIC X(9)    VALUE 'PHYSICAL '. PHYSINV
00109   006100       10   FILLER               PIC X(10)   VALUE 'INVENTORY '. PHYSINV
00110   006110       10   FILLER               PIC X(6)    VALUE 'REPORT'. PHYSINV
00111   006120       10   FILLER               PIC X(16)   VALUE SPACES.  PHYSINV
00112   006130       10   FILLER               PIC X(5)    VALUE 'PAGE '. PHYSINV
00113   006140       10   PAGE-HEADING         PIC ZZ9.                    PHYSINV
00114   006150       10   FILLER               PIC X(57)   VALUE SPACES.  PHYSINV
00115   006160     05   SECOND-HEADING-LINE.                               PHYSINV
00116   006170       10   CARRIAGE-CONTROL     PIC X.                      PHYSINV
00117   006180       10   FILLER               PIC X(4)    VALUE 'DEPT'.  PHYSINV
00118   006190       10   FILLER               PIC X(6)    VALUE SPACES.  PHYSINV
00119   006200       10   FILLER               PIC X(4)    VALUE 'PART'.  PHYSINV
00120   007010       10   FILLER               PIC X(30)   VALUE SPACES.  PHYSINV
00121   007020       10   FILLER               PIC X(8)    VALUE 'QUANTITY'. PHYSINV
00122   007030       10   FILLER               PIC X(4)    VALUE SPACES.  PHYSINV
00123   007040       10   FILLER               PIC X(4)    VALUE 'UNIT'.  PHYSINV
00124   007050       10   FILLER               PIC X(6)    VALUE SPACES.  PHYSINV
00125   007060       10   FILLER               PIC X(9)    VALUE 'INVENTORY'. PHYSINV
00126   007070       10   FILLER               PIC X(57)   VALUE SPACES.  PHYSINV
```

Figure 8-32 Source Listing [Part 2 of 4]

```
      3
 00127   007080      05  THIRD-HEADING-LINE.                                 PHYSINV
 00128   007090          10  CARRIAGE-CONTROL    PIC X.                      PHYSINV
 00129   007100          10  FILLER              PIC X       VALUE SPACE.    PHYSINV
 00130   007110          10  FILLER              PIC XX      VALUE 'NO'.     PHYSINV
 00131   007120          10  FILLER              PIC X(6)    VALUE SPACES.   PHYSINV
 00132   007130          10  FILLER              PIC X(6)    VALUE 'NUMBER'. PHYSINV
 00133   007140          10  FILLER              PIC X(9)    VALUE SPACES.   PHYSINV
 00134   007150          10  FILLER              PIC X(11)   VALUE 'DESCRIPTION'. PHYSINV
 00135   007160          10  FILLER              PIC X(9)    VALUE SPACES.   PHYSINV
 00136   007170          10  FILLER              PIC X(7)    VALUE 'ON HAND'. PHYSINV
 00137   007180          10  FILLER              PIC X(5)    VALUE SPACES.   PHYSINV
 00138   007190          10  FILLER              PIC X(4)    VALUE 'COST'.   PHYSINV
 00139   007200          10  FILLER              PIC X(8)    VALUE SPACES.   PHYSINV
 00140   008010          10  FILLER              PIC X(5)    VALUE 'VALUE'.  PHYSINV
 00141   008020          10  FILLER              PIC X(59)   VALUE SPACES.   PHYSINV
 00142   008030                                                             PHYSINV
 00143   008040  01  TOTAL-LINES.                                           PHYSINV
 00144   008050      05  DEPARTMENT-TOTAL-LINE.                             PHYSINV
 00145   008060          10  CARRIAGE-CONTROL    PIC X.                      PHYSINV
 00146   008070          10  FILLER              PIC X(32)   VALUE SPACES.   PHYSINV
 00147   008080          10  FILLER              PIC X(6)    VALUE 'TOTAL '. PHYSINV
 00148   008090          10  FILLER              PIC X(8)    VALUE 'VALUE - '. PHYSINV
 00149   008100          10  FILLER              PIC X(11)   VALUE 'DEPARTMENT '. PHYSINV
 00150   008110          10  DEPT-NUMBER-TOTAL-LINE PIC ZZZ9.               PHYSINV
 00151   008120          10  FILLER              PIC X       VALUE SPACE.    PHYSINV
 00152   008130          10  DEPT-VALUE-TOTAL-LINE PIC $$,$$$,$$$.99.        PHYSINV
 00153   008140          10  FILLER              PIC X       VALUE '*'.      PHYSINV
 00154   008150          10  FILLER              PIC X(56)   VALUE SPACES.   PHYSINV
 00155   008160      05  FINAL-TOTAL-LINE.                                  PHYSINV
 00156   008170          10  FILLER              PIC X.                      PHYSINV
 00157   008180          10  FILLER              PIC X(33)   VALUE SPACES.   PHYSINV
 00158   008190          10  FILLER              PIC X(11)   VALUE 'FINAL TOTAL'. PHYSINV
 00159   008200          10  FILLER              PIC X(17)   VALUE          PHYSINV
 00160   009010                                      ' INVENTORY VALUE '.   PHYSINV
 00161   009020          10  INVENTORY-VALUE-FINAL-TOTAL PIC $$$,$$$,$$$.99. PHYSINV
 00162   009030          10  FILLER              PIC XX      VALUE '**'.     PHYSINV
 00163   009040          10  FILLER              PIC X(55)   VALUE SPACES.   PHYSINV
```

```
      4
 00164   009060  PROCEDURE DIVISION.                                        PHYSINV
 00165   009070                                                             PHYSINV
 00166   009080  ************************************************************* PHYSINV
 00167   009090*                                                          * PHYSINV
 00168   009100*   THIS MODULE CONTROLS THE PROCESSING OF THE DETAIL RECORDS. * PHYSINV
 00169   009110*   WHEN A CONTROL BREAK OCCURS ON DEPARTMENT NUMBER, CONTROL * PHYSINV
 00170   009120*   IS TRANSFERRED TO A MODULE TO PRINT THE DEPARTMENT TOTALS. * PHYSINV
 00171   009130*   FINAL TOTALS ARE PRINTED AFTER ALL RECORDS HAVE BEEN    * PHYSINV
 00172   009140*   PROCESSED.  THIS MODULE IS ENTERED FROM AND             * PHYSINV
 00173   009150*   EXITS TO THE OPERATING SYSTEM.                          * PHYSINV
 00174   009160*                                                          * PHYSINV
 00175   009170  ************************************************************* PHYSINV
 00176   009180                                                             PHYSINV
 00177   009190  A000-CREATE-INVENTORY-REPORT.                             PHYSINV
 00178   009200                                                             PHYSINV
 00179   010010      OPEN INPUT  INVENTORY-INPUT-FILE                       PHYSINV
 00180   010020           OUTPUT INVENTORY-REPORT-FILE.                     PHYSINV
 00181   010030      READ INVENTORY-INPUT-FILE                              PHYSINV
 00182   010040          AT END                                            PHYSINV
 00183   010050              MOVE 'NO ' TO ARE-THERE-MORE-RECORDS.          PHYSINV
 00184   010060      IF THERE-IS-A-RECORD                                   PHYSINV
 00185   010070          MOVE DEPT-NUMBER-INPUT TO PREVIOUS-DEPT-NUMBER     PHYSINV
 00186   010080          PERFORM A001-COMPARE-AND-PROCESS                   PHYSINV
 00187   010090              UNTIL THERE-ARE-NO-MORE-RECORDS                PHYSINV
 00188   010100          PERFORM B010-PROCESS-DEPT-CHANGE                   PHYSINV
 00189   010110          PERFORM B020-PRINT-FINAL-TOTALS.                   PHYSINV
 00190   010120      CLOSE INVENTORY-INPUT-FILE                             PHYSINV
 00191   010130            INVENTORY-REPORT-FILE.                           PHYSINV
 00192   010140      STOP RUN..                                             PHYSINV
 00193   010150                                                             PHYSINV
 00194   010160                                                             PHYSINV
 00195   010170                                                             PHYSINV
 00196   010180  A001-COMPARE-AND-PROCESS.                                  PHYSINV
 00197   010190                                                             PHYSINV
 00198   010200      IF DEPT-NUMBER-INPUT IS NOT = PREVIOUS-DEPT-NUMBER     PHYSINV
 00199   011010          PERFORM B010-PROCESS-DEPT-CHANGE.                  PHYSINV
 00200   011020      PERFORM B000-PROCESS-DETAIL-RECORD.                    PHYSINV
 00201   011030      READ INVENTORY-INPUT-FILE                              PHYSINV
 00202   011040          AT END                                            PHYSINV
 00203   011050              MOVE 'NO ' TO ARE-THERE-MORE-RECORDS.          PHYSINV
```

Figure 8-33 Source Listing [Page 3 of 4]

```
   5
00204  011060*********************************************************  PHYSINV
00205  011070*                                                      *  PHYSINV
00206  011080*  THIS MODULE IS ENTERED TO PRINT THE DETAIL LINE FOR THE *  PHYSINV
00207  011090*  REPORT.  IF NECESSARY, IT CAUSES THE HEADINGS TO BE PRINTED *  PHYSINV
00208  011100*  AND THEN FORMATS THE DETAIL LINE, CALCULATES THE INVENTORY *  PHYSINV
00209  011110*  VALUE, AND PRINTS THE DETAIL LINE.  DEPARTMENT AND FINAL  *  PHYSINV
00210  011120*  TOTALS ARE ALSO ACCUMULATED.  THIS MODULE IS ENTERED FROM *  PHYSINV
00211  011130*  AND EXITS TO THE A000-CREATE-INVENTORY-REPORT MODULE.  *  PHYSINV
00212  011140*                                                      *  PHYSINV
00213  011150*********************************************************  PHYSINV
00214  011160                                                         PHYSINV
00215  011170 B000-PROCESS-DETAIL-RECORD.                             PHYSINV
00216  011180                                                         PHYSINV
00217  011190     IF LINES-PRINTED IS EQUAL TO PAGE-SIZE OR           PHYSINV
00218  011200        IS GREATER THAN PAGE-SIZE OR                     PHYSINV
00219  012010        FIRST-PAGE                                       PHYSINV
00220  012020        PERFORM C000-PRINT-HEADINGS.                     PHYSINV
00221  012030     MOVE SPACES TO INVENTORY-REPORT-LINE.               PHYSINV
00222  012040     MOVE DEPT-NUMBER-INPUT TO DEPT-NUMBER-REPORT.       PHYSINV
00223  012050     MOVE PART-NUMBER-INPUT TO PART-NUMBER-REPORT.       PHYSINV
00224  012060     MOVE DESCRIPTION-INPUT TO DESCRIPTION-REPORT.       PHYSINV
00225  012070     MOVE QUANTITY-INPUT TO QUANTITY-REPORT.             PHYSINV
00226  012080     MOVE UNIT-COST-INPUT TO UNIT-COST-REPORT.           PHYSINV
00227  012090     MULTIPLY QUANTITY-INPUT BY UNIT-COST-INPUT GIVING   PHYSINV
00228  012100        INVENTORY-VALUE-WORK.                            PHYSINV
00229  012110     MOVE INVENTORY-VALUE-WORK TO INVENTORY-VALUE-REPORT. PHYSINV
00230  012120     ADD INVENTORY-VALUE-WORK TO DEPT-TOTAL-ACCUM        PHYSINV
00231  012130                                FINAL-TOTAL-ACCUM.       PHYSINV
00232  012140     WRITE INVENTORY-REPORT-LINE                         PHYSINV
00233  012150        AFTER PROPER-SPACING.                            PHYSINV
00234  012160     MOVE SPACE-ONE-LINE TO PROPER-SPACING.              PHYSINV
00235  012170     ADD 1 TO LINES-PRINTED.                             PHYSINV

   6
00236  012190*********************************************************  PHYSINV
00237  012200*                                                      *  PHYSINV
00238  013010*  THIS MODULE PROCESSES A CHANGE IN DEPARTMENT NUMBER.  THE *  PHYSINV
00239  013020*  DEPARTMENT TOTAL IS PRINTED AND THE ACCUMULATOR AND COMPARE *  PHYSINV
00240  013030*  AREAS ARE RESET.  THIS MODULE IS ENTERED FROM AND EXITS TO *  PHYSINV
00241  013040*  THE A000-CREATE-INVENTORY-REPORT MODULE.             *  PHYSINV
00242  013050*                                                      *  PHYSINV
00243  013060*********************************************************  PHYSINV
00244  013070                                                         PHYSINV
00245  013080 B010-PROCESS-DEPT-CHANGE.                               PHYSINV
00246  013090                                                         PHYSINV
00247  013100     MOVE PREVIOUS-DEPT-NUMBER TO DEPT-NUMBER-TOTAL-LINE. PHYSINV
00248  013110     MOVE DEPT-TOTAL-ACCUM TO DEPT-VALUE-TOTAL-LINE.     PHYSINV
00249  013120     WRITE INVENTORY-REPORT-LINE FROM DEPARTMENT-TOTAL-LINE PHYSINV
00250  013130        AFTER ADVANCING 2 LINES.                         PHYSINV
00251  013140     MOVE SPACE-THREE-LINES TO PROPER-SPACING.           PHYSINV
00252  013150     ADD 4 TO LINES-PRINTED.                             PHYSINV
00253  013160     MOVE ZEROS TO DEPT-TOTAL-ACCUM.                     PHYSINV
00254  013170     MOVE DEPT-NUMBER-INPUT TO PREVIOUS-DEPT-NUMBER.     PHYSINV

   7
00255  013190*********************************************************  PHYSINV
00256  013200*                                                      *  PHYSINV
00257  014010*  THIS MODULE PRINTS THE FINAL TOTALS.  IT IS ENTERED FROM *  PHYSINV
00258  014020*  AND EXITS TO THE A000-CREATE-INVENTORY-REPORT MODULE. *  PHYSINV
00259  014030*                                                      *  PHYSINV
00260  014040*********************************************************  PHYSINV
00261  014050                                                         PHYSINV
00262  014060 B020-PRINT-FINAL-TOTALS.                                PHYSINV
00263  014070                                                         PHYSINV
00264  014080     MOVE FINAL-TOTAL-ACCUM TO INVENTORY-VALUE-FINAL-TOTAL. PHYSINV
00265  014090     WRITE INVENTORY-REPORT-LINE FROM FINAL-TOTAL-LINE   PHYSINV
00266  014100        AFTER ADVANCING 3 LINES.                         PHYSINV

   8
00267  014120*********************************************************  PHYSINV
00268  014190*                                                      *  PHYSINV
00269  014140*  THIS MODULE IS ENTERED TO PRINT THE HEADINGS ON THE REPORT. *  PHYSINV
00270  014150*  IT IS ENTERED FROM AND EXITS TO THE B000-PROCESS-DETAIL- *  PHYSINV
00271  014160*  RECORD MODULE.                                       *  PHYSINV
00272  014170*                                                      *  PHYSINV
00273  014180*********************************************************  PHYSINV
00274  014190                                                         PHYSINV
00275  014200 C000-PRINT-HEADINGS.                                    PHYSINV
00276  015010                                                         PHYSINV
00277  015020     MOVE CURRENT-DATE TO DATE-HEADING.                  PHYSINV
00278  015030     MOVE PAGE-COUNT TO PAGE-HEADING.                    PHYSINV
00279  015040     WRITE INVENTORY-REPORT-LINE FROM FIRST-HEADING-LINE PHYSINV
00280  015050        AFTER ADVANCING TO-TOP-OF-PAGE.                  PHYSINV
00281  015060     ADD 1 TO PAGE-COUNT.                                PHYSINV
00282  015070     WRITE INVENTORY-REPORT-LINE FROM SECOND-HEADING-LINE PHYSINV
00283  015080        AFTER ADVANCING 2 LINES.                         PHYSINV
00284  015090     WRITE INVENTORY-REPORT-LINE FROM THIRD-HEADING-LINE PHYSINV
00285  015100        AFTER ADVANCING 1 LINES.                         PHYSINV
00286  015110     MOVE SPACE-TWO-LINES TO PROPER-SPACING.             PHYSINV
00287  015120     MOVE ZERO TO LINES-PRINTED.                         PHYSINV
```

Figure 8-34 Source Listing [Part 4 of 4]

CHAPTER 8

REVIEW QUESTIONS

1. What is meant by ''Detail Printing''.

2. Explain the term ''Control Break''.

3. Briefly explain the processing that must occur when the first record is read in a program involving a control break.

4. Briefly explain the processing that must occur in a program involving a control break when a control break occurs.

CHAPTER 8

DEBUGGING COBOL PROGRAMS

PROBLEM 1

INSTRUCTIONS

The following COBOL program contains an error or errors which occurred during execution. Circle each error and record the corrected entries directly on the listing. Explain the error and method of correction in the space provided below.

```
      1                           IBM DOS AMERICAN NATIONAL STANDARD COBOL        CBF CL3-4        07/05/77

   00001    001010 IDENTIFICATION DIVISION.                                     PHYSINV
   00002    001020                                                              PHYSINV
   00003    001030 PROGRAM-ID.    PHYSINV.                                      PHYSINV
   00004    001040 AUTHOR.        SHELLY AND CASHMAN.                           PHYSINV
   00005    001050 INSTALLATION.  ANAHEIM.                                      PHYSINV
   00006    001060 DATE-WRITTEN.  07/05/77.                                     PHYSINV
   00007    001070 DATE-COMPILED. 07/05/77                                      PHYSINV
   00008    001080 SECURITY.      UNCLASSIFIED.                                 PHYSINV
   00009    001090                                                              PHYSINV
   00010    001100********************************************************       PHYSINV
   00011    001110*                                                      *      PHYSINV
   00012    001120*  THIS PROGRAM PRODUCES A PHYSICAL INVENTORY REPORT.  FOR EACH* PHYSINV
   00013    001130*  ITEM NUMBER IN INVENTORY THE QUANTITY ON HAND IS MULTIPLIED * PHYSINV
   00014    001140*  BY THE UNIT COST TO OBTAIN THE INVENTORY VALUE.  WHEN THERE * PHYSINV
   00015    001150*  IS A CHANGE IN DEPARTMENT NUMBER A TOTAL IS PRINTED LISTING * PHYSINV
   00016    001160*  THE INVENTORY VALUE FOR THE DEPARTMENT.  AFTER ALL CARDS  * PHYSINV
   00017    001170*  HAVE BEEN PROCESSED A FINAL TOTAL IS PRINTED.            * PHYSINV
   00018    001180*                                                      *      PHYSINV
   00019    001190********************************************************       PHYSINV
   00020    001200                                                              PHYSINV
   00021    002010                                                              PHYSINV
   00022    002020                                                              PHYSINV
   00023    002030 ENVIRONMENT DIVISION.                                        PHYSINV
   00024    002040                                                              PHYSINV
   00025    002050 CONFIGURATION SECTION.                                       PHYSINV
   00026    002060                                                              PHYSINV
   00027    002070 SOURCE-COMPUTER. IBM-370.                                    PHYSINV
   00028    002080 OBJECT-COMPUTER. IBM-370.                                    PHYSINV
   00029    002090 SPECIAL-NAMES.   C01 IS TO-TOP-OF-PAGE.                      PHYSINV
   00030    002100                                                              PHYSINV
   00031    002110 INPUT-OUTPUT SECTION.                                        PHYSINV
   00032    002120                                                              PHYSINV
   00033    002130 FILE-CONTROL.                                                PHYSINV
   00034    002140     SELECT INVENTORY-INPUT-FILE                              PHYSINV
   00035    002150         ASSIGN TO SYS007-UR-2540R-S.                         PHYSINV
   00036    002160     SELECT INVENTORY-REPORT-FILE                             PHYSINV
   00037    002170         ASSIGN TO SYS013-UR-1403-S.                          PHYSINV
```

```
      2

   00038    002190 DATA DIVISION.                                               PHYSINV
   00039    002200                                                              PHYSINV
   00040    003010 FILE SECTION.                                                PHYSINV
   00041    003020                                                              PHYSINV
   00042    003030 FD  INVENTORY-INPUT-FILE                                     PHYSINV
   00043    003040     RECORD CONTAINS 80 CHARACTERS                            PHYSINV
   00044    003050     LABEL RECORDS ARE OMITTED                                PHYSINV
   00045    003060     DATA RECORD IS INVENTORY-INPUT-RECORD.                   PHYSINV
   00046    003070 01  INVENTORY-INPUT-RECORD.                                  PHYSINV
   00047    003080     05  DEPT-NUMBER-INPUT       PIC 9(4).                    PHYSINV
   00048    003090     05  PART-NUMBER-INPUT       PIC 9(6).                    PHYSINV
   00049    003100     05  DESCRIPTION-INPUT       PIC X(20).                   PHYSINV
   00050    003110     05  QUANTITY-INPUT          PIC 9(4).                    PHYSINV
   00051    003120     05  UNIT-COST-INPUT         PIC 99V99.                   PHYSINV
   00052    003130     05  FILLER                  PIC X(42).                   PHYSINV
   00053    003140                                                              PHYSINV
   00054    003150 FD  INVENTORY-REPORT-FILE                                    PHYSINV
   00055    003160     RECORD CONTAINS 133 CHARACTERS                           PHYSINV
   00056    003170     LABEL RECORDS ARE OMITTED                                PHYSINV
   00057    003180     DATA RECORD IS INVENTORY-REPORT-LINE.                    PHYSINV
   00058    003190 01  INVENTORY-REPORT-LINE.                                   PHYSINV
   00059    003200     05  CARRIAGE-CONTROL        PIC X.                       PHYSINV
   00060    004010     05  DEPT-NUMBER-REPORT      PIC ZZZ9.                    PHYSINV
   00061    004020     05  FILLER                  PIC X(5).                    PHYSINV
   00062    004030     05  PART-NUMBER-REPORT      PIC ZZZZZ9.                  PHYSINV
   00063    004040     05  FILLER                  PIC X(5).                    PHYSINV
   00064    004050     05  DESCRIPTION-REPORT      PIC X(20).                   PHYSINV
   00065    004060     05  FILLER                  PIC X(5).                    PHYSINV
   00066    004070     05  QUANTITY-REPORT         PIC Z,ZZ9.                   PHYSINV
   00067    004080     05  FILLER                  PIC X(5).                    PHYSINV
   00068    004090     05  UNIT-COST-REPORT        PIC ZZ.99.                   PHYSINV
   00069    004100     05  FILLER                  PIC X(5).                    PHYSINV
   00070    004110     05  INVENTORY-VALUE-REPORT  PIC ZZZ,ZZZ.99.             PHYSINV
   00071    004120     05  FILLER                  PIC X(57).                   PHYSINV
   00072    004130                                                              PHYSINV
```

Control Breaks

8.37

```
   3
00073  004140 WORKING-STORAGE SECTION.                              PHYSINV
00074  004150                                                       PHYSINV
00075  004160 01  PROGRAM-INDICATORS.                               PHYSINV
00076  004170     05  ARE-THERE-MORE-RECORDS  PIC XXX    VALUE 'YES'. PHYSINV
00077  004180         88  THERE-IS-A-RECORD              VALUE 'YES'. PHYSINV
00078  004190         88  THERE-ARE-NO-MORE-RECORDS      VALUE 'NO '. PHYSINV
00079  004200                                                       PHYSINV
00080  005010 01  PROGRAM-COMPARE-AREAS.                            PHYSINV
00081  005020     05  PREVIOUS-DEPT-NUMBER  PIC 9(4)   USAGE IS COMP-3. PHYSINV
00082  005030                                                       PHYSINV
00083  005040 01  WORK-AREAS.                                       PHYSINV
00084  005050     05  INVENTORY-VALUE-WORK  PIC S9(6)V99 USAGE IS COMP-3. PHYSINV
00085  005060                                                       PHYSINV
00086  005070 01  TOTAL-ACCUMULATORS           USAGE IS COMP-3.     PHYSINV
00087  005080     05  DEPT-TOTAL-ACCUM  PIC S9(7)V99 VALUE ZERO.    PHYSINV
00088  005090     05  FINAL-TOTAL-ACCUM PIC S9(8)V99 VALUE ZERO.    PHYSINV
00089  005100                                                       PHYSINV
00090  005110 01  PRINTER-CONTROL.                                  PHYSINV
00091  005120     05  PROPER-SPACING       PIC 9.                   PHYSINV
00092  005130     05  SPACE-ONE-LINE       PIC 9      VALUE 1.      PHYSINV
00093  005140     05  SPACE-TWO-LINES      PIC 9      VALUE 2.      PHYSINV
00094  005150     05  SPACE-THREE-LINES    PIC 9      VALUE 3.      PHYSINV
00095  005160     05  LINES-PRINTED        PIC S999   VALUE ZERO    PHYSINV
00096  005170                                   USAGE IS COMP-3.    PHYSINV
00097  005180     05  PAGE-SIZE            PIC 999    VALUE 50      PHYSINV
00098  005190                                   USAGE IS COMP-3.    PHYSINV
00099  005200     05  PAGE-COUNT           PIC S999   VALUE +1      PHYSINV
00100  006010                                   USAGE IS COMP-3.    PHYSINV
00101  006020         88  FIRST-PAGE                  VALUE +1.     PHYSINV
00102  006030                                                       PHYSINV
00103  006040 01  REPORT-HEADINGS.                                  PHYSINV
00104  006050     05  FIRST-HEADING-LINE.                           PHYSINV
00105  006060         10  CARRIAGE-CONTROL  PIC X.                  PHYSINV
00106  006070         10  DATE-HEADING      PIC X(8).               PHYSINV
00107  006080         10  FILLER            PIC X(18)  VALUE SPACES. PHYSINV
00108  006090         10  FILLER            PIC X(9)   VALUE 'PHYSICAL '. PHYSINV
00109  006100         10  FILLER            PIC X(10)  VALUE 'INVENTORY '. PHYSINV
00110  006110         10  FILLER            PIC X(6)   VALUE 'REPORT'. PHYSINV
00111  006120         10  FILLER            PIC X(16)  VALUE SPACES. PHYSINV
00112  006130         10  FILLER            PIC X(5)   VALUE 'PAGE '. PHYSINV
00113  006140         10  PAGE-HEADING      PIC ZZ9.                PHYSINV
00114  006150         10  FILLER            PIC X(57)  VALUE SPACES. PHYSINV
00115  006160     05  SECOND-HEADING-LINE.                          PHYSINV
00116  006170         10  CARRIAGE-CONTROL  PIC X.                  PHYSINV
00117  006180         10  FILLER            PIC X(4)   VALUE 'DEPT'. PHYSINV
00118  006190         10  FILLER            PIC X(6)   VALUE SPACES. PHYSINV
00119  006200         10  FILLER            PIC X(4)   VALUE 'PART'. PHYSINV
00120  007010         10  FILLER            PIC X(30)  VALUE SPACES. PHYSINV
00121  007020         10  FILLER            PIC X(8)   VALUE 'QUANTITY'. PHYSINV
00122  007030         10  FILLER            PIC X(4)   VALUE SPACES. PHYSINV
00123  007040         10  FILLER            PIC X(4)   VALUE 'UNIT'. PHYSINV
00124  007050         10  FILLER            PIC X(6)   VALUE SPACES. PHYSINV
00125  007060         10  FILLER            PIC X(9)   VALUE 'INVENTORY'. PHYSINV
00126  007070         10  FILLER            PIC X(57)  VALUE SPACES. PHYSINV
00127  007080     05  THIRD-HEADING-LINE.                           PHYSINV
00128  007090         10  CARRIAGE-CONTROL  PIC X.                  PHYSINV
00129  007100         10  FILLER            PIC X      VALUE SPACE.  PHYSINV
00130  007110         10  FILLER            PIC XX     VALUE 'NO'.   PHYSINV
00131  007120         10  FILLER            PIC X(6)   VALUE SPACES. PHYSINV
00132  007130         10  FILLER            PIC X(6)   VALUE 'NUMBER'. PHYSINV
00133  007140         10  FILLER            PIC X(9)   VALUE SPACES. PHYSINV
00134  007150         10  FILLER            PIC X(11)  VALUE 'DESCRIPTION'. PHYSINV
00135  007160         10  FILLER            PIC X(9)   VALUE SPACES. PHYSINV
00136  007170         10  FILLER            PIC X(7)   VALUE 'ON HAND'. PHYSINV
00137  007180         10  FILLER            PIC X(5)   VALUE SPACES. PHYSINV
00138  007190         10  FILLER            PIC X(4)   VALUE 'COST'. PHYSINV
00139  007200         10  FILLER            PIC X(8)   VALUE SPACES. PHYSINV
00140  008010         10  FILLER            PIC X(5)   VALUE 'VALUE'. PHYSINV
00141  008020         10  FILLER            PIC X(59)  VALUE SPACES. PHYSINV
00142  008030                                                       PHYSINV
00143  008040 01  TOTAL-LINES.                                      PHYSINV
00144  008050     05  DEPARTMENT-TOTAL-LINE.                        PHYSINV
00145  008060         10  CARRIAGE-CONTROL  PIC X.                  PHYSINV
00146  008070         10  FILLER            PIC X(32)  VALUE SPACES. PHYSINV
00147  008080         10  FILLER            PIC X(6)   VALUE 'TOTAL '. PHYSINV
00148  008090         10  FILLER            PIC X(8)   VALUE 'VALUE - '. PHYSINV
00149  008100         10  FILLER            PIC X(11)  VALUE 'DEPARTMENT '. PHYSINV
00150  008110         10  DEPT-NUMBER-TOTAL-LINE PIC ZZZ9.          PHYSINV
00151  008120         10  FILLER            PIC X      VALUE SPACE.  PHYSINV
00152  008130         10  DEPT-VALUE-TOTAL-LINE PIC $$$,$$$,$$$.99.  PHYSINV
00153  008140         10  FILLER            PIC X      VALUE '*'.    PHYSINV
00154  008150         10  FILLER            PIC X(56)  VALUE SPACES. PHYSINV
00155  008160     05  FINAL-TOTAL-LINE.                             PHYSINV
00156  008170         10  CARRIAGE-CONTROL  PIC X.                  PHYSINV
00157  008180         10  FILLER            PIC X(33)  VALUE SPACES. PHYSINV
00158  008190         10  FILLER            PIC X(11)  VALUE 'FINAL TOTAL'. PHYSINV
00159  008200         10  FILLER            PIC X(17)  VALUE         PHYSINV
00160  009010                                   ' INVENTORY VALUE '. PHYSINV
00161  009020         10  INVENTORY-VALUE-FINAL-TOTAL PIC $$$,$$$,$$$.99. PHYSINV
00162  009030         10  FILLER            PIC XX     VALUE '**'.   PHYSINV
00163  009040         10  FILLER            PIC X(55)  VALUE SPACES. PHYSINV
```

```
     4

00164  009060 PROCEDURE DIVISION.                                         PHYSINV
00165  009070                                                             PHYSINV
00166  009080*****************************************************************  PHYSINV
00167  009090*                                                         *   PHYSINV
00168  009100*  THIS MODULE CONTROLS THE PROCESSING OF THE DETAIL RECORDS. * PHYSINV
00169  009110*  WHEN A CONTROL BREAK OCCURS ON DEPARTMENT NUMBER, CONTROL  * PHYSINV
00170  009120*  IS TRANSFERRED TO A MODULE TO PRINT THE DEPARTMENT TOTALS. * PHYSINV
00171  009130*  FINAL TOTALS ARE PRINTED AFTER ALL RECORDS HAVE BEEN     * PHYSINV
00172  009140*  PROCESSED.  THIS MODULE IS ENTERED FROM AND EXITS TO THE  * PHYSINV
00173  009150*  EXITS TO THE OPERATING SYSTEM.                           * PHYSINV
00174  009160*                                                         *   PHYSINV
00175  009170*****************************************************************  PHYSINV
00176  009180                                                             PHYSINV
00177  009190 A000-CREATE-INVENTORY-REPORT.                               PHYSINV
00178  009200                                                             PHYSINV
00179  010010     OPEN INPUT  INVENTORY-INPUT-FILE                        PHYSINV
00180  010020          OUTPUT INVENTORY-REPORT-FILE.                      PHYSINV
00181  010030     READ INVENTORY-INPUT-FILE                               PHYSINV
00182  010040        AT END                                               PHYSINV
00183  010050           MOVE 'NO ' TO ARE-THERE-MORE-RECORDS.             PHYSINV
00184  010060     IF THERE-IS-A-RECORD                                    PHYSINV
00185  010070        MOVE DEPT-NUMBER-INPUT TO PREVIOUS-DEPT-NUMBER        PHYSINV
00186  010080        PERFORM A001-COMPARE-AND-PROCESS                     PHYSINV
00187  010090           UNTIL THERE-ARE-NO-MORE-RECORDS                   PHYSINV
00188  010100        PERFORM B010-PROCESS-DEPT-CHANGE                     PHYSINV
00189  010110        PERFORM B020-PRINT-FINAL-TOTALS.                    PHYSINV
00190  010120     CLOSE INVENTORY-INPUT-FILE                              PHYSINV
00191  010130           INVENTORY-REPORT-FILE.                            PHYSINV
00192  010140     STOP RUN.                                               PHYSINV
00193  010150                                                             PHYSINV
00194  010160                                                             PHYSINV
00195  010170                                                             PHYSINV
00196  010180 A001-COMPARE-AND-PROCESS.                             (1)   PHYSINV
00197  010190                                                             PHYSINV
00198  010200     IF DEPT-NUMBER-INPUT IS NOT = PREVIOUS-DEPT-NUMBER       PHYSINV
00199  011010        PERFORM B010-PROCESS-DEPT-CHANGE.                   PHYSINV
00200  011020     PERFORM B000-PROCESS-DETAIL-RECORD.                     PHYSINV
00201  011030     READ INVENTORY-INPUT-FILE                               PHYSINV
00202  011040        AT END                                               PHYSINV
00203  011050           MOVE 'NO ' TO ARE-THERE-MORE-RECORDS.             PHYSINV

     5

00204  011060*****************************************************************  PHYSINV
00205  011070*                                                         *   PHYSINV
00206  011080*  THIS MODULE IS ENTERED TO PRINT THE DETAIL LINE FOR THE  * PHYSINV
00207  011090*  REPORT.  IF NECESSARY, IT CAUSES THE HEADINGS TO BE PRINTED * PHYSINV
00208  011100*  AND THEN FORMATS THE DETAIL LINE, CALCULATES THE INVENTORY * PHYSINV
00209  011110*  VALUE, AND PRINTS THE DETAIL LINE.  DEPARTMENT AND FINAL  * PHYSINV
00210  011120*  TOTALS ARE ALSO ACCUMULATED.  THIS MODULE IS ENTERED FROM * PHYSINV
00211  011130*  AND EXITS TO THE A000-CREATE-INVENTORY-REPORT MODULE.     * PHYSINV
00212  011140*                                                         *   PHYSINV
00213  011150*****************************************************************  PHYSINV
00214  011160                                                             PHYSINV
00215  011170 B000-PROCESS-DETAIL-RECORD.                                 PHYSINV
00216  011180                                                             PHYSINV
00217  011190     IF LINES-PRINTED IS EQUAL TO PAGE-SIZE OR               PHYSINV
00218  011200        IS GREATER THAN PAGE-SIZE OR                         PHYSINV
00219  012010        FIRST-PAGE                                           PHYSINV
00220  012020        PERFORM C000-PRINT-HEADINGS.                         PHYSINV
00221  012030     MOVE SPACES TO INVENTORY-REPORT-LINE.                   PHYSINV
00222  012040     MOVE DEPT-NUMBER-INPUT TO DEPT-NUMBER-REPORT.           PHYSINV
00223  012050     MOVE PART-NUMBER-INPUT TO PART-NUMBER-REPORT.           PHYSINV
00224  012060     MOVE DESCRIPTION-INPUT TO DESCRIPTION-REPORT.           PHYSINV
00225  012070     MOVE QUANTITY-INPUT TO QUANTITY-REPORT.                 PHYSINV
00226  012080     MOVE UNIT-COST-INPUT TO UNIT-COST-REPORT.               PHYSINV
00227  012090     MULTIPLY QUANTITY-INPUT BY UNIT-COST-INPUT GIVING       PHYSINV
00228  012100        INVENTORY-VALUE-WORK.                                PHYSINV
00229  012110     MOVE INVENTORY-VALUE-WORK TO INVENTORY-VALUE-REPORT.    PHYSINV
00230  012120     ADD INVENTORY-VALUE-WORK TO DEPT-TOTAL-ACCUM            PHYSINV
00231  012130                                FINAL-TOTAL-ACCUM.           PHYSINV
00232  012140     WRITE INVENTORY-REPORT-LINE                             PHYSINV
00233  012150        AFTER PROPER-SPACING.                                PHYSINV
00234  012160     MOVE SPACE-ONE-LINE TO PROPER-SPACING.                  PHYSINV
00235  012170     ADD 1 TO LINES-PRINTED.                                 PHYSINV

     6

00236  012190*****************************************************************  PHYSINV
00237  012200*                                                         *   PHYSINV
00238  013010*  THIS MODULE PROCESSES A CHANGE IN DEPARTMENT NUMBER.  THE * PHYSINV
00239  013020*  DEPARTMENT TOTAL IS PRINTED AND THE ACCUMULATOR AND COMPARE * PHYSINV
00240  013030*  AREAS ARE RESET.  THIS MODULE IS ENTERED FROM AND EXITS TO * PHYSINV
00241  013040*  THE A000-CREATE-INVENTORY-REPORT MODULE.                 * PHYSINV
00242  013050*                                                         *   PHYSINV
00243  013060*****************************************************************  PHYSINV
00244  013070                                                             PHYSINV
00245  013080 B010-PROCESS-DEPT-CHANGE.                                   PHYSINV
00246  013090                                                             PHYSINV
00247  013100     MOVE PREVIOUS-DEPT-NUMBER TO DEPT-NUMBER-TOTAL-LINE.    PHYSINV
00248  013110     MOVE DEPT-TOTAL-ACCUM TO DEPT-VALUE-TOTAL-LINE.         PHYSINV
00249  013120     WRITE INVENTORY-REPORT-LINE FROM DEPARTMENT-TOTAL-LINE  PHYSINV
00250  013130        AFTER ADVANCING 2 LINES.                             PHYSINV
00251  013140     MOVE SPACE-THREE-LINES TO PROPER-SPACING.               PHYSINV
00252  013150     ADD 4 TO LINES-PRINTED.                                 PHYSINV
00253  013160     MOVE ZEROS TO DEPT-TOTAL-ACCUM.                         PHYSINV
```

```
     7
00254  013190*********************************************************  PHYSINV
00255  013200*                                                       *  PHYSINV
00256  014010*  THIS MODULE PRINTS THE FINAL TOTALS.  IT IS ENTERED FROM *  PHYSINV
00257  014020*  AND EXITS TO THE A000-CREATE-INVENTORY-REPORT MODULE.  *  PHYSINV
00258  014030*                                                       *  PHYSINV
00259  014040*********************************************************  PHYSINV
00260  014050                                                           PHYSINV
00261  014060  B020-PRINT-FINAL-TOTALS.                                 PHYSINV
00262  014070                                                           PHYSINV
00263  014080      MOVE FINAL-TOTAL-ACCUM TO INVENTORY-VALUE-FINAL-TOTAL. PHYSINV
00264  014090      WRITE INVENTORY-REPORT-LINE FROM FINAL-TOTAL-LINE     PHYSINV
00265  014100          AFTER ADVANCING 3 LINES.                         PHYSINV
```

```
     8
00266  014120*********************************************************  PHYSINV
00267  014130*                                                       *  PHYSINV
00268  014140*  THIS MODULE IS ENTERED TO PRINT THE HEADINGS ON THE REPORT. *  PHYSINV
00269  014150*  IT IS ENTERED FROM AND EXITS TO THE B000-PROCESS-DETAIL- *  PHYSINV
00270  014160*  RECORD MODULE.                                         *  PHYSINV
00271  014170*                                                       *  PHYSINV
00272  014180*********************************************************  PHYSINV
00273  014190                                                           PHYSINV
00274  014200  C000-PRINT-HEADINGS.                                     PHYSINV
00275  015010                                                           PHYSINV
00276  015020      MOVE CURRENT-DATE TO DATE-HEADING.                   PHYSINV
00277  015030      MOVE PAGE-COUNT TO PAGE-HEADING.                     PHYSINV
00278  015040      WRITE INVENTORY-REPORT-LINE FROM FIRST-HEADING-LINE  PHYSINV
00279  015050          AFTER ADVANCING TO-TOP-OF-PAGE.                  PHYSINV
00280  015060      ADD 1 TO PAGE-COUNT.                                 PHYSINV
00281  015070      WRITE INVENTORY-REPORT-LINE FROM SECOND-HEADING-LINE PHYSINV
00282  015080          AFTER ADVANCING 2 LINES.                         PHYSINV
00283  015090      WRITE INVENTORY-REPORT-LINE FROM THIRD-HEADING-LINE  PHYSINV
00284  015100          AFTER ADVANCING 1 LINES.                         PHYSINV
00285  015110      MOVE SPACE-TWO-LINES TO PROPER-SPACING.              PHYSINV
00286  015120      MOVE ZERO TO LINES-PRINTED.                          PHYSINV
```

```
07/05/77              PHYSICAL INVENTORY REPORT              PAGE   1

DEPT     PART                        QUANTITY   UNIT     INVENTORY
NO       NUMBER    DESCRIPTION       ON HAND    COST     VALUE

1000     110025    SKI SOCKS            100      3.00      300.00
1000     110723    SKI JACKET            30     20.00      600.00

                    TOTAL VALUE - DEPARTMENT 1000     $900.00*


2010     22050     TENNIS SOCKS         100      1.25      125.00

                    TOTAL VALUE - DEPARTMENT 1000     $125.00*


2010     22444     TENNIS SHIRT          50     15.00      750.00

                    TOTAL VALUE - DEPARTMENT 1000     $750.00*


3011     30009     GOLF TEES            900       .05       45.00

                    TOTAL VALUE - DEPARTMENT 1000     $45.00*


3011     30009     GOLF TEES            900       .05       45.00

                    TOTAL VALUE - DEPARTMENT 1000     $45.00*


3011     30115     GOLF CLUBS             5     99.00      495.00

                    TOTAL VALUE - DEPARTMENT 1000     $495.00*


4012     42113     BASEBALLS            200      1.75      350.00

                    TOTAL VALUE - DEPARTMENT 1000     $350.00*
```

EXPLANATION

CHAPTER 8

PROGRAMMING ASSIGNMENT 1

INSTRUCTIONS

A Sales Analysis Report is to be prepared. Write the COBOL program to prepare the required report. An IPO Chart and Pseudocode Specifications should be used when designing the program. Use Test Data Set 1 in Appendix A.

INPUT

The input is to consist of Sales Cards that contain a Store Number, a Salesman Number, a Salesman Name and the Current Sales. The cards must be sorted in ascending sequence by Store Number prior to processing. The format of the cards is illustrated below.

OUTPUT

The output is to consist of a Sales Analysis Report by Store. When there is a change in Store Number, the total sales for each store are to be printed. After all cards have been processed, a final total of the sales for all stores is to be printed. A printer spacing chart of the report that is to be prepared is illustrated below.

CHAPTER 8

PROGRAMMING ASSIGNMENT 2

INSTRUCTIONS

An Invoice Register is to be prepared. Write the COBOL program to prepare the required report. An IPO Chart and Pseudocode Specifications should be used when designing the program. Use Test Data Set 2 in Appendix A.

INPUT

Input consists of Sales Cards that contain the Invoice Number, the Branch Number, the Salesman Number, Customer Number, the Quantity Sold, the Item Description, the Item Number and the Unit Price. The cards must be sorted in ascending sequence by Invoice Number prior to processing. The format of the cards is illustrated below.

OUTPUT

The output is to consist of an Invoice Register. The Sales Amount is calculated by multiplying the Quantity Sold by the Unit Price. When there is a change in Invoice Number, a total for the Invoice should be printed. After all cards have been processed, a "record count" should be taken, and a final total printed of the total sales amount for all invoices. A printer spacing chart of the report is illustrated below.

CHAPTER 8

PROGRAMMING ASSIGNMENT 3

INSTRUCTIONS

An Order Register Summary is to be prepared. Write the COBOL program to prepare the required report. An IPO Chart and Pseudocode Specifications should be used when designing the program. Use Test Data Set 2 in Appendix A.

INPUT

Input consists of Order Cards containing the Order Date, the Order Number, the Customer Number, the Description, the Item Number, Sales Amount and a Credit Limit Code. The cards must be sorted in ascending sequence by Order Number prior to processing. There will be one or more cards with different item numbers for each order number. The format of the cards is illustrated below.

OUTPUT

Output is to consist of an Order Register Summary. The report is to be a GROUP PRINTED report; that is, one line is to be printed for each order (there will be one or more cards for each order). When there is a change in Order Number, the accumulated sales for each order is to be printed. If the accumulated Sales Amount for any order is greater than $1,000.00, the message *OBTAIN CREDIT APPROVAL* should be printed. If the accumulated Sales Amount for any order is greater than $300.00 and the character "L" appears in the Credit Limit Code field (column 80), the message *OBTAIN CREDIT APPROVAL* should be printed. After all records have been processed, the total number of orders processed and the total sales for all orders should be printed. It should be noted that the date, the customer number, and the credit limit indicator found in the first record for a new order will be the same as values found in all subsequent records for the same order.

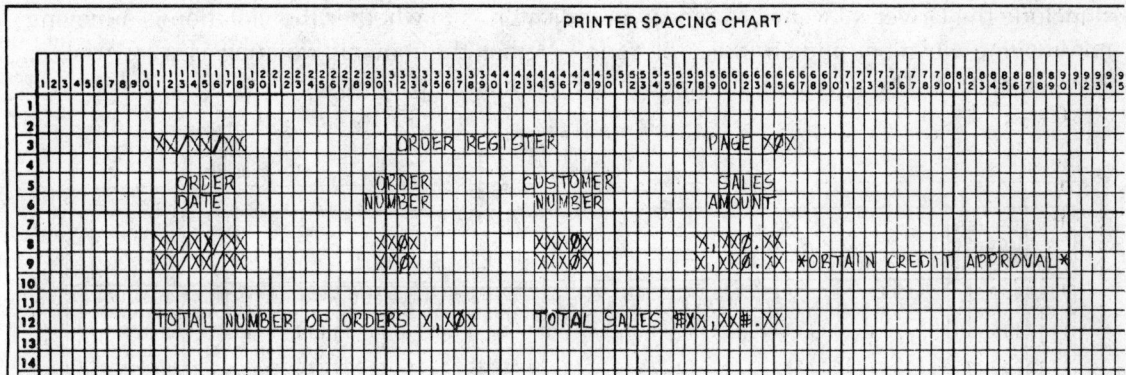

CHAPTER 8

PROGRAMMING ASSIGNMENT 4

INSTRUCTIONS

A Confidential Traffic Violation Report is to be prepared. Write the COBOL program to produce the required report. An IPO Chart and Pseudocode Specifications should be used when designing the program. Use Test Data Set 1 in Appendix A.

INPUT

Input consists of the Violator Input File, which is stored on punched cards. The fields in the card include the Driver's License Number, an indicator as to whether the violation is a moving or non-moving violation, and an indicator as to whether the moving violation is a low-risk or high-risk violation. The format of the input record is illustrated below.

Violation Type
0 = Non-Moving
1 = Moving

Risk
0 = Low Risk
1 = High Risk

DRIVER LICENSE NUMBER   TYPE   RISK

Note that for the Violation Type (column 49), the value 0 indicates that the violation was a Non-Moving Violation on which the violator failed to appear in court or pay the fine. The value 1 indicates that the violator was convicted of or pleaded guilty to a Moving Violation. The Risk field, in column 74, can have two meanings: the value 0 indicates a Low-Risk moving violation while the value 1 indicates a High-Risk moving violation.

OUTPUT

The output of the program is the Confidential Traffic Violation Report. The format of the report is illustrated on page 8.45.

PRINTER SPACING CHART

```
XX/XX/XX                    CONFIDENTIAL TRAFFIC VIOLATION REPORT                    PAGE XØX

LICENSE     NON-MOVING      MOVING          HIGH-RISK       LOW-RISK        TOTAL       ACTION
NUMBER      VIOLATIONS      VIOLATIONS      VIOLATIONS      VIOLATIONS      POINTS      TAKEN

XXXXXX          ØX              ØX              ØX              ØX              ØX      WARRANT ISSUED
                                                                                      SCHOOL ENROLLMENT
XXXXXX          ØX              ØX              ØX              ØX              ØX      NOTICE OF VIOLATIONS
XXXXXX          ØX              ØX              ØX              ØX              ØX      LICENSE SUSPENSION
XXXXXX          ØX              ØX              ØX              ØX              ØX      SUSPENSION WARNING


PAGE TOTALS

NON-MOVING VIOLATIONS XØX
MOVING-VIOLATIONS     XØX
HIGH-RISK VIOLATIONS  XØX
LOW-RISK VIOLATIONS   XØX




FINAL TOTALS

NON-MOVING VIOLATIONS X,XØX
MOVING VIOLATIONS     X,XØX
HIGH-RISK VIOLATIONS  X,XØX
LOW-RISK VIOLATIONS   X,XØX
```

Note that the report contains the License Number, the number of Non-Moving Violations, the number of Moving Violations, the number of High-Risk Violations, the number of Low-Risk Violations, the Total Points, and the Action Taken. The report is a group-printed report; that is, there may be one or more input cards for the same driver (ie, the same driver's license number).

The following is the explanation of the processing which is to take place in the program:

1. The report is group-printed. More than one input card may be read for each driver, but only one line for moving violations and/or one line for non-moving violations is to be printed.

2. The non-moving violations and the moving violations are to be totaled for each driver. In addition, the number of high-risk violations and the number of low-risk violations for each driver are to be totaled.

3. For each driver, the total points are to be printed. Points are calculated for moving violations in the following manner: one point for each low-risk violation; three points for each high-risk violation.

4. When the total points are known, the following message should be printed in the Action Taken position, depending upon the number of points:

Points	Message
3 or less	NOTICE OF VIOLATIONS
4 - 5	SCHOOL ENROLLMENT
6 - 8	SUSPENSION WARNING
Over 8	LICENSE SUSPENSION

5. Non-moving violations for which the driver has failed to appear do not count in the point calculation. However, if the number of non-moving violations is greater than 1, then the message WARRANT ISSUED should be printed in the Action Taken portion of the report.

6. It should be noted that a single driver could have both moving violations and more than one non-moving violation. In that case, both the appropriate point message and the WARRANT ISSUED message should be printed for the driver. The second line should have just the Action Taken message (see the printer spacing chart).

7. There are to be four drivers per each page of the report.

8. Page totals for the number of Non-Moving Violations, the number of Moving Violations, the number of High-Risk Violations, and the number of Low-Risk Violations should be printed on each page for the drivers on that page. These totals should be printed after the four drivers on a page have been printed but before the headings on a new page are printed.

9. Final totals should be printed after all records have been processed.

MULTIPLE LEVEL CONTROL BREAKS

9

INTRODUCTION

The previous chapter introduced the concept of single level control breaks and the printing of totals when a control break occurred. In some applications it may be desirable to take more than one level of totals when processing records. For example, in the Sales Report illustrated in Figure 9-1, when there is a change in Customer Number, a total for the customer is printed; when there is a change in Salesman Number, the total for the customer and the total for the salesman is printed; and, when there is a change in Branch Number, the total for the customer, the total for the salesman, and the total for the branch is printed. In addition, after all records have been processed, the final total is printed.

Note in the report that the Branch Number, the Salesman Number, and the Customer Number are GROUP INDICATED; that is, these numbers are printed only for the first record of the group. Group Indication refers to the process of suppressing the printing of repetitive information and is used to improve the readability of a report.

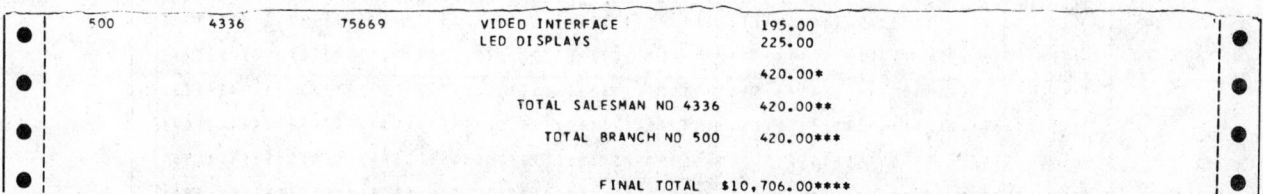

```
07/21/77                         SALES REPORT                      PAGE   1

BRANCH      SALESMAN       CUSTOMER          PRODUCT                SALES
  NO          NO             NO            DESCRIPTION             AMOUNT

 100         1225          32911        AUDIO INTERFACE            500.00
                                        KEYBOARD                   100.00
                                        POWER SUPPLY                50.00

                                                                   650.00*

                           40015        CRT INTERFACE               75.00
                                        FLOPPY CONTROLLER          125.00
                                        POWER TRANSFORMER           50.00

                                                                   250.00*

                                        TOTAL SALESMAN NO 1225     900.00**

             4199          27663        4K RAM                     330.00
                                        ROM MEMORY                  30.00

                                                                   360.00*

                                        TOTAL SALESMAN NO 4199     360.00**

                                        TOTAL BRANCH NO 100      1,260.00***
```
```
 500         4336          75669        VIDEO INTERFACE            195.00
                                        LED DISPLAYS               225.00

                                                                   420.00*

                                        TOTAL SALESMAN NO 4336     420.00**

                                        TOTAL BRANCH NO 500        420.00***

                                        FINAL TOTAL    $10,706.00****
```

Figure 9-1 Multiple Level Control Break Report with Group Indication

1 H. D. Mills, *HOW TO WRITE CORRECT PROGRAMS AND KNOW IT, IBM Federal Systems Division, IBM, February 1973.*

It is important to note that whenever a control break occurs on Salesman Number, a control break must automatically occur on Customer Number. Thus, when there is a change in Salesman Number, both the customer total and the salesman total are printed. Similarly, whenever a change occurs on Branch Number, a control break automatically occurs on Salesman Number and Customer Number. Therefore, on a change in Branch Number, the customer total, salesman total, and branch total are printed.

When processing records containing multiple level control breaks, the records must be properly sorted prior to producing the required report. Note in the report in Figure 9-1 that the Customer Numbers are arranged in an ascending sequence within each Salesman, the Salesman Numbers are arranged in an ascending sequence within each Branch, and all of the Branch Numbers are arranged in an ascending sequence.

SAMPLE PROGRAM

This chapter discusses the technique of designing and programming an application in which there are multiple level control breaks. The printer spacing chart and the format of the input records are illustrated below.

OUTPUT

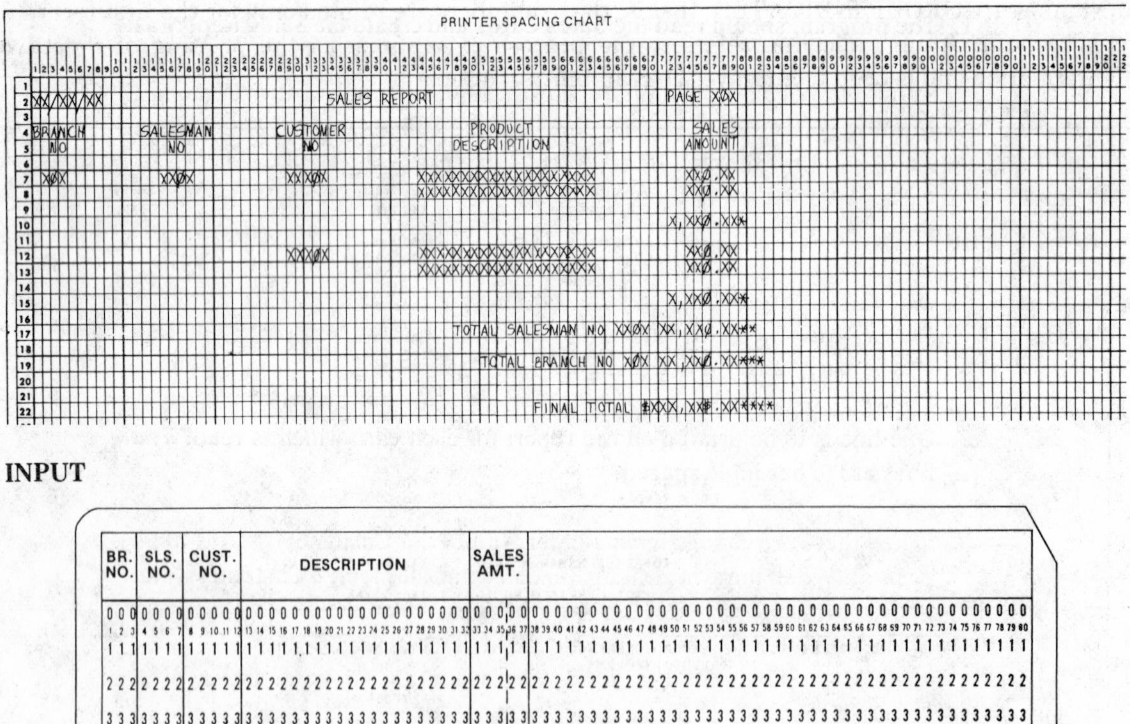

INPUT

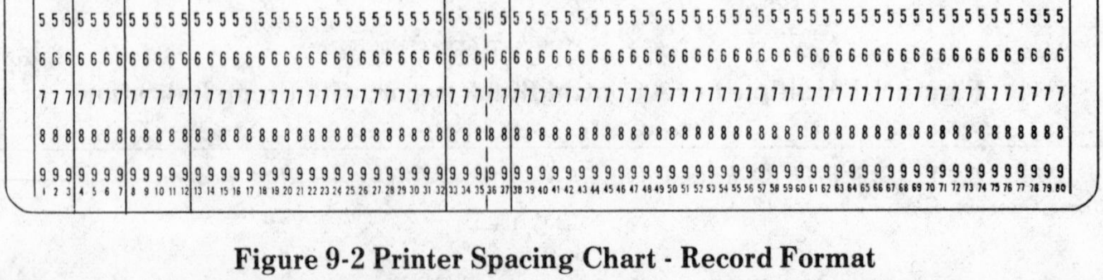

Figure 9-2 Printer Spacing Chart - Record Format

Note in the record format illustrated in Figure 9-2 that the input cards contain the Branch Number, the Salesman Number, the Customer Number, the Description, and the Sales Amount; and that the report that is to be produced contains Customer Totals, Salesman Totals, Branch Totals, and a Final Total.

Programming Specifications

The programming specifications for the sample problem are illustrated below.

PROGRAMMING SPECIFICATIONS		
SUBJECT Sales Report	**DATE** June 16	**PAGE** 1 **OF** 1
TO Programmer	**FROM** Systems Analyst	

A program is to be written to prepare a Sales Report. The format of the input card file and the printer spacing chart are included as a part of this narative. The program should include the following processing.

1. The program should read the Sales Cards and create the Sales Report as per the format illustrated on the printer spacing chart. The report shall contain the Branch Number, the Salesman Number, the Customer Number, the Product Description, and the Sales Amount. The Branch Number, the Salesman Number, and the Customer Number are to be group indicated.

2. Headings should be printed on the first and subsequent pages of the report. The heading is to contain the current date and the page number. Fifty-five detail and total lines are to appear on each page before skipping to a new page.

3. One line is to be printed on the report for each card which is read. The lines are to be single spaced.

4. When there is a change in Customer Number, a Customer Total is to be printed. When there is a change in Salesman Number, a Customer Total and Salesman Total are to be printed; and when there is a change in Branch Number, Customer, Salesman, and Branch Totals are to be printed. A Final Total is to be printed after all cards have been processed.

5. The program is to be written in COBOL.

6. Input records must be sorted by Customer Number within Salesman Number within Branch Number prior to processing.

Figure 9-3 Programming Specifications

MULTIPLE LEVEL CONTROL BREAK PROCESSING

Prior to beginning the design of a program involving the use of multiple level control breaks, it is important to have an overall understanding of the processing that must take place. The processing of multiple level control breaks is very similar to the processing that must occur for single level control breaks as illustrated in the previous chapter. That is, records are read, the control fields are moved to a compare area, and the control fields on subsequent input records are compared to the values in the compare area. If the values are equal, a detail record is processed and printed. If the values are not equal, control break processing occurs to print the appropriate totals.

Initial Processing

Figure 9-4 illustrates a diagram of storage and the processing that occurs for the first record in an application involving multiple level control breaks. Note in the example, in step 1, that when the first record is read into the input area, the Branch Number, Customer Number, and Salesman Number are moved to individual compare areas. Each of the fields in the compare areas are then compared to the corresponding fields in the input area. When processing the first card, all fields will be equal and the processing of the first detail record will occur.

Processing Detail Records

When processing the detail record (step 2), a heading is printed on the first page of the report; the fields in the input area are moved to the output area; the Sales Amount from the input record is added into a Branch Total Accumulator, a Salesman Total Accumulator, a Customer Total Accumulator, and a Final Total Accumulator; and a detail line is then printed.

As long as the records read contain a Branch Number, Salesman Number, and Customer Number that are equal to the related numbers in the compare areas, processing of the detail records will occur; that is, the fields in the input area are moved to the output area, the Sales Amount is added to the accumulators, and a line is printed.

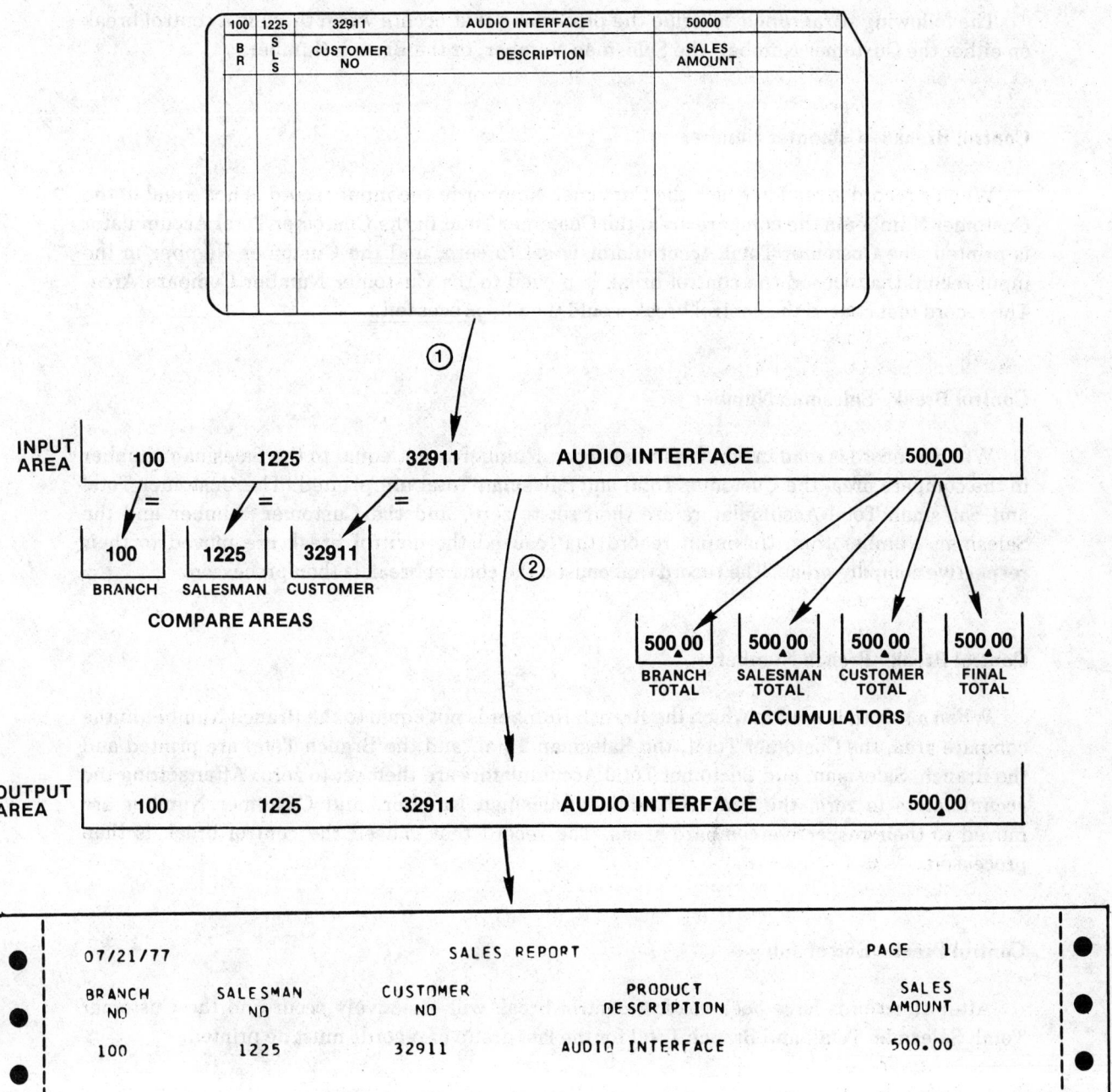

Figure 9-4 Processing the First Card

The following paragraphs describe the processing that occurs when there is a control break on either the Customer Number, the Salesman Number, or the Branch Number.

Control Breaks - Customer Number

When a record is read in which the Customer Number in the input record is not equal to the Customer Number in the compare area, the Customer Total in the Customer Total Accumulator is printed, the Customer Total Accumulator is set to zero, and the Customer Number in the input record that caused the control break is moved to the Customer Number Compare Area. The record that caused the control break would then be processed.

Control Break - Salesman Number

When a record is read in which the Salesman Number is not equal to the Salesman Number in the compare area, the Customer Total and Salesman Total are printed. The Customer Total and Salesman Total Accumulators are then set to zero, and the Customer Number and the Salesman Number from the input record that caused the control break are moved to their respective compare areas. The record that caused the control break is then processed.

Control Break - Branch Number

When a record is read in which the Branch Number is not equal to the Branch Number in the compare area, the Customer Total, the Salesman Total, and the Branch Total are printed and the Branch, Salesman, and Customer Total Accumulators are then set to zero. After setting the accumulators to zero, the Branch Number, Salesman Number, and Customer Number are moved to their respective compare areas. The record that caused the control break is then processed.

Control Break - End of Job

After all records have been read, a control break will effectively occur and the Customer Total, Salesman Total, and Branch Total for the last group of records must be printed.

Final Total Processing

Prior to terminating processing, a Final Total is printed. The program is then terminated.

It is important for the programmer to have a thorough understanding of the processing of records that contain multiple level control breaks in order to be able to properly design a program which includes multiple level control break processing.

PROGRAM DESIGN

IPO Chart - Create Sales Report

An analysis of the printer spacing chart, the format of the input records, and the programming specifications provides the programmer with the information needed for the development of the control module for the program. The IPO Chart for the Create Sales Report Module is illustrated below.

IPO CHART					
PROGRAM: Sales Report		**PROGRAMMER:** Shelly/Cashman			**DATE:** June 17
MODULE NAME: Create Sales Report		**REF:** A000	**MODULE FUNCTION:** Create the Sales Report		
INPUT	**PROCESSING**		**REF:**	**OUTPUT**	
1. Sales Input File	1. Initialization			1. Sales Report	
	2. Obtain the input data				
	3. Process detail records		B000		
	4. Process customer changes		B010		
	5. Process salesman changes		B020		
	6. Process branch changes		B030		
	7. Print the final totals		B040		
	8. Termination				

Figure 9-5 IPO Chart - Create Sales Report

Note from the IPO Chart that the output to be produced is the Sales Report and the input is the Sales Input File. From the processing section of the IPO Chart it can be seen that in addition to Initialization, Obtaining the input data, and Processing the detail records, other major processing tasks include the processing that must occur when there is a change in Customer Number, a change in Salesman Number, and a change in Branch Number. The final entries on the IPO Chart are the major processing tasks of Printing the final total and Termination of the program.

An analysis of the major processing tasks specified on the Create Sales Report IPO Chart must be performed next to determine if any of the tasks define a specific function to be performed by the program and are of such a size and complexity as to justify another module.

As a result of this analysis, it can be determined that the program can logically consist of five additional modules. These modules are illustrated in the hierarchy chart in Figure 9-6.

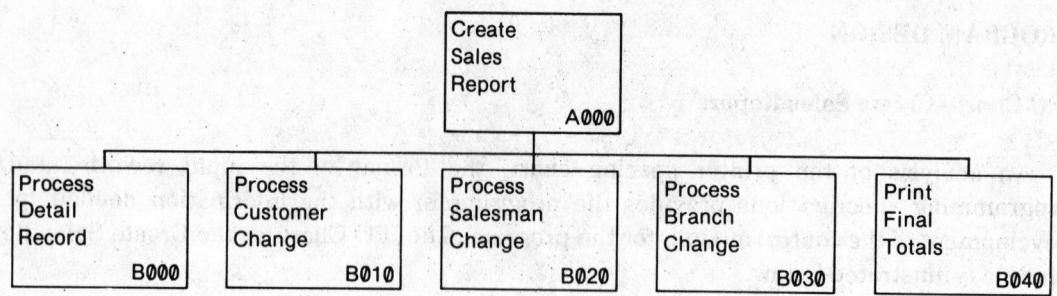

Figure 9-6 Hierarchy Chart

From the hierarchy chart it can be seen that the major processing tasks defined in the Create Sales Report Module that warrant separate modules include processing the detail records, processing the customer changes, processing the salesman changes, processing the branch changes, and printing the final totals.

After the relationship of the modules has been defined through the hierarchy chart, the next step in the design of the program is to define the major processing tasks associated with each module through the use of additional IPO Charts.

IPO Chart - Process Detail Records

The IPO Chart for the Process Detail Record Module is illustrated below.

IPO CHART				
PROGRAM: Sales Report		**PROGRAMMER:** Shelly/Cashman		**DATE:** June 17
MODULE NAME: Process Detail Record	**REF:** B000	**MODULE FUNCTION:** Process the Detail Record		
INPUT	**PROCESSING**		**REF:**	**OUTPUT**
1. Sales Input Record	1. Print headings when required		C000	1. Detail Print Line
2. Accumulators	2. Format detail line			2. Updated Accumulators
a. Customer Total	3. Update accumulators			a. Customer Total
b. Salesman Total	a. Customer total			b. Salesman Total
c. Branch Total	b. Salesman total			c. Branch Total
d. Final Total	c. Branch total			d. Final Total
	d. Final total			
	4. Write the detail line			

Figure 9-7 IPO Chart - Process Detail Records

The output of the module which processes the detail records is the detail print line and the updated total accumulators. The accumulators are considered output because the Sales Amount from the input record must be added to the total accumulators and the accumulators are to be used in another module of the program.

The input to the module consists of the Sales Input Record, and the Customer, Salesman, Branch, and Final Total Accumulators.

The major processing tasks necessary to convert the input to the required output consist of printing the heading on the report when needed, formatting the detail line, updating the Customer, Salesman, Branch, and Final Total Accumulators, and writing the detail line.

As with all IPO Charts, the major processing tasks specified within this module must be analyzed to determine if any of the tasks justifies the creation of an additional module. In analyzing the major processing tasks for this module, it can be seen that the printing of the heading on the report contains significiant enough processing to justify a separate module; therefore, this requirement for an additional module should be reflected on the hierarchy chart, as illustrated below.

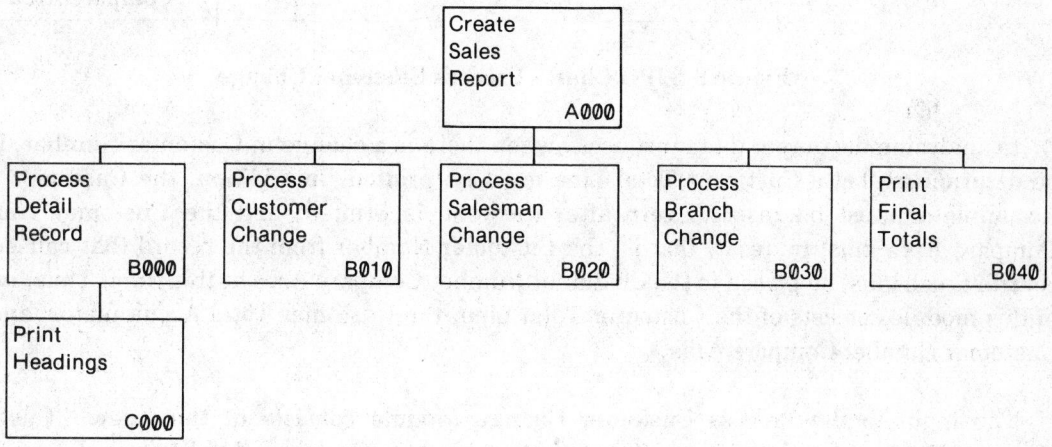

Figure 9-8 Hierarchy Chart

Note that the Print Headings Module is a sub-module of the Process Detail Record Module.

IPO Chart - Process Customer Change

The next IPO Chart which must be prepared is the IPO Chart to define the major processing tasks that must take place when there is a change in Customer Number. This IPO Chart is illustrated in Figure 9-9.

IPO CHART

PROGRAM: Sales Report		PROGRAMMER: Shelly/Cashman		DATE: June 17
MODULE NAME: Process Customer Change	REF: B010	MODULE FUNCTION: Process Customer Change		

INPUT	PROCESSING	REF:	OUTPUT
1. New Customer Number	1. Format customer total line		1. Customer Total Line
2. Customer Total	2. Write the customer total line		2. Customer Total
Accumulator	3. Reset customer total accumulator		Accumulator
	4. Reset customer number compare area		3. Customer Number
			Compare Area

Figure 9-9 IPO Chart - Process Customer Change

In analyzing the output that must occur when there is a change in Customer Number, it can be determined that a Customer Total Line must be printed. In addition, the Customer Total Accumulator must be reset to zero after the total is printed; and the Customer Number Compare Area must be reset, that is, the Customer Number from the record that caused the control break must be placed in the Customer Number Compare Area at this time. Thus, output of this module consists of the Customer Total Line, the Customer Total Accumulator, and the Customer Number Compare Area.

The input to the Process Customer Change Module consists of the ''new'' Customer Number that must be placed in the Compare Area, and the Customer Total Accumulator.

The major processing tasks required to produce the output of the module include the formatting of the customer total line; writing the customer total line; resetting the customer total accumulator to zero, and resetting the customer compare area so that the compare area contains the Customer Number of the input record that caused the control break.

None of these major processing tasks is of such size or complexity so as to justify a lower-level module.

IPO Chart - Process Salesman Change

The next IPO Chart to be developed is the IPO Chart which defines the output, input, and major processing tasks that are required when there is a change in Salesman Number. This IPO Chart is illustrated in Figure 9-10.

IPO CHART

PROGRAM: Sales Report		PROGRAMMER: Shelly/Cashman		DATE: June 17
MODULE NAME: Process Salesman Change		REF: B020	MODULE FUNCTION: Process Salesman Change	

INPUT	PROCESSING	REF:	OUTPUT
1. Old Salesman Number	1. Format salesman total line		1. Salesman Total Line
2. New Salesman Number	2. Write the salesman total line		2. Salesman Total
3. Salesman Total	3. Reset salesman total accumulator		Accumulator
Accumulator	4. Reset salesman number compare area		3. Salesman Number
			Compare Area

Figure 9-10 IPO Chart - Process Salesman Change

The output of the Process Salesman Change Module is very similar to the output from the Customer Change Module. In an analysis of the output that occurs when there is a change in Salesman Number, it can be seen that a Salesman Total Line must be printed, the Salesman Total Accumulator must be reset to zero, and the Salesman Number from the input record that caused the control break must be moved to the Salesman Compare Area. Thus, the output of the Salesman Change Module consists of the Salesman Total Line, the Salesman Total Accumulator, and the Salesman Number Compare Area.

Input to the module consists of both the "old" Salesman Number and the "new" Salesman Number. The old Salesman Number is required because the Salesman Number from the group of records just processed is to be printed on the salesman total line (see Figure 9-1). The new Salesman Number is the Salesman Number that caused the control break to occur. This Salesman Number must be placed in the Salesman Number Compare Area. Other input to the module consists of the Salesman Total Accumulator, which is to be moved to the output area and printed on the report.

The processing to produce that output consists of formatting and printing the Salesman Total Line, resetting the Salesman Total Accumulator to zero, and resetting the Salesman Compare Area so that the compare area contains the Salesman Number of the record that caused the control break. None of these major processing tasks justifies a lower-level module.

IPO Chart - Process Branch Change

The IPO Chart for the Process Branch Change Module is illustrated below.

IPO CHART

PROGRAM: Sales Report		PROGRAMMER: Shelly/Cashman		DATE: June 17
MODULE NAME: Process Branch Change	REF: B030	MODULE FUNCTION: Process Branch Change		

INPUT	PROCESSING	REF:	OUTPUT
1. Old Branch Number	1. Format branch total line		1. Branch Total Line
2. New Branch Number	2. Write the branch total line		2. Branch Total
3. Branch Total	3. Reset the branch total accumulator		Accumulator
Accumulator	4. Reset the branch number compare area		3. Branch Number
			Compare Area

Figure 9-11 IPO Chart - Process Branch Change

From the IPO Chart for the Process Branch Change Module, it can be seen that the output of this module consists of: a Branch Total Line, the Branch Total Accumulator, and the Branch Number Compare Area. Input to the module consists of the "old" Branch Number, the "new" Branch Number, and the Branch Total Accumulator. The major processing tasks that must occur to transform the input to the output consist of formatting and writing the Branch Total Line, resetting the Branch Total Accumulator, and resetting the Branch Number Compare Area. No lower-level modules are required.

IPO Chart - Print the Final Total

The IPO Chart for the module whose function is to print the Final Total is illustrated in Firuge 9-12.

IPO CHART

PROGRAM: Sales Report		PROGRAMMER: Shelly/Cashman		DATE: June 17
MODULE NAME: Print Final Total	REF: B040	MODULE FUNCTION: Print the Final Total		

INPUT	PROCESSING	REF:	OUTPUT
1. Final Total Accumulators	1. Format final total line		1. Final Total Line
	2. Write the final total line		

Figure 9-12 IPO Chart - Print the Final Total

As can be seen, the output from the module is the Final Total Line and the input is the Final Total Accumulator. The major processing tasks consist of formatting the total line and writing the total line. Neither of these tasks justifies a lower-level module.

IPO Chart - Print the Headings

After the IPO Charts for the modules of the second level of the program have been designed, the programmer would review them and then design the modules on the third level. In the sample program, there is only one module on the third level—the module to print the headings. The IPO Chart for this module is illustrated below.

IPO CHART

PROGRAM: Sales Report		PROGRAMMER: Shelly/Cashman		DATE: June 17
MODULE NAME: Print Headings	REF: C000	MODULE FUNCTION: Print the Headings		

INPUT	PROCESSING	REF:	OUTPUT
1. Heading Lines	1. Format heading lines		1. Heading Lines.
	2. Write the heading lines		

Figure 9-13 IPO Chart - Print the Headings

The output from the module which is to print the headings is the Heading Lines that appear on the report. The input to the module is the Heading Lines. The major processing tasks are to format the heading lines and write the heading lines, neither of which justify a lower-level module.

Since there is not a lower-level module required for this module, the design of the program on the IPO Chart is completed. The programmer would normally review this design with the analysts, other programmers, or the user in order to ensure that a viable solution to the problem has been designed. After everyone is agreed that the solution is correct, the programmer would proceed to the next level of design—that of developing the pseudocode for the program.

PSEUDOCODE SPECIFICATIONS

It should be noted from the previous explanations of the IPO Charts for the program that although the complexity of this program has increased over previous programs, through the use of the IPO Charts each element of the program is broken down into a relatively simple form that is easy to understand. The pseudocode which must be developed for the program must specify only the processing which is to take place within each of the relatively simple modules, not the entire program.

The pseudocode specifications for the module whose function is to create the sales report are illustrated in Figure 9-14.

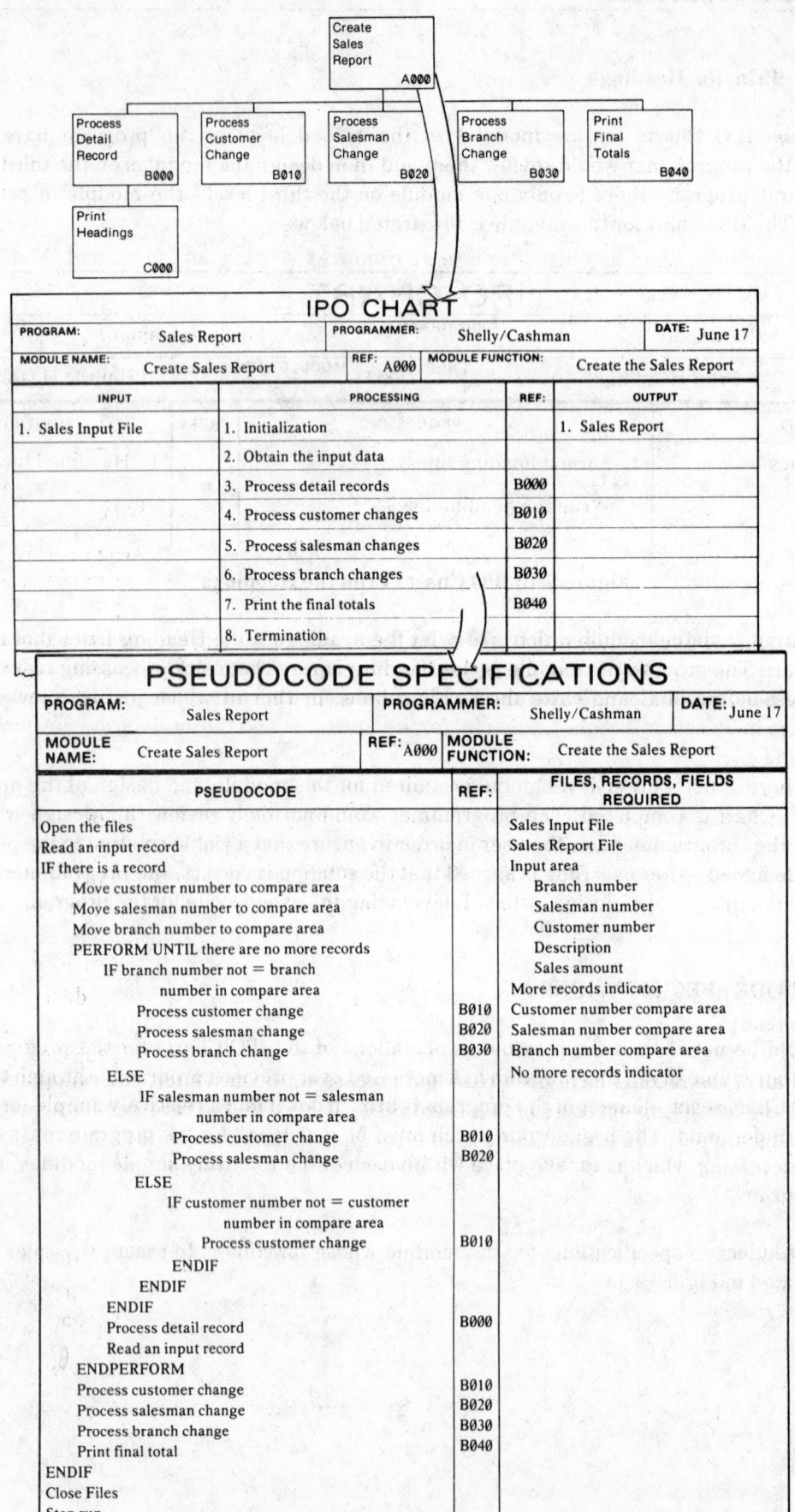

Figure 9-14 Pseudocode for Create Sales Report Module

From the Pseudocode Specifications in Figure 9-14, it can be seen that the files are opened and the first record is read. If there is a record to be processed, the Customer Number, Salesman Number, and Branch Number are moved to individual compare areas, where each of the control fields will be compared when additional records are read to determine if a control break has occurred.

In reviewing the pseudocode statements, it can be seen that when the Branch Number, Salesman Number, and Customer Number are compared and the data in each of the fields are EQUAL to the data in their respective compare areas, a detail record will be processed, and another input record will be read.

It is important to note that when comparing to determine if a control break has occurred, the Branch Number is compared first. This is because when there is a change in Branch Number, there is also a change in Salesman Number and Customer Number. Thus, as can be seen from Figure 9-14, if there is a change in the Branch Number, the module which processes a Customer Change will be executed first, followed by the module which processes the Salesman Change, and then the module which processes the Branch Change. Therefore, when there is a change in the Branch Number, the Customer Total will be printed first, followed by the Salesman Total, and then the Branch Total.

Similarly, it should be noted that when the Salesman Number in the record just read is not equal to the Salesman Number in the compare area, the Process Customer Change Module and the Process Salesman Change Module are both executed. This is necessary because when there is a change in Salesman Number, the total for the Customer and the total for the Salesman must be printed.

Lastly, when the Customer Number is compared and the Customer Number in the input record is not equal to the Customer Number in the compare area, the Process Customer Change Module is executed to print the total for the customer.

It is important to note that after any control break occurs, the statement "PROCESS DETAIL RECORD" will be performed next. This is necessary because the record that caused the control break to occur must be processed. After this record is processed, another input record is read.

After all of the records have been read and processed, the customer, salesman, and branch totals for the last group of records must be printed. Therefore, the modules for accomplishing this printing are performed when there is no more input data. The module to print the final total is then performed.

In addition to the pseudocode, the entries for the Files, Records, and Fields required for the module are specified on the Pseudocode Specifications in Figure 9-14. Also, the REF column includes the reference numbers for the lower level modules. These reference numbers correspond to the reference numbers given to the modules when the Hierarchy Chart is designed.

Pseudocode Specifications - Process Detail Record

The Pseudocode Specifications for the module whose function is to process the detail records are illustrated in Figure 9-15.

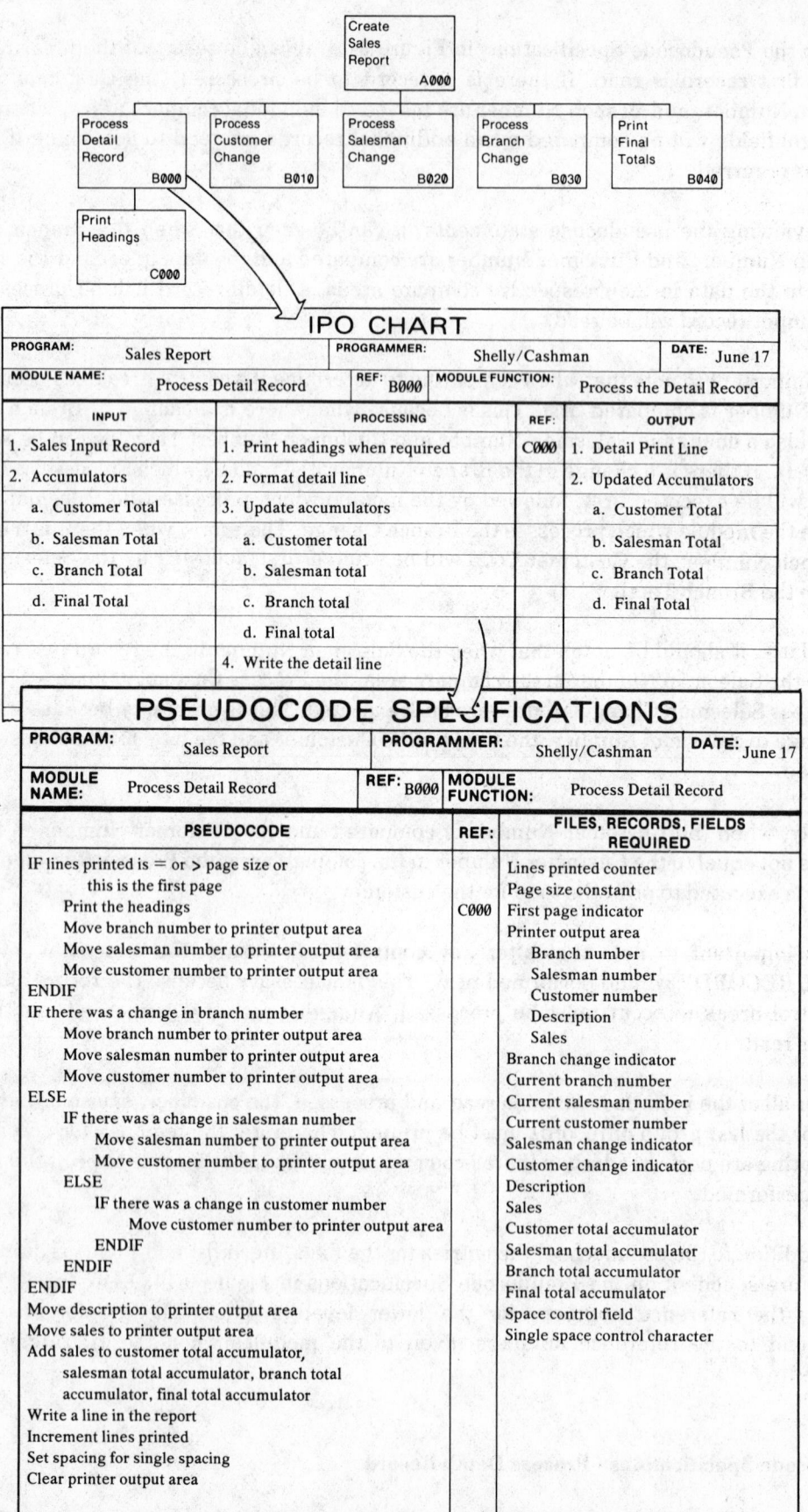

Figure 9-15 Pseudocode Specifications for Process Detail Record Module

The specifications for the module to process the detail records contain the logic required for the processing that occurs when each record is read, processed, and printed. This module controls the printing of the headings on the first page and on subsequent pages of the report, formats the detail print line, writes the line, and adds the Sales Amount into the Customer Total, Salesman Total, Branch Total, and Final Total Accumulators.

The pseudocode for the Process Detail Record Module also contains statements which provide for group indicating the Branch Number, the Salesman Number, and the Customer Number on the Report. A sample of the group indicated report is illustrated below.

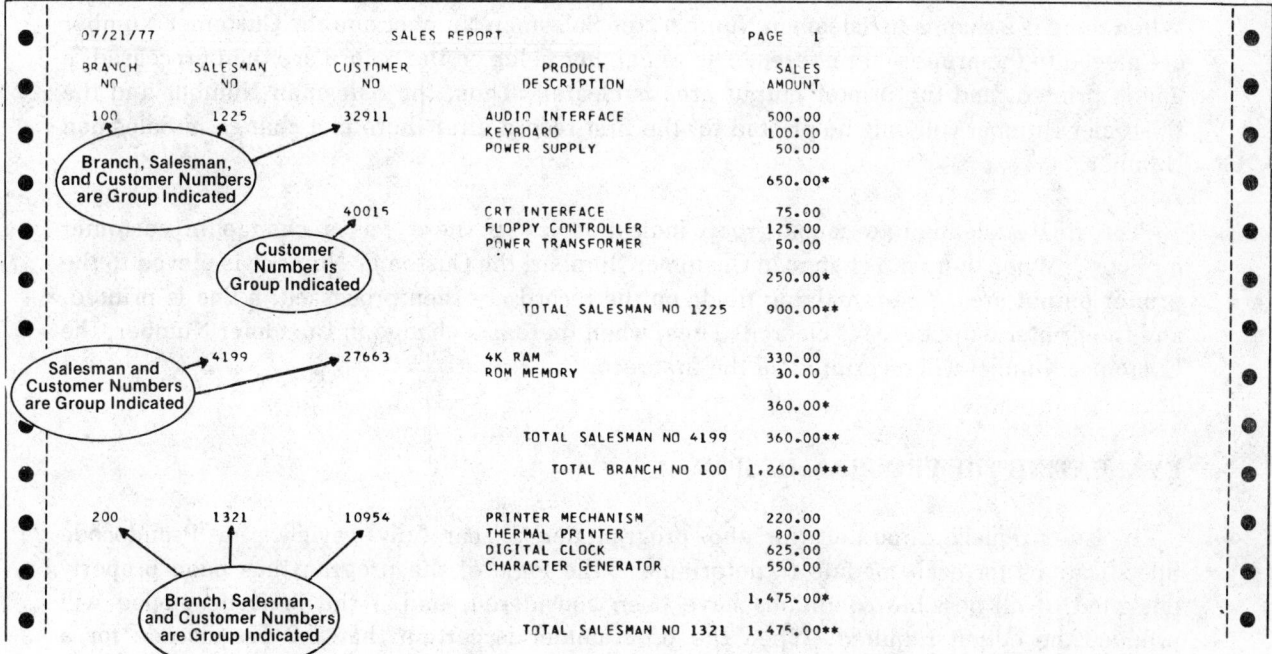

Figure 9-16 Group Indicated Report

From the sample report above it can be seen that after the heading is printed, the Branch Number, the Salesman Number, and the Customer Number are printed; but the printing of these fields is suppressed on subsequent lines until a control break occurs. Also, when there is a change in Branch Number, the Branch Number, Salesman Number, and Customer Number are printed on the first line only. When there is a change in Salesman Number, the Salesman Number and Customer Number are printed; and, when there is a change in Customer Number, the Customer Number is printed. The entries on the Pseudocode Specifications must provide for the printing of the various fields on the report, dependent upon whether there is a change in Branch Number, Salesman Number, or Customer Number.

Note in the Pseudocode Specifications that for the first page of the report, the headings are printed and then the Branch Number, Salesman Number, and Customer Number are moved to the output area. A test is then performed to determine if there were any control breaks. If not, the Description and Sales are moved to the output area, the total accumulators are incremented by the Sales Amount, and the line is printed. The number of lines printed is then added to the line counter and the spacing is set for single spacing. The last statement is to clear the printer output area. It will be recalled that in previous programs, the printer output area was cleared to spaces before any data was moved to it. In this program, the printer output area is cleared to spaces after the first line is printed. This is necessary because the report is group indicated; the technique in COBOL to cause the printer output area to be initialized to spaces before processing the first record, which involves the Value Clause, is illustrated later in this chapter.

Note that the Pseudocode Specifications in Figure 9-15 contain the statement "If there was a change in branch number". When there is a change in Branch Number, the Branch Number, the Salesman Number, and the Customer Number are moved to the printer output area. After the processing for a change in Branch Number has been completed, the remaining fields in the input record are moved to the output area, the calculations are performed, a line is printed, and the printer output area is cleared. Thus, the Branch Number, the Salesman Number, and the Customer Number will only print for the first record following a change in Branch Number; this is the group indication which is required for the report.

The pseudocode also contains the statement "If there was a change in salesman number". When there is a change in Salesman Number, the Salesman Number and the Customer Number are moved to the printer output area. The remaining fields on the record are then processed, a line is printed, and the printer output area is cleared. Thus, the Salesman Number and the Customer Number will only be printed for the first record after there is a change in Salesman Number.

The final statement to cause group indication is "If there was a change in customer number". When there is a change in Customer Number, the Customer Number is moved to the printer output area. The remaining fields on the record are then processed, a line is printed, and the printer output area is cleared. Thus, when there is a change in Customer Number, the Customer Number will be printed for the first record.

EVALUATING THE PROGRAM DESIGN

It is extremely important for the programmer to carefully review the Pseudocode Specifications for each module to determine if the logic of the program has been properly designed, if all possible conditions have been considered, and if the logic developed will produce the output required. When the programmer is certain that the pseudocode for a module is correct and no revisions are necessary, the pseudocode for the next module may be written.

In reviewing the pseudocode for the module which processes the detail records, several potential problems become apparent. The statements "IF THERE WAS A CHANGE IN BRANCH NUMBER", "IF THERE WAS A CHANGE IN SALESMAN NUMBER", and "IF THERE WAS A CHANGE IN CUSTOMER NUMBER" imply the need for a means to determine in this module that a control break has occurred. The means, however, has not been established. Thus, the programmer is faced with the task of modifying or adding to the existing design which was initially developed.

It is important to understand that THE PROCESS OF DESIGNING A PROGRAM IS OFTEN AN ITERATIVE PROCESS; that is, the basic design that is initially developed through the Hierarchy Chart, IPO Charts, and Pseudocode Specifications may need to be repeatedly refined as the programmer moves further into the design process and as the initial design is evaluated and reviewed.

As the programming specifications for a problem become increasingly complex, the first pass through the design phase of program development may not yield the best design, or in fact, even produce the anticipated results. This does not mean that the problem was approached incorrectly or that the programmer has done a ''poor'' job in designing the program. It merely means that additional refinements of the program design are required.

It is important to note that using the techniques of Top-Down Development, through the use of IPO Charts and Pseudocode, the programmer is able to produce the best design before entering the COBOL coding phase of the program development process. This is an extremely important concept; for once the coding phase is begun, it is extremely costly, in terms of programming time, to make changes in the coding. In addition, changes during the coding phase lead to ''patched'' programs that frequently defeat the purpose of structured programming, that is, to develop programs that are easy to modify and maintain. Thus, these changes which are found in the design phase should be made to the pseudocode prior to undertaking any coding of the program.

EVALUATING PROGRAM DESIGN - SAMPLE PROGRAM

As noted previously, the Branch Number, Salesman Number, and Customer Number are to be group indicated on the report. In addition, in the pseudocode for the module whose function is to process the detail records (see Figure 9-15), a test is made to determine if any control breaks have occurred; this is done so that the proper group indication can take place. It has become apparent upon review of the pseudocode of this module, however, that no provision has been made to indicate that a control break has occurred so that this module can test for it. When this type of problem happens, the programmer must review the existing design of the program to determine three things: First, if the control of the group indication should be in the module whose function is to process the detail records, as it currently is; second, how to indicate that a control break has occurred; and third, once a means has been determined, it must be decided which module is to pass the information to the Detail Processing Module.

In order to determine which module should handle the processing of the group indication, a basic concept of program design must be applied. This concept states that each module should perform a single function, if possible. For example, the Process Branch Change module should only be concerned with the processing that occurs when there is a change in the Branch Number; it is not concerned with the format of the detail printed lines on the report.

Similarly, the Process Salesman Change Module is concerned only with the processing that occurs when the Salesman Number changes; and the Process Customer Change Module is concerned only with the processing which occurs when the Customer Number changes. Thus, each of the modules will perform a specific function and they are not concerned with the format of the detail report line and whether the report is group indicated or not.

With this concept in mind, it becomes apparent that the module which should be concerned with the group indication is the module whose function is to process the detail records. As will be recalled, one of the major processing tasks for this module is to format the report; and clearly, the group indication of certain fields on a report is a part of formatting the report line. Thus, this analysis reveals that the module which processes the detail records as illustrated in Figure 9-15 is the proper place for these checks and the appropriate processing to take place.

The second problem is how to "tell" the detail record processing module that a control break has occurred. In many programs, the method used for passing information such as this is an indicator. It will be recalled in previous programs that indicators have been used to indicate that there are no more records to be processed. In this program, indicators can be used to indicate that a branch control break, a salesman control break, or a customer control break has occurred. It should be recalled, however, that no provision has been made for these indicators to be defined and set when a control break does occur. Therefore, the programmer must analyze the modules which have been defined thus far to determine if any of them is the place in which the indicators should be set.

The module whose function is to create the Sales Report is the module that controls which lower level modules will be executed and when they will be executed. When the pseudocode for this module was designed (see Figure 9-14), the test for a control break was included so that the proper control break module would be entered when a control break occurred. Because the determination of a control break is a proper function of the top level module, and because the function of the top level module is to control the processing of the lower level modules, this top level module is a logical place in the program to define and set the indicators which indicate there has been a control break. Thus, the programmer must evaluate the processing which is to take place in the module as a result of the pseudocode which has been designed to determine what changes are necessary in order to set these indicators.

A review of the Pseudocode Specifications in Figure 9-14 reveals that the only change required to set the indicators is to indicate that the control breaks have occurred in the appropriate place. These changes, together with the entries in the Files, Records, and Fields portion of the form to point out the need for the indicators are illustrated in Figure 9-17. With these changes, the module whose function is to process the detail records now has the information needed to group indicate the data as required on the report. It must also be noted that after the processing of a control break in the detail module is complete, the appropriate indicator is reset so that the control break processing will not occur for every detail record.

Revised Pseudocode Specifications

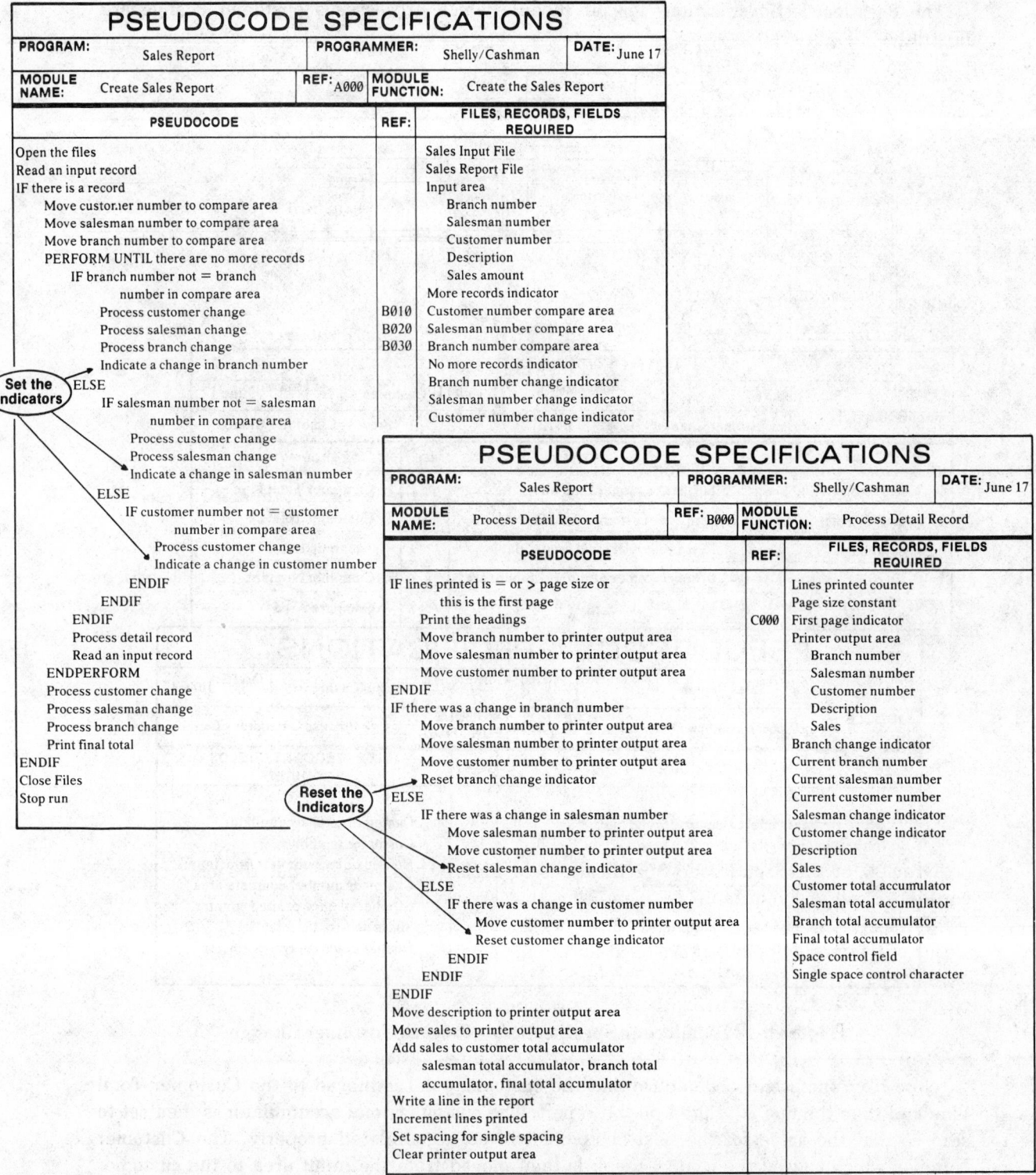

Figure 9-17 Revised Pseudocode Specifications

Pseudocode Specifications - Process Customer Change

The Pseudocode Specifications for the module which processes a customer change are illustrated in Figure 9-18.

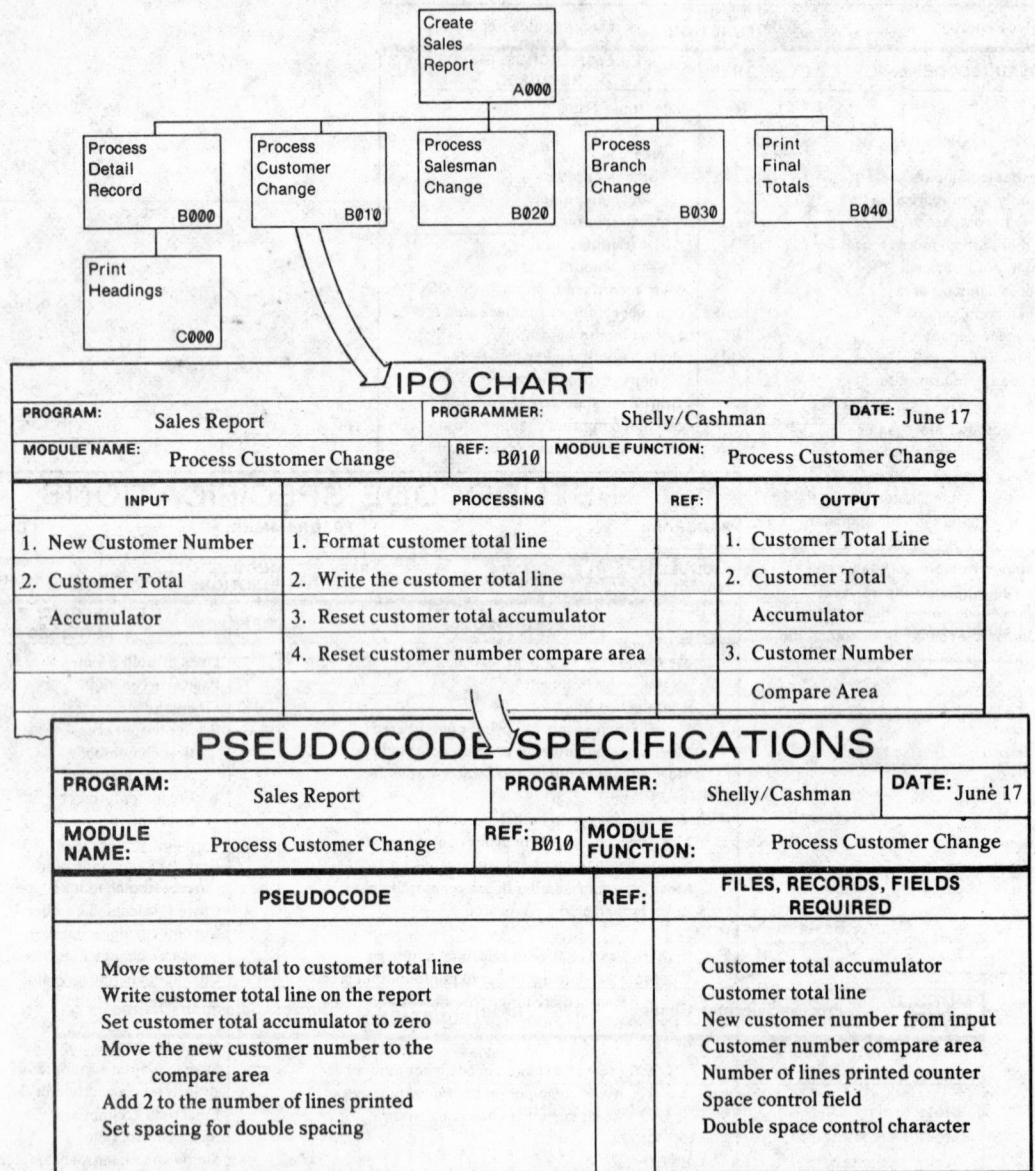

Figure 9-18 Pseudocode Specifications - Process Customer Change

Note from the pseudocode above that the customer total is moved to the Customer Total Line and then the line is printed on the report. The customer total accumulator is then set to zero so that the value for the next customer will be accumulated properly. The Customer Number which caused the control break is then moved from the input area to the customer number compare area. The last two statements are used to accumulate the proper number of lines printed, and to set the space control so that the next detail record will be double spaced following the total line. Note that the value "2" is added to the lines printed counter because the total line is printed after two lines are spaced on the printer.

Pseudocode Specifications - Process Salesman Change

The Pseudocode Specifications for the Process Salesman Change Module are illustrated in Figure 9-19. It can be seen that in the first statement, the "previous" Salesman Number is moved to the Salesman Total Line. This statement is for the purpose of having the Salesman Number from the previous group of cards print on the Salesman Total Line (see the sample report in Figure 9-1). The Salesman Total is then moved to the Salesman Total Line and a line is printed. After the total line is printed, the Salesman Total Accumulator is reset to zero, and the "new" Salesman Number, that is, the Salesman Number that caused the control change to occur, is moved to the compare area. A "2" is added to the number of lines printed counter, and the space control is set for triple spacing.

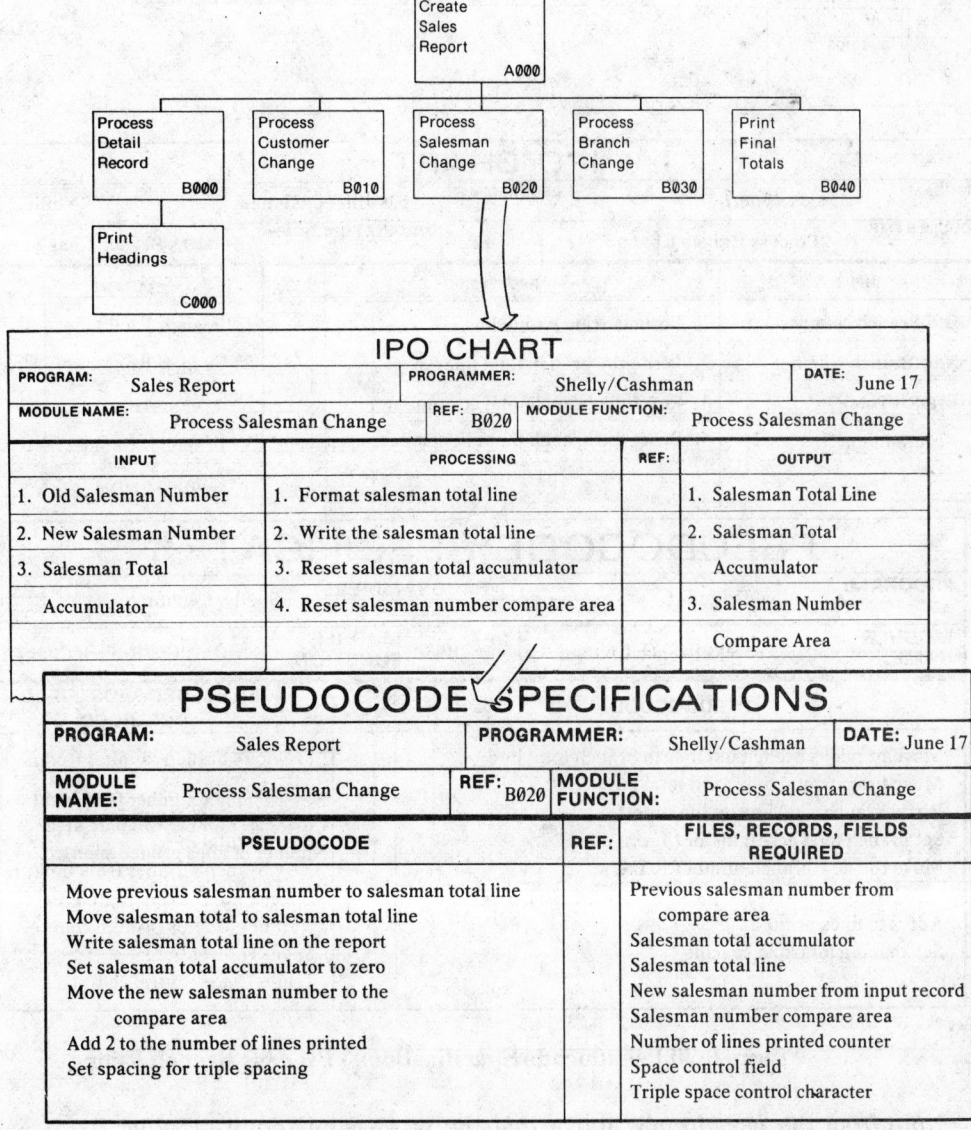

Figure 9-19 Pseudocode Specifications - Process Salesman Change

Pseudocode Specifications - Process Branch Change

Figure 9-20 illustrates the Pseudocode Specifications for the module which processes a change in Branch Number.

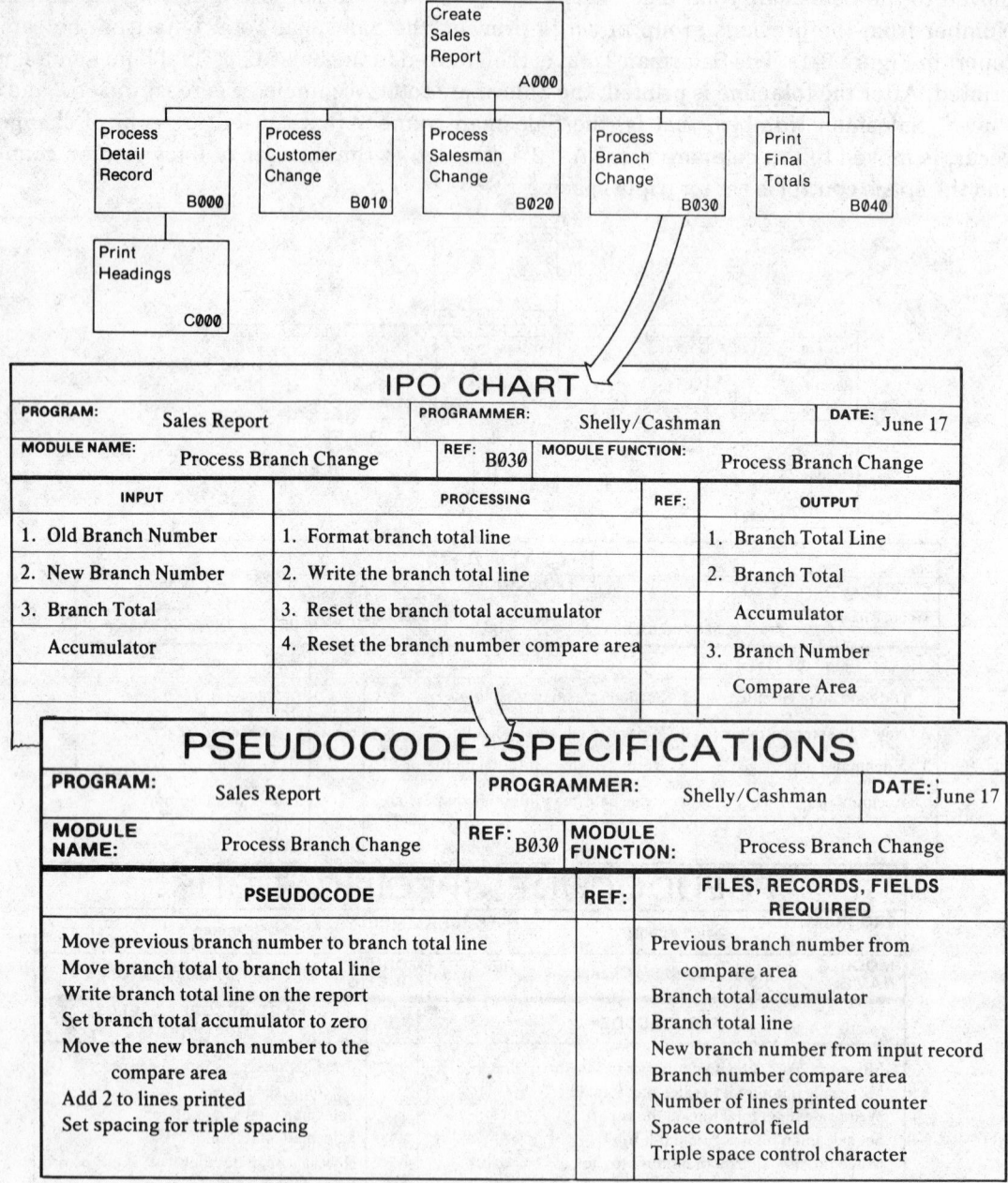

Figure 9-20 Pseudocode Specifications - Process Branch Change

Note from the pseudocode above that the processing required when the Branch Number changes is quite similar to the processing which occurs when the Salesman Number changes. The previous Branch Number and the branch total are moved to the branch total line, which is then written. The branch total accumulator is set to zero and the new Branch Number is moved to the branch compare area. The lines printed counter is then incremented and the spacing is set for triple spacing, as is required.

Pseudocode Specifications - Print Final Totals

The Pseudocode Specifications for the module which prints the final totals are shown in Figure 9-21.

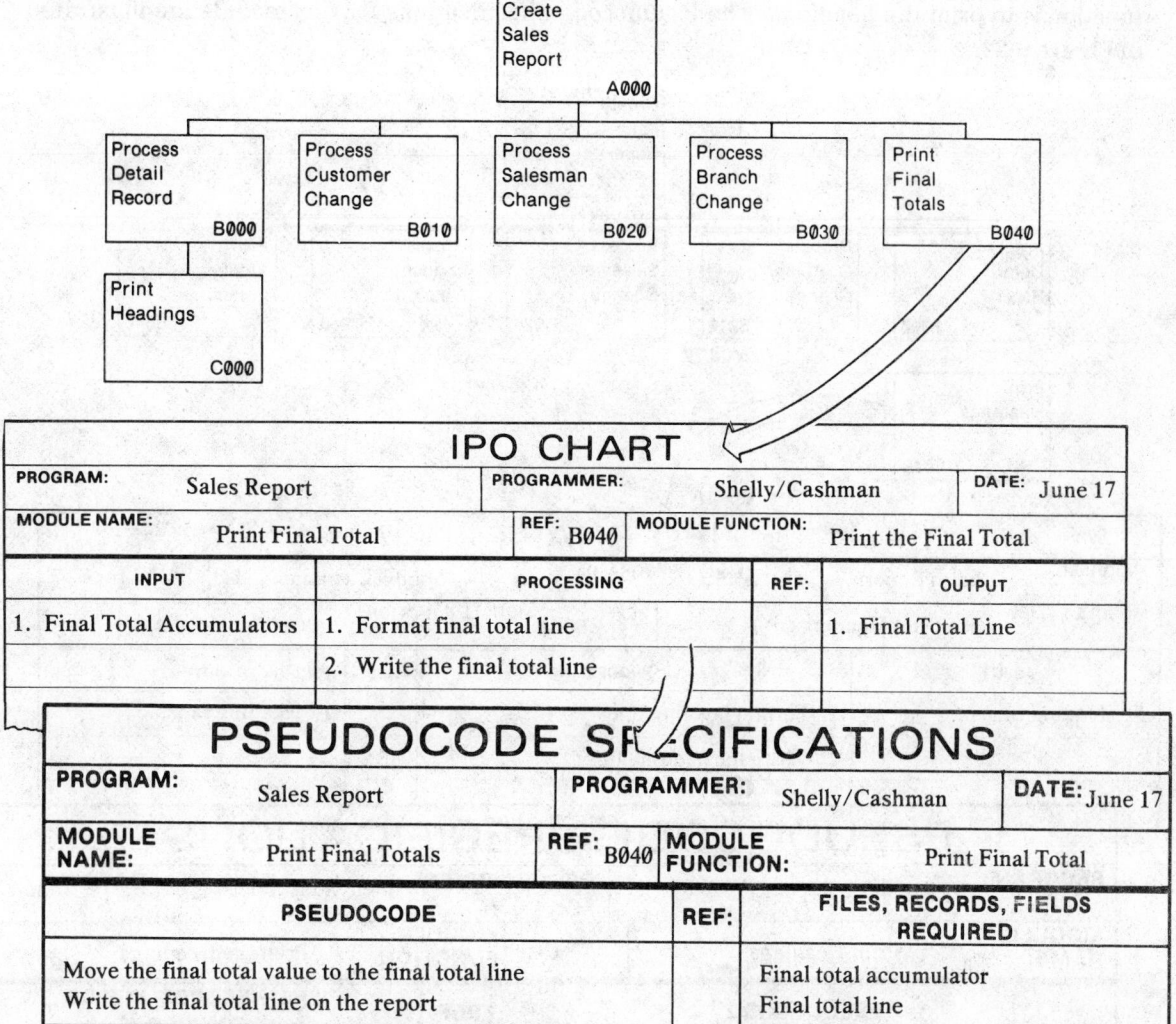

Figure 9-21 Pseudocode Specifications - Print Final Totals

Note from Figure 9-21 that in order to print the final totals, the final total value is moved from the final total accumulator to the final total line and then the line is printed. This is similar to the processing which has been seen in previous programs.

Pseudocode Specifications - Print the Headings

After the pseudocode for the modules on the second level of the program is complete, the programmer would normally begin the pseudocode for modules on the third level of the Hierarchy Chart. The only module on the third level in this program is the module whose function is to print the headings. The Pseudocode Specifications for this module are illustrated in Figure 9-22.

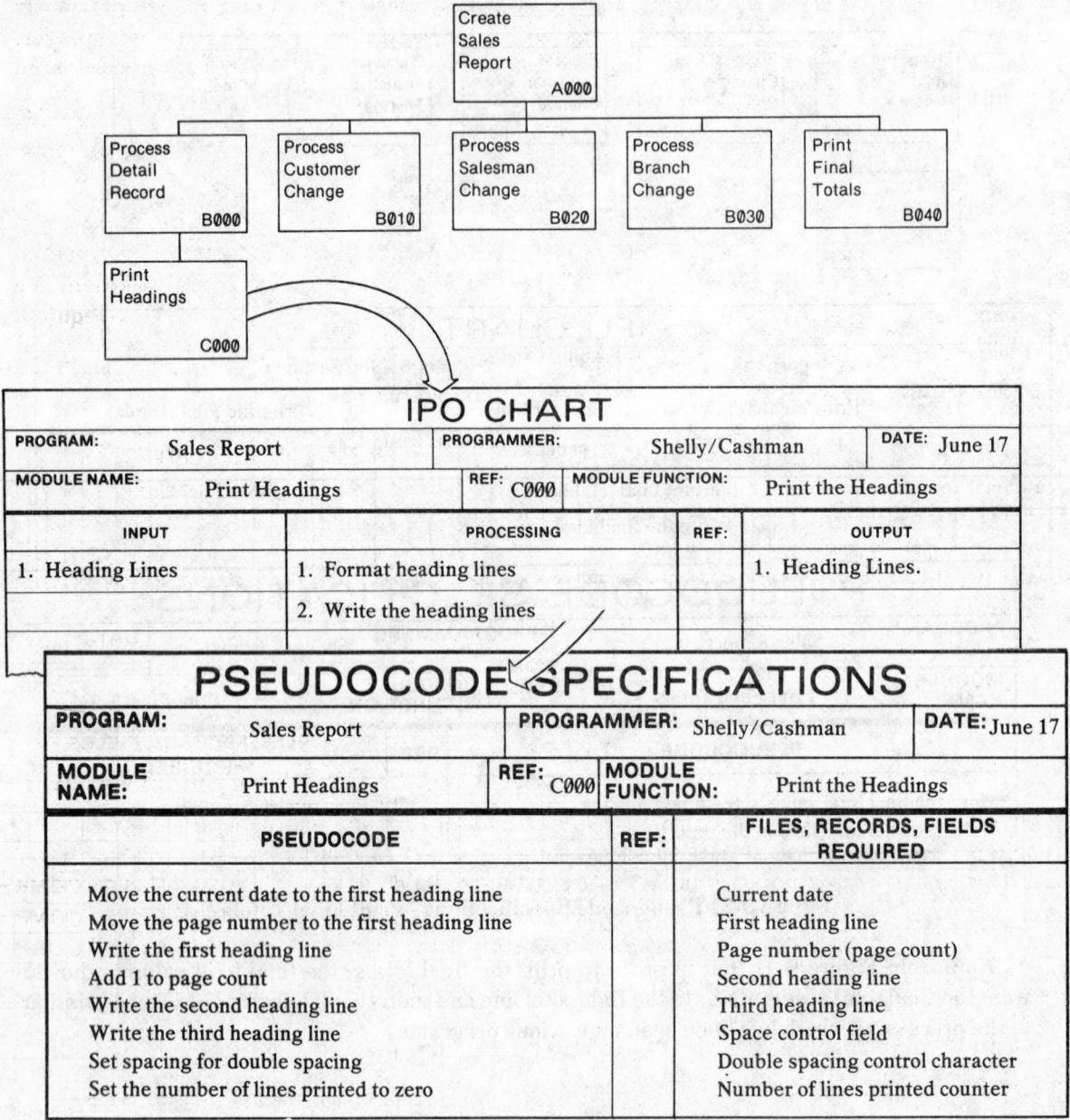

Figure 9-22 Pseudocode Specifications - Print the Headings

Note from Figure 9-22 that the headings are formatted and printed in the same manner as has been seen in previous programs.

SUMMARY

As can be seen from the program design, when the major processing tasks are decomposed into lower-level modules, the development of the logical steps to accomplish the task is not an overly difficult job. It must be remembered, however, that the review, such as was conducted when the group indication was required, is an extremely important part of program design. Without the review and the flexibility at the design stage to go back and change previously defined modules, there is a good chance that a program will not be designed properly; however, when the programmer recognizes that changes will occur and that the design process is an iterative process, then there is every likelihood that good programs will be produced.

SOURCE CODING - SAMPLE PROGRAM

It will be recalled from the Pseudocode Specifications that a series of indicators is required in the sample program to indicate when there is a change in Branch Number, when there is a change in Salesman Number, and when there is a change in Customer Number. The required Working-Storage entries are illustrated in the coding below.

EXAMPLE

```
003200 WORKING-STORAGE SECTION.
004010
004020 01  PROGRAM-INDICATORS.
004030     05  ARE-THERE-MORE-RECORDS     PIC XXX        VALUE 'YES'.
004040         88  THERE-IS-A-RECORD                     VALUE 'YES'.
004050         88  THERE-ARE-NO-MORE-RECORDS             VALUE 'NO '.
004060     05  WAS-THERE-A-BRANCH-CHANGE   PIC XXX       VALUE 'NO '.
004070         88  THERE-WAS-A-BRANCH-CHANGE             VALUE 'YES'.
004080     05  WAS-THERE-A-SALESMAN-CHANGE PIC XXX       VALUE 'NO '.
004090         88  THERE-WAS-A-SALESMAN-CHANGE           VALUE 'YES'.
004100     05  WAS-THERE-A-CUSTOMER-CHANGE PIC XXX       VALUE 'NO '.
004110         88  THERE-WAS-A-CUSTOMER-CHANGE           VALUE 'YES'.
004120
004130 01  PROGRAM-COMPARE-AREAS.
004140     05  PREVIOUS-CUSTOMER-NUMBER PIC 9(5)         USAGE IS COMP-3.
004150     05  PREVIOUS-SALESMAN-NUMBER PIC 9(4)         USAGE IS COMP-3.
004160     05  PREVIOUS-BRANCH-NUMBER   PIC 9(3)         USAGE IS COMP-3.
004170
004180 01  TOTAL-ACCUMULATORS                            USAGE IS COMP-3.
004190     05  CUSTOMER-TOTAL-ACCUM      PIC S9(4)V99    VALUE ZERO.
004200     05  SALESMAN-TOTAL-ACCUM      PIC S9(5)V99    VALUE ZERO.
005010     05  BRANCH-TOTAL-ACCUM        PIC S9(5)V99    VALUE ZERO.
005020     05  FINAL-TOTAL-ACCUM         PIC S9(6)V99    VALUE ZERO.
```

Figure 9-23 Working-Storage Coding

Note in Figure 9-23 that the indicators are defined together with condition names which can be tested in the Procedure Division. In addition, the compare areas for the Customer Number, the Salesman Number, and the Branch Number are shown, as well as the accumulators for the Customer Total, the Salesman Total, the Branch Total, and the Final Total.

COBOL Coding - Create Sales Report Module

The COBOL coding for the Create Sales Report module is illustrated in Figure 9-24.

EXAMPLE

```
010160 A000-CREATE-SALES-REPORT.
010170
010180     OPEN INPUT   SALES-INPUT-FILE
010190          OUTPUT  SALES-REPORT-FILE.
010200     READ SALES-INPUT-FILE
011010          AT END
011020              MOVE 'NO ' TO ARE-THERE-MORE-RECORDS.
011030     IF THERE-IS-A-RECORD
011040         MOVE CUSTOMER-NO-INPUT TO PREVIOUS-CUSTOMER-NUMBER
011050         MOVE SALESMAN-NO-INPUT TO PREVIOUS-SALESMAN-NUMBER
011060         MOVE BRANCH-NO-INPUT TO PREVIOUS-BRANCH-NUMBER
011070         PERFORM A001-PROCESS-AND-READ
011080             UNTIL THERE-ARE-NO-MORE-RECORDS
011090         PERFORM B010-PROCESS-CUSTOMER-CHANGE
011100         PERFORM B020-PROCESS-SALESMAN-CHANGE
011110         PERFORM B030-PROCESS-BRANCH-CHANGE
011120         PERFORM B040-PRINT-FINAL-TOTAL.
011130     CLOSE SALES-INPUT-FILE
011140           SALES-REPORT-FILE.
011150     STOP RUN.
011160
011170
011180
011190 A001-PROCESS-AND-READ.
011200
012010     IF BRANCH-NO-INPUT NOT = PREVIOUS-BRANCH-NUMBER
012020         PERFORM B010-PROCESS-CUSTOMER-CHANGE
012030         PERFORM B020-PROCESS-SALESMAN-CHANGE
012040         PERFORM B030-PROCESS-BRANCH-CHANGE
012050         MOVE 'YES' TO WAS-THERE-A-BRANCH-CHANGE
012060     ELSE
012070         IF SALESMAN-NO-INPUT NOT = PREVIOUS-SALESMAN-NUMBER
012080             PERFORM B010-PROCESS-CUSTOMER-CHANGE
012090             PERFORM B020-PROCESS-SALESMAN-CHANGE
012100             MOVE 'YES' TO WAS-THERE-A-SALESMAN-CHANGE
012110         ELSE
012120             IF CUSTOMER-NO-INPUT NOT = PREVIOUS-CUSTOMER-NUMBER
012130                 PERFORM B010-PROCESS-CUSTOMER-CHANGE
012140                 MOVE 'YES' TO WAS-THERE-A-CUSTOMER-CHANGE.
012150     PERFORM B000-PROCESS-DETAIL-RECORD.
012160     READ SALES-INPUT-FILE
012170          AT END
012180              MOVE 'NO ' TO ARE-THERE-MORE-RECORDS.
```

Figure 9-24 COBOL Coding - Create Sales Report Module

Note from Figure 9-24 that after the files are opened and the Read Statement on line 010200 is executed, a test is made to determine if there is a record to process (line 011030). If there is, the Customer Number, the Salesman Number, and the Branch Number are moved to their respective compare areas (see Figure 9-23). This is necessary in order to initialize the compare areas prior to processing the first record.

After the moves to the compare areas, the A001-PROCESS-AND-READ routine is executed until there are no more records. The first statements in the A001-READ-AND-PROCESS routine determine if a control break has occurred for the Branch Number (line 012010), the Salesman Number (line 012070), or the Customer Number (line 012120). When the first record is being processed, there will be no control breaks because the values from the first record were moved to the compare areas immediately before entering this module. Therefore, the statement on line 012150 will be executed, which will result in the execution of the routine which processes the detail records. Following the processing of the first input record, another input record is read by the Read Statement on line 012160; and the comparing operation to determine if a control break has occured (which begins on line 012010) will be repeated. This processing will occur so long as there are more input records to process.

When a record is read and there is a control break on the Branch Number, that is, when the Branch Number in the input area is NOT equal to the Branch Number in the compare area, the modules which process a Customer Change, a Salesman Change, and a Branch Change are performed. This causes the customer total, the salesman total, and the branch total to be printed on the report. The statement on line 012050 is used to set the branch change indicator to specify that a change in Branch Number has occurred. It is necessary to set the indicator at this time because it is tested in the module which processes the detail records to determine if group indication is required for the Branch Number, the Salesman Number, and the Customer Number.

On line 012070, the Salesman Number in the input record is compared to the Salesman Number in the compare area. If these number are NOT equal, the Customer Change module and the Salesman Change module are executed. This results in the customer total and the salesman total being printed on the report. The entry on line 012100 sets the salesman change indicator to specify that a change in Salesman Number has occurred; again, this is required for group indication.

It should be noted that the IF Statement beginning on line 012010 is a Nested IF Statement. Therefore, if there is a change in the Branch Number, the test for a change in the Salesman Number or Customer Number will not take place. Similarly, if there is not a change in the Branch Number but there is a change in the Salesman Number, the test for a change in the Customer Number will not occur.

If there is not a change in the Branch Number or the Salesman Number but there is a change in the Customer Number, the module to print the customer total is performed and the indicator is set to indicate that a customer change has occurred.

Regardless of whether there were any control breaks, the module to process the detail records is performed and then another input record is read. This processing will continue until there are no more input records. When there are no more input records, the modules to print the control break totals will be performed (lines 011090 - 011110) so that the totals for the last group of records will be printed, and then the final totals will be printed (line 011120). The files are then closed and the program is terminated.

Thus, from the entries in the Create Sales Report module, it can be seen that this module controls when processing is to occur within the program. This is normally the function of the highest level module in a program.

COBOL Coding - Process Detail Record Module

The COBOL coding in Figure 9-25 contains the entries for the module which processes the detail records.

EXAMPLE

```
013100  B000-PROCESS-DETAIL-RECORD.
013110
013120      IF LINES-PRINTED IS EQUAL TO PAGE-SIZE OR
013130              IS GREATER THAN PAGE-SIZE OR
013140              FIRST-PAGE
013150          PERFORM C000-PRINT-HEADINGS
013160          MOVE PREVIOUS-BRANCH-NUMBER TO BRANCH-NO-REPORT
013170          MOVE PREVIOUS-SALESMAN-NUMBER TO SALESMAN-NO-REPORT
013180          MOVE PREVIOUS-CUSTOMER-NUMBER TO CUSTOMER-NO-REPORT.
013190      IF THERE-WAS-A-BRANCH-CHANGE
013200          MOVE BRANCH-NO-INPUT TO BRANCH-NO-REPORT
014010          MOVE SALESMAN-NO-INPUT TO SALESMAN-NO-REPORT
014020          MOVE CUSTOMER-NO-INPUT TO CUSTOMER-NO-REPORT
014030          MOVE 'NO ' TO WAS-THERE-A-BRANCH-CHANGE
014040      ELSE
014050          IF THERE-WAS-A-SALESMAN-CHANGE
014060              MOVE SALESMAN-NO-INPUT TO SALESMAN-NO-REPORT
014070              MOVE CUSTOMER-NO-INPUT TO CUSTOMER-NO-REPORT
014080              MOVE 'NO ' TO WAS-THERE-A-SALESMAN-CHANGE
014090          ELSE
014100              IF THERE-WAS-A-CUSTOMER-CHANGE
014110                  MOVE CUSTOMER-NO-INPUT TO CUSTOMER-NO-REPORT
014120                  MOVE 'NO ' TO WAS-THERE-A-CUSTOMER-CHANGE.
014130      MOVE DESCRIPTION-INPUT TO DESCRIPTION-REPORT.
014140      MOVE SALES-INPUT TO SALES-REPORT.
014150      ADD SALES-INPUT TO CUSTOMER-TOTAL-ACCUM
014160                        SALESMAN-TOTAL-ACCUM
014170                        BRANCH-TOTAL-ACCUM
014180                        FINAL-TOTAL-ACCUM.
014190      WRITE SALES-REPORT-LINE FROM DETAIL-LINE
014200              AFTER PROPER-SPACING.
015010      ADD PROPER-SPACING TO LINES-PRINTED.
015020      MOVE SPACE-ONE-LINE TO PROPER-SPACING.
015030      MOVE SPACES TO DETAIL-LINE.
```

Figure 9-25 COBOL Coding - Process Detail Record Module

The first entries in the module which processes the detail records are used to determine if a heading should be printed. If so, the headings are printed and then the Branch Number, the Salesman Number, and the Customer Number are moved to the printer output area. When a report is group indicated, those fields which are group indicated will normally be printed when a new page is begun, for ease of reading the report. The Move Statements on lines 013160 - 013180 will place the group indicated fields in the detail output area so that they will be printed on the first line of the new page.

The IF Statement on line 013190 tests the condition of whether a control break has occurred (the condition name THERE-WAS-A-BRANCH-CHANGE is defined in Figure 9-23). The indicator is set to indicate a branch change in the Create Sales Report module (see Figure 9-24). If there is a change, then the Branch Number, the Salesman Number, and the Customer Number are moved to the detail report line. In addition, the indicator is reset by the Move Statement on line 014030. It must be reset because the processing that is to occur in the module when there is a change in the Branch Number has been completed (the moving of the Branch Number, Salesman Number, and Customer Number to the output area). After the branch change processing is done, the statements on lines 014130 through 015030 would be executed to process the detail record.

If there is not a change in branch number, then a test is made to determine if there was a change in Salesman Number (line 014050). If so, the Salesman Number and Customer Number would be moved to the detail print line and the salesman change indicator is reset.

If there is no change in the Salesman Number, the test is performed to determine if there was a change in the Customer Number (line 014100). If so, the Customer Number is moved to the printer report line and the customer change indicator is reset (line 014120). It will be noted that all of these checks for a control break are a part of a Nested IF Statement and if any one of them is true, the remaining tests will not be made.

After the checking for control breaks is completed, each detail record will be printed. It will be noted in Figure 9-25 that the Write Statement on line 014190 uses the "Write . . . From" form of the Write verb. Thus, DETAIL-LINE must be defined in the Working-Storage Section of the Data Division rather than the File Section of the Data Division. The field SALES-REPORT-LINE, however, must be defined in the File Section. This coding is illustrated in Figure 9-26.

EXAMPLE

File Section

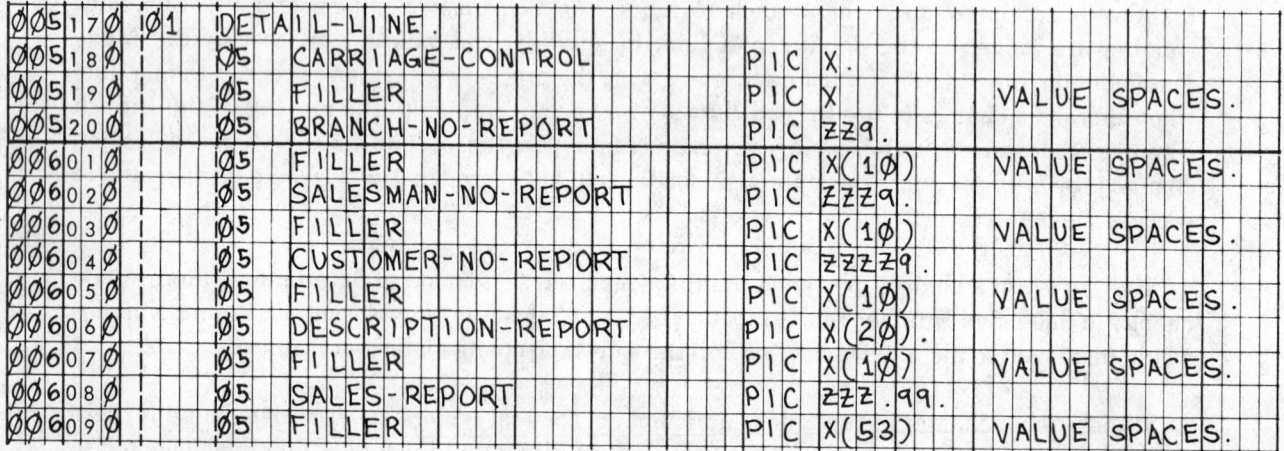

```
003140 FD  SALES-REPORT-FILE
003150         RECORD CONTAINS 133 CHARACTERS
003160         LABEL RECORDS ARE OMITTED
003170         DATA RECORD IS SALES-REPORT-LINE.
003180 01  SALES-REPORT-LINE              PIC X(133).
```

Working-Storage Section

```
005170 01  DETAIL-LINE.
005180     05  CARRIAGE-CONTROL           PIC X.
005190     05  FILLER                     PIC X          VALUE SPACES.
005200     05  BRANCH-NO-REPORT           PIC ZZ9.
006010     05  FILLER                     PIC X(10)      VALUE SPACES.
006020     05  SALESMAN-NO-REPORT         PIC ZZZ9.
006030     05  FILLER                     PIC X(10)      VALUE SPACES.
006040     05  CUSTOMER-NO-REPORT         PIC ZZZZ9.
006050     05  FILLER                     PIC X(10)      VALUE SPACES.
006060     05  DESCRIPTION-REPORT         PIC X(20).
006070     05  FILLER                     PIC X(10)      VALUE SPACES.
006080     05  SALES-REPORT               PIC ZZZ.99.
006090     05  FILLER                     PIC X(53)      VALUE SPACES.
```

Procedure Division

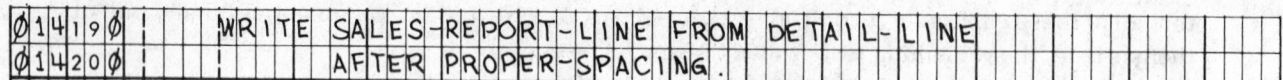

```
014190     WRITE SALES-REPORT-LINE FROM DETAIL-LINE
014200         AFTER PROPER-SPACING.
```

Figure 9-26 Example of Detail-Line

Note in the example of the File Section of the Data Division that the SALES-REPORT-FILE is defined in the same manner as in previous programs. The output area, however, is defined with a PIC X(133), instead of each individual field. This is because each individual field is to be defined in the Working-Storage Section of the Data Division as a part of the output record. In Working-Storage, the DETAIL-LINE is defined with each field. It should be noted that the FILLERs which will not contain data are given the value Spaces through the use of the Value Clause. This is necessary so that the first time the line is printed, these Filler fields will not contain "garbage." After the first line is printed, spaces will be moved to the DETAIL-LINE and subsequent lines will contain only valid data. This technique is required when the report is group indicated.

When preparing a report involving multiple level control breaks, it is important to keep an accurate count of the number of detail and total lines printed, including the spaces before and after these lines, so that proper page overflow will take place. The example in Figure 9-27 illustrates the report from the sample program and the spacing with which the programmer must be concerned.

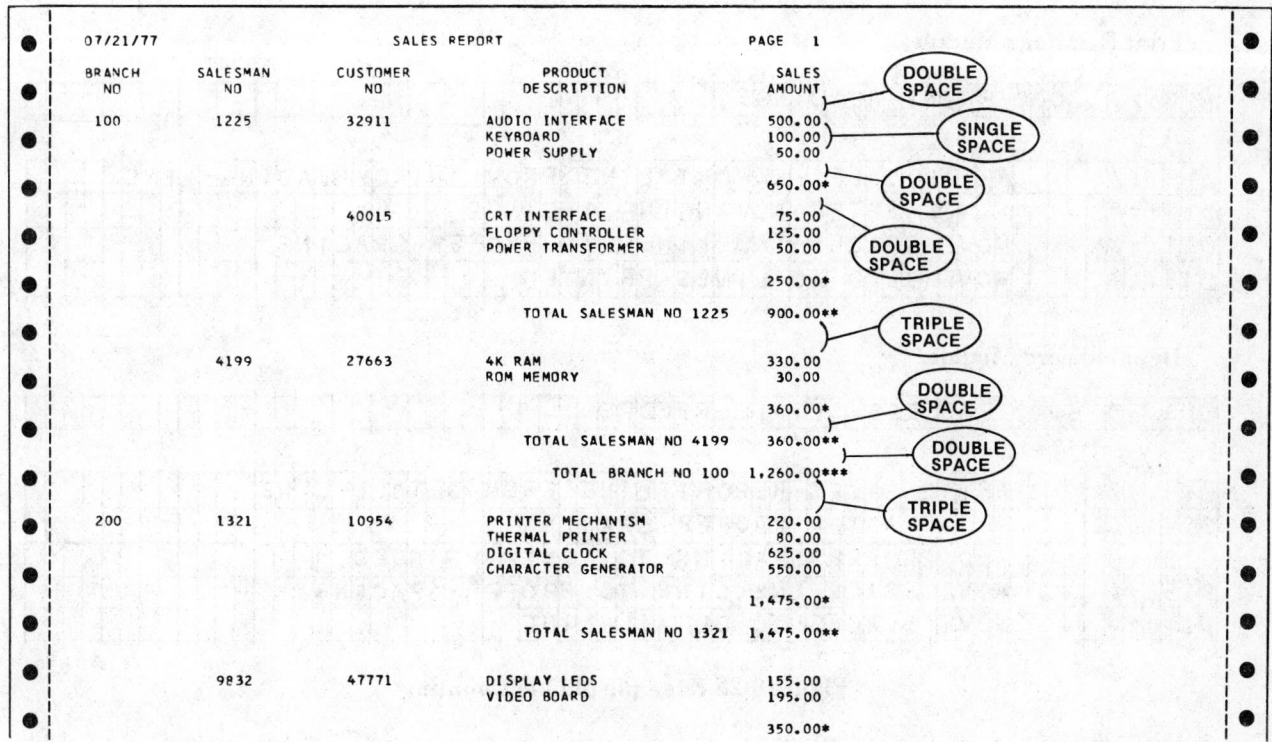

Figure 9-27 Example of Spacing on Report

Note in the report above that after the heading is printed, the report is double spaced. The detail lines are single spaced. There is double spacing before the customer total is printed and before the salesman total is printed. There is double spacing after the customer total is printed. There is triple spacing after the salesman total is printed unless the branch total is printed immediately after it. If the branch total is printed, there is double spacing following the salesman total and triple spacing following the branch total. It should be noted that double spacing means there is one blank line with the data being printed on the second line; and triple spacing means there are two blank lines with the data being printed on the third line.

As noted, it is important for the programmer to be aware of the spacing so that the lines printed can be counted properly. The following segments of coding from the sample program illustrate how the lines printed counter is updated after printing the headings on a page.

EXAMPLE

Print Headings Module

```
019070  CØØØ-PRINT-HEADINGS.
```

```
019160      WRITE SALES-REPORT-LINE FROM THIRD-HEADING-LINE
019170          AFTER ADVANCING 1 LINES.
019180      MOVE SPACES-TWO-LINES TO PROPER-SPACING.
019190      MOVE ZERO TO LINES-PRINTED.
```

Detail Record Module

```
013100  BØØØ-PROCESS-DETAIL-RECORD.
```

```
014190      WRITE SALES-REPORT-LINE FROM DETAIL-LINE
014200          AFTER PROPER-SPACING.
015010      ADD PROPER-SPACING TO LINES-PRINTED.
015020      MOVE SPACE-ONE-LINE TO PROPER-SPACING.
015030      MOVE SPACES TO DETAIL-LINE.
```

Figure 9-28 Example of Line Counting

In the example it can be seen that after the third heading line is written by means of the Write Statement on Line 019160, the statement MOVE SPACE-TWO-LINES TO PROPER-SPACING is specified. This statement results in the constant "2" being moved to PROPER-SPACING. Note that when the first detail line is written in the Process Detail Record module, as indicated by the Write Statement on line 014190, the line is written after PROPER-SPACING. As PROPER-SPACING contains the constant "2", the first detail line is double spaced. The next statement specifies ADD PROPER-SPACING TO LINES-PRINTED and the value 2 is added to the LINES-PRINTED counter. Thus, the two lines on the page which were used for double spacing are accounted for in the count of the number of lines printed on the page.

The statement on line 015020, MOVE SPACE-ONE-LINE TO PROPER-SPACING, moves the constant "1" to PROPER-SPACING so that when the next detail line is printed, the line will be single spaced. Note also that because the statement following the write statement is ADD PROPER-SPACING TO LINES-PRINTED, a 1 will then be added to the lines printed counter for each detail line, thus accounting for the single spacing of the detail lines. This coding technique results in the proper number of lines being accumulated in the lines printed counter.

This same basic technique is utilized to handle the variable spacing that occurs when there is a change in Branch Number, Salesman Number, and Customer Number.

SOURCE LISTING

The following pages contain the source listing of the sample program in this chapter.

```
   1                              IBM DOS AMERICAN NATIONAL STANDARD COBOL        CBF CL3-4        07/21/77

00001   001010 IDENTIFICATION DIVISION.                                          SALESRPT
00002   001020                                                                   SALESRPT
00003   001030 PROGRAM-ID.   SALESRPT.                                           SALESRPT
00004   001040 AUTHOR.       SHELLY AND CASHMAN.                                 SALESRPT
00005   001050 INSTALLATION. ANAHEIM.                                            SALESRPT
00006   001060 DATE-WRITTEN. 07/21/77.                                           SALESRPT
00007   001070 DATE-COMPILED. 07/21/77                                           SALESRPT
00008   001080 SECURITY.     UNCLASSIFIED.                                       SALESRPT
00009   001090                                                                   SALESRPT
00010   001100**************************************************************   * SALESRPT
00011   001110*                                                              * SALESRPT
00012   001120*  THIS PROGRAM PREPARES A SALES REPORT. THE REPORT CONTAINS  * SALESRPT
00013   001130*  SALES INFORMATION FOR EACH BRANCH, SALESMAN, AND CUSTOMER. * SALESRPT
00014   001140*  TOTALS ARE TAKEN FOR A CHANGE IN CUSTOMER, A CHANGE IN     * SALESRPT
00015   001150*  SALESMAN, AND A CHANGE IN BRANCH. FINAL TOTALS ARE ALSO    * SALESRPT
00016   001160*  PRINTED.                                                   * SALESRPT
00017   001170*                                                             * SALESRPT
00018   001180**************************************************************   * SALESRPT
00019   001190                                                                   SALESRPT
00020   001200                                                                   SALESRPT
00021   002010                                                                   SALESRPT
00022   002020 ENVIRONMENT DIVISION.                                             SALESRPT
00023   002030                                                                   SALESRPT
00024   002040 CONFIGURATION SECTION.                                            SALESRPT
00025   002050                                                                   SALESRPT
00026   002060 SOURCE-COMPUTER. IBM-370.                                         SALESRPT
00027   002070 OBJECT-COMPUTER. IBM-370.                                         SALESRPT
00028   002080 SPECIAL-NAMES.   C01 IS TO-TOP-OF-PAGE.                           SALESRPT
00029   002090                                                                   SALESRPT
00030   002100 INPUT-OUTPUT SECTION.                                             SALESRPT
00031   002110                                                                   SALESRPT
00032   002120 FILE-CONTROL.                                                     SALESRPT
00033   002130     SELECT SALES-INPUT-FILE                                       SALESRPT
00034   002140         ASSIGN TO SYS007-UR-2540R-S.                              SALESRPT
00035   002150     SELECT SALES-REPORT-FILE                                      SALESRPT
00036   002160         ASSIGN TO SYS013-UR-1403-S.                               SALESRPT
```

Figure 9-29 Source Listing [Part 1 of 5]

```
      2
00037  002180 DATA DIVISION.                                              SALESRPT
00038  002190                                                            SALESRPT
00039  002200 FILE SECTION.                                              SALESRPT
00040  003010                                                            SALESRPT
00041  003020 FD   SALES-INPUT-FILE                                      SALESRPT
00042  003030      RECORD CONTAINS 80 CHARACTERS                         SALESRPT
00043  003040      LABEL RECORDS ARE OMITTED                             SALESRPT
00044  003050      DATA RECORD IS SALES-INPUT-RECORD.                    SALESRPT
00045  003060 01   SALES-INPUT-RECORD.                                   SALESRPT
00046  003070      05  BRANCH-NO-INPUT        PIC 999.                   SALESRPT
00047  003080      05  SALESMAN-NO-INPUT      PIC 9999.                  SALESRPT
00048  003090      05  CUSTOMER-NO-INPUT      PIC 9(5).                  SALESRPT
00049  003100      05  DESCRIPTION-INPUT      PIC X(20).                 SALESRPT
00050  003110      05  SALES-INPUT            PIC 999V99.                SALESRPT
00051  003120      05  FILLER                 PIC X(43).                 SALESRPT
00052  003130                                                            SALESRPT
00053  003140 FD   SALES-REPORT-FILE                                     SALESRPT
00054  003150      RECORD CONTAINS 133 CHARACTERS                        SALESRPT
00055  003160      LABEL RECORDS ARE OMITTED                             SALESRPT
00056  003170      DATA RECORD IS SALES-REPORT-LINE.                     SALESRPT
00057  003180 01   SALES-REPORT-LINE          PIC X(133).                SALESRPT
00058  003190                                                            SALESRPT
00059  003200 WORKING-STORAGE SECTION.                                   SALESRPT
00060  004010                                                            SALESRPT
00061  004020 01   PROGRAM-INDICATORS.                                   SALESRPT
00062  004030      05  ARE-THERE-MORE-RECORDS  PIC XXX    VALUE 'YES'.   SALESRPT
00063  004040          88  THERE-IS-A-RECORD              VALUE 'YES'.   SALESRPT
00064  004050          88  THERE-ARE-NO-MORE-RECORDS      VALUE 'NO '.   SALESRPT
00065  004060      05  WAS-THERE-A-BRANCH-CHANGE PIC XXX  VALUE 'NO '.   SALESRPT
00066  004070          88  THERE-WAS-A-BRANCH-CHANGE      VALUE 'YES'.   SALESRPT
00067  004080      05  WAS-THERE-A-SALESMAN-CHANGE PIC XXX VALUE 'NO '.  SALESRPT
00068  004090          88  THERE-WAS-A-SALESMAN-CHANGE    VALUE 'YES'.   SALESRPT
00069  004100      05  WAS-THERE-A-CUSTOMER-CHANGE PIC XXX VALUE 'NO '.  SALESRPT
00070  004110          88  THERE-WAS-A-CUSTOMER-CHANGE    VALUE 'YES'.   SALESRPT
00071  004120                                                            SALESRPT
00072  004130 01   PROGRAM-COMPARE-AREAS.                                SALESRPT
00073  004140      05  PREVIOUS-CUSTOMER-NUMBER PIC 9(5)   USAGE IS COMP-3. SALESRPT
00074  004150      05  PREVIOUS-SALESMAN-NUMBER PIC 9(4)   USAGE IS COMP-3. SALESRPT
00075  004160      05  PREVIOUS-BRANCH-NUMBER   PIC 9(3)   USAGE IS COMP-3. SALESRPT
00076  004170                                                            SALESRPT
00077  004180 01   TOTAL-ACCUMULATORS                      USAGE IS COMP-3. SALESRPT
00078  004190      05  CUSTOMER-TOTAL-ACCUM   PIC S9(4)V99 VALUE ZERO.   SALESRPT
00079  004200      05  SALESMAN-TOTAL-ACCUM   PIC S9(5)V99 VALUE ZERO.   SALESRPT
00080  005010      05  BRANCH-TOTAL-ACCUM     PIC S9(5)V99 VALUE ZERO.   SALESRPT
00081  005020      05  FINAL-TOTAL-ACCUM      PIC S9(6)V99 VALUE ZERO.   SALESRPT
00082  005030                                                            SALESRPT
00083  005040 01   PRINTER-CONTROL.                                      SALESRPT
00084  005050      05  PROPER-SPACING         PIC 9.                     SALESRPT
00085  005060      05  SPACE-ONE-LINE         PIC 9      VALUE 1.        SALESRPT
00086  005070      05  SPACE-TWO-LINES        PIC 9      VALUE 2.        SALESRPT
00087  005080      05  SPACE-THREE-LINES      PIC 9      VALUE 3.        SALESRPT
00088  005090      05  LINES-PRINTED          PIC S999   VALUE ZERO.     SALESRPT
00089  005100                                            USAGE COMP-3.   SALESRPT
00090  005110      05  PAGE-SIZE              PIC S999   VALUE +50.      SALESRPT
00091  005120                                            USAGE COMP-3.   SALESRPT
00092  005130      05  PAGE-NUMBER            PIC S999   VALUE +1.       SALESRPT
00093  005140                                            USAGE COMP-3.   SALESRPT
00094  005150          88  FIRST-PAGE                    VALUE +1.       SALESRPT
00095  005160                                                            SALESRPT
00096  005170 01   DETAIL-LINE.                                          SALESRPT
00097  005180      05  CARRIAGE-CONTROL       PIC X.                     SALESRPT
00098  005190      05  FILLER                 PIC X      VALUE SPACES.   SALESRPT
00099  005200      05  BRANCH-NO-REPORT       PIC ZZ9.                   SALESRPT
00100  006010      05  FILLER                 PIC X(10)  VALUE SPACES.   SALESRPT
00101  006020      05  SALESMAN-NO-REPORT     PIC ZZZ9.                  SALESRPT
00102  006030      05  FILLER                 PIC X(10)  VALUE SPACES.   SALESRPT
00103  006040      05  CUSTOMER-NO-REPORT     PIC ZZZZ9.                 SALESRPT
00104  006050      05  FILLER                 PIC X(10)  VALUE SPACES.   SALESRPT
00105  006060      05  DESCRIPTION-REPORT     PIC X(20).                 SALESRPT
00106  006070      05  FILLER                 PIC X(10)  VALUE SPACES.   SALESRPT
00107  006080      05  SALES-REPORT           PIC ZZZ.99.                SALESRPT
00108  006090      05  FILLER                 PIC X(53)  VALUE SPACES.   SALESRPT
00109  006100                                                            SALESRPT
00110  006110 01   HEADING-LINES.                                        SALESRPT
00111  006120      05  FIRST-HEADING-LINE.                               SALESRPT
00112  006130          10  CARRIAGE-CONTROL   PIC X.                     SALESRPT
00113  006140          10  DATE-HDG1          PIC X(8).                  SALESRPT
00114  006150          10  FILLER             PIC X(25)  VALUE SPACES.   SALESRPT
00115  006160          10  FILLER             PIC X(12)  VALUE           SALESRPT
00116  006170                                            'SALES REPORT'. SALESRPT
00117  006180          10  FILLER             PIC X(26)  VALUE SPACES.   SALESRPT
00118  006190          10  FILLER             PIC X(5)   VALUE 'PAGE '.  SALESRPT
00119  006200          10  PAGE-NUMBER-HDG1   PIC ZZ9.                   SALESRPT
00120  007010          10  FILLER             PIC X(53)  VALUE SPACES.   SALESRPT
00121  007020      05  SECOND-HEADING-LINE.                              SALESRPT
00122  007030          10  CARRIAGE-CONTROL   PIC X.                     SALESRPT
00123  007040          10  FILLER             PIC X(6)   VALUE 'BRANCH'. SALESRPT
00124  007050          10  FILLER             PIC X(6)   VALUE SPACES.   SALESRPT
00125  007060          10  FILLER             PIC X(8)   VALUE 'SALESMAN'. SALESRPT
00126  007070          10  FILLER             PIC X(7)   VALUE SPACES.   SALESRPT
00127  007080          10  FILLER             PIC X(8)   VALUE 'CUSTOMER'. SALESRPT
00128  007090          10  FILLER             PIC X(14)  VALUE SPACES.   SALESRPT
00129  007100          10  FILLER             PIC X(7)   VALUE 'PRODUCT'. SALESRPT
00130  007110          10  FILLER             PIC X(18)  VALUE SPACES.   SALESRPT
00131  007120          10  FILLER             PIC X(5)   VALUE 'SALES'.  SALESRPT
00132  007130          10  FILLER             PIC X(53)  VALUE SPACES.   SALESRPT
```

Figure 9-30 Source Listing [Part 2 of 5]

```
3

00133  007140  05  THIRD-HEADING-LINE.                              SALESRPT
00134  007150      10  CARRIAGE-CONTROL  PIC X.                      SALESRPT
00135  007160      10  FILLER            PIC XX        VALUE SPACES. SALESRPT
00136  007170      10  FILLER            PIC XX        VALUE 'NO'.   SALESRPT
00137  007180      10  FILLER            PIC X(11)     VALUE SPACES. SALESRPT
00138  007190      10  FILLER            PIC XX        VALUE 'NO'.   SALESRPT
00139  007200      10  FILLER            PIC X(13)     VALUE SPACES. SALESRPT
00140  008010      10  FILLER            PIC XX        VALUE 'NO'.   SALESRPT
00141  008020      10  FILLER            PIC X(15)     VALUE SPACES. SALESRPT
00142  008030      10  FILLER            PIC X(11)     VALUE 'DESCRIPTION'.SALESRPT
00143  008040      10  FILLER            PIC X(15)     VALUE SPACES. SALESRPT
00144  008050      10  FILLER            PIC X(6)      VALUE 'AMOUNT'.SALESRPT
00145  008060      10  FILLER            PIC X(53)     VALUE SPACES. SALESRPT
00146  008070                                                       SALESRPT
00147  008080  01  TOTAL-LINES.                                     SALESRPT
00148  008090  05  CUSTOMER-TOTAL-LINE.                             SALESRPT
00149  008100      10  CARRIAGE-CONTROL  PIC X.                      SALESRPT
00150  008110      10  FILLER            PIC X(71)     VALUE SPACES. SALESRPT
00151  008120      10  CUSTOMER-TOTAL-CUSTOT PIC Z,ZZZ.99.          SALESRPT
00152  008130      10  FILLER            PIC X         VALUE '*'.   SALESRPT
00153  009140      10  FILLER            PIC X(52)     VALUE SPACES. SALESRPT
00154  008150  05  SALESMAN-TOTAL-LINE.                             SALESRPT
00155  008160      10  CARRIAGE-CONTROL  PIC X.                      SALESRPT
00156  009170      10  FILLER            PIC X(47)     VALUE SPACES. SALESRPT
00157  008180      10  FILLER            PIC X(6)      VALUE 'TOTAL '.SALESRPT
00158  008190      10  FILLER            PIC X(12)     VALUE        SALESRPT
00159  008200                                         'SALESMAN NO '.SALESRPT
00160  009010      10  SALESMAN-NO-SMTOT PIC ZZZ9.                   SALESRPT
00161  009020      10  FILLER            PIC X         VALUE SPACE.  SALESRPT
00162  009030      10  SALESMAN-TOTAL-SMTOT PIC ZZ,ZZZ.99.          SALESRPT
00163  009040      10  FILLER            PIC XX        VALUE '**'.   SALESRPT
00164  009050      10  FILLER            PIC X(51)     VALUE SPACES. SALESRPT
00165  009060  05  BRANCH-TOTAL-LINE.                               SALESRPT
00166  009070      10  CARRIAGE-CONTROL  PIC X.                      SALESRPT
00167  009080      10  FILLER            PIC X(50)     VALUE SPACES. SALESRPT
00168  009090      10  FILLER            PIC X(16)     VALUE        SALESRPT
00169  009100                                         'TOTAL BRANCH NO '.SALESRPT
00170  009110      10  BRANCH-NO-BRTOT   PIC ZZ9.                    SALESRPT
00171  009120      10  FILLER            PIC X         VALUE SPACE.  SALESRPT
00172  009130      10  BRANCH-TOTAL-BRTOT PIC ZZ,ZZZ.99.            SALESRPT
00173  009140      10  FILLER            PIC XXX       VALUE '***'.  SALESRPT
00174  009150      10  FILLER            PIC X(50)     VALUE SPACES. SALESRPT
00175  009160  05  FINAL-TOTAL-LINE.                                SALESRPT
00176  009170      10  CARRIAGE-CONTROL  PIC X.                      SALESRPT
00177  009180      10  FILLER            PIC X(56)     VALUE SPACES. SALESRPT
00178  009190      10  FILLER            PIC X(12)     VALUE        SALESRPT
00179  009200                                         'FINAL TOTAL '.SALESRPT
00180  010010      10  FINAL-TOTAL-FINTOT PIC $$$$,$$$.99.          SALESRPT
00181  010020      10  FILLER            PIC X(4)      VALUE '****'. SALESRPT
00182  010030      10  FILLER            PIC X(49)     VALUE SPACES. SALESRPT


4

00183  010050  PROCEDURE DIVISION.                                 SALESRPT
00184  010060                                                       SALESRPT
00185  010070***********************************************************SALESRPT
00186  010080*                                                    * SALESRPT
00187  010090*  THIS MODULE INITIALIZES THE FILES AND THEN DETERMINES WHEN * SALESRPT
00188  010100*  CONTROL BREAKS HAVE OCCURRED AND CAUSES THE APPROPRIATE    * SALESRPT
00189  010110*  PROCESSING TO OCCUR. IT ALSO CAUSES THE DETAIL LINES TO    * SALESRPT
00190  010120*  BE PRINTED. IT IS ENTERED FROM THE OPERATING SYSTEM AND    * SALESRPT
00191  010130*  EXITS TO THE OPERATING SYSTEM.                     * SALESRPT
00192  010140*                                                    * SALESRPT
00193  010150***********************************************************SALESRPT
00194  010160                                                       SALESRPT
00195  010170  A000-CREATE-SALES-REPORT.                           SALESRPT
00196  010180                                                       SALESRPT
00197  010190      OPEN INPUT  SALES-INPUT-FILE                     SALESRPT
00198  010200           OUTPUT SALES-REPORT-FILE.                   SALESRPT
00199  011010      READ SALES-INPUT-FILE                            SALESRPT
00200  011020          AT END                                       SALESRPT
00201  011030              MOVE 'NO ' TO ARE-THERE-MORE-RECORDS.    SALESRPT
00202  011040      IF THERE-IS-A-RECORD                             SALESRPT
00203  011050          MOVE CUSTOMER-NO-INPUT TO PREVIOUS-CUSTOMER-NUMBER SALESRPT
00204  011060          MOVE SALESMAN-NO-INPUT TO PREVIOUS-SALESMAN-NUMBER SALESRPT
00205  011070          MOVE BRANCH-NO-INPUT TO PREVIOUS-BRANCH-NUMBER SALESRPT
00206  011080          PERFORM A001-PROCESS-AND-READ               SALESRPT
00207  011090              UNTIL THERE-ARE-NO-MORE-RECORDS.        SALESRPT
00208  011100          PERFORM B010-PROCESS-CUSTOMER-CHANGE        SALESRPT
00209  011110          PERFORM B020-PROCESS-SALESMAN-CHANGE        SALESRPT
00210  011120          PERFORM B030-PROCESS-BRANCH-CHANGE          SALESRPT
00211  011130          PERFORM B040-PRINT-FINAL-TOTAL.             SALESRPT
00212  011140      CLOSE SALES-INPUT-FILE                          SALESRPT
00213  011150            SALES-REPORT-FILE.                        SALESRPT
00214  011160      STOP RUN.                                       SALESRPT
00215  011170                                                       SALESRPT
00216  011180                                                       SALESRPT
00217  011190                                                       SALESRPT
```

Figure 9-31 Source Listing [Part 3 of 5]

```
    5
00218  011200  A001-PROCESS-AND-READ.                                        SALESRPT
00219  012010                                                                SALESRPT
00220  012020      IF BRANCH-NO-INPUT NOT = PREVIOUS-BRANCH-NUMBER           SALESRPT
00221  012030          PERFORM B010-PROCESS-CUSTOMER-CHANGE                  SALESRPT
00222  012040          PERFORM B020-PROCESS-SALESMAN-CHANGE                  SALESRPT
00223  012050          PERFORM B030-PROCESS-BRANCH-CHANGE                    SALESRPT
00224  012060          MOVE 'YES' TO WAS-THERE-A-BRANCH-CHANGE               SALESRPT
00225  012070      ELSE                                                      SALESRPT
00226  012080          IF SALESMAN-NO-INPUT NOT = PREVIOUS-SALESMAN-NUMBER   SALESRPT
00227  012090              PERFORM B010-PROCESS-CUSTOMER-CHANGE              SALESRPT
00228  012100              PERFORM B020-PROCESS-SALESMAN-CHANGE              SALESRPT
00229  012110              MOVE 'YES' TO WAS-THERE-A-SALESMAN-CHANGE         SALESRPT
00230  012120          ELSE                                                  SALESRPT
00231  012130              IF CUSTOMER-NO-INPUT NOT = PREVIOUS-CUSTOMER-NUMBER  SALESRPT
00232  012140                  PERFORM B010-PROCESS-CUSTOMER-CHANGE          SALESRPT
00233  012150                  MOVE 'YES' TO WAS-THERE-A-CUSTOMER-CHANGE.    SALESRPT
00234  012160      PERFORM B000-PROCESS-DETAIL-RECORDS.                      SALESRPT
00235  012170      READ SALES-INPUT-FILE                                     SALESRPT
00236  012180          AT END                                                SALESRPT
00237  012190              MOVE 'NO ' TO ARE-THERE-MORE-RECORDS.             SALESRPT
```

```
    6
00238  013010**************************************************************  SALESRPT
00239  013020*                                                            *  SALESRPT
00240  013030*  THIS MODULE IS ENTERED TO PRINT THE DETAIL LINE FOR THE   *  SALESRPT
00241  013040*  REPORT.  IF NECESSARY, IT CAUSES THE HEADINGS TO BE PRINTED*  SALESRPT
00242  013050*  AND THEN FORMATS AND PRINTS THE DETAIL LINE. TOTALS ARE ALSO*  SALESRPT
00243  013060*  ACCUMULATED.  THIS MODULE IS ENTERED FROM THE             *  SALESRPT
00244  013070*  A000-CREATE-SALES-REPORT MODULE AND EXITS BACK TO IT.     *  SALESRPT
00245  013080*                                                            *  SALESRPT
00246  013090**************************************************************  SALESRPT
00247  013100                                                                SALESRPT
00248  013110  B000-PROCESS-DETAIL-RECORDS.                                  SALESRPT
00249  013120                                                                SALESRPT
00250  013130      IF LINES-PRINTED IS EQUAL TO PAGE-SIZE OR                 SALESRPT
00251  013140            IS GREATER THAN PAGE-SIZE OR                        SALESRPT
00252  013150            FIRST-PAGE                                          SALESRPT
00253  013160          PERFORM C000-PRINT-HEADINGS                           SALESRPT
00254  013170          MOVE PREVIOUS-BRANCH-NUMBER TO BRANCH-NO-REPORT       SALESRPT
00255  013180          MOVE PREVIOUS-SALESMAN-NUMBER TO SALESMAN-NO-REPORT   SALESRPT
00256  013190          MOVE PREVIOUS-CUSTOMER-NUMBER TO CUSTOMER-NO-REPORT.  SALESRPT
00257  013200      IF THERE-WAS-A-BRANCH-CHANGE                              SALESRPT
00258  014010          MOVE BRANCH-NO-INPUT TO BRANCH-NO-REPORT              SALESRPT
00259  014020          MOVE SALESMAN-NO-INPUT TO SALESMAN-NO-REPORT          SALESRPT
00260  014030          MOVE CUSTOMER-NO-INPUT TO CUSTOMER-NO-REPORT          SALESRPT
00261  014040          MOVE 'NO ' TO WAS-THERE-A-BRANCH-CHANGE               SALESRPT
00262  014050      ELSE                                                      SALESRPT
00263  014060          IF THERE-WAS-A-SALESMAN-CHANGE                        SALESRPT
00264  014070              MOVE SALESMAN-NO-INPUT TO SALESMAN-NO-REPORT      SALESRPT
00265  014080              MOVE CUSTOMER-NO-INPUT TO CUSTOMER-NO-REPORT      SALESRPT
00266  014090              MOVE 'NO ' TO WAS-THERE-A-SALESMAN-CHANGE         SALESRPT
00267  014100          ELSE                                                  SALESRPT
00268  014110              IF THERE-WAS-A-CUSTOMER-CHANGE                    SALESRPT
00269  014120                  MOVE CUSTOMER-NO-INPUT TO CUSTOMER-NO-REPORT  SALESRPT
00270  014130                  MOVE 'NO ' TO WAS-THERE-A-CUSTOMER-CHANGE.    SALESRPT
00271  014140      MOVE DESCRIPTION-INPUT TO DESCRIPTION-REPORT.             SALESRPT
00272  014150      MOVE SALES-INPUT TO SALES-REPORT.                         SALESRPT
00273  014160      ADD SALES-INPUT TO CUSTOMER-TOTAL-ACCUM                   SALESRPT
00274  014170                        SALESMAN-TOTAL-ACCUM                    SALESRPT
00275  014180                        BRANCH-TOTAL-ACCUM                      SALESRPT
00276  014190                        FINAL-TOTAL-ACCUM.                      SALESRPT
00277  014200      WRITE SALES-REPORT-LINE FROM DETAIL-LINE                  SALESRPT
00278  015010          AFTER PROPER-SPACING.                                 SALESRPT
00279  015020      ADD PROPER-SPACING TO LINES-PRINTED.                      SALESRPT
00280  015030      MOVE SPACE-ONE-LINE TO PROPER-SPACING.                    SALESRPT
00281  015040      MOVE SPACES TO DETAIL-LINE.                               SALESRPT
```

```
    7
00282  015060**************************************************************  SALESRPT
00283  015070*                                                            *  SALESRPT
00284  015080*  THIS MODULE IS ENTERED TO PROCESS A CHANGE IN CUSTOMER    *  SALESRPT
00285  015090*  NUMBER.  IT PRINTS THE CUSTOMER TOTAL AND RESETS THE      *  SALESRPT
00286  015100*  COMPARE AREA AND COUNTER.  IT IS ENTERED FROM THE         *  SALESRPT
00287  015110*  A000-CREATE-SALES-REPORT MODULE AND EXITS BACK TO IT.     *  SALESRPT
00288  015120*                                                            *  SALESRPT
00289  015130**************************************************************  SALESRPT
00290  015140                                                                SALESRPT
00291  015150  B010-PROCESS-CUSTOMER-CHANGE.                                 SALESRPT
00292  015160                                                                SALESRPT
00293  015170      MOVE CUSTOMER-TOTAL-ACCUM TO CUSTOMER-TOTAL-CUSTOT.       SALESRPT
00294  015180      WRITE SALES-REPORT-LINE FROM CUSTOMER-TOTAL-LINE          SALESRPT
00295  015190          AFTER ADVANCING 2 LINES.                              SALESRPT
00296  015200      MOVE ZEROS TO CUSTOMER-TOTAL-ACCUM                        SALESRPT
00297  016010      MOVE CUSTOMER-NO-INPUT TO PREVIOUS-CUSTOMER-NUMBER.       SALESRPT
00298  016020      ADD 2 TO LINES-PRINTED.                                   SALESRPT
00299  016030      MOVE SPACE-TWO-LINES TO PROPER-SPACING.                   SALESRPT
```

Figure 9-32 Source Listing [Part 4 of 5]

```
  8
00300   016050**************************************************************   SALESRPT
00301   016060*                                                          *   SALESRPT
00302   016070*   THIS MODULE IS ENTERED TO PROCESS A CHANGE IN SALESMAN *   SALESRPT
00303   016080*   NUMBER.  IT PRINTS THE SALESMAN TOTAL AND RESETS THE   *   SALESRPT
00304   016090*   COMPARE AREA AND COUNTER.  IT IS ENTERED FROM THE      *   SALESRPT
00305   016100*   A000-CREATE-SALES-REPORT MODULE AND EXITS TO IT.       *   SALESRPT
00306   016110*                                                          *   SALESRPT
00307   016120**************************************************************   SALESRPT
00308   016130                                                              SALESRPT
00309.  016140   B020-PROCESS-SALESMAN-CHANGE.                              SALESRPT
00310   016150                                                              SALESRPT
00311   016160       MOVE PREVIOUS-SALESMAN-NUMBER TO SALESMAN-NO-SMTOT.    SALESRPT
00312   016170       MOVE SALESMAN-TOTAL-ACCUM TO SALESMAN-TOTAL-SMTOT.     SALESRPT
00313   016180       WRITE SALES-REPORT-LINE FROM SALESMAN-TOTAL-LINE       SALESRPT
00314   016190           AFTER ADVANCING 2 LINES.                          SALESRPT
00315   016200       MOVE ZEROS TO SALESMAN-TOTAL-ACCUM.                    SALESRPT
00316   017010       MOVE SALESMAN-NO-INPUT TO PREVIOUS-SALESMAN-NUMBER.    SALESRPT
00317   017020       ADD 2 TO LINES-PRINTED.                                SALESRPT
00318   017030       MOVE SPACE-THREE-LINES TO PROPER-SPACING.             SALESRPT
```

```
  9
00319   017050**************************************************************   SALESRPT
00320   017060*                                                          *   SALESRPT
00321   017070*   THIS MODULE IS ENTERED TO PROCESS A CHANGE IN BRANCH NUMBER.*  SALESRPT
00322   017080*   IT PRINTS THE BRANCH TOTAL AND RESETS THE COMPARE AREA AND  *  SALESRPT
00323   017090*   COUNTER.  IT IS ENTERED FROM THE A000-CREATE-SALES-REPORT   *  SALESRPT
00324   017100*   MODULE AND EXITS BACK TO IT.                           *   SALESRPT
00325   017110*                                                          *   SALESRPT
00326   017120**************************************************************   SALESRPT
00327   017130                                                              SALESRPT
00328   017140   B030-PROCESS-BRANCH-CHANGE.                                SALESRPT
00329   017150                                                              SALESRPT
00330   017160       MOVE PREVIOUS-BRANCH-NUMBER TO BRANCH-NO-BRTOT.        SALESRPT
00331   017170       MOVE BRANCH-TOTAL-ACCUM TO BRANCH-TOTAL-BRTOT.         SALESRPT
00332   017180       WRITE SALES-REPORT-LINE FROM BRANCH-TOTAL-LINE         SALESRPT
00333   017190           AFTER ADVANCING 2 LINES.                          SALESRPT
00334   017200       MOVE ZEROS TO BRANCH-TOTAL-ACCUM.                      SALESRPT
00335   018010       MOVE BRANCH-NO-INPUT TO PREVIOUS-BRANCH-NUMBER.        SALESRPT
00336   018020       ADD 2 TO LINES-PRINTED.                                SALESRPT
00337   018030       MOVE SPACE-THREE-LINES TO PROPER-SPACING.             SALESRPT
```

```
  10
00338   018050**************************************************************   SALESRPT
00339   018060*                                                          *   SALESRPT
00340   018070*   THIS MODULE IS ENTERED TO PROCESS THE FINAL TOTAL.  THE  *   SALESRPT
00341   018080*   FINAL TOTAL IS MOVED TO THE OUTPUT AREA AND PRINTED.  THIS *  SALESRPT
00342   018090*   MODULE IS ENTERED FROM THE A000-CREATE-SALES-REPORT MODULE *  SALESRPT
00343   018100*   AND EXITS BACK TO IT.                                  *   SALESRPT
00344   018110*                                                          *   SALESRPT
00345   018120**************************************************************   SALESRPT
00346   018130                                                              SALESRPT
00347   018140   B040-PRINT-FINAL-TOTAL.                                    SALESRPT
00348   018150                                                              SALESRPT
00349   018160       MOVE FINAL-TOTAL-ACCUM TO FINAL-TOTAL-FINTOT.          SALESRPT
00350   018170       WRITE SALES-REPORT-LINE FROM FINAL-TOTAL-LINE          SALESRPT
00351   018180           AFTER ADVANCING 3 LINES.                          SALESRPT
```

```
  11
00352   019200**************************************************************   SALESRPT
00353   019010*                                                          *   SALESRPT
00354   019020*   THIS MODULE PRINTS THE HEADINGS ON THE REPORT.  IT IS  *   SALESRPT
00355   019030*   ENTERED FROM THE B000-PROCESS-DETAIL-RECORDS MODULE AND *   SALESRPT
00356   019040*   EXITS TO THE SAME MODULE.                              *   SALESRPT
00357   019050*                                                          *   SALESRPT
00358   019060**************************************************************   SALESRPT
00359   019070                                                              SALESRPT
00360   019080   C000-PRINT-HEADINGS.                                       SALESRPT
00361   019090                                                              SALESRPT
00362   019100       MOVE CURRENT-DATE TO DATE-HDG1.                        SALESRPT
00363   019110       MOVE PAGE-NUMBER TO PAGE-NUMBER-HDG1.                  SALESRPT
00364   019120       WRITE SALES-REPORT-LINE FROM FIRST-HEADING-LINE        SALESRPT
00365   019130           AFTER ADVANCING TO-TOP-OF-PAGE.                   SALESRPT
00366   019140       ADD 1 TO PAGE-NUMBER.                                  SALESRPT
00367   019150       WRITE SALES-REPORT-LINE FROM SECOND-HEADING-LINE       SALESRPT
00368   019160           AFTER ADVANCING 2 LINES.                          SALESRPT
00369   019170       WRITE SALES-REPORT-LINE FROM THIRD-HEADING-LINE        SALESRPT
00370   019180           AFTER ADVANCING 1 LINES.                          SALESRPT
00371   019190       MOVE SPACE-TWO-LINES TO PROPER-SPACING.               SALESRPT
00372   019200       MOVE ZERO TO LINES-PRINTED.                           SALESRPT
```

Figure 9-33 Source Listing [Part 5 of 5]

CHAPTER 9

REVIEW QUESTIONS

1. What is meant by the term GROUP INDICATION?

2. To perform group indication on a report, a programmer designed the program so that the Branch Number, Salesman Number, and Customer Number were moved to the detail output area in their respective ''Change Modules''. This would result in group indication. Why is this a poor program design?

3. What changes would have to be made in the sample program if a change in programming specifications were received that stated that the Customer Number was not to be group indicated on subsequent reports?

CHAPTER 9

DEBUGGING COBOL PROGRAMS

PROBLEM 1

INSTRUCTIONS

The following COBOL program contains an error or errors which occurred during execution. Circle each error and record the corrected entries directly on the listing. Explain the error and method of correction in the space provided below.

```
   1                          IBM DOS AMERICAN NATIONAL STANDARD COBOL         CBF CL3-4        07/21/77

   00001   001010 IDENTIFICATION DIVISION.                                   SALESRPT
   00002   001020                                                            SALESRPT
   00003   001030 PROGRAM-ID.    SALESRPT.                                   SALESRPT
   00004   001040 AUTHOR.        SHELLY AND CASHMAN.                         SALESRPT
   00005   001050 INSTALLATION.  ANAHEIM.                                    SALESRPT
   00006   001060 DATE-WRITTEN.  07/21/77.                                   SALESRPT
   00007   001070 DATE-COMPILED. 07/21/77                                    SALESRPT
   00008   001080 SECURITY.      UNCLASSIFIED.                               SALESRPT
   00009   001090                                                            SALESRPT
   00010   001100**************************************************************  SALESRPT
   00011   001110*                                                          *  SALESRPT
   00012   001120*   THIS PROGRAM PREPARES A SALES REPORT. THE REPORT CONTAINS * SALESRPT
   00013   001130*   SALES INFORMATION FOR EACH BRANCH, SALESMAN, AND CUSTOMER.* SALESRPT
   00014   001140*   TOTALS ARE TAKEN FOR A CHANGE IN CUSTOMER, A CHANGE IN   * SALESRPT
   00015   001150*   SALESMAN, AND A CHANGE IN BRANCH. FINAL TOTALS ARE ALSO  * SALESRPT
   00015   001160*   PRINTED.                                                *  SALESRPT
   00017   001170*                                                          *  SALESRPT
   00018   001180**************************************************************  SALESRPT
   00019   001190                                                            SALESRPT
   00020   001200                                                            SALESRPT
   00021   002010                                                            SALESRPT
   00022   002020 ENVIRONMENT DIVISION.                                      SALESRPT
   00023   002030                                                            SALESRPT
   00024   002040 CONFIGURATION SECTION.                                     SALESRPT
   00025   002050                                                            SALESRPT
   00026   002060 SOURCE-COMPUTER. IBM-370.                                  SALESRPT
   00027   002070 OBJECT-COMPUTER. IBM-370.                                  SALESRPT
   00028   002080 SPECIAL-NAMES.   C01 IS TO-TOP-OF-PAGE.                    SALESRPT
   00029   002090                                                            SALESRPT
   00030   002100 INPUT-OUTPUT SECTION.                                      SALESRPT
   00031   002110                                                            SALESRPT
   00032   002120 FILE-CONTROL.                                              SALESRPT
   00033   002130     SELECT SALES-INPUT-FILE                                SALESRPT
   00034   002140         ASSIGN TO SYS007-UR-2540R-S.                       SALESRPT
   00035   002150     SELECT SALES-REPORT-FILE                               SALESRPT
   00036   002160         ASSIGN TO SYS013-UR-1403-S.                        SALESRPT

   2

   00037   002180 DATA DIVISION.                                             SALESRPT
   00038   002190                                                            SALESRPT
   00039   002200 FILE SECTION.                                              SALESRPT
   00040   003010                                                            SALESRPT
   00041   003020 FD  SALES-INPUT-FILE                                       SALESRPT
   00042   003030     RECORD CONTAINS 80 CHARACTERS                          SALESRPT
   00043   003040     LABEL RECORDS ARE OMITTED                              SALESRPT
   00044   003050     DATA RECORD IS SALES-INPUT-RECORD.                     SALESRPT
   00045   003060 01  SALES-INPUT-RECORD.                                    SALESRPT
   00046   003070     05  BRANCH-NO-INPUT          PIC 999.                  SALESRPT
   00047   003080     05  SALESMAN-NO-INPUT        PIC 9999.                 SALESRPT
   00048   003090     05  CUSTOMER-NO-INPUT        PIC 9(5).                 SALESRPT
   00049   003100     05  DESCRIPTION-INPUT        PIC X(20).                SALESRPT
   00050   003110     05  SALES-INPUT              PIC 999V99.               SALESRPT
   00051   003120     05  FILLER                   PIC X(43).                SALESRPT
   00052   003130                                                            SALESRPT
   00053   003140 FD  SALES-REPORT-FILE                                      SALESRPT
   00054   003150     RECORD CONTAINS 133 CHARACTERS                         SALESRPT
   00055   003160     LABEL RECORDS ARE OMITTED                              SALESRPT
   00056   003170     DATA RECORD IS SALES-REPORT-LINE.                      SALESRPT
   00057   003180 01  SALES-REPORT-LINE            PIC X(133).               SALESRPT
   00058   003190                                                            SALESRPT
   00059   003200 WORKING-STORAGE SECTION.                                   SALESRPT
   00060   004010                                                            SALESRPT
   00061   004020 01  PROGRAM-INDICATORS.                                    SALESRPT
   00062   004030     05  ARE-THERE-MORE-RECORDS PIC XXX    VALUE 'YES'.     SALESRPT
   00063   004040         88  THERE-IS-A-RECORD             VALUE 'YES'.     SALESRPT
   00064   004050         88  THERE-ARE-NO-MORE-RECORDS     VALUE 'NO '.     SALESRPT
   00065   004060     05  WAS-THERE-A-BRANCH-CHANGE PIC XXX VALUE 'NO '.     SALESRPT
   00066   004070         88  THERE-WAS-A-BRANCH-CHANGE     VALUE 'YES'.     SALESRPT
   00067   004080     05  WAS-THERE-A-SALESMAN-CHANGE PIC XXX VALUE 'NO '.   SALESRPT
   00068   004090         88  THERE-WAS-A-SALESMAN-CHANGE   VALUE 'YES'.     SALESRPT
   00069   004100     05  WAS-THERE-A-CUSTOMER-CHANGE PIC XXX VALUE 'NO '.   SALESRPT
   00070   004110         88  THERE-WAS-A-CUSTOMER-CHANGE   VALUE 'YES'.     SALESRPT
   00071   004120                                                            SALESRPT
   00072   004130 01  PROGRAM-COMPARE-AREAS.                                 SALESRPT
   00073   004140     05  PREVIOUS-CUSTOMER-NUMBER PIC 9(5)  USAGE IS COMP-3. SALESRPT
   00074   004150     05  PREVIOUS-SALESMAN-NUMBER PIC 9(4)  USAGE IS COMP-3. SALESRPT
   00075   004160     05  PREVIOUS-BRANCH-NUMBER   PIC 9(3)  USAGE IS COMP-3. SALESRPT
   00076   004170                                                            SALESRPT
```

```
        3
00077  004180 01  TOTAL-ACCUMULATORS                        USAGE IS COMP-3.   SALESRPT
00078  004190    05  CUSTOMER-TOTAL-ACCUM   PIC S9(4)V99 VALUE ZERO.           SALESRPT
00079  004200    05  SALESMAN-TOTAL-ACCUM   PIC S9(5)V99 VALUE ZERO.           SALESRPT
00080  005010    05  BRANCH-TOTAL-ACCUM     PIC S9(5)V99 VALUE ZERO.           SALESRPT
00081  005020    05  FINAL-TOTAL-ACCUM      PIC S9(6)V99 VALUE ZERO.           SALESRPT
00082  005030                                                                  SALESRPT
00083  005040 01  PRINTER-CONTROL.                                             SALESRPT
00084  005050    05  PROPER-SPACING         PIC 9.                             SALESRPT
00085  005060    05  SPACE-ONE-LINE         PIC 9        VALUE 1.              SALESRPT
00086  005070    05  SPACE-TWO-LINES        PIC 9        VALUE 2.              SALESRPT
00087  005080    05  SPACE-THREE-LINES      PIC 9        VALUE 3.              SALESRPT
00088  005090    05  LINES-PRINTED          PIC S999     VALUE ZERO.           SALESRPT
00089  005100                                            USAGE COMP-3.         SALESRPT
00090  005110    05  PAGE-SIZE              PIC S999     VALUE +50             SALESRPT
00091  005120                                            USAGE COMP-3.         SALESRPT
00092  005130    05  PAGE-NUMBER            PIC S999     VALUE +1              SALESRPT
00093  005140                                            USAGE COMP-3.         SALESRPT
00094  005150        88  FIRST-PAGE                      VALUE +1.             SALESRPT
00095  005160                                                                  SALESRPT
00096  005170 01  DETAIL-LINE.                                                 SALESRPT
00097  005180    05  CARRIAGE-CONTROL       PIC X.                             SALESRPT
00098  005190    05  FILLER                 PIC X        VALUE SPACES.         SALESRPT
00099  005200    05  BRANCH-NO-REPORT       PIC ZZ9.                           SALESRPT
00100  006010    05  FILLER                 PIC X(10)    VALUE SPACES.         SALESRPT
00101  006020    05  SALESMAN-NO-REPORT     PIC ZZZ9.                          SALESRPT
00102  006030    05  FILLER                 PIC X(10)    VALUE SPACES.         SALESRPT
00103  006040    05  CUSTOMER-NO-REPORT     PIC ZZZZ9.                         SALESRPT
00104  006050    05  FILLER                 PIC X(10)    VALUE SPACES.         SALESRPT
00105  006060    05  DESCRIPTION-REPORT     PIC X(20).                         SALESRPT
00106  006070    05  FILLER                 PIC X(10)    VALUE SPACES.         SALESRPT
00107  006080    05  SALES-REPORT           PIC ZZZ.99.                        SALESRPT
00108  006090    05  FILLER                 PIC X(53)    VALUE SPACES.         SALESRPT
00109  006100 01  HEADING-LINES.                                               SALESRPT
00110  006110    05  FIRST-HEADING-LINE.                                       SALESRPT
00111  006120        10  CARRIAGE-CONTROL   PIC X.                             SALESRPT
00112  006130        10  DATE-HDG1          PIC X(8).                          SALESRPT
00113  006140        10  FILLER             PIC X(25)    VALUE SPACES.         SALESRPT
00114  006150        10  FILLER             PIC X(12)    VALUE                 SALESRPT
00115  006160                                            'SALES REPORT'.       SALESRPT
00116  006170        10  FILLER             PIC X(26)    VALUE SPACES.         SALESRPT
00117  006180        10  FILLER             PIC X(5)     VALUE 'PAGE '.        SALESRPT
00118  006190        10  PAGE-NUMBER-HDG1   PIC ZZ9.                           SALESRPT
00119  006200        10  FILLER             PIC X(53)    VALUE SPACES.         SALESRPT
00120  007010    05  SECOND-HEADING-LINE.                                      SALESRPT
00121  007020        10  CARRIAGE-CONTROL   PIC X.                             SALESRPT
00122  007030        10  FILLER             PIC X(6)     VALUE 'BRANCH'.       SALESRPT
00123  007040        10  FILLER             PIC X(6)     VALUE SPACES.         SALESRPT
00124  007050        10  FILLER             PIC X(8)     VALUE 'SALESMAN'.     SALESRPT
00125  007060        10  FILLER             PIC X(7)     VALUE SPACES.         SALESRPT
00126  007070        10  FILLER             PIC X(8)     VALUE 'CUSTOMER'.     SALESRPT
00127  007080        10  FILLER             PIC X(14)    VALUE SPACES.         SALESRPT
00128  007090        10  FILLER             PIC X(7)     VALUE 'PRODUCT'.      SALESRPT
00129  007100        10  FILLER             PIC X(18)    VALUE SPACES.         SALESRPT
00130  007110        10  FILLER             PIC X(5)     VALUE 'SALES'.        SALESRPT
00131  007120        10  FILLER             PIC X(53)    VALUE SPACES.         SALESRPT
00132  007130    05  THIRD-HEADING-LINE.                                       SALESRPT
00133  007140        10  CARRIAGE-CONTROL   PIC X.                             SALESRPT
00134  007150        10  FILLER             PIC XX       VALUE SPACES.         SALESRPT
00135  007160        10  FILLER             PIC XX       VALUE 'NO'.           SALESRPT
00136  007170        10  FILLER             PIC X(11)    VALUE SPACES.         SALESRPT
00137  007180        10  FILLER             PIC XX       VALUE 'NO'.           SALESRPT
00138  007190        10  FILLER             PIC X(13)    VALUE SPACES.         SALESRPT
00139  007200        10  FILLER             PIC XX       VALUE 'NO'.           SALESRPT
00140  008010        10  FILLER             PIC X(15)    VALUE SPACES.         SALESRPT
00141  008020        10  FILLER             PIC X(11)    VALUE 'DESCRIPTION'.  SALESRPT
00142  008030        10  FILLER             PIC X(15)    VALUE SPACES.         SALESRPT
00143  008040        10  FILLER             PIC X(6)     VALUE 'AMOUNT'.       SALESRPT
00144  008050        10  FILLER             PIC X(53)    VALUE SPACES.         SALESRPT
00145  008060                                                                  SALESRPT
00146  008070 01  TOTAL-LINES.                                                 SALESRPT
00147  008080    05  CUSTOMER-TOTAL-LINE.                                      SALESRPT
00148  008090        10  CARRIAGE-CONTROL   PIC X.                             SALESRPT
00149  008100        10  FILLER             PIC X(71)    VALUE SPACES.         SALESRPT
00150  008110        10  CUSTOMER-TOTAL-CUSTOT PIC Z,ZZZ.99.                   SALESRPT
00151  008120        10  FILLER             PIC X        VALUE '*'.            SALESRPT
00152  008130        10  FILLER             PIC X(52)    VALUE SPACES.         SALESRPT
00153  008140    05  SALESMAN-TOTAL-LINE.                                      SALESRPT
00154  008150        10  CARRIAGE-CONTROL   PIC X.                             SALESRPT
00155  008160        10  FILLER             PIC X(47)    VALUE SPACES.         SALESRPT
00156  008170        10  FILLER             PIC X(6)     VALUE 'TOTAL '.       SALESRPT
00157  008180        10  FILLER             PIC X(12)    VALUE                 SALESRPT
00158  008190                                            'SALESMAN NO '.       SALESRPT
00159  008200        10  SALESMAN-NO-SMTOT  PIC ZZZ9.                          SALESRPT
00160  009010        10  FILLER             PIC X        VALUE SPACE.          SALESRPT
00161  009020        10  SALESMAN-TOTAL-SMTOT PIC ZZ,ZZZ.99.                   SALESRPT
00162  009030        10  FILLER             PIC XX       VALUE '**'.           SALESRPT
00163  009040        10  FILLER             PIC X(51)    VALUE SPACES.         SALESRPT
00164  009050    05  BRANCH-TOTAL-LINE.                                        SALESRPT
00165  009060        10  CARRIAGE-CONTROL   PIC X.                             SALESRPT
00166  009070        10  FILLER             PIC X(50)    VALUE SPACES.         SALESRPT
00167  009080        10  FILLER             PIC X(16)    VALUE                 SALESRPT
00168  009090                                            'TOTAL BRANCH NO '.   SALESRPT
00169  009100        10  BRANCH-NO-BRTOT    PIC ZZ9.                           SALESRPT
00170  009110        10  FILLER             PIC X        VALUE SPACE.          SALESRPT
00171  009120        10  BRANCH-TOTAL-BRTOT PIC ZZ,ZZZ.99.                     SALESRPT
00172  009130        10  FILLER             PIC XXX      VALUE '***'.          SALESRPT
00173  009140        10  FILLER             PIC X(50)    VALUE SPACES.         SALESRPT
00174  009150    05  FINAL-TOTAL-LINE.                                         SALESRPT
00175  009160        10  CARRIAGE-CONTROL   PIC X.                             SALESRPT
00176  009170        10  FILLER             PIC X(56)    VALUE SPACES.         SALESRPT
00177  009180        10  FILLER             PIC X(12)    VALUE                 SALESRPT
00178  009190                                            'FINAL TOTAL '.       SALESRPT
00179  009200        10  FINAL-TOTAL-FINTOT PIC $$$$,$$$.99.                   SALESRPT
00180  010010        10  FILLER             PIC X(4)     VALUE '****'.         SALESRPT
00181  010020        10  FILLER             PIC X(49)    VALUE SPACES.         SALESRPT
```

```
     4
00182   010040 PROCEDURE DIVISION.                                            SALESRPT
00183   010050                                                               SALESRPT
00184   010060*********************************************************************   SALESRPT
00185   010070*                                                          *   SALESRPT
00186   010080*   THIS MODULE INITIALIZES THE FILES AND THEN DETERMINES WHEN  *   SALESRPT
00187   010090*   CONTROL BREAKS HAVE OCCURRED AND CAUSES THE APPROPRIATE     *   SALESRPT
00188   010100*   PROCESSING TO OCCUR. IT ALSO CAUSES THE DETAIL LINES TO     *   SALESRPT
00189   010110*   BE PRINTED. IT IS ENTERED FROM THE OPERATING SYSTEM AND     *   SALESRPT
00190   010120*   EXITS TO THE OPERATING SYSTEM.                             *   SALESRPT
00191   010130*                                                          *   SALESRPT
00192   010140*********************************************************************   SALESRPT
00193   010150                                                               SALESRPT
00194   010160 A000-CREATE-SALES-REPORT.                                      SALESRPT
00195   010170                                                               SALESRPT
00196   010180     OPEN INPUT  SALES-INPUT-FILE                               SALESRPT
00197   010190          OUTPUT SALES-REPORT-FILE.                             SALESRPT
00198   010200     READ SALES-INPUT-FILE                                      SALESRPT
00199   011010         AT END                                                SALESRPT
00200   011020             MOVE 'NO ' TO ARE-THERE-MORE-RECORDS.              SALESRPT
00201   011030     IF THERE-IS-A-RECORD                                       SALESRPT
00202   011040         MOVE CUSTOMER-NO-INPUT TO PREVIOUS-CUSTOMER-NUMBER     SALESRPT
00203   011050         MOVE SALESMAN-NO-INPUT TO PREVIOUS-SALESMAN-NUMBER     SALESRPT
00204   011060         MOVE BRANCH-NO-INPUT TO PREVIOUS-BRANCH-NUMBER         SALESRPT
00205   011070         PERFORM A001-PROCESS-AND-READ                          SALESRPT
00206   011080             UNTIL THERE-ARE-NO-MORE-RECORDS                    SALESRPT
00207   011090         PERFORM B010-PROCESS-CUSTOMER-CHANGE                   SALESRPT
00208   011100         PERFORM B020-PROCESS-SALESMAN-CHANGE                   SALESRPT
00209   011110         PERFORM B030-PROCESS-BRANCH-CHANGE                     SALESRPT
00210   011120         PERFORM B040-PRINT-FINAL-TOTAL.                        SALESRPT
00211   011130     CLOSE SALES-INPUT-FILE                                     SALESRPT
00212   011140           SALES-REPORT-FILE.                                   SALESRPT
00213   011150     STOP RUN.                                                  SALESRPT
00214   011160                                                               SALESRPT
00215   011170                                                               SALESRPT
00216   011180                                                               SALESRPT
00217   011190 A001-PROCESS-AND-READ.                                         SALESRPT
00218   011200                                                               SALESRPT
00219   012010     IF BRANCH-NO-INPUT NOT = PREVIOUS-BRANCH-NUMBER            SALESRPT
00220   012020         PERFORM B010-PROCESS-CUSTOMER-CHANGE                   SALESRPT
00221   012030         PERFORM B020-PROCESS-SALESMAN-CHANGE                   SALESRPT
00222   012040         PERFORM B030-PROCESS-BRANCH-CHANGE                     SALESRPT
00223   012050         MOVE 'YES' TO WAS-THERE-A-BRANCH-CHANGE                SALESRPT
00224   012060     ELSE                                                       SALESRPT
00225   012070         IF SALESMAN-NO-INPUT NOT = PREVIOUS-SALESMAN-NUMBER    SALESRPT
00226   012080             PERFORM B010-PROCESS-CUSTOMER-CHANGE               SALESRPT
00227   012090             PERFORM B020-PROCESS-SALESMAN-CHANGE               SALESRPT
00228   012110         ELSE                                                   SALESRPT
00229   012120             IF CUSTOMER-NO-INPUT NOT = PREVIOUS-CUSTOMER-NUMBER SALESRPT
00230   012130                 PERFORM B010-PROCESS-CUSTOMER-CHANGE           SALESRPT
00231   012140                 MOVE 'YES' TO WAS-THERE-A-CUSTOMER-CHANGE.     SALESRPT
00232   012150     PERFORM B000-PROCESS-DETAIL-RECORDS.                       SALESRPT
00233   012160     READ SALES-INPUT-FILE                                      SALESRPT
00234   012170         AT END                                                SALESRPT
00235   012180             MOVE 'NO ' TO ARE-THERE-MORE-RECORDS.              SALESRPT
```

```
     5
00236   012200*********************************************************************   SALESRPT
00237   013010*                                                          *   SALESRPT
00238   013020*   THIS MODULE IS ENTERED TO PRINT THE DETAIL LINE FOR THE   *   SALESRPT
00239   013030*   REPORT.  IF NECESSARY, IT CAUSES THE HEADINGS TO BE PRINTED *   SALESRPT
00240   013040*   AND THEN FORMATS AND PRINTS THE DETAIL LINE. TOTALS ARE ALSO* SALESRPT
00241   013050*   ACCUMULATED.  THIS MODULE IS ENTERED FROM THE            *   SALESRPT
00242   013060*   A000-CREATE-SALES-REPORT MODULE AND EXITS BACK TO IT.     *   SALESRPT
00243   013070*                                                          *   SALESRPT
00244   013080*********************************************************************   SALESRPT
00245   013090                                                               SALESRPT
00246   013100 B000-PROCESS-DETAIL-RECORDS.                                   SALESRPT
00247   013110                                                               SALESRPT
00248   013120     IF LINES-PRINTED IS EQUAL TO PAGE-SIZE OR                  SALESRPT
00249   013130         IS GREATER THAN PAGE-SIZE OR                           SALESRPT
00250   013140         FIRST-PAGE                                             SALESRPT
00251   013150         PERFORM C000-PRINT-HEADINGS                            SALESRPT
00252   013160         MOVE PREVIOUS-BRANCH-NUMBER TO BRANCH-NO-REPORT        SALESRPT
00253   013170         MOVE PREVIOUS-SALESMAN-NUMBER TO SALESMAN-NO-REPORT    SALESRPT
00254   013180         MOVE PREVIOUS-CUSTOMER-NUMBER TO CUSTOMER-NO-REPORT.   SALESRPT
00255   013190     IF THERE-WAS-A-BRANCH-CHANGE                               SALESRPT
00256   013200         MOVE BRANCH-NO-INPUT TO BRANCH-NO-REPORT               SALESRPT
00257   014010         MOVE SALESMAN-NO-INPUT TO SALESMAN-NO-REPORT           SALESRPT
00258   014020         MOVE CUSTOMER-NO-INPUT TO CUSTOMER-NO-REPORT           SALESRPT
00259   014030         MOVE 'NO ' TO WAS-THERE-A-BRANCH-CHANGE                SALESRPT
00260   014040     ELSE                                                       SALESRPT
00261   014050         IF THERE-WAS-A-SALESMAN-CHANGE                         SALESRPT
00262   014060             MOVE SALESMAN-NO-INPUT TO SALESMAN-NO-REPORT       SALESRPT
00263   014070             MOVE CUSTOMER-NO-INPUT TO CUSTOMER-NO-REPORT       SALESRPT
00264   014080             MOVE 'NO ' TO WAS-THERE-A-SALESMAN-CHANGE          SALESRPT
00265   014090         ELSE                                                   SALESRPT
00266   014100             IF THERE-WAS-A-CUSTOMER-CHANGE                     SALESRPT
00267   014110                 MOVE CUSTOMER-NO-INPUT TO CUSTOMER-NO-REPORT   SALESRPT
00268   014120                 MOVE 'NO ' TO WAS-THERE-A-CUSTOMER-CHANGE.     SALESRPT
00269   014130     MOVE DESCRIPTION-INPUT TO DESCRIPTION-REPORT.              SALESRPT
00270   014140     MOVE SALES-INPUT TO SALES-REPORT.                          SALESRPT
00271   014150     ADD SALES-INPUT TO CUSTOMER-TOTAL-ACCUM                    SALESRPT
00272   014160                        SALESMAN-TOTAL-ACCUM                    SALESRPT
00273   014170                        BRANCH-TOTAL-ACCUM                      SALESRPT
00274   014180                        FINAL-TOTAL-ACCUM.                      SALESRPT
00275   014190     WRITE SALES-REPORT-LINE FROM DETAIL-LINE                   SALESRPT
00276   014200         AFTER PROPER-SPACING.                                  SALESRPT
00277   015010     ADD PROPER-SPACING TO LINES-PRINTED.                       SALESRPT
00278   015020     MOVE SPACE-ONE-LINE TO PROPER-SPACING.                     SALESRPT
00279   015030     MOVE SPACES TO DETAIL-LINE.                                SALESRPT
```

```
   6
00280   015040*****************************************************************  SALESRPT
00281   015050*                                                              *  SALESRPT
00282   015060*   THIS MODULE IS ENTERED TO PROCESS A CHANGE IN CUSTOMER     *  SALESRPT
00283   015070*   NUMBER.  IT PRINTS THE CUSTOMER TOTAL AND RESETS THE       *  SALESRPT
00284   015080*   COMPARE AREA AND COUNTER.  IT IS ENTERED FROM THE          *  SALESRPT
00285   015090*   A000-CREATE-SALES-REPORT MODULE AND EXITS BACK TO IT.      *  SALESRPT
00286   015100*                                                              *  SALESRPT
00287   015110*****************************************************************  SALESRPT
00288   015120                                                                  SALESRPT
00289   015130 B010-PROCESS-CUSTOMER-CHANGE.                                    SALESRPT
00290   015140                                                                  SALESRPT
00291   015150     MOVE CUSTOMER-TOTAL-ACCUM TO CUSTOMER-TOTAL-CUSTOT.          SALESRPT
00292   015160     WRITE SALES-REPORT-LINE FROM CUSTOMER-TOTAL-LINE             SALESRPT
00293   015170        AFTER ADVANCING 2 LINES.                                  SALESRPT
00294   015180     MOVE ZEROS TO CUSTOMER-TOTAL-ACCUM                           SALESRPT
00295   015190     MOVE CUSTOMER-NO-INPUT TO PREVIOUS-CUSTOMER-NUMBER.          SALESRPT
00296   015200     ADD 2 TO LINES-PRINTED.                                      SALESRPT
00297   016010     MOVE SPACE-TWO-LINES TO PROPER-SPACING.                      SALESRPT
```

```
   7
00298   016030*****************************************************************  SALESRPT
00299   016040*                                                              *  SALESRPT
00300   016050*   THIS MODULE IS ENTERED TO PROCESS A CHANGE IN SALESMAN     *  SALESRPT
00301   016060*   NUMBER.  IT PRINTS THE SALESMAN TOTAL AND RESETS THE       *  SALESRPT
00302   016070*   COMPARE AREA AND COUNTER.  IT IS ENTERED FROM THE          *  SALESRPT
00303   016080*   A000-CREATE-SALES-REPORT MODULE AND EXITS TO IT.           *  SALESRPT
00304   016090*                                                              *  SALESRPT
00305   016100*****************************************************************  SALESRPT
00306   016110                                                                  SALESRPT
00307   016120 B020-PROCESS-SALESMAN-CHANGE.                                    SALESRPT
00308   016130                                                                  SALESRPT
00309   016140     MOVE PREVIOUS-SALESMAN-NUMBER TO SALESMAN-NO-SMTOT.          SALESRPT
00310   016150     MOVE SALESMAN-TOTAL-ACCUM TO SALESMAN-TOTAL-SMTOT.           SALESRPT
00311   016160     WRITE SALES-REPORT-LINE FROM SALESMAN-TOTAL-LINE             SALESRPT
00312   016170        AFTER ADVANCING 2 LINES.                                  SALESRPT
00313   016180     MOVE ZEROS TO SALESMAN-TOTAL-ACCUM.                          SALESRPT
00314   016190     MOVE SALESMAN-NO-INPUT TO PREVIOUS-SALESMAN-NUMBER.          SALESRPT
00315   016200     ADD 2 TO LINES-PRINTED.                                      SALESRPT
00316   017010     MOVE SPACE-THREE-LINES TO PROPER-SPACING.                    SALESRPT
```

```
   8
00317   017030*****************************************************************  SALESRPT
00318   017040*                                                              *  SALESRPT
00319   017050*   THIS MODULE IS ENTERED TO PROCESS A CHANGE IN BRANCH NUMBER.*  SALESRPT
00320   017060*   IT PRINTS THE BRANCH TOTAL AND RESETS THE COMPARE AREA AND *  SALESRPT
00321   017070*   COUNTER.  IT IS ENTERED FROM THE A000-CREATE-SALES-REPORT  *  SALESRPT
00322   017080*   MODULE AND EXITS BACK TO IT.                               *  SALESRPT
00323   017090*                                                              *  SALESRPT
00324   017100*****************************************************************  SALESRPT
00325   017110                                                                  SALESRPT
00326   017120 B030-PROCESS-BRANCH-CHANGE.                                      SALESRPT
00327   017130                                                                  SALESRPT
00328   017140     MOVE PREVIOUS-BRANCH-NUMBER TO BRANCH-NO-BRTOT.              SALESRPT
00329   017150     MOVE BRANCH-TOTAL-ACCUM TO BRANCH-TOTAL-BRTOT.               SALESRPT
00330   017160     WRITE SALES-REPORT-LINE FROM BRANCH-TOTAL-LINE               SALESRPT
00331   017170        AFTER ADVANCING 2 LINES.                                  SALESRPT
00332   017180     MOVE ZEROS TO BRANCH-TOTAL-ACCUM.                            SALESRPT
00333   017190     MOVE BRANCH-NO-INPUT TO PREVIOUS-BRANCH-NUMBER.              SALESRPT
00334   017200     ADD 2 TO LINES-PRINTED.                                      SALESRPT
00335   018010     MOVE SPACE-THREE-LINES TO PROPER-SPACING.                    SALESRPT
```

```
   9
00336   018030*****************************************************************  SALESRPT
00337   018040*                                                              *  SALESRPT
00338   018050*   THIS MODULE IS ENTERED TO PROCESS THE FINAL TOTAL.  THE    *  SALESRPT
00339   018060*   FINAL TOTAL IS MOVED TO THE OUTPUT AREA AND PRINTED.  THIS *  SALESRPT
00340   018070*   MODULE IS ENTERED FROM THE A000-CREATE-SALES-REPORT MODULE *  SALESRPT
00341   018080*   AND EXITS BACK TO IT.                                      *  SALESRPT
00342   018090*                                                              *  SALESRPT
00343   018100*****************************************************************  SALESRPT
00344   018110                                                                  SALESRPT
00345   018120 B040-PRINT-FINAL-TOTAL.                                          SALESRPT
00346   018130                                                                  SALESRPT
00347   018140     MOVE FINAL-TOTAL-ACCUM TO FINAL-TOTAL-FINTOT.                SALESRPT
00348   018150     WRITE SALES-REPORT-LINE FROM FINAL-TOTAL-LINE                SALESRPT
00349   018160        AFTER ADVANCING 3 LINES.                                  SALESRPT
```

```
    10
00350   018190*******************************************************   SALESRPT
00351   018200*                                                     *   SALESRPT
00352   019010*  THIS MODULE PRINTS THE HEADINGS ON THE REPORT.  IT IS   *   SALESRPT
00353   019020*  ENTERED FROM THE 8000-PROCESS-DETAIL-RECORDS MODULE AND  *   SALESRPT
00354   019030*  EXITS TO THE SAME MODULE.                           *   SALESRPT
00355   019040*                                                     *   SALESRPT
00356   019050*******************************************************   SALESRPT
00357   019060                                                         SALESRPT
00358   019070 C000-PRINT-HEADINGS.                                    SALESRPT
00359   019080                                                         SALESRPT
00360   019090     MOVE CURRENT-DATE TO DATE-HDG1.                     SALESRPT
00361   019100     MOVE PAGE-NUMBER TO PAGE-NUMBER-HDG1.               SALESRPT
00362   019110     WRITE SALES-REPORT-LINE FROM FIRST-HEADING-LINE     SALESRPT
00363   019120         AFTER ADVANCING TO-TOP-OF-PAGE.                 SALESRPT
00364   019130     ADD 1 TO PAGE-NUMBER.                               SALESRPT
00365   019140     WRITE SALES-REPORT-LINE FROM SECOND-HEADING-LINE    SALESRPT
00366   019150         AFTER ADVANCING 2 LINES.                        SALESRPT
00367   019160     WRITE SALES-REPORT-LINE FROM THIRD-HEADING-LINE     SALESRPT
00368   019170         AFTER ADVANCING 1 LINES.                        SALESRPT
00369   019180     MOVE SPACE-TWO-LINES TO PROPER-SPACING.             SALESRPT
00370   019190     MOVE ZERO TO LINES-PRINTED.                         SALESRPT
```

```
07/21/77                    SALES REPORT                    PAGE   1

BRANCH      SALESMAN      CUSTOMER      PRODUCT              SALES
NO          NO            NO            DESCRIPTION          AMOUNT

100         1225          32911         AUDIO INTERFACE      500.00
                                        KEYBOARD             100.00
                                        POWER SUPPLY          50.00

                                                             650.00*

                          40015         CRT INTERFACE         75.00
                                        FLOPPY CONTROLLER    125.00
                                        POWER TRANSFORMER     50.00

                                                             250.00*

                                        TOTAL SALESMAN NO 1225   900.00**


                                        4K RAM               330.00
                                        ROM MEMORY            30.00

                                                             360.00*

                                        TOTAL SALESMAN NO 4199   360.00**

                                        TOTAL BRANCH NO 100   1,260.00***

200         1321          10954         PRINTER MECHANISM    220.00
                                        THERMAL PRINTER       80.00
                                        DIGITAL CLOCK        625.00
                                        CHARACTER GENERATOR  550.00

                                                           1,475.00*

                                        TOTAL SALESMAN NO 1321  1,475.00**


                                        DISPLAY LEDS         155.00
                                        VIDEO BOARD          195.00

                                                             350.00*

                                        TOTAL SALESMAN NO 9832   350.00**

                                        TOTAL BRANCH NO 200   1,825.00***
```

EXPLANATION

_____

_____

_____

_____

CHAPTER 9

PROGRAMMING ASSIGNMENT 1

INSTRUCTIONS

A Sales Commission report is to be prepared. Write the COBOL program to prepare the required report. An IPO Chart and Pseudocode Specifications should be used when designing the program. Use Test Data Set 1 in Appendix A.

INPUT

The input is to consist of Sales Commission Cards that contain the Date, the Store Number, the Department Number, the Salesman Number, the Salesman Name, and the Sales Commission. The cards must be sorted in ascending sequence by Department Number, within Store Number, within Date prior to processing the records.

OUTPUT

The output is to consist of a Sales Commission report. Only the Date is to be group indicated. When there is a change in Department Number, the total commissions paid within the department is to be printed. When there is a change in Store Number, the total commissions paid within the Department and the Store are to be printed. When there is a change in Date, the total commissions for the Department, Store, and Date are to be printed. After all records have been processed, a final total is to be printed. The printer spacing chart is illustrated on page 9.47.

PRINTER SPACING CHART

```
         1111111111222222222233333333334444444444555555555566666666667777777777888888888
123456789012345678901234567890123456789012345678901234567890123456789012345678901234567890123456789
```

Line						
4	XX/XX/XX			SALES COMMISSION REPORT		PAGE XØX
6	DATE	STORE	DEPT.	SALESMAN	NAME	COMMISSION
8	XX/XX/XX	ØX	ØX	XØX	XXXXXXXXXXXXXXXXXXXXX	X,XXØ.XX
9		ØX	ØX	XØX	XXXXXXXXXXXXXXXXXXXX	X,XXØ.XX
11					DEPARTMENT ØX TOTAL	XX,XXØ.XX
14		ØX	ØX	XØX	XXXXXXXXXXXXXXXXXXXX	X,XXØ.XX
16					DEPARTMENT ØX TOTAL	XX,XXØ.XX
18					STORE ØX TOTAL	XX,XXØ.XX
21		ØX	ØX	XØX	XXXXXXXXXXXXXXXXXXXX	X,XXØ.XX
23					DEPARTMENT ØX TOTAL	XX,XXØ.XX
25					STORE ØX TOTAL	XX,XXØ.XX
27					TOTAL SALES XX/XX/XX	XX,XXØ.XX
29					FINAL TOTAL $XXX,XX#.XX	

CHAPTER 9

PROGRAMMING ASSIGNMENT 2

INSTRUCTIONS

A Sales Analysis Report is to be prepared. Write the COBOL program to prepare the required report. An IPO Chart and Pseudocode Specifications should be used when designing the program. Use Test Data Set 2 in Appendix A.

INPUT

Input consists of Sales Cards that contain a District Number, a Branch Number, Salesman Number, a Store Name, and a Sales Amount. The cards must be sorted by Salesman Number, within Branch Number, within District Number prior to processing the records. The format of the cards is illustrated below.

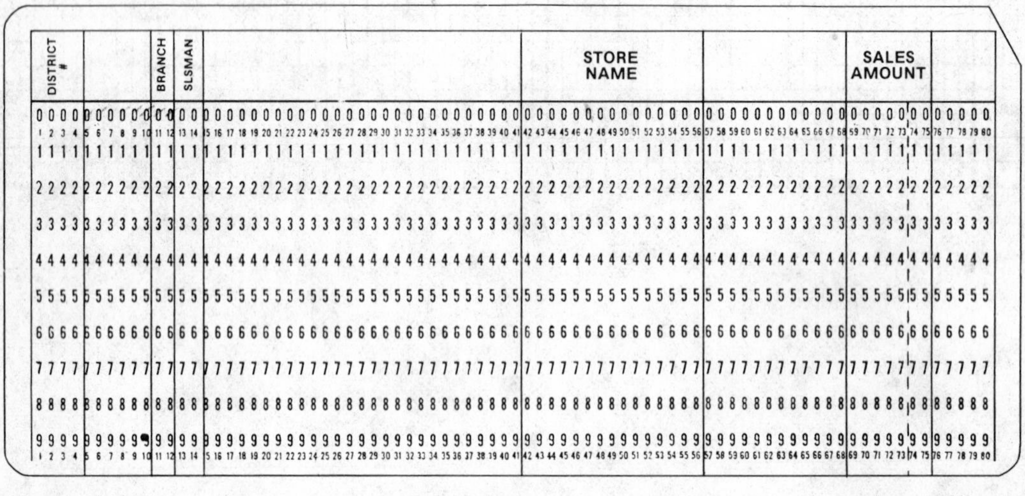

OUTPUT

The output is to consist of a Sales Analysis Report. The printer spacing chart is illustrated on page 9.49.

PRINTER SPACING CHART

```
         1111111111222222222233333333334444444444555555555566666666667777777777888888888899999999990000000001111111111
 1234567890123456789012345678901234567890123456789012345678901234567890123456789012345678901234567890123456789012345678 9
4      XX/XX/XX                                    SALES  REPORT                                    PAGE XØX
6     DISTRICT  BRANCH    SALESMAN           STORE              SALES AMOUNT
8      XXØX        ØX         ØX             XXXXXXXXXXXXXXX          XX,XXØ.XX
9                                           XXXXXXXXXXXXXX           XX,XXØ.XX  BELOW QUOTA BY $X,XXØ.XX
11                                       SALESMAN ØX TOTAL XXX,XXØ.XX
14                        ØX             XXXXXXXXXXXXXXX          XX,XXØ.XX
15                                       XXXXXXXXXXXXXXX          XX,XXØ.XX
17                                    SALESMAN ØX TOTAL XXX,XXØ.XX
19                                     BRANCH ØX TOTAL XXX,XXØ.XX
22           ØX           ØX             XXXXXXXXXXXXXXX          XX,XXØ.XX
24                                    SALESMAN ØX TOTAL XXX,XXØ.XX
26                                     BRANCH ØX TOTAL XXX,XXØ.XX
28                                   DISTRICT XXØX TOTAL X,XXX,XXØ.XX
30 TOTAL STORES BELOW QUOTA XØX                                FINAL TOTAL $X,XXX,XXØ.XX
```

When there is a change in Salesman Number, the total sales for the salesman is to be printed. When there is a change in Branch Number, the total sales for the salesman is to be printed and the total sales for the branch is to be printed. When there is a change in District, the total sales for the salesman, the total sales for the branch, and the total sales for the district are to be printed.

Salesmen have a Sales Quota of $5,000.00 for EACH store. For salesmen with sales less than $5,000.00 for a given store, the message "BELOW QUOTA" together with the amount below quota should be printed on the report.

After all cards have been processed, a final total of sales and a count of the number of stores below quota is to be printed.

Note that the District Number, the Branch Number, and the Salesman Number are to be group indicated.

CHAPTER 9

PROGRAMMING ASSIGNMENT 3

INSTRUCTIONS

An Intelligence Quotient Test Results report is to be prepared. Write the COBOL program to produce the required report. An IPO Chart and Pseudocode Specifications should be used when designing the program. Use Test Data Set 1 in Appendix A.

INPUT

Input consists of Student IQ Cards that contain a School Number, a Teacher Number, a Student Name, and the Student's IQ. The cards should be sorted by Teacher Number within School Number prior to processing the records.

OUTPUT

Output is to consist of an Intelligence Quotient Test Results report. A printer spacing chart is illustrated on page 9.51.

PRINTER SPACING CHART

```
XX/XX/XX        INTELLIGENCE QUOTIENT TEST RESULTS                PAGE XØX

    SCHOOL    TEACHER        NAME              I.Q.

      XØX        ØX     XXXXXXXXXXXXXXXXXXXXX   XØX
                        XXXXXXXXXXXXXXXXXXXXX   XØX
                        XXXXXXXXXXXXXXXXXXXXX   XØ   **IQ NOT IN VALID RANGE**
                        XXXXXXXXXXXXXXXXXXXX    XØX

                               AVERAGE I.Q.     XØX


                 ØX     XXXXXXXXXXXXXXXXXXXXX    XØX
                        XXXXXXXXXXXXXXXXXXXX     XØX

                               AVERAGE I.Q.     XØX

                        SCHOOL XØX - AVERAGE I.Q.  XØX

      TOTAL NUMBER OF STUDENTS XØX - AVERAGE I.Q.  XØX
```

There is one input record for each student. One or more students will be found for each teacher, and one or more teachers will be found for each school. A control break is to be taken whenever there is a change in teacher, and whenever there is a change in school. When there is a change in teacher, the IQs for all students associated with that teacher are to be divided by the number of students in the group to determine the average IQ of the students associated with a particular teacher. When there is a change in school, the processing occurring when there is a change in teacher must take place; and then the IQ's of all of the students in that school are to be divided by the number of students in that school to determine the average IQ of the students in the school.

The School Number and Teacher Number are to be group indicated on the report.

After all records have been processed the average IQ of all students in the district (all schools) is to be calculated and printed.

If the IQ recorded on the input record is greater than 150 or less than 60, the message **IQ NOT IN VALID RANGE** is to be printed on the report and these IQs are not to be included when computing the average IQ.

CHAPTER 9

PROGRAMMING ASSIGNMENT 4

INSTRUCTIONS

A Quality Control Report is to be prepared. Write the COBOL program to prepare the required report. An IPO Chart and Pseudocode Specifications should be used when designing the program. Use Test Data Set 2 in Appendix A.

INPUT

The input consists of Quality Control Cards containing the Date, the Plant Number, the Part Number, the Quantity Manufactured, the Lot Number, and the Quantity Rejected. There will be one or more cards for each lot number. The format of the input cards is illustrated below.

OUTPUT

The output of the program is the Quality Control Report. The report contains the Date, the Plant Number, the Part Number, the Lot Number, the Quantity Manufactured, the Quantity Rejected, the Usable Quantity (Quantity Manufactured - Quantity Rejected), and the Percent Usable (Quantity Usable divided by Quantity Manufactured). The format of the report is illustrated on page 9.53.

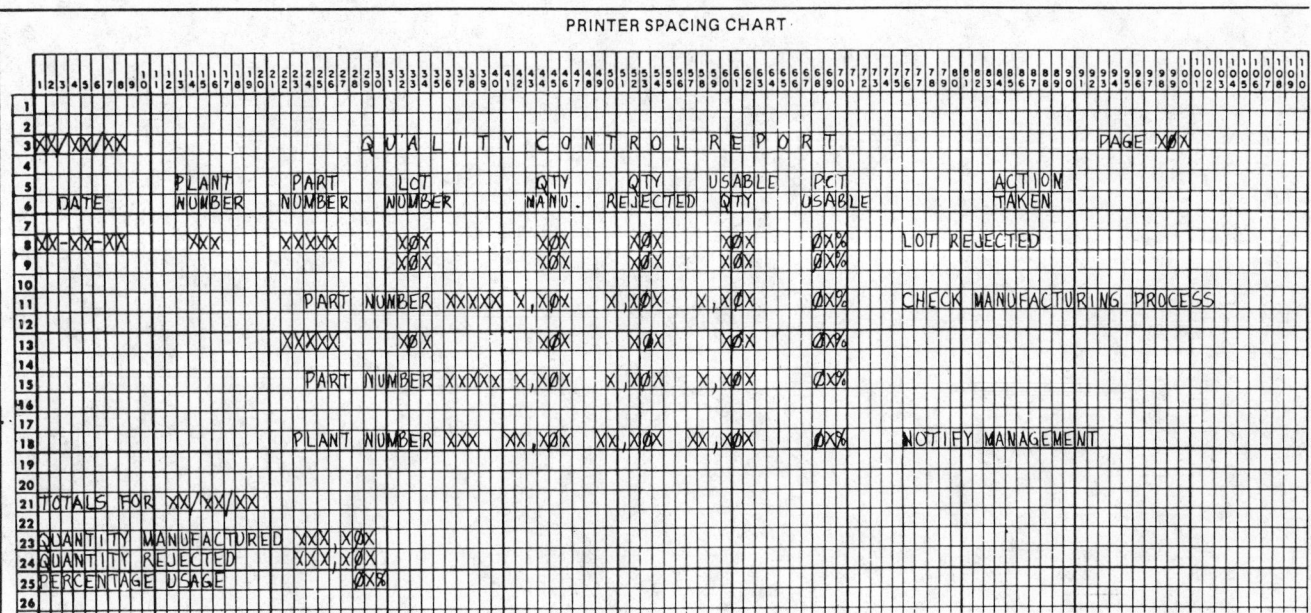

The report is group printed on Lot Number; that is, more than one input record may be read for a given Lot Number, but only one line is printed for each Lot Number. The Quantity Manufactured is the total quantity for one lot number. The Quantity Rejected which is printed is the total quantity rejected for one Lot Number. For each lot, if the Percentage Usable is less than 80%, the message LOT REJECTED should be printed in the Action Taken portion of the report.

When there is a change in Part Number, the totals for Quantity Manufactured, Quantity Rejected, and Usable Quantity should be printed. In addition, the Percent Usable should be calculated for the Part Number. If the percent usable for the Part Number is less than 90%, the message CHECK MANUFACTURING PROCESS should be printed in the Action Taken portion of the report.

When there is a change in Plant Number, the totals for the plant should be printed. The Percent Usable for the plant should be calculated. If the Percent Usable for the plant is less than 95%, the message NOTIFY MANAGEMENT should be printed in the Action Taken portion of the report.

When the Date changes, the totals for the date should be printed as illustrated on the printer spacing chart. The next date should begin on a new page; that is, whenever the Date changes, the date totals are printed and then a new page should be begun for the next date.

The Date, Plant Number, and Part Number should be group indicated.

TABLE PROCESSING

10

10

INTRODUCTION

There are a number of methods in the COBOL language that provide the ability to process data stored in the form of large lists in which adjacent data fields contain similar characteristics. An example of such a list is an input record that is designed to contain an historical record of the sales of a product for the months of January, February, March, April, May, June, July, August, September, October, November, and December; that is, the sales for an entire year. One approach to processing such data would be to define a separate field for each of the months of the year, give each field an individual name, and reference each name as required in the Procedure Division.

COBOL, however, provides a facility within the language to define the list of fields by a single name and to reference each individual field through the use of the single name and a value called a SUBSCRIPT. A subscript is merely a number which indicates which of the fields within the list is to be referenced. This number can be specified either as a literal or as the data-name of a field containing the number. For example, if the sales for the months throughout the year were defined in this manner, the entry SALES-INPUT (1) could reference the sales for January; the entry SALES-INPUT (2) could reference the sales for February, etc.

Another technique commonly used in computer programming for defining data is the use of TABLES. A table is merely a series of related data items that are stored in consecutive locations in computer storage. The data stored in the tables may be extracted from the table for use in the program. For example, one of the tables illustrated in the sample program in this chapter contains the names of the months of the year. When processing the detail records, the proper name of the month is extracted from the table, based upon the number of the month of the year. For example, the number 01 would extract the name JANUARY from the table, the number 02 would extract the name FEBRUARY from the table, etc.

In order to illustrate the processing of lists of repeated data items and the use of tables, a sample program is illustrated in this chapter which prepares a Sales Analysis Report from a group of Sales Input Cards. The format of the input data and a sample of the report are illustrated in Figure 10-1.

---

1 Kernighan, B.W., and Plauger, P.J., *THE ELEMENTS OF PROGRAMMING STYLE*, McGraw-Hill Book Company, 1974

INPUT

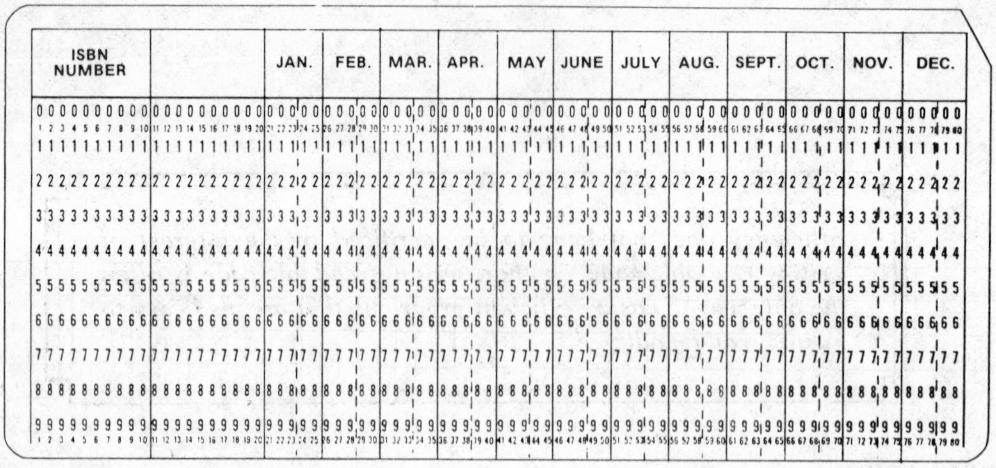

OUTPUT

```
07/21/77                              SALES ANALYSIS REPORT                                                  PAGE   1
    ISBN                                          LOWEST MONTHLY SALES    HIGHEST MONTHLY SALES        YEARLY       AVERAGE
   NUMBER            BOOK TITLE                     MONTH       SALES        MONTH       SALES          SALES         SALES

0 88236 111 2   STRUCTURED COBOL                  JANUARY      100.00     DECEMBER      900.00      $6,000.00      $500.00
0 88236 043 4   SYSTEMS ANALYSIS AND DESIGN       DECEMBER     100.00     JANUARY       900.00      $6,200.00      $516.67
0 88236 226 7   COMPUTER PROGRAMMING RPG II       SEPTEMBER    120.00     JANUARY       985.00      $5,850.00      $487.50
0 88236 103 1   ANSI COBOL                        FEBRUARY     239.50     AUGUST        899.00      $5,138.50      $428.21
0 78236 103 1   UNKNOWN                           MARCH        300.00     OCTOBER       818.25      $6,418.25      $534.85
0 88236 151 1   BASIC FORTRAN IV                  OCTOBER      195.10     JULY          900.00      $6,095.10      $507.93

FINAL TOTALS

TOTAL SALES  $35,701.85
AVERAGE SALES    $495.86
```

Figure 10-1 Sales Input Card and Sales Report

It can be seen from the input record above that the format of the input card consists of an ISBN Number (book number) and the Sales Amounts for the months of January through December. These amounts represent the monthly sales of a given book for each of the 12 months of the year.

Note that printed on each line of the output report is the ISBN Number, the Book Title, the name of the month with the lowest sales amount for the year, the lowest sales amount for the year, the name of the month with the highest sales amount for the year, the highest sales amount for the year, the yearly sales, and the average sales. The Book Title is extracted from a table in the program. The Yearly Sales is obtained by adding the sales for each of the months from January through December. The Average Sales is obtained by adding the sales for each of the months from January through December, and dividing by 12.

After all the cards have been processed, a final total of the Yearly Sales is to be printed; and the average monthly sales of all books is to be calculated and printed. The Average Sales printed when there is a final total represents the monthly average sales of all books sold and is obtained by accumulating the total sales and dividing by the total number of months accumulated. For example, if there were 10 input records, the Total Sales would be divided by 120 (12 months on each record times 10 records) to obtain the average sales.

DEFINING LISTS OF RELATED ITEMS

The format of the input record for the sample program is illustrated in Figure 10-1. Note that each of the sales amount fields on the card for the months of January through December contains five digits. As previously mentioned, one method of defining these fields in COBOL is to assign individual data names to each of the fields. The COBOL coding below illustrates this technique.

EXAMPLE

```
004040  01  SALES-INPUT-RECORD.
004050      05  ISBN-NUMBER-INPUT        PIC X(10).
004060      05  FILLER                   PIC X(10).
004070      05  JANUARY-INPUT            PIC 999V99.
004080      05  FEBRUARY-INPUT           PIC 999V99.
004090      05  MARCH-INPUT              PIC 999V99.
004100      05  APRIL-INPUT              PIC 999V99.
004110      05  MAY-INPUT                PIC 999V99.
004120      05  JUNE-INPUT               PIC 999V99.
004130      05  JULY-INPUT               PIC 999V99.
004140      05  AUGUST-INPUT             PIC 999V99.
004150      05  SEPTEMBER-INPUT          PIC 999V99.
004160      05  OCTOBER-INPUT            PIC 999V99.
004170      05  NOVEMBER-INPUT           PIC 999V99.
004180      05  DECEMBER-INPUT           PIC 999V99.
```

Figure 10-2 Example of Definition of Input Record

As can be seen from the example above, each of the twelve fields is given an individual name. Although this technique will work, the referencing of each individual name in the Procedure Division is a cumbersome method of processing these fields, particularly, for example, if all of the values in the fields were to be added together in order to determine the yearly sales.

OCCURS CLAUSE

In order to overcome this difficulty, the OCCURS Clause can be used to define a list of related items, all of which have the same format. An example of the Occurs Clause is illustrated in Figure 10-3.

EXAMPLE

0 0 3 0 8 0	0 1	SALES-INPUT-RECORD.			
0 0 3 0 9 0		0 5	ISBN-NUMBER-INPUT	PIC X(10).	
0 0 3 1 0 0		0 5	FILLER	PIC X(10).	
0 0 3 1 1 0		0 5	SALES-INPUT	PIC 999V99	OCCURS 12 TIMES.

```
OCCURS  integer-2 TIMES
```

Figure 10-3 Example of OCCURS Clause

The Occurs Clause specifies the number of times a field is repeated. In the example above, it can be seen that the field SALES-INPUT, with a Picture 999V99, occurs 12 times. Thus, the twelve Sales fields as illustrated in Figure 10-2 are defined with one entry in the definition of the input record, instead of the twelve entries which are required in the Figure 10-2. As can be seen, the Occurs Clause can be used to define the repeated occurrences of adjacent fields with the same attributes, that is, the same size with the same number of digits to the right of the decimal place.

When a series of fields is defined using the Occurs Clause, the individual fields are called Elements of the list. The following diagram illustrates this concept.

EXAMPLE

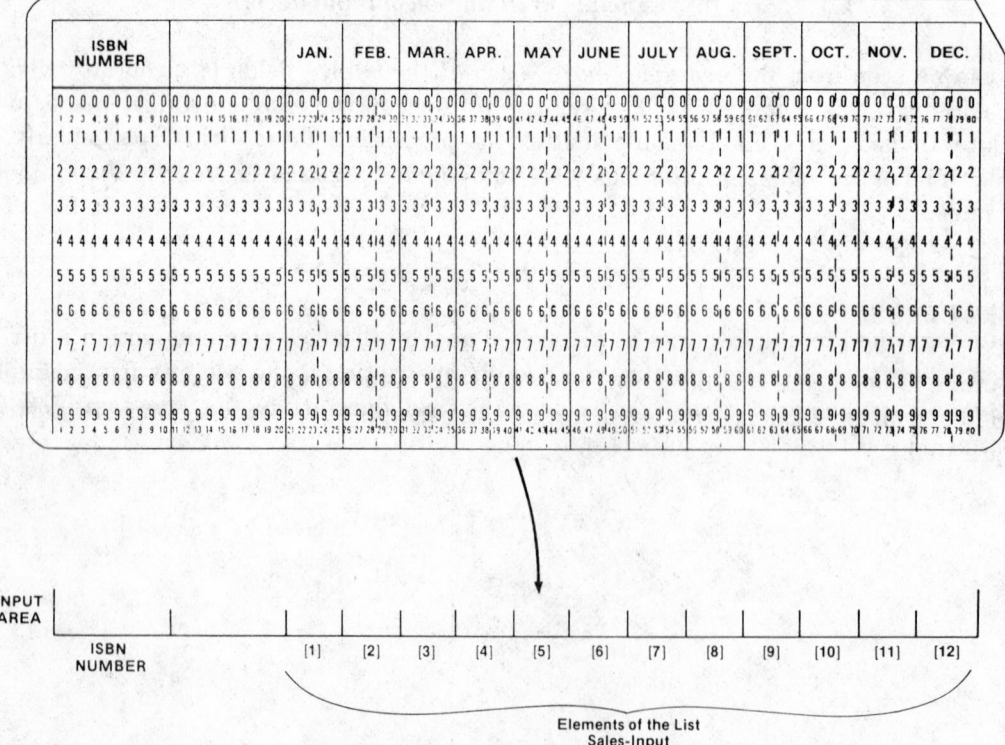

Figure 10-4 Elements of a List

Note in the example in Figure 10-4 that when an input record is read into an input area with the record defined as illustrated in Figure 10-3, each of the fields defined by the Occurs Clause is considered to be an individual element within the list, or series of fields.

Each element within the list can be referenced only by means of the name given to the list and a subscript that identifies which element within the list is to be referenced. For example, to reference the first element within the list (the sales for January), the following COBOL statement could be used.

EXAMPLE

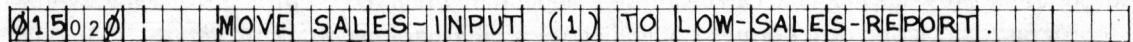

Figure 10-5 Example of Use of Subscript

In the example above, a subscript of 1 is used to specify that the first element of the list SALES-INPUT is to be moved to the LOW-SALES-REPORT field. Note that the subscript must be contained within parentheses, and that there is a space before the left parenthesis and a space after the right parenthesis. There are no spaces within the parentheses. Thus, as a result of the statement in Figure 10-5, the sales for January, which are stored in the SALES-INPUT list, would be moved to the report area.

In order to move the sales for April (the fourth month) to the output area, the Move Statement below could be used.

EXAMPLE

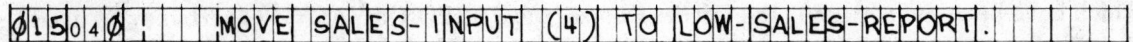

Figure 10-6 Example of Use of Subscript

In the example in Figure 10-6, the value 4 is used as the subscript for the SALES-INPUT list; therefore, the fourth element within the list would be extracted and moved to the LOW-SALES-REPORT field. Since the fourth element of the list contains the sales for April, the April sales would be moved to the report field.

Although the literal subscripts as illustrated above will allow elements within a list to be referenced properly, a more practical method of subscripting is the use of a data-name being specified within the parentheses. The value in the field identified by the data-name acts as the subscript. This is illustrated in the example in Figure 10-7.

EXAMPLE

| Ø | 1 | 7 | 0 | 6 | Ø | | | | | | MOVE | SALES-INPUT | (LOW-SUBSCRIPT) | TO | LOW-SALES-REPORT. | | | |

Figure 10-7 Example of Data-Name Used as a Subscript

In the example in Figure 10-7, the element to be moved depends upon the value found in the field LOW-SUBSCRIPT. If the value is equal to 1, then the first element of the list SALES-INPUT will be moved; if the value in the LOW-SUBSCRIPT field is equal to 2, then the second element will be moved; if the value is equal to 12, then the twelfth element will be moved. Since the value in a field can be altered, depending upon the required processing within the program, subscripts are normally specified as a data-name such as in Figure 10-7; this allows any element within the table to be referenced, depending upon the value which is placed in the field referenced by the data-name.

Because subscripts are used to refer to the position of the elements within the list, the use of zero as a subscript is not permitted; and, the highest permissible subscript value in any given case is the maximum number of elements in the list as specified in the Occurs Clause.

PERFORM VARYING

In the sample program, the sales for each month of the year are contained in the input record and are defined in the Data Division using the Occurs Clause (see Figure 10-3). One of the requirements of the sample program is that these sales be added together in order to obtain the Yearly Sales which is to be printed on the report (see Figure 10-1). To add a series of fields which have been defined using the Occurs Clause, the PERFORM VARYING verb may be used. The Perform Varying Statement used to add the monthly sales in the sample program is illustrated in Figure 10-8.

EXAMPLE

```
Ø1 6 0 4 Ø          PERFORM B001-CALCULATE-TOTAL-SALES
Ø1 6 0 5 Ø              VARYING SALES-SUBSCRIPT FROM 1 BY 1
Ø1 6 0 6 Ø              UNTIL SALES-SUBSCRIPT IS GREATER THAN 12.
```

```
Ø1 6 1 2 Ø   B001-CALCULATE-TOTAL-SALES.
Ø1 6 1 3 Ø
Ø1 6 1 4 Ø       ADD SALES-INPUT (SALES-SUBSCRIPT) TO
Ø1 6 1 5 Ø           YEARLY-SALES-WORK.
```

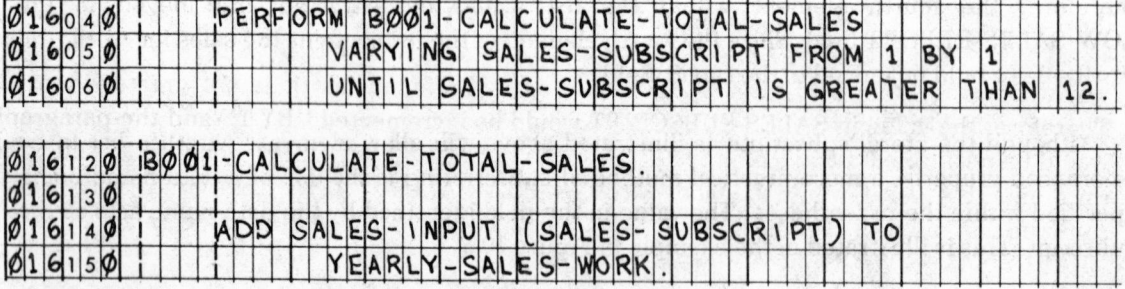

Figure 10-8 Example of Perform Varying Statement

Procedure-name-1 in the Perform Varying Statement specifies the name of the paragraph to be performed. The Varying Clause is used to vary the value in a field FROM a given value BY a given value. Thus, in the example in Figure 10-8, the value in the field SALES-SUBSCRIPT will be varied from the value 1 by the value 1. This means that the first time the B001-CALCULATE-TOTAL-SALES paragraph is performed, the value in SALES-SUBSCRIPT will be 1. The second time the B001-CALCULATE-TOTAL-SALES paragraph is performed by this Perform Statement, the value in SALES-SUBSCRIPT will be 2, since the value has been varied "by 1". The third time the paragraph is performed by this Perform Statement, the value in SALES-SUBSCRIPT will be 3. Thus it can be seen that the Varying Clause is used to establish an initial value in a field ("FROM 1"), and to specify the value which is to be added to the field each time the paragraph is performed ("BY 1"). It should be noted that the "BY" value may be negative as well as positive, so that the effect would be to subtract a value from the field rather than adding a value to the field.

As noted, this varying the value in a field will be done each time the paragraph is performed. When this format of the Perform Statement is used, there must be a condition specified which will indicate when this "looping" effect of the Perform Statement will be terminated. This condition is indicated through the Until Clause. In the example, the loop will be executed until the value in the SALES-SUBSCRIPT field is greater than 12. When that condition occurs, the performing of the B001-CALCULATE-TOTAL-SALES paragraph will be terminated.

The effect of the Perform Statement and the Add Statement in Figure 10-8 is to add all of the monthly sales in the SALES-INPUT list and store the sum in the YEARLY-SALES-WORK field. This occurs in the following manner: The first time the paragraph is performed, the value in the field SALES-SUBSCRIPT will be one because of the Varying Clause. Therefore, the value in the first element of the list SALES-INPUT will be added to the YEARLY-SALES-WORK field. This value is the sales for the first month. After the paragraph is performed one time, the condition specified will be tested and it would be found that the value in SALES-SUBSCRIPT is not greater than 12. Therefore, the value in SALES-SUBSCRIPT would be incremented "BY 1" and the paragraph be performed again. The second time, the value in SALES-SUBSCRIPT is 2; therefore, the second element in the SALES-INPUT list would be added to YEARLY-SALES-WORK. After the paragraph is performed, the value in SALES-SUBSCRIPT would again be compared to 12 and it would again be found that it is not greater than 12. Therefore, the value in SALES-SUBSCRIPT would be incremented "BY 1" and the paragraph would be performed a third time, with the value in SALES-SUBSCRIPT equal to 3. Thus, the third month's sales would be added to YEARLY-SALES-WORK. This processing would continue until all twelve of the monthly sales values in the SALES-INPUT list were added to the YEARLY-SALES-WORK field.

The Perform Varying Statement is commonly used in problems involving lists and tables.

TABLES

In many business applications, it is desirable to organize some types of data in the form of a TABLE, store the table in main storage, and retrieve those portions of the table which are needed in the solution of the problem. A table is merely a series of similar types of data which are stored in consecutive locations within main storage. The example below illustrates the use of a table in which an input record containing a month number is used to extract the name of the related month from a table.

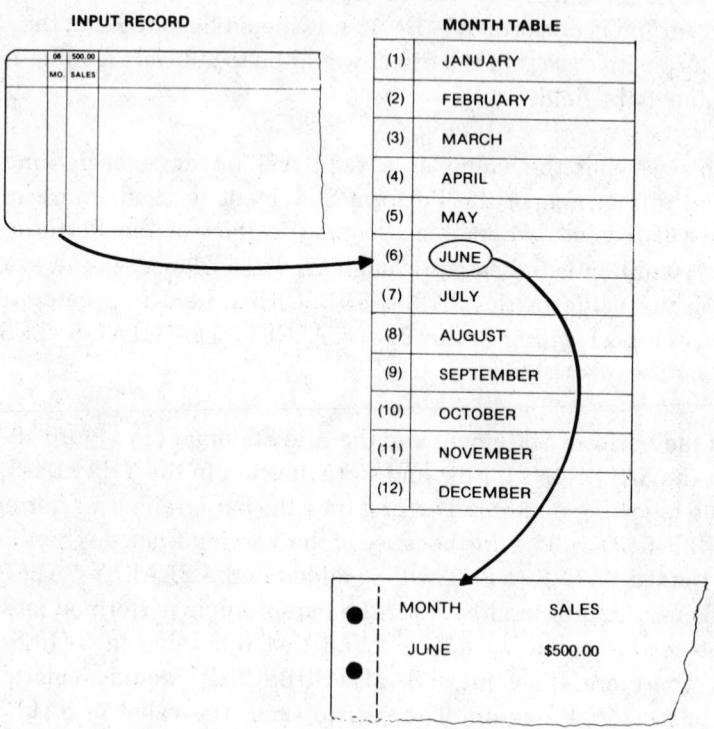

Figure 10-9 Example of Table Lookup

Note in the example above that the input record contains the value 06 in the Month field. This value indicates which month is to be processed (June). In order to print the month on the report, this number is used to extract the sixth name from the Month Table. As can be seen, the values 01 through 12 in the input record could be used to extract the corresponding month name from the Month Table. This technique is commonly called Table Lookup.

The example in Figure 10-10 illustrates the COBOL coding required to define a "Name of the Months" Table in Working-Storage from which the name of the month can be extracted, based upon the month numbers 01 through 12.

EXAMPLE

```
005010  01  PROGRAM-TABLES.
005020      05  MONTHS-TABLE.
005030          10  MONTH-CONSTANTS.
005040              15  FILLER      PIC X(9)      VALUE 'JANUARY   '.
005050              15  FILLER      PIC X(9)      VALUE 'FEBRUARY  '.
005060              15  FILLER      PIC X(9)      VALUE 'MARCH     '.
005070              15  FILLER      PIC X(9)      VALUE 'APRIL     '.
005080              15  FILLER      PIC X(9)      VALUE 'MAY       '.
005090              15  FILLER      PIC X(9)      VALUE 'JUNE      '.
005100              15  FILLER      PIC X(9)      VALUE 'JULY      '.
005110              15  FILLER      PIC X(9)      VALUE 'AUGUST    '.
005120              15  FILLER      PIC X(9)      VALUE 'SEPTEMBER'.
005130              15  FILLER      PIC X(9)      VALUE 'OCTOBER   '.
005140              15  FILLER      PIC X(9)      VALUE 'NOVEMBER  '.
005150              15  FILLER      PIC X(9)      VALUE 'DECEMBER  '.
005160          10  MONTH-TABLE REDEFINES MONTH-CONSTANTS
005170                          PIC X(9)      OCCURS 12 TIMES.
```

Figure 10-10 Example of Coding to Define Table

In the example above, the level 01 entry, PROGRAM-TABLES, is used to document the fact that the lower level entries following it comprise the tables which are to be used in the program. The level 05 entry, MONTHS-TABLE, documents the fact that the table following it is the table for the month names.

A table which is given its values in the source program, such as this table, normally consists of two separate entities when being defined in the Data Division. The first entity is the constant values which are to comprise the table. This entity must be specified as a group item, and in the example above, the group name given to the constant values which will be stored in the table is MONTH-CONSTANTS. Within this group are the level 15 entries which define the constant values which are to be in the table. In the example, these constant values are the names of the months. Note that each of the names of the months are defined by the Filler data-name.

It should be noted that the names of the months cannot be referenced in the group item MONTH-CONSTANTS because each of the names are defined as Filler. Therefore, in order to reference each of the names of the months, a REDEFINES Clause must be used together with an Occurs Clause. This is the second entity required when defining a table.

A Redefines Clause is used to give a single area of computer storage a different name or different attributes or both. In the example in Figure 10-10, it can be seen that the statement MONTH-TABLE REDEFINES MONTH-CONSTANTS is specified on line 005160. This statement states that the area in storage with the name MONTH-CONSTANTS is to be given another name, MONTH-TABLE. This concept is illustrated in the following diagram.

EXAMPLE

MONTH-CONSTANTS Group	MONTH-TABLE Redefinition
JANUARY	MONTH-TABLE (1)
FEBRUARY	MONTH-TABLE (2)
MARCH	MONTH-TABLE (3)
APRIL	MONTH-TABLE (4)
MAY	MONTH-TABLE (5)
JUNE	MONTH-TABLE (6)
JULY	MONTH-TABLE (7)
AUGUST	MONTH-TABLE (8)
SEPTEMBER	MONTH-TABLE (9)
OCTOBER	MONTH-TABLE (10)
NOVEMBER	MONTH-TABLE (11)
DECEMBER	MONTH-TABLE (12)

Figure 10-11 Example of Redefines Statement

Note in the diagram above that the MONTH-CONSTANTS group consists of twelve areas, each of which is nine characters in length and each of which contains the name of a month. The MONTH-TABLE redefinition, on the other hand, gives a different name to the area of computer storage. Note from Figure 10-10 that MONTH-TABLE consists of 12 occurrences (OCCURS 12 TIMES) of a field with the PICTURE X(9). Thus, through the use of the REDEFINES Clause, the values in the table are able to be referenced by the name MONTH-TABLE and a subscript in the same manner as was illustrated for the SALES-INPUT list. This is illustrated in Figure 10-12.

EXAMPLE

```
019090      MOVE MONTH-TABLE (LOW-SUBSCRIPT) TO LOW-MONTH-REPORT.
```

Figure 10-12 Example of Extracting an Element from a Table

Note in the example above that the data-name MONTH-TABLE, together with a subscript (LOW-SUBSCRIPT), is used in the Move Statement to reference a given month name within the table. If the subscript contains the value ''1'', the name JANUARY would be extracted from the table and moved to LOW-MONTH-REPORT. If the subscript contains the value ''2'', the name FEBRUARY would be extracted from the table and moved to LOW-MONTH-REPORT, etc.

Thus, it can be seen that constant data can be stored in a table within computer storage and then each element within the table can extracted for use within the program.

TABLE SEARCH

In the previous example, there is a direct relationship between the value in the subscript and the element which is extracted from the table. For example, the first entry in the table is JANUARY and it is referenced by the subscript 01; the second entry in the table is FEBRUARY and it is referenced by the subscript 02, etc.

In many applications there may not be a direct relationship between the numbers used to reference the elements within a table and the actual entries within the table. When this type of problem occurs, a procedure called TABLE SEARCH is commonly used.

The diagram below illustrates the concept of a table search.

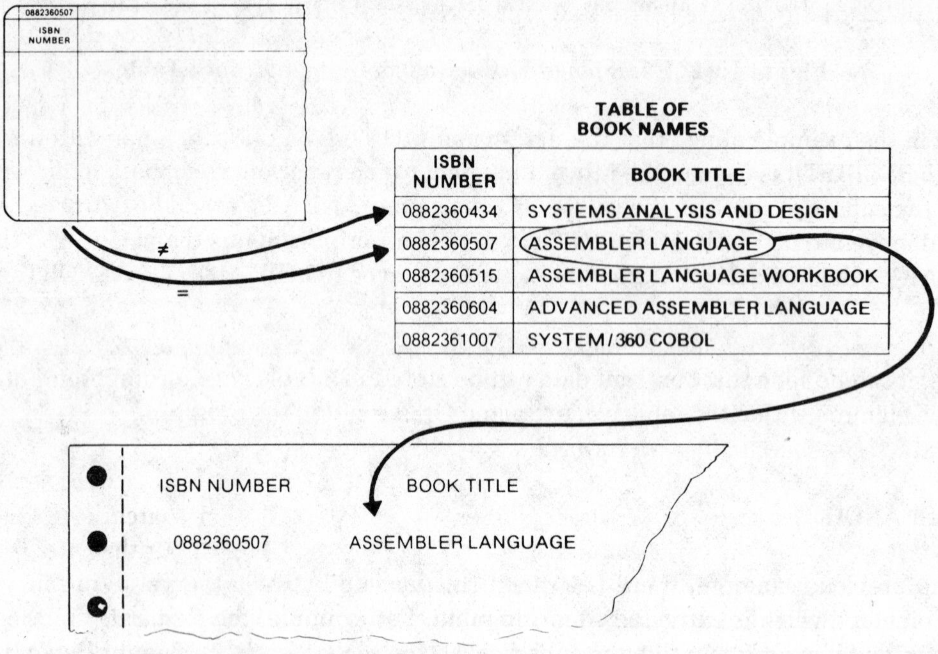

Figure 10-13 Example of a Table Search

In this example above, the table consists of a series of entries within the table that contain an ISBN Number (book number) and a related book title. The input record contains only the ISBN Number and the position of the ISBN Number in the table, and that the ISBN Numbers in title of the book must be extracted from the table. Note that there is no relationship between the ISBN Number and the position of the ISBN Number in the table, and that the ISBN Number in the table are not consecutive; therefore, a table search must be used.

One method of performing a table search involves the comparing of the number in the input record to the first number in the table to determine if they are equal. If the numbers are equal, the appropriate Book Title would be extracted from the table. If the numbers are not equal, the next entry in the table would be examined to determine if this number is equal to the number in the input record. If this number is not equal, the next entry in the table would be examined, etc.. This process would continue until an equal condition was found or until all entries in the table had been examined. If all entries had been examined and the entry in the input record was not equal to any of the entries in the table, an error message would normally be printed.

Note in the example in Figure 10-13, that the ISBN Number on the card is 0882360507. The first step in the table search procedure is to compare the entry in the input record to the first entry in the table. In the example, the first entry in the table is not equal to the ISBN Number 0882360507 found in the input record; therefore, the next entry in the table is examined. Note that the second entry in the table is ISBN Number 0882360507. As this number is equal to the ISBN Number in the input record, the related book title is extracted from the table and moved to the output area for printing on the report. Thus, the "table search" procedure is completed, and the remainder of the processing within the program would occur.

BINARY SEARCH

In the previous example, the comparison of the number in the input record began with the first entry in the table, followed by a comparison with the second entry in the table, etc., until an equal condition was found or all of the entries in the table had been compared. Thus, a "sequential table search" was performed.

Another technique called a BINARY SEARCH is often used when searching a table. In a binary search, the entry in the middle of the table is examined first, rather than the first entry as with the sequential search. If the entry in the middle of the table is lower than the value in the input record that is being searched for, then it is known that the information to be retrieved from the table must reside in the upper half of the table. By the same token, if the entry in the middle of the table is higher than the value in the input record, then it is known that the information to be retrieved from the table must reside in the lower half of the table.

The middle entry in the proper half of the table is then examined to determine if it is greater than, less than, or equal to the value in the input record. Depending upon the result of the comparison, the table is again split in half and the middle entry of the remaining "half" is examined. This process of reducing the size of the table in half each time a comparison is made continues until the desired entry in the table is located.

When searching large tables, the binary search technique can substantially reduce the search time as compared to the sequential search technique. It is important to note, however, that when the binary search technique is used, the value in the table which is compared must be arranged in either an ascending or descending sequence, while with the sequential search technique, the values do not have to be in a particular sequence.

DEFINING A TABLE - TABLE SEARCH

In the sample program, a Book Title is to be printed on a report, but the input record contains only the ISBN Number. Therefore, a table containing the ISBN Number and the Book Title must be established and a table search performed to extract the proper Book Title from the table. The COBOL coding to establish the table is illustrated in Figure 10-14.

EXAMPLE

```
006140      05  BOOK-TABLE.
006150          10  BOOK-CONSTANTS.
006160              15  FILLER          PIC X(40)    VALUE
006170                  '0882360434SYSTEMS ANALYSIS AND DESIGN            '.
006180              15  FILLER          PIC X(40)    VALUE
006190                  '0882360507ASSEMBLER LANGUAGE                     '.
006200              15  FILLER          PIC X(40)    VALUE
007010                  '0882360515ASSEMBLER LANGUAGE WORKBOOK            '.
007020              15  FILLER          PIC X(40)    VALUE
007030                  '0882360604ADVANCED ASSEMBLER LANGUAGE            '.
007040              15  FILLER          PIC X(40)    VALUE
007050                  '0882361007SYSTEM 360 COBOL                       '.
007060              15  FILLER          PIC X(40)    VALUE
007070                  '0882361015SYSTEM 360 COBOL PROBLEM TEXT          '.
007080              15  FILLER          PIC X(40)    VALUE
007090                  '0882361031ANSI COBOL                            '.
007100              15  FILLER          PIC X(40)    VALUE
007110                  '088236104XANSI COBOL WORKBOOK                    '.
007120              15  FILLER          PIC X(40)    VALUE
007130                  '0882361058ADVANCED ANSI COBOL                    '.
007140              15  FILLER          PIC X(40)    VALUE
007150                  '0882361104ADVANCED SYSTEM/360 COBOL              '.
007160              15  FILLER          PIC X(40)    VALUE
007170                  '0882361112STRUCTURED COBOL                       '.
007180              15  FILLER          PIC X(40)    VALUE
007190                  '0882361511BASIC FORTRAN IV                       '.
007200              15  FILLER          PIC X(40)    VALUE
008010                  '0882361775 COMPUTERS IN OUR SOCIETY             '.
008020              15  FILLER          PIC X(40)    VALUE
008030                  '0882361783COMPUTERS IN OUR SOC. WORKBOOK'
008040              15  FILLER          PIC X(40)    VALUE
008050                  '0882361791PROGRAMMING IN BASIC                   '.
008060              15  FILLER          PIC X(40)    VALUE
008070                  '0882361805BASIC WITH APPLICATIONS                '.
008080              15  FILLER          PIC X(40)    VALUE
008090                  '0882361902SYSTEM/360 PL/I                        '.
008100              15  FILLER          PIC X(40)    VALUE
008110                  '0882362259INTRODUCTION TO RPG                    '.
008120              15  FILLER          PIC X(40)    VALUE
008130                  '0882362267COMPUTER PROGRAMMING RPG II            '.
008140          10  BOOK-CONSTANTS-TABLE REDEFINES BOOK-CONSTANTS
008150                                              OCCURS 19 TIMES
008160                                              ASCENDING KEY IS
008170                                                  ISBN-TABLE
008180                                              INDEXED BY BOOK-IND.
008190              15  ISBN-TABLE      PIC X(10).
008200              15  BOOK-TITLE-TABLE PIC X(30).
```

Figure 10-14 COBOL Coding to Define the Book Table

In the example in Figure 10-14, it can be seen that the name of the entire table is BOOK-TABLE (line 006140). The group item BOOK-CONSTANTS contains all of the constants which are to be in the table. Note that each level 15 Filler has a PIC X(40) entry. The constant for each Filler contains 10 characters for the ISBN Number and 30 characters for the title of the book. There are nineteen separate elements in the table.

Beginning on line 008140 are the entries to redefine the table so that each element in the table may be referenced in the Procedure Division. As can be seen, the group item BOOK-CONSTANTS-TABLE redefines BOOK-CONSTANTS and it occurs 19 times. Thus, each element within the table is defined with the group item BOOK-CONSTANTS-TABLE. Two other phrases are included for the BOOK-CONSTANTS-TABLE group item. The first phrase is the ASCENDING KEY IS ISBN-TABLE phrase. The words ASCENDING KEY IS are required to define the value in the table which is to be compared and which must be in an ascending sequence. In the example, this field is the ISBN-Table field which is defined on line 008190. Therefore, the data-name ISBN-TABLE must be specified. The second phrase is the INDEXED BY phrase. This phrase specifies the data-name of a field which will be used as the index for the table search. An index operates in the same fashion as a subscript; that is, it contains a value which references a particular element within the table. When a table is to be searched, the index to be used must be defined by using the INDEXED BY phrase. The name chosen for the index, in this case BOOK-IND, is a programmer-chosen name. The index should not be defined elsewhere in the program; the only place it should appear in the Data Division is in the INDEXED BY phrase.

The group item BOOK-CONSTANTS-TABLE is followed by two elementary items—ISBN-TABLE and BOOK-TITLE-TABLE. These two items reference each of the elements within the table. Thus, the first ten characters of each element within the table will be referenced by the name ISBN-TABLE and the next thirty characters of each element will be referenced by the name BOOK-TITLE-TABLE. For example, if the index BOOK-IND contained the value 1, the entry ISBN-TABLE (BOOK-IND) would reference the first ten characters of the first element of the table while the entry BOOK-TITLE-TABLE (BOOK-IND) would reference the next thirty characters of the first element of the table. Similarly, if the index BOOK-IND contained the value 13, the entry ISBN-TABLE (BOOK-IND) would reference the first ten characters of the 13th element in the table, and the entry BOOK-TITLE-TABLE would reference the next thirty characters of the 13th element of the table.

SEARCH ALL STATEMENT

After the table is defined in the Working-Storage Section of the Data Division, statements in the Procedure Division must be executed in order to search the table. COBOL provides two verbs to perform the search activity—the SEARCH ALL verb is used when a binary search is to be performed and the SEARCH verb is used when a sequential search is to be performed.

In the sample program, a binary search is to be conducted. The Search All Statement used in the sample program to search the Book Table is illustrated in Figure 10-15.

EXAMPLE

```
Ø15120        SEARCH ALL BOOK-CONSTANTS-TABLE
Ø15130            AT END
Ø15140                MOVE 'UNKNOWN' TO BOOK-TITLE-REPORT
Ø15150            WHEN ISBN-TABLE (BOOK-IND) = ISBN-NUMBER-INPUT
Ø15160                MOVE BOOK-TITLE-TABLE (BOOK-IND)
Ø15170                    TO BOOK-TITLE-REPORT.
```

```
SEARCH ALL identifier-1 [ ; AT END imperative-statement-1 ]

                   ⎧ data-name-1      ⎧ IS EQUAL TO ⎫   ⎧ identifier-3           ⎫ ⎫
   ; WHEN          ⎨                  ⎨ IS =        ⎬   ⎨ literal-1              ⎬ ⎬
                   ⎩ condition-name-1 ⎩             ⎭   ⎩ arithmetic-expression-1 ⎭ ⎭

         ⎡       ⎧ data-name-2      ⎧ IS EQUAL TO ⎫   ⎧ identifier-4           ⎫ ⎫ ⎤
         ⎢ AND   ⎨                  ⎨ IS =        ⎬   ⎨ literal-2              ⎬ ⎬ ⎥ ...
         ⎣       ⎩ condition-name-2 ⎩             ⎭   ⎩ arithmetic-expression-2 ⎭ ⎭ ⎦

         ⎧ imperative-statement-2 ⎫
         ⎨ NEXT SENTENCE          ⎬
         ⎩                        ⎭
```

Figure 10-15 Example of Search Statement

The statement above is used to search a table that contains an ISBN Number and a related Book Title. This table was previously illustrated in Figure 10-14. As a result of the search, the appropriate Book Title will be extracted from the table and moved to the report output area; or an error message will be printed if the ISBN Number is not found in the table.

The words SEARCH ALL are required when a binary search is to be performed. Identifier-1 in the format notation must be the name of the item in the Data Division which contains the Occurs Clause, the Indexed By Clause, and the Ascending Key Is Clause. In the example, this name is BOOK-CONSTANTS-TABLE. The AT END portion of the Search All Statement specifies the processing which is to occur if the entire table is searched and the condition specified is not found. In the example, the statement MOVE 'UNKNOWN' to BOOK-TITLE-REPORT will be executed so that the value "UNKNOWN" will appear on the report instead of the Book Title. It should be noted that any imperative statement could have been specified following the AT END portion of the Search All Statement.

The word WHEN is required in the Search All Statement to indicate that the statements following it are to specify the conditions which are to be satisfied in order to successfully complete the table search operation. The "condition-1" entry should be an expression which uses the "equal to" condition operator. In the sample program, it is desired to extract a Book Title from the table when a match is found between the ISBN Number in the input record and the ISBN Number in the table; therefore, the condition WHEN ISBN-TABLE (BOOK-IND) = ISBN-NUMBER-INPUT is specified. When this condition occurs, that is, when the ISBN Number in the input record is equal to the ISBN Number in the table, then the imperative statement following the word WHEN is executed. In the example, the Book Title from the table will be moved to the report output area. It should be noted in the condition specified that some compilers require the data-name with the index to be on the left of the equal sign, while it does not matter with other compilers. Therefore, the safest way to write the condition in the When Clause is to place the table name with the index name on the left side of the equal sign.

SET AND SEARCH STATEMENTS

In the previous example, the Search All Statement was used to conduct a binary search of the table. If a sequential search of the table is required, the Search Statement is used. In conjunction with the Search Statement, however, the Set Statement must be used to give the index an initial value before the table search begins. The following example illustrates the Set and Search Statements which could be used to perform a sequential search on the Book Table.

EXAMPLE

```
023020      SET BOOK-IND TO 1.
023030      SEARCH BOOK-CONSTANTS-TABLE
023040          AT END
023050          MOVE 'UNKNOWN' TO BOOK-TITLE-REPORT
023060          WHEN ISBN-TABLE (BOOK-IND) = ISBN-NUMBER-INPUT
023070          MOVE BOOK-TITLE-TABLE (BOOK-IND)
023080              TO BOOK-TITLE-REPORT.
```

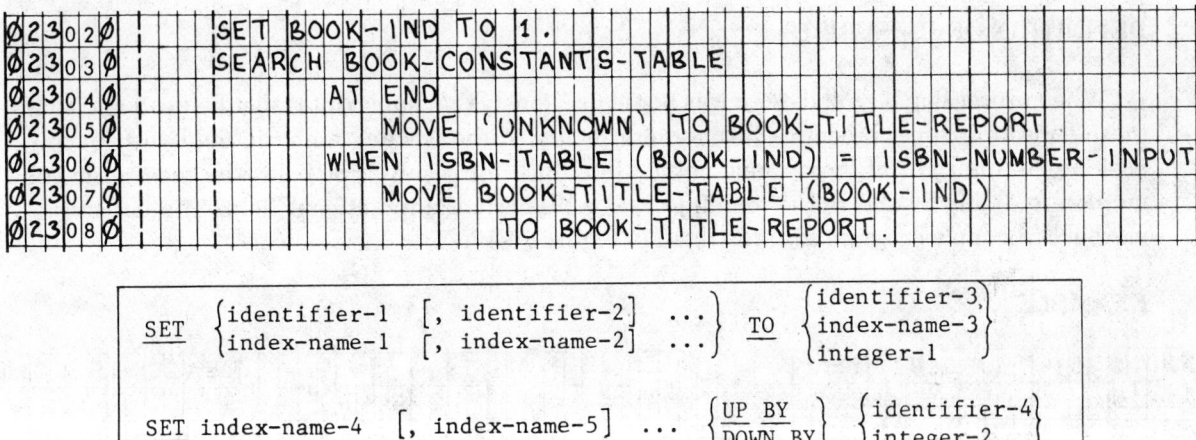

Figure 10-16 Example of Set and Search Statements

In the example in Figure 10-16, the Set Statement on line 023020 is used to set the index BOOK-IND to the value 1. The Set Statement will set the value of identifier-1, identifier-2, ... to the value in either identifier-3, index-name-3, or integer-1. In this case a numeric integer is used in the Set Statement. It must be noted that before the Search Statement can be used to perform the table search, the index associated with the table must be set to the number of the first element to be examined. Thus, if the programmer wishes the search to begin with first element in the table, then the index must be set to the value 1, such as in the example. If the program required that the search begin with the tenth element in the table, then the index must be set to the value 10 prior to beginning the search operation. It will be recalled that the setting of the index is not required for the Search All Statement because it searches the entire table using the binary search technique.

The Search Statement itself appears to be the same as the Search All Statement except that the word ALL is not used. There are, however, several differences. First, the conditions specified for the termination of the search (condition-1, condition-2, etc.) do not have to be equal conditions; they can be any allowable relation conditions. Secondly, it will be noted from the format notation of the Search All Statement in Figure 10-15 that more than one condition can be specified, that is, two or more conditions may have to be true before the search is terminated. In the Search All Statement, these conditions are in an AND relationship; that is, all of the conditions specified must be true before the Search All Statement will be stopped and the "When" portion of the statement executed. With the Search Statement, on the other hand, the conditions specified are in an OR relationship; that is, if any of the conditions specified is true, the search is terminated and the "When" portion of the statement is executed.

DEFINITION OF SUBSCRIPTS

When processing lists of data, it was noted previously that subscripts must be used and that these subscripts must be defined as numeric fields. Although any numeric field without any positions to the right of the decimal point will suffice for a subscript field, the most efficient method to define a subscript is to define it as a numeric Computational field. The subscripts used in the sample program are illustrated in Figure 10-17.

EXAMPLE

```
005110 01  SUBSCRIPTS                              USAGE IS COMP.
005120     05  LOW-SUBSCRIPT         PIC S9(8)     SYNC.
005130     05  SEARCH-SUBSCRIPT      PIC S9(8)     SYNC.
005140     05  HIGH-SUBSCRIPT        PIC S9(8)     SYNC.
005150     05  SALES-SUBSCRIPT       PIC S9(8)     SYNC.
```

Figure 10-17 Definition of Subscripts

Note from Figure 10-17 that the Usage Is Comp Clause is specified for the group of elementary numeric items which follow. The COMP (or COMPUTATIONAL) word indicates that the numeric fields are to be defined in the Binary format, that is, the values will be represented by binary numbers in these fields. On many computers, a subscript must be in the binary format before it can be used as a subscript; if it were not defined as binary, the compiler would generate instructions to transform it to binary. Therefore, if possible, the subscript fields should be defined as COMP or COMPUTATIONAL fields.

Each of the subscripts is defined with PIC S9(8) SYNC. All Computational fields must be signed; therefore the "S" is required. On many computer systems, the binary subscript will be contained in a "fullword", that is, four bytes, when it is used. In order to initially define the subscript as a fullword and avoid any compiler-generated conversion instructions, the field should be defined with 8 numeric characters, even though the value of the subscript will never require a field this large.

The SYNC (or SYNCHRONIZED) Clause is used to align the binary numeric field on the required boundaries of the computer system being used. These boundaries are certain addresses which must be used for binary fields. For example, it may be required that a fullword begin on an address ending in 0, 4, 8, or C (hexadecimal values). The SYNC Clause will ensure that this occurs when the program is compiled. If the SYNC Clause is not used, the compiler may have to generate instructions which would be executed in order to align the field. These needless instructions can be avoided by specifying the SYNC Clause.

SUMMARY

The use of lists of data and tables finds many applications in business data processing. The COBOL programmer should have thorough grasp of the methods and techniques associated with programming tables and lists.

SAMPLE PROGRAM

The design and programming of the sample problem to produce the Sales Analysis report illustrated in Figure 10-1 is explained on the following pages. The printer spacing chart and the format of the input records are illustrated in Figure 10-18.

OUTPUT

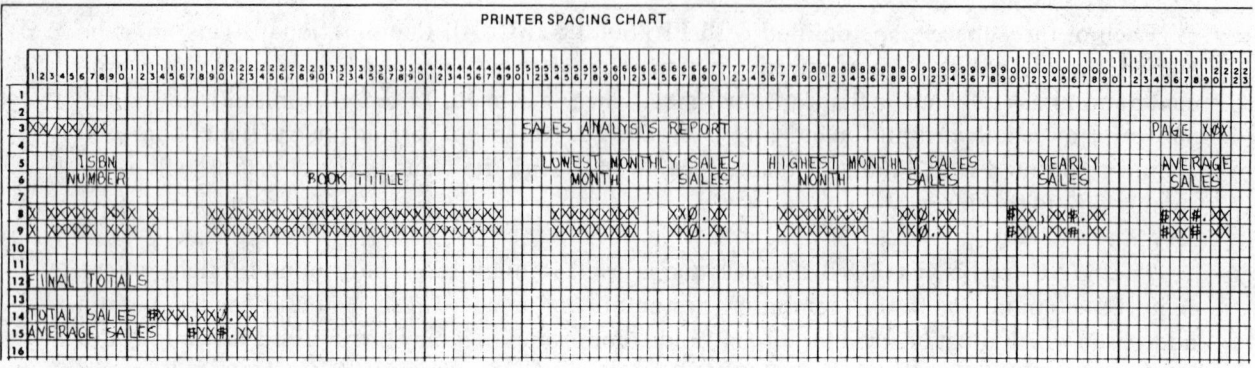

INPUT

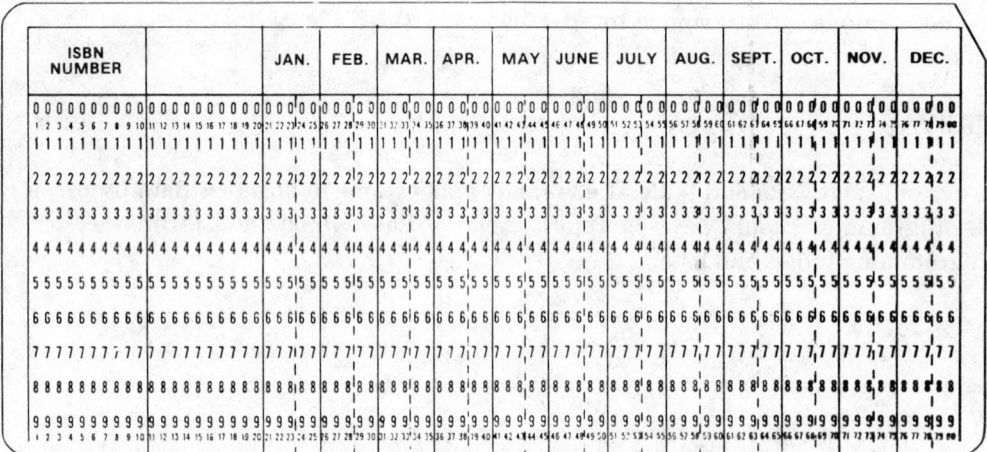

Figure 10-18 Printer Spacing Chart and Program Input

The Programming Specifications for the sample program are illustrated in Figure 10-19.

Programming Specifications

The Programming Specifications for the sample program are illustrated below.

PROGRAMMING SPECIFICATIONS				
SUBJECT	Sales Analysis Report	**DATE** June 20	**PAGE** 1 OF 1	
TO	Programmer	**FROM**	Systems Analyst	

A program is to be written to prepare a Sales Analysis Report. The formats of the input card file and the printer spacing chart are included as a part of this narrative. The program should include the following processing.

1. The program should read the input cards and create the Sales Analysis Report as per the format illustrated on the printer spacing chart.

2. The title of the book is to be extracted from a table based upon the ISBN Number contained in the input record.

3. The total sales and average sales for the year for each product are to be calculated.

4. For each product the name of the month in which the lowest monthly sales occurred is to be printed. In addition, the lowest Sales Amount is also to be printed. The name of the month with the lowest sales is to be extracted from a table.

5. For each product the name of the month in which the highest sales occurred is to be printed. In addition, the highest Sales Amount is also to be printed. The name of the month with the highest sales is to be extracted from a table.

6. If any of the months has sales that are equal, the first occurrence of the lowest and highest sales are to be printed on the report.

7. Headings should be printed on the first page and on each subsequent page of the report. Fifty-five detail and total lines are to appear on a page.

8. Final totals for the total sales and also the average monthly sales for all books are to be printed after all input records have been processed.

9. The program is to be written in COBOL.

Figure 10-19 Programming Specifications

PROGRAM DESIGN

As with all programs, the first step in program design is to analyze the output, input, and programming specifications, and determine the major processing tasks that are necessary to transform the input to output. The IPO Chart below illustrates the major processing tasks for the control module.

IPO Chart - Create Sales Report

IPO CHART					
PROGRAM: Sales Analysis		**PROGRAMMER:** Shelly/Cashman			**DATE:** June 25
MODULE NAME: Create Sales Report		**REF:** A000	**MODULE FUNCTION:** Create Sales Report		
INPUT		PROCESSING	REF:	OUTPUT	
1. Sales Cards		1. Initialization		1. Sales Analysis Report	
		2. Obtain input data			
		3. Process detail records	B000		
		4. Print the final totals	B010		
		5. Termination			

Figure 10-20 IPO Chart - Create Sales Report

It can be seen from the IPO Chart that the output is to consist of the Sales Analysis Report, and the input is the Sales Cards. The major processing tasks consist of initialization, obtaining the input data, processing the detail records, printing the final totals, and termination of the program. From an analysis of these major processing tasks, it would appear that both the tasks of "Process Detail Records" and "Print Final Totals" could be considered for possible development as separate modules.

Thus, a Hierarchy Chart showing the relationship of these modules should be developed at this time. This Hierarchy Chart is illustrated in Figure 10-21.

Hierarchy Chart

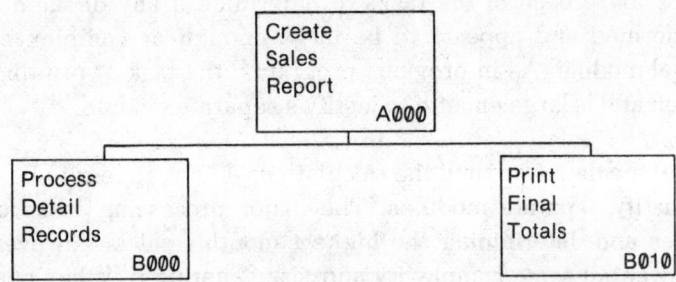

Figure 10-21 Hierarchy Chart

From the Hierarchy Chart in Figure 10-21 it can be seen that at this point in the design process, the program is to consist of three modules: the Create Sales Report module, the Process Detail Records module, and the Process Final Totals module. The next step in the design process is to design the IPO Charts for the modules on the second level of the hierarchy chart.

IPO Chart - Process Detail Records

The IPO Chart for the module whose function is to process the detail records is illustrated in Figure 10-22.

IPO CHART

PROGRAM: Sales Analysis		PROGRAMMER: Shelly/Cashman		DATE: June 25
MODULE NAME: Process Detail Records	REF: B000	MODULE FUNCTION: Process Detail Records		

INPUT	PROCESSING	REF:	OUTPUT	
1. Sales Input Record	1. Print heading when required	C000	1. Detail Print Line	
2. Name of Month Table	2. Format detail line		2. Updated Final Total Sales	
3. Name of Book Table	3. Perform calculations		Accumulator	
4. Final Total Accumulator	4. Determine lowest monthly sales	C010	3. Updated Number of	
5. Number of Months	5. Determine highest monthly sales	C020	Months Accumulator	
Accumulator	6. Update final total accumulators			
	7. Write the detail line			

Figure 10-22 IPO Chart - Process Detail Records

The output from this module includes a Detail Print Line, an Updated Final Total Sales Accumulator, and an Updated Number of Months Accumulator. Input consists of the Sales Input record, the Name of the Month Table, the Name of the Book Table, the Final Total Accumulator, and the Number of Months Accumulator.

After the major processing tasks of the module have been specified on the IPO Chart, the programmer must analyze each of the tasks to determine if any of them specifies a specific function to be performed and appears to be large enough or complex enough to justify a separate, lower-level module. As in previous programs, the task of printing the headings is a well-defined function and is large enough to justify a separate module.

The formatting of the detail line and the calculations do not appear to be of sufficient size or complexity as to justify separate modules. The major processing tasks of determining the lowest monthly sales and determining the highest monthly sales, however, are well defined functions which may entail some complexity and size. Therefore, it has been determined that these two major processing tasks should become lower-level modules.

The tasks of updating the final total accumulators and writing the detail line do not justify lower-level modules. As a result of this analysis, the Hierarchy Chart would have three lower-level modules from the module which processes the detail records. This is illustrated in the Hierarchy Chart in Figure 10-23.

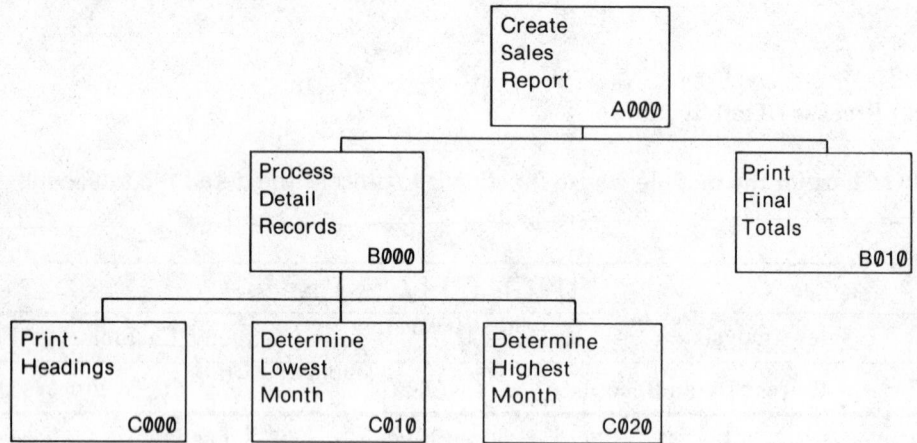

Figure 10-23 Hierarchy Chart

As can be seen from Figure 10-23, the three modules which are to be lower-level modules from the module which processes the detail records are illustrated on the Hierarchy Chart.

After these modules have been placed on the Hierarchy Chart, the programmer would continue the design of the IPO Charts by designing the IPO Chart for the module which prints the final totals.

IPO Chart - Print Final Totals

The IPO Chart for the module which prints the final totals is illustrated in Figure 10-24.

IPO CHART					
PROGRAM: Sales Analysis		**PROGRAMMER:** Shelly/Cashman			**DATE:** June 25
MODULE NAME: Print Final Totals		**REF:** B010	**MODULE FUNCTION:** Print Final Totals		
INPUT	**PROCESSING**		**REF:**	**OUTPUT**	
1. Final Total Sales	1. Format final total lines			1. Final Total Lines	
Accumulator	2. Calculate average monthly sales				
2. Total Number of Months	3. Write the final total lines				
Accumulator					

Figure 10-24 IPO Chart - Print Final Totals

From the sample of the report illustrated in Figure 10-1, it can be seen that two values are to be printed after all of the input records have been processed: A final total of all sales for all books and the average monthly sales for all books. Thus, the output of this module are the Final Total Lines which contain the Total Sales and the Average Monthly Sales for all of the books.

The input consists of the Final Total Sales Accumulator and the Total Number of Months Accumulator which is used in the calcualtion to determine the Monthly Average for all books. The major processing tasks consist of formatting the final total lines, calculating the average monthly sales, and writing the final total lines. None of these tasks justifies a lower-level module.

Thus, the IPO Charts for the modules on the second level of the program are complete. The programmer would then turn to the design of the IPO Charts on the third level of the program. These modules consist of the print the headings module, the module to determine the lowest sales, and the module to determine the highest sales (see Figure 10-23).

IPO Chart - Print the Headings

The IPO Chart for the module which prints the headings is illustrated in Figure 10-25.

IPO CHART					
PROGRAM: Sales Analysis		**PROGRAMMER:** Shelly/Cashman			**DATE:** June 25
MODULE NAME: Print Headings		**REF:** C000	**MODULE FUNCTION:** Print Headings		
INPUT	**PROCESSING**		**REF:**	**OUTPUT**	
1. Heading Lines	1. Format headings			1. Heading Lines	
	2. Write the heading				

Figure 10-25 IPO Chart - Print the Headings

As can be seen from the IPO Chart, the output from the module are the heading lines and the input to the module are the heading lines. The major processing tasks are to format the heading lines and to write the heading lines. Neither of these tasks requires a lower-level module.

IPO Chart - Determine Lowest Month

The second module which is a submodule to the module which processes the detail records is the module whose function is to determine the month in which the lowest sales of the year took place. The IPO Chart for this module is illustrated below.

IPO CHART					
PROGRAM: Sales Analysis		**PROGRAMMER:** Shelly/Cashman			**DATE:** June 25
MODULE NAME: Determine Lowest Month		**REF:** C010	**MODULE FUNCTION:** Determine Lowest Month		
INPUT	**PROCESSING**		**REF:**	**OUTPUT**	
1. Monthly Sales Fields	1. Examine monthly sales fields to			1. Lowest Month	
	determine lowest monthly sales				

Figure 10-26 IPO Chart - Determine Lowest Month

From the IPO Chart it can be seen that the output of the module which determines the lowest month is the month with the lowest sales. The input is the sales for each month of the year. The major processing task which must be performed involves examining the sales for each month of the year, determining the lowest sales, and determining the month which corresponds to the lowest sales.

IPO Chart - Determine Highest Month

The IPO Chart for the module which determines the highest month is similar to the IPO Chart for the module which determines the lowest month except that the monthly sales fields are analyzed to determine which month has the highest monthly sales. The IPO Chart for the module which determines the highest sales is illustrated in Figure 10-27.

IPO CHART					
PROGRAM: Sales Analysis		**PROGRAMMER:** Shelly/Cashman			**DATE:** June 25
MODULE NAME: Determine Highest Month		**REF:** C020	**MODULE FUNCTION:** Determine Highest Month		
INPUT	**PROCESSING**		**REF:**	**OUTPUT**	
1. Monthly Sales Fields	1. Examine monthly sales fields to			1. Highest Month	
	determine highest monthly sales				

Figure 10-27 IPO Chart - Determine Highest Month

SUMMARY - Hierarchy Chart and IPO Charts

The Hierarchy Chart and the IPO Charts for the program are illustrated below.

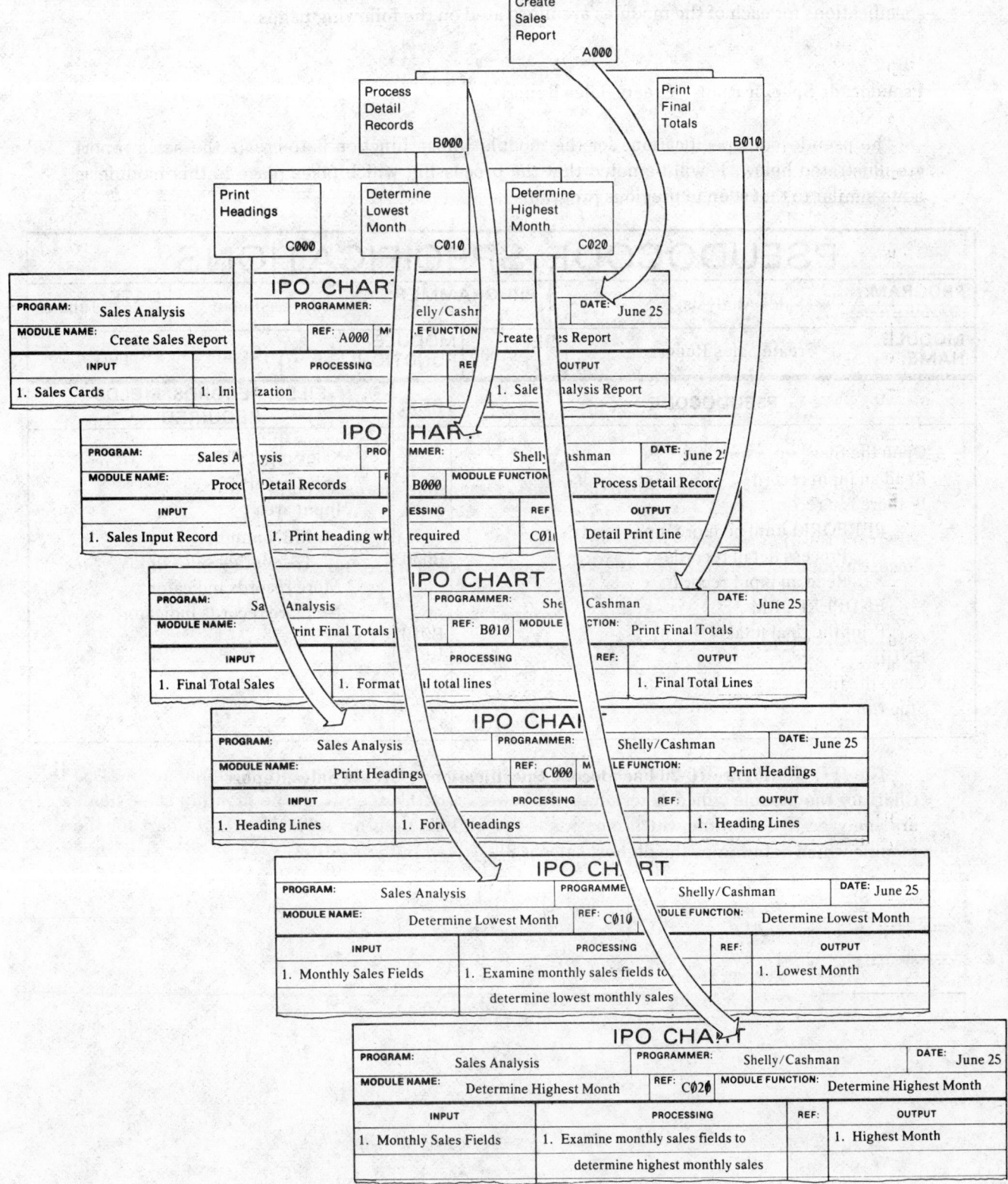

Figure 10-28 Hierarchy Chart and IPO Charts

PSEUDOCODE SPECIFICATIONS

After the IPO Charts have been designed and reviewed to ensure a viable solution to the problem, the pseudocode specifications for each module must be developed. The pseudocode specifications for each of the modules are illustrated on the following pages.

Pseudocode Specifications - Create Sales Report

The pseudocode specifications for the module whose function is to create the sales report are illustrated below. It will be noted that the processing which takes place in this module is quite similar to that seen in previous programs.

PSEUDOCODE SPECIFICATIONS

PROGRAM: Sales Analysis	PROGRAMMER: Shelly/Cashman	DATE: June 25
MODULE NAME: Create Sales Report	REF: A000 MODULE FUNCTION:	Create Sales Report

PSEUDOCODE	REF:	FILES, RECORDS, FIELDS REQUIRED

Open the files
Read an input record
IF there is a record
   PERFORM until no more input records
     Process detail records
     Read an input record
   ENDPERFORM
   Print the final totals
ENDIF
Close the files
Stop run
	
	B000
	
	B010
		Sales input file
		Sales report file
		Input area
		  ISBN number
		  12 monthly sales fields
		More records indicator
		No more records indicator

Figure 10-29 Pseudocode Specifications - Create Sales Report

Pseudocode Specifications - Process Detail Records

The pseudocode specifications for the Process Detail Records module are illustrated in Figure 10-30. This module contains the detailed steps necessary to produce the detail line. Note that the steps necessary to determine the lowest month and to determine the highest month are not specified in this module. This is because these operations will be performed in separate modules that are subfunctions of the Process Detail Records module.

PSEUDOCODE SPECIFICATIONS

PROGRAM: Sales Analysis	PROGRAMMER: Shelly/Cashman	DATE: June 25
MODULE NAME: Process Detail Record	REF: B000	MODULE FUNCTION: Process Detail Record

PSEUDOCODE	REF:	FILES, RECORDS, FIELDS REQUIRED
IF number of lines printed is = or > page size or this is the first page Print the headings ENDIF Clear the printer area Move ISBN number to printer output area Search book table to find book title IF ISBN number in record = ISBN number in table Move book title to output area ELSE Move unknown message to output area ENDIF Determine month with lowest sales Move name of month with lowest sales to printer output area Move lowest sales to printer output area Determine month with highest sales Move name of month with highest sales to printer output area Move highest sales to printer output area Calculate total yearly sales Move yearly sales to printer output area Calculate average monthly sales Add yearly sales to final total Add 12 to total months accumulator Set yearly sales to zero Write a line on the report Set spacing for single spacing Add 1 to number of lines printed	C000 C010 C020	Number of lines printed counter Page size constant First page indicator Printer output area ISBN number Book title Name of month with lowest sales Lowest sales Name of month with highest sales Highest sales Yearly sales Average sales Input area ISBN number Monthly sales fields Tables Name of months table Name of book table Yearly sales work area Final total accumulator Total months accumulator Space control field Single space control character

Figure 10-30 Pseudocode Specifications - Process Detail Records

Pseudocode Specifications - Print Final Totals

The pseudocode specifications for the Print Final Totals module are illustrated below. The steps in processing the final total consist of moving the totals sales which have been accumulated to the final total line, calculating the average monthly sales of all items sold, and writing the final total line.

PSEUDOCODE SPECIFICATIONS

PROGRAM: Sales Analysis	PROGRAMMER: Shelly/Cashman	DATE: June 25
MODULE NAME: Print Final Totals	REF: B010 MODULE FUNCTION: Print Final Totals	

PSEUDOCODE	REF:	FILES, RECORDS, FIELDS REQUIRED

Write final total constant line
Move final total sales to final total line
Write final total sales on report
Calculate average sales = total sales / number of mos.
Write average sales on report
		Final total constant line
		Final total sales line
		Final total average line
		Total sales in final
		  total accumulator
		Total number of months in
		  months accumulator

Figure 10-31 Pseudocode Specifications - Print Final Totals

Pseudocode Specifications - Print Headings

The pseudocode specifications for the Print Headings module are very similar to those used in previous programs; and they are illustrated below.

PSEUDOCODE SPECIFICATIONS

PROGRAM: Sales Analysis	PROGRAMMER: Shelly/Cashman	DATE: June 25
MODULE NAME: Print Headings	REF: C000 MODULE FUNCTION: Print Headings	

PSEUDOCODE	REF:	FILES, RECORDS, FIELDS REQUIRED
Move current date to heading line Move page count to heading line Write first heading line Add 1 to page count Write second heading line Write third heading line Set space control for double spacing Set number of lines printed to zero		Current date First heading line Page number (page count) Second heading line Third heading line Space control field Double space control character Number of lines printed counter

Figure 10-32 Pseudocode Specifications - Print Headings

STUB TESTING

In sample programs in the previous chapters of the text, the design of the entire program has been completed and then the program would be coded, compiled, and tested. However, an important testing technique often used in structured programming allows a program to be partially coded and tested before the entire program is designed. This technique, which is possible because of Top-Down Design, is called STUB TESTING.

When stub testing is used, one or more modules in the higher levels of the Hierarchy Chart are designed and coded. Those modules which are submodules to the modules which are designed and coded are established as "stubs" in the program which is tested. A stub is merely a submodule which will not at this time be coded to perform the processing it is supposed to perform, but which will allow reference to it. For example, in the sample program, the modules which create the sales report, process the detail records, print the final totals, and print the headings have been designed. The modules which determine the lowest monthly sales and determine the highest monthly sales, however, have not yet been designed. The relationships of these modules are illustrated in the hierarchy chart below.

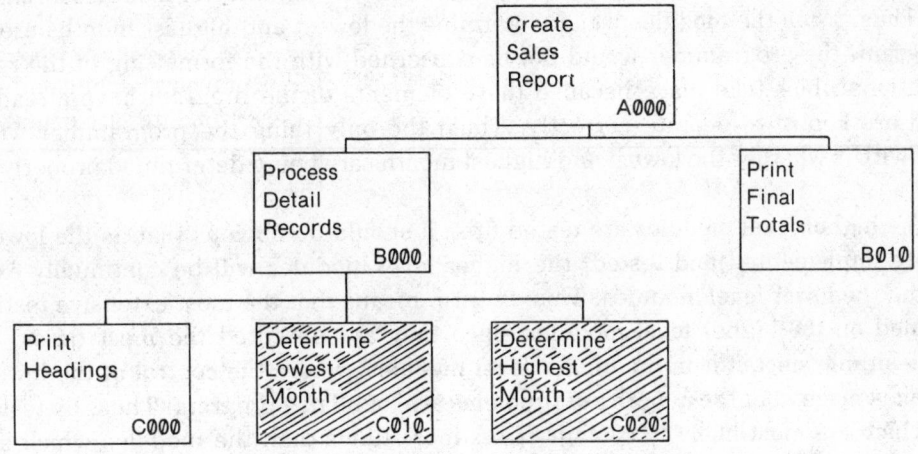

Figure 10-33 Example of Hierarchy Chart with "Stubs"

In the hierarchy chart above, the modules which determine the lowest month and determine the highest month have not yet been designed at the pseudocode level. The modules which have been designed, however, will allow the program to read input data and create the output report; that is, the data is read in the module which creates the sales report (see Figure 10-29), the detail records on the report are written in the module which processes the detail records (see Figure 10-30), and the final totals are written by the module which prints the final totals (see Figure 10-31). Therefore, meaningful data can be produced from the modules which are currently designed. The only elements which would be missing from the report are the name and sales of the highest and lowest months. Thus, the program could be written with these two modules as stubs and could be completely tested except for determining the name and sales of the highest and lowest months.

Why Stub Testing

Stub testing offers several advantages over waiting until the entire program is designed and coded before beginning testing. First, debugging the program is normally made easier than when the entire program is tested. This is because the programmer can concentrate on debugging only several modules within the program instead of attempting to debug all of the modules within the program. Since the programmer is concentrating on only several modules, it is likely that fewer errors will occur and that they will be easier to identify and correct than if the entire program were being tested. For example, in the sample program, the programmer would be able to test whether the report format and the calculations within the program were being done properly without worrying about whether or not the lowest and highest months were determined properly. By being able to narrow the elements of the program which are being tested, the programmer would be able to isolate and correct errors without trying to correct an entire program.

In addition, since the higher-level modules are tested and made correct before the "stubs" are actually implemented within the program, the testing of the stub modules is made easier, since when they are tested, the programmer knows that the higher level modules already work properly. Thus, when the modules which determine the lowest and highest months are placed in the program, the programmer would not be concerned with the formatting of the report or the calculations which take place because these elements of the program have already been tested and are known to operate correctly. Thus, the only thing the programmer would be concerned with is whether the lowest and highest months are being determined properly.

Since the higher level modules are tested first, it should be obvious that as the lower level modules are implemented and tested, the higher level modules will be continually executed when testing the lower level modules. This, in turn, means that the most extensive testing will be performed on the higher level modules since they are executed the most times. This is normally desirable since it is in the higher level modules, where the control of the lower level modules takes place, that the majority of problems are found in a program. Thus, by testing the modules which are most likely to contain errors more times than the modules which are less likely to contain errors, the program is more thoroughly tested than if all modules were tested the same number of times.

Another great advantage is that output is produced from the program sooner than if testing waited for the entire program to be completed. Thus, the user of the program will be able to review output from the program and, if there are errors in the output design, these errors can be corrected immediately instead of late in the programming project. In addition, the programmer "looks good" because her program is producing good output. To users of data processing systems, this may be an important factor because without stub testing, a user may not receive any output for a long time and she may wonder what the programming staff is doing. If output is received early in the project, the user is satisfied that progress is being made on the project. Also, by producing some type of results early in the programming project, the morale of the programmer is many times raised, since he can see progress on the project.

Another advantage that may be critical when attempting to finish a programming project on time is that the testing of the program is distributed over a longer period of time. Prior to top-down design and stub testing, a large programming project would normally show very little computer usage until toward the end of the project, when the need for computer use would jump quite high. If the machine were not available, then typically the entire project stopped while waiting for the machine. With stub testing, the use of the machine begins early in the project and is more evenly distributed over the life of the project. In this manner, there is not the frantic use of the computer at the end of the project as so often happens without stub testing.

Types of Stubs

The modules which are stubs can be written in several different ways, depending upon the needs of the higher-level modules which are being tested. One method which can be used is for the stub module to do nothing — it is placed in the program only so that the higher-level module can reference it, but it does no actual processing. The coding to accomplish this type of activity is illustrated in Figure 10-34.

EXAMPLE

High-Level Module

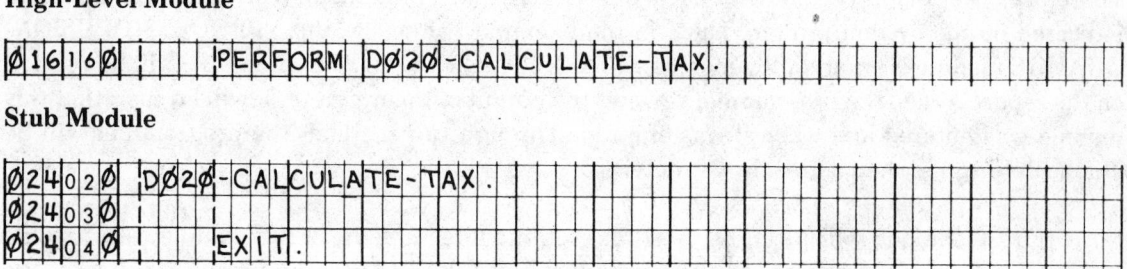

Stub Module

Figure 10-34 Example of Program Stub - Return Control

In the example above it can be seen that the Perform Statement in the high-level module references the module with the name D020-CALCULATE-TAX. Therefore, the module name must be included in the program in order for the program to compile properly. However, it has been decided that the module should do no processing. Thus, merely the name and the EXIT Statement are included in the paragraph. The Exit Statement does no processing; it merely returns control to the statement following the Perform Statement which called the paragraph. As a result of this type of stub, the high-level module can be tested because the program will compile properly.

A more useful stub is one which indicates in some manner that it has been entered, that is, that control has been passed to the module. A method which can be used in this type of stub module is illustrated in Figure 10-35.

EXAMPLE

High-Level Module

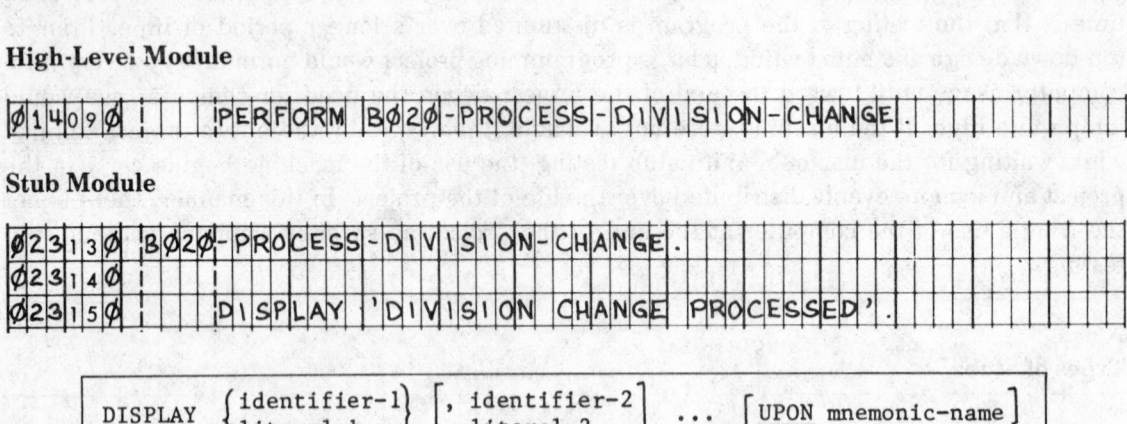

Stub Module

DISPLAY $\left\{\begin{array}{l}\text{identifier-1}\\\text{literal-1}\end{array}\right\}$ $\left[\begin{array}{l},\text{ identifier-2}\\,\text{ literal-2}\end{array}\right]$ ... $\left[\underline{\text{UPON}}\text{ mnemonic-name}\right]$

Figure 10-35 Example of Program Stub

Note in the example above that the high-level module contains the Perform Statement which will cause the B020-PROCESS-DIVISION-CHANGE module to be performed. This lower-level module is to be a stub module. In this program, however, it has been decided by the programmer that the stub module should give some indication that it has been entered. Therefore, the Display Statement is used. The Display Statement will write the message indicated on the system printer. Thus, in the example, when the B020-PROCESS-DIVISION-CHANGE module is entered, the message "DIVISION CHANGE PROCESSED" will be printed on the report. When the programmer reviews the output of the program, it will be seen that this module was entered and when it was entered. Through this method, the programmer will be able to determine when a module was entered.

A third technique which can be used for stub modules is to have the module return some form of data which can be used in the higher-level module. For example, if the function of the module was to calculate the income tax, a value of $10.00 could be returned to the higher-level module each time the stub module was entered. The higher-level module could then operate on this value even though it may not be the correct value.

In the sample program, the modules which determine the lowest month and the highest month are to be stub tested. It has been decided to have the modules return data to the higher-level module which processes the detail records. The coding for the two stub modules, together with the applicable coding in the module which processes the detail records, is illustrated in Figure 10-36.

EXAMPLE

Process Detail Records Module

```
Ø16Ø1Ø        PERFORM CØ1Ø-DETERMINE-LOWEST-MONTH.
Ø16Ø2Ø        MOVE MONTH-TABLE (LOW-SUBSCRIPT) TO LOW-MONTH-REPORT.
Ø16Ø3Ø        MOVE SALES-INPUT (LOW-SUBSCRIPT) TO LOW-SALES-REPORT.
Ø16Ø4Ø        PERFORM CØ2Ø-DETERMINE-HIGHEST-MONTH.
Ø16Ø5Ø        MOVE MONTH-TABLE (HIGH-SUBSCRIPT) TO HIGH-MONTH-REPORT.
Ø16Ø6Ø        MOVE SALES-INPUT (HIGH-SUBSCRIPT) TO HIGH-SALES-REPORT.
```

Determine Lowest Month Module

```
Ø191 8Ø   CØ1Ø-DETERMINE-LOWEST-MONTH.
Ø191 9Ø
Ø192 ØØ       MOVE 1 TO LOW-SUBSCRIPT.
```

Determine Highest Month Module

```
Ø21Ø9Ø    CØ2Ø-DETERMINE-HIGHEST-MONTH.
Ø211ØØ
Ø211 1Ø       MOVE 1 TO HIGH-SUBSCRIPT.
```

Figure 10-36 Example of Stub Coding in Sample Program

Note from the example above that on line 016010 of the module which processes the detail records, the C010-DETERMINE-LOWEST-MONTH module is performed. The only entry in the module which determines the lowest month is the Move Statement on line 019200 that moves the value 1 to the LOW-SUBSCRIPT field. The effect of this Move Statement is to indicate that the first month of the year is the lowest month. The statements on line 016020 and line 016030 would then be executed and the month name (JANUARY) and sales for the first month would be moved to the output area.

When the C020-DETERMINE-HIGHEST-MONTH module is entered from the Perform Statement on line 016040, the Move Statement on line 021110 is executed, which moves the value 1 to the HIGH-SUBSCRIPT field. Thus, the highest month is also indicated as month 1. It should be noted, however, that this is perfectly valid since the lowest and highest month modules are stub modules and, at this time, are not supposed to return the actual low and high months.

After these stub modules are coded, the program would be compiled and executed. The Procedure Division for the sample program with the stub modules and the output from this run are illustrated on the following pages.

Source Listing - Stub Testing

Note from Figure 10-38 that the output of the program is correct except that the lowest and highest months are always January, regardless of the sales for the month. This is because the stub modules move the value 1 to the subscript fields for each record.

```
6

00240   013020 PROCEDURE DIVISION.                                               SALESANA
00241   013030                                                                   SALESANA
00242   013040*************************************************************      SALESANA
00243   013050*                                                            *     SALESANA
00244   013060*  THIS MODULE OBTAINS THE INPUT DATA AND CAUSES THE DETAIL  *     SALESANA
00245   013070*  PROCESSING AND FINAL TOTAL PROCESSING TO OCCUR. IT IS     *     SALESANA
00246   013080*  ENTERED FROM AND EXITS TO THE OPERATING SYSTEM.           *     SALESANA
00247   013090*                                                            *     SALESANA
00248   013100*************************************************************      SALESANA
00249   013110                                                                   SALESANA
00250   013120 A000-CREATE-SALES-REPORT.                                         SALESANA
00251   013130                                                                   SALESANA
00252   013140     OPEN INPUT  SALES-INPUT-FILE                                  SALESANA
00253   013150          OUTPUT SALES-ANALYSIS-REPORT-FILE.                       SALESANA
00254   013160     READ SALES-INPUT-FILE                                         SALESANA
00255   013170          AT END                                                   SALESANA
00256   013180              MOVE 'NO ' TO ARE-THERE-MORE-RECORDS.                 SALESANA
00257   013190     IF THERE-IS-A-RECORD                                          SALESANA
00258   013200         PERFORM A001-PROCESS-AND-READ                             SALESANA
00259   014010              UNTIL THERE-ARE-NO-MORE-RECORDS                       SALESANA
00260   014020         PERFORM B010-PRINT-FINAL-TOTALS.                          SALESANA
00261   014030     CLOSE SALES-INPUT-FILE                                        SALESANA
00262   014040          SALES-ANALYSIS-REPORT-FILE.                              SALESANA
00263   014050     STOP RUN.                                                     SALESANA
00264   014060                                                                   SALESANA
00265   014070 A001-PROCESS-AND-READ.                                            SALESANA
00266   014080                                                                   SALESANA
00267   014090                                                                   SALESANA
00268   014100     PERFORM B000-PROCESS-DETAIL-RECORDS.                          SALESANA
00269   014110     READ SALES-INPUT-FILE                                         SALESANA
00270   014120          AT END                                                   SALESANA
00271   014130              MOVE 'NO ' TO ARE-THERE-MORE-RECORDS.                 SALESANA
```

```
7

00272   014150*************************************************************      SALESANA
00273   014160*                                                            *     SALESANA
00274   014170*  THIS MODULE PROCESSES THE DETAIL RECORDS BY FORMATTING THE *    SALESANA
00275   014180*  REPORT LINE.  A TABLE IS SEARCHED FOR THE BOOK TITLE, THE  *    SALESANA
00276   014190*  LOWEST AND HIGHEST SALES ARE DETERMINED, THE YEARLY SALES  *    SALESANA
00277   014200*  AND AVERAGE SALES CALCULATED, AND FINAL TOTAL ACCUMULATED. *    SALESANA
00278   015010*  IT IS ENTERED AND EXITS TO THE A000-CREATE-SALES-REPORT    *    SALESANA
00279   015020*  MODULE.                                                    *    SALESANA
00280   015030*                                                            *     SALESANA
00281   015040*************************************************************      SALESANA
00282   015050                                                                   SALESANA
00283   015060 B000-PROCESS-DETAIL-RECORDS.                                      SALESANA
00284   015070                                                                   SALESANA
00285   015080     IF LINES-PRINTED IS EQUAL TO PAGE-SIZE OR                     SALESANA
00286   015090        IS GREATER THAN PAGE-SIZE OR                               SALESANA
00287   015100        FIRST-PAGE                                                 SALESANA
00288   015110         PERFORM C000-PRINT-HEADINGS.                              SALESANA
00289   015120     MOVE SPACES TO SALES-ANALYSIS-REPORT-LINE.                    SALESANA
00290   015130     MOVE ISBN-NUMBER-INPUT TO ISBN-NUMBER-REPORT.                 SALESANA
00291   015140     SEARCH ALL BOOK-CONSTANTS-TABLE                               SALESANA
00292   015150          AT END                                                   SALESANA
00293   015160              MOVE 'UNKNOWN' TO BOOK-TITLE-REPORT                  SALESANA
00294   015170          WHEN ISBN-TABLE (BOOK-IND) = ISBN-NUMBER-INPUT           SALESANA
00295   015180              MOVE BOOK-TITLE-TABLE (BOOK-IND)                     SALESANA
00296   015190                  TO BOOK-TITLE-REPORT.                           SALESANA
00297   015200     PERFORM C010-DETERMINE-LOWEST-MONTH.                          SALESANA
00298   016010     MOVE MONTH-TABLE (LOW-SUBSCRIPT) TO LOW-MONTH-REPORT.         SALESANA
00299   016020     MOVE SALES-INPUT (LOW-SUBSCRIPT) TO LOW-SALES-REPORT.         SALESANA
00300   016030     PERFORM C020-DETERMINE-HIGHEST-MONTH.                         SALESANA
00301   016040     MOVE MONTH-TABLE (HIGH-SUBSCRIPT) TO HIGH-MONTH-REPORT.       SALESANA
00302   016050     MOVE SALES-INPUT (HIGH-SUBSCRIPT) TO HIGH-SALES-REPORT.       SALESANA
00303   016060     PERFORM B001-CALCULATE-TOTAL-SALES                           SALESANA
00304   016070          VARYING SALES-SUBSCRIPT FROM 1 BY 1                      SALESANA
00305   016080          UNTIL SALES-SUBSCRIPT IS GREATER THAN 12.               SALESANA
00306   016090     MOVE YEARLY-SALES-WORK TO YEARLY-SALES-REPORT.                SALESANA
00307   016100     COMPUTE AVERAGE-MONTHLY-SALES-REPORT ROUNDED =                SALESANA
00308   016110          YEARLY-SALES-WORK / 12.                                  SALESANA
00309   016120     ADD YEARLY-SALES-WORK TO TOTAL-SALES-ACCUM.                   SALESANA
00310   016130     ADD 12 TO NUMBER-OF-MONTHS-ACCUM.                             SALESANA
00311   016140     MOVE ZEROS TO YEARLY-SALES-WORK.                              SALESANA
00312   016150     WRITE SALES-ANALYSIS-REPORT-LINE                             SALESANA
00313   016160          AFTER PROPER-SPACING.                                    SALESANA
00314   016170     MOVE SPACE-ONE-LINE TO PROPER-SPACING.                        SALESANA
00315   016180     ADD 1 TO LINES-PRINTED.                                       SALESANA
00316   016190                                                                   SALESANA
00317   016200                                                                   SALESANA
00318   017010                                                                   SALESANA
00319   017020 B001-CALCULATE-TOTAL-SALES.                                       SALESANA
00320   017030                                                                   SALESANA
00321   017040     ADD SALES-INPUT (SALES-SUBSCRIPT) TO                         SALESANA
00322   017050          YEARLY-SALES-WORK.                                       SALESANA
```

Figure 10-37 Source Listing - Stub Testing [Part 1 of 2]

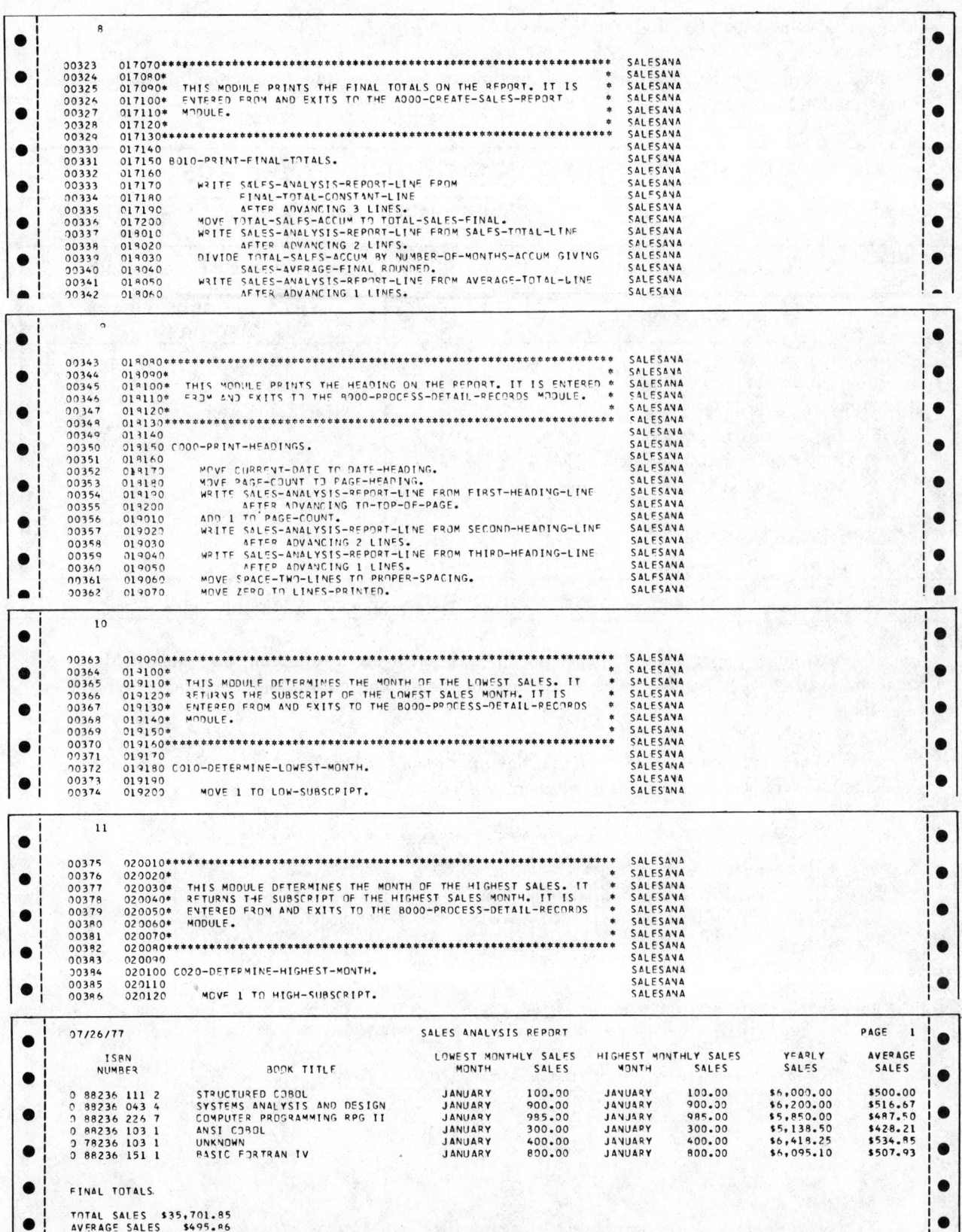

```
    8
00323    017070***********************************************************    SALESANA
00324    01708O*                                                         *    SALESANA
00325    017090*   THIS MODULE PRINTS THE FINAL TOTALS ON THE REPORT. IT IS  *    SALESANA
00326    017100*   ENTERED FROM AND EXITS TO THE A000-CREATE-SALES-REPORT    *    SALESANA
00327    017110*   MODULE.                                                *    SALESANA
00328    017120*                                                         *    SALESANA
00329    017130***********************************************************    SALESANA
00330    017140                                                              SALESANA
00331    017150 B010-PRINT-FINAL-TOTALS.                                     SALESANA
00332    017160                                                              SALESANA
00333    017170     WRITE SALES-ANALYSIS-REPORT-LINE FROM                    SALESANA
00334    017180         FINAL-TOTAL-CONSTANT-LINE                            SALESANA
00335    017190         AFTER ADVANCING 3 LINES.                             SALESANA
00336    017200     MOVE TOTAL-SALES-ACCUM TO TOTAL-SALES-FINAL.             SALESANA
00337    018010     WRITE SALES-ANALYSIS-REPORT-LINE FROM SALES-TOTAL-LINE   SALESANA
00338    018020         AFTER ADVANCING 2 LINES.                             SALESANA
00339    018030     DIVIDE TOTAL-SALES-ACCUM BY NUMBER-OF-MONTHS-ACCUM GIVING SALESANA
00340    018040         SALES-AVERAGE-FINAL ROUNDED.                         SALESANA
00341    018050     WRITE SALES-ANALYSIS-REPORT-LINE FROM AVERAGE-TOTAL-LINE  SALESANA
00342    018060         AFTER ADVANCING 1 LINES.                             SALESANA
```

```
    9
00343    018080***********************************************************    SALESANA
00344    018090*                                                         *    SALESANA
00345    018100*   THIS MODULE PRINTS THE HEADING ON THE REPORT. IT IS ENTERED *    SALESANA
00346    018110*   FROM AND EXITS TO THE B000-PROCESS-DETAIL-RECORDS MODULE.  *    SALESANA
00347    018120*                                                         *    SALESANA
00348    018130***********************************************************    SALESANA
00349    018140                                                              SALESANA
00350    018150 C000-PRINT-HEADINGS.                                         SALESANA
00351    018160                                                              SALESANA
00352    018170     MOVE CURRENT-DATE TO DATE-HEADING.                       SALESANA
00353    018180     MOVE PAGE-COUNT TO PAGE-HEADING.                         SALESANA
00354    018190     WRITE SALES-ANALYSIS-REPORT-LINE FROM FIRST-HEADING-LINE  SALESANA
00355    018200         AFTER ADVANCING TO-TOP-OF-PAGE.                      SALESANA
00356    019010     ADD 1 TO PAGE-COUNT.                                     SALESANA
00357    019020     WRITE SALES-ANALYSIS-REPORT-LINE FROM SECOND-HEADING-LINE SALESANA
00358    019030         AFTER ADVANCING 2 LINES.                             SALESANA
00359    019040     WRITE SALES-ANALYSIS-REPORT-LINE FROM THIRD-HEADING-LINE  SALESANA
00360    019050         AFTER ADVANCING 1 LINES.                             SALESANA
00361    019060     MOVE SPACE-TWO-LINES TO PROPER-SPACING.                  SALESANA
00362    019070     MOVE ZERO TO LINES-PRINTED.                              SALESANA
```

```
    10
00363    019080***********************************************************    SALESANA
00364    019100*                                                         *    SALESANA
00365    019110*   THIS MODULE DETERMINES THE MONTH OF THE LOWEST SALES. IT  *    SALESANA
00366    019120*   RETURNS THE SUBSCRIPT OF THE LOWEST SALES MONTH. IT IS    *    SALESANA
00367    019130*   ENTERED FROM AND EXITS TO THE B000-PROCESS-DETAIL-RECORDS *    SALESANA
00368    019140*   MODULE.                                                *    SALESANA
00369    019150*                                                         *    SALESANA
00370    019160***********************************************************    SALESANA
00371    019170                                                              SALESANA
00372    019180 C010-DETERMINE-LOWEST-MONTH.                                 SALESANA
00373    019190                                                              SALESANA
00374    019200     MOVE 1 TO LOW-SUBSCRIPT.                                 SALESANA
```

```
    11
00375    020010***********************************************************    SALESANA
00376    020020*                                                         *    SALESANA
00377    020030*   THIS MODULE DETERMINES THE MONTH OF THE HIGHEST SALES. IT *    SALESANA
00378    020040*   RETURNS THE SUBSCRIPT OF THE HIGHEST SALES MONTH. IT IS   *    SALESANA
00379    020050*   ENTERED FROM AND EXITS TO THE B000-PROCESS-DETAIL-RECORDS *    SALESANA
00380    020060*   MODULE.                                                *    SALESANA
00381    020070*                                                         *    SALESANA
00382    020080***********************************************************    SALESANA
00383    020090                                                              SALESANA
00384    020100 C020-DETERMINE-HIGHEST-MONTH.                                SALESANA
00385    020110                                                              SALESANA
00386    020120     MOVE 1 TO HIGH-SUBSCRIPT.                                SALESANA
```

```
07/26/77                        SALES ANALYSIS REPORT                                    PAGE  1

     ISBN                                 LOWEST MONTHLY SALES    HIGHEST MONTHLY SALES     YEARLY      AVERAGE
    NUMBER          BOOK TITLE            MONTH      SALES         MONTH      SALES         SALES        SALES

 0 88236 111 2   STRUCTURED COBOL         JANUARY    100.00       JANUARY    100.00       $6,000.00    $500.00
 0 88236 043 4   SYSTEMS ANALYSIS AND DESIGN   JANUARY  900.00    JANUARY    900.00       $6,200.00    $516.67
 0 88236 226 7   COMPUTER PROGRAMMING RPG II   JANUARY  985.00    JANUARY    985.00       $5,850.00    $487.50
 0 88236 103 1   ANSI COBOL               JANUARY    300.00       JANUARY    300.00       $5,138.50    $428.21
 0 78236 103 1   UNKNOWN                  JANUARY    400.00       JANUARY    400.00       $6,418.25    $534.85
 0 88236 151 1   BASIC FORTRAN IV         JANUARY    800.00       JANUARY    800.00       $6,095.10    $507.93

FINAL TOTALS.

TOTAL SALES   $35,701.85
AVERAGE SALES    $495.86
```

Figure 10-38 Source Listing and Output - Stub Testing [Part 2 of 2]

Pseudocode Specifications - Determine Lowest Month

The pseudocode specifications for the module to determine the lowest monthly sales are illustrated in Figure 10-39.

PSEUDOCODE SPECIFICATIONS

PROGRAM: Sales Analysis	PROGRAMMER: Shelly/Cashman	DATE: June 25

MODULE NAME: Determine Lowest Month	REF: C010	MODULE FUNCTION: Determine Lowest Month

PSEUDOCODE	REF:	FILES, RECORDS, FIELDS REQUIRED

Set low subscript to 1
Set search subscript to 2
PERFORM UNTIL all fields are examined
    IF sales (low subscript) is greater than
        sales (search subscript)
      Move search subscript to low subscript
    ENDIF
    Add 1 to search subscript
ENDPERFORM
		Sales fields
		Low subscript
		Search subscript

Figure 10-39 Pseudocode Specifications - Determine Lowest Monthly Sales

It is extremely important to understand the logic involved in searching the Sales fields to determine the lowest monthly sales. The diagrams below and on the following pages explain this logic.

In the diagram below it can be seen that the input record is read into storage and each of the Sales fields on the card is stored as an element in a list.

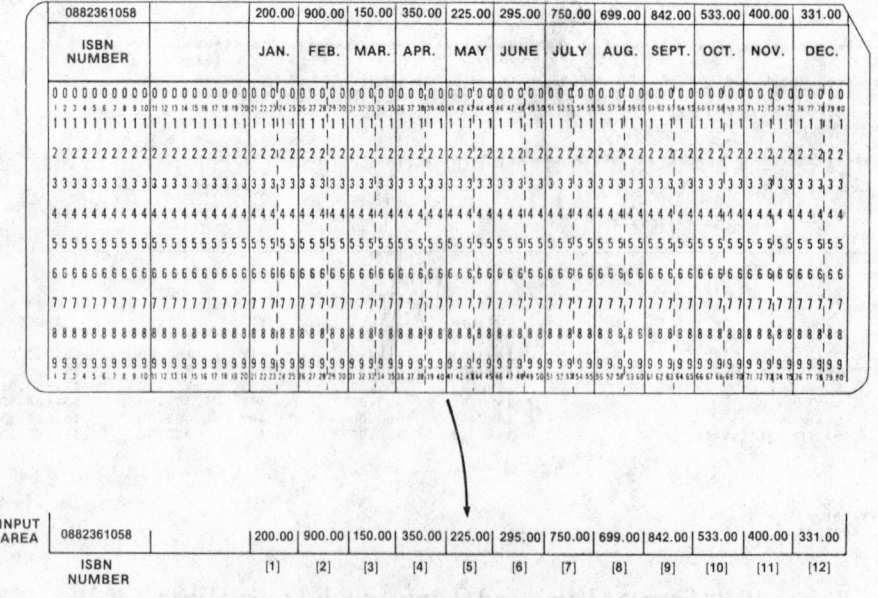

Figure 10-40 Reading and Storing an Input Record

1. The Low Subscript is initialized to the value 1 and the Search Subscript is initialized to the value 2. Then, the sales for the first month, as referenced by the Low Subscript, are compared to the sales for the second month, as referenced by the Search Subscript. This is illustrated below.

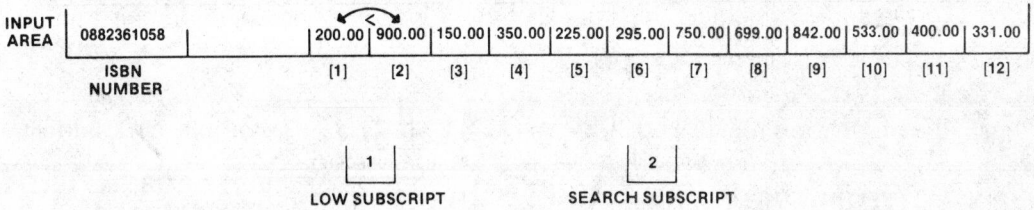

Figure 10-41 Example of List Search

Note in the example above that the value in the first Sales input field, as referenced by the Low Subscript, is compared to the value in the second Sales input field, as referenced by the Search Subscript. As can be seen, the value in the first field is less than the value in the second field. Therefore, according to the pseudocode in Figure 10-39, the only processing which will occur is that the value in the Search Subscript is incremented by 1. Since all of the elements in the Sales input field have not yet been examined, the loop will be performed again.

2. The value in the third element of the Sales input field is compared to the value in the first Sales input field.

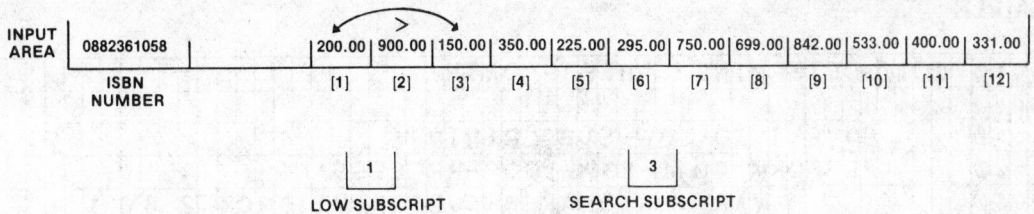

Figure 10-42 Example of List Search

Note in the example above that the value in the first element is compared to the value in the third element of the Sales input field. In this case, the value in the first element, which is referenced by the Low Subscript, is greater than the value in the third element, referenced by Search Subscript. Therefore, according to the pseudocode in Figure 10-39, the value in the Search Subscript would be moved to the Low Subscript field. As a result of this move, it can be seen that the Low Subscript field contains the number of the lowest sales value which has been found thus far in the search of the Sales input fields. The value in the Search Subscript field would be incremented by 1 and, since there are more fields to be examined, the loop would be performed again.

3. The value in the third element of the Sales input field is compared to the value in the fourth element of the Sales input field.

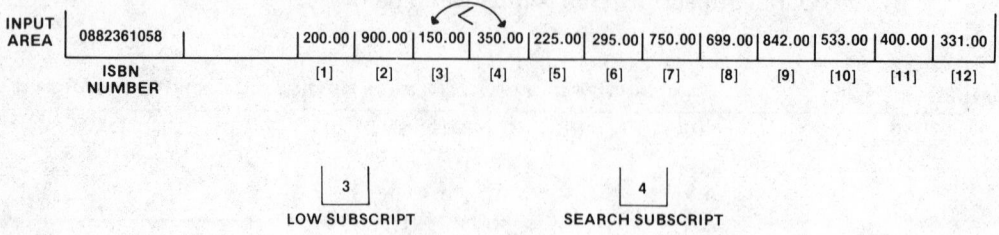

Figure 10-43 Example of List Search

Note from Figure 10-43 that the third element, as referenced by the Low Subscript, is compared to the fourth element, as referenced by the Search Subscript. Since the third element is less than the fourth element, the Search Subscript would be incremented by one; and the loop would continue, searching for the lowest Sales value. After all elements in the list have been examined in this fashion, the value in the Low Subscript field would reference the lowest sales in the list. This value would be returned to the Process Detail Record module, where the name of the month with the lowest sales and the Sales Amount will be moved to the printer output area.

The COBOL coding to implement this processing is illustrated in Figure 10-44.

EXAMPLE

```
019010  CØ1Ø-DETERMINE-LOWEST-MONTH.
019020
019030      MOVE 1 TO LOW-SUBSCRIPT.
019040      PERFORM CØ11-LOW-LOOP-PROCESSING
019050          VARYING SEARCH-SUBSCRIPT FROM 2 BY 1
019060          UNTIL SEARCH-SUBSCRIPT IS GREATER THAN 12.
019070
019080
019090
019100  CØ11-LOW-LOOP-PROCESSING.
019110
019120      IF SALES-INPUT (LOW-SUBSCRIPT) IS GREATER THAN
019130          SALES-INPUT (SEARCH-SUBSCRIPT)
019140      MOVE SEARCH-SUBSCRIPT TO LOW-SUBSCRIPT.
```

Figure 10-44 Example of Coding for List Search

Note in the example that the Move Statement on line 019030 sets the LOW-SUBSCRIPT to the value 1. The Perform Varying Statement then initializes the SEARCH-SUBSCRIPT to the value 2 (FROM 2) and indicates that the SEARCH-SUBSCRIPT is to be incremented by 1 (BY 1). The loop is then performed.

Pseudocode Specifications - Determine Highest Month

The steps involved in determining the month with the highest sales are quite similar to the steps involved in determining the month with the lowest sales. To determine the month with the highest sales, a High Subscript and a Search Subscript are used as pointers to allow the fields in the input record to be compared to one another. When the comparing process begins, the first month is compared to the second month. The subscript of the higher field is placed in the High Subscript field and then the next field is compared to the field referenced by the High Subscript. This processing continues until all of the fields have been compared and the subscript of the highest field has been placed in the High Subscript field. The pseudocode specifications for the module which determines the highest month are illustrated below.

PSEUDOCODE SPECIFICATIONS

PROGRAM: Sales Analysis		PROGRAMMER: Shelly/Cashman	DATE: June 25
MODULE NAME: Determine Highest Month	REF: C020	MODULE FUNCTION: Determine Highest Month	

PSEUDOCODE	REF:	FILES, RECORDS, FIELDS REQUIRED

Set high subscript to 1
Set search subscript to 2
PERFORM UNTIL all fields are examined
    IF sales (high subscript) is less than
        sales (search subscript)
      Move search subscript to high subscript
    ENDIF
    Add 1 to search subscript
ENDPERFORM
		Sales fields
		High subscript
		Search subscript

Figure 10-45 Pseudocode Specifications - Determine Highest Month

Note from the pseudocode specifications in Figure 10-45 that the only difference between the technique used to determine the highest month and that used when determining the lowest month (see Figure 10-39) is the compare statement within the Perform loop. In the determination of the highest month, if the sales referenced by the High Subscript are less than the sales referenced by the Search Subscript, then the Search Subscript is moved to the High Subscript. This ensures that when the loop is completed, the High Subscript field contains the subscript of the field containing the highest monthly sales.

SUMMARY

The use of tables and lists play an important part in business application programming. The programmer should have a good command of the COBOL statements necessary to effectively use tables and lists.

SOURCE LISTING

The following pages contain the source listing of the sample program.

```
    1                          IBM DOS AMERICAN NATIONAL STANDARD COBOL          CBF CL3-4        07/21/77

00001    001010 IDENTIFICATION DIVISION.                                                SALESANA
00002    001020                                                                         SALESANA
00003    001030 PROGRAM-ID.     SALESANA.                                               SALESANA
00004    001040 AUTHOR.         SHELLY AND CASHMAN.                                     SALESANA
00005    001050 INSTALLATION. ANAHEIM.                                                  SALESANA
00006    001060 DATE-WRITTEN. 07/21/77.                                                 SALESANA
00007    001070 DATE-COMPILED. 07/21/77                                                 SALESANA
00008    001080 SECURITY.       SECRET.                                                 SALESANA
00009    001090                                                                         SALESANA
00010    001100*********************************************************** *            SALESANA
00011    001110*                                                          *            SALESANA
00012    001120*  THIS PROGRAM PRODUCES A SALES ANALYSIS REPORT. FOR EACH *            SALESANA
00013    001130*  BOOK, THE MONTHLY SALES VALUES ARE COMPARED TO DETERMINE *           SALESANA
00014    001140*  THE MONTH IN WHICH SALES WERE LOWEST AND THE MONTH IN WHICH *         SALESANA
00015    001150*  SALES WERE HIGHEST. THESE VALUES ARE PRINTED, TOGETHER WITH *         SALESANA
00016    001160*  THE TOTAL SALES FOR THE YEAR AND THE AVERAGE MONTHLY SALES. *         SALESANA
00017    001170*  AFTER ALL OF THE DATA IS PROCESSED, THE TOTAL OF ALL SALES *          SALESANA
00018    001180*  AND THE MONTHLY AVERAGE FOR ALL SALES ARE PRINTED.        *           SALESANA
00019    001190*                                                          *            SALESANA
00020    001200*********************************************************** *            SALESANA
00021    002010                                                                         SALESANA
00022    002020                                                                         SALESANA
00023    002030                                                                         SALESANA
00024    002040 ENVIRONMENT DIVISION.                                                   SALESANA
00025    002050                                                                         SALESANA
00026    002060 CONFIGURATION SECTION.                                                  SALESANA
00027    002070                                                                         SALESANA
00028    002080 SOURCE-COMPUTER. IBM-370.                                               SALESANA
00029    002090 OBJECT-COMPUTER. IBM-370.                                               SALESANA
00030    002100 SPECIAL-NAMES.   C01 IS TO-TOP-OF-PAGE.                                 SALESANA
00031    002110                                                                         SALESANA
00032    002120 INPUT-OUTPUT SECTION.                                                   SALESANA
00033    002130                                                                         SALESANA
00034    002140 FILE-CONTROL.                                                           SALESANA
00035    002150     SELECT SALES-INPUT-FILE                                             SALESANA
00036    002160         ASSIGN TO SYS007-UR-2540R-S.                                    SALESANA
00037    002170     SELECT SALES-ANALYSIS-REPORT-FILE                                   SALESANA
00038    002180         ASSIGN TO SYS013-UR-1403-S.                                     SALESANA
```

Figure 10-46 Source Listing [Part 1 of 5]

```
      2
00039  002200 DATA DIVISION.                                          SALESANA
00040  003010                                                         SALESANA
00041  003020 FILE SECTION.                                           SALESANA
00042  003030                                                         SALESANA
00043  003040 FD  SALES-INPUT-FILE                                    SALESANA
00044  003050      RECORD CONTAINS 80 CHARACTERS                      SALESANA
00045  003060      LABEL RECORDS ARE OMITTED                          SALESANA
00046  003070      DATA RECORD IS SALES-INPUT-RECORD.                 SALESANA
00047  003080 01  SALES-INPUT-RECORD.                                 SALESANA
00048  003090     05  ISBN-NUMBER-INPUT        PIC X(10).             SALESANA
00049  003100     05  FILLER                   PIC X(10).             SALESANA
00050  003110     05  SALES-INPUT              PIC 999V99   OCCURS 12 TIMES.  SALESANA
00051  003120                                                         SALESANA
00052  003130 FD  SALES-ANALYSIS-REPORT-FILE                          SALESANA
00053  003140      RECORD CONTAINS 133 CHARACTERS                     SALESANA
00054  003150      LABEL RECORDS ARE OMITTED                          SALESANA
00055  003160      DATA RECORD IS SALES-ANALYSIS-REPORT-LINE.         SALESANA
00056  003170 01  SALES-ANALYSIS-REPORT-LINE.                         SALESANA
00057  003180     05  CARRIAGE-CONTROL         PIC X.                 SALESANA
00058  003190     05  ISBN-NUMBER-REPORT       PIC XBXXXXBXXXBX.      SALESANA
00059  003200     05  FILLER                   PIC X(5).              SALESANA
00060  004010     05  BOOK-TITLE-REPORT        PIC X(30).             SALESANA
00061  004020     05  FILLER                   PIC X(5).              SALESANA
00062  004030     05  LOW-MONTH-REPORT         PIC X(9).              SALESANA
00063  004040     05  FILLER                   PIC XXX.               SALESANA
00064  004050     05  LOW-SALES-REPORT         PIC ZZZ.99.            SALESANA
00065  004060     05  FILLER                   PIC X(5).              SALESANA
00066  004070     05  HIGH-MONTH-REPORT        PIC X(9).              SALESANA
00067  004080     05  FILLER                   PIC XXX.               SALESANA
00068  004090     05  HIGH-SALES-REPORT        PIC ZZZ.99.            SALESANA
00069  004100     05  FILLER                   PIC X(5).              SALESANA
00070  004110     05  YEARLY-SALES-REPORT      PIC $$$,$$$.99.        SALESANA
00071  004120     05  FILLER                   PIC X(5).              SALESANA
00072  004130     05  AVERAGE-MONTHLY-SALES-REPORT PIC $$$$.99.       SALESANA
00073  004140     05  FILLER                   PIC X(11).             SALESANA
00074  004150                                                         SALESANA
00075  004160 WORKING-STORAGE SECTION.                                SALESANA
00076  004170                                                         SALESANA
00077  004180 01  PROGRAM-INDICATORS.                                 SALESANA
00078  004190     05  ARE-THERE-MORE-RECORDS   PIC XXX     VALUE 'YES'.  SALESANA
00079  004200        88  THERE-IS-A-RECORD                VALUE 'YES'.  SALESANA
00080  005010        88  THERE-ARE-NO-MORE-RECORDS        VALUE 'NO '.  SALESANA
00081  005020                                                         SALESANA
00082  005030 01  WORK-AREAS.                                         SALESANA
00083  005040     05  YEARLY-SALES-WORK        PIC S9(5)V99 VALUE ZERO  SALESANA
00084  005050                                                USAGE IS COMP-3.  SALESANA
00085  005060                                                         SALESANA
00086  005070 01  TOTAL-ACCUMULATORS                       USAGE IS COMP-3.  SALESANA
00087  005080     05  NUMBER-OF-MONTHS-ACCUM   PIC S9(5)    VALUE ZERO.  SALESANA
00088  005090     05  TOTAL-SALES-ACCUM        PIC S9(6)V99 VALUE ZERO.  SALESANA
00089  005100                                                         SALESANA
00090  005110 01  SUBSCRIPTS                               USAGE IS COMP.  SALESANA
00091  005120     05  LOW-SUBSCRIPT            PIC S9(8)   SYNC.       SALESANA
00092  005130     05  SEARCH-SUBSCRIPT         PIC S9(8)   SYNC.       SALESANA
00093  005140     05  HIGH-SUBSCRIPT           PIC S9(8)   SYNC.       SALESANA
00094  005150     05  SALES-SUBSCRIPT          PIC S9(8)   SYNC.       SALESANA
00095  005160                                                         SALESANA
00096  005170 01  PROGRAM-TABLES.                                     SALESANA
00097  005180     05  MONTHS-TABLE.                                   SALESANA
00098  005190        10  MONTH-CONSTANTS.                             SALESANA
00099  005200            15  FILLER           PIC X(9)    VALUE 'JANUARY   '.  SALESANA
00100  006010            15  FILLER           PIC X(9)    VALUE 'FEBRUARY  '.  SALESANA
00101  006020            15  FILLER           PIC X(9)    VALUE 'MARCH     '.  SALESANA
00102  006030            15  FILLER           PIC X(9)    VALUE 'APRIL     '.  SALESANA
00103  006040            15  FILLER           PIC X(9)    VALUE 'MAY       '.  SALESANA
00104  006050            15  FILLER           PIC X(9)    VALUE 'JUNE      '.  SALESANA
00105  006060            15  FILLER           PIC X(9)    VALUE 'JULY      '.  SALESANA
00106  006070            15  FILLER           PIC X(9)    VALUE 'AUGUST    '.  SALESANA
00107  006080            15  FILLER           PIC X(9)    VALUE 'SEPTEMBER '.  SALESANA
00108  006090            15  FILLER           PIC X(9)    VALUE 'OCTOBER   '.  SALESANA
00109  006100            15  FILLER           PIC X(9)    VALUE 'NOVEMBER  '.  SALESANA
00110  006110            15  FILLER           PIC X(9)    VALUE 'DECEMBER  '.  SALESANA
00111  006120        10  MONTH-TABLE REDEFINES MONTH-CONSTANTS        SALESANA
00112  006130                                 PIC X(9)    OCCURS 12 TIMES.  SALESANA
00113  006140     05  BOOK-TABLE.                                     SALESANA
00114  006150        10  BOOK-CONSTANTS.                              SALESANA
00115  006160            15  FILLER           PIC X(40)   VALUE       SALESANA
00116  006170                 '0882360434SYSTEMS ANALYSIS AND DESIGN     '.SALESANA
00117  006180            15  FILLER           PIC X(40)   VALUE       SALESANA
00118  006190                 '0882360507ASSEMBLER LANGUAGE              '.SALESANA
00119  006200            15  FILLER           PIC X(40)   VALUE       SALESANA
00120  007010                 '0882360515ASSEMBLER LANGUAGE WORKBOOK     '.SALESANA
00121  007020            15  FILLER           PIC X(40)   VALUE       SALESANA
00122  007030                 '0882360604ADVANCED ASSEMBLER LANGUAGE     '.SALESANA
00123  007040            15  FILLER           PIC X(40)   VALUE       SALESANA
00124  007050                 '0882361007SYSTEM/360 COBOL               '.SALESANA
00125  007060            15  FILLER           PIC X(40)   VALUE       SALESANA
00126  007070                 '0882361015SYSTEM/360 COBOL PROBLEM TEXT   '.SALESANA
00127  007080            15  FILLER           PIC X(40)   VALUE       SALESANA
00128  007090                 '0882361031ANSI COBOL                     '.SALESANA
00129  007100            15  FILLER           PIC X(40)   VALUE       SALESANA
00130  007110                 '088236104XANSI COBOL WORKBOOK            '.SALESANA
00131  007120            15  FILLER           PIC X(40)   VALUE       SALESANA
00132  007130                 '0882361058ADVANCED ANSI COBOL            '.SALESANA
00133  007140            15  FILLER           PIC X(40)   VALUE       SALESANA
00134  007150                 '0882361104ADVANCED SYSTEM/360 COBOL       '.SALESANA
00135  007160            15  FILLER           PIC X(40)   VALUE       SALESANA
00136  007170                 '0882361112STRUCTURED COBOL               '.SALESANA
00137  007180            15  FILLER           PIC X(40)   VALUE       SALESANA
00138  007190                 '0882361511BASIC FORTRAN IV               '.SALESANA
00139  007200            15  FILLER           PIC X(40)   VALUE       SALESANA
00140  008010                 '0882361775COMPUTERS IN OUR SOCIETY        '.SALESANA
```

Figure 10-47 Source Listing [Part 2 of 5]

```
 3
00141  008020           15  FILLER        PIC X(40)     VALUE                    SALESANA
00142  008030                       '0882361783COMPUTERS IN OUR SOC. WORKBOOK'.SALESANA
00143  008040           15  FILLER        PIC X(40)     VALUE                    SALESANA
00144  008050                       '0882361791PROGRAMMING IN BASIC            '.SALESANA
00145  008060           15  FILLER        PIC X(40)     VALUE                    SALESANA
00146  008070                       '0882361805BASIC WITH APPLICATIONS         '.SALESANA
00147  008080           15  FILLER        PIC X(40)     VALUE                    SALESANA
00148  008090                       '0882361902SYSTEM/360 PL/I                 '.SALESANA
00149  008100           15  FILLER        PIC X(40)     VALUE                    SALESANA
00150  008110                       '0882362259INTRODUCTION TO RPG             '.SALESANA
00151  008120           15  FILLER        PIC X(40)     VALUE                    SALESANA
00152  008130                       '0882362267COMPUTER PROGRAMMING RPG II     '.SALESANA
00153  008140       10  BOOK-CONSTANTS-TABLE REDEFINES BOOK-CONSTANTS           SALESANA
00154  008150                                   OCCURS 19 TIMES                  SALESANA
00155  008160                                   ASCENDING KEY IS                 SALESANA
00156  008170                                   ISBN-TABLE                       SALESANA
00157  008180                                   INDEXED BY BOOK-IND.SALESANA
00158  008190           15  ISBN-TABLE       PIC X(10).                          SALESANA
00159  008200           15  BOOK-TITLE-TABLE PIC X(30).                          SALESANA
00160  009010                                                                    SALESANA
00161  009020 01  PRINTER-CONTROL.                                               SALESANA
00162  009030     05  PROPER-SPACING        PIC 9.                               SALESANA
00163  009040     05  SPACE-ONE-LINE        PIC 9       VALUE 1.                 SALESANA
00164  009050     05  SPACE-TWO-LINES       PIC 9       VALUE 2.                 SALESANA
00165  009060     05  LINES-PRINTED         PIC S999    VALUE ZERO               SALESANA
00166  009070                                           USAGE IS COMP-3.         SALESANA
00167  009080     05  PAGE-SIZE             PIC 999     VALUE 50                 SALESANA
00168  009090                                           USAGE IS COMP-3.         SALESANA
00169  009100     05  PAGE-COUNT            PIC S999    VALUE +1                 SALESANA
00170  009110                                           USAGE IS COMP-3.         SALESANA
00171  009120         88  FIRST-PAGE                    VALUE +1.                SALESANA
00172  009130                                                                    SALESANA
00173  009140 01  REPORT-HEADINGS.                                               SALESANA
00174  009150     05  FIRST-HEADING-LINE.                                        SALESANA
00175  009160         10  CARRIAGE-CONTROL  PIC X.                               SALESANA
00176  009170         10  DATE-HEADING      PIC X(8).                            SALESANA
00177  009180         10  FILLER            PIC X(42)   VALUE SPACES.            SALESANA
00178  009190         10  FILLER            PIC X(6)    VALUE 'SALES '.          SALESANA
00179  009200         10  FILLER            PIC X(9)    VALUE 'ANALYSIS '.       SALESANA
00180  010010         10  FILLER            PIC X(6)    VALUE 'REPORT'.          SALESANA
00181  010020         10  FILLER            PIC X(42)   VALUE SPACES.            SALESANA
00182  010030         10  FILLER            PIC X(5)    VALUE 'PAGE '.           SALESANA
00183  010040         10  PAGE-HEADING      PIC ZZ9.                             SALESANA
00184  010050         10  FILLER            PIC X(11)   VALUE SPACES.            SALESANA
00185  010060     05  SECOND-HEADING-LINE.                                       SALESANA
00186  010070         10  CARRIAGE-CONTROL  PIC X.                               SALESANA
00187  010080         10  FILLER            PIC X(5)    VALUE SPACES.            SALESANA
00188  010090         10  FILLER            PIC X(4)    VALUE 'ISBN'.            SALESANA
00189  010100         10  FILLER            PIC X(43)   VALUE SPACES.            SALESANA
00190  010110         10  FILLER            PIC X(7)    VALUE 'LOWEST '.         SALESANA
00191  010120         10  FILLER            PIC X(8)    VALUE 'MONTHLY '.        SALESANA
00192  010130         10  FILLER            PIC X(5)    VALUE 'SALES'.           SALESANA
00193  010140         10  FILLER            PIC XXX     VALUE SPACES.            SALESANA
00194  010150         10  FILLER            PIC X(9)    VALUE 'HIGHEST '.        SALESANA
00195  010160         10  FILLER            PIC X(8)    VALUE 'MONTHLY '.        SALESANA
00196  010170         10  FILLER            PIC X(5)    VALUE 'SALES'.           SALESANA
00197  010180         10  FILLER            PIC X(6)    VALUE SPACES.            SALESANA
00198  010190         10  FILLER            PIC X(5)    VALUE 'YEARLY'.          SALESANA
00199  010200         10  FILLER            PIC X(6)    VALUE SPACES.            SALESANA
00200  011010         10  FILLER            PIC X(7)    VALUE 'AVERAGE'.         SALESANA
00201  011020         10  FILLER            PIC X(11)   VALUE SPACES.            SALESANA
00202  011030     05  THIRD-HEADING-LINE.                                        SALESANA
00203  011040         10  CARRIAGE-CONTROL  PIC X.                               SALESANA
00204  011050         10  FILLER            PIC X(4)    VALUE SPACE.             SALESANA
00205  011060         10  FILLER            PIC X(6)    VALUE 'NUMBER'.          SALESANA
00206  011070         10  FILLER            PIC X(18)   VALUE SPACES.            SALESANA
00207  011080         10  FILLER            PIC X(10)   VALUE 'BOOK TITLE'.      SALESANA
00208  011090         10  FILLER            PIC X(17)   VALUE SPACES.            SALESANA
00209  011100         10  FILLER            PIC X(5)    VALUE 'MONTH'.           SALESANA
00210  011110         10  FILLER            PIC X(6)    VALUE SPACES.            SALESANA
00211  011120         10  FILLER            PIC X(5)    VALUE 'SALES'.           SALESANA
00212  011130         10  FILLER            PIC X(7)    VALUE SPACES.            SALESANA
00213  011140         10  FILLER            PIC X(5)    VALUE 'MONTH'.           SALESANA
00214  011150         10  FILLER            PIC X(6)    VALUE SPACES.            SALESANA
00215  011160         10  FILLER            PIC X(5)    VALUE 'SALES'.           SALESANA
00216  011170         10  FILLER            PIC X(8)    VALUE SPACES.            SALESANA
00217  011180         10  FILLER            PIC X(5)    VALUE 'SALES'.           SALESANA
00218  011190         10  FILLER            PIC X(8)    VALUE SPACES.            SALESANA
00219  011200         10  FILLER            PIC X(5)    VALUE 'SALES'.           SALESANA
00220  012010         10  FILLER            PIC X(12)   VALUE SPACES.            SALESANA
00221  012020                                                                    SALESANA
00222  012030 01  TOTAL-LINES.                                                   SALESANA
00223  012040     05  FINAL-TOTAL-CONSTANT-LINE.                                 SALESANA
00224  012050         10  CARRIAGE-CONTROL  PIC X.                               SALESANA
00225  012060         10  FILLER            PIC X(12)   VALUE                    SALESANA
00226  012070                                           'FINAL TOTALS'.          SALESANA
00227  012080         10  FILLER            PIC X(120)  VALUE SPACES.            SALESANA
00228  012090     05  SALES-TOTAL-LINE.                                          SALESANA
00229  012100         10  CARRIAGE-CONTROL  PIC X.                               SALESANA
00230  012110         10  FILLER            PIC X(11)   VALUE 'TOTAL SALES'.     SALESANA
00231  012120         10  FILLER            PIC X       VALUE SPACE.             SALESANA
00232  012130         10  TOTAL-SALES-FINAL PIC $$$$,$$$.99.                     SALESANA
00233  012140         10  FILLER            PIC X(109)  VALUE SPACES.            SALESANA
00234  012150     05  AVERAGE-TOTAL-LINE.                                        SALESANA
00235  012160         10  CARRIAGE-CONTROL  PIC X.                               SALESANA
00236  012170         10  FILLER            PIC X(16)   VALUE                    SALESANA
00237  012180                                           'AVERAGE SALES  '.       SALESANA
00238  012190         10  SALES-AVERAGE-FINAL PIC $$$.99.                        SALESANA
00239  012200         10  FILLER            PIC X(109)  VALUE SPACES.            SALESANA
```

Figure 10-48 Source Listing [Part 3 of 5]

```
    4
00240  013020 PROCEDURE DIVISION.                                              SALESANA
00241  013030                                                                  SALESANA
00242  013040*************************************************************     SALESANA
00243  013050*                                                           *     SALESANA
00244  013060* THIS MODULE OBTAINS THE INPUT DATA AND CAUSES THE DETAIL  *     SALESANA
00245  013070* PROCESSING AND FINAL TOTAL PROCESSING TO OCCUR. IT IS     *     SALESANA
00246  013080* ENTERED FROM AND EXITS TO THE OPERATING SYSTEM.           *     SALESANA
00247  013090*                                                           *     SALESANA
00248  013100*************************************************************     SALESANA
00249  013110                                                                  SALESANA
00250  013120 A000-CREATE-SALES-REPORT.                                        SALESANA
00251  013130                                                                  SALESANA
00252  013140     OPEN INPUT  SALES-INPUT-FILE                                 SALESANA
00253  013150          OUTPUT SALES-ANALYSIS-REPORT-FILE.                      SALESANA
00254  013160     READ SALES-INPUT-FILE                                        SALESANA
00255  013170         AT END                                                   SALESANA
00256  013180             MOVE 'NO ' TO ARE-THERE-MORE-RECORDS.                SALESANA
00257  013190     IF THERE-IS-A-RECORD                                         SALESANA
00258  013200         PERFORM A001-PROCESS-AND-READ                            SALESANA
00259  014010             UNTIL THERE-ARE-NO-MORE-RECORDS.                     SALESANA
00260  014020     PERFORM B010-PRINT-FINAL-TOTALS.                             SALESANA
00261  014030     CLOSE SALES-INPUT-FILE                                       SALESANA
00262  014040           SALES-ANALYSIS-REPORT-FILE.                            SALESANA
00263  014050     STOP RUN.                                                    SALESANA
00264  014060                                                                  SALESANA
00265  014070                                                                  SALESANA
00266  014080 A001-PROCESS-AND-READ.                                           SALESANA
00267  014090                                                                  SALESANA
00268  014100     PERFORM B000-PROCESS-DETAIL-RECORDS.                         SALESANA
00269  014110     READ SALES-INPUT-FILE                                        SALESANA
00270  014120         AT END                                                   SALESANA
00271  014130             MOVE 'NO ' TO ARE-THERE-MORE-RECORDS.                SALESANA

    5
00272  014150*************************************************************     SALESANA
00273  014160*                                                           *     SALESANA
00274  014170* THIS MODULE PROCESSES THE DETAIL RECORDS BY FORMATTING THE*     SALESANA
00275  014180* REPORT LINE.  A TABLE IS SEARCHED FOR THE BOOK TITLE, THE *     SALESANA
00276  014190* LOWEST AND HIGHEST SALES ARE DETERMINED, THE YEARLY SALES *     SALESANA
00277  014200* AND AVERAGE SALES CALCULATED, AND FINAL TOTAL ACCUMULATED.*     SALESANA
00278  015010* IT IS ENTERED AND EXITS TO THE A000-CREATE-SALES-REPORT   *     SALESANA
00279  015020* MODULE.                                                   *     SALESANA
00280  015030*                                                           *     SALESANA
00281  015040*************************************************************     SALESANA
00282  015050                                                                  SALESANA
00283  015060 B000-PROCESS-DETAIL-RECORDS.                                     SALESANA
00284  015070                                                                  SALESANA
00285  015080     IF LINES-PRINTED IS EQUAL TO PAGE-SIZE OR                    SALESANA
00286  015090        IS GREATER THAN PAGE-SIZE OR                              SALESANA
00287  015100        FIRST-PAGE                                                SALESANA
00288  015110         PERFORM C000-PRINT-HEADINGS.                             SALESANA
00289  015120     MOVE SPACES TO SALES-ANALYSIS-REPORT-LINE.                   SALESANA
00290  015130     MOVE ISBN-NUMBER-INPUT TO ISBN-NUMBER-REPORT.                SALESANA
00291  015140     SEARCH ALL BOOK-CONSTANTS-TABLE                              SALESANA
00292  015150         AT END                                                   SALESANA
00293  015160             MOVE 'UNKNOWN' TO BOOK-TITLE-REPORT                  SALESANA
00294  015170         WHEN ISBN-TABLE (BOOK-IND) = ISBN-NUMBER-INPUT           SALESANA
00295  015180             MOVE BOOK-TITLE-TABLE (BOOK-IND)                     SALESANA
00296  015190                 TO BOOK-TITLE-REPORT.                            SALESANA
00297  015200     PERFORM C010-DETERMINE-LOWEST-MONTH.                         SALESANA
00298  016010     MOVE MONTH-TABLE (LOW-SUBSCRIPT) TO LOW-MONTH-REPORT.        SALESANA
00299  016020     MOVE SALES-INPUT (LOW-SUBSCRIPT) TO LOW-SALES-REPORT.        SALESANA
00300  016030     PERFORM C020-DETERMINE-HIGHEST-MONTH.                        SALESANA
00301  016040     MOVE MONTH-TABLE (HIGH-SUBSCRIPT) TO HIGH-MONTH-REPORT.      SALESANA
00302  016050     MOVE SALES-INPUT (HIGH-SUBSCRIPT) TO HIGH-SALES-REPORT.      SALESANA
00303  016060     PERFORM B001-CALCULATE-TOTAL-SALES                           SALESANA
00304  016070         VARYING SALES-SUBSCRIPT FROM 1 BY 1                      SALESANA
00305  016080             UNTIL SALES-SUBSCRIPT IS GREATER THAN 12.            SALESANA
00306  016090     MOVE YEARLY-SALES-WORK TO YEARLY-SALES-REPORT.               SALESANA
00307  016100     COMPUTE AVERAGE-MONTHLY-SALES-REPORT ROUNDED =               SALESANA
00308  016110             YEARLY-SALES-WORK / 12.                              SALESANA
00309  016120     ADD YEARLY-SALES-WORK TO TOTAL-SALES-ACCUM.                  SALESANA
00310  016130     ADD 12 TO NUMBER-OF-MONTHS-ACCUM.                            SALESANA
00311  016140     MOVE ZEROS TO YEARLY-SALES-WORK.                             SALESANA
00312  016150     WRITE SALES-ANALYSIS-REPORT-LINE                             SALESANA
00313  016160             AFTER PROPER-SPACING.                                SALESANA
00314  016170     MOVE SPACE-ONE-LINE TO PROPER-SPACING.                       SALESANA
00315  016180     ADD 1 TO LINES-PRINTED.                                      SALESANA
00316  016190                                                                  SALESANA
00317  016200                                                                  SALESANA
00318  017010                                                                  SALESANA
00319  017020 B001-CALCULATE-TOTAL-SALES.                                      SALESANA
00320  017030                                                                  SALESANA
00321  017040     ADD SALES-INPUT (SALES-SUBSCRIPT) TO                         SALESANA
00322  017050             YEARLY-SALES-WORK.                                   SALESANA
```

Figure 10-49 Source Listing [Part 4 of 5]

```
    6
00323   017070***************************************************  SALESANA
00324   017080*                                                 *  SALESANA
00325   017090*   THIS MODULE PRINTS THE FINAL TOTALS ON THE REPORT. IT IS  *  SALESANA
00326   017100*   ENTERED FROM AND EXITS TO THE A000-CREATE-SALES-REPORT    *  SALESANA
00327   017110*   MODULE.                                       *  SALESANA
00328   017120*                                                 *  SALESANA
00329   017130***************************************************  SALESANA
00330   017140                                                     SALESANA
00331   017150 B010-PRINT-FINAL-TOTALS.                            SALESANA
00332   017160                                                     SALESANA
00333   017170     WRITE SALES-ANALYSIS-REPORT-LINE FROM           SALESANA
00334   017180         FINAL-TOTAL-CONSTANT-LINE                   SALESANA
00335   017190         AFTER ADVANCING 3 LINES.                    SALESANA
00336   017200     MOVE TOTAL-SALES-ACCUM TO TOTAL-SALES-FINAL.    SALESANA
00337   018010     WRITE SALES-ANALYSIS-REPORT-LINE FROM SALES-TOTAL-LINE  SALESANA
00338   018020         AFTER ADVANCING 2 LINES.                    SALESANA
00339   018030     DIVIDE TOTAL-SALES-ACCUM BY NUMBER-OF-MONTHS-ACCUM GIVING  SALESANA
00340   018040         SALES-AVERAGE-FINAL ROUNDED.                SALESANA
00341   018050     WRITE SALES-ANALYSIS-REPORT-LINE FROM AVERAGE-TOTAL-LINE  SALESANA
00342   018060         AFTER ADVANCING 1 LINES.                    SALESANA

    7
00343   018080***************************************************  SALESANA
00344   018090*                                                 *  SALESANA
00345   018100*   THIS MODULE PRINTS THE HEADING ON THE REPORT. IT IS ENTERED  *  SALESANA
00346   018110*   FROM AND EXITS TO THE B000-PROCESS-DETAIL-RECORDS MODULE.    *  SALESANA
00347   018120*                                                 *  SALESANA
00348   018130***************************************************  SALESANA
00349   018140                                                     SALESANA
00350   018150 C000-PRINT-HEADINGS.                                SALESANA
00351   018160                                                     SALESANA
00352   018170     MOVE CURRENT-DATE TO DATE-HEADING.              SALESANA
00353   018180     MOVE PAGE-COUNT TO PAGE-HEADING.                SALESANA
00354   018190     WRITE SALES-ANALYSIS-REPORT-LINE FROM FIRST-HEADING-LINE  SALESANA
00355   018200         AFTER ADVANCING TO-TOP-OF-PAGE.             SALESANA
00356   019010     ADD 1 TO PAGE-COUNT.                            SALESANA
00357   019020     WRITE SALES-ANALYSIS-REPORT-LINE FROM SECOND-HEADING-LINE  SALESANA
00358   019030         AFTER ADVANCING 2 LINES.                    SALESANA
00359   019040     WRITE SALES-ANALYSIS-REPORT-LINE FROM THIRD-HEADING-LINE  SALESANA
00360   019050         AFTER ADVANCING 1 LINES.                    SALESANA
00361   019060     MOVE SPACE-TWO-LINES TO PROPER-SPACING.         SALESANA
00362   019070     MOVE ZERO TO LINES-PRINTED.                     SALESANA

    8
00363   019090***************************************************  SALESANA
00364   019100*                                                 *  SALESANA
00365   019110*   THIS MODULE DETERMINES THE MONTH OF THE LOWEST SALES. IT  *  SALESANA
00366   019120*   RETURNS THE SUBSCRIPT OF THE LOWEST SALES MONTH. IT IS  *  SALESANA
00367   019130*   ENTERED FROM AND EXITS TO THE B000-PROCESS-DETAIL-RECORDS  *  SALESANA
00368   019140*   MODULE.                                       *  SALESANA
00369   019150*                                                 *  SALESANA
00370   019160***************************************************  SALESANA
00371   019170                                                     SALESANA
00372   019180 C010-DETERMINE-LOWEST-MONTH.                        SALESANA
00373   019190                                                     SALESANA
00374   019200     MOVE 1 TO LOW-SUBSCRIPT.                        SALESANA
00375   020010     PERFORM C011-LOW-LOOP-PROCESSING                SALESANA
00376   020020         VARYING SEARCH-SUBSCRIPT FROM 2 BY 1        SALESANA
00377   020030         UNTIL SEARCH-SUBSCRIPT IS GREATER THAN 12.  SALESANA
00378   020040                                                     SALESANA
00379   020050                                                     SALESANA
00380   020060                                                     SALESANA
00381   020070 C011-LOW-LOOP-PROCESSING.                           SALESANA
00382   020080                                                     SALESANA
00383   020090     IF SALES-INPUT (LOW-SUBSCRIPT) IS GREATER THAN  SALESANA
00384   020100         SALES-INPUT (SEARCH-SUBSCRIPT)              SALESANA
00385   020110         MOVE SEARCH-SUBSCRIPT TO LOW-SUBSCRIPT.     SALESANA

    9
00386   020130***************************************************  SALESANA
00387   020140*                                                 *  SALESANA
00388   020150*   THIS MODULE DETERMINES THE MONTH OF THE HIGHEST SALES. IT  *  SALESANA
00389   020160*   RETURNS THE SUBSCRIPT OF THE HIGHEST SALES MONTH. IT IS  *  SALESANA
00390   020170*   ENTERED FROM AND EXITS TO THE B000-PROCESS-DETAIL-RECORDS  *  SALESANA
00391   020180*   MODULE.                                       *  SALESANA
00392   020190*                                                 *  SALESANA
00393   020200***************************************************  SALESANA
00394   021010                                                     SALESANA
00395   021020 C020-DETERMINE-HIGHEST-MONTH.                       SALESANA
00396   021030                                                     SALESANA
00397   021040     MOVE 1 TO HIGH-SUBSCRIPT.                       SALESANA
00398   021050     PERFORM C021-HIGH-LOOP-PROCESSING               SALESANA
00399   021060         VARYING SEARCH-SUBSCRIPT FROM 2 BY 1        SALESANA
00400   021070         UNTIL SEARCH-SUBSCRIPT IS GREATER THAN 12.  SALESANA
00401   021080                                                     SALESANA
00402   021090                                                     SALESANA
00403   021100                                                     SALESANA
00404   021110 C021-HIGH-LOOP-PROCESSING.                          SALESANA
00405   021120                                                     SALESANA
00406   021130     IF SALES-INPUT (HIGH-SUBSCRIPT) IS LESS THAN    SALESANA
00407   021140         SALES-INPUT (SEARCH-SUBSCRIPT)              SALESANA
00408   021150         MOVE SEARCH-SUBSCRIPT TO HIGH-SUBSCRIPT.    SALESANA
```

Figure 10-50 Source Listing [Part 5 of 5]

CHAPTER 10

REVIEW QUESTIONS

1. What are the advantages of defining adjacent fields with the same attributes with the Occurs Clause rather than giving them separate names?

2. What are the advantages of the SEARCH ALL Statement over the SEARCH Statement?

3. What are the advantages of the SEARCH Statement over the SEARCH ALL Statement?

4. Explain the differences between a sequential table search and a binary table search.

5. What are the advantages of Stub Testing?

CHAPTER 10

DEBUGGING COBOL PROGRAMS

PROBLEM 1

INSTRUCTIONS

The following COBOL program contains an error or errors which occurred during execution. Circle each error and record the corrected entries directly on the listing. Explain the error and method of correction in the space provided below.

```
1                        IBM DOS AMERICAN NATIONAL STANDARD COBOL        CBF CL3-4        07/21/77

00001   001010 IDENTIFICATION DIVISION.                                   SALESANA
00002   001020                                                            SALESANA
00003   001030 PROGRAM-ID.    SALESANA.                                   SALESANA
00004   001040 AUTHOR.        SHELLY AND CASHMAN.                         SALESANA
00005   001050 INSTALLATION.  ANAHEIM.                                    SALESANA
00006   001060 DATE-WRITTEN.  07/21/77.                                   SALESANA
00007   001070 DATE-COMPILED. 07/21/77                                    SALESANA
00008   001080 SECURITY.      SECRET.                                     SALESANA
00009   001090                                                            SALESANA
00010   001100*************************************************************SALESANA
00011   001110*                                                          *SALESANA
00012   001120*  THIS PROGRAM PRODUCES A SALES ANALYSIS REPORT. FOR EACH *SALESANA
00013   001130*  BOOK, THE MONTHLY SALES VALUES ARE COMPARED TO DETERMINE*SALESANA
00014   001140*  THE MONTH IN WHICH SALES WERE LOWEST AND THE MONTH IN WHICH *SALESANA
00015   001150*  SALES WERE HIGHEST. THESE VALUES ARE PRINTED, TOGETHER WITH *SALESANA
00016   001160*  THE TOTAL SALES FOR THE YEAR AND THE AVERAGE MONTHLY SALES. *SALESANA
00017   001170*  AFTER ALL OF THE DATA IS PROCESSED, THE TOTAL OF ALL SALES *SALESANA
00018   001180*  AND THE MONTHLY AVERAGE FOR ALL SALES ARE PRINTED.       *SALESANA
00019   001190*                                                          *SALESANA
00020   001200*************************************************************SALESANA
00021   002010                                                            SALESANA
00022   002020                                                            SALESANA
00023   002030                                                            SALESANA
00024   002040 ENVIRONMENT DIVISION.                                      SALESANA
00025   002050                                                            SALESANA
00026   002060 CONFIGURATION SECTION.                                     SALESANA
00027   002070                                                            SALESANA
00028   002080 SOURCE-COMPUTER. IBM-370.                                  SALESANA
00029   002090 OBJECT-COMPUTER. IBM-370.                                  SALESANA
00030   002100 SPECIAL-NAMES.   C01 IS TO-TOP-OF-PAGE.                    SALESANA
00031   002110                                                            SALESANA
00032   002120 INPUT-OUTPUT SECTION.                                      SALESANA
00033   002130                                                            SALESANA
00034   002140 FILE-CONTROL.                                              SALESANA
00035   002150     SELECT SALES-INPUT-FILE                                SALESANA
00036   002160         ASSIGN TO SYS007-UR-2540R-S.                       SALESANA
00037   002170     SELECT SALES-ANALYSIS-REPORT-FILE                      SALESANA
00038   002180         ASSIGN TO SYS013-UR-1403-S.                        SALESANA

2

00039   002200 DATA DIVISION.                                             SALESANA
00040   003010                                                            SALESANA
00041   003020 FILE SECTION.                                              SALESANA
00042   003030                                                            SALESANA
00043   003040 FD  SALES-INPUT-FILE                                       SALESANA
00044   003050     RECORD CONTAINS 80 CHARACTERS                          SALESANA
00045   003060     LABEL RECORDS ARE OMITTED                              SALESANA
00046   003070     DATA RECORD IS SALES-INPUT-RECORD.                     SALESANA
00047   003080 01  SALES-INPUT-RECORD.                                    SALESANA
00048   003090     05  ISBN-NUMBER-INPUT       PIC X(10).                 SALESANA
00049   003100     05  FILLER                  PIC X(10).                 SALESANA
00050   003110     05  SALES-INPUT             PIC 999V99  OCCURS 12 TIMES. SALESANA
00051   003120                                                            SALESANA
00052   003130 FD  SALES-ANALYSIS-REPORT-FILE                             SALESANA
00053   003140     RECORD CONTAINS 133 CHARACTERS                         SALESANA
00054   003150     LABEL RECORDS ARE OMITTED                              SALESANA
00055   003160     DATA RECORD IS SALES-ANALYSIS-REPORT-LINE.             SALESANA
00056   003170 01  SALES-ANALYSIS-REPORT-LINE.                            SALESANA
00057   003180     05  CARRIAGE-CONTROL        PIC X.                     SALESANA
00058   003190     05  ISBN-NUMBER-REPORT      PIC XBXXXXXBXXXBX.         SALESANA
00059   003200     05  FILLER                  PIC X(5).                  SALESANA
00060   004010     05  BOOK-TITLE-REPORT       PIC X(30).                 SALESANA
00061   004020     05  FILLER                  PIC X(5).                  SALESANA
00062   004030     05  LOW-MONTH-REPORT        PIC X(9).                  SALESANA
00063   004040     05  FILLER                  PIC XXX.                   SALESANA
00064   004050     05  LOW-SALES-REPORT        PIC ZZZ.99.                SALESANA
00065   004060     05  FILLER                  PIC X(5).                  SALESANA
00066   004070     05  HIGH-MONTH-REPORT       PIC X(9).                  SALESANA
00067   004080     05  FILLER                  PIC XXX.                   SALESANA
00068   004090     05  HIGH-SALES-REPORT       PIC ZZZ.99.                SALESANA
00069   004100     05  FILLER                  PIC X(5).                  SALESANA
00070   004110     05  YEARLY-SALES-REPORT     PIC $$$,$$$.99.            SALESANA
00071   004120     05  FILLER                  PIC X(5).                  SALESANA
00072   004130     05  AVERAGE-MONTHLY-SALES-REPORT PIC $$$$.99.          SALESANA
00073   004140     05  FILLER                  PIC X(11).                 SALESANA
00074   004150                                                            SALESANA
```

```
     3
00075    004160 WORKING-STORAGE SECTION.                                      SALESANA
00076    004170                                                              SALESANA
00077    004180 01  PROGRAM-INDICATORS.                                       SALESANA
00078    004190     05  ARE-THERE-MORE-RECORDS   PIC XXX      VALUE 'YES'.    SALESANA
00079    004200         88  THERE-IS-A-RECORD                 VALUE 'YES'.    SALESANA
00080    005010         88  THERE-ARE-NO-MORE-RECORDS         VALUE 'NO '.    SALESANA
00081    005020                                                              SALESANA
00082    005030 01  WORK-AREAS.                                              SALESANA
00083    005040     05  YEARLY-SALES-WORK        PIC S9(5)V99 VALUE ZERO     SALESANA
00084    005050                                              USAGE IS COMP-3. SALESANA
00085    005060                                                              SALESANA
00086    005070 01  TOTAL-ACCUMULATORS                       USAGE IS COMP-3. SALESANA
00087    005080     05  NUMBER-OF-MONTHS-ACCUM   PIC S9(5)   VALUE ZERO.     SALESANA
00088    005090     05  TOTAL-SALES-ACCUM        PIC S9(6)V99 VALUE ZERO.     SALESANA
00089    005100                                                              SALESANA
00090    005110 01  SUBSCRIPTS                               USAGE IS COMP.   SALESANA
00091    005120     05  LOW-SUBSCRIPT            PIC S9(8)   SYNC.           SALESANA
00092    005130     05  SEARCH-SUBSCRIPT         PIC S9(8)   SYNC.           SALESANA
00093    005140     05  HIGH-SUBSCRIPT           PIC S9(8)   SYNC.           SALESANA
00094    005150     05  SALES-SUBSCRIPT          PIC S9(8)   SYNC.           SALESANA
00095    005160                                                              SALESANA
00096    005170 01  PROGRAM-TABLES.                                          SALESANA
00097    005180     05  MONTHS-TABLE.                                        SALESANA
00098    005190         10  MONTH-CONSTANTS.                                 SALESANA
00099    005200             15  FILLER          PIC X(9)    VALUE 'JANUARY  '. SALESANA
00100    006010             15  FILLER          PIC X(9)    VALUE 'FEBRUARY '. SALESANA
00101    006020             15  FILLER          PIC X(9)    VALUE 'MARCH    '. SALESANA
00102    006030             15  FILLER          PIC X(9)    VALUE 'APRIL    '. SALESANA
00103    006040             15  FILLER          PIC X(9)    VALUE 'MAY      '. SALESANA
00104    006050             15  FILLER          PIC X(9)    VALUE 'JUNE     '. SALESANA
00105    006060             15  FILLER          PIC X(9)    VALUE 'JULY     '. SALESANA
00106    006070             15  FILLER          PIC X(9)    VALUE 'AUGUST   '. SALESANA
00107    006080             15  FILLER          PIC X(9)    VALUE 'SEPTEMBER'. SALESANA
00108    006090             15  FILLER          PIC X(9)    VALUE 'OCTOBER  '. SALESANA
00109    006100             15  FILLER          PIC X(9)    VALUE 'NOVEMBER '. SALESANA
00110    006110             15  FILLER          PIC X(9)    VALUE 'DECEMBER '. SALESANA
00111    006120         10  MONTH-TABLE REDEFINES MONTH-CONSTANTS            SALESANA
00112    006130                             PIC X(9)    OCCURS 12 TIMES.     SALESANA
00113    006140     05  BOOK-TABLE.                                          SALESANA
00114    006150         10  BOOK-CONSTANTS.                                  SALESANA
00115    006160             15  FILLER          PIC X(40)   VALUE            SALESANA
00116    006170               '0882360434SYSTEMS ANALYSIS AND DESIGN      '.SALESANA
00117    006180             15  FILLER          PIC X(40)   VALUE            SALESANA
00118    006190               '0882360507ASSEMBLER LANGUAGE               '.SALESANA
00119    006200             15  FILLER          PIC X(40)   VALUE            SALESANA
00120    007010               '0882360515ASSEMBLER LANGUAGE WORKBOOK      '.SALESANA
00121    007020             15  FILLER          PIC X(40)   VALUE            SALESANA
00122    007030               '0882360604ADVANCED ASSEMBLER LANGUAGE      '.SALESANA
00123    007040             15  FILLER          PIC X(40)   VALUE            SALESANA
00124    007050               '0882361007SYSTEM/360 COBOL                 '.SALESANA
00125    007060             15  FILLER          PIC X(40)   VALUE            SALESANA
00126    007070               '0882361015SYSTEM/360 COBOL PROBLEM TEXT    '.SALESANA
00127    007080             15  FILLER          PIC X(40)   VALUE            SALESANA
00128    007090               '0882361031ANSI COBOL                       '.SALESANA
00129    007100             15  FILLER          PIC X(40)   VALUE            SALESANA
00130    007110               '0892361040ANSI COBOL WORKBOOK              '.SALESANA
00131    007120             15  FILLER          PIC X(40)   VALUE            SALESANA
00132    007130               '0882361058ADVANCED ANSI COBOL              '.SALESANA
00133    007140             15  FILLER          PIC X(40)   VALUE            SALESANA
00134    007150               '0882361104ADVANCED SYSTEM/360 COBOL        '.SALESANA
00135    007160             15  FILLER          PIC X(40)   VALUE            SALESANA
00136    007170               '0882361112STRUCTURED COBOL                 '.SALESANA
00137    007180             15  FILLER          PIC X(40)   VALUE            SALESANA
00138    007190               '0882361511BASIC FORTRAN IV                 '.SALESANA
00139    007200             15  FILLER          PIC X(40)   VALUE            SALESANA
00140    008010               '0882361775COMPUTERS IN OUR SOCIETY         '.SALESANA
00141    008020             15  FILLER          PIC X(40)   VALUE            SALESANA
00142    008030               '0882361783COMPUTERS IN OUR SOC. WORKBOOK'.SALESANA
00143    008040             15  FILLER          PIC X(40)   VALUE            SALESANA
00144    008050               '0882361791PROGRAMMING IN BASIC             '.SALESANA
00145    008060             15  FILLER          PIC X(40)   VALUE            SALESANA
00146    008070               '0882361805BASIC WITH APPLICATIONS          '.SALESANA
00147    008080             15  FILLER          PIC X(40)   VALUE            SALESANA
00148    008090               '0882361902SYSTEM/360 PL/I                  '.SALESANA
00149    008100             15  FILLER          PIC X(40)   VALUE            SALESANA
00150    008110               '0882362259INTRODUCTION TO RPG              '.SALESANA
00151    008120             15  FILLER          PIC X(40)   VALUE            SALESANA
00152    008130               '0882362267COMPUTER PROGRAMMING RPG II      '.SALESANA
00153    008140         10  BOOK-CONSTANTS-TABLE REDEFINES BOOK-CONSTANTS    SALESANA
00154    008150                                     OCCURS 19 TIMES          SALESANA
00155    008160                                     ASCENDING KEY IS         SALESANA
00156    008170                                        ISBN-TABLE            SALESANA
00157    008180                                     INDEXED BY BOOK-IND.SALESANA
00158    008190             15  ISBN-TABLE      PIC X(10).                   SALESANA
00159    008200             15  BOOK-TITLE-TABLE PIC X(30).                  SALESANA
00160    009010                                                              SALESANA
00161    009020 01  PRINTER-CONTROL.                                         SALESANA
00162    009030     05  PROPER-SPACING           PIC 9.                      SALESANA
00163    009040     05  SPACE-ONE-LINE           PIC 9       VALUE 1.        SALESANA
00164    009050     05  SPACE-TWO-LINES          PIC 9       VALUE 2.        SALESANA
00165    009060     05  LINES-PRINTED            PIC S999    VALUE ZERO      SALESANA
00166    009070.                                             USAGE IS COMP-3. SALESANA
00167    009080     05  PAGE-SIZE                PIC 999     VALUE 50        SALESANA
00168    009090                                             USAGE IS COMP-3. SALESANA
00169    009100     05  PAGE-COUNT               PIC S999    VALUE +1        SALESANA
00170    009110                                             USAGE IS COMP-3. SALESANA
00171    009120         88  FIRST-PAGE                       VALUE +1.       SALESANA
00172    009130                                                              SALESANA
```

```
    4

00173   009140 01  REPORT-HEADINGS.                                          SALESANA
00174   009150     05  FIRST-HEADING-LINE.                                   SALESANA
00175   009160         10  CARRIAGE-CONTROL      PIC X.                       SALESANA
00176   009170         10  DATE-HEADING          PIC X(8).                    SALESANA
00177   009180         10  FILLER                PIC X(42)    VALUE SPACES.   SALESANA
00178   009190         10  FILLER                PIC X(6)     VALUE 'SALES '. SALESANA
00179   009200         10  FILLER                PIC X(9)     VALUE 'ANALYSIS '. SALESANA
00180   010010         10  FILLER                PIC X(6)     VALUE 'REPORT'. SALESANA
00181   010020         10  FILLER                PIC X(42)    VALUE SPACES.   SALESANA
00182   010030         10  FILLER                PIC X(5)     VALUE 'PAGE '.  SALESANA
00183   010040         10  PAGE-HEADING          PIC ZZ9.                     SALESANA
00184   010050         10  FILLER                PIC X(11)    VALUE SPACES.   SALESANA
00185   010060     05  SECOND-HEADING-LINE.                                  SALESANA
00186   010070         10  CARRIAGE-CONTROL      PIC X.                       SALESANA
00187   010080         10  FILLER                PIC X(5)     VALUE SPACES.   SALESANA
00188   010090         10  FILLER                PIC X(4)     VALUE 'ISBN'.   SALESANA
00189   010100         10  FILLER                PIC X(43)    VALUE SPACES.   SALESANA
00190   010110         10  FILLER                PIC X(7)     VALUE 'LOWEST '. SALESANA
00191   010120         10  FILLER                PIC X(8)     VALUE 'MONTHLY '. SALESANA
00192   010130         10  FILLER                PIC X(5)     VALUE 'SALES'.  SALESANA
00193   010140         10  FILLER                PIC XXX      VALUE SPACES.   SALESANA
00194   010150         10  FILLER                PIC X(8)     VALUE 'HIGHEST '. SALESANA
00195   010160         10  FILLER                PIC X(8)     VALUE 'MONTHLY '. SALESANA
00196   010170         10  FILLER                PIC X(5)     VALUE 'SALES'.  SALESANA
00197   010180         10  FILLER                PIC X(6)     VALUE SPACES.   SALESANA
00198   010190         10  FILLER                PIC X(6)     VALUE 'YEARLY'. SALESANA
00199   010200         10  FILLER                PIC X(6)     VALUE SPACES.   SALESANA
00200   011010         .0  FILLER                PIC X(7)     VALUE 'AVERAGE'. SALESANA
00201   011020         10  FILLER                PIC X(11)    VALUE SPACES.   SALESANA
00202   011030     05  THIRD-HEADING-LINE.                                   SALESANA
00203   011040         10  CARRIAGE-CONTROL      PIC X.       VALUE SPACE.    SALESANA
00204   011050         10  FILLER                PIC X(4)     VALUE 'NUMBER'. SALESANA
00205   011060         10  FILLER                PIC X(6)     VALUE SPACES.   SALESANA
00206   011070         10  FILLER                PIC X(18)    VALUE 'BOOK TITLE'. SALESANA
00207   011080         10  FILLER                PIC X(10)    VALUE SPACES.   SALESANA
00208   011090         10  FILLER                PIC X(17)    VALUE 'MONTH'.  SALESANA
00209   011100         10  FILLER                PIC X(5)     VALUE SPACES.   SALESANA
00210   011110         10  FILLER                PIC X(6)     VALUE 'SALES'.  SALESANA
00211   011120         10  FILLER                PIC X(5)     VALUE SPACES.   SALESANA
00212   011130         10  FILLER                PIC X(7)     VALUE 'MONTH'.  SALESANA
00213   011140         10  FILLER                PIC X(5)     VALUE SPACES.   SALESANA
00214   011150         10  FILLER                PIC X(6)     VALUE 'SALES'.  SALESANA
00215   011160         10  FILLER                PIC X(5)     VALUE SPACES.   SALESANA
00216   011170         10  FILLER                PIC X(8)     VALUE 'SALES'.  SALESANA
00217   011180         10  FILLER                PIC X(5)     VALUE SPACES.   SALESANA
00218   011190         10  FILLER                PIC X(8)     VALUE 'SALES'.  SALESANA
00219   011200         10  FILLER                PIC X(5)     VALUE SPACES.   SALESANA
00220   012010         10  FILLER                PIC X(12)    VALUE SPACES.   SALESANA
00221   012020                                                                SALESANA
00222   012030 01  TOTAL-LINES.                                              SALESANA
00223   012040     05  FINAL-TOTAL-CONSTANT-LINE.                            SALESANA
00224   012050         10  CARRIAGE-CONTROL      PIC X.                       SALESANA
00225   012060         10  FILLER                PIC X(12)    VALUE           SALESANA
00226   012070                                                'FINAL TOTALS'. SALESANA
00227   012080         10  FILLER                PIC X(120)   VALUE SPACES.   SALESANA
00228   012090     05  SALES-TOTAL-LINE.                                     SALESANA
00229   012100         10  CARRIAGE-CONTROL      PIC X.                       SALESANA
00230   012110         10  FILLER                PIC X(11)    VALUE 'TOTAL SALES'. SALESANA
00231   012120         10  FILLER                PIC X        VALUE SPACE.    SALESANA
00232   012130         10  TOTAL-SALES-FINAL     PIC $$$$,$$$.99.             SALESANA
00233   012140         10  FILLER                PIC X(109)   VALUE SPACES.   SALESANA
00234   012150     05  AVERAGE-TOTAL-LINE.                                   SALESANA
00235   012160         10  CARRIAGE-CONTROL      PIC X.                       SALESANA
00236   012170         10  FILLER                PIC X(16)    VALUE           SALESANA
00237   012180                                                'AVERAGE SALES '. SALESANA
00238   012190         10  SALES-AVERAGE-FINAL PIC $$$$.99.                   SALESANA
00239   012200         10  FILLER                PIC X(109)   VALUE SPACES.   SALESANA
```

```
    5

00240   013020 PROCEDURE DIVISION.                                          SALESANA
00241   013030                                                               SALESANA
00242   013040 ************************************************************** SALESANA
00243   013050*                                                           *  SALESANA
00244   013060*  THIS MODULE OBTAINS THE INPUT DATA AND CAUSES THE DETAIL *  SALESANA
00245   013070*  PROCESSING AND FINAL TOTAL PROCESSING TO OCCUR. IT IS    *  SALESANA
00246   013080*  ENTERED FROM AND EXITS TO THE OPERATING SYSTEM.          *  SALESANA
00247   013090*                                                           *  SALESANA
00248   013100 ************************************************************** SALESANA
00249   013110                                                               SALESANA
00250   013120 A000-CREATE-SALES-REPORT.                                    SALESANA
00251   013130                                                               SALESANA
00252   013140     OPEN INPUT  SALES-INPUT-FILE                             SALESANA
00253   013150          OUTPUT SALES-ANALYSIS-REPORT-FILE.                  SALESANA
00254   013160     READ SALES-INPUT-FILE                                    SALESANA
00255   013170         AT END                                              SALESANA
00256   013180             MOVE 'NO ' TO ARE-THERE-MORE-RECORDS.           SALESANA
00257   013190     IF THERE-IS-A-RECORD                                    SALESANA
00258   013200         PERFORM A001-PROCESS-AND-READ                       SALESANA
00259   014010             UNTIL THERE-ARE-NO-MORE-RECORDS                 SALESANA
00260   014020     PERFORM B010-PRINT-FINAL-TOTALS.                        SALESANA
00261   014030     CLOSE SALES-INPUT-FILE                                  SALESANA
00262   014040           SALES-ANALYSIS-REPORT-FILE.                       SALESANA
00263   014050     STOP RUN.                                               SALESANA
00264   014060                                                               SALESANA
00265   014070                                                               SALESANA
00266   014080 A001-PROCESS-AND-READ.                                      SALESANA
00267   014090                                                               SALESANA
00268   014100     PERFORM B000-PROCESS-DETAIL-RECORDS.                    SALESANA
00269   014110     READ SALES-INPUT-FILE                                   SALESANA
00270   014120         AT END                                              SALESANA
00271   014130             MOVE 'NO ' TO ARE-THERE-MORE-RECORDS.           SALESANA
```

```
     6
00272  014150********************************************************  SALESANA
00273  014160*                                                     *  SALESANA
00274  014170*  THIS MODULE PROCESSES THE DETAIL RECORDS BY FORMATTING THE  *  SALESANA
00275  014180*  REPORT LINE.  A TABLE IS SEARCHED FOR THE BOOK TITLE, THE  *  SALESANA
00276  014190*  LOWEST AND HIGHEST SALES ARE DETERMINED, THE YEARLY SALES  *  SALESANA
00277  014200*  AND AVERAGE SALES CALCULATED, AND FINAL TOTAL ACCUMULATED.  *  SALESANA
00278  015010*  IT IS ENTERED AND EXITS TO THE A000-CREATE-SALES-REPORT  *  SALESANA
00279  015020*  MODULE.                                            *  SALESANA
00280  015030*                                                     *  SALESANA
00281  015040********************************************************  SALESANA
00282  015050                                                         SALESANA
00283  015060 B000-PROCESS-DETAIL-RECORDS.                             SALESANA
00284  015070                                                         SALESANA
00285  015080     IF LINES-PRINTED IS EQUAL TO PAGE-SIZE OR            SALESANA
00286  015090        IS GREATER THAN PAGE-SIZE OR                      SALESANA
00287  015100        FIRST-PAGE                                        SALESANA
00288  015110        PERFORM C000-PRINT-HEADINGS.                      SALESANA
00289  015120     MOVE SPACES TO SALES-ANALYSIS-REPORT-LINE.           SALESANA
00290  015130     MOVE ISBN-NUMBER-INPUT TO ISBN-NUMBER-REPORT.        SALESANA
00291  015140     SEARCH BOOK-CONSTANTS-TABLE                          SALESRPT
00292  015150        AT END                                            SALESANA
00293  015160           MOVE 'UNKNOWN' TO BOOK-TITLE-REPORT            SALESANA
00294  015170        WHEN ISBN-TABLE (BOOK-IND) = ISBN-NUMBER-INPUT    SALESANA
00295  015180           MOVE BOOK-TITLE-TABLE (BOOK-IND)               SALESANA
00296  015190              TO BOOK-TITLE-REPORT.                       SALESANA
00297  015200     PERFORM C010-DETERMINE-LOWEST-MONTH.                 SALESANA
00298  016010     MOVE MONTH-TABLE (LOW-SUBSCRIPT) TO LOW-MONTH-REPORT. SALESANA
00299  016020     MOVE SALES-INPUT (LOW-SUBSCRIPT) TO LOW-SALES-REPORT. SALESANA
00300  016030     PERFORM C020-DETERMINE-HIGHEST-MONTH.                SALESANA
00301  016040     MOVE MONTH-TABLE (HIGH-SUBSCRIPT) TO HIGH-MONTH-REPORT. SALESANA
00302  016050     MOVE SALES-INPUT (HIGH-SUBSCRIPT) TO HIGH-SALES-REPORT. SALESANA
00303  016060     PERFORM B001-CALCULATE-TOTAL-SALES                   SALESANA
00304  016070        VARYING SALES-SUBSCRIPT FROM 1 BY 1               SALESANA
00305  016080        UNTIL SALES-SUBSCRIPT IS GREATER THAN 12.         SALESANA
00306  016090     MOVE YEARLY-SALES-WORK TO YEARLY-SALES-REPORT.       SALESANA
00307  016100     COMPUTE AVERAGE-MONTHLY-SALES-REPORT ROUNDED =       SALESANA
00308  016110        YEARLY-SALES-WORK / 12.                           SALESANA
00309  016120     ADD YEARLY-SALES-WORK TO TOTAL-SALES-ACCUM.          SALESANA
00310  016130     ADD 12 TO NUMBER-OF-MONTHS-ACCUM.                    SALESANA
00311  016140     MOVE ZEROS TO YEARLY-SALES-WORK.                     SALESANA
00312  016150     WRITE SALES-ANALYSIS-REPORT-LINE                     SALESANA
00313  016160        AFTER PROPER-SPACING.                             SALESANA
00314  016170     MOVE SPACE-ONE-LINE TO PROPER-SPACING.               SALESANA
00315  016180     ADD 1 TO LINES-PRINTED.                              SALESANA
00316  016190                                                         SALESANA
00317  016200                                                         SALESANA
00318  017010                                                         SALESANA
00319  017020 B001-CALCULATE-TOTAL-SALES.                              SALESANA
00320  017030                                                         SALESANA
00321  017040     ADD SALES-INPUT (SALES-SUBSCRIPT) TO                 SALESANA
00322  017050        YEARLY-SALES-WORK.                                SALESANA

     7
00323  017070********************************************************  SALESANA
00324  017080*                                                     *  SALESANA
00325  017090*  THIS MODULE PRINTS THE FINAL TOTALS ON THE REPORT. IT IS  *  SALESANA
00326  017100*  ENTERED FROM AND EXITS TO THE A000-CREATE-SALES-REPORT  *  SALESANA
00327  017110*  MODULE.                                            *  SALESANA
00328  017120*                                                     *  SALESANA
00329  017130********************************************************  SALESANA
00330  017140                                                         SALESANA
00331  017150 B010-PRINT-FINAL-TOTALS.                                 SALESANA
00332  017160                                                         SALESANA
00333  017170     WRITE SALES-ANALYSIS-REPORT-LINE FROM               SALESANA
00334  017180        FINAL-TOTAL-CONSTANT-LINE                         SALESANA
00335  017190        AFTER ADVANCING 3 LINES.                          SALESANA
00336  017200     MOVE TOTAL-SALES-ACCUM TO TOTAL-SALES-FINAL.         SALESANA
00337  018010     WRITE SALES-ANALYSIS-REPORT-LINE FROM SALES-TOTAL-LINE SALESANA
00338  018020        AFTER ADVANCING 2 LINES.                          SALESANA
00339  018030     DIVIDE TOTAL-SALES-ACCUM BY NUMBER-OF-MONTHS-ACCUM GIVING SALESANA
00340  018040        SALES-AVERAGE-FINAL ROUNDED.                      SALESANA
00341  018050     WRITE SALES-ANALYSIS-REPORT-LINE FROM AVERAGE-TOTAL-LINE SALESANA
00342  018060        AFTER ADVANCING 1 LINES.                          SALESANA

     8
00343  018080********************************************************  SALESANA
00344  018090*                                                     *  SALESANA
00345  018100*  THIS MODULE PRINTS THE HEADING ON THE REPORT. IT IS ENTERED *  SALESANA
00346  018110*  FROM AND EXITS TO THE B000-PROCESS-DETAIL-RECORDS MODULE.  *  SALESANA
00347  018120*                                                     *  SALESANA
00348  018130********************************************************  SALESANA
00349  018140                                                         SALESANA
00350  018150 C000-PRINT-HEADINGS.                                     SALESANA
00351  018160                                                         SALESANA
00352  018170     MOVE CURRENT-DATE TO DATE-HEADING.                   SALESANA
00353  018180     MOVE PAGE-COUNT TO PAGE-HEADING.                     SALESANA
00354  018190     WRITE SALES-ANALYSIS-REPORT-LINE FROM FIRST-HEADING-LINE SALESANA
00355  018200        AFTER ADVANCING TO-TOP-OF-PAGE.                   SALESANA
00356  019010     ADD 1 TO PAGE-COUNT.                                 SALESANA
00357  019020     WRITE SALES-ANALYSIS-REPORT-LINE FROM SECOND-HEADING-LINE SALESANA
00358  019030        AFTER ADVANCING 2 LINES.                          SALESANA
00359  019040     WRITE SALES-ANALYSIS-REPORT-LINE FROM THIRD-HEADING-LINE SALESANA
00360  019050        AFTER ADVANCING 1 LINES.                          SALESANA
00361  019060     MOVE SPACE-TWO-LINES TO PROPER-SPACING.              SALESANA
00362  019070     MOVE ZERO TO LINES-PRINTED.                          SALESANA
```

```
      9
00363  019090*********************************************************  SALESANA
00364  019100*                                                      *  SALESANA
00365  019110*  THIS MODULE DETERMINES THE MONTH OF THE LOWEST SALES. IT  *  SALESANA
00366  019120*  RETURNS THE SUBSCRIPT OF THE LOWEST SALES MONTH. IT IS  *  SALESANA
00367  019130*  ENTERED FROM AND EXITS TO THE B000-PROCESS-DETAIL-RECORDS  *  SALESANA
00368  019140*  MODULE.                                              *  SALESANA
00369  019150*                                                      *  SALESANA
00370  019160*********************************************************  SALESANA
00371  019170                                                          SALESANA
00372  019180 C010-DETERMINE-LOWEST-MONTH.                             SALESANA
00373  019190                                                          SALESANA
00374  019200     MOVE 1 TO LOW-SUBSCRIPT.                             SALESANA
00375  020010     PERFORM C011-LOW-LOOP-PROCESSING                     SALESANA
00376  020020         VARYING SEARCH-SUBSCRIPT FROM 2 BY 1             SALESANA
00377  020030         UNTIL SEARCH-SUBSCRIPT IS GREATER THAN 12.       SALESANA
00378  020040                                                          SALESANA
00379  020050                                                          SALESANA
00380  020060                                                          SALESANA
00381  020070 C011-LOW-LOOP-PROCESSING.                                SALESANA
00382  020080                                                          SALESANA
00383  020090     IF SALES-INPUT (LOW-SUBSCRIPT) IS GREATER THAN       SALESANA
00384  020100         SALES-INPUT (SEARCH-SUBSCRIPT)                   SALESANA
00385  020110     MOVE SEARCH-SUBSCRIPT TO LOW-SUBSCRIPT.              SALESANA
```

```
      10
00386  020130*********************************************************  SALESANA
00387  020140*                                                      *  SALESANA
00388  020150*  THIS MODULE DETERMINES THE MONTH OF THE HIGHEST SALES. IT  *  SALESANA
00389  020160*  RETURNS THE SUBSCRIPT OF THE HIGHEST SALES MONTH. IT IS  *  SALESANA
00390  020170*  ENTERED FROM AND EXITS TO THE B000-PROCESS-DETAIL-RECORDS  *  SALESANA
00391  020180*  MODULE.                                              *  SALESANA
00392  020190*                                                      *  SALESANA
00393  020200*********************************************************  SALESANA
00394  021010                                                          SALESANA
00395  021020 C020-DETERMINE-HIGHEST-MONTH.                            SALESANA
00396  021030                                                          SALESANA
00397  021040     MOVE 1 TO HIGH-SUBSCRIPT.                            SALESANA
00398  021050     PERFORM C021-HIGH-LOOP-PROCESSING                    SALESANA
00399  021060         VARYING SEARCH-SUBSCRIPT FROM 2 BY 1             SALESANA
00400  021070         UNTIL SEARCH-SUBSCRIPT IS GREATER THAN 12.       SALESANA
00401  021080                                                          SALESANA
00402  021090                                                          SALESANA
00403  021100                                                          SALESANA
00404  021110 C021-HIGH-LOOP-PROCESSING.                               SALESANA
00405  021120                                                          SALESANA
00406  021130     IF SALES-INPUT (HIGH-SUBSCRIPT) IS LESS THAN         SALESANA
00407  021140         SALES-INPUT (SEARCH-SUBSCRIPT)                   SALESANA
00408  021150     MOVE SEARCH-SUBSCRIPT TO HIGH-SUBSCRIPT.             SALESANA
```

```
07/21/77                          SALES ANALYSIS REPORT                                    PAGE   1

   ISBN                              LOWEST MONTHLY SALES   HIGHEST MONTHLY SALES    YEARLY      AVERAGE
  NUMBER          BOOK TITLE         MONTH       SALES      MONTH       SALES        SALES        SALES

0 88236 111 2    UNKNOWN            JANUARY     100.00     DECEMBER    900.00    $6,000.00     $500.00
0 88236 043 4    UNKNOWN            DECEMBER    100.00     JANUARY     900.00    $6,200.00     $516.67
0 88236 226 7    UNKNOWN            SEPTEMBER   120.00     JANUARY     985.00    $5,850.00     $487.50
0 88236 103 1    UNKNOWN            FEBRUARY    239.50     AUGUST      899.00    $5,138.50     $428.21
0 78236 103 1    UNKNOWN            MARCH       300.00     OCTOBER     818.25    $6,418.25     $534.85
0 88236 151 1    UNKNOWN            OCTOBER     195.10     JULY        900.00    $6,095.10     $507.93

FINAL TOTALS

TOTAL SALES   $35,701.85
AVERAGE SALES    $495.86
```

EXPLANATION

CHAPTER 10

PROGRAMMING ASSIGNMENT 1

INSTRUCTIONS

A report of Test Results is to be prepared. Write the COBOL program to prepare the report. An IPO Chart and Pseudocode Specifications should be used when designing the report. Use Test Data Set 1 in Appendix A.

INPUT

Input consists of Test Result Cards that contain the Class Number, the Student Name, and the number of points scored on a series of eight tests. The format of the cards is illustrated below.

OUTPUT

Output is to consist of a Test Results Report that contains the Class Number, the Class Name, the Total Points scored on six out of eight of the tests, and the Average Test Score. When computing the Average Test Score, the lowest test grade and the highest test grade are not to be counted. The Average Test Score is computed by dividing the Total Points scored on the six middle tests by the value 6. The Class Name is to be extracted from a table and printed on the report. The contents of the table are illustrated on page 10.54.

Class Number	Class Name
71001	Survey of Data Processing
71002	Intro to Data Processing
71003	COBOL Programming
71005	FORTRAN Programming
71008	Advanced COBOL
71009	Assembler Language
72002	Adv. Assembler Language
72004	RPG Programming
72007	Systems Analysis
72010	Data Base Design

If a Class Number that is contained in the input record is not contained in the table, the message UNKNOWN is to print on the report in place of the Class Name.

After all records have been processed, the total number of students and the average test score are to be printed. There are to be 40 detail lines per page. The printer spacing chart is illustrated below.

PRINTER SPACING CHART

```
     1234567890123456789012345678901234567890123456789012345678901234567890123456789012345678
 1
 2
 3
 4  XX XX XX                          CLASS TEST RESULTS                          PAGE XØX
 5
 6  CLASS NO.        CLASS NAME                    STUDENT NAME          TOTAL PTS.  AVERAGE
 7
 8  XXXXX    XXXXXXXXXXXXXXXXXXXXXXXXX     XXXXXXXXXXXXXXXXXXXXXXX        XXX        XX
 9  XXXXX    UNKNOWN                       XXXXXXXXXXXXXXXXXXXXXXX        XXX        XX
10
11
12  TOTAL STUDENT XØX
13
14  AVERAGE TEST SCORE ØX
```

Write the program using Stub Testing. Test and debug all modules except the modules to determine the lowest and highest test scores. When all modules are correct, add the modules to determine the lowest and highest test scores, so that these scores may be utilized as required in the program.

CHAPTER 10

PROGRAMMING ASSIGNMENT 2

INSTRUCTIONS

An Athlete Recruiting Report is to be prepared. Design and write the COBOL program to produce the required report. An IPO Chart and Pseudocode Specifications should be used when designing the program. Use Test Data Set 1 in Appendix A.

INPUT

Input consists of a series of Athlete Evaluation Cards that contain a School Number, the Athlete's Name, and a series of two digit Code Numbers, from 00-99, which rate each athlete on a numeric scale for Speed, Endurance, Agility, Aggressiveness, Size, and Attitude. The format of the input record is illustrated below.

OUTPUT

Output is to consist of a Recruiting Report that lists the Name of the School the athlete is attending, the Athlete's Name, his Total Score in all six categories, the name of the category in which the athlete rated the lowest, and the name of the category in which the athlete rated the highest. The printer spacing chart is illustrated on page 10.56.

PRINTER SPACING CHART

```
         1111111111222222222233333333334444444444555555555566666666667777777777888888888
123456789012345678901234567890123456789012345678901234567890123456789012345678
 1
 2
 3
 4 XX/XX/XX                        RECRUITING REPORT                              PAGE XØX
 5
 6        SCHOOL                   NAME                SCORE      LOW RATING         HIGH RATING
 7
 8 XXXXXXXXXXXXXXXXXXXXXX   XXXXXXXXXXXXXXXXXXXXXXX   XØX    XXXXXXXXXXXXXXX    XXXXXXXXXXXXXXX
 9                         XXXXXXXXXXXXXXXXXXXXXXX   XØX    XXXXXXXXXXXXXXX    XXXXXXXXXXXXXXX
10
11
12 TOTAL ATHLETES EVALUATED XØX
13
14 XXXXXXXXXXXXXXXXXXXXXX   XXXXXXXXXXXXXXXXXXXXXX   XØX    XXXXXXXXXXXXXXX    XXXXXXXXXXXXXXX
15                                                         XXXXXXXXXXXXXXX    XXXXXXXXXXXXXXX
16
17 TOTAL ATHLETES EVALUATED XØX
18
19 TOTAL SCHOOLS XØX
20
21 TOTAL ATHLETES - ALL SCHOOLS XØX
```

Note on the printer spacing chart that when there is a change in school, the total number of athletes evaluated at that school is to be printed. The School Name is group indicated on the report. After all records have been processed, a final total of the number of schools represented and a final total of the number of athletes evaluated is to be printed.

The chart listing the skills to be evaluated is illustrated below.

RATING CHART

All athletes are to be rated on a scale of 00 - 99 in the following categories.

Speed
Endurance
Agility
Aggressiveness
Size
Attitude

The following is a list of the schools which are visited in recruiting athletes.

School Number	School Name
1010	Cleat College
1012	Hahtewtraht State
1014	Run and Bump U.
1015	Animal A & M.
1016	Tricknee Tech
1017	Jacquetche J.C.
1020	Psuentt Polytech

If the input record contains an invalid School Number, the message UNIDENTIFIED SCHOOL is to print on the report in place of the school name.

CHAPTER 10

PROGRAMMING ASSIGNMENT 3

INSTRUCTIONS

A Production Report is to be prepared. Write the COBOL program to prepare the report. An IPO Chart and Pseudocode Specifications should be used when designing the report. Use Test Data Set 1 in Appendix A.

INPUT

Input consists of input records containing the Employee Number, Employee Name, the Item Number, and the number of Units Manufactured on Monday, Tuesday, Wednesday, Thursday, and Friday. The format of the input record is illustrated below.

OUTPUT

Output is to consist of a Production Report listing the Employee Number, the Employee Name, a Description of the Item Manufactured, the total number of Items Manufactured for the week, the highest number of Units Manufactured on a given day in the week, the Day of the Week on which the highest number of units were manufactured, and the "Production Range." The Production Range is obtained by subtracting the lowest number of units manufactured on any given day from the highest number of units manufactured on any given day. For example, if the highest number of units manufactured was 25, and the lowest number of units manufactured was 20, the Production Range would be 5. The printer spacing chart is illustrated on page 10.59.

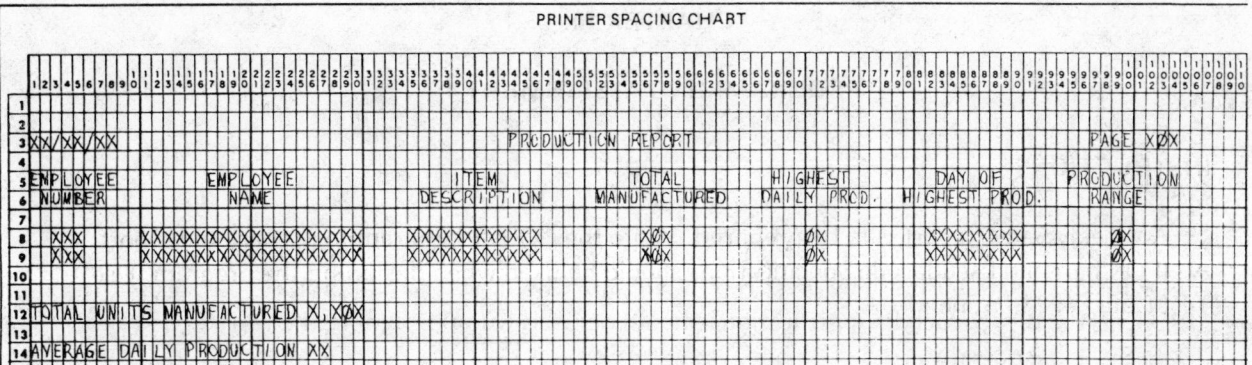

After all records have been processed, the total number of Units Manufactured and the Average Daily Production is to be printed.

The Item Description is extracted from the following table, based upon the Item Number.

Item Number	Item Description
050	Door Frame
100	Screen Panel
120	Screen Guard
125	Kick Plate
131	Door Lock
150	Door Closer
151	Door Hinges

If an Item Number is contained on an input record that is not contained in the table, the message INVALID ITEM is to print on the report.

Design and write the program and use Stub Testing.

CHAPTER 10

PROGRAMMING ASSIGNMENT 4

INSTRUCTIONS

A Weekly Sales Report is to be prepared. Write the COBOL program to prepare the report. An IPO Chart and Pseudocode Specifications should be used when designing the program. Use Test Data Set 2 in Appendix A.

INPUT

Input is to consist of Weekly Sales records that contain a Company Number, an Item Number, and the Quantity Sold for Sunday, Monday, Tuesday, Wednesday, Thursday, Friday, and Saturday. The format of the records is illustrated below.

OUTPUT

The Weekly Sales Report is to be a group-printed report, that is, when there is a change in Item Number, daily totals are to be printed. There are one or more input records per Item Number, and the input records are arranged in Item Number sequence.

The report is to contain the Item Number, the Item Description, and the Quantity Sold for Sunday, Monday, Tuesday, Wednesday, Thursday, Friday, and Saturday, and the Total Quantity Sold. In addition, the day of the week of the Highest Sales is to be printed on the report. After all records have been processed, Final Totals are to be printed. The printer spacing chart is illustrated below.

The Item Description is to be extracted from a table. The Item Number and related Item Description are illustrated in the table below.

Item Number	Item Description
2401241	File, 3 Drawer
2402243	File, Legal
2403394	File, Caddy
2403395	File, Lock
2406396	Desk, Economy
2407457	Bookcase, Open
2408457	Book Shelves
2409508	Chairs, Swivel
2410508	Chairs, Side Arm

The report is run for a single company at a time. The report heading is to contain the Company Name. The Company Name is to be extracted from a table using the Company Number contained in the input record.

The Company Name Table is illustrated below.

Company Number	Company Name
01	Stationers Inc.
02	Busmart Supply
03	Office Supplies Inc.
04	Johnns Supplies co.
05	McMahon Stores
06	Business Mart
07	School Supply Co.
08	College Stores
09	Numart Supplies

Write the program using Stub Testing.

ADDITIONAL COBOL STATEMENTS

11

> *The GO TO Statement, as it stands, is just too primitive; it is too much of an invitation to make a mess of one's program.* [1]
>
> *What we really want is to conceive of our program in such a way that we rarely even think about go to statements because the real need for them hardly ever arises . . . [BUT] the use of four-letter words like go to can occasionally be justified even in the best of company.* [2]

INTRODUCTION

The previous chapters have covered the major elements of the COBOL language. There are, however, some elements of the language which have not been discussed and which, in some applications, can prove useful. This chapter will summarize these additional capabilities of the COBOL language.

DATA DIVISION

The following segments of the language are used in the Data Division.

Level 77 Entries

In the definitions of data which have appeared in the previous programs, the level numbers 01, 05, 10, etc. have been used to present the group and elementary items. Another method which may be used is the level 77 data item. The use of level 77 data items is illustrated in Figure 11-1.

EXAMPLE

```
004020  77   SALES-TOTAL-ACCUM           PIC S9(5)V99 VALUE ZERO
004030                                                USAGE IS COMP-3.
004040  77   ARE-THERE-MORE-RECORDS      PIC XXX     VALUE 'YES'.
004050       88   THERE-ARE-NO-MORE-RECORDS          VALUE 'NO'.
```

Figure 11-1 Example of Level 77 Entries

---

1 Dijkstra, E., ''GO TO Statement Considered Harmful,'' COMMUNICATIONS OF THE ACM, Vol. 11, No. 3, March 1968

2 Knuth, Don ''Structured Programming With Go To Statements'', ACM COMPUTING SURVEYS, Vol. 6, No. 4, December 1974

Note from Figure 11-1 that the level number 77 appears in columns 8-9 of the coding form. A level 77 data item allows a single data item to be defined without it being a member of a group, such as was seen in the previous programs. Although a level 77 data item can be defined, it is a better programming technique not to use them because an 01 group level item can be used to identify the use of each of the elementary items within a section of the Data Division, leading to a more easily read Data Division. Therefore, it is suggested that the use of group and elementary items as illustrated in previous programs be used instead of level 77 data items.

Level 66 Renames Clause

The following example illustrates the use of a level 66 data item to rename other data items within the Data Division.

EXAMPLE

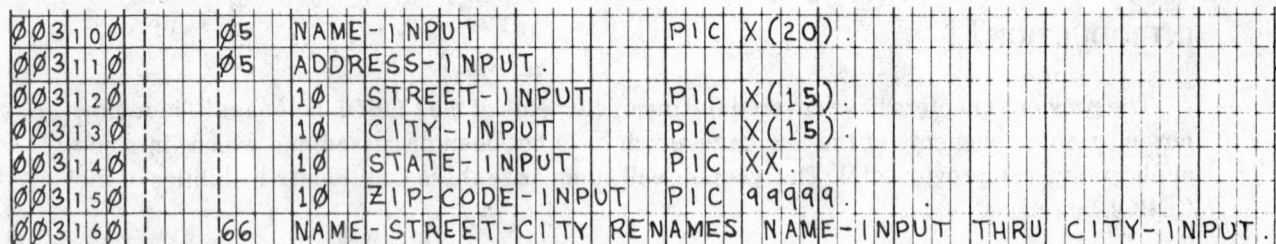

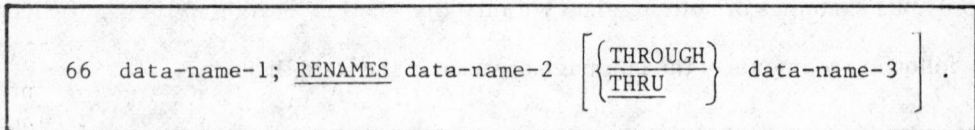

Figure 11-2 Example of Renames Clause

Note in the example above that on line 003160 a level 66 item is included. This item renames the fields NAME-INPUT through CITY-INPUT to the name NAME-STREET-CITY. The data-name-1 in the Renames Statement (NAME-STREET-CITY) is treated as a group item which includes all of the data items from data-name-2 through data-name-3. Thus, when NAME-STREET-CITY is referenced in the Procedure Division of the program, it refers to the fields NAME-INPUT, STREET-INPUT, and CITY-INPUT. In some applications, this can be a useful tool, but the programmer must be careful when using it to ensure that the correct data items are renamed. In addition, meaningful names should be chosen when renaming other data items.

Condition Names with Group Level Items

The use of condition names for elementary data items has been extensively illustrated in previous chapters. Condition names can also be used for group items. This is illustrated in Figure 11-3.

EXAMPLE

```
004120        05  ADDRESS-INPUT.
004130            88  ADDRESS-IS-NOT-IN-RECORD          VALUE SPACES.
004140            10  STREET-INPUT        PIC X(15).
004150            10  CITY-INPUT          PIC X(15).
004160            10  STATE-INPUT         PIC XX.
004170            10  ZIP-CODE-INPUT      PIC 99999.
```

Figure 11-3 Example of Condition Name with Group Item

Note in the example in Figure 11-3 that the 88 Level Condition Name is specified immediately following the group name ADDRESS-INPUT. Therefore, the condition name ADDRESS-IS-NOT-IN-RECORD applies to the entire group as defined by ADDRESS-INPUT. If the entire field contains spaces, then the condition will be true; if any of the elementary items contains non-spaces, then the condition will be false.

Name Qualification

In previous examples of defining data within either the File Section of the Data Division or the Working-Storage Section, all data-names and identifiers which have been referenced have been unique, that is, each has been different. It is allowable, however, to have the same data-names reference different areas of main storage. The requirement is that there be some higher-level name which is unique and which will Qualify the data-name, and therefore make it unique.

The ability to qualify names is illustrated in Figure 11-4.

```
003020  01  TRANSACTION-RECORD.
003030        05  NAME-EMPLOYEE.
003040            10  FIRST-NAME       PIC X(10).
003050            10  LAST-NAME        PIC X(15).
003060        05  ADDRESS-EMPLOYEE.
003070            10  STREET-NUMBER    PIC X(5).
003080            10  STREET-NAME      PIC X(10).
003090        05  CITY-EMPLOYEE        PIC X(20).
003100        05  STATE-EMPLOYEE       PIC X(15).
003110
003120  01  MASTER-RECORD.
003130        05  NAME-EMPLOYEE.
003140            10  FIRST-NAME       PIC X(10).
003150            10  LAST-NAME        PIC X(15).
003160        05  ADDRESS-EMPLOYEE     PIC X(15).
003170        05  CITY-EMPLOYEE        PIC X(20).
003180        05  STATE-EMPLOYEE       PIC X(15).
```

Figure 11-4 Example of Name Qualification

In the example in Figure 11-4, it can be seen that there are two 01 level data-names—TRANSACTION-RECORD and MASTER-RECORD. Within these record descriptions there are both group and elementary items with identical names; that is, both records have a NAME-EMPLOYEE group field, a FIRST-NAME elementary item, etc. In order to reference these different fields with the same names, each of the identical names must be "qualified" up to a point where they become unique. Thus, if one were to reference the name NAME-EMPLOYEE as belonging to the group TRANSACTION-RECORD or belonging to the group MASTER-RECORD, then these data-names would become unique. This process is known as qualification.

The example in Figure 11-5 illustrates a Move Statement which could be used to move the NAME-EMPLOYEE field in the TRANSACTION-RECORD to the NAME-EMPLOYEE field in the MASTER-RECORD.

EXAMPLE

```
014020      MOVE NAME-EMPLOYEE IN TRANSACTION-RECORD TO
014030           NAME-EMPLOYEE IN MASTER-RECORD.
```

Figure 11-5 Example of Move Statement with Name Qualification

Note in the example in Figure 11-5 that the field to be moved is identified as NAME-EMPLOYEE IN TRANSACTION-RECORD. This is known as name qualification because NAME-EMPLOYEE is used for more than one field in the program. The term "IN TRANSACTION-RECORD" uniquely identifies which NAME-EMPLOYEE field is being referenced. Thus, the compiler will be able to determine that the NAME-EMPLOYEE field within the group item TRANSACTION-RECORD is the sending field in the Move Statement.

Similarly, the term "NAME-EMPLOYEE IN MASTER-RECORD" identifies the receiving field in the Move Statement. It should be noted that the word "OF" is logically the same as the word "IN" when identifying qualified names. Thus, the data-name NAME-EMPLOYEE OF TRANSACTION-RECORD would also identify the NAME-EMPLOYEE field in the group item TRANSACTION-RECORD as the sending field in the Move Statement.

It must be noted that whenever the same data-names are used to define different areas in main storage, they must never be used as identifiers within an imperative statement without some qualification which will make them unique. It should also be noted that more than one level of qualification may be used. The following example illustrates this.

EXAMPLE

```
021050      MOVE LAST-NAME IN NAME-EMPLOYEE IN TRANSACTION-RECORD TO
021060           LAST-NAME IN NAME-EMPLOYEE IN MASTER-RECORD.
```

Figure 11-6 Example of Multi-Level Name Qualification

Note in Figure 11-6 that there are two names, NAME-EMPLOYEE and TRANSACTION-RECORD, qualifying the data-name LAST-NAME for the sending field. The only requirement when specifying qualified names is that the name be qualified to a point where it is unique and can be identified by the COBOL compiler.

Justified Right Clause

In some applications it may be desirable to have alphabetic data right justified. Normally an alphabetic move is left justified. For example, in the following segment of the printer spacing chart illustrated below, the words "DISCOUNT" and "TOTAL" are right justified. This may be accomplished by use of the Justified Right Clause in the Data Division. The following segment of a program illustrates the use of the Justified Right Clause.

PRINTER SPACING CHART

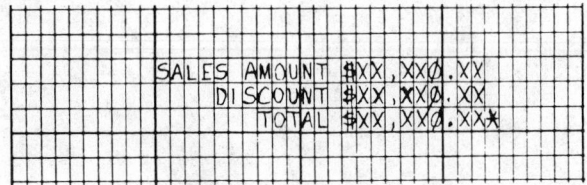

CODING

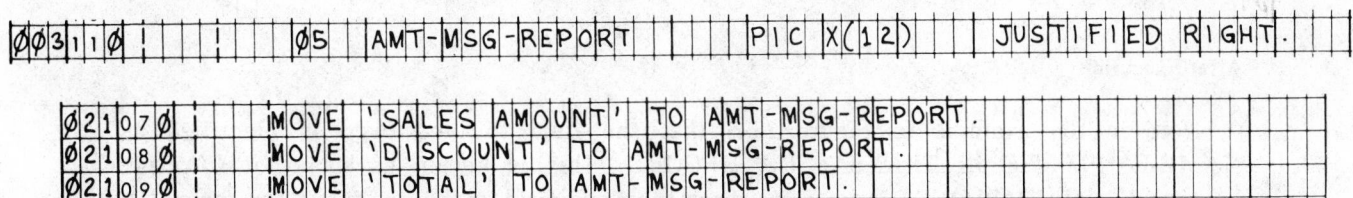

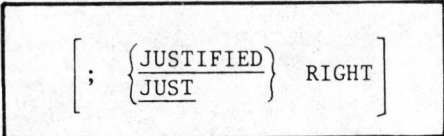

Figure 11-7 Example of Justified Right Clause

The Justified Right Clause may be written only for an elementary alphabetic or alphanumeric item. When non-numeric data is moved to a field for which JUSTIFIED RIGHT has been specified, the rightmost character of the source field is placed in the rightmost position of the receiving field. The moving of characters continues from right to left until the receiving field is filled. If the length of the source field is greater than that of the receiving field, truncation terminates the move after the leftmost position of the receiving field is filled. If the source field is shorter, the remaining leftmost positions of the receiving field are filled with spaces.

Blank When Zero Clause

The Blank When Zero Clause can be used to permit the blanking of a field when its value is zero. This is illustrated in Figure 11-8.

EXAMPLE

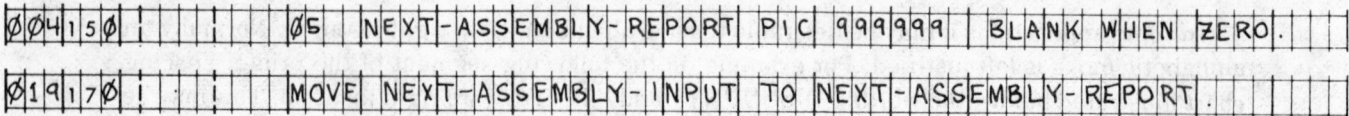

Before Execution

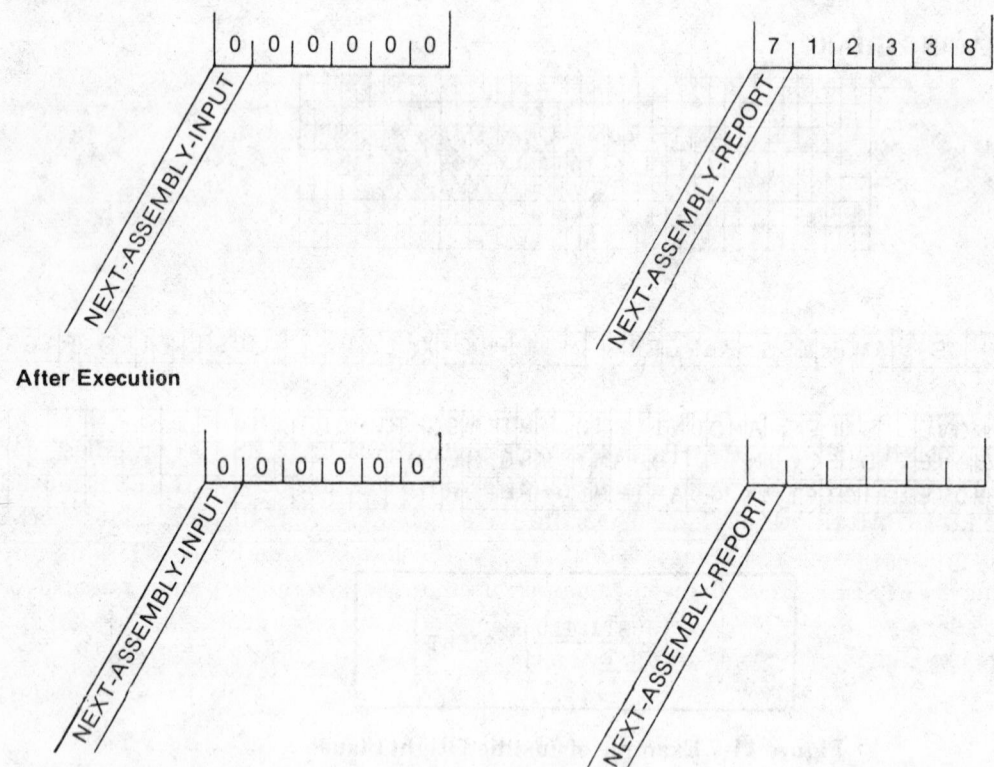

After Execution

Figure 11-8 Example of Blank When Zero Clause

Note in the example above that the NEXT-ASSEMBLY-REPORT field is defined as a numeric field with the BLANK WHEN ZERO Clause. When the value in the NEXT-ASSEMBLY-INPUT field, which is zero, is moved to the report field, blanks will be placed in the field instead of zeros. The Blank When Zero Clause can be used only for an elementary item whose Picture is specified as numeric or numeric edited.

Low-Values and High-Values

The figurative constants LOW-VALUES and HIGH-VALUES can be used to place the lowest character and highest character, respectively, of the collating sequence of a computer into an alphanumeric field. These values may be placed in a field through the use of either the Value Clause when defining the field in the Data Division or through the use of the Move Statement in the Procedure Division. These two methods are illustrated in Figure 11-9.

EXAMPLE

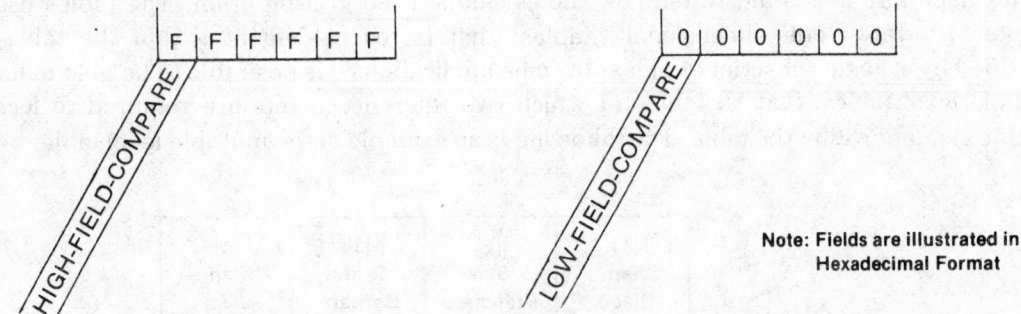

After Execution

Note: Fields are illustrated in
Hexadecimal Format

Figure 11-9 Example of High Values and Low Values

In the example above, the figurative constant HIGH-VALUES is specified for HIGH-FIELD-COMPARE in the Value Clause. The figurative constant LOW-VALUES is moved to LOW-FIELD-COMPARE through the use of the Move Statement. Note that the values stored in the fields are represented in a hexadecimal format. The lowest value is 000000, while the highest value is FFFFFF. Although these values are used on the System/360 and System/370, as well as other computers, some machines may have other values which represent the high and low values in the collating sequence on the machine.

ALL Figurative Constant

In order to give an alphanumeric field a repetitive sequence of one or more values, the ALL figurative constant can be used. This is illustrated in Figure 11-10.

EXAMPLE

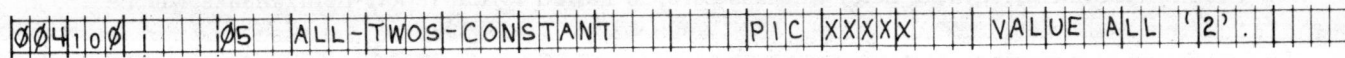

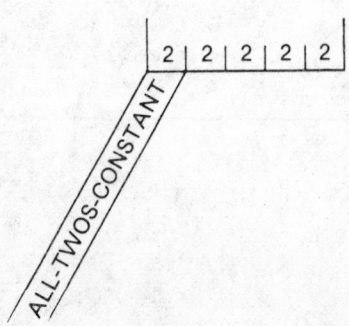

Figure 11-10 Example of ALL Figurative Constant

Note from Figure 11-10 that the field ALL-TWOS-CONSTANT contains the value 2 in each position even though only one "2" is specified in the Value Clause. This is because the figurative constant ALL is specified; when the figurative constant ALL is specified, the one or more constant values within the apostrophes are repeated as many times as necessary to fill the field defined with the Picture Clause.

Multiple Level Tables

In Chapter 10 it was illustrated how tables can be used in a program. The tables used in Chapter 10 were "one dimensional" tables; that is, each element within the table was identified by a single subscript or index. In some applications it is desirable to be able to handle multiple level tables; that is, tables in which two reference points are required to locate a specific element within the table. The following is an example of the multiple level table.

	[1] San Diego	[2] San Francisco	[3] Santa Barbara	[4] San Jose
ECONOMY [1]	12.50	28.00	14.00	26.00
FIRST CLASS [2]	14.50	35.00	17.00	33.00

Figure 11-11 Example of Multiple Level Table

In the table above, the air fare from Los Angeles to the cities listed across the top of the chart is specified for both economy class and first class. In order to find the proper air fare, it is necessary to know both the destination city and whether the flight is economy class or first class. For example, a first class ticket to San Jose is $33.00. This is determined by first locating the first class line and then looking along that line until the San Jose column is located. Thus, as can be seen, two points of reference are required—one for the class of the flight and one for the destination.

The entries in the Data Division to define the above table are illustrated in Figure 11-12.

EXAMPLE

006020	01	PROGRAM-TABLES.				
006030		05 AIR-FARE-TABLE.				
006040		10 AIR-FARE-CONSTANTS.				
006050		15 FILLER	PIC 99V99	VALUE 12.50.		
006060		15 FILLER	PIC 99V99	VALUE 28.00.		
006070		15 FILLER	PIC 99V99	VALUE 14.00.		
006080		15 FILLER	PIC 99V99	VALUE 26.00.		
006090		15 FILLER	PIC 99V99	VALUE 14.50.		
006100		15 FILLER	PIC 99V99	VALUE 35.00.		
006110		15 FILLER	PIC 99V99	VALUE 17.00.		
006120		15 FILLER	PIC 99V99	VALUE 33.00.		
006130		10 CLASS-TABLE REDEFINES				
006140		AIR-FARE-CONSTANTS		OCCURS 2 TIMES.		
006150		15 FARE-TABLE	PIC 99V99	OCCURS 4 TIMES.		

Figure 11-12 Example of Definition of Two-Dimensional Table

Note in the example above that the constant values which are to be placed in the table are defined in the same manner as the single level table in Chapter 10. The CLASS-TABLE entry on line 006130 redefines the entire constant field and it is specified as occuring two times (OCCURS 2 TIMES). Thus, through this entry it can be seen that the table is divided into two elements. The FARE-TABLE entry on line 006150 divides each of the two elements into four more elements, each of which is a field with the Picture 99V99. Thus, the eight constants in the AIR-FARE-CONSTANTS group are accounted for by the two elements of the CLASS-TABLE, each of which contains four elements of the FARE-TABLE.

This arrangement is illustrated in Figure 11-13.

EXAMPLE

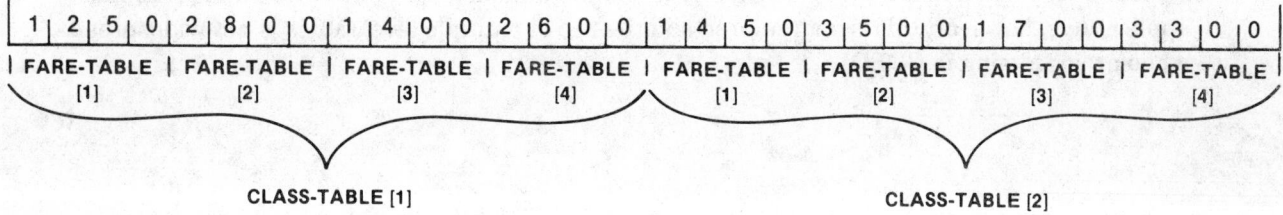

Figure 11-13 Example of Table Layout

Note in Figure 11-13 that CLASS-TABLE consists of two elements. FARE-TABLE consists of four elements and is repeated two times because it is a part of the CLASS-TABLE.

In order to reference an element within the table, a double subscript must be used. The first subscript references the highest level table and the second subscript references the lowest level table. In the sample table, the highest level is the CLASS-TABLE and the lowest is the FARE-TABLE. This is illustrated in the example below.

EXAMPLE

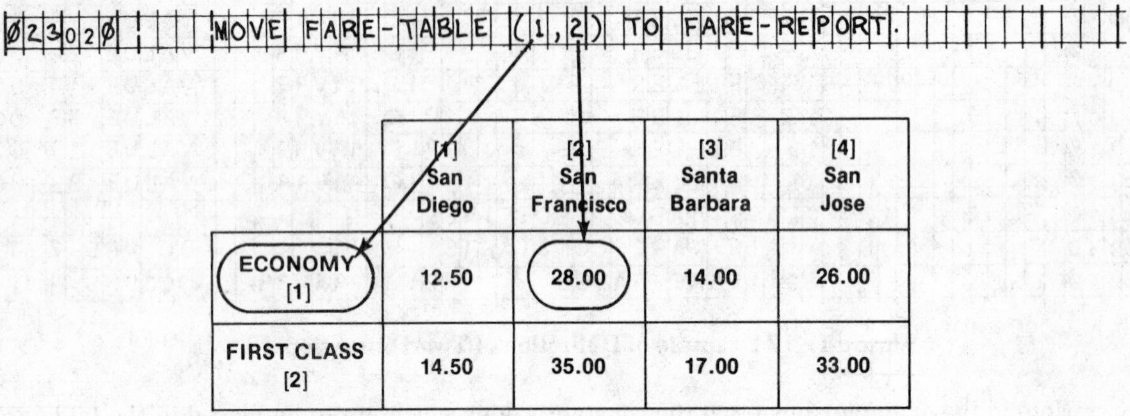

Figure 11-14 MOVE Statement to Reference Two Dimension Table

In the example above, it can be seen that the second element in the economy section is being referenced by the subscripts (1,2). The first subscript specifies whether economy or first class is to be referenced. The second subscript specifies which element within the proper class is to be referenced.

As can be seen from Figure 11-14, a literal subscript is used to specify which element is to be processed. Variable-names can also be used to reference the elements within a table in the same manner as was illustrated for single level tables in Chapter 10.

It should also be noted that COBOL allows a three dimensional table to be defined. In most applications, however, this is not required and the use of multiple level tables is not widespread when programming in COBOL.

PROCEDURE DIVISION

As with the Data Division, there are some statements that can be used within the Procedure Division which are useful in some applications. These statements are explained below.

Go To Statement

The Go To Statement is used to pass control from one paragraph to another. This is illustrated in the following example.

EXAMPLE

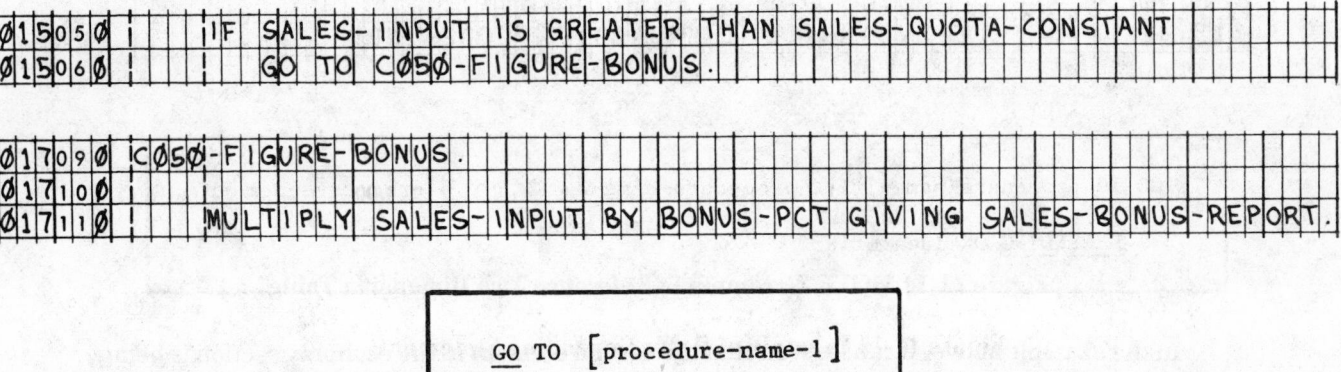

```
015050        IF SALES-INPUT IS GREATER THAN SALES-QUOTA-CONSTANT
015060           GO TO C050-FIGURE-BONUS.
```

```
017090 C050-FIGURE-BONUS.
017100
017110        MULTIPLY SALES-INPUT BY BONUS-PCT GIVING SALES-BONUS-REPORT.
```

```
GO TO [procedure-name-1]
```

Figure 11-15 Example of Go To Statement

In the example above, the Go To Statement is used to transfer control to the first statement in the C050-FIGURE-BONUS paragraph. Thus, as a result of the Go To Statement on line 015060, the next statement to be executed in the program is the Multiply Statement on line 017110 of the program.

The Go To Statement as illustrated in Figure 11-15 is not a useful statement in COBOL for two major reasons: First, if the program and logic of the program are designed properly, there is normally no reason to even use the Go To Statement; and second, with the use of the Go To Statement there is the distinct possibility that the program will violate the rules of the three control structures which are used to arrive at a ''proper program''. Therefore, the Go To Statement is a dangerous statement in that it will likely lead to a program which is not easily read and maintained. As a consequence, it is suggested that the Go To Statement not be used in a program unless there is an overwhelming and thoroughly thought-out reason for doing so. As Dijkstra says, ''it [Go To Statement] is too much of an invitation to make a mess of one's program.''

Go To Depending Statement

A variation of the Go To Statement which finds a more useful and practical application in a well-designed structured COBOL program is the Go To Depending Statement. An example of the Go To Depending Statement is illustrated below.

EXAMPLE

```
Ø18130        GO TO CØØ1-ADD-A-RECORD
Ø18140              CØØ2-DELETE-A-RECORD
Ø18150              CØØ3-CHANGE-SALES-AMOUNT
Ø18160              CØØ4-CHANGE-CUSTOMER-ADDRESS
Ø18170              CØØ5-CHANGE-CREDIT-LIMIT
Ø18180        DEPENDING ON TRANSACTION-CODE-INPUT.
```

```
GO TO procedure-name-1  [, procedure-name-2]  ...   , procedure-name-n

DEPENDING ON identifier
```

Figure 11-16 Example of Go To Depending Statement

In the example above, the Go To Depending Statement will cause control to be passed to one of the five paragraphs specified, depending upon the value found in the TRANSACTION-CODE-INPUT field. If the value in the field is equal to 1, then the C001-ADD-A-RECORD paragraph would be entered. If the value is equal to 2, then C002-DELETE-A-RECORD paragraph would be entered. If the value is equal to 3, C003-CHANGE-SALES-AMOUNT would receive control, etc. Thus, if the value in the field is equal to 1, 2, 3, 4, or 5, the appropriate paragraph would receive control. If the value in the field was not equal to 1, 2, 3, 4, or 5, then the statement following line 018180 would be executed.

The identifier in the Go To Depending Statement must be an elementary numeric field which contains positive integers. If the field contains a negative number, zero, or a number greater than the number of paragraph names specified, then control passes to the statement following the Go To Depending Statement.

Case Structure

The Go To Depending Statement finds application in the Case Structure, which is a control structure which has been introduced to Structured Programming in addition to the three major structures illustrated previously (Sequence, If-Then-Else, and Perform Until). The Case Structure is used when there are a number of "cases" which must be processed, depending upon the value in a given field.

In order to illustrate the Case Structure, assume that a transaction record is to be read which contains a numeric code to specify the type of processing which is to take place. The codes are summarized below.

Code 1 - Add a record
Code 2 - Delete a record
Code 3 - Change the Sales Amount
Code 4 - Change the Customer Address
Code 5 - Change the Credit Limit

The coding to process the Case Structure through the use of the Go To Depending statement is illustrated below.

EXAMPLE

```
015020     PERFORM B000-PROCESS-TRANSACTIONS THRU B000-EXIT.

016060 B000-PROCESS-TRANSACTIONS.
016070
016080     GO TO B001-ADD-A-RECORD
016090        B002-DELETE-A-RECORD
016100        B003-CHANGE-SALES-AMOUNT
016110        B004-CHANGE-CUSTOMER-ADDRESS
016120        B005-CHANGE-CREDIT-LIMIT
016130        DEPENDING ON TRANSACTION-CODE-INPUT.
016140     GO TO B006-PRINT-ERROR-MESSAGE.

017160 B001-ADD-A-RECORD.
         .
         .
018180     GO TO B000-EXIT.

019020 B002-DELETE-A-RECORD.
         .
         .
019140     GO TO B000-EXIT.

020070 B003-CHANGE-SALES-AMOUNT.
         .
         .
021090     GO TO B000-EXIT.

021110 B004-CHANGE-CUSTOMER-ADDRESS.
         .
         .
022130     GO TO B000-EXIT.

022150 B005-CHANGE-CREDIT-LIMIT.
         .
         .
023170     GO TO B000-EXIT.

023190 B006-PRINT-ERROR-MESSAGE.
         .
         .
025010     GO TO B000-EXIT.

025030 B000-EXIT.
025040
025050     EXIT.
```

Figure 11-17 Example of Case Structure with Go To Depending Statement

In the example in Figure 11-17, it can be seen that the processing of the Case Structure is initiated with the Perform Statement on line 015020. Note that this Perform Statement includes the THRU Clause. When the THRU Clause is used, control does not return to the statement following the Perform Statement when a single paragraph has been performed; rather, control is returned only after the paragraph whose name is specified following the word THRU is executed. Thus, in the example, control would be returned to the statement following the Perform Statement on line 015020 only after the B000-EXIT paragraph is executed.

The B000-PROCESS-TRANSACTIONS paragraph, which is the first one performed, contains the Go To Depending Statement. This statement will direct control to one of the named paragraphs, depending upon the value found in the field TRANSACTION-CODE-INPUT. If the value 1-5 is not found, then the B006-PRINT-ERROR-MESSAGE paragraph will be entered. Regardless of which paragraph is entered as a result of the Go To Depending Statement, the appropriate processing will take place and then a Go To Statement at the end of each of the paragraphs will direct control to the B000-EXIT paragraph. It will be recalled that this is the named paragraph in the Thru Clause of the Perform Statement (see line 015020). The only statement in the B000-EXIT paragraph is the EXIT Statement. The Exit Statement accomplishes no processing; it merely specifies that control is to be returned to the statement following the Perform Statement.

Therefore, as a result of the coding illustrated in Figure 11-17, the Go To Depending statement will be executed to direct control to the proper processing paragraph. After the proper paragraph has been executed, control is passed to the B000-EXIT paragraph which in turn returns control to the statement following the Perform Statement which initiated the processing.

Alternate Method for Case Structure

The previous example illustrated one method which can be used to process the case structure. It will be noted, however, that the use of the Go To Depending Statement depends upon the code field containing a numeric value. If the field does not contain a numeric value, then the Go To Depending Statement cannot be used.

If the code field does not contain a numeric field, or even when the code field does contain numeric data, the technique illustrated in Figure 11-18 can be used to process the case structure.

EXAMPLE

Data Division

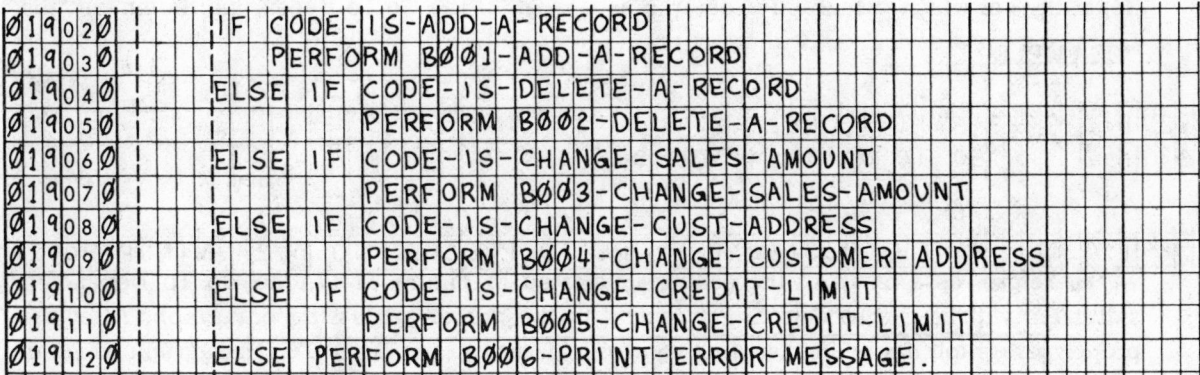

0|0|4|0|2|0			|0|5	|T|R|A|N|S|A|C|T|I|O|N|-|C|O|D|E|-|I|N|P|U|T|	|P|I|C| |9|.|												

```
004020        05  TRANSACTION-CODE-INPUT   PIC 9.
004030            88  CODE-IS-ADD-A-RECORD                    VALUE 1.
004040            88  CODE-IS-DELETE-A-RECORD                 VALUE 2.
004050            88  CODE-IS-CHANGE-SALES-AMOUNT             VALUE 3.
004060            88  CODE-IS-CHANGE-CUST-ADDRESS             VALUE 4.
004070            88  CODE-IS-CHANGE-CREDIT-LIMIT             VALUE 5.
```

Procedure Division

```
019020     IF  CODE-IS-ADD-A-RECORD
019030         PERFORM B001-ADD-A-RECORD
019040     ELSE IF  CODE-IS-DELETE-A-RECORD
019050              PERFORM B002-DELETE-A-RECORD
019060     ELSE IF  CODE-IS-CHANGE-SALES-AMOUNT
019070              PERFORM B003-CHANGE-SALES-AMOUNT
019080     ELSE IF  CODE-IS-CHANGE-CUST-ADDRESS
019090              PERFORM B004-CHANGE-CUSTOMER-ADDRESS
019100     ELSE IF  CODE-IS-CHANGE-CREDIT-LIMIT
019110              PERFORM B005-CHANGE-CREDIT-LIMIT
019120     ELSE PERFORM B006-PRINT-ERROR-MESSAGE.
```

Figure 11-18 Example of IF-THEN-ELSE for Case Structure

Note from Figure 11-18 that a Nested IF Statement is used to check for the appropriate code in the record and, therefore, solves the case structure problem. The Nested IF Statement in Figure 11-18 is different from those which have been seen previously in several respects. First, once one of the conditions is true, there will never have to be a check for a further condition; that is, once the code for Delete A Record is found, there will never have to be a further check of any of the other codes. Thus, instead of checking further conditions when one condition is true, as has been done in previous Nested IF Statements, the proper paragraph is performed and control will pass to·the statement following the Nested IF Statement. Second, this Nested IF Statement is written on the coding forms in a different manner than previous Nested IF Statements. Note that the phrase "ELSE IF" is written on the same coding line and there is no indentation of each Else Statement as was done previously. The reason for this is that if the condition is true, there are no further IF Statements which must be executed. If the condition is not true, then the next IF Statement must be executed. Thus, there is no danger that the person reading the program will be misled by applying an ELSE Clause to the wrong IF Statement. Whenever the case structure is to be implemented using the Nested IF technique, the statement should normally be written as illustrated in Figure 11-18.

Although both the Go To Depending technique and the Nested IF technique can be used for the case structure, the Nested IF technique offers more flexibility, since it can be used with alphanumeric as well as numeric fields. In addition, when used in conjuction with condition names, the Nested IF technique will normally be clearer to the reader than the Go To Depending technique.

Alter Statement

Although some persons will argue that the Go To Statement should be used in certain circumstances within a program, there is universal agreement that the Alter Statement should NEVER be used in a program. In the past, however, programs have been written with this statement in them, so the Alter Statement is presented here merely for general information. Again, the Alter Statement should NEVER be used in a COBOL program.

The ALTER Statement is used to modify an unconditional GO TO Statement elsewhere in the Procedure Division, thus changing the sequence in which programs steps are to be executed. The following example illustrates the Alter Statement.

EXAMPLE

```
Ø2714Ø  CØ23-SWITCH-ONE.
Ø2715Ø      GO TO DØ11-SWITCH-ON.
```

```
Ø2917Ø      ALTER CØ23-SWITCH-ONE TO PROCEED TO DØ24-MINOR-ROUTINE.
```

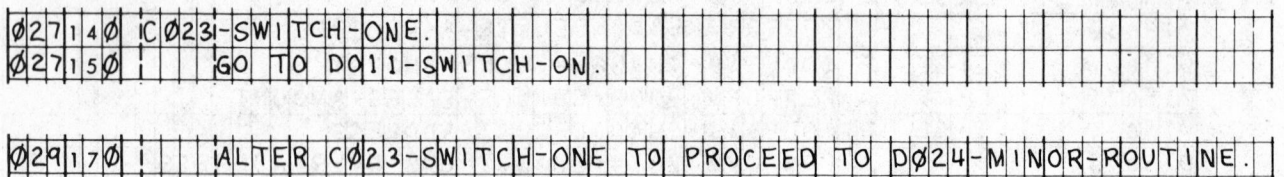

```
ALTER procedure-name-1 TO [ PROCEED TO ] procedure-name-2

    [, procedure-name-3 TO [ PROCEED TO ] procedure-name-4 ] ...
```

Figure 11-19 Example of Alter Statement

''Procedure-name-1'' designates a paragraph containing a single sentence consisting only of a Go To Statement. The effect of the Alter Statement is to replace the procedure-name specified in the Go To Statement with ''Procedure-name-2'' of the Alter Statement. Thus, in the example above, before the Alter Statement is executed, the Go To Statement on line 027150 will cause control to be passed to the D011-SWITCH-ON paragraph. After the execution of the Alter Statement, control will be passed to the D024-MINOR-ROUTINE paragraph.

Again, the Alter Statement will appear in some programs which were written in the past, but should never be used in a program.

Accept Statement

The function of the Accept Statement is to obtain data from the system logical input device or from the console.

The format of the Accept Statement is:

ACCEPT identifier [FROM mnemonic-name]

Figure 11-20 Format Notation-ACCEPT Statement

"Identifier" may be either a fixed-length group item or an elementary alphabetic, alphanumeric, or external decimal item. One logical record is read and the appropriate number of characters are transferred from left to right into the area reserved for "identifier". No editing or error checking on the incoming data is performed. If the input/output device used with the Accept Statement is the same as the device designated for a Read Statement, the results may be unpredictable.

"Mnemonic-name" will normally assume the meaning CONSOLE. Mnemonic-name must be specified in the Special-Names paragraph of the Environment Division. If mnemonic-name is associated with CONSOLE, identifier must not exceed 225 character positions in length. The following is an example of the Accept Statement.

EXAMPLE

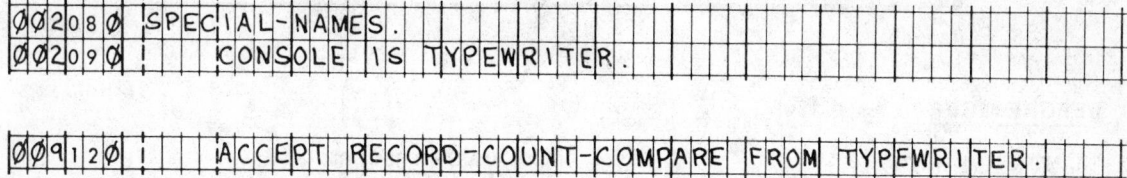

```
002080  SPECIAL-NAMES.
002090      CONSOLE IS TYPEWRITER.


009120      ACCEPT RECORD-COUNT-COMPARE FROM TYPEWRITER.
```

Figure 11-21 Example of the Accept Statement

Move Corresponding Statement

In a previous example of name qualification, it was seen that the same data-name could be used for an elementary data item as long as it belonged to a group item with a unique name. It should be noted also that each Move Statement which used name-qualification referenced only one data item within the group.

The Corresponding option may be used to reference all fields with common data names within two different groups. The following example illustrates the use of the Corresponding option when used with the Move Statement.

EXAMPLE

```
003020  01  TRANSACTION-RECORD.
003030      05  NAME                    PIC X(25).
003040      05  ADDRESS                 PIC X(25).
003050      05  CITY                    PIC X(25).
003060      05  FILLER                  PIC X(4).
003070      05  CODE                    PIC X.
003080
003090  01  MASTER-RECORD.
003100      05  COUNT                   PIC XXX.
003110      05  NAME                    PIC X(25).
003120      05  ADDRESS                 PIC X(25).
003130      05  CITY                    PIC X(25).
003140      05  FILLER                  PIC XX.
```

```
019170      MOVE CORRESPONDING TRANSACTION-RECORD TO MASTER-RECORD.
```

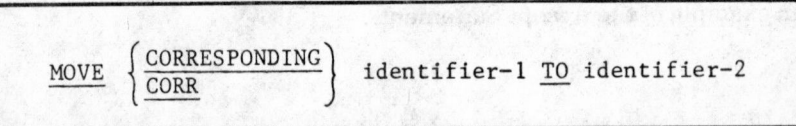

```
        ⎧ CORRESPONDING ⎫
MOVE    ⎨               ⎬  identifier-1  TO  identifier-2
        ⎩ CORR          ⎭
```

BEFORE MOVE

TRANSACTION-RECORD

NAME   ALFRED R. JOHONSKI
ADDRESS   7245 DRUMMOND AVE
CITY   NORTH LAKE, NEW YORK
CODE   3

MASTER-RECORD

COUNT   275
NAME   JAMES JILLIAN
ADDRESS   1927 HIWAY 37
CITY   BRUSHVILLE, TEXAS

AFTER MOVE

TRANSACTION-RECORD

NAME   ALFRED R. JOHONSKI
ADDRESS   7245 DRUMMOND AVE
CITY   NORTH LAKE, NEW YORK
CODE   3

MASTER-RECORD

COUNT   275
NAME   ALFRED R. JOHONSKI
ADDRESS   7245 DRUMMOND AVE
CITY   NORTH LAKE, NEW YORK

Figure 11-22 Example of MOVE CORRESPONDING

As can be seen, the verb MOVE must be stated the same as in Move Statements illustrated previously. The word CORRESPONDING or the abbreviation CORR must immediately follow the Move verb, separated by one or more blanks.

Identifier-1 is used to specify a group-item name which contains the sending fields to be moved in the Move Statement. Identifier-2 specifies the group-item data name which contains the receiving fields. When the Move Corresponding instruction is executed, as illustrated in Figure 11-22, all data stored in fields within the group-item specified by Identifier-1 with the same data names as data stored in the fields within the group-item specified by Identifier-2 are moved. Thus, for example, since the name NAME appears both in the group specified by Identifier-1 and in the group specified by Identifier-2, the data in the field NAME is moved from the sending group-item (TRANSACTION-RECORD) to the receiving group-item (MASTER-RECORD). The same is true for the fields ADDRESS and CITY, which are specified in both the TRANSACTION-RECORD group and the MASTER-RECORD group. It should be noted that the individual names of the fields need not be specified in order to move the data from one field to another. The use of the Corresponding entry causes these moves to take place by merely specifying the group-item data names.

It should be noted also that names within either group which do not have a corresponding name in the other group are not affected by the Move Corresponding Statement. Thus, in the example in Figure 11-22, the field CODE, for which there is not a corresponding name in the MASTER-RECORD group, is not moved; and the field COUNT in the MASTER-RECORD group is not altered because there is no correspondingly-named field in the TRANSACTION-RECORD group. Any Fillers which are defined in either of the group-items are not moved even though the names are the same.

The Corresponding option may be used with other instructions as well as the Move instruction. For example, it may be used with the Add Statement in order to add the values in fields with corresponding names within a group item. It must be remembered, however, that when the Add Corresponding Statement is utilized, all of the fields which are to be added within the group item must be validly signed numeric fields, the same as when the simple Add Statement is used, or there may be a cancellation of the program or other unpredictable results.

On Size Error Processing

It will be recalled from previous chapters that the On Size Error option can be used with various arithmetic statements. When used, it tests if the answer developed from the arithmetic operation is too large to fit into the field which was defined for it. If so, then an ''on size error'' is said to have occurred. In addition, when it is used with the Divide Statement, it can also mean that the divisor is zero.

The On Size Error option does present some problems, however, because it is a conditional statement which does not have an "else" possibility. This is illustrated in the following example, which is an INCORRECT EXAMPLE of the way in which to write the On Size Error.

EXAMPLE - INCORRECT

```
015070        IF PERCENTAGE-INPUT IS GREATER THAN .10
015080           DIVIDE SALES-INPUT BY SALES-RETURNS-INPUT GIVING
015090              RATIO-WORK
015100              ON SIZE ERROR
015110                 MOVE 'ZERO DIVISOR' TO MESSAGE-OUTPUT
015120        MOVE SALESMAN-NAME-INPUT TO SALESMEN-OVER-10-OUTPUT
015130        MOVE RATIO-WORK TO RATIO-OUTPUT.
```

Figure 11-23 Example of Incorrect Use of On Size Error Option

Note from the example above that if the Percentage is greater than .10, then the Divide Statement is to be executed. It also appears that after the Divide Statement is executed, the programmer intends that the Move Statements on lines 015120 and 015130 should be executed. These statements, however will be executed ONLY if an "on size error" occurs. This is because they follow the On Size Error statement within the Divide Statement. Any statement following the On Size Error option in an arithmetic statement will be executed only if the size error occurs. The only way to end the effect of the On Size Error option is to place a period in the coding.

Thus, the programmer must be careful when using the On Size Error option so that the program will do what was intended. In order to have the above statement work properly, an indicator should be set. This is illustrated below.

EXAMPLE - CORRECT

```
015020        IF PERCENTAGE-INPUT IS GREATER THAN .10
015030           DIVIDE SALES-INPUT BY SALES-RETURNS-INPUT GIVING
015040              RATIO-WORK
015050              ON SIZE ERROR
015060                 MOVE 'YES' TO WAS-THERE-A-SIZE-ERROR.
015070        IF THERE-WAS-A-SIZE-ERROR
015080           MOVE 'ZERO DIVISOR' TO MESSAGE-OUTPUT
015090           MOVE 'NO ' TO WAS-THERE-A-SIZE-ERROR
015100        ELSE
015110           MOVE SALESMAN-NAME-INPUT TO SALESMEN-OVER-10-OUTPUT
015120           MOVE RATIO-WORK TO RATIO-OUTPUT.
```

Figure 11-24 Example of Correct Use of On Size Error Option

Note in the example above that when an On Size Error occurs, the indicator WAS-THERE-A-SIZE-ERROR is set to the value "YES". The IF Statement on line 015070 then checks if there was an error—if so, the error message is moved to the output area and then the indicator is reset to the value "NO". It will be recalled that whenever an indicator is set to indicate a condition, it must be reset after that condition has been processed. If there is no size error, then the Salesman Name and Ratio are moved to the output area. Thus, the required processing is accomplished despite the limitations of the On Size Error option.

Inspect Statement

The Inspect Statement is used to examine fields and to either count the number of occurrences of certain characters within the field, or to replace certain characters within a field with other characters, or both.

The following are the general formats of the Inspect Statement.

Format 1

```
INSPECT identifier-1 TALLYING

     ⎧                  ⎧  ⎧ALL      ⎫ ⎧identifier-3⎫⎫ ⎡⎧BEFORE⎫          ⎧identifier-4⎫⎤⎫   ⎫
     ⎨, identifier-2 FOR ⎨, ⎨LEADING  ⎬ ⎨literal-1   ⎬⎬ ⎢⎨AFTER ⎬ INITIAL ⎨literal-2   ⎬⎥⎬...⎬...
     ⎩                  ⎩  ⎩CHARACTERS⎭ ⎩           ⎭⎭ ⎣⎩      ⎭          ⎩           ⎭⎦⎭   ⎭
```

Format 2

```
INSPECT identifier-1 REPLACING

⎧ CHARACTERS BY ⎧identifier-6⎫ ⎡⎧BEFORE⎫ INITIAL ⎧identifier-7⎫⎤                                                    ⎫
⎪               ⎨literal-4   ⎬ ⎢⎨AFTER ⎬         ⎨literal-5   ⎬⎥                                                    ⎪
⎨               ⎩           ⎭ ⎣⎩      ⎭          ⎩           ⎭⎦                                                    ⎬
⎪ ⎧  ⎧ALL    ⎫ ⎧  ⎧identifier-5⎫    ⎧identifier-6⎫ ⎡⎧BEFORE⎫ INITIAL ⎧identifier-7⎫⎤⎫   ⎫                           ⎪
⎩ ⎨, ⎨LEADING⎬ ⎨, ⎨literal-3   ⎬ BY ⎨literal-4   ⎬ ⎢⎨AFTER ⎬         ⎨literal-5   ⎬⎥⎬...⎬...                        ⎭
  ⎩  ⎩FIRST  ⎭ ⎩  ⎩           ⎭    ⎩           ⎭ ⎣⎩      ⎭          ⎩           ⎭⎦⎭   ⎭
```

Format 3

```
INSPECT identifier-1 TALLYING

     ⎧                  ⎧  ⎧ALL      ⎫ ⎧identifier-3⎫⎫ ⎡⎧BEFORE⎫          ⎧identifier-4⎫⎤⎫   ⎫
     ⎨, identifier-2 FOR ⎨, ⎨LEADING  ⎬ ⎨literal-1   ⎬⎬ ⎢⎨AFTER ⎬ INITIAL ⎨literal-2   ⎬⎥⎬...⎬...
     ⎩                  ⎩  ⎩CHARACTERS⎭ ⎩           ⎭⎭ ⎣⎩      ⎭          ⎩           ⎭⎦⎭   ⎭

REPLACING

⎧ CHARACTERS BY ⎧identifier-6⎫ ⎡⎧BEFORE⎫ INITIAL ⎧identifier-7⎫⎤                                                    ⎫
⎪               ⎨literal-4   ⎬ ⎢⎨AFTER ⎬         ⎨literal-5   ⎬⎥                                                    ⎪
⎨               ⎩           ⎭ ⎣⎩      ⎭          ⎩           ⎭⎦                                                    ⎬
⎪ ⎧  ⎧ALL    ⎫ ⎧  ⎧identifier-5⎫    ⎧identifier-6⎫ ⎡⎧BEFORE⎫ INITIAL ⎧identifier-7⎫⎤⎫   ⎫                           ⎪
⎩ ⎨, ⎨LEADING⎬ ⎨, ⎨literal-3   ⎬ BY ⎨literal-4   ⎬ ⎢⎨AFTER ⎬         ⎨literal-5   ⎬⎥⎬...⎬...                        ⎭
  ⎩  ⎩FIRST  ⎭ ⎩  ⎩           ⎭    ⎩           ⎭ ⎣⎩      ⎭          ⎩           ⎭⎦⎭   ⎭
```

Figure 11-25 General Formats of Inspect Statement

In each of the three formats, Identifier-1 must be a data item whose Usage is Display. It may also be a group item. Identifier-3 through identifier-n must reference either an elementary alphabetic, alphanumeric, or numeric item described as Usage is Display. Each literal must be nonnumeric and may be any figurative constant except ALL. In formats 1 and 3, identifier-2 must be an elementary numeric data item.

The following examples illustrate the use of the Inspect Statement.

EXAMPLE 1

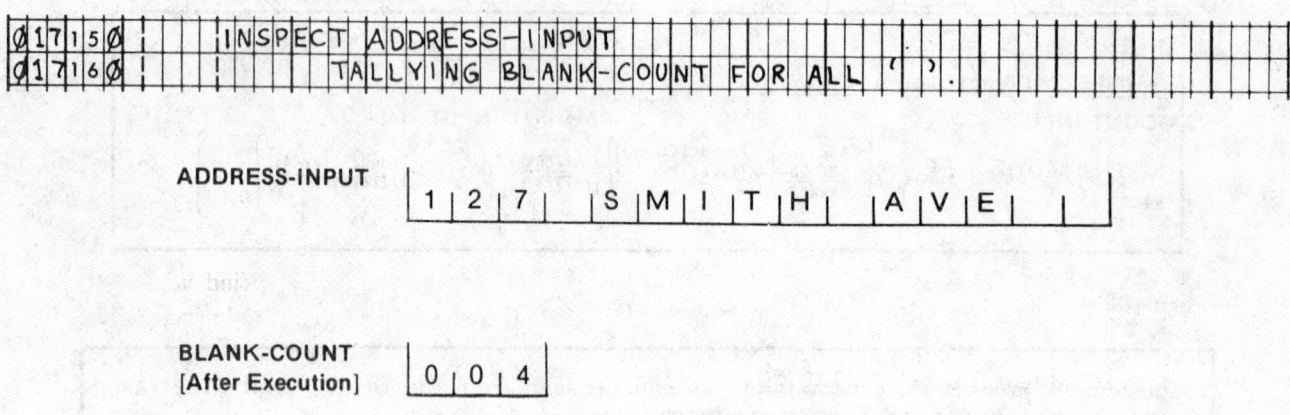

Figure 11-26 Example of Inspect Statement

Note in the example above that the ADDRESS-INPUT field is to be inspected. The word TALLYING indicates that all of a certain character within the field are to be counted. The identifier-2 field, BLANK-COUNT, is where the count will be stored. The "For All" phrase says that a count is to be taken for all of the character ' ' which is found, that is, all of the blanks which are found in the field. As can be seen, after the statement is executed, the field BLANK-COUNT contains the value 004, which is the number of blanks in the field.

EXAMPLE 2

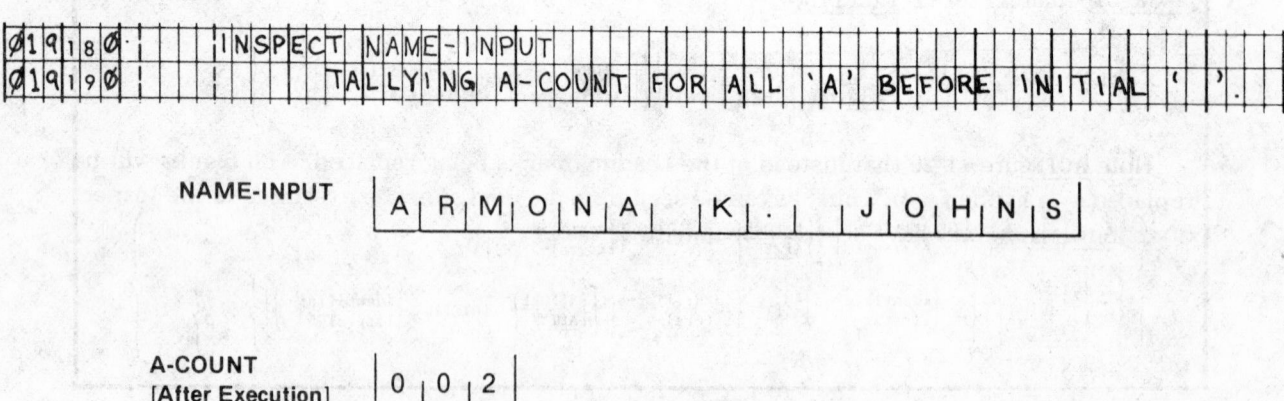

Figure 11-27 Example of Inspect Statement

In Figure 11-27 the Inspect Statement is used to examine the NAME-INPUT field. A count is to be taken for all of the character "A" which is found in the field before the initial (first) blank (' ') is found. As can be seen, there are two A's in the field before the first blank is found. Therefore, the value in the field A-COUNT after the execution of the Inspect Statement is 002.

EXAMPLE 3

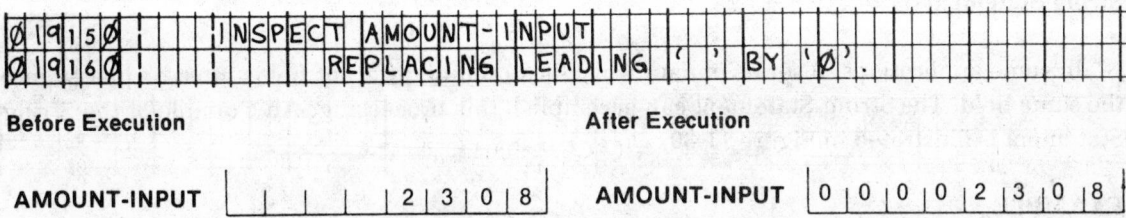

Before Execution   **After Execution**

AMOUNT-INPUT | | | |2|3|0|8| **AMOUNT-INPUT** |0|0|0|0|2|3|0|8|

Figure 11-28 Example of Inspect Statement

In the example above, the AMOUNT-INPUT field is to be inspected and all leading blanks (' ') are to be replaced by zeros (0). The word REPLACING must be specified when one character is to be replaced by another. The word LEADING indicates that the blanks in the field are to be replaced by zeros until a non-blank character is found in the field. At that point, the replacement process is to terminate. As can be seen from the fields, before the Inspect Statement is executed, the AMOUNT-INPUT field contains four blanks in the leading positions of the field. After the execution of the Inspect Statement, these leading blanks have been replaced by zeros. This technique is useful where numeric fields are not zero-filled when punched in the record. It ensures that the field contains no leading blanks.

EXAMPLE 4

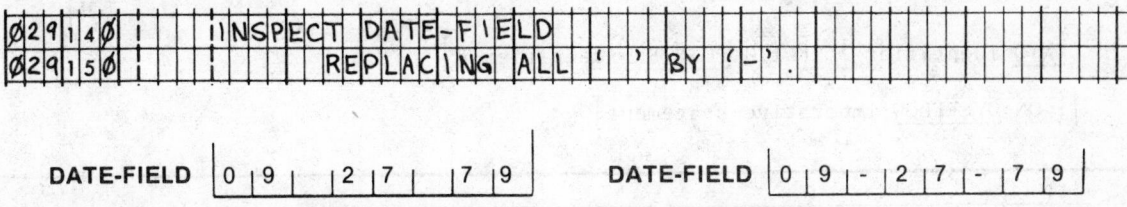

DATE-FIELD |0|9| |2|7| |7|9| **DATE-FIELD** |0|9|-|2|7|-|7|9|

Figure 11-29 Example of Inspect Statement

Note in Figure 11-29 that instead of the Leading blanks being replaced, ALL blanks will be replaced by a hyphen ('-'). Thus, as can be seen from the field after the execution of the Inspect Statement, the blanks have been replaced by hyphens.

The previous examples have illustrated Format 1 and Format 2 of the Inspect Statement. Format 3 works just as if a Format 1 statement were written followed immediately by a Format 2 statement. The Inspect Statement can be useful in some applications, particularly where checking and editing of data is required.

String Statement

In some applications, a series of data which is stored in different fields must be placed into the same field. The String Statement can accomplish this processing. An example of the String Statement is illustrated in Figure 11-30.

EXAMPLE

```
028020          STRING NAME-INPUT DELIMITED BY ','
028030                 SOCIAL-SECURITY-INPUT DELIMITED BY '-'
028040
028050                 ADDRESS-INPUT DELIMITED BY SIZE
028060                 CITY-INPUT DELIMITED BY ','
028070                 INTO IDENTIFICATION-LINE.
```

STRING {identifier-1 / literal-1} [, identifier-2 / , literal-2] ... DELIMITED BY {identifier-3 / literal-3 / SIZE}

[, {identifier-4 / literal-4} [, identifier-5 / , literal-5] ... DELIMITED BY {identifier-6 / literal-6 / SIZE}] ...

INTO identifier-7 [WITH POINTER identifier-8]

[; ON OVERFLOW imperative-statement]

NAME-INPUT   J O N E S , _ P .

SOCIAL-SECURITY-INPUT   6 5 3 - 6 4 - 1 3 7 9

ADDRESS-INPUT   1 7 4 _ A M E S

CITY-INPUT   C H I C A G O , _ I L

IDENTIFICATION-LINE   J O N E S 6 5 3 _ _ _ _ _ 1 7 4 _ A M E S C H I C A G O

Figure 11-30 Example of String Statement

Note from Figure 11-30 that the verb STRING must be specified first. Next come the name or names of the fields whose contents are to be placed into a single field. The first field specified is NAME-INPUT. The entry DELIMITED BY ',' indicates that the contents of the NAME-INPUT field are to be moved until the first comma is found in the field. The comma is not to be moved.

The data is to be moved to the field identified on line 028070 by the "INTO" phrase. Thus, in the example, all of the data is to be moved to the IDENTIFICATION-LINE field. As can be seen, the first five characters in the Identification Line field after execution of the statement is the word JONES, which is the word found in NAME-INPUT before the first comma.

Next, the value in the SOCIAL-SECURITY-INPUT field is to be moved to IDENTIFICATION-LINE until a hyphen is found. This has taken place, since the value 653 immediately follows JONES in the Identification Line field. The next values to be moved are five blanks, which are indicated by the alphanumeric literal. Since no "delimited" phrase is used, the entire five characters are moved.

The value in ADDRESS-INPUT is moved in its entirety to the Identification Line since the DELIMITED BY SIZE phrase is used. Whenever SIZE is used, it means to move the entire field. The last entry moves the city name to the Identification Line.

Thus, as can be seen, the String Statement can be used to join two or more fields into a single field.

Unstring Statement

The Unstring Statement will take data which is in a single field and distribute the data to two or more other fields. Thus, it is the opposite of the String Statement. The example in Figure 11-31 illustrates the use of the Unstring Statement.

EXAMPLE

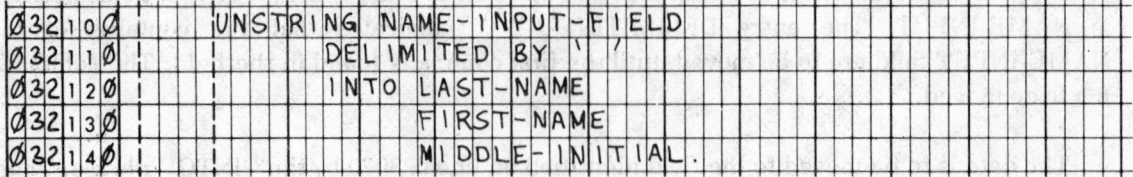

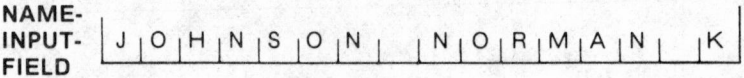

UNSTRING identifier-1

$$\left[\underline{\text{DELIMITED}} \text{ BY } \left[\underline{\text{ALL}}\right] \left\{ \begin{array}{l} \text{identifier-2} \\ \text{literal-1} \end{array} \right\} \left[, \underline{\text{OR}} \left[\underline{\text{ALL}}\right] \left\{ \begin{array}{l} \text{identifier-3} \\ \text{literal-2} \end{array} \right\} \right] \dots \right]$$

$$\underline{\text{INTO}} \text{ identifier-4} \left[, \underline{\text{DELIMITER}} \text{ IN identifier-5}\right] \left[, \underline{\text{COUNT}} \text{ IN identifier-6}\right]$$

$$\left[, \text{ identifier-7} \left[, \underline{\text{DELIMITER}} \text{ IN identifier-8}\right] \left[, \underline{\text{COUNT}} \text{ IN identifier-9}\right]\right] \dots$$

$$\left[\text{WITH } \underline{\text{POINTER}} \text{ identifier-10}\right] \left[\underline{\text{TALLYING}} \text{ IN identifier-11}\right]$$

$$\left[; \text{ ON } \underline{\text{OVERFLOW}} \text{ imperative-statement}\right]$$

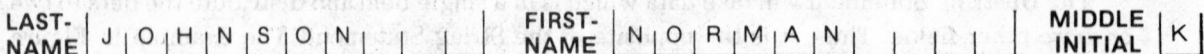

Figure 11-31 Example of Unstring Statement

The field which contains the data to be moved to separate fields is specified as identifier-1; thus, in the example, the field is NAME-INPUT-FIELD. The DELIMITED BY phrase is used to specify the character which, when found in the identifier-1 field, will terminate the search and cause the data to be moved from the identifier-1 field to the identifier-4, identifier-7, . . . fields. Thus, in the example, when a blank is encountered in the NAME-INPUT-FIELD, the characters to the left of the blank will be moved to LAST-NAME. As can be seen, the first blank occurs after the "N" in Johnson. Therefore, the characters J-O-H-N-S-O-N are moved to the output area. The search then continues for the next blank character. This is found after the word NORMAN. Therefore, the letters N-O-R-M-A-N are moved to the FIRST-NAME field. This type of search and move activity will continue until either there are no more receiving fields or until the last character in the sending field has been moved.

CASE
STUDIES

> *Resist the urge to code.*
> Mills

┌─────────────────────────────┐
│ CASE STUDY 1 │
│ AUTOMOBILE WARRANTY REPORT │
└─────────────────────────────┘

INSTRUCTIONS

The Automobile Warranty Report illustrated below is currently being prepared manually. This report indicates the number of new and used cars that have been repaired under warranty. The report contains the Dealer Number, a Repair Code, and the Type of Repair. For new cars, the report lists the number of new cars repaired, the amount of the total bill charged to a Parts Account, the amount of the total bill charged to a Labor Account, and the Total Amount of the bill. The percent charged to the Parts Account is dependent upon the type of repair. These percentages are listed in the chart on page 11.31. For used cars under warranty, similar calculations are performed.

In the report below it can be seen that Dealer 851 serviced three new automobiles requiring transmission repairs. The total amount of the charge was $22.00. From the chart it can be determined that for transmission repairs (Repair Code 09), 30% of the total amount is to be charged to the Parts Account ($6.60) and the balance is to be charged to the Labor Account ($15.40). There were no transmission repairs for used cars for Dealer 851.

07/22/77 — AUTOMOBILE WARRANTY REPORT — PAGE 1

DEALER NO.	REPAIR CODE	TYPE OF REPAIR	NEW CARS REPAIRED	NEW CARS PARTS	NEW CARS LABOR	TOTAL AMOUNT	USED CARS REPAIRED	USED CARS PARTS	USED CARS LABOR	TOTAL AMOUNT
851	09	TRANSMISSION	3	6.60	15.40	22.00				
	22	BRAKES	2	6.98	27.92	34.90				
	26	FUEL SYSTEM	18	125.82	503.28	629.10	5	14.95	59.80	74.75
	44	UNKNOWN	1	2.00	8.00	10.00				
	46	INTERIOR	3	7.62	37.23	44.85	2	4.92	24.03	28.95
	47	AIR CONDITIONING	1	1.43	10.52	11.95	1	1.55	11.40	12.95
	57	ELECTRICAL	14	21.77	413.53	435.30	10	9.80	186.15	195.95
	65	COOLING SYSTEM	1	5.99	13.96	19.95	1	4.49	10.46	14.95
		DEALER 851 TOTALS	43	178.21	1,029.84	1,208.05	19	35.71	291.84	327.55
852	13	SUSPENSION	2	21.76	106.24	128.00				
	24	ENGINE	1	13.97	79.13	93.10				
	46	INTERIOR	3	6.81	33.25	40.06				
		DEALER 852 TOTALS	6	42.54	218.62	261.16	0	.00	.00	.00
		FINAL TOTALS	49	$220.75*	$1,248.46*	$1,469.21*	19	$35.71*	$291.84*	$327.55*

Note that each line on the report represents one or more input records, that is, there is one record for each car repaired. Therefore, the values on each line represent totals which have been accumulated and group printed. When there is a change in Dealer Number, totals are to be printed; and after all records have been processed, final totals are to be printed.

INPUT

It has been decided to convert this application to a computer prepared report. The card format for each transaction is illustrated below.

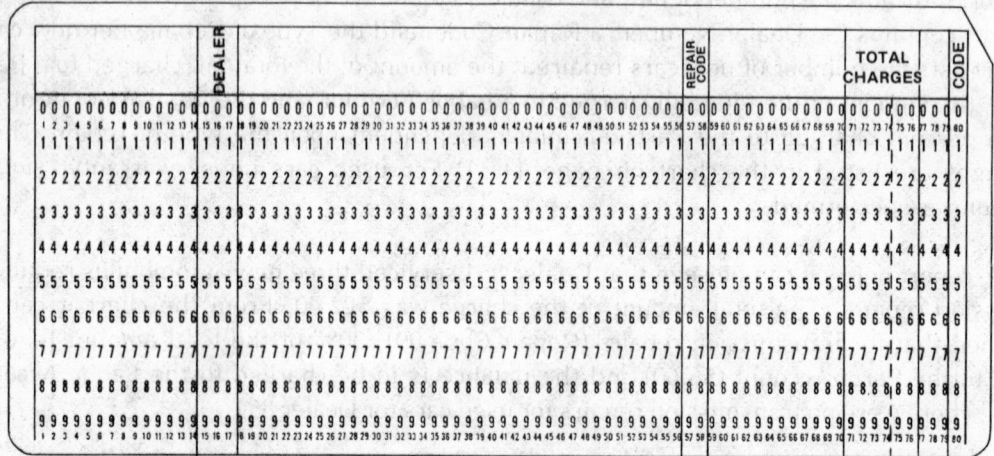

Note that each card contains a Dealer Number, a Repair Code, the Total Amount of the charges, and a type code in card column 80.

Card column 80 contains the following type codes:

    Code N — New car in warranty
    Code U — Used car with warranty
    Code O — Other - automobiles not in warranty

Thus, three different card types will be utilized when processing the records. Only those cards with a code of "N" or "U" will be printed on the Automobile Warranty Report. No processing is to occur if the input record contains an "O" in card column 80.

The percentage charged to parts is contained in the chart illustrated below. The **Repair Code** and related name are also illustrated in this chart.

REPAIR CODE	TYPE OF REPAIR	PERCENTAGE (PARTS)
09	Transmission	30.0
13	Suspension	17.0
18	Paint/Body	23.0
22	Brakes	20.0
24	Engine	15.0
26	Fuel System	20.0
32	Tires	30.0
42	Steering	15.0
46	Interior	17.0
47	Air Conditioning	12.0
49	Drive Train	34.6
57	Electrical	05.0
65	Cooling System	30.0

If a Repair Code is contained in an input record that does not appear in the chart above, the message "UNKNOWN" should appear on the report, and 20% should be used for the percentage for parts.

OUTPUT

The printer spacing chart is illustrated below.

Write the COBOL program to prepare the required report. An IPO Chart and Pseudocode Specifications should be used when designing the program.

The test data to be used is illustrated below.

```
                          TEST DATA - CASE STUDY I
              851                      09        000350   N
              851                      09        000450   N
              851                      09        001400   N
              851                      22        001490   N
              851                      22        002000   N
              851                      26        000475   N
              851                      26        002945   N
              851                      26        003150   N
              851                      26        003200   N
              851                      26        003330   N
              851                      26        003390   N
              851                      26        003600   N
              851                      26        003794   N
              851                      26        003800   N
              851                      26        004080   N
              851                      26        004500   N
              851                      26        005892   N
              851                      26        006055   N
              851                      26        002295   N
              851                      26        002720   N
              851                      26        003000   N
              851                      26        003189   N
              851                      26        003495   N
              851                      26        001222   U
              851                      26        001432   U
              851                      26        001891   U
              851                      26        002107   U
              851                      26        000823   U
              851                      32        001000   U
              851                      44        001000   N
              851                      46        000706   N
              851                      46        001483   N
              851                      46        002296   N
              851                      46        001395   U
              851                      46        001500   U
              851                      47        001195   N
              851                      47        001295   U
              851                      57        000999   N
              851                      57        001000   N
              851                      57        001332   N
              851                      57        001625   N
              851                      57        001986   N
              851                      57        002342   N
              851                      57        002451   N
              851                      57        003150   N
              851                      57        003222   N
              851                      57        003841   N
              851                      57        004083   N
              851                      57        004533   N
              851                      57        005968   N
              851                      57        006998   N
              851                      57        000895   U
              851                      57        001125   U
              851                      57        001382   U
              851                      57        001445   U
              851                      57        001529   U
              851                      57        001896   U
              851                      57        002103   U
              851                      57        002448   U
              851                      57        003030   U
              851                      57        003742   U
              851                      65        001995   N
              851                      65        001495   U
              852                      13        005207   N
              852                      13        007593   N
              852                      24        009310   N
              852                      46        001003   N
              852                      46        001475   N
              852                      46        001528   N
```

TOTAL CARDS 69

```
┌─────────────────────────────────────────┐
│                                           │
│              CASE STUDY 2                  │
│                                           │
│          COST DISTRIBUTION REPORT         │
│                                           │
└─────────────────────────────────────────┘
```

INSTRUCTIONS

A Faculty Cost Distribution Report is to be prepared which lists the members of the faculty of a school and related information, such as the number of teaching hours, the number of research hours, the faculty member's yearly salary, the amount of salary assigned to teaching, and the amount of salary assigned to research.

INPUT

The input records to produce the report contain a Division Number, a Department Number, the faculty member's name, a code to signify professional title, and the yearly salary. The format of the input records is illustrated below.

PRINTER SPACING CHART

The printer spacing chart is illustrated below. Note that two reports are to be prepared - a Faculty Cost Distribution Report and a School Summary Report. The School Summary Report lists the total number of faculty members and the totals of the various professional titles. In addition, total teaching hours, total research hours, and the salary totals for the various categories are to be printed.

PRINTER SPACING CHART

```
XX/XX/XX                    FACULTY COST DISTRIBUTION                                    PAGE XØX
DIVISION   DEPARTMENT     FACULTY          FACULTY          TEACHING  RESEARCH   YEARLY      SALARY      SALARY
NAME       NAME           NAME             TITLE            HOURS     HOURS      SALARY      TEACHING    RESEARCH
XXXXXXXXX  XXXXXXXXX      XXXXXXXXXXXXXX   XXXXXXXXXXXXXXXX   ØX       ØX       XX,XXØ.XX   XX,XXØ.XX   XX,XXØ.XX
                          XXXXXXXX XXXX XX XXXXXXXXXXXXXXXX   ØX       ØX       XX,XXØ.XX   XX,XXØ.XX   XX,XXØ.XX
                          DEPARTMENT TOTALS - XXXXXXXXXX    XØX      XØX      XXX,XXØ.XX  XXX,XXØ.XX  XXX,XXØ.XX

                          XXXXXXXXX      XXXXXXXXXXXXXXX   XXXXXXXXXXXXXXXX   ØX    ØX   XX,XXØ.XX   XX,XXØ.XX   XX,XXØ.XX
                          DEPARTMENT TOTALS - XXXXXXXXXX    XØX      XØX      XXX,XXØ.XX  XXX,XXØ.XX  XXX,XXØ.XX
                          DIVISION TOTALS - XXXXXXXXXX  X,XØX   X,XØX   XXX,XXØ.XX  XXX,XXØ.XX  XXX,XXØ.XX EXC. RSRH.

                                           NEW PAGE

XX/XX/XX                         SCHOOL SUMMARY                                          PAGE ØX
TOTAL                  ASSISTANT     ASSOCIATE             TEACHING  RESEARCH  TOTAL   TEACHING    RESEARCH      TOTAL
FACULTY   INSTRUCTORS  PROFESSORS    PROFESSORS  PROFESSORS  HOURS   HOURS    HOURS   SALARIES    SALARIES     SALARIES
XØX        XØX          XØX           XØX         XØX       X,XØX   X,XØX  X,XØX  $X,XXX,XXØ.XX $X,XXX,XXØ.XX $X,XXX,XXØ.XX
```

PROCESSING

The report is to contain the Division Name, the Department Name, the Faculty Member's Name, and the Faculty Title. Information for the Division Name, Department Name, and Faculty Title are contained in the charts on the following pages. The number of hours that the faculty member is assigned to teaching and the number of hours that a faculty member is assigned to research are also to be printed. These figures are calculated based upon the information contained in the Faculty Title Chart. The Yearly Salary is to be printed and also is to be broken down into the amount of the Yearly Salary which is to be charged to teaching responsibilities and the amount of the yearly salary which is to be charged to research. The percent of salary assigned to teaching and the percent of salary assigned to research is also based upon the information contained in the Faculty Title Chart.

When there is a change in Department Number, Department Totals are to be printed. In addition, the name of the department is to print on the department total line. If an invalid department number is contained in the input record, the message "UNKNOWN" should print on the report in place of the department name.

When there is a change in Division, both Department Totals and Division Totals are to be printed. Note that the Division Name Chart contains the information relative to the maximum time that a Division is to spend in research. If the total hours charged to research for a division exceeds the amount specified in the chart, the message "EXC. RSRH." should be printed adjacent to the Division Total.

Note that the Division Name and the Department Name are to be group indicated.

After all records have been processed, a School Summary Report is to be printed. The contents of the School Summary Report are illustrated on the printer spacing chart. The page number on the School Summary Report should be 01.

ADDITIONAL INFORMATION

There are five Divisions in the school. The Division Codes and the Division Names are illustrated in the chart below. The chart also indicates the maximum percentage of time that may be alloted to research by a division.

DIVISION NAME CHART

Division Code	Division Name	Research Percentage
01	Business	40%
02	English	30%
03	Fine Arts	30%
04	Humanities	30%
05	Science	50%

Each Division contains one or more Departments. The Department Numbers and the Department Names are illustrated on the following chart.

DEPARTMENT NAME CHART

Department Number	Department Name
030	Accounting
041	Art
048	Anatomy
053	Biology
057	Botany
065	Chemistry
071	Journalism
073	Literature
077	History
082	Marketing
088	Math
099	Music
101	Philosophy
111	Physics
140	Management

The Faculty Code in the input record designates the faculty member's title, and also designates the time to be assigned to teaching and the time to be assigned to research. The Faculty Code and the related Faculty Title and Percentages to be spent in teaching and research are contained in the Faculty Title Chart below.

FACULTY TITLE CHART

Faculty Code	Faculty Title	Time To Be Spent In The Classroom	Time In Research
01	Instructor	100%	0%
02	Assistant Professor	80%	20%
03	Associate Professor	60%	40%
04	Professor	40%	60%

The time spent in the classroom and the time spent in research are to be based upon a maximum teaching load of 15 hours per week. For example, an Assistant Professor with 80% of his time to be spent in the classroom would have a teaching load of 12 hours, and would be required to spend 3 hours in research.

Write the COBOL program to produce the required reports. IPO Charts and Pseudocode Specifications should be used when designing the program. The test data to be used is illustrated below.

```
            TEST DATA - CASE STUDY II

    01030SUSAN CAIN      01        1200000
    01030GERALDINE SHOCK02         1500000
    01030BILL URALEE     03        1800000
    01030BARBARA CORRY   04        2400000
    01140RICHARD DANIS   03        1850000
    01140CORREA RAY      03        1800000
    01082BARBARA BECKMAN01         1200000
    01082JOE LASHMET     02        1500000
    01082BUZZ BETHBY     03        1850000
    01082DON BUSGLETON   02        1650000
    02071JUNE DUNSTON    02        1575000
    02071PAUL FRITZ      01        1250000
    02071ROBERT GARRET   01        1300000
    02071BETTY GULLS     03        1875000
    02073MARK HARRIS     02        1550000
    02073RUTH HARMS      02        1600000
    02073BILL HOWS       01        1350000
    02073WILLIAM KEELS   01        1375000
    03041MARY JOY        03        1850000
    03041CHARLES DIRK    02        1550000
    03099ROBERT LITE     01        1250000
    03099LENA LEEPER     01        1275000
    03099PETE LEESON     02        1550000
    03099DALE LOPEZ      03        1825000
    04077FAYE MANN       04        2400000
    04077DARREL MAJORS   04        2000000
    04077MARCIA MOLDON   04        2450000
    04077STEVE MURTH     03        1850000
    04077JOHN PRYS       03        1800000
    04101EDMOND RICHARDS03         2400000
    04101JOE ROSS        03        1825000
    04101KATHY ROSS      04        2400000
    04101PAUL SACKETT    04        2400000
    04101YVONNE ELLIS    04        2400000
    05053MELVA EVANS     02        1200000
    05053DAVID FORSYTHE  03        1800000
    05065PEGGY GERMAIN   04        2400000
    05065PEGGY JOHNSON   03        1850000
    05111DELPHINE LONG   04        2425000
    05111CECIL HOODSMITH01         1250000

    TOTAL CARDS  40
```

```
┌──────────────────────────────────────────┐
│                                            │
│              CASE STUDY 3                  │
│                                            │
│          STOCK PURCHASE REPORT             │
│                                            │
└──────────────────────────────────────────┘
```

INSTRUCTIONS

A Stock Purchase Report is to be prepared. Write the COBOL program to prepare the required report. An IPO Chart and Pseudocode Specifications should be used when designing the program. Use Test Data Set 2 in Appendix A.

INPUT

The input consists of Stock Purchase Transaction Cards which contain a Branch Number, a Customer Number, the Number of Shares Purchased, and the Price per Share. There will be one or more transaction cards for each customer and one or more customers for each branch. The format of the input cards is illustrated below.

OUTPUT

The output of the program is the Stock Purchase Report. The format of the report is illustrated below.

The Stock Purchase Report is Group-Indicated and Group-Printed. The Branch Name is group-indicated, that is, there will be one or more customers for each branch but the Branch Name is printed only on the line for the first Customer. There will be one or more input cards for each customer, but only one line is printed for each customer (ie., the customer is group-printed).

The Branch Name is extracted from the following table, based upon the Branch Number:

Branch Number	Branch Name
12	Atlanta
24	Chicago
30	Denver
39	Los Angeles
45	New York
50	Philadelphia
54	San Francisco

The calculations required to determine the values on the report are explained below:

1. Total Stock Purchases (each transaction) - This value is calculated by multiplying the quantity of shares purchased by the price per share.

2. Total Stock Purchases (each customer) - This value, which is printed, is the sum of the stock purchases for each transaction of the customer.

3. Broker's Commission (each transaction) - The Broker's Commission is calculated for each individual stock transaction for a customer in the following manner:

   (a) For Round Lots (Purchases of 100 shares or in 100 share increments) - The commission is 1.5% of the stock purchase price.
   (b) For Odd Lots (Purchases of less than 100 shares) - The commission is 2% of the stock purchase price.
   (c) For Mixed Round and Odd Lots (Example 345 shares) - The commission is 1.8% of the stock purchase price.
   (d) Minimum Commission - The minimum commission for each transaction is $12.00.
   (e) Maximum Commission - For round lots, the maximum commission is $83.00 per one hundred shares purchased. For odd lots, the maximum commission is $83.00. For mixed lots, the maximum commission is $83.00 per one hundred shares purchased, based upon the next higher even hundred quantity. For example, if the customer purchased 345 shares, the maximum commission is $332.00 ($83.00 x 4).

4. Broker's Commission (each customer) - This value, which is printed, is the sum of the commissions for each transaction.

5. Total Due (each customer) - This value, which is printed, is the sum of the Total Stock Purchases for a customer plus the Broker's Commissions for the customer.

6. Minimum Deposit (each transaction) - The minimum deposit for each transaction is based upon the following table:

Total Stock Purchase (for one transaction)	Percent of Total Stock Purchase
$ 0.00 - 999.99	31%
1,000.00 - 2,999.99	32%
3,000.00 - 9,999.99	34%
10,000.00 - 29,999.99	36%
30,000.00 - 69,999.99	42%
70,000.00 - 99,999.99	52%

The minimum deposit for each transaction is calculated by multiplying the Total Stock Purchases for the transaction by the appropriate Percent.

7. Minimum Deposit (each customer) - This value, which is printed, is the sum of the mimimum deposit values for each transaction, except that it cannot be less than 33% of the Total Stock Purchase for the customer. If it is less, the Minimum Deposit for the customer is 33% of the Total Stock Purchase.

8. Minimum Due (each customer) - This value, which is printed, is the sum of the Broker's Commission for the customer plus the Minimum Deposit for the customer.

Branch Totals for all fields indicated on the printer spacing chart are to be printed when the Branch Number changes. Final totals are to be printed when all of the input records have been processed.

APPENDIX

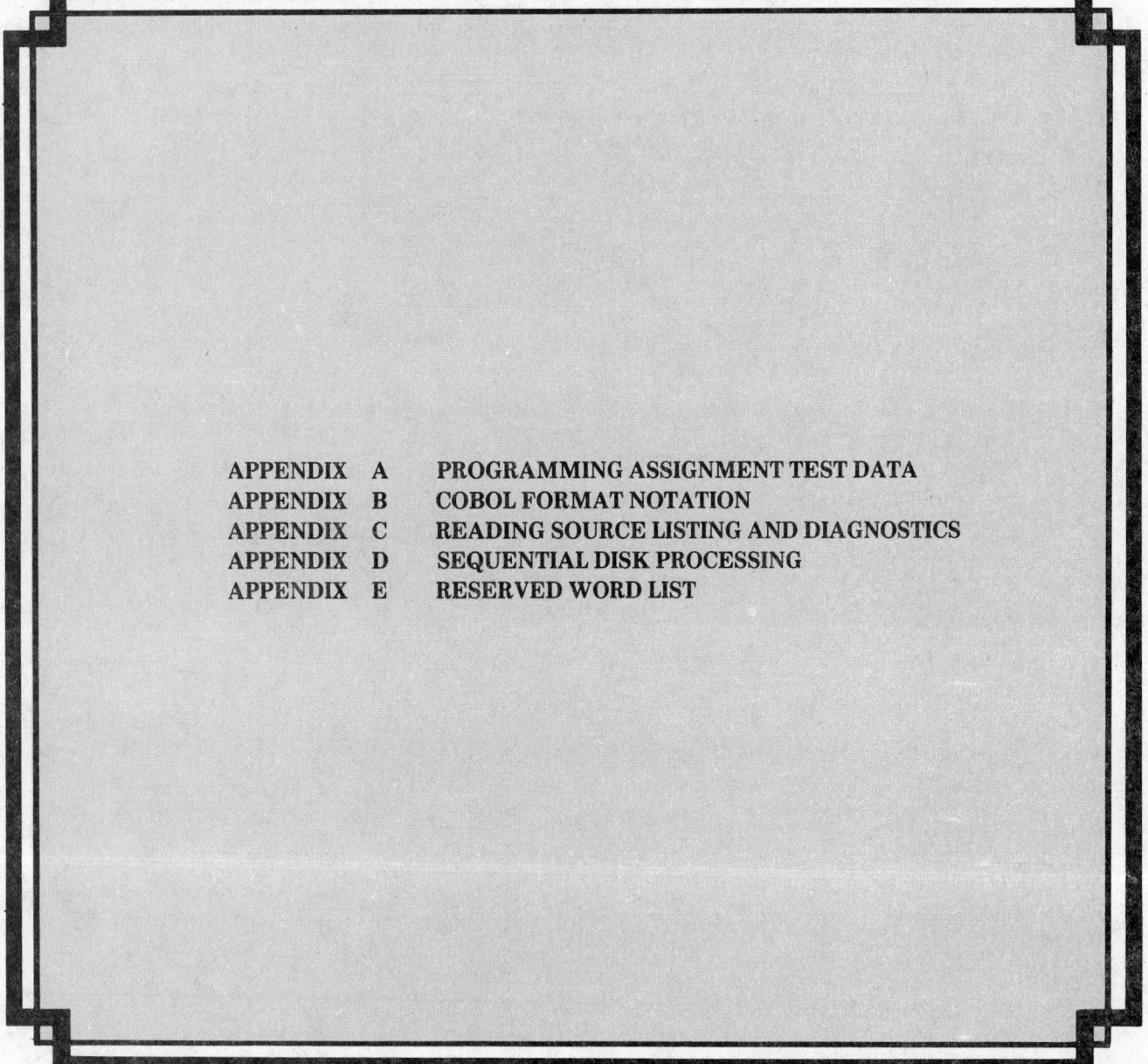

APPENDIX A

PROGRAMMING ASSIGNMENT TEST DATA

TEST DATA SET 1

Note: All data is presorted and need not be sorted to be used.

```
                              TEST DATA SET 1
1015771001004ACTION, JOHN C.      BINDER, 3 RING 100301940260057524000000000019100
1015771001185DONNEGER, THOMAS N.  FLIP FILES     100706504230090019001020000012700
1015771001730REEDE, OWEN W.        DEC RIBBON     100809035550115144002310000012900
1015771001960WINGLAND, KEITH E.    EXTERNAL CABLE 100201500050035025051000000017500
1015771003111CARTOLER, VIOLET B.   FICHE FILES    120402809980075016001140000022320
1015771003304FROMM, STEVE V.       ROTARY STANDS  120506500050120000001823000028040
1015771003030ALLOREN, RUTH W.      FLEXIBLE DISK  151021320250050090020933000359380
1015771003181DELBERT, EDWARD D.    TRAVEL CASE    150912506590130554000000000021450
1015771003487KING, MILDRED J.      CONTROL BOARDS 151018538960180429005322201513473
1016771003027ALHOUER, ELAINE E.    INDEX TABS     120501125730022066000400000005280
1016771003171COSTA, NAN S.         ALBUMS         121005803560056092000903011200000
1016771005308GLEASON, JAMES E.     DISK HOLDER    100401450030030390000000000000009700
1016771005568LYNNE, GERALD H.      MCA BINDERS    100709244870133311001428000018800
1016771005909UDSON, DORIS M.       MYLAR TAPE     100401544990030325000000000007500
1016771006292EVERLEY, DONNA M.     FICHE MAILERS  060203320020177500000032200043700
1016771006409ICK, MICK W.          REFERENCE RACK 050701131220195080014500000013900
1016771006607ODELLE, NICHOLAS P.   MCA PORTA DISK 060305825070018750700622000030700
1016771006825TILLMAN, DON M.       PAPER TAPE TRAY050512344440199509004665000019450
1016771008214EDMONSON, RICK T.     FICHE BINDERS  100301740670033057000000000010900
1016771008310GORMALLY, MARIE N.    MULTI-DISK RACK100603830220064055000866000010600
1016771008322HARLETON, JEAN H.     DATA BATCH BAGS150607848990120089000000000029550
1016771008505LAMBERT, JERRY D.     REPORT COVERS  150401540010040745000000000015150
1016771008921ULL, GEORGE          DEC CONNECTORS 150918020050270025012080000032550
1017771009105BOYLE, RALPH P.       FICHE PANELS   120608740440143055007787000028200
1017771009215EDSON, WILBUR S.      FICHE PAGES    120706040510082015001575000013920
1017771009574MELTZ, FRANK K.       CODING FORMS   121007543660059030000000001020272
1017771009820TELLER, STEPHEN U.    DISK FILTER    121019530440177019032222201127236
1017772002300FELDMAN, MIKE R.      MAG CARD PANELS100902500010030000000000000003300
1017772002325HATFIELD, MARK I.     CLAMP BINDERS  100701511220020539012220000002900
1017772002590NEIL, CLARENCE N.     PRINTOUT DESIGN120807500650090230023240014040
1017772002801SCHEIBER, HARRY R.    CASSETTE STAND 120301952370032508300052000012960
1017772002956WANGLEY, THEO A.      INTERNAL CABLE 120701200050015000000275000002520
1017772004311GROLER, GRACE B.      CARD HOLDER    151023036430215420018369013485810
1017772004318HANEY, CAROL S.       PUNCH TAPE     150509750010145000000601900042600
1017772004834TRAWLEY, HARRIS T.    TAPE WINDER    151005723260055000000132901661000
1017772004317HANABEE, ALETA O.     PLASTIC FILES  121003850010039500001180015930860
1017772004721RASSMUSEN, JOHN J.    LINE CANISTERS 120808100010110000000234600014760
1018722004739RIDEL, ROBERT R.      SILK RIBBON    120705545040082571007224000014040
1018772004806STOCKTON, NORMAN Q.   DISK CARTRIDGES120906725070070725880133800000096000
1018772007122CENNA, DICK L.        DESK PADS      100803537770044201000000000005400
1018772007207EBERHARDT, RON G.     EASEL BINDERS  100605640070090409900098000012700
1018772007100BATES, TONY F.        RULER, FORMS   050408140660217645005170000254000
1018772007179DAMSON, ERIC C.       MINI BINDERS   050203525020180888000223000044550
1018772007332HELD, ANNA J.         FORMS CARRIERS 100902440050029500000092600003200
1018772007689OWNEY, REED M.        BOT MARKERS    100904347880053066001132000005800
1018772007802SHEA, MICHAEL H.      CASSETTE BOX   100806420330082089004680000010100
1018772010102BELLSLEY, ARTHUR A.   TEMPLATE       150908830010099015002762000005450
1018772010282ESTABAN, JUAN L.      VINYL POCKETS  151019840550050000000505000397281
1018772010315HALE, ALAN A.         MAGNETIC SHIELD120812741050168000003829000024720
1018772010740RIDGEFIELD, SUZY S.   HANGING FILES  121018041780190506002310012805430

TOTAL CARDS  50
```

TEST DATA SET 2

Note: All data is presorted and need not be sorted to be used.

```
                          TEST DATA SET 2

0608772401241910017483016BROOMS          FUTURE FOODS     6513531015000496000031 25
0608772401241910017483045CIDER           HAW'S BURGERS     19216140050006300000 3528D
0608772401241905017483300COFFEE          KEY'S SLIMRITE   25263288210086400003 6288D
0608772401241910017483150CONDENSED MILK  SEA SUPPLIES     7627226011003900000 24570L
0608772402243415021229007AMMONIA         CALICO INC        630150930100006510 00527L
0608772402243420021229016APPLE SAUCE     AMERICAN STORES 220321601250025600 001613L
0608772402243410021229009APPLES          STEAK HOUSE      65135310150004960 0003125L
0608772402243415021229008APRICOTS        PEDRO'S TACOS    22048370230002960 0001865L
0608772402243405021229010CEYLON TEA      RUSSEL'S         45169480250004800 0003024L
0608772403394210052224088DRIED PEACHES   MICKY'S INN      52359082070007216 004546
0608772403394220052224009FLOUR           FUNGUS FOODS     11383810470007290 004593
0608772403394215052224030GINGER SNAPS    VITA VILLAGE     48424350220010500 0066150
0608772403394215052224015MATCHES         ROBIN'S INN      65537094025001410 000888D
0608772403394210052240125ONIONS          SAM'S GROCERY    20583017012002125 001339D
0608772404395105060663008ANIMAL CRACKERSBURGER BUN       48024050030004000 002520L
0608772404395120060663003GELATINE        NUMART GROCERY  49408145044004350 002741L
0608772404395105060663007GINGER SNAPS    QUEEN'S MART     48424350220002450 001544L
0608772404395125060663052LEMON SODA      RIO-RITA FOODS  36480075050039000 024570L
0608772404395120060663020PORK AND BEANS  SIZZLER HUT     27697305150016000 038430L
0608772405395205062206ASPARAGUS         DON'S DRIVE IN   23056560210033600 021168D
0608772405395220061522011COFFEE          LAKE'S HAVEN     45263288210031680 019958
0608772405395205061522095DRIED PEACHES   NANNY'S EATERY  52359082070007790 004908D
0608772405395215061522092ONIONS          SAVMOR MARKETS  20583017012001564 000985
0608772405395205061522090HORSE RADISH    RECTOR'S        32456042039003780 0023810
0608772406396610077156176COCOA           CHICKEN HUT      46257083050014608 009203D
0608772406396600577156020CRACKERS        MARTIN'S MARKET483123101500062000 003906D
0608772406396605771560097NUTMEG          RED BARN INN     43560550500053500 033610
0608772406396615077156130PAPRIKA         SUKO STEAK'S     43632060050007800 004914
0609772407457120093823020ANIMAL CRACKERSBEELINE INC      48024050030001000 000630L
0609772407457105093823017FLOUR           NONO'S          11383810470013770 008675D
0609772407457120093823040RAISINS         SEYOR STORES    21744054022002160 001361D
0609772407457120093823050STOVE BLACK     PAYMORE         66864060035003000 0001890L
0609722407457105093923017OVEN CLEANER    ZAMBY'S BBQ      6301509304000083700 0527L
0609722407457115093923017FLOOR WAX       ZUZU MART       14008080500056000 003528D
0609722407457105093823021BLEACH          YARMY'S INC      67875020010004200 0002100D
0609722407457115093823011DISH SOAP       COFFEE HOURS    68890100050011200 0056000
0609722407457110093823025DFTERGENT       YANCY'S MARKET  67871050025011500 006250
0609722407457120093823095BRILLO PADS     SANDWICH SHOP   66870100050009500 0047500
0609722407457120093823025SOAP            VIMVIM FOODS    66869015010000375 0002500
0609722407457120093823100SHOE POLISH     SCANLON'S INN   66865020010002000 0001000D
0609772408457405096401003BROOMS          FLAGGS INC       6513531015000961 00060540
0609772408457405096401029CHOW CHOW       HARVEY'S HUT    23207034019000986 0000621
0609772408457415096401025CIDER           HILLVIEW MARKET19216140050003500 0022050
0609772408457410096401016COFFEE          LARK STORES INC45263288210046080 0290300
0610772409508105097485007CELERY          GEORGIA INN     20161100800077000 0048510
0610772409508115097485005CORN            YUMMY YAMS      23289240110012000 007560
0610772409508110097485031COCOA           KINZER'S CAVES  46257083050025730 016210
0610772410508220097447007AMERICAN CHEESEACME STORES INC140080800500056000 03528D
0610772410508215097447006CLAM BROTH      JACKS PLACE     74233015010000900 00001 89D
0610772410508205097447005CHICKEN SOUP    MAYNARD'S MANOR74192378205018900 0014288D

TOTAL CARDS  50
```

COBOL FORMAT NOTATION

The following are the general formats for all COBOL Statements used in this text.

Identification Division

GENERAL FORMAT FOR IDENTIFICATION DIVISION

IDENTIFICATION DIVISION.

PROGRAM-ID. program-name.

[AUTHOR. [comment-entry] ...]

[INSTALLATION. [comment-entry] ...]

[DATE-WRITTEN. [comment-entry] ...]

[DATE-COMPILED. [comment-entry] ...]

[SECURITY. [comment-entry] ...]

<u>GENERAL FORMAT FOR ENVIRONMENT DIVISION</u>

<u>ENVIRONMENT</u> <u>DIVISION</u>.

<u>CONFIGURATION</u> <u>SECTION</u>.

<u>SOURCE-COMPUTER</u>.   computer-name $\left[\text{WITH} \underline{\text{DEBUGGING}} \underline{\text{MODE}}\right]$.

<u>OBJECT-COMPUTER</u>.   computer-name

$$\left[, \underline{\text{MEMORY}} \text{ SIZE integer} \left\{\begin{array}{l} \underline{\text{WORDS}} \\ \underline{\text{CHARACTERS}} \\ \underline{\text{MODULES}} \end{array}\right\}\right]$$

$$\left[, \text{PROGRAM COLLATING} \underline{\text{SEQUENCE}} \text{ IS alphabet-name}\right]$$

$$\left[, \underline{\text{SEGMENT-LIMIT}} \underline{\text{IS}} \text{ segment-number}\right] \; .$$

$\left[\underline{\text{SPECIAL-NAMES}}. \; \left[, \text{ implementor-name} \right.\right.$

$$\left\{\begin{array}{l} \underline{\text{IS}} \text{ mnemonic-name} \left[, \underline{\text{ON}} \text{ STATUS} \underline{\text{IS}} \text{ condition-name-1} \left[, \underline{\text{OFF}} \text{ STATUS} \underline{\text{IS}} \text{ condition-name-2}\right]\right]\right) \\ \underline{\text{IS}} \text{ mnemonic-name} \left[, \underline{\text{OFF}} \text{ STATUS} \underline{\text{IS}} \text{ condition-name-2} \left[, \underline{\text{ON}} \text{ STATUS} \underline{\text{IS}} \text{ condition-name-1}\right]\right] \\ \underline{\text{ON}} \text{ STATUS} \underline{\text{IS}} \text{ condition-name-1} \left[, \underline{\text{OFF}} \text{ STATUS} \underline{\text{IS}} \text{ condition-name-2}\right] \\ \underline{\text{OFF}} \text{ STATUS} \underline{\text{IS}} \text{ condition-name-2} \left[, \underline{\text{ON}} \text{ STATUS} \underline{\text{IS}} \text{ condition-name-1}\right] \end{array}\right\} \dots$$

$$\left[, \text{ alphabet-name IS} \left\{\begin{array}{l} \underline{\text{STANDARD-1}} \\ \underline{\text{NATIVE}} \\ \text{implementor-name} \\ \text{literal-1} \left[\left\{\begin{array}{l}\underline{\text{THROUGH}}\\\underline{\text{THRU}}\end{array}\right\} \text{literal-2} \\ \underline{\text{ALSO}} \text{ literal-3} \left[, \underline{\text{ALSO}} \text{ literal-4}\right]\dots\right] \\ \left[\text{literal-5} \left[\left\{\begin{array}{l}\underline{\text{THROUGH}}\\\underline{\text{THRU}}\end{array}\right\} \text{literal-6} \\ \underline{\text{ALSO}} \text{ literal-7} \left[, \underline{\text{ALSO}} \text{ literal-8}\right]\dots\right]\right]\dots \end{array}\right\}\dots\right.$$

$$\left[, \underline{\text{CURRENCY}} \text{ SIGN} \underline{\text{IS}} \text{ literal-9}\right]$$

$$\left.\left[, \underline{\text{DECIMAL-POINT}} \underline{\text{IS}} \underline{\text{COMMA}}\right] \; . \right]$$

[INPUT-OUTPUT SECTION.

FILE-CONTROL.

    {file-control-entry} ...

[I-O-CONTROL.

    [; RERUN [ON {file-name-1 / implementor-name}]

        EVERY { { [END OF] {REEL / UNIT} } OF file-name-2 }] ...
               { integer-1 RECORDS }
               integer-2 CLOCK-UNITS
               condition-name

    [; SAME [RECORD / SORT / SORT-MERGE] AREA FOR file-name-3 {, file-name-4} ...] ...

    [; MULTIPLE FILE TAPE CONTAINS file-name-5 [POSITION integer-3]

        [, file-name-6 [POSITION integer-4]] ...] ... .]]

<u>GENERAL FORMAT FOR FILE CONTROL ENTRY</u>

<u>FORMAT 1</u>:

<u>SELECT</u> [<u>OPTIONAL</u>] file-name

    <u>ASSIGN</u> TO implementor-name-1 [, implementor-name-2] ...

    [; <u>RESERVE</u> integer-1 $\begin{bmatrix} \text{AREA} \\ \text{AREAS} \end{bmatrix}$]

    [; <u>ORGANIZATION</u> IS <u>SEQUENTIAL</u>]

    [; <u>ACCESS</u> MODE IS <u>SEQUENTIAL</u>]

    [; FILE <u>STATUS</u> IS data-name-1] .

<u>FORMAT 2</u>:

<u>SELECT</u> file-name

    <u>ASSIGN</u> TO implementor-name-1 [, implementor-name-2] ...

    [; <u>RESERVE</u> integer-1 $\begin{bmatrix} \text{AREA} \\ \text{AREAS} \end{bmatrix}$]

    ; <u>ORGANIZATION</u> IS <u>RELATIVE</u>

    $\left[; \underline{\text{ACCESS}} \text{ MODE IS} \left\{ \begin{array}{l} \underline{\text{SEQUENTIAL}} \quad [, \underline{\text{RELATIVE}} \text{ KEY IS data-name-1}] \\ \left\{ \begin{array}{l} \underline{\text{RANDOM}} \\ \underline{\text{DYNAMIC}} \end{array} \right\} , \underline{\text{RELATIVE}} \text{ KEY IS data-name-1} \end{array} \right\} \right]$

    [; FILE <u>STATUS</u> IS data-name-2] .

FORMAT 3:

SELECT file-name

    ASSIGN TO implementor-name-1 [, implementor-name-2] ...

    [; RESERVE integer-1 [AREA / AREAS]]

    ; ORGANIZATION IS INDEXED

    [; ACCESS MODE IS { SEQUENTIAL / RANDOM / DYNAMIC }]

    ; RECORD KEY IS data-name-1

    [; ALTERNATE RECORD KEY IS data-name-2 [WITH DUPLICATES]] ...

    [; FILE STATUS IS data-name-3] .

FORMAT 4:

SELECT file-name ASSIGN TO implementor-name-1 [, implementor-name-2] ...

<u>GENERAL FORMAT FOR DATA DIVISION</u>

```
DATA DIVISION.

[ FILE SECTION.

[ FD  file-name

    [ ; BLOCK CONTAINS [integer-1 TO] integer-2 { RECORDS   } ]
                                               { CHARACTERS }

    [ ; RECORD CONTAINS [integer-3 TO] integer-4 CHARACTERS ]

      ; LABEL { RECORD IS   } { STANDARD }
              { RECORDS ARE  } { OMITTED  }

    [ ; VALUE OF implementor-name-1 IS { data-name-1 }
                                       { literal-1   }

         [ , implementor-name-2 IS { data-name-2 } ] ... ]
                                   { literal-2   }

    [ ; DATA { RECORD IS   } data-name-3 [ , data-name-4] ... ]
             { RECORDS ARE  }

    [ ; LINAGE IS { data-name-5 } LINES [ , WITH FOOTING AT { data-name-6 } ]
                  { integer-5   }                           { integer-6   }

         [ , LINES AT TOP { data-name-7 } ] [ , LINES AT BOTTOM { data-name-8 } ] ]
                          { integer-7   }                       { integer-8   }

    [ ; CODE-SET IS alphabet-name ]

    [ ; { REPORT IS   } report-name-1 [ , report-name-2] ... ] .
        { REPORTS ARE  }

[record-description-entry] ... ] ...


[ SD  file-name

    [ ; RECORD CONTAINS [integer-1 TO] integer-2 CHARACTERS ]

    [ ; DATA { RECORD IS   } data-name-1 [ , data-name-2] ... ] .
             { RECORDS ARE  }

{record-description-entry} ... ] ... ]


[ WORKING-STORAGE SECTION.

[ 77-level-description-entry ] ...
  record-description-entry

[ LINKAGE SECTION.

[ 77-level-description-entry ] ...
  record-description-entry
```

Data Division

GENERAL FORMAT FOR DATA DESCRIPTION ENTRY

FORMAT 1:

```
level-number   {data-name-1}
               {FILLER    }

[; REDEFINES data-name-2]

[; {PICTURE}  IS character-string]
   {PIC    }

[; [USAGE IS]  {COMPUTATIONAL}]
               {COMP         }
               {DISPLAY      }
               {INDEX        }

[; [SIGN IS]  {LEADING }  [SEPARATE CHARACTER]]
              {TRAILING}

[; OCCURS  {integer-1 TO integer-2 TIMES DEPENDING ON data-name-3}
           {integer-2 TIMES                                      }

      [{ASCENDING }  KEY IS data-name-4  [, data-name-5]  ...]  ...
       {DESCENDING}

      [INDEXED BY index-name-1  [, index-name-2]  ...]]

[; {SYNCHRONIZED}  [LEFT ]]
   {SYNC        }  [RIGHT]

[; {JUSTIFIED}  RIGHT]
   {JUST     }

[; BLANK WHEN ZERO]

[; VALUE IS literal] .
```

FORMAT 2:

```
66 data-name-1; RENAMES data-name-2  [{THROUGH}  data-name-3] .
                                      [{THRU   }             ]
```

FORMAT 3:

```
88 condition-name; {VALUE IS  }  literal-1  [{THROUGH}  literal-2]
                   {VALUES ARE}              [{THRU   }          ]

      [, literal-3  [{THROUGH}  literal-4]]  ...  .
                    [{THRU   }           ]
```

GENERAL FORMAT FOR PROCEDURE DIVISION

FORMAT 1:

PROCEDURE DIVISION [USING data-name-1 [, data-name-2] ...] .

[DECLARATIVES.

{ section-name SECTION [segment-number] .   declarative-sentence

[paragraph-name. [sentence] ...] ... } ...

END DECLARATIVES.]

{ section-name SECTION [segment-number] .

[paragraph-name. [sentence] ...] ... } ...

FORMAT 2:

PROCEDURE DIVISION [USING data-name-1 [, data-name-2] ...] .

{ paragraph-name. [sentence] ... } ...

COBOL Verb Formats

GENERAL FORMAT FOR VERBS

<u>ACCEPT</u> identifier [<u>FROM</u> mnemonic-name]

<u>ACCEPT</u> identifier <u>FROM</u> $\left\{ \begin{array}{l} \underline{DATE} \\ \underline{DAY} \\ \underline{TIME} \end{array} \right\}$

<u>ACCEPT</u> cd-name MESSAGE <u>COUNT</u>

<u>ADD</u> $\left\{ \begin{array}{l} \text{identifier-1} \\ \text{literal-1} \end{array} \right\}$ $\left[\begin{array}{l} \text{, identifier-2} \\ \text{, literal-2} \end{array} \right]$ ... <u>TO</u> identifier-m [<u>ROUNDED</u>]

    [, identifier-n [<u>ROUNDED</u>]] ... [; ON <u>SIZE</u> <u>ERROR</u> imperative-statement]

<u>ADD</u> $\left\{ \begin{array}{l} \text{identifier-1} \\ \text{literal-1} \end{array} \right\}$, $\left\{ \begin{array}{l} \text{identifier-2} \\ \text{literal-2} \end{array} \right\}$ $\left[\begin{array}{l} \text{, identifier-3} \\ \text{, literal-3} \end{array} \right]$ ...

    <u>GIVING</u> identifier-m [<u>ROUNDED</u>] [, identifier-n [<u>ROUNDED</u>]] ...

    [; ON <u>SIZE</u> <u>ERROR</u> imperative-statement]

<u>ADD</u> $\left\{ \begin{array}{l} \underline{CORRESPONDING} \\ \underline{CORR} \end{array} \right\}$ identifier-1 <u>TO</u> identifier-2 [<u>ROUNDED</u>]

    [; ON <u>SIZE</u> <u>ERROR</u> imperative-statement]

<u>ALTER</u> procedure-name-1 <u>TO</u> [<u>PROCEED</u> <u>TO</u>] procedure-name-2

    [, procedure-name-3 <u>TO</u> [<u>PROCEED</u> <u>TO</u>] procedure-name-4] ...

<u>CALL</u> $\left\{ \begin{array}{l} \text{identifier-1} \\ \text{literal-1} \end{array} \right\}$ [<u>USING</u> data-name-1 [, data-name-2] ...]

    [; ON <u>OVERFLOW</u> imperative-statement]

<u>CANCEL</u> $\left\{ \begin{array}{l} \text{identifier-1} \\ \text{literal-1} \end{array} \right\}$ $\left[\begin{array}{l} \text{, identifier-2} \\ \text{, literal-2} \end{array} \right]$ ...

<u>CLOSE</u> file-name-1 $\left[\begin{array}{l} \left\{ \begin{array}{l} \underline{REEL} \\ \underline{UNIT} \end{array} \right\} \left[\begin{array}{l} \text{WITH } \underline{NO} \ \underline{REWIND} \\ \text{FOR } \underline{REMOVAL} \end{array} \right] \\ \\ \text{WITH} \left\{ \begin{array}{l} \underline{NO} \ \underline{REWIND} \\ \underline{LOCK} \end{array} \right\} \end{array} \right]$

$\left[, \text{file-name-2} \left[\begin{array}{l} \left\{ \begin{array}{l} \underline{REEL} \\ \underline{UNIT} \end{array} \right\} \left[\begin{array}{l} \text{WITH } \underline{NO} \ \underline{REWIND} \\ \text{FOR } \underline{REMOVAL} \end{array} \right] \\ \\ \text{WITH} \left\{ \begin{array}{l} \underline{NO} \ \underline{REWIND} \\ \underline{LOCK} \end{array} \right\} \end{array} \right] \right]$ ...

<u>CLOSE</u> file-name-1 [WITH <u>LOCK</u>] [, file-name-2 [WITH <u>LOCK</u>]] ...

COMPUTE identifier-1 [ROUNDED] [, identifier-2 [ROUNDED]] ...

   = arithmetic-expression [; ON SIZE ERROR imperative-statement]

DELETE file-name RECORD [; INVALID KEY imperative-statement]

DISABLE { INPUT / OUTPUT [TERMINAL] } cd-name WITH KEY { identifier-1 / literal-1 }

DISPLAY { identifier-1 / literal-1 } [, identifier-2 / , literal-2] ... [UPON mnemonic-name]

DIVIDE { identifier-1 / literal-1 } INTO identifier-2 [ROUNDED]

   [, identifier-3 [ROUNDED]] ... [; ON SIZE ERROR imperative-statement]

DIVIDE { identifier-1 / literal-1 } INTO { identifier-2 / literal-2 } GIVING identifier-3 [ROUNDED]

   [, identifier-4 [ROUNDED]] ... [; ON SIZE ERROR imperative-statement]

DIVIDE { identifier-1 / literal-1 } BY { identifier-2 / literal-2 } GIVING identifier-3 [ROUNDED]

   [, identifier-4 [ROUNDED]] ... [; ON SIZE ERROR imperative-statement]

DIVIDE { identifier-1 / literal-1 } INTO { identifier-2 / literal-2 } GIVING identifier-3 [ROUNDED]

   REMAINDER identifier-4 [; ON SIZE ERROR imperative-statement]

DIVIDE { identifier-1 / literal-1 } BY { identifier-2 / literal-2 } GIVING identifier-3 [ROUNDED]

   REMAINDER identifier-4 [; ON SIZE ERROR imperative-statement]

ENABLE { INPUT / OUTPUT [TERMINAL] } cd-name WITH KEY { identifier-1 / literal-1 }

ENTER language-name [routine-name] .

EXIT [PROGRAM] .

GENERATE { data-name / report-name }

GO TO [procedure-name-1]

GO TO procedure-name-1 [, procedure-name-2] ... , procedure-name-n

DEPENDING ON identifier

IF condition; $\begin{Bmatrix} \text{statement-1} \\ \underline{\text{NEXT}}\ \underline{\text{SENTENCE}} \end{Bmatrix} \begin{Bmatrix} ;\ \underline{\text{ELSE}}\ \text{statement-2} \\ ;\ \underline{\text{ELSE}}\ \underline{\text{NEXT}}\ \underline{\text{SENTENCE}} \end{Bmatrix}$

INITIATE report-name-1 [, report-name-2] ...

INSPECT identifier-1 TALLYING

$$\left\{ ,\ \text{identifier-2}\ \underline{\text{FOR}} \left\{ ,\ \begin{Bmatrix} \underline{\text{ALL}} \\ \underline{\text{LEADING}} \\ \text{CHARACTERS} \end{Bmatrix} \begin{Bmatrix} \text{identifier-3} \\ \text{literal-1} \end{Bmatrix} \left[\begin{Bmatrix} \underline{\text{BEFORE}} \\ \underline{\text{AFTER}} \end{Bmatrix} \text{INITIAL} \begin{Bmatrix} \text{identifier-4} \\ \text{literal-2} \end{Bmatrix} \right] \right\} \dots \right\} \dots$$

INSPECT identifier-1 REPLACING

$$\left\{ \begin{matrix} \text{CHARACTERS}\ \underline{\text{BY}} \begin{Bmatrix} \text{identifier-6} \\ \text{literal-4} \end{Bmatrix} \left[\begin{Bmatrix} \underline{\text{BEFORE}} \\ \underline{\text{AFTER}} \end{Bmatrix} \text{INITIAL} \begin{Bmatrix} \text{identifier-7} \\ \text{literal-5} \end{Bmatrix} \right] \\ \left\{ ,\ \begin{Bmatrix} \underline{\text{ALL}} \\ \underline{\text{LEADING}} \\ \underline{\text{FIRST}} \end{Bmatrix} \left\{ ,\ \begin{Bmatrix} \text{identifier-5} \\ \text{literal-3} \end{Bmatrix} \underline{\text{BY}} \begin{Bmatrix} \text{identifier-6} \\ \text{literal-4} \end{Bmatrix} \left[\begin{Bmatrix} \underline{\text{BEFORE}} \\ \underline{\text{AFTER}} \end{Bmatrix} \text{INITIAL} \begin{Bmatrix} \text{identifier-7} \\ \text{literal-5} \end{Bmatrix} \right] \right\} \dots \right\} \dots \end{matrix} \right\}$$

INSPECT identifier-1 TALLYING

$$\left\{ ,\ \text{identifier-2}\ \underline{\text{FOR}} \left\{ ,\ \begin{Bmatrix} \underline{\text{ALL}} \\ \underline{\text{LEADING}} \\ \text{CHARACTERS} \end{Bmatrix} \begin{Bmatrix} \text{identifier-3} \\ \text{literal-1} \end{Bmatrix} \left[\begin{Bmatrix} \underline{\text{BEFORE}} \\ \underline{\text{AFTER}} \end{Bmatrix} \text{INITIAL} \begin{Bmatrix} \text{identifier-4} \\ \text{literal-2} \end{Bmatrix} \right] \right\} \dots \right\} \dots$$

REPLACING

$$\left\{ \begin{matrix} \text{CHARACTERS}\ \underline{\text{BY}} \begin{Bmatrix} \text{identifier-6} \\ \text{literal-4} \end{Bmatrix} \left[\begin{Bmatrix} \underline{\text{BEFORE}} \\ \underline{\text{AFTER}} \end{Bmatrix} \text{INITIAL} \begin{Bmatrix} \text{identifier-7} \\ \text{literal-5} \end{Bmatrix} \right] \\ \left\{ ,\ \begin{Bmatrix} \underline{\text{ALL}} \\ \underline{\text{LEADING}} \\ \underline{\text{FIRST}} \end{Bmatrix} \left\{ ,\ \begin{Bmatrix} \text{identifier-5} \\ \text{literal-3} \end{Bmatrix} \underline{\text{BY}} \begin{Bmatrix} \text{identifier-6} \\ \text{literal-4} \end{Bmatrix} \left[\begin{Bmatrix} \underline{\text{BEFORE}} \\ \underline{\text{AFTER}} \end{Bmatrix} \text{INITIAL} \begin{Bmatrix} \text{identifier-7} \\ \text{literal-5} \end{Bmatrix} \right] \right\} \dots \right\} \dots \end{matrix} \right\}$$

MERGE file-name-1 ON $\left\{\begin{array}{l}\underline{ASCENDING}\\ \underline{DESCENDING}\end{array}\right\}$ KEY data-name-1 [, data-name-2] ...

$\left[\text{ON} \left\{\begin{array}{l}\underline{ASCENDING}\\ \underline{DESCENDING}\end{array}\right\} \text{KEY data-name-3} \left[, \text{data-name-4}\right] ... \right]$ ...

$\left[\underline{COLLATING} \ \underline{SEQUENCE} \ \text{IS alphabet-name}\right]$

$\underline{USING}$ file-name-2, file-name-3 [, file-name-4] ...

$\left\{\begin{array}{l}\underline{OUTPUT} \ \underline{PROCEDURE} \ \text{IS section-name-1} \left[\left\{\begin{array}{l}\underline{THROUGH}\\ \underline{THRU}\end{array}\right\} \text{section-name-2}\right]\\ \\ \underline{GIVING} \ \text{file-name-5}\end{array}\right\}$

$\underline{MOVE} \left\{\begin{array}{l}\text{identifier-1}\\ \text{literal}\end{array}\right\} \underline{TO}$ identifier-2 [, identifier-3] ...

$\underline{MOVE} \left\{\begin{array}{l}\underline{CORRESPONDING}\\ \underline{CORR}\end{array}\right\}$ identifier-1 $\underline{TO}$ identifier-2

$\underline{MULTIPLY} \left\{\begin{array}{l}\text{identifier-1}\\ \text{literal-1}\end{array}\right\} \underline{BY}$ identifier-2 $\left[\underline{ROUNDED}\right]$

$\left[, \text{identifier-3} \left[\underline{ROUNDED}\right]\right]$ ... $\left[; \text{ON} \ \underline{SIZE} \ \underline{ERROR} \ \text{imperative-statement}\right]$

$\underline{MULTIPLY} \left\{\begin{array}{l}\text{identifier-1}\\ \text{literal-1}\end{array}\right\} \underline{BY} \left\{\begin{array}{l}\text{identifier-2}\\ \text{literal-2}\end{array}\right\} \underline{GIVING}$ identifier-3 $\left[\underline{ROUNDED}\right]$

$\left[, \text{identifier-4} \left[\underline{ROUNDED}\right]\right]$ ... $\left[; \text{ON} \ \underline{SIZE} \ \underline{ERROR} \ \text{imperative-statement}\right]$

$\underline{OPEN} \left\{\begin{array}{l}\underline{INPUT} \ \text{file-name-1} \left[\begin{array}{l}\underline{REVERSED}\\ \underline{WITH} \ \underline{NO} \ \underline{REWIND}\end{array}\right]\left[, \text{file-name-2} \left[\begin{array}{l}\underline{REVERSED}\\ \underline{WITH} \ \underline{NO} \ \underline{REWIND}\end{array}\right]\right] ...\\ \underline{OUTPUT} \ \text{file-name-3} \left[\underline{WITH} \ \underline{NO} \ \underline{REWIND}\right]\left[, \text{file-name-4} \left[\underline{WITH} \ \underline{NO} \ \underline{REWIND}\right]\right] ...\\ \underline{I-O} \ \text{file-name-5} \ [, \text{file-name-6}] ...\\ \underline{EXTEND} \ \text{file-name-7} \ [, \text{file-name-8}] ...\end{array}\right\}$ ...

$\underline{OPEN} \left\{\begin{array}{l}\underline{INPUT} \ \text{file-name-1} \ [, \text{file-name-2}] ...\\ \underline{OUTPUT} \ \text{file-name-3} \ [, \text{file-name-4}] ...\\ \underline{I-O} \ \text{file-name-5} \ [, \text{file-name-6}] ...\end{array}\right\}$ ...

$\underline{PERFORM}$ procedure-name-1 $\left[\left\{\begin{array}{l}\underline{THROUGH}\\ \underline{THRU}\end{array}\right\} \text{procedure-name-2}\right]$

$\underline{PERFORM}$ procedure-name-1 $\left[\left\{\begin{array}{l}\underline{THROUGH}\\ \underline{THRU}\end{array}\right\} \text{procedure-name-2}\right] \left\{\begin{array}{l}\text{identifier-1}\\ \text{integer-1}\end{array}\right\} \underline{TIMES}$

$\underline{PERFORM}$ procedure-name-1 $\left[\left\{\begin{array}{l}\underline{THROUGH}\\ \underline{THRU}\end{array}\right\} \text{procedure-name-2}\right] \underline{UNTIL}$ condition-1

PERFORM procedure-name-1 $\left[\left\{ \begin{matrix} \underline{THROUGH} \\ \underline{THRU} \end{matrix} \right\} \text{procedure-name-2} \right]$

        <u>VARY</u>ING $\left\{ \begin{matrix} \text{identifier-2} \\ \text{index-name-1} \end{matrix} \right\}$ <u>FROM</u> $\left\{ \begin{matrix} \text{identifier-3} \\ \text{index-name-2} \\ \text{literal-1} \end{matrix} \right\}$

            <u>BY</u> $\left\{ \begin{matrix} \text{identifier-4} \\ \text{literal-3} \end{matrix} \right\}$ <u>UNTIL</u> condition-1

$\left[\underline{AFTER} \left\{ \begin{matrix} \text{identifier-5} \\ \text{index-name-3} \end{matrix} \right\} \underline{FROM} \left\{ \begin{matrix} \text{identifier-6} \\ \text{index-name-4} \\ \text{literal-3} \end{matrix} \right\} \right.$

            <u>BY</u> $\left\{ \begin{matrix} \text{identifier-7} \\ \text{literal-4} \end{matrix} \right\}$ <u>UNTIL</u> condition-2

$\left[\underline{AFTER} \left\{ \begin{matrix} \text{identifier-8} \\ \text{index-name-5} \end{matrix} \right\} \underline{FROM} \left\{ \begin{matrix} \text{identifier-9} \\ \text{index-name-6} \\ \text{literal-5} \end{matrix} \right\} \right.$

            $\left. \left. \underline{BY} \left\{ \begin{matrix} \text{identifier-10} \\ \text{literal-6} \end{matrix} \right\} \underline{UNTIL} \text{ condition-3} \right] \right]$

<u>READ</u> file-name RECORD $\left[\underline{INTO} \text{ identifier} \right]$ $\left[\text{; AT } \underline{END} \text{ imperative-statement} \right]$

<u>READ</u> file-name $\left[\underline{NEXT} \right]$ RECORD $\left[\underline{INTO} \text{ identifier} \right]$

  $\left[\text{; AT } \underline{END} \text{ imperative-statement} \right]$

<u>READ</u> file-name RECORD $\left[\underline{INTO} \text{ identifier} \right]$ $\left[\text{; } \underline{INVALID} \text{ KEY imperative-statement} \right]$

<u>READ</u> file-name RECORD $\left[\underline{INTO} \text{ identifier} \right]$

  $\left[\text{; } \underline{KEY} \text{ IS data-name} \right]$

  $\left[\text{; } \underline{INVALID} \text{ KEY imperative-statement} \right]$

<u>RECEIVE</u> cd-name $\left\{ \begin{matrix} \underline{MESSAGE} \\ \underline{SEGMENT} \end{matrix} \right\}$ <u>INTO</u> identifier-1 $\left[\text{; } \underline{NO} \underline{DATA} \text{ imperative-statement} \right]$

<u>RELEASE</u> record-name $\left[\underline{FROM} \text{ identifier} \right]$

<u>RETURN</u> file-name RECORD $\left[\underline{INTO} \text{ identifier} \right]$; AT <u>END</u> imperative-statement

<u>REWRITE</u> record-name $\left[\underline{FROM} \text{ identifier} \right]$

<u>REWRITE</u> record-name $\left[\underline{FROM} \text{ identifier} \right]$ $\left[\text{; } \underline{INVALID} \text{ KEY imperative-statement} \right]$

$$\underline{\text{SEARCH}} \text{ identifier-1} \left[\underline{\text{VARYING}} \begin{Bmatrix} \text{identifier-2} \\ \text{index-name-1} \end{Bmatrix} \right] \left[; \text{ AT } \underline{\text{END}} \text{ imperative-statement-1} \right]$$

$$; \underline{\text{WHEN}} \text{ condition-1} \begin{Bmatrix} \text{imperative-statement-2} \\ \underline{\text{NEXT}} \ \underline{\text{SENTENCE}} \end{Bmatrix}$$

$$\left[; \underline{\text{WHEN}} \text{ condition-2} \begin{Bmatrix} \text{imperative-statement-3} \\ \underline{\text{NEXT}} \ \underline{\text{SENTENCE}} \end{Bmatrix} \right] \ \ldots$$

$$\underline{\text{SEARCH}} \ \underline{\text{ALL}} \text{ identifier-1} \left[; \text{ AT } \underline{\text{END}} \text{ imperative-statement-1} \right]$$

$$; \underline{\text{WHEN}} \begin{Bmatrix} \text{data-name-1} \begin{Bmatrix} \text{IS } \underline{\text{EQUAL}} \text{ TO} \\ \text{IS } = \end{Bmatrix} \begin{Bmatrix} \text{identifier-3} \\ \text{literal-1} \\ \text{arithmetic-expression-1} \end{Bmatrix} \\ \text{condition-name-1} \end{Bmatrix}$$

$$\left[\underline{\text{AND}} \begin{Bmatrix} \text{data-name-2} \begin{Bmatrix} \text{IS } \underline{\text{EQUAL}} \text{ TO} \\ \text{IS } = \end{Bmatrix} \begin{Bmatrix} \text{identifier-4} \\ \text{literal-2} \\ \text{arithmetic-expression-2} \end{Bmatrix} \\ \text{condition-name-2} \end{Bmatrix} \right] \ \ldots$$

$$\begin{Bmatrix} \text{imperative-statement-2} \\ \underline{\text{NEXT}} \ \underline{\text{SENTENCE}} \end{Bmatrix}$$

$$\underline{\text{SEND}} \text{ cd-name } \underline{\text{FROM}} \text{ identifier-1}$$

$$\underline{\text{SEND}} \text{ cd-name } \left[\underline{\text{FROM}} \text{ identifier-1} \right] \begin{Bmatrix} \text{WITH identifier-2} \\ \text{WITH } \underline{\text{ESI}} \\ \text{WITH } \underline{\text{EMI}} \\ \text{WITH } \underline{\text{EGI}} \end{Bmatrix}$$

$$\left[\begin{Bmatrix} \underline{\text{BEFORE}} \\ \underline{\text{AFTER}} \end{Bmatrix} \text{ ADVANCING} \begin{Bmatrix} \begin{Bmatrix} \text{identifier-3} \\ \text{integer} \end{Bmatrix} \begin{bmatrix} \text{LINE} \\ \text{LINES} \end{bmatrix} \\ \begin{Bmatrix} \text{mnemonic-name} \\ \underline{\text{PAGE}} \end{Bmatrix} \end{Bmatrix} \right]$$

$$\underline{\text{SET}} \begin{Bmatrix} \text{identifier-1} \ [, \text{ identifier-2}] \ \ldots \\ \text{index-name-1} \ [, \text{ index-name-2}] \ \ldots \end{Bmatrix} \underline{\text{TO}} \begin{Bmatrix} \text{identifier-3} \\ \text{index-name-3} \\ \text{integer-1} \end{Bmatrix}$$

$$\underline{\text{SET}} \text{ index-name-4} \ [, \text{ index-name-5}] \ \ldots \begin{Bmatrix} \underline{\text{UP}} \ \underline{\text{BY}} \\ \underline{\text{DOWN}} \ \underline{\text{BY}} \end{Bmatrix} \begin{Bmatrix} \text{identifier-4} \\ \text{integer-2} \end{Bmatrix}$$

SORT file-name-1 ON $\left\{ \begin{array}{l} \underline{ASCENDING} \\ \underline{DESCENDING} \end{array} \right\}$ KEY data-name-1 $\left[, \text{ data-name-2} \right]$ ...

$\left[\text{ON } \left\{ \begin{array}{l} \underline{ASCENDING} \\ \underline{DESCENDING} \end{array} \right\} \text{ KEY data-name-3 } \left[, \text{ data-name-4} \right] ... \right]$ ...

$\left[\text{COLLATING } \underline{SEQUENCE} \text{ IS alphabet-name} \right]$

$\left\{ \begin{array}{l} \underline{INPUT} \ \underline{PROCEDURE} \text{ IS section-name-1 } \left[\left\{ \begin{array}{l} \underline{THROUGH} \\ \underline{THRU} \end{array} \right\} \text{ section-name-2} \right] \\ \underline{USING} \text{ file-name-2 } \left[, \text{ file-name-3} \right] ... \end{array} \right\}$

$\left\{ \begin{array}{l} \underline{OUTPUT} \ \underline{PROCEDURE} \text{ IS section-name-3} \left[\left\{ \begin{array}{l} \underline{THROUGH} \\ \underline{THRU} \end{array} \right\} \text{ section-name-4} \right] \\ \underline{GIVING} \text{ file-name-4} \end{array} \right\}$

$\underline{START}$ file-name $\left[\underline{KEY} \left\{ \begin{array}{l} \text{IS } \underline{EQUAL} \text{ TO} \\ \text{IS } = \\ \text{IS } \underline{GREATER} \text{ THAN} \\ \text{IS } > \\ \text{IS } \underline{NOT} \ \underline{LESS} \text{ THAN} \\ \text{IS } \underline{NOT} < \end{array} \right\} \text{data-name} \right]$

$\left[; \ \underline{INVALID} \text{ KEY imperative-statement} \right]$

$\underline{STOP}$ $\left\{ \begin{array}{l} \underline{RUN} \\ \text{literal} \end{array} \right\}$

$\underline{STRING}$ $\left\{ \begin{array}{l} \text{identifier-1} \\ \text{literal-1} \end{array} \right\}$ $\left[\begin{array}{l} , \text{ identifier-2} \\ , \text{ literal-2} \end{array} \right]$ ... $\underline{DELIMITED}$ BY $\left\{ \begin{array}{l} \text{identifier-3} \\ \text{literal-3} \\ \underline{SIZE} \end{array} \right\}$

$\left[, \left\{ \begin{array}{l} \text{identifier-4} \\ \text{literal-4} \end{array} \right\} \left[\begin{array}{l} , \text{ identifier-5} \\ , \text{ literal-5} \end{array} \right] ... \underline{DELIMITED} \text{ BY } \left\{ \begin{array}{l} \text{identifier-6} \\ \text{literal-6} \\ \underline{SIZE} \end{array} \right\} \right]$ ...

$\underline{INTO}$ identifier-7 $\left[\text{WITH } \underline{POINTER} \text{ identifier-8} \right]$

$\left[; \text{ ON } \underline{OVERFLOW} \text{ imperative-statement} \right]$

$\underline{SUBTRACT}$ $\left\{ \begin{array}{l} \text{identifier-1} \\ \text{literal-1} \end{array} \right\}$ $\left[\begin{array}{l} , \text{ identifier-2} \\ , \text{ literal-2} \end{array} \right]$ ... $\underline{FROM}$ identifier-m $\left[\underline{ROUNDED} \right]$

$\left[, \text{ identifier-n } \left[\underline{ROUNDED} \right] \right]$ ... $\left[; \text{ ON } \underline{SIZE} \ \underline{ERROR} \text{ imperative-statement} \right]$

GENERAL FORMAT FOR VERBS

SUBTRACT $\begin{Bmatrix} \text{identifier-1} \\ \text{literal-1} \end{Bmatrix}$ $\begin{bmatrix} , \text{ identifier-2} \\ , \text{ literal-2} \end{bmatrix}$ ... FROM $\begin{Bmatrix} \text{identifier-m} \\ \text{literal-m} \end{Bmatrix}$

    GIVING identifier-n [ROUNDED] [, identifier-o [ROUNDED]] ...

    [; ON SIZE ERROR imperative-statement]

SUBTRACT $\begin{Bmatrix} \underline{\text{CORRESPONDING}} \\ \underline{\text{CORR}} \end{Bmatrix}$ identifier-1 FROM identifier-2 [ROUNDED]

    [; ON SIZE ERROR imperative-statement]

SUPPRESS PRINTING

TERMINATE report-name-1 [, report-name-2] ...

UNSTRING identifier-1

    $\left[\text{DELIMITED BY } [\text{ALL}] \begin{Bmatrix} \text{identifier-2} \\ \text{literal-1} \end{Bmatrix} \left[, \text{ OR } [\text{ALL}] \begin{Bmatrix} \text{identifier-3} \\ \text{literal-2} \end{Bmatrix} \right] ... \right]$

      INTO identifier-4 [, DELIMITER IN identifier-5] [, COUNT IN identifier-6]

        [, identifier-7 [, DELIMITER IN identifier-8] [, COUNT IN identifier-9]] ...

    [WITH POINTER identifier-10] [TALLYING IN identifier-11]

    [; ON OVERFLOW imperative-statement]

USE AFTER STANDARD $\begin{Bmatrix} \text{EXCEPTION} \\ \text{ERROR} \end{Bmatrix}$ PROCEDURE ON $\begin{Bmatrix} \text{file-name-1 } [, \text{ file-name-2}] ... \\ \text{INPUT} \\ \text{OUTPUT} \\ \text{I-O} \\ \text{EXTEND} \end{Bmatrix}$.

USE AFTER STANDARD $\begin{Bmatrix} \text{EXCEPTION} \\ \text{ERROR} \end{Bmatrix}$ PROCEDURE ON $\begin{Bmatrix} \text{file-name-1 } [, \text{ file-name-2}] ... \\ \text{INPUT} \\ \text{OUTPUT} \\ \text{I-O} \end{Bmatrix}$.

USE BEFORE REPORTING identifier.

$$\underline{USE} \text{ FOR } \underline{DEBUGGING} \text{ ON } \begin{Bmatrix} \text{cd-name-1} \\ [\underline{ALL} \text{ REFERENCES OF}] \text{ identifier-1} \\ \text{file-name-1} \\ \text{procedure-name-1} \\ \underline{ALL} \text{ } \underline{PROCEDURES} \end{Bmatrix}$$

$$\left[, \begin{matrix} \text{cd-name-2} \\ [\underline{ALL} \text{ REFERENCES OF}] \text{ identifier-2} \\ \text{file-name-2} \\ \text{procedure-name-2} \\ \underline{ALL} \text{ } \underline{PROCEDURES} \end{matrix} \right] \text{ ... } .$$

$$\underline{WRITE} \text{ record-name } \left[\underline{FROM} \text{ identifier-1} \right]$$

$$\left[\begin{Bmatrix} \underline{BEFORE} \\ \underline{AFTER} \end{Bmatrix} \text{ ADVANCING } \begin{Bmatrix} \begin{Bmatrix} \text{identifier-2} \\ \text{integer} \end{Bmatrix} \begin{bmatrix} \text{LINE} \\ \text{LINES} \end{bmatrix} \\ \begin{Bmatrix} \text{mnemonic-name} \\ \underline{PAGE} \end{Bmatrix} \end{Bmatrix} \right]$$

$$\left[\text{ ; AT } \begin{Bmatrix} \text{END-OF-PAGE} \\ \underline{EOP} \end{Bmatrix} \text{ imperative-statement} \right]$$

$$\underline{WRITE} \text{ record-name } \left[\underline{FROM} \text{ identifier} \right] \left[\text{ ; } \underline{INVALID} \text{ KEY imperative-statement} \right]$$

GENERAL FORMAT FOR CONDITIONS

RELATION CONDITION:

$$
\left\{ \begin{array}{l} \text{identifier-1} \\ \text{literal-1} \\ \text{arithmetic-expression-1} \\ \text{index-name-1} \end{array} \right\}
\left\{ \begin{array}{l} \text{IS [NOT] \underline{GREATER} THAN} \\ \text{IS [NOT] \underline{LESS} THAN} \\ \text{IS [NOT] \underline{EQUAL} TO} \\ \text{IS [NOT] >} \\ \text{IS [NOT] <} \\ \text{IS [NOT] =} \end{array} \right\}
\left\{ \begin{array}{l} \text{identifier-2} \\ \text{literal-2} \\ \text{arithmetic-expression-2} \\ \text{index-name-2} \end{array} \right\}
$$

CLASS CONDITION:

$$
\text{identifier IS [\underline{NOT}]} \left\{ \begin{array}{l} \underline{\text{NUMERIC}} \\ \underline{\text{ALPHABETIC}} \end{array} \right\}
$$

SIGN CONDITION:

$$
\text{arithmetic-expression is [\underline{NOT}]} \left\{ \begin{array}{l} \underline{\text{POSITIVE}} \\ \underline{\text{NEGATIVE}} \\ \underline{\text{ZERO}} \end{array} \right\}
$$

CONDITION-NAME CONDITION:

condition-name

SWITCH-STATUS CONDITION:

condition-name

NEGATED SIMPLE CONDITION:

<u>NOT</u> simple-condition

COMBINED CONDITION:

$$
\text{condition} \left\{ \left\{ \begin{array}{l} \underline{\text{AND}} \\ \underline{\text{OR}} \end{array} \right\} \text{condition} \right\} \ldots
$$

ABBREVIATED COMBINED RELATION CONDITION:

$$
\text{relation-condition} \left\{ \left\{ \begin{array}{l} \underline{\text{AND}} \\ \underline{\text{OR}} \end{array} \right\} [\underline{\text{NOT}}] \ [\text{relational-operator}] \ \text{object} \right\} \ldots
$$

Miscellaneous Formats

MISCELLANEOUS FORMATS

QUALIFICATION:

$$\left\{ \begin{array}{l} \text{data-name-1} \\ \text{condition-name} \end{array} \right\} \left[\left\{ \begin{array}{l} \underline{\text{OF}} \\ \underline{\text{IN}} \end{array} \right\} \text{data-name-2} \right] \cdots$$

$$\text{paragraph-name} \left[\left\{ \begin{array}{l} \underline{\text{OF}} \\ \underline{\text{IN}} \end{array} \right\} \text{section-name} \right]$$

$$\text{text-name} \left[\left\{ \begin{array}{l} \underline{\text{OF}} \\ \underline{\text{IN}} \end{array} \right\} \text{library-name} \right]$$

SUBSCRIPTING:

$$\left\{ \begin{array}{l} \text{data-name} \\ \text{condition-name} \end{array} \right\} (\text{subscript-1} \left[, \text{subscript-2} \left[, \text{subscript-3} \right] \right])$$

INDEXING:

$$\left\{ \begin{array}{l} \text{data-name} \\ \text{condition-name} \end{array} \right\} \left(\left\{ \begin{array}{l} \text{index-name-1} \left[\{\pm\} \text{ literal-2} \right] \\ \text{literal-1} \end{array} \right\} \right.$$

$$\left[, \left\{ \begin{array}{l} \text{index-name-2} \left[\{\pm\} \text{ literal-4} \right] \\ \text{literal-3} \end{array} \right\} \left[, \left\{ \begin{array}{l} \text{index-name-3} \left[\{\pm\} \text{ literal-6} \right] \\ \text{literal-5} \end{array} \right\} \right] \right])$$

IDENTIFIER: FORMAT 1

$$\text{data-name-1} \left[\left\{ \begin{array}{l} \underline{\text{OF}} \\ \underline{\text{IN}} \end{array} \right\} \text{data-name-2} \right] \cdots \left[(\text{subscript-1} \left[, \text{subscript-2} \right. \right.$$

$$\left. \left. \left[, \text{subscript-3} \right] \right) \right]$$

IDENTIFIER: FORMAT 2

$$\text{data-name-1} \left[\left\{ \begin{array}{l} \underline{\text{OF}} \\ \underline{\text{IN}} \end{array} \right\} \text{data-name-2} \right] \cdots \left[\left(\left\{ \begin{array}{l} \text{index-name-1} \left[\{\pm\} \text{ literal-2} \right] \\ \text{literal-1} \end{array} \right\} \right. \right.$$

$$\left[, \left\{ \begin{array}{l} \text{index-name-2} \left[\{\pm\} \text{ literal-4} \right] \\ \text{literal-3} \end{array} \right\} \left[, \left\{ \begin{array}{l} \text{index-name-3} \left[\{\pm\} \text{ literal-6} \right] \\ \text{literal-5} \end{array} \right\} \right] \right]) \right]$$

GENERAL FORMAT FOR COPY STATEMENT

```
COPY text-name  [ { OF } library-name ]
                  { IN }

 [                  ( ( ==pseudo-text-1== )      ( ==pseudo-text-2== )      )
  REPLACING  { , {  ( identifier-1       )  BY  ( identifier-2       ) } ... }
                   ( literal-1           )      ( literal-2           )
                   ( word-1              )      ( word-2              )
 ]
```

READING SOURCE LISTING AND DIAGNOSTICS

The compiler and related software of the computer system used for COBOL programs can produce output in the form of printed listings. In addition, the printed listings may contain "diagnostics" and informative messages when errors are detected in the source program. An explanation of the contents of the listing is given below.

SOURCE LISTING

Figures C-1 and C-2 contain an example of a source listing from the IBM DOS COBOL compiler.

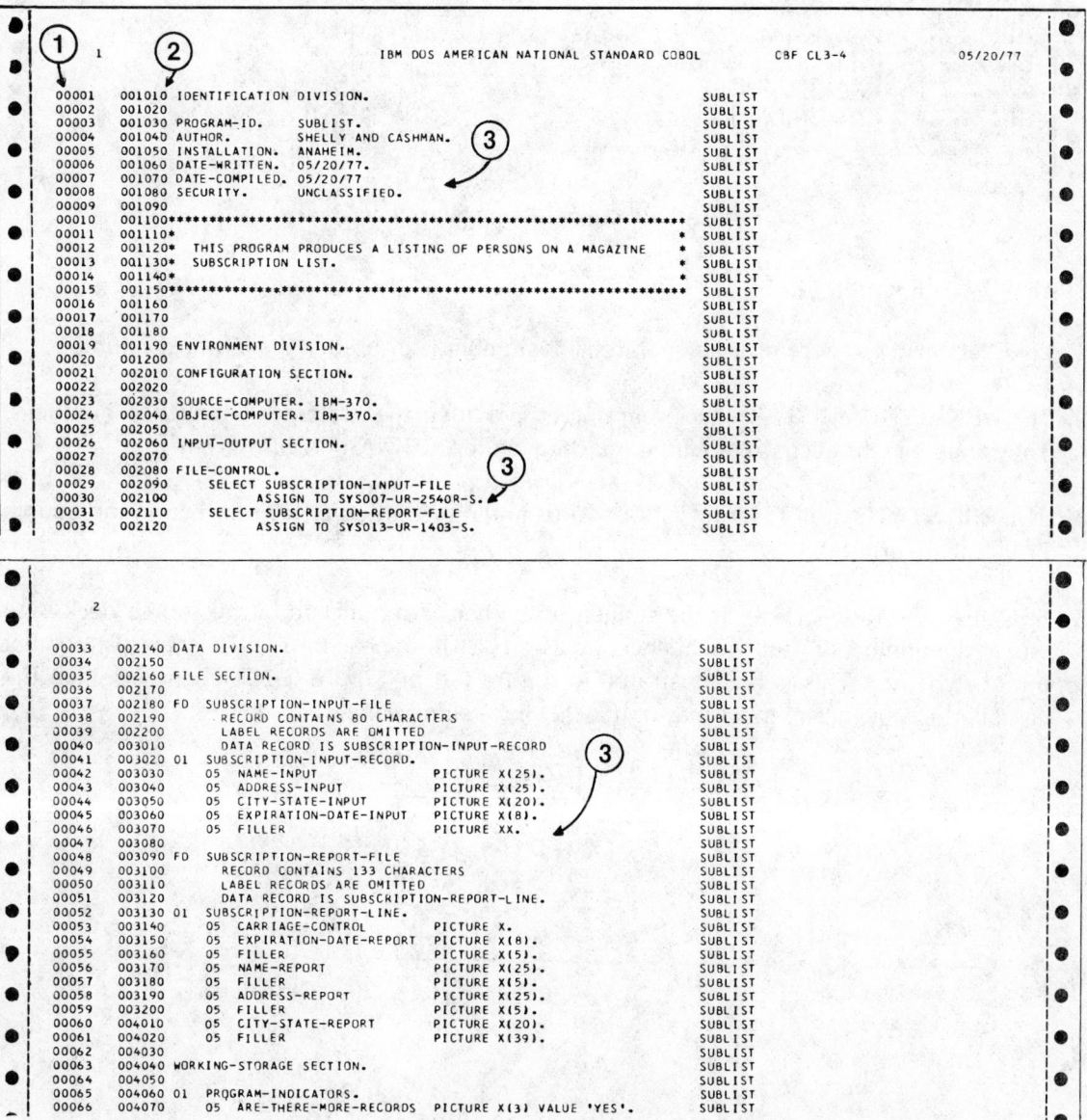

Figure C-1 Source Listing [Part 1 of 2]

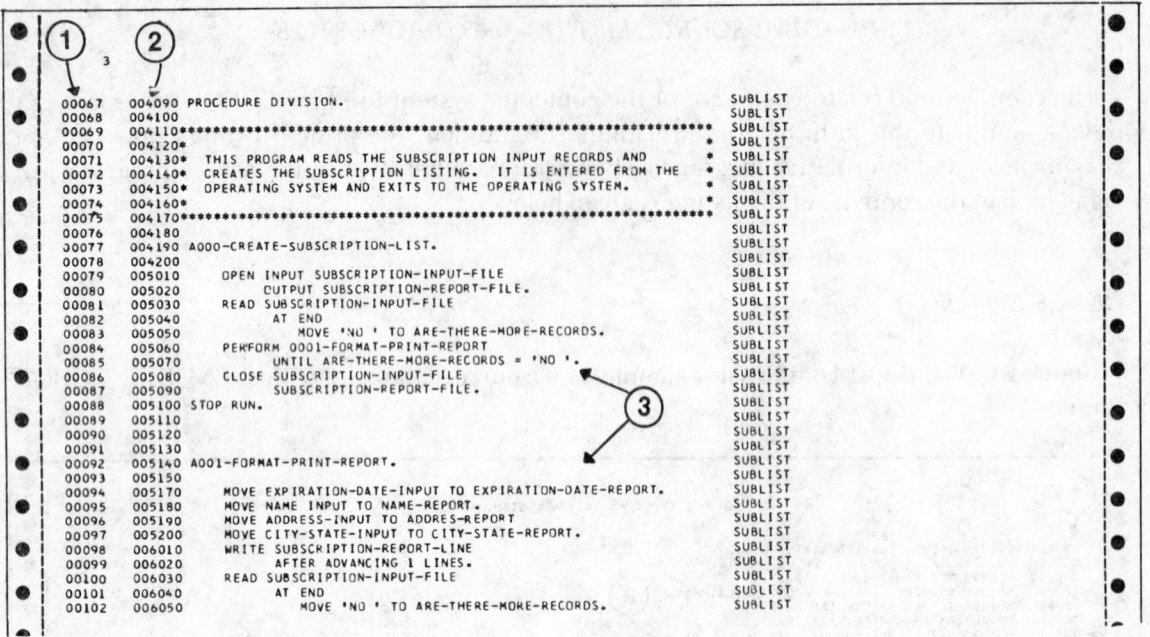

```
00067   004090 PROCEDURE DIVISION.                                        SUBLIST
00068   004100                                                           SUBLIST
00069   004110*********************************************************  SUBLIST
00070   004120*                                                       *  SUBLIST
00071   004130*  THIS PROGRAM READS THE SUBSCRIPTION INPUT RECORDS AND *  SUBLIST
00072   004140*  CREATES THE SUBSCRIPTION LISTING.  IT IS ENTERED FROM THE *  SUBLIST
00073   004150*  OPERATING SYSTEM AND EXITS TO THE OPERATING SYSTEM.   *  SUBLIST
00074   004160*                                                       *  SUBLIST
00075   004170*********************************************************  SUBLIST
00076   004180                                                           SUBLIST
00077   004190 A000-CREATE-SUBSCRIPTION-LIST.                            SUBLIST
00078   004200                                                           SUBLIST
00079   005010      OPEN INPUT SUBSCRIPTION-INPUT-FILE                   SUBLIST
00080   005020           OUTPUT SUBSCRIPTION-REPORT-FILE.                SUBLIST
00081   005030      READ SUBSCRIPTION-INPUT-FILE                         SUBLIST
00082   005040           AT END                                         SUBLIST
00083   005050               MOVE 'NO ' TO ARE-THERE-MORE-RECORDS.       SUBLIST
00084   005060      PERFORM 0001-FORMAT-PRINT-REPORT                     SUBLIST
00085   005070           UNTIL ARE-THERE-MORE-RECORDS = 'NO '.           SUBLIST
00086   005080      CLOSE SUBSCRIPTION-INPUT-FILE                        SUBLIST
00087   005090           SUBSCRIPTION-REPORT-FILE.                       SUBLIST
00088   005100 STOP RUN.                                                 SUBLIST
00089   005110                                                           SUBLIST
00090   005120                                                           SUBLIST
00091   005130                                                           SUBLIST
00092   005140 A001-FORMAT-PRINT-REPORT.                                 SUBLIST
00093   005150                                                           SUBLIST
00094   005170      MOVE EXPIRATION-DATE-INPUT TO EXPIRATION-DATE-REPORT. SUBLIST
00095   005180      MOVE NAME-INPUT TO NAME-REPORT.                      SUBLIST
00096   005190      MOVE ADDRESS-INPUT TO ADDRES-REPORT                  SUBLIST
00097   005200      MOVE CITY-STATE-INPUT TO CITY-STATE-REPORT.          SUBLIST
00098   006010      WRITE SUBSCRIPTION-REPORT-LINE                       SUBLIST
00099   006020           AFTER ADVANCING 1 LINES.                        SUBLIST
00100   006030      READ SUBSCRIPTION-INPUT-FILE                         SUBLIST
00101   006040           AT END                                         SUBLIST
00102   006050               MOVE 'NO ' TO ARE-THERE-MORE-RECORDS.       SUBLIST
```

Figure C-2 Source Listing [Part 2 of 2]

The source listing consists of:

1. LINE NUMBER — A compiler-generated line number is printed in the leftmost column.

2. SEQUENCE NUMBER — The programmer provides the statement sequence numbers. They appear in the second column, if punched in the COBOL Source Program.

3. SOURCE STATEMENT — All COBOL words and punctuation as keypunched in the Source Program are printed.

4. SEQUENCE ERROR (*) — If the sequence numbers are punched in the source deck, and one of the numbers is out of sequence, an asterisk will appear beside the source statement out of sequence. This is not illustrated in Figure C-1 or Figure C-2. Depending upon the compiler, a sequence number may or may not have significance.

DIAGNOSTIC MESSAGES

The segment of the listing in Figure C-3 is an example of a list of error messages. These diagnostic messages were generated by the DOS COBOL compiler for the program shown in Figure C-1 and Figure C-2. It should be noted that the format of the diagnostics and the diagnostic identification numbers will vary, dependent upon the compiler and machine used. An explanation of diagnostic messages follows.

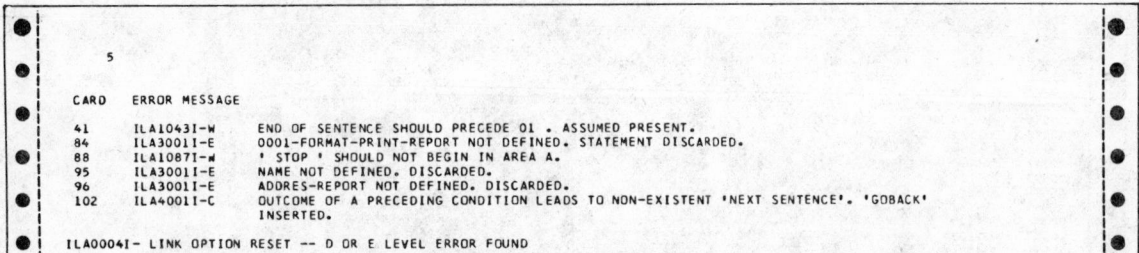

```
     5

CARD    ERROR MESSAGE

 41     ILA1043I-W     END OF SENTENCE SHOULD PRECEDE 01 . ASSUMED PRESENT.
 84     ILA3001I-E     0001-FORMAT-PRINT-REPORT NOT DEFINED. STATEMENT DISCARDED.
 88     ILA1087I-W     ' STOP ' SHOULD NOT BEGIN IN AREA A.
 95     ILA3001I-E     NAME NOT DEFINED. DISCARDED.
 96     ILA3001I-E     ADDRES-REPORT NOT DEFINED. DISCARDED.
102     ILA4001I-C     OUTCOME OF A PRECEDING CONDITION LEADS TO NON-EXISTENT 'NEXT SENTENCE'. 'GOBACK'
                       INSERTED.

ILA0004I- LINK OPTION RESET -- D OR E LEVEL ERROR FOUND
```

Figure C-3 Diagnostics

1. CARD — This value contains the internal line number of the source statement where the error was detected.

2. ERROR MESSAGE — This line contains a message number and the severity of the error.

MESSAGE NUMBER	All message numbers and the associated messages are described in the appropriate programmer's guide.

Severity Code	Explanation
W = WARNING	This code indicates that an error was made in the source program. However, it is not serious enough to hinder the execution of the program.
C = CONDITIONAL	This indicates that an error was made but the compiler usually makes a corrective assumption. The statement containing the error is retained. Execution can be attempted for the debugging value.
E = ERROR	This indicates that a serious error was made. Usually the compiler makes no corrective assumption. The statement containing the error is dropped. Execution of the program should not be attempted.
D = DISASTER	This indicates that a serious error was made. Compilation is not completed and the results are unpredictable.

3. MESSAGE — Following the message number and the code is a sentence which indicates the nature of the error.

SEQUENTIAL DISK PROCESSING

INTRODUCTION

The use of direct-access (disk) devices is widespread in industry. Although there is very little difference between using a sequential disk file and a card file, as is illustrated in the sample programs throughout the book, the following is an explanation of several basic concepts which pertain to disk files and the COBOL entries required to write and read sequential disk files.

BLOCKING

When records are stored on a disk in a sequential mode, they are stored one after the other on the surface of the disk. This is illustrated in Figure D-1.

EXAMPLE

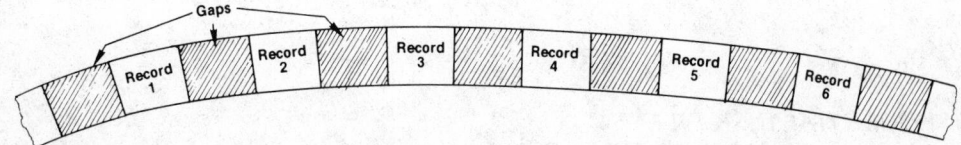

Figure D-1 Example of Sequentially Stored Records

Note in Figure D-1 that the records are stored one after another on the surface of the disk. Between each record is a "gap", which is required so that the computer hardware can distinguish one record from another.

In many instances, it is advantageous to BLOCK the records. Blocking refers to the process in which two or more individual records (referred to as "logical records") are grouped together and written on a disk, creating a "physical record" or "block". This is illustrated in Figure D-2.

EXAMPLE

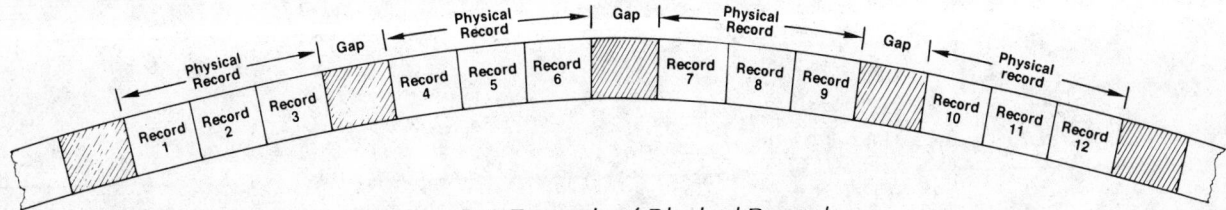

Figure D-2 Example of Blocked Records

Note in Figure D-2 that three logical records (Record 1, Record 2, and Record 3) are placed adjacent to each other without a gap between them. These three records form a physical record or block.

Blocking has two major advantages: 1) More records can be written in the same space on a disk because a number of records are recorded between each gap, thus reducing the number of gaps on the disk; 2) The records can be read faster because two or more records can be read before the read operation is terminated by the gap. It should be noted that the software of the operating system is used to determine where a logical record begins and ends within the physical record which is read from the disk.

The limiting factor in blocking records is the amount of computer storage available for input/output operations, as there must be enough room in storage to store the complete block of data to be processed. Thus, the larger the block of records, the more computer storage that must be allocated for storing the block. For example, if fifty 80 character records comprise the physical record, then 4,000 positions of computer storage are required when the physical record is transferred from disk to computer storage or from computer storage to disk. The programmer or analyst must make the determination as to what size block can be used so that there is enough storage available and the blocking is as efficient as possible.

The number of logical records comprising the "physical record" is called the BLOCKING FACTOR.

WRITING SEQUENTIAL DISK FILES

In order to write records on a disk file, entries must be made in the Environment Division, the Data Division, and the Procedure Division. The entries required in these portions of the COBOL program are illustrated in Figure D-3.

Environment-Division

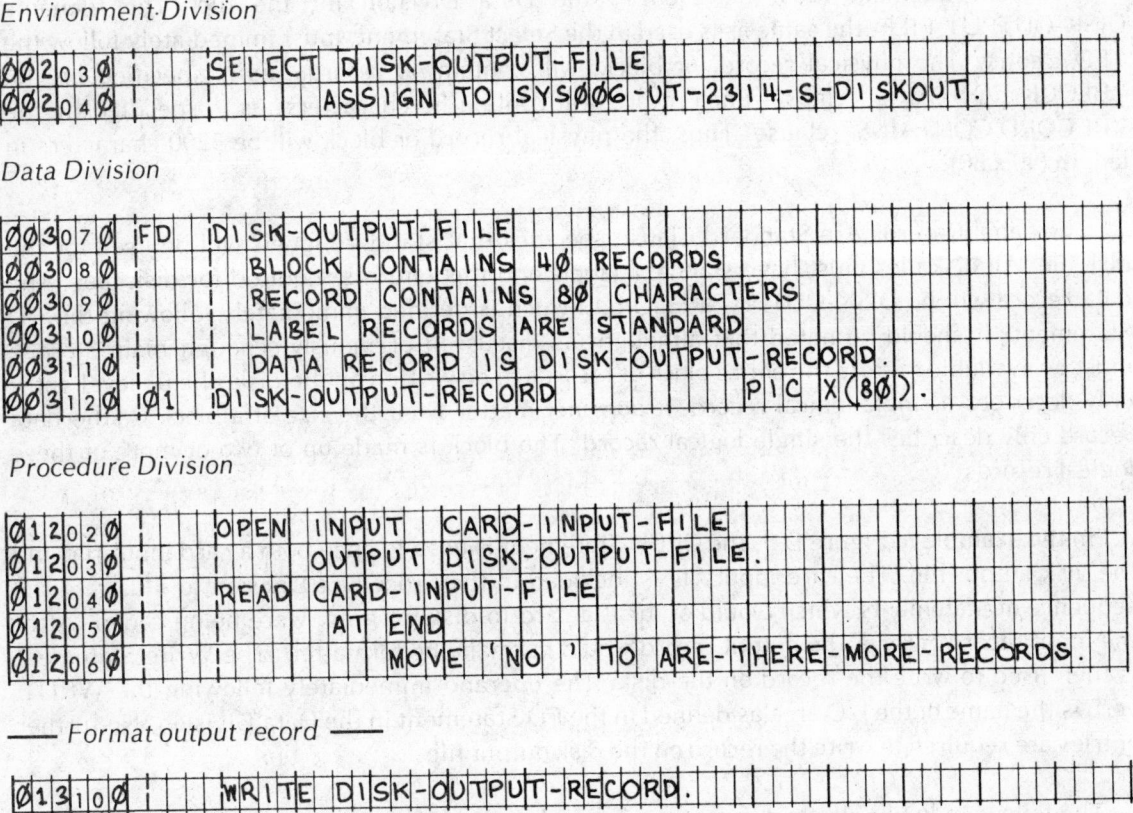

```
0 0 2 0 3 0        SELECT DISK-OUTPUT-FILE
0 0 2 0 4 0           ASSIGN TO SYS006-UT-2314-S-DISKOUT.
```

Data Division

```
0 0 3 0 7 0  FD   DISK-OUTPUT-FILE
0 0 3 0 8 0        BLOCK CONTAINS 40 RECORDS
0 0 3 0 9 0        RECORD CONTAINS 80 CHARACTERS
0 0 3 1 0 0        LABEL RECORDS ARE STANDARD
0 0 3 1 1 0        DATA RECORD IS DISK-OUTPUT-RECORD.
0 0 3 1 2 0  01   DISK-OUTPUT-RECORD            PIC X(80).
```

Procedure Division

```
0 1 2 0 2 0       OPEN INPUT CARD-INPUT-FILE
0 1 2 0 3 0            OUTPUT DISK-OUTPUT-FILE.
0 1 2 0 4 0       READ CARD-INPUT-FILE
0 1 2 0 5 0            AT END
0 1 2 0 6 0              MOVE 'NO ' TO ARE-THERE-MORE-RECORDS.
```

——— *Format output record* ———

```
0 1 3 1 0 0       WRITE DISK-OUTPUT-RECORD.
```

Figure D-3 Entries to Write a Sequential Disk File

The Select Statement is required for sequential disk files in the same manner it is required for all files defined in a COBOL program. The filename DISK-OUTPUT-FILE immediately follows the Select Statement in the same manner as is used for card and printer files. The Assign Statement assigns the output file to the device assigned to "SYS006" at the time the program is executed. The letters "UT" specify that the file is a sequential file on a device that is not considered a unit-record device. The entry 2314 states that the file will be contained on a 2314 disk drive. The file is sequential as defined by the "S", and the file will be referenced by the name DISKOUT in job control statements. This last statement is called the "system name" and should be used with sequential disk files. The name can be any programmer-chosen name of eight or fewer characters.

The FD Statement must be used in the Data Division for the file. The filename DISK-OUTPUT-FILE, the same as is used in the Select Statement, must immediately follow the "FD" entry. The physical record, or block, will contain 40 records, as is specified by the "BLOCK CONTAINS" clause. Each record will contain 80 characters, as is specified by the "RECORD CONTAINS" clause. Thus, the physical record or block will be 3200 characters in length (40 x 80).

The Label Records Are Standard Clause specifies that standard labels will be used for the disk file. All disk files must have standard labels and this entry is required for disk files. The data record will be DISK-OUTPUT-RECORD, which is defined immediately following the FD Statement. It should be noted that although, as discussed previously, enough main storage must be available to store the entire block of records to be written on the disk, the 01 level entry only describes a single logical record. It does not matter what the size of a block is; the data record only describes the single logical record. The block is made up of two or more of these logical records.

In the example in Figure D-3, the OPEN Statement is used to open both a card input file and the disk output file. The card input file is included in the Procedure Division to illustrate the sequence of statements which would occur if a card-to-disk program were being coded. After the input record is read, the output record would normally be formatted. The Write Statement is then used to write the record on the disk. The operand immediately following the WRITE verb is the name of the I/O area as defined in the FD Statement in the Data Division. No further entries are required to write the record on the disk output file.

The following listing illustrates a program which creates a sequential disk output file. This program could be used to load the test data for the programming assignments, which is contained in Appendix A, onto a disk file so that all students could reference that one disk input file rather than having to prepare and use punched cards.

```
        1                               IBM DOS AMERICAN NATIONAL STANDARD COBOL        CBF CL3-4        07/25/77

    00001   001010 IDENTIFICATION DIVISION.                                              DISKOUT
    00002   001020                                                                       DISKOUT
    00003   001030 PROGRAM-ID.    DISKOUT.                                               DISKOUT
    00004   001040 AUTHOR.        SHELLY AND CASHMAN.                                    DISKOUT
    00005   001050 INSTALLATION.  ANAHEIM.                                               DISKOUT
    00006   001060 DATE-WRITTEN.  07/25/77.                                              DISKOUT
    00007   001070 DATE-COMPILED. 07/25/77                                               DISKOUT
    00008   001080 SECURITY.      UNCLASSIFIED.                                          DISKOUT
    00009   001090                                                                       DISKOUT
    00010   001100*********************************************************************   DISKOUT
    00011   001110*                                                                  *   DISKOUT
    00012   001120*   THIS PROGRAM READS A FILE OF CARDS AND STORES THE CARDS        *   DISKOUT
    00013   001130*   SEQUENTIALLY ON DISK.                                          *   DISKOUT
    00014   001140*                                                                  *   DISKOUT
    00015   001150*********************************************************************   DISKOUT
    00016   001160                                                                       DISKOUT
    00017   001170                                                                       DISKOUT
    00018   001180                                                                       DISKOUT
    00019   001190 ENVIRONMENT DIVISION.                                                 DISKOUT
    00020   001200                                                                       DISKOUT
    00021   002010 CONFIGURATION SECTION.                                                DISKOUT
    00022   002020                                                                       DISKOUT
    00023   002030 SOURCE-COMPUTER. IBM-370.                                             DISKOUT
    00024   002040 OBJECT-COMPUTER. IBM-370.                                             DISKOUT
    00025   002050                                                                       DISKOUT
    00026   002060 INPUT-OUTPUT SECTION.                                                 DISKOUT
    00027   002070                                                                       DISKOUT
    00028   002080 FILE-CONTROL.                                                         DISKOUT
    00029   002090     SELECT CARD-INPUT-FILE                                            DISKOUT
    00030   002100           ASSIGN TO SYS007-UR-2540R-S.                                DISKOUT
    00031   002110     SELECT DISK-OUTPUT-FILE                                           DISKOUT
    00032   002120           ASSIGN TO SYS006-UT-2314-S-DISKOUT.                         DISKOUT


        2

    00033   002140 DATA DIVISION.                                                        DISKOUT
    00034   002150                                                                       DISKOUT
    00035   002160 FILE SECTION.                                                         DISKOUT
    00036   002170                                                                       DISKOUT
    00037   002180 FD  CARD-INPUT-FILE                                                   DISKOUT
    00038   002190     RECORD CONTAINS 80 CHARACTERS                                     DISKOUT
    00039   002200     LABEL RECORDS ARE OMITTED                                         DISKOUT
    00040   003010     DATA RECORD IS CARD-INPUT-RECORD.                                 DISKOUT
    00041   003020 01  CARD-INPUT-RECORD         PIC X(80).                              DISKOUT
    00042   003030                                                                       DISKOUT
    00043   003040 FD  DISK-OUTPUT-FILE                                                  DISKOUT
    00044   003050     BLOCK CONTAINS 40 RECORDS                                         DISKOUT
    00045   003060     RECORD CONTAINS 80 CHARACTERS                                     DISKOUT
    00046   003070     LABEL RECORDS ARE STANDARD                                        DISKOUT
    00047   003080     DATA RECORD IS DISK-OUTPUT-RECORD.                                DISKOUT
    00048   003090 01  DISK-OUTPUT-RECORD        PIC X(80).                              DISKOUT
    00049   003100                                                                       DISKOUT
    00050   003110 WORKING-STORAGE SECTION.                                              DISKOUT
    00051   003120                                                                       DISKOUT
    00052   003130 01  PROGRAM-INDICATORS.                                               DISKOUT
    00053   003140     05  ARE-THERE-MORE-RECORDS  PICTURE X(3) VALUE 'YES'.             DISKOUT
```

Figure D-4 Source Listing - Disk Output File (Part 1 of 2)

```
   3
00054  004010 PROCEDURE DIVISION.                                       DISKOUT
00055  004020                                                           DISKOUT
00056  004030*******************************************************************  DISKOUT
00057  004040*                                                       *  DISKOUT
00058  004050*  THIS PROGRAM READS THE SUBSCRIPTION INPUT RECORDS AND *  DISKOUT
00059  004060*  CREATES A SEQUENTIAL DISK FILE.  IT IS ENTERED FROM THE *  DISKOUT
00060  004070*  OPERATING SYSTEM AND EXITS TO THE OPERATING SYSTEM.   *  DISKOUT
00061  004080*                                                       *  DISKOUT
00062  004090*******************************************************************  DISKOUT
00063  004100                                                           DISKOUT
00064  004110 A000-CREATE-DISK-OUTPUT-FILE.                             DISKOUT
00065  004120                                                           DISKOUT
00066  004130     OPEN INPUT  CARD-INPUT-FILE                           DISKOUT
00067  004140          OUTPUT DISK-OUTPUT-FILE.                         DISKOUT
00068  004150     READ CARD-INPUT-FILE                                  DISKOUT
00069  004160         AT END                                           DISKOUT
00070  004170             MOVE 'NO ' TO ARE-THERE-MORE-RECORDS.        DISKOUT
00071  004180     PERFORM A001-PROCESS-RECORDS                          DISKOUT
00072  004190         UNTIL ARE-THERE-MORE-RECORDS = 'NO '.            DISKOUT
00073  004200     CLOSE CARD-INPUT-FILE                                 DISKOUT
00074  005010           DISK-OUTPUT-FILE.                              DISKOUT
00075  005020     STOP RUN.                                             DISKOUT
00076  005030                                                           DISKOUT
00077  005040                                                           DISKOUT
00078  005050                                                           DISKOUT
00079  005060 A001-PROCESS-RECORDS.                                     DISKOUT
00080  005070                                                           DISKOUT
00081  005080     MOVE CARD-INPUT-RECORD TO DISK-OUTPUT-RECORD.         DISKOUT
00082  005090     WRITE DISK-OUTPUT-RECORD.                             DISKOUT
00083  005100     READ CARD-INPUT-FILE                                  DISKOUT
00084  005110         AT END                                           DISKOUT
00085  005120             MOVE 'NO ' TO ARE-THERE-MORE-RECORDS.        DISKOUT
```

Figure D-5 Source Listing - Disk Output File [Part 2 of 2]

READING SEQUENTIAL DISK FILES

In order to read a sequential disk file, entries must be made in the Environment Division, the Data Division, and the Procedure Division in the same manner as when writing a file. The entries in the Environment Division and the Data Division are identical to those required when writing a file. It should be noted that the Blocking Factor and Record Size which are specified must be the same as when the file was created.

The entries to read a sequential disk input file are illustrated in Figure D-6.

Environment Division

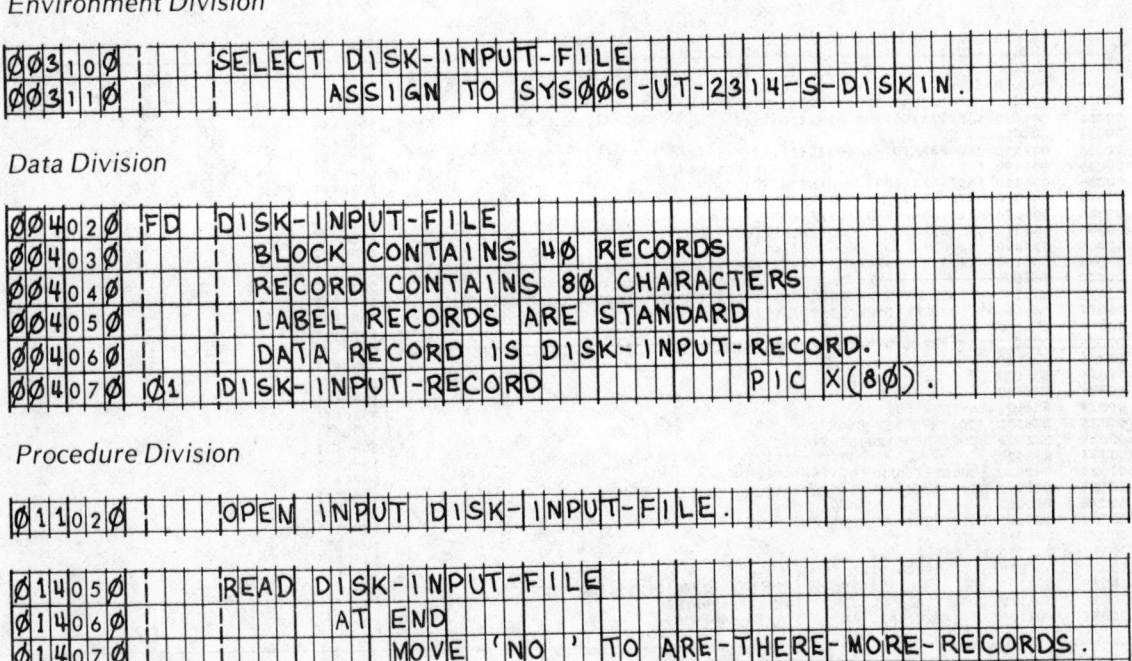

Data Division

Procedure Division

Figure D-6 Example of Entries to Read Sequential Disk File

Note from the above statements that the Environment and Data Division Statements are virtually the same as those required for writing a disk file. The disk input file must be opened as an input file. The READ Statement which is used to read the input file operates in exactly the same way as a Read Statement which is used to read a card input file.

SAMPLE PROGRAM

In order to illustrate the reading of a sequential disk file, the program presented in Chapter 3 has been altered to allow for reading a sequential disk file instead of a card input file. The small arrows on the following listing point out the changes which were made.

SOURCE LISTING

```
    1                         IBM DOS AMERICAN NATIONAL STANDARD COBOL        C8F CL3-4        07/25/77

  00001   001010 IDENTIFICATION DIVISION.                                           SUBLIST
  00002   001020                                                                    SUBLIST
  00003   001030 PROGRAM-ID.    SUBLIST.                                            SUBLIST
  00004   001040 AUTHOR.        SHELLY AND CASHMAN.                                 SUBLIST
  00005   001050 INSTALLATION.  ANAHEIM.                                            SUBLIST
  00006   001060 DATE-WRITTEN.  07/25/77.                                           SUBLIST
  00007   001070 DATE-COMPILED. 07/25/77                                            SUBLIST
  00008   001080 SECURITY.      UNCLASSIFIED.                                       SUBLIST
  00009   001090                                                                    SUBLIST
  00010   001100************************************************************         SUBLIST
  00011   001110*                                                          *        SUBLIST
  00012   001120*  THIS PROGRAM PRODUCES A LISTING OF PERSONS ON A MAGAZINE *        SUBLIST
  00013   001130*  SUBSCRIPTION LIST.                                       *        SUBLIST
  00014   001140*                                                          *        SUBLIST
  00015   001150************************************************************         SUBLIST
  00016   001160                                                                    SUBLIST
  00017   001170                                                                    SUBLIST
  00018   001180                                                                    SUBLIST
  00019   001190 ENVIRONMENT DIVISION.                                              SUBLIST
  00020   001200                                                                    SUBLIST
  00021   002010 CONFIGURATION SECTION.                                             SUBLIST
  00022   002020                                                                    SUBLIST
  00023   002030 SOURCE-COMPUTER. IBM-370.                                          SUBLIST
  00024   002040 OBJECT-COMPUTER. IBM-370.                                          SUBLIST
  00025   002050                                                                    SUBLIST
  00026   002060 INPUT-OUTPUT SECTION.                                              SUBLIST
  00027   002070                                                                    SUBLIST
  00028   002080 FILE-CONTROL.                                                      SUBLIST
  00029   002090     SELECT DISK-INPUT-FILE                                         SUBLIST
  00030   002100         ASSIGN TO SYS006-UT-2314-S-DISKIN.   ←                     SUBLIST
  00031   002110     SELECT SUBSCRIPTION-REPORT-FILE                                SUBLIST
  00032   002120         ASSIGN TO SYS013-UR-1403-S.                                SUBLIST


    2

  00033   002130 DATA DIVISION.                                                     SUBLIST
  00034   002140                                                                    SUBLIST
  00035   002150 FILE SECTION.                                                      SUBLIST
  00036   002160                                                                    SUBLIST
  00037   002170 FD  DISK-INPUT-FILE                                              ⎫ SUBLIST
  00038   002180     BLOCK CONTAINS 40 RECORDS                                    ⎬ SUBLIST
  00039   002190     RECORD CONTAINS 80 CHARACTERS                          ←     ⎪ SUBLIST
  00040   002200     LABEL RECORDS ARE STANDARD                                   ⎭ SUBLIST
  00041   003010     DATA RECORD IS DISK-INPUT-RECORD.                              SUBLIST
  00042   003020 01  DISK-INPUT-RECORD.                                             SUBLIST
  00043   003030     05  NAME-INPUT            PICTURE X(25).                       SUBLIST
  00044   003040     05  ADDRESS-INPUT         PICTURE X(25).                       SUBLIST
  00045   003050     05  CITY-STATE-INPUT      PICTURE X(20).                       SUBLIST
  00046   003060     05  EXPIRATION-DATE-INPUT PICTURE X(8).                        SUBLIST
  00047   003070     05  FILLER                PICTURE XX.                          SUBLIST
  00048   003080                                                                    SUBLIST
  00049   003090 FD  SUBSCRIPTION-REPORT-FILE                                       SUBLIST
  00050   003100     RECORD CONTAINS 133 CHARACTERS                                 SUBLIST
  00051   003110     LABEL RECORDS ARE OMITTED                                      SUBLIST
  00052   003120     DATA RECORD IS SUBSCRIPTION-REPORT-LINE.                       SUBLIST
  00053   003130 01  SUBSCRIPTION-REPORT-LINE.                                      SUBLIST
  00054   003140     05  CARRIAGE-CONTROL      PIC X.                               SUBLIST
  00055   003150     05  EXPIRATION-DATE-REPORT PICTURE X(8).                       SUBLIST
  00056   003160     05  FILLER                PICTURE X(5).                        SUBLIST
  00057   003170     05  NAME-REPORT           PICTURE X(25).                       SUBLIST
  00058   003180     05  FILLER                PICTURE X(5).                        SUBLIST
  00059   003190     05  ADDRESS-REPORT        PICTURE X(25).                       SUBLIST
  00060   003200     05  FILLER                PICTURE X(5).                        SUBLIST
  00061   004010     05  CITY-STATE-REPORT     PICTURE X(20).                       SUBLIST
  00062   004020     05  FILLER                PICTURE X(39).                       SUBLIST
  00063   004030                                                                    SUBLIST
  00064   004040 WORKING-STORAGE SECTION.                                           SUBLIST
  00065   004050                                                                    SUBLIST
  00066   004060 01  PROGRAM-INDICATORS.                                            SUBLIST
  00067   004070     05  ARE-THERE-MORE-RECORDS PICTURE X(3) VALUE 'YES'.           SUBLIST
```

Figure D-7 Source Listing - Disk Input File [Part 1 of 2]

```
   3
00068  004090 PROCEDURE DIVISION.                                          SUBLIST
00069  004100                                                             SUBLIST
00070  004110**********************************************************    SUBLIST
00071  004120*                                                       *    SUBLIST
00072  004130*  THIS PROGRAM READS THE SUBSCRIPTION INPUT RECORDS AND  *  SUBLIST
00073  004140*  CREATES THE SUBSCRIPTION LISTING.  IT IS ENTERED FROM THE *  SUBLIST
00074  004150*  OPERATING SYSTEM AND EXITS TO THE OPERATING SYSTEM.    *  SUBLIST
00075  004160*                                                       *    SUBLIST
00076  004170**********************************************************    SUBLIST
00077  004180                                                             SUBLIST
00078  004190 A000-CREATE-SUBSCRIPTION-LIST.                              SUBLIST
00079  004200                                                             SUBLIST
00080  005010     OPEN INPUT  DISK-INPUT-FILE                             SUBLIST
00081  005020          OUTPUT SUBSCRIPTION-REPORT-FILE.                   SUBLIST
00082  005030     READ DISK-INPUT-FILE                                    SUBLIST
00083  005040         AT END                                             SUBLIST
00084  005050             MOVE 'NO ' TO ARE-THERE-MORE-RECORDS.          SUBLIST
00085  005060     PERFORM A001-FORMAT-PRINT-REPORT                        SUBLIST
00086  005070         UNTIL ARE-THERE-MORE-RECORDS = 'NO '.              SUBLIST
00087  005080     CLOSE DISK-INPUT-FILE                                   SUBLIST
00088  005090           SUBSCRIPTION-REPORT-FILE.                         SUBLIST
00089  005100     STOP RUN.                                               SUBLIST
00090  005110                                                             SUBLIST
00091  005120                                                             SUBLIST
00092  005130                                                             SUBLIST
00093  005140 A001-FORMAT-PRINT-REPORT.                                   SUBLIST
00094  005150                                                             SUBLIST
00095  005160     MOVE SPACES TO SUBSCRIPTION-REPORT-LINE.                SUBLIST
00096  005170     MOVE EXPIRATION-DATE-INPUT TO EXPIRATION-DATE-REPORT.   SUBLIST
00097  005180     MOVE NAME-INPUT TO NAME-REPORT.                         SUBLIST
00098  005190     MOVE ADDRESS-INPUT TO ADDRESS-REPORT                    SUBLIST
00099  005200     MOVE CITY-STATE-INPUT TO CITY-STATE-REPORT.             SUBLIST
00100  006010     WRITE SUBSCRIPTION-REPORT-LINE                          SUBLIST
00101  006020         AFTER ADVANCING 1 LINES.                           SUBLIST
00102  006030     READ DISK-INPUT-FILE                                    SUBLIST
00103  006040         AT END                                             SUBLIST
00104  006050             MOVE 'NO ' TO ARE-THERE-MORE-RECORDS.          SUBLIST
```

Figure D-8 Source Listing - Disk Input File [Part 2 of 2]

Note that the only changes necessary to read a sequential disk input file are changes to the Select Statement and the FD Statement. The example program assumes there are 40 records in each physical block in the file which is to be read.

RESERVED WORD LIST

The following is a list of the reserved words used in the COBOL language.

ACCEPT	CORRESPONDING	EXTEND	LESS
ACCESS	COUNT		LIMIT
ADD	CURRENCY	FD	LIMITS
ADVANCING		FILE	LINAGE
AFTER	DATA	FILE-CONTROL	LINAGE-COUNTER
ALL	DATE	FILLER	LINE
ALPHABETIC	DATE-COMPILED	FINAL	LINE-COUNTER
ALSO	DATE-WRITTEN	FIRST	LINES
ALTER	DAY	FOOTING	LINKAGE
ALTERNATE	DE	FOR	LOCK
AND	DEBUG-CONTENTS	FROM	LOW-VALUE
ARE	DEBUG-ITEM		LOW-VALUES
AREA	DEBUG-LINE	GENERATE	
AREAS	DEBUG-NAME	GIVING	MEMORY
ASCENDING	DEBUG-SUB-1	GO	MERGE
ASSIGN	DEBUG-SUB-2	GREATER	MESSAGE
AT	DEBUG-SUB-3	GROUP	MODE
AUTHOR	DEBUGGING		MODULES
	DECIMAL-POINT	HEADING	MOVE
	DECLARATIVES	HIGH-VALUE	MULTIPLE
BEFORE	DELETE	HIGH-VALUES	MULTIPLY
BLANK	DELIMITED		
BLOCK	DELIMITER	I-O	NATIVE
BOTTOM	DEPENDING	I-O-CONTROL	NEGATIVE
BY	DESCENDING	IDENTIFICATION	NEXT
	DESTINATION	IF	NO
CALL	DETAIL	IN	NOT
CANCEL	DISABLE	INDEX	NUMBER
CD	DISPLAY	INDEXED	NUMERIC
CF	DIVIDE	INDICATE	
CH	DIVISION	INITIAL	OBJECT-COMPUTER
CHARACTER	DOWN	INITIATE	OCCURS
CHARACTERS	DUPLICATES	INPUT	OF
CLOCK-UNITS	DYNAMIC	INPUT-OUTPUT	OFF
CLOSE		INSPECT	OMITTED
COBOL		INSTALLATION	ON
CODE	EGI	INTO	OPEN
CODE-SET	ELSE	INVALID	OPTIONAL
COLLATING	EMI	IS	OR
COLUMN	ENABLE		ORGANIZATION
COMMA	END		OUTPUT
COMMUNICATION	END-OF-PAGE	JUST	OVERFLOW
COMP	ENTER	JUSTIFIED	
COMPUTATIONAL	ENVIRONMENT		
COMPUTE	EOP	KEY	PAGE
CONFIGURATION	EQUAL		PAGE-COUNTER
CONTAINS	ERROR	LABEL	PERFORM
CONTROL	ESI	LAST	PF
CONTROLS	EVERY	LEADING	PH
COPY	EXCEPTION	LEFT	PIC
CORR	EXIT	LENGTH	PICTURE

PLUS	RERUN	SPACE	TYPE
POINTER	RESERVE	SPACES	
POSITION	RESET	SPECIAL-NAMES	UNIT
POSITIVE	RETURN	STANDARD	UNSTRING
PRINTING	REVERSED	STANDARD-1	UNTIL
PROCEDURE	REWIND	START	UP
PROCEDURES	REWRITE	STATUS	UPON
PROCEED	RF	STOP	USAGE
PROGRAM	RH	STRING	USE
PROGRAM-ID	RIGHT	SUB-QUEUE-1	USING
	ROUNDED	SUB-QUEUE-2	
QUEUE	RUN	SUB-QUEUE-3	VALUE
QUOTE		SUBTRACT	VALUES
QUOTES	SAME	SUM	VARYING
	SD	SUPPRESS	
RANDOM	SEARCH	SYMBOLIC	WHEN
RD	SECTION	SYNC	WITH
READ	SECURITY	SYNCHRONIZED	WORDS
RECEIVE	SEGMENT		WORKING-STORAGE
RECORD	SEGMENT-LIMIT	TABLE	WRITE
RECORDS	SELECT	TALLYING	
REDEFINES	SEND	TAPE	ZERO
REEL	SENTENCE	TERMINAL	ZEROES
REFERENCES	SEPARATE	TERMINATE	ZEROS
RELATIVE	SEQUENCE	TEXT	
RELEASE	SEQUENTIAL	THAN	+
REMAINDER	SET	THROUGH	-
REMOVAL	SIGN	THRU	*
RENAMES	SIZE	TIME	/
REPLACING	SORT	TIMES	**
REPORT	SORT-MERGE	TO	>
REPORTING	SOURCE	TOP	<
REPORTS	SOURCE-COMPUTER	TRAILING	=

INDEX

-T-

TABLES, 10.1
TABLE DEFINITION, 10.9
TABLE LOOKUP, 10.8
TABLE SEARCH, 10.11
TABLES, MULTIPLE LEVEL, 11.8

-U-

USAGE CLAUSE, 5.28
USAGE IS COMPUTATIONAL, 10.19
USAGE IS COMPUTATIONAL-3, 5.28

-V-

VALUE CLAUSE, 3.31, 4.33
VALUE SPACES, 4.31

VALUE ZERO, 6.32
VARIABLE LINE SPACING, 4.33
VERBS, COBOL, 3.34

-W-

WORKING-STORAGE SECTION, 3.29
WRITE FROM, 4.32
WRITE STATEMENT, 3.49

-Z-

ZERO, FIGURATIVE CONSTANT, 6.32
ZERO CHARACTER, EDITING, 4.25
ZERO SUPPRESSION, ASTERISK FILL, 4.20
ZERO SUPPRESSION, EDITING, 4.19